Praise for
A HISTORY OF OPERA

"[*A History of Opera*] will surely become essential reading for anyone seeking an engaging and highly informed chronicle of the great composers and their works." —*Opera* magazine

"Writers on opera tend to fall into two mutually hostile camps: the mind people and the body people, the Kermans and the Koestenbaums. Abbate and Parker are in possession of minds *and* bodies, alive to pleasures rational as well as sensual. Their take on opera is generous—singers and audiences and directors claim their attention and people their pages, alongside composers and librettists—and their prose is gorgeous, combining scholarly precision with the ardor of true lovers. Their history is elegiac: their beloved genre, they acknowledge, is dying, living off its past. But what a past it is, and the book pays it fitting tribute: it sings."
—Richard Taruskin, author of
Oxford History of Western Music

"A highly idiosyncratic and personal history of opera . . . exciting and wide-ranging." —G. W. Bowersock, *New Republic*

"This book is not only a total delight to read, but its insights are so varied, its arguments so wonderfully precise and unpredictable, its prose so generous and engaging, that it is an utter delight to *re*-read." —David J. Levin, executive editor, *Opera Quarterly*

"A virtuoso performance . . . fantastically clear-sighted and down-to-earth." —*Telegraph* (UK)

"Essential reading for all who love this most ambitious of art forms." —Daniel Snowman, author of *The Gilded Stage: A Social History of Opera*

"An interesting and alert history of the art form." —Philip Hensher, *Guardian* (UK)

"An extended duet of intertwined voices, this inspiring book is at once a history of opera and a poetic meditation on the genre itself, its complexity, depth, and allure." —Ellen Rosand, George A. Saden Professor of Music, Yale University

"A revealing genealogy of a living tradition that will speak vividly to those who continue to fall for opera's mad charms, and entice those who might be about to." —Christopher Morris, author of *Reading Opera between the Lines*

"Experts and beginners alike will enjoy what is sure to become a classic work." —Andrew Moravcsik, director, European Union Program, Princeton University

Also by Carolyn Abbate

Unsung Voices
In Search of Opera

Also by Roger Parker

Leonora's Last Act
Remaking the Song

ABOUT THE AUTHORS

Carolyn Abbate is Professor of Music at Harvard University and the author of *Unsung Voices* and *In Search of Opera*. Her work has been translated into many languages. She herself is a translator, and has been involved in theatre as a dramaturge and director.

Roger Parker is Professor of Music at King's College London and the author of *Leonora's Last Act* and *Remaking the Song*. He is founding co-editor of the Donizetti critical edition, and editor of *The Oxford Illustrated History of Opera*.

CAROLYN ABBATE
AND ROGER PARKER

A History of Opera

W. W. NORTON & COMPANY
Independent Publishers Since 1923
New York • London

First published in Great Britain in 2012 by Allen Lane, an imprint of Penguin Books, under the title *A History of Opera: The Last Four Hundred Years*

Printed in the United States of America
First published as a Norton paperback 2015

Manufacturing by RR Donnelley Westford
Production manager: Anna Oler

Library of Congress Cataloging-in-Publication Data

Abbate, Carolyn.
A history of opera / Carolyn Abbate and Roger Parker. — 1st ed.
p. cm.
Includes bibliographical references and index.
ISBN 978-0-393-05721-8 (hardcover)
1. Opera. I. Parker, Roger, 1951– II. Title.
ML1700.A22 2012
782.1—dc23
2012031546

ISBN 978-0-393-34895-8 pbk.

W. W. Norton & Company, Inc.
500 Fifth Avenue, New York, N.Y. 10110
www.wwnorton.com

W. W. Norton & Company Ltd.
Castle House, 75/76 Wells Street, London W1T 3QT

1 2 3 4 5 6 7 8 9 0

In memoriam

Joseph Kerman (1924–2014)

Contents

Illustrations

Preface to the Paperback Edition

We have only a few words to add to the precautions, homilies, and – heartfelt – thanks that appear in our original Preface. The world of opera has changed even in the three or so years that have passed since this book first appeared. At least one new opera house has opened: in Linz, and thus in the already super-saturated operatic climate of Austria. Another has been mooted, much mooted, in Perth, in Western Australia, but the design and the estimated $1.2bn cost have together conspired to put the project in limbo. New productions of hallowed classics have continued to astound and sometimes enrage the operatic faithful. We've attended many performances on two continents – *I puritani, Les Vêpres siciliennes, Billy Budd* and *Parsifal* stay especially in the mind – in which we encountered marvellous singing and orchestral playing, and immense directorial verve: cause for continued rejoicing. What is more, many new operatic works have been written and produced: often at great expense and with brief afterlives, but that has always been the case during opera's long history. On the other hand, some opera houses have gone permanently dark, including the New York City Opera (1943–2013), while the situation in recession-plagued Italy seems to become ever more parlous. The general mood about opera's theatrical future, at least in the US and Europe, has darkened in response. Some trends, though, point upwards: YouTube as a source of video and audio documentation for opera has grown again, and again, with recent statistics suggesting 1bn users for the site, and new material appearing at 100 hours per minute. A tiny proportion of this is operatic, of course, but a tiny proportion is still enormous by any previous standards of opera's dissemination via mass media. In particular, the number of forgotten operatic rarities now restored and available to all has ascended, probably into the thousands. Our publisher's generosity in allowing us to expand an already-long book has meant that we have been able to account for some of these very recent developments. In doing so we have recast our original final chapter as two, adding new material on opera and operatic culture in recent decades. We have also taken the opportunity to correct a few errors, with gratitude due to those who pointed them out. We are especially indebted to the meticulous work of our German translators, Karl Heinz Siber and Nikolaus de Palézieux, whose attentive reading of the original text often encouraged us to clarify our own thinking.

The passage of time has brought one loss that is immeasurable. Joseph Kerman, to whom we dedicated our book in 2012, died in March 2014. This new edition is re-dedicated, now to his memory.

Carolyn Abbate
Roger Parker

Preface and acknowledgements

A history of opera is not lightly undertaken in this Age of Information, particularly when it attempts to survey the entire 400-year period. But while the footsteps of those who have trodden the path before are of course daunting, recent competition is not as intense as it might once have been. Although histories of opera were common a century ago (when Richard Wagner was a convenient and attractively all-embracing endpoint), modern retellings are surprisingly few. This is true of all general histories of music, at least of those emerging from the academy. As information has accumulated, authors used to professing, which means professing authority, have become cautious: their 'special fields' have shrunk inexorably. What is more, the subject of opera offers further difficulties, not least that some of its major practitioners still have shaky academic reputations. Puccini is the classic example here: hugely, inescapably popular, for many almost defining what is meant by opera in the early twentieth century; but with a musicological literature that, at least until very recently, looked thin even in comparison with early symphonists or earnest serialists.

There is also the persistent issue, now more than a century old, of 'opera crisis': of how to assess the future of an art form that, at best, has had a troubled relationship with modernity. If histories always tell us a good deal about the present, even as they explicitly concern themselves with the past, then this one needs to reflect the fact that one obvious feature of opera today is an obsession – at least among critics – with viability and vitality. In one sense, opera is thriving. The sheer volume of live opera taking place around the world is far greater now than it was fifty years ago, and this expansion shows little sign of abatement. There is also the remarkable way in which modern technology (recordings and broadcasts, both of them now expanding through the internet as well as through more traditional means) has made operatic performances of both the past and present newly available to vast global audiences. Unless one is a diehard elitist, this proliferation would seem an obvious cause for rejoicing. But celebratory hymns are muted by one glaring circumstance: opera's expansion has overwhelmingly involved performances of works from the past, often works that were blithely cast aside by the people for whom they were produced – by societies who were confident that more operas, and probably better ones, were just around the corner. The present situation is often the subject of elaborate lament: many of those residing otherwise happily in the opera museum are prone to recite mantras about how urgently we need *new* operas, that modern additions to the repertory are critical to the health or even the survival of the art form.

Our stance in this debate is laid out clearly enough in the last chapter; we need not anticipate it here. But it may be worth stressing that the two elements of operatic change – the establishment of a repertory and its expansion backwards on the one hand, and the gradual dwindling of new works on the other – have been moving in tandem for more than a century now, and are clearly related. To put this another way, it is sentimental, probably downright utopian, to believe that we can lovingly preserve and continue to add to opera's repertory of historical objects while at the same time providing the best possible environment for the emergence of new work. The key aspect here, one we will mention more than once in what follows, is the cultural pessimism that now fuels the repertory, an attitude which makes the operatic scene so different from that in cognate forms such as the novel, or film, or visual art, where the new is in constant and lively competition with the old. The energies we devote to careful preservation and renewal of opera's past glories are now enormous, and quite possibly overwhelming. Think of the emulative competitions engaged in by performers and audiences over their favourite roles and operas; the constant rethinking of stage technologies and modes of presentation; the endless historical research and proliferation of new critical editions, either to restore unknown works or to repackage ones we know well, making them more authoritative and imposing. All these endeavours, laudable in themselves, raise the bar ever higher where new work is concerned. How can it hope to compete? If we really wanted a present in which the new was more exciting than the old, in which the world premiere took precedence over the revival, then we would need to learn to discard at least a part of the past, to recapture some of that now-ancient belief in artistic progress. We would also need to forget the nineteenth century's elevation of music's importance among the arts, to recover an earlier attitude in which music was almost always new because past efforts were almost always cast aside, being thought of little lasting value. This would be a radical future indeed; but it is one that hardly anyone seems to want.

One further issue needs some discussion, as it has obvious consequences for the content and tone of the book. At a very early stage, and in no sense at the urging of our editors, we decided that this history would contain no musical examples. We did so because, at the same stage, it became obvious to us that – as far as possible – we wanted to write the book without reference to musical scores. This was a more radical gesture than banning musical examples from the printed book, and might seem a wilful renunciation of precisely the expertise that many see as the musicologist's greatest strength. Why, after all, ignore such rich repositories of musical detail? In part, we did so out of a desire to find a broader audience, one not involved in the disciplinary habits of musicology. But mostly it was because scores encourage elaborate attention to particular aspects of a strictly musical argument, above all those involving harmonic and melodic detail on the small and the large scale, aspects that have tended to figure too prominently in musicological writings about opera. In other words, scores encourage the idea of opera as a text rather than as an event. Memory, on the other hand, goes back to an event – something heard out loud, possibly also seen on stage. Hence the musical descriptions in this book were written almost entirely on the basis of memory, whether in response to a recording, or – far more often – from the repositories of our personal operatic experiences. This in turn engendered a certain style of musical description, one in which various stalwarts of the musicological lexicon are almost entirely absent. Readers will look in vain for abstract structural analyses of music, or extended descriptions of notes interacting with each other: that kind of information, although relatively easy – with training – to extract from a score, is virtually impossible to extract from listening to or attending an opera. On the other hand, room is then available for other details to emerge: sometimes those involving orchestral effects; above all those involving the singing voice, its heft and colour and power. Whether anything has been gained, whether relying on acoustic memory has enabled us to talk more persuasively about opera as presence and material sound, will of course be for the reader to judge. Although it was sometimes frustrating, and although we transgressed occasionally (at a late stage, for example, a triple-metre passage from *Tristan* Act 2 was aurally present, but its notated time signature remained fugitive to recollection), on the whole we kept to our decision, and found the resulting experiment constantly challenging and liberating.

An important corollary of the renunciation of scores, and the attendant reliance on musical memory, is that this book mostly deals with operas that are firmly in the present-day repertory. Fifty years ago, that restriction would have been much more drastic than it is today, when operas available at least in recordings are more numerous than ever before. However, and despite this new availability, the composers we discuss at greatest length are those most often performed in today's global repertory: in numerical order of ubiquity, Verdi, Mozart, Puccini, Rossini, Wagner, Donizetti, Strauss, Bizet and Handel. We have not artfully corralled for consideration multiple works outside opera's central repertories. Rather, we have tried to present ways of hearing and understanding that can, we hope, be extended beyond the usual national traditions, to rich repertories in a host of less likely places. True, we do pay attention to several composers whose historical importance far outweighs their presence in today's opera houses – the most obvious cases are Monteverdi and, in particular, Meyerbeer, whose most influential works are now very rarely heard, but who figures prominently here. We have also tried hard to consider composers, or even entire genres, that were once famous but now forgotten, and to explain why their fame did not survive. We have, in short, aimed to be responsible in our duty as historians. But it is also true that those nine composers mentioned above had distinctly variable influences on the broad stream of operatic history, from the negligible (Handel, Mozart) to the all-but overwhelming (Rossini, Wagner); concentrating on them is, then, bound to distort the historical narrative. At the least, though, our emphases result in an operatic history that gives due attention to a considerable number of works (the operas of Puccini and those of the later Strauss are the most obvious) which are generally ignored in music histories, even those of recent vintage.

This book, the product of four hands, has had a complicated genesis. We had written articles and edited a book together before, and knew that the collaboration itself would work. What's more, our particular combination of interests and specialist knowledge probably did no harm, and in some ways mirrored happily the collaborative energies that have forever fuelled our subject. But it soon became clear, somewhat to our surprise in this age of instant digital communication, that we needed to be in the same town and have daily, face-to-face conversations in order to begin the book in earnest, and then – more surprising still – needed to repeat that face-to-face contact in order to contribute anything more than trivial updates to its contents. When homes are separated by thousands of miles, and when writing such a book can never be one's sole occupation, these requirements presented logistical obstacles. But it also seemed to make sense both of the project and of our collaboration. We have, over the course of almost thirty years of occasional teamwork, often been asked – sometimes incredulously – how we manage to write together. It's usually assumed that we must agree to divide up the responsibilities by chapter or verse; that one of us does Italy and the other does Germany, with France and the remaining bits parcelled off in smaller assignments. As it happens, though, the *modus scribendi* is quite different. For better or worse, we end up writing almost everything together, starting with a paragraph tossed across the court, which seems to attract another paragraph or two, and things branch out from there. Because of this odd method, there is hardly a sentence in the book – this one included – without the material traces of both writers. In most instances the original author of this or that paragraph has disappeared entirely, replaced by a composite voice whose personality seems gradually and quite mysteriously to emerge. Such collaboration needs many circumstances to sustain it, not least a willingness to abandon personal control over what writers, even non-fiction writers, often consider paramount: individual prejudices and opinions, firm convictions, habits of punctuation and vocabulary, many other features of style. But that very abandonment can also be liberating and stimulating.

We have, in the time it took us to write this book, frequently had to rely on others, in particular those who were experts in the many unfamiliar fields we occasionally traversed. Many of these are duly mentioned in the bibliography and references. But some did us the good service of reading our work in progress. Thanks, then, to a gentle host of interlocutors. Harriet Boyd, Chris Chowrimootoo, Elaine Combs-Schilling, Lynden Cranham, Martin Deasy, John Deathridge, Marina Frolova-Walker, Katherine Hambridge, Matthew Head, Ellen Lockhart, Marian Read, Susan Rutherford, Arman Schwartz, Emanuele Senici, David Trippett,

Laura Tunbridge, Ben Walton and Heather Wiebe all read chapters (some of them several chapters) and commented with great generosity. Flora Willson gave us invaluable assistance with picture research, in the process reading and then responding critically to almost the entire book. A special tribute is owed to Gary Tomlinson, who was kind enough to lend us his unparalleled knowledge of opera's beginnings, and then went on to read large portions of the remainder of the book, in the process leaving welcome traces of his uniquely broad and encompassing purview. We have also been exceptionally lucky in our editors, Stuart Proffitt at Penguin and Maribeth Payne at Norton; their patience and persistence were remarkable, as was their intellectual engagement in the entire enterprise. In Stuart's case this involvement started at the very beginning, and included enormously detailed editorial comments that were inspiring enough to change our first draft in fundamental ways.

Most of the book was written at Princeton's Institute for Advanced Study, a venue famous for its mathematicians and physicists, but one also proving a congenial and hospitable setting for operatic fantasy. Our particular thanks go to the Institute's Director, Peter Goddard, for his exceptional generosity in accommodating us both for prolonged periods; and to Walter Lippincott, long-time Institute habitué and long-time friend, whose enthusiasm for opera and conviviality knows no bounds. Lastly, we want to thank our students over the years. Our graduate seminars and their derivatives – those halfway houses between reading and writing, in which people of different ages share and sometimes create ideas, a miniature society with all its complications and joyous communication – have been central to the ideas that emerge in this book.

One moment made doubly complex by a collaborative enterprise might come when choosing the dedication. In some shared ventures the act is strangely revealing. F. R. and Q. D. Leavis proudly dedicated their joint volume on Dickens 'to each other'; but they also signed chapters individually and so were perhaps justified in this disconcertingly inward turn. For us, though, agreement on the matter was immediate. We have long been aware that our collaborations are facilitated partly by the fact that we grew up as writers under many of the same critical influences. Among these the most significant has always been Joseph Kerman. His monograph *Opera as Drama*, written in the 1950s, was still *the* operatic book for our generation, and has – quite remarkably – remained in currency, challenging readers to this day. Joe himself then presided benignantly over both our apprenticeships, as he did over those of so many others. He published each of our earliest scholarly essays on opera in *19th-Century Music*; and he then applied his legendary editorial hand to our first collaborative book. His presence is everywhere in the chapters that follow. If even a few of their pages manage distantly to recall the wit and critical edge of his writings on opera, or suggest the generosity of his intellectual spirit, then – for the authors at least – the project will have reached a happy end.

Carolyn Abbate, Princeton, NJ (40° 37′ N, 74° 35′ W)
Roger Parker, Havant, Hants (50° 85 N, 0° 96′ W)
Distance: 3483 miles

1
Introduction

Opera is a type of theatre in which most or all of the characters sing most or all of the time. In that very obvious sense it is not realistic, and has, through most of its 400-year history, often been thought exotic and strange. What's more, it is almost always ridiculously expensive to stage and to attend. At no time in history has society at large managed to sustain easily opera's outrageous cost. Why, then, do so many people love it so deeply? Why do they devote their lives to performing it, writing about it, watching it? Why do some opera fans travel the world to watch a new production or hear a favourite singer, paying huge sums for the fleeting privilege? And why is opera the one form of classical music still developing significant new audiences in spite of the fact that, in the last century or so, the stream of new works that was once its lifeblood has dried to a trickle?

These questions are mostly about opera as it is today: about what opera has become at the start of the twenty-first century. In what follows we will have much to say about the history of our subject, about the ways opera has developed during its 400-year journey towards us; but our emphasis will also be on the present, on the effect opera continues to have on audiences around the world. Our aim is to get to grips with an art form whose most popular and enduring works were almost all written in a distant European past, and so were created in cultures very different from our own, but whose hold over many of us – whose meaning in our lives today – is still palpable. Opera can change us: physically, emotionally, intellectually. We want to explore why.

WORDS AND MUSIC

It is often said that opera, being in essence sung theatre, involves a battle between words and music. Whole operas have been written about this supposed battle. One of the more famous (at least in the history books) is Antonio Salieri's little comic work, *Prima la musica, dopo le parole* (First the Music, Then the Words), which was premiered in 1786 amid the opulence of the Orangerie, a deluxe greenhouse-cum-conservatory at the Schönbrunn Palace in Vienna. A poet and a composer must complete an opera within four days. The poet complains about the indignity of being asked to concoct words to fit pre-existing music; the composer replies that the poet's angst is trivial – no one cares about the words anyway. The basic terms of this tussle – the battle-lines between words and music – are drawn up again and again in the history of opera: Richard Strauss's *Capriccio*, premiered at the Munich Staatsoper during one of Germany's darkest years, 1942, deals with the same theme in an understandably more world-weary manner.

On the surface, this sense of a continuing competition might seem strange: the words, after all, supply the basic story; the music then gives that story added impact and aura. While it's little wonder that operatic poets and composers occasionally get into arguments (for one thing, the relative prestige of their professions has changed a great deal through the centuries), they need each other and always have done. As soon as we press a little, though, the reason why the words/music opposition is often so tense and anxious becomes clearer. In a libretto there are at least two separate domains. The first involves the narrative element, basically the plot and its characters; the second involves the representation of this narrative in text, in specific (almost always poetic) words. While the first domain has tended to remain stable when operas are performed, the second is often highly variable. Operatic poetry, the libretto text, is rarely thought so exquisite as literature that it commands reverent handling at every turn. There is, for example, a continuing and heated contemporary debate about whether we should hear opera in translation, in the language of the audience rather than the language of the original work. Those who want translations are in effect arguing that the first of the libretto's domains, the one involving plot and characters, is more important than the second, in which individual words reside. Muddying the waters of this debate, though, is a further circumstance, one that Salieri's composer points out rather cruelly: that words set to music tend to lose a good deal of their semantic force, and that this loss can be at its most extreme in opera.

The reasons for this loss are many. The musical surroundings – the instrumental forces, as well as the kind of music they play – can overwhelm as well as accompany the human voice. Composers can also use words as a kind of roughage: in coloratura singing, cascades of vocal ornament on an open vowel reduce the verbal element to mere sound, almost like an instrumental tone colour. But the voice itself, specifically the operatic voice, contributes in its own way to the disappearance of linguistic sense. Opera singers, given the requirements for volume and pitch, must at times produce sound in ways that will force verbal articulation to take a back seat. The words will be obscured no matter what the language of the libretto. Even in languages we know well, listening to opera's verbal text can be frustrating: single words or phrases – 'la vendetta', 'das Schwert', 'j'ai peur', 'I am bad' – will swim briefly to the surface of comprehension, but what follows will again be drowned in musical activity. Avid listeners may memorize long stretches of libretto poetry and then, during the act of listening, supply from memory the words that lie underneath the babble. But even this doesn't mean that they necessarily understand the words they have by heart, just as singers, in some cases, learn their parts phonetically without having more than a general sense of what they're actually saying when they sing.

Some singers are much better at verbal articulation than others – in German, Franz Mazura comes to mind, in Italian, Giuseppe di Stefano – but the counterexamples, singers who are famous for their wooliness in this department, are probably more numerous and include revered superstars such as Joan Sutherland. (It's no accident that our examples of clear-articulators are both men and the non-articulator is a woman renowned for her elaborate feats of coloratura singing: the higher the voice and the more elaborate the ornamental flights, the less chance there is of understanding the words.) Some listeners don't care if words are fuzzy; but for others the sense that language is being enunciated with intent, passion and conviction is crucial even if they don't always recognize or understand what they hear. The latter position is powerfully articulated by the historian Paul Robinson, who points out that while the specific words of the libretto often seem of little moment among the pleasures opera can bring, it is still true that three hours of drama in which the characters sang 'la, la, la, la' would be intolerable.[1] In other words, it matters a great deal that verbal meaning is embedded somewhere in opera, even if the listener can't always hear exactly what the words are at the moment the singing takes place.

The debate about the role of words in the experience of opera has taken a further, specifically contemporary form in today's endless debates about super- or surtitles. When opera houses perform works in the original language, should they provide audiences with translations (displayed above the stage or in the back of the next row's seat) so that *all* the words can be clearly understood? Many think this is plainly an advance, giving us back the words' second domain, their specific meaning. But others remain passionately opposed, arguing that too detailed an exposure to the semantic aspect of words will take attention away from what is most important in the operatic experience. As the British critic Rodney Milnes put it, 'You go to opera to listen and to watch, not to read.' Before surtitles a neophyte was often expected to work: knowing something of both the story and the poetry beforehand was deemed a necessary preparation for taking pleasure in the operatic experience (as Milnes wrote, 'You read beforehand'). But Milnes represents an historically limited attitude. For one thing, reading the libretto *during* the performance was standard practice in many theatres from the seventeenth to the nineteenth centuries. As Samuel Sharp wrote from Naples in 1767, complaining of a lack of candles in the auditorium, 'dark as the boxes are, they would be still darker, if those who sit in them did not, at their expense, put up a couple of candles, without which it would be impossible to read the opera'.[2] This applied even more forcibly to the experience of foreign works: when Handel's Italian operas were performed in eighteenth-century London, dual-language libretti were published in conjunction with productions. What is more, reading the libretto was just one of the alternative activities available to the operagoer of the past; there was also gambling, chess-playing, eating, talking, ogling one's fellow attendees and, in the so-called *loges grillées* (shuttered boxes), quite possibly things a gentleman never mentions. In other words, an all-absorbing devotion to what was happening onstage – the attitude represented by 'you go to opera to listen and to watch' – was not the historical norm and, for much of opera's history, the experience of the event was not exclusively focused on the stage world, or indeed even on documents related to that world such as a libretto translation in a book.

This debate about understanding the words and the plot in opera can even take on ethical overtones. The notion that pleasure is based on or at least enhanced by knowledge (and hence a prior expenditure of labour) crops up again and again in opera's history. When Carl Maria von Weber's *Der Freischütz* was first performed in French, in Paris in the early 1840s, Richard Wagner thought the Parisians so incapable of uninformed delight in the work that he wrote an elaborate essay instructing them on the opera's background, plot and cultural significance.[3] In other words, the fact that the audience in Paris were hearing an opera in French was, to Wagner, no guarantee that they would understand the words, thus understand the story, thus understand the work's meaning and thus take delight in the whole package. Surtitles seem to short-circuit preparatory labour of the kind Wagner prescribed; they provide – in the form of verbal comprehensibility – easy access to the story, and hence a kind of instant cultural connection, a sense of belonging.

Perhaps, then, understanding specific words is not as critical as it might seem in the experience of opera. Opponents of surtitling claim that such understanding could even become a distortion, counterproductive of the theatrical absorption or attention to music and voice that are a specifically operatic ideal. They may have a point; but again operatic history will not always support them. In what follows, for example, we will have a great deal to say about absorption and detachment, but it will soon be clear that, historically, theatre audiences have been prone to these experiences in different ways at different times. Certain aspects of opera are now routinely – and uncritically – assumed to transfix the soul (usually the musical components), while others are assumed to produce disenchantment or distraction ('bad poetry', or an unpleasing performance). Hence, perhaps, the persistence in different periods of the idea of opera as a *Gesamtkunstwerk* – Wagner's famous word – meaning a total work of art, multi-media (words, music, scenery), the simultaneous experience of several registers and kinds of art-work.

We can examine the case further by looking at some examples of real violence to the integrity of the word–music bond. We're not talking here about opera performed in translation – even though the very practice goes some way to demonstrating that the words of the original libretto often count for little. There are, though, well-known instances of substitute aria texts being written for existing music, and succeeding indecently well in their transposed state. This shows that at least some operatic music is potentially mutable and non-specific in its content, and that music which would seem to correspond to an aria text about (let's say) a lost beloved – to express the emotion to perfection, to set the specific words with subtlety and art – may work just as well with a different aria text about something else. There are notorious examples in Rossini's operas, perhaps the most famous being his revision of his Italian *Mosè in Egitto* (1818) for the Paris stage, as *Moïse et Pharaon* (1827). In *Mosè* the soprano, Elcia, sings a cabaletta 'Tormenti! affanni! e smanie!' about the torments that afflict her wounded heart. But when Rossini recycled the piece for *Moïse* (admittedly with some changes) he gave it to another character, one joyfully celebrating a happy turn in the plot: the opening words are 'Qu'entends-je! ô douce ivresse!' (What do I hear! oh sweet bliss!). Those tempted to argue that this kind of switch would only be possible in Italian opera *d'un certain âge* need to explain how music that Wagner sketched in 1856–7, which ended up in *Siegfried* Act 3, was labelled in the sketch 'Act 3. Or Tristan', indicating that this particular music might do perfectly well for either piece.[4] But even substitute aria texts for identical music do not go as far as the most radical cases. In the early nineteenth century, the libretto of Mozart's German opera *Die Zauberflöte* (1791) went through an unpopular phase, being thought inane or ludicrous. The music, though, was standing the test of time: indeed, Mozart was already beginning to be canonized. The solution was to graft on to the music an entirely new libretto: new narrative, characters and words. Anton Wilhelm Florentin von Zuccalmaglio (1803–69), a literary polymath whose work included several volumes of poetry and folk song collections, wrote new libretti for several Mozart operas. In 1834, he turned *Die Zauberflöte* into *Der Kederich* (the 'Kederich' is a cliff high above the Rhine). The opera now takes place on the Rhine and involves water nixies, *Nibelungenlied* (The Song of the Nibelung) references and 'Rudhelm' (he used to be called Tamino), a Crusader back from the Holy Land. The Speaker (the Priest who enlightens Tamino in Act 1) becomes 'Sibo, Lord of Lorch', and Pamina, now renamed 'Garlina', is his daughter rather than the Queen of the Night's. The Queen becomes 'Lore von Lurlei', a sylph who floats around in white veils.[5] On the whole, the alternate libretto works very well. Are those who thought up or those who enjoyed this new opera to be condemned, or did they know something that we've now lost about how opera can communicate?

That question is interesting most of all because it invokes an historical era, now almost 200 years past, whose cultural attitudes retain the power to surprise us. We need to ask why we are so shocked: why our present fear of loss, our cultural pessimism, has turned operatic performance into an activity policed by a reverence for the work as a well nigh sacred object – a reverence in almost all cases not present at the time it was created. Addressing such issues may in turn encourage us to ask radical questions about the supposed fusion of, or perfect correspondence between, the components of opera (the *Gesamtkunstwerk* issue again), even in canonic masterpieces. It may ultimately suggest that historically informed performances of opera could include far more creative licence with the published text – far more irreverence – than anything seen nowadays. For example, almost all eighteenth-century opera composers spent time writing substitute arias for their own or other composers' operas: when a work was revived with new singers, what would be more natural than to throw out some of the old arias and write some new ones, better adapted to the skills of the new cast? But who would dare take such an attitude today; even – or, in the case of Mozart, especially – to operas written during that precise period?

The more specifically musical side of opera is also split in a way we will often return to during this book. On the one hand is what we might call the 'composer's music', what's notated in the score, a document that could be reproduced on this page or, more important, that could form the basis of a keyboard-and-voice performance in our living room. Before recordings, such living-room performances were the most common way people enjoyed opera when not in the theatre, which was most of the time. This score, this composer's music, is an essential blueprint, but it doesn't constitute what most people understand as, and love about, opera: it gives us something more like a reminder of the operatic experience. To get at the real thing, we need a lot more – the sound of a live orchestra, the view of the stage, and so on. Most important of all, what's missing is *voice*, the specific, irreplaceable quality of human vocal cords, membrane stretched across the larynx, vibrating in song. Voice is much harder to talk about than 'composer's music', partly because it's not reproducible in symbols and thus fixable on the page. But that mustn't deter us. We need to keep in mind that the human voice has almost always been at the centre of operatic experience. And so, while we'll be talking often – as historians should – about 'composer's music' in this book, we'll also keep reminding ourselves that the voices carrying the music are quite rightly essential to most people's operatic experience.

An example may help here. At the end of Act 3 of Verdi's *Il trovatore* (1853), Manrico's aria 'Di quella pira' features within it and then closes with high Cs from the tenor, notes quite out of keeping with the rest of the role, and ones long known to have had nothing to do with the composer. No score near to the time of the first performance has a trace of them. Despite these circumstances, those high Cs are the most famous utterances in the entire work. When the conductor Riccardo Muti, who is famed for his adherence to the exact musical text and nothing more, opened the 2000–2001 La Scala season with *Il trovatore*, he instructed the tenor on no account to sing those offending high Cs. The tenor trembled and obeyed. The *loggionisti*, opera fans who haunt the upper reaches of the theatre and who know every recording intimately, went mad with rage, cries of 'Vergogna' (shame) rained down on the stage.[6] Why was there so much passion? One waggish critic had earlier tried to defend the note, suggesting that if it wasn't by Verdi, then it was best thought of as a gift *to* Verdi from the Italian people. It would be easy to dismiss this as sentimentality, or even as wilful disregard for the composer's intentions. But the formulation could also say something basic about the operatic experience, suggesting that opera fans can grow to feel that they have a right to particular notes, or rather to the particular extremes of voice occasioned by those notes.

Precisely because it is an experience so difficult to put into words, the emotions aroused by hearing operatic voices can be enormously powerful and can lead to feelings of devotion that will seem irrational to others, those untouched by opera. It's important to bear this extreme devotion in mind, because the story of opera and how it communicates can otherwise seem inexplicable. Important aspects of the operatic experience may matter very little for those in the grip of voice-generated emotion. They may not understand the plot. They may not even understand the words (and, as mentioned a moment ago, at extreme vocal moments the words almost always disappear, as if they have been consumed). Yet the power of the human voice still holds them.

A potent exploration of this irrational devotion to voice occurs in a 1981 French-language film by Jean-Jacques Beineix called, simply, *Diva*. The film has a strange mixture of styles, part comedy, part thriller – it's famous to some primarily for its spectacular motorcycle chase. An excerpt near the start shows a young Parisian mail courier, Jules, attending the concert of an American opera star whose peculiarity is that she refuses to make recordings. His devotion to her voice is so profound that he smuggles a tape recorder into the concert hall. The star appears, and once she starts singing Jules enters a state of trance-like bliss, forgetting what he's doing: the voice washes over him. What's interesting from our point of view is how this act of singing is treated in the film. We hear an aria from a late nineteenth-century Italian opera ('Ebben? ne andrò lontana' from Alfredo Catalani's *La Wally*, 1892). The aria obviously has a text, but the film doesn't bother to subtitle the words; we have no idea what she's singing about, and may suspect that Jules is equally ignorant – that he doesn't care, and neither do we. What's more, this isn't an operatic performance: the aria is out of context, out of its plot environment, sung by someone not in costume, not pretending to play a part. None of this seems to matter. What captivates Jules is pure operatic singing, devoid of narrative and perhaps even of language. It's an extreme case, of course, the far end of the spectrum; but the scene serves as a reminder of how this enormously powerful aspect of opera's music can function, of what voice *doesn't* need in order to make its impact.

The word *impact* is justified. Typically, operatic heroines will be sung by a high soprano voice. The singer may be required to make herself heard above an orchestra of up to 100 players, including (in the nineteenth century and beyond) many instruments that have steadily evolved with a view to producing an increased volume of sound, not least a formidable phalanx of newly invented, acoustically aggressive brass. Microphones and discreet amplification are sometimes used, but this is almost always regarded as shameful, a crutch that real opera singers would never need. So the singer, unaided, may have to make herself heard in all corners of an auditorium seating more than 3000 people – that is, in a cavernous place where the back balcony is many, many metres from the stage. At the Metropolitan Opera in New York, the seats farthest from the stage are about 150ft away, a distance one expert on theatrical acoustics has called 'staggering'.[7]

Admittedly, since the nineteenth century the orchestra has tended to play in a sunken area in front of (and partly underneath) the stage, a position that serves to dull the sound somewhat. But the presence of this 'pit', and the economic need to cram more and more seats into modern theatres, has also meant that the stage now rarely comes out into the auditorium, as it typically did in earlier times. The singer thus has to project from a recessed space whose proscenium arch tends implacably to block the sound. Depending on theatre size, that feat of projection can approach the miraculous.

When a new Metropolitan Opera house opened in New York in 1883, the architectural critic for the *New York Times* took the occasion to marvel at its 'vast auditorium' and to compare the sizes of contemporary opera houses worldwide, giving us a snapshot of the building's dimensions alongside those of its biggest European relatives in the late nineteenth century.[8] As the *Times* reported, the auditorium at Covent Garden was 78ft deep and 62ft wide; at the 'new' Paris Opera House (this meant the Palais Garnier on the Place de l'Opéra), it was 90 by 67ft. The auditorium at the 1883 Met was described as 95 by 89ft. At Munich (the Nationaltheater, destroyed in 1943 and reconstructed in the early 1960s) the auditorium space was smaller, 68 by 61ft; at Vienna the proportions were (and are) 83 by 67ft. What stands out at the 1883 Met is also the *height* of the auditorium. At 82ft, it was 15–20ft higher than any other mentioned, with the exception of San Carlo in Naples, a notorious barn. This height makes for an increase in capacity and a larger distance from the stage in the highest regions: on the hypotenuse of the triangle, about 100ft away for Covent Garden, as opposed to about 125ft at the 1883 Met. Covent Garden seats a little over 2000; the 1883 Met seated about 3000. These differences in size will of course have acoustic consequences, no matter how the interior might be sculpted. What is more they have perceptual consequences for one's experience of the event: as near and overwhelming, or as faraway and imbued with (perhaps magical) distance.

The new Metropolitan Opera, which opened in 1966, is bigger still, although its seating capacity at about 3800 is less than that of the Chicago Lyric Opera, which can hold 4300. But things can, it seems, still be extremely loud, even far away from the stage. In December

2006, the Metropolitan put on special performances of Mozart's *Die Zauberflöte* in an English-language abridged version for young people. When the *New York Times* music critic Anthony Tommasini interviewed these junior listeners about their reactions, he was told repeatedly that the voices were loud, unpleasantly so.[9] Struck by such comments from an audience accustomed to powerful stage amplifiers and high-volume headphones, he reasoned that the perception of loudness wasn't a matter of decibels per se but of raw *human* decibels: of loudness without crutches; of a sense of what the sound must be like close to. The physiology of this feat of human decibels is worth pausing over. The singer uses her diaphragm to draw air into the lungs and then push it out, projecting her voice (produced by the larynx) into various resonating chambers in the skull. At the same time, she uses her throat muscles, jaw, lips and tongue to vary the sound, which then radiates out through the mouth and nose. This process is common to the production of all human vocal sound; but people who sing opera generate it on an unparalleled scale, letting loose huge acoustic forces; if they turn their voices on you at close range, you have to retreat and cover your ears. There are very few people who have the basic bodily equipment – the sheer muscular strength and flexibility – to do this; there are fewer still who succeed in mastering such tasks well enough to give others musical pleasure.

It's a commonplace that those who can are by no means always able to impersonate an operatic heroine convincingly from a visual point of view. They may, for example, be large in all directions. Indeed, another common caricature of opera (one that goes back long into its history) is of a grotesque mismatch between the singer and the physical image intended dramatically. The surprising thing is that such mismatches don't seem to matter very much; or at least they haven't for large stretches of operatic history, even at the times when the caricatures were in circulation. Opera is the one spectacle – the one 'something you look at' – in which conventional physical attractiveness counts for relatively little. The comparison with theatre or film is obvious; and it's also a different story in ballet, which is as artificial as opera in other ways, but in which an unusually tall female dancer, or an unusually short male one, would not be tolerated. Opera alone can trade in imperfect faces and unfashionable forms, such offences against our visual expectations being overlooked or even celebrated in the roar of singing. Of course, there have been fluctuations in tolerance. It may be that our contemporary culture, so dominated by the visual, and in which a particular image of physical perfection is so obsessively valued, is among the most intolerant of the 'wrong' bodily shapes. But it's still a matter of degree. Today's opera houses are places where the look of a character is rarely dominant. In that sense, opera may provide a space in which we can appreciate an alternate and valuable truth.

TELLING THE STORY, THE REALITY ISSUE

We wrote at the start of this chapter that opera was non-realistic. This is as much true of its narrative capabilities as of its performers. There is, for example, often a lack of verisimilitude even within the rational element of the action, the part taken directly from a literary source (very often a pre-existing play). Because characters spend their time singing, they get through relatively few words, so plots and sentiments have to be condensed: the source text is sometimes so compressed that it seems ridiculous when removed from its operatic environment. A good question for an opera buffs' party game might be: narrate the plot of Verdi's *La forza del destino* (first version in 1862; Verdi then revised it in 1869) in one coherent sentence. Denis Forman's attempt in *The Good Opera Guide* goes like this: it's 'the one where a marquis is killed by an exploding pistol and his daughter in monk's costume finds her lover has murdered her brother just outside the front door of her cave'.[10] Admittedly, this passes over large swathes in the middle (most of the opera, in fact). It also omits the fact that the daughter dies too, murdered by her brother just before he expires; and that, in the first version, the lover responds to all this carnage by calling down a curse of mankind and throwing himself off a nearby precipice. But the missing bits aren't really essential. *La forza del destino* is what Verdi called 'an opera of ideas',[11] one in which crowd-pleasing musical numbers are less important than impressive human subjects and abstract themes such as 'fate' (the *destino* of the title). What emerged was close to a sprawling historical novel put on stage, with all sorts of extravagant gestures that lead nowhere. It's an extreme case of narrative wildness, but by no means the most improbable. Indeed, among the essentials of an operatic drama seem to be exaggerated coincidence, obscure motivations and (if it's tragic) multiple deaths. If you take away the music, the plots are ripe for parody or kitsch; and the poetic text is usually second-class, formulaic at best. Thus denuded, there's very little left to explain why opera is worth loving, a sentiment that forms the basis for a famous comic animated film by Kim Thompson, *All the Great Operas in Ten Minutes* (1992). The essence of Wagner's epic, *Der Ring des Nibelungen* (1876), which lasts around sixteen hours in performance over four nights, is covered in less than two minutes. Here are just the first two operas:

> The Ring of the Nibelungs is actually more of a miniseries 'cos it's four full operas. These girls in a river have this gold and a dwarf steals it and makes a ring from it. The head guy Wotan gets the gold back but there's a death curse on the ring and these two giants get the gold and one kills the other and then turns into a dragon to guard it. Wotan wants the ring so he decides that his illegitimate human son Siegmund will get it for him. Siegmund meanwhile falls in love with his long-lost sister Sieglinde. He picks a fight with her husband so Wotan gets Brünnhilde to protect him, then changes his mind and orders her to kill Siegmund instead, but she doesn't want to so Wotan gets Sieglinde's husband to kill him and then Wotan kills the husband too just for the hell of it. He punishes Brünnhilde by putting her to sleep on a mountain in a ring of fire.

At the end of the film, the narrator says: 'That's it. That's opera. Nothing else you need to know. Just a lot of people in costumes falling in love and dying. Yup, that's pretty much it. Oh, except for the music. There's singing too? See, they don't actually say anything, so they sing everything. Lots of music. Yup. Some of it's kind of nice, too.'

But before we laugh and move on, we should acknowledge that there's a problem here. All lovers of opera will agree that the story, the narrative element, can often be ludicrous; but it's also essential. We can't seem to live comfortably with it; but we can't live without it. Narrative and opera are, in other words, locked together in an uneasy embrace. Neither wants divorce, but untroubled cohabitation is almost always out of the question. In this sense, the narrative dimension is rather like the verbal dimension as a whole. It's another example of the fact that opera can make us forget: forget that we don't understand the language being sung; forget the size of the singer, and the fact that he's impersonating an ardent and athletic young troubadour although patently nearer sixty-two than twenty-six; forget the fact we have only a shaky idea of what on earth is happening on stage. Opera communicates in strange, unpredictable ways; it appeals to something beyond the narrow cognitive dimension.

All of which brings us to what is probably *the* central improbability about opera: the fact that most of the characters sing most of the time. We have to be careful not to exaggerate here: after all, drama that is sung or chanted is probably more the rule than the exception throughout world history. But the brand of sung drama that emerged in Western Europe around 1600 was nevertheless a peculiarly dense and radical one, and it caused consternation from the very start. These debates about opera, although often intense, never managed to curb opera's excesses, or at least not for long. Pretty soon opera was too widespread for philosophical scruples to prevail. Pretty soon everyone could be impersonated on the operatic stage: gods and coachmen, pirates and vestal virgins all sang away, happily accepted or at least tolerated. Yet elements of unease about singing recur throughout opera's history. This discomfort accounts for the fact that operatic characters throughout history – starting with Orpheus, one of the first – have readily embraced moments that would have been sung even in a spoken drama or, if it's possible to imagine, in real life. Opera is bestrewn with serenades to the distant beloved and with drinking songs shared by confederates in crime or love; any tenor or baritone worth his fee will know how to enter the stage winningly with guitar in hand. The fact that these moments are operatic commonplaces is significant, suggesting that we all need reality checks – times during which we can relax our (willing) suspension of disbelief, for an instant or two ceasing to maintain the fiction of all these characters singing at each other. But such moments of pause shouldn't deflect us from confronting what, in the end, opera asks us to believe.

We might make an imaginative leap and think for a moment about what it would be like to inhabit a world that is operatic; a world in which everyday life takes place and ordinary time passes, but in which everything – every action, every thought, every utterance – is geared to never-ending music. It's similar to the kind of thought-experiment explored in Peter Weir's film *The Truman Show* (1998), in which Jim Carrey gradually becomes aware that his entire life is being played out for the benefit of a TV reality-show. How would we figure in another kind of man-made fantasy, one in which everything surrounding us was opera?

Think of the metaphysical questions that this state-of-opera would raise. First, and most important: who is making the music? Do we know we are singing, that we are constantly swimming in musical sound? Or do we maintain the illusion that the stage world is really quite ordinary and that we hear music in some magical way? When the music seems omniscient or prescient, whose mind is telling us its secrets? Such speculations may seem fanciful, or even idle; but pondering their significance turns out to be important to our understanding of opera. Filmmakers have constantly made artistic capital from playing with audience expectations about the origins of sound in film: does it spring from the world of the characters or is it a commentary on that world? Can our attitude to the narrative be made more interestingly complex if these two sources are sometimes confused? In just the same way, opera composers (and not just those of the recent past) have played with the idea of a mutable musical source, of exploring and enriching the operatic experience by making us ponder that basic question: *where does the music come from?*

Thinking about these issues also stresses the existence of the 'marvellous' in opera: the fact that the whole business is in so many ways fundamentally unrealistic, and can't be presented as a sensible model for leading one's life or understanding human behaviour. No one conducts her life in song and continuously hears fabulous music around her. This is a critical point, since this basic lack of verisimilitude, while it didn't end up restricting opera to certain exceptional character types (gods or elves or water-nymphs), in broad ways determined opera's liking for narrative extremes: moments of extraordinary passion and impossible dilemma; magic and the irrational; world-historical events. Spoken theatre can also be extreme in its plot material, populated by ghosts and improbable turns of fate. But it can never match the central unrealism of opera, the fact of continual singing. And this foundational trait has tended to guarantee that opera libretti almost never deal with the *ordinary*, while spoken theatre can thrive on it. Even when libretti (briefly) marched under the banner of 'realism' in the nineteenth century, their reality was an immensely charged affair. Modernist works like Ernst Krenek's *Jonny spielt auf* (1927) or Francis Poulenc's *La*

Voix humaine (1959) don't contradict this, instead playing against opera's historical taste for the extraordinary by including scenes of self-conscious banality, everyday life made into art: *La Voix humaine*, after all, stages nothing more than a telephone call. The first recitative in Stravinsky's *The Rake's Progress* (1951) tries something similar. It begins with the (sung) words 'Anne, my dear, your advice is needed in the kitchen', a sentence that is surely a deliberate ploy to estrange us, to tell us that *The Rake* will be a very knowing opera. A different case is Berg's *Lulu* (1937), where the petty rituals of the high bourgeois co-exist in a dissociated fugue with acts of murder and betrayal. In *Lulu*, as in other examples of German modernism, the impulse to put mundane events on stage was aligned during the Weimar era (1918–33) with a much-theorized and politicized aesthetic populism: with the idea that art composers should produce *Gebrauchsmusik*, music for everyday use, or *Zeitopern*, operas on contemporary, topical themes.

But these are exceptions. For most of its history opera has disdained ordinary events and actions; or, as *Lulu* did famously, it has treated them as a surreal counterpoint to a more dramatic and violent hyper-existence. Hardly any operatic character makes a cup of tea, or reads the newspaper, or puts on his socks; those who did so would be embedded in a comic reversal of normality or would have been deliberately trivialized. In Wagner's *Ring*, the dwarf Mime is made ludicrous when he cooks a good breakfast for the imperious young hero Siegfried, the implication being that cooks, like newspaper-readers, tea-drinkers and sock-wearers, are by their ordinariness excluded from the heights of true passion or mythic significance. The irony in *Siegfried* (hardly intended by Wagner) is that Siegfried's own efforts to re-forge his father Siegmund's magical sword, accompanied as they are by much filing, pouring, stoking of fires and measuring of temperatures, can in performance easily slide into a parody of domesticity: breakfast-making while high on excess testosterone.

Nowhere is opera's affinity for the unreal more obvious than in its ways and means of manipulating time. That high-C-laden Act 3 aria for Manrico in *Il trovatore* again provides a classic instance. Manrico is about to marry his beloved Leonora when a messenger enters to inform him that his mother has been captured by a deadly enemy and is about to be burnt at the stake. He calls his companions in arms together and draws his sword; they must go to rescue her *immediately*. But then, instead of rushing off, Manrico faces the audience and sings two (quite long) verses of the cabaletta 'Di quella pira', prolonged high Cs and elaborate cadential writing for the chorus not excluded. Act 2 of Gilbert and Sullivan's *The Pirates of Penzance* (1880), which like all their operettas uses Italian serious opera as the primary butt for its satire, has an apt parody. A small regiment of police gears up for battle in the chorus 'When the foeman bares his steel', a number that ends with endless repetitions of 'Yes forward on the foe, yes forward on the foe'. The major-general steps out of the opera to comment caustically: 'Yes, but you *don't* go'.

Related but even more spectacular examples of opera's cavalier way with the realistic often occur when its major characters are constrained to die onstage. A classic example here is the last scene of Verdi's *La traviata* (1853), in which the courtesan Violetta succumbs to tuberculosis. In the plot, the character's lungs have been destroyed; but operatic Violetta sings on without evident trouble, producing well-supported, beautiful sound. A soprano who dared to make Violetta's affliction realistic by croaking and coughing would have left opera behind. Mortally wounded people who nevertheless sing on and on mellifluously are inhabitants of opera in its normal mode; we accept the fantasy without resistance; indeed, it is reality that would be shocking. Violetta's case shows that opera involves perpetual mismatches between assumptions about real-world plausibility based on human characters, and demands that musical performance will make on both singers and audiences.

We can take this further. The idea that opera puts a dying, literary Violetta comfortably aside in favour of a flourishing, powerful operatic Violetta brings us to a critical distinction, one that will reappear several times in this book: the difference between the character as she exists in words, what we could call the *plot-character*, and the corresponding character that exists in music, the *voice-character*.

Plot-character could, for instance, be Wolfram von Eschenbach in Wagner's *Tannhäuser* (1845), a tedious and uninteresting suitor who preaches chaste devotion. In Wagner's libretto, he's a sidekick and foil to Tannhäuser (tenor), the erotically sophisticated anti-hero whom the heroine cannot resist. But as voice-character Wolfram (baritone) is not simply parallel or equivalent; he is constructed by means of an amalgam of the music assigned to the plot-character and the feats of performance that music elicits from the singer. In the Act 2 singing contest between Tannhäuser and Wolfram, there's an odd moment during Wolfram's decorous serenade. Praising the grandeur of the scene, he sings 'my gaze grows drunk from seeing' to an exotic harmonic progression accompanying a long lyric fall in the baritone's melody. This is the only truly sensual passage in the entire song contest, outdoing anything by Tannhäuser. It marks the appearance of a voice-character, an alternative Wolfram with attributes beyond, even at odds with, the plot-character. The same contrast appears in Wolfram's famous 'Evening Star' aria in Act 3. The words are studiously poetic, about a character with a good soul, but the sensuality elicited from the voice tells another story entirely. Perhaps we should think of the strange verbal turn in Wolfram's Act 2 serenade – the line about growing intoxicated through sensation – as a slip in the plot-character's language, a place where the voice-character, for an instant, works his way into words.

One could quite rightly argue that this same distinction between plot-character and voice-character also occurs in spoken drama; anyone who has attended a Shakespeare soliloquy or a Hugolian tirade will know that the speaker in question is engaging a different register at these points. But in opera the distinction is so much more extreme, so much more *spectacular*. The Manrico who must rush off to rescue his mother is plot-Manrico; the one who remains centre-stage singing high Cs is voice-Manrico. Plot-Violetta is dying of tuberculosis and desperately fights for breath; voice-Violetta sings robustly, lamenting but also, in a sense, *celebrating* in song her imminent death. And the difference emphasizes once again that the tension between representations of human reality amid omnipresent music is a basic characteristic of opera. Concerns about verisimilitude are behind opera's general tendency for libretti with mythic or divine characters, or ones that invoke magic or emotional overload or other extremes: the theory is that music belongs or is somehow more explicable in such cases. In the end, though, verisimilitude gets discarded no matter what. In the end, opera can't ever be anything other than unreal.

POPULARITY AND CONVENTION

As mentioned already, opera has for most of its history seemed strange and exotic to most of its audience. It is important to realize that this was the case even in Italy, which was the home of opera, and where for this reason it is sometimes thought to be, or at least to have been, a natural form of expression. And although its financial basis has gradually broadened – from the court-sponsored private entertainments of the seventeenth century, to the (almost) free capitalist enterprises of the nineteenth century, to the often precarious state- or corporate-funded institutions of the present – opera in its primary, theatrical form has typically been the province of elite groups, only becoming more broadly popular when technologies of various kinds allowed it to spread from the opera house into the streets and into people's homes. It is arguably only in the last thirty or so years, the era of the Three Tenors all singing 'O sole mio' together on the eve of a soccer World Cup, that opera has become popular in the modern sense, and it's probably more accurate to say that, in this case, particles of opera have now become iconic (if also ironic) objects in mass culture.

In Hollywood, for example, opera-going has often stood for Italianness and emotional excitability or prone-ness, as in *Moonstruck* (1987), where Ronny Cammareri (Nicolas Cage) wins the love of fellow working-class Italian-American Loretta Castorini (Cher) by taking her to see Puccini's *La bohème*. In some films, opera houses become places where different classes and characters can meet as if in a goldfish bowl, pursuing their many agendas and pleasures. In Billy Wilder's *Love in the Afternoon* (1957) the major characters show up for a performance of *Tristan und Isolde* at the Paris Opéra: spoiled playboy Gary Cooper, dragged along by a socialite friend, clowns around with his programme book; earnest composition students from the Conservatoire conduct along with the Prelude while sneering at the common audience; only Audrey Hepburn, terribly in love, seems wholly lost in a sensual experience – but it's less *Tristan* than Gary Cooper who is doing the business (see Figure 2). The irony is that no one is represented as properly or truly moved by the opera itself, something hardly unexpected given Wilder's proclaimed disdain for Wagner.

Love in the Afternoon also shows how popular culture can make opera a sign for upper-class privilege. The opening scene of Martin Scorsese's *The Age of Innocence* (1993) centres on a performance of Gounod's *Faust* at the old Met in New York. This establishes a milieu for the plot, but with a camera that swoops drunkenly and supernaturally everywhere around the house: the upper classes, he tells us, get derailed by passions, just like everyone else. In the Marx Brothers' *A Night at the Opera* (1935), the running joke is how a stiff, old-money audience can be outraged by low-life antics from the brothers. At one point the latter infiltrate the pit, switch the orchestra's parts and cause the players (ostensibly against their will, of course) to strike up with 'Take me out to the ball game'; the clash of high and low culture couldn't be clearer. A more insidiously sentimental example comes in Garry Marshall's film *Pretty Woman* (1990), in which Julia Roberts plays a prostitute picked up by Richard Gere (a 'handsome corporate mogul' according to the publicity flier) on Hollywood Boulevard, and is then given the Cinderella treatment. During their week-long affair Gere flies Roberts (private jet) up the coast to the San Francisco opera, where she makes all kinds of gaffes among fan-fluttering socialites, but eventually shows that she is more open than them, more sensitive to what she sees on stage (the opera in question is, of course, *La traviata*).

These scenes may also reinforce a contradiction in the way we approach opera today. On the one hand is its age-old identification with aristocracy, ostentatious wealth and exclusivity. Running parallel, though, is a sense that opera can appeal directly to our emotions. Both attitudes are given voice in *A Night at the Opera*: socialites go to the opera as a duty, and are outraged when decorum is assailed. But the movie's hero and heroine – an underdog tenor and soprano helped by the brothers into their starring roles – are shown singing triumphantly in the final reel of the film, with immense joy and glorious smiles (and this even though it's the 'Miserere' scene from *Il trovatore*). They are, quite properly, moved by opera: not by a silly operatic plot but by singing itself. This scene of underdogs and comic outsiders, transformed by singing, shows opera as having a powerful effect on people who are different in some way – on Julia Roberts's character (who is stubbornly herself no matter what the opulence of the surroundings, and who sings Prince in the bath), or on large Italians with white handkerchiefs – people who have declared their diversity, their distance from the everyday, emotionally constricted life we think we now lead.

For at least its first 250 years, the opera industry (just like the film industry today) was sustained by a steady stream of new works. There was no repertory to speak of, no body of familiar, endlessly repeated works such as we find in every opera house today. Because of this, operas (like films) needed to make their impact immediately. One way they did this was through using a set of conventions: working practices common from opera to opera, readily understood and appreciated. And so emerged different operatic types, usually dictated by language and register (Italian *opera seria* or *opera buffa*, French *grand opéra* or *opéra comique*, German *Singspiel* or *romantische Oper*), each with its own peculiarities, its own codes of communication.

More basically still, though, operatic character types gradually evolved into voice types, the register and weight of the voice belonging to a particular character who could then pass from opera to opera, and eventually into operetta and musical theatre. A repertoire of operatic characters emerged: the female lead (soprano), the woman of advanced age or little virtue or touched by sorcery (mezzo-soprano or contralto), the heroic male lead (in the eighteenth century usually castrato, after that tenor), the villain or father or loyal-unto-death companion (baritone), the grandfather or priest or other symbol of patriarchal authority (bass). Although all these types were liable to variation (there have been soprano priests, but not many), it is often important to know what was conventional, in particular to appreciate how turning convention on its head is itself a form of drama. One instance of voice cast against character type is Mephistopheles (the devil in the Faust legend: he of the pact signed in blood, a favourite operatic subject). Most Mephistopheles characters of the nineteenth century (there are several) are basses, but in Busoni's *Doktor Faust* (1925) Mephistopheles is a tenor; he is heard first calling Faust's name from offstage, and he does so on a high A♮ – in a whisper. It is knowledge of the going-against-type that makes the effect so striking.

The question arises whether these choices of voice type are the product of nature or convention. Some (the bass authority figure) might be thought natural – both men and women are encouraged to lower their voices when they want to be deemed especially worthy of attention and respect – and it's probably significant that this character/voice type has been around throughout the operatic centuries. For the most part, though, history suggests that simple convention is at work. For example, in early eighteenth-century serious opera (so-called *opera seria*), almost all characters, male or female, sang in high voices. It was quite common for male roles to be sung by females, or by castrated males whose voices remained ever high. There are various explanations for the demise of the castrato and the rise of the heroic tenor in the nineteenth century, and some plausibly invoke changes in ideas about human subjectivity (about what we think makes us who we are). But it's likely that even tenor heroes were never experienced as normal. The notion of aberration, of opera's strangeness, is always there.

Conventions track deep into opera. Through most of its long history (until at least the mid nineteenth century), composers tended to write several operas each year. They did so out of financial necessity. Works were rarely revived (and, if they were, were generally unprotected by copyright), and it was only by writing new works that composers could earn a living from their art. The consequent need for instant communication with an audience tended to make both libretto and music formulaic. The word 'formulaic' now sounds pejorative: in our culturally pessimistic state, we tend to think that only the startlingly original can be artistically worthy. We shouldn't forget, though, that formulas can be a source of pleasure, not (as usual these days) from knowing a piece backwards and forwards through recordings, but from harbouring expectations about how operas usually work. Expectations can give comfort and furnish ready understanding, and can also be productive of a *frisson* when something happens against type, when a convention is creatively manipulated, as in Busoni's upsetting of voice-type associations.

Because the structural formulas of opera are important, we should introduce some of the basic ones immediately. They didn't emerge simultaneously, and some got much weaker in the nineteenth century. But, for all that, they have been surprisingly long-lived and malleable, some of them adapting to radical changes elsewhere in verbal and musical language. The two most basic terms involve both words and music: 'recitative' versus 'aria' or 'number'. These distinguish between two kinds of poetry in the libretto and two kinds of music that sets that poetry. The dualism existed from opera's beginnings, wasn't broken down until the mid nineteenth century, and still to some extent exists in operas written today. A brief scene from the first act of Mozart's *Don Giovanni* (1787) offers an illustration of the two at work. The scene involves the lecherous aristocrat Don Giovanni (baritone) and his servant Leporello (bass). The libretto starts with dialogue. Leporello is becoming exasperated with the various risky stratagems he is obliged to carry out in his master's name:

LEPORELLO
Io deggio ad ogni patto
Per sempre abbandonar questo bel matto!
Eccolo qui: guardate
Con qual indifferenza se ne viene!

DON GIOVANNI
Oh, Leporello mio! va tutto bene.

LEPORELLO
Don Giovannino mio! va tutto male!

[LEPORELLO: Whatever happens, I must / abandon for ever this fine madman! / Here he is: look / at the nonchalance with which he comes and goes! DON GIOVANNI: Oh, my Leporello! everything's going well. LEPORELLO: My dear little Don Giovanni! everything's going badly!]

This is intended as a typical passage of recitative. It's written in the Italian equivalent of blank verse (so-called *versi sciolti*), a free mixture of seven- and eleven-syllable lines, with only a few, sporadic rhymes, and with no fixed accents within the lines. Meant to approximate ordinary speech rhythms, it's also quite ordinary in the lexicon it uses, with few poetic words or conceits. This conversation continues for some time, as Don Giovanni and Leporello prepare for a banquet that night in which Don Giovanni will (he hopes) be able to have his wicked way with a peasant girl called Zerlina. He ends the recitative in jubilant mood and then launches into an aria, 'Fin ch'han dal vino' ('So long as there's wine'). This number is often called 'the champagne aria', but although wine is mentioned in the very first line, Don Giovanni is overwhelmingly concerned with the women who will attend the banquet. In a wild fantasy, he imagines how he will vary the dances so that they succeed each other chaotically; in the mêlée thus created he will, he hopes, add 'at least ten' to his already considerable list of conquests. Here are the last five lines of recitative and then, indented, the aria text:

DON GIOVANNI
Bravo, bravo, arcibravo!
L'affar non può andar meglio. Incominciasti,
io saprò terminar. Troppo mi premono
queste contadinotte;
le voglio divertir finché vien notte.

Finch'han dal vino
Calda la testa
Una gran festa
Fa preparar.
Se trovi in piazza
Qualche ragazza,
Teco ancor quella
Cerca menar.
Senza alcun ordine
La danza sia;
Chi 'l minuetto,
Chi la follia,
Chi l'alemanna
Farai ballar.
Ed io fra tanto
Dall'altro canto
Con questa, e quella
Vo' amoreggiar.
Ah! la mia lista
Doman mattina
D'una decina
Devi aumentar!
(They leave.)

[DON GIOVANNI: Bravo, bravo, bravissimo! / This business couldn't go better. You begin it, / and I'll finish it off. These peasant girls / urge me on too much. / I want to enjoy them as night falls. /

> While they have their heads / warm with wine / you must prepare / a grand party. / If you find around the place / any girls, / try to get them / to come along with you. / The dances should be / without any order; / one a minuet, / one a *follia*, / one an allemande / I'll make dance. / And in the meantime, / on the side / I'll make love / to this one and that one. / Ah! By tomorrow morning / my list / must be longer / by at least ten!]

It's easy to see that the start of the aria is marked by a change in the poetry. Now all the lines are of equal length and have a common stress; there is also a fixed rhyme scheme outlining a four-line verse structure; in other words, the poetic register has made a decisive appearance.

These are the most elementary differences between 'recitative' and 'aria' as we see them from the libretto; but embedded within such differences are important distinctions having to do with content. The most basic is that recitative is the place for narrative, informal dialogue, stage action: moments in which the plot moves forward. The aria, on the other hand, is a static mode. It is fundamentally about contemplation, and through contemplation the communication of mood to the audience; it is what the poets call 'musing'. In this aria, as in most others, nothing external, nothing plot-related happens; what the aria does instead is characterize Don Giovanni, making us aware of his desire to mix dances 'without any order', to create chaos, which is the medium in which he, an anarchic force, can flourish. In some sense, then, arias stop time – they let nothing else happen while they unfold, allowing us to sample a kind of internal time, one in which the character's mind reveals itself. And what is said here about arias goes equally for all the contemplative parts of the opera: the duets, trios and bigger ensembles. Admittedly, one of the great departures of nineteenth-century opera is that all these fixed forms may be liable to injections of outside action; but even then there remain frequent occasions during which time seems to be arrested. The presence of singing of a particular kind will brook no competition. Singing that would not take place in the fictional world still has the capacity to exclude other events from that world.

The musical distinctions between recitative, on the one hand, and arias as well as 'numbers' for more than one voice, on the other, are obvious and immediately audible. In the simplest kinds of recitative, found mostly in the late seventeenth and eighteenth centuries, the vocal line is 'recited', usually with great rapidity, accompanied or punctuated by a simple succession of chords on what is often called the 'continuo': usually a harpsichord, with its bass strengthened by a lower string instrument, usually a cello. Although such simple recitative (sometimes called by its Italian name, *secco recitativo*) tends to be notated in a fixed time signature, it is typically performed very freely, with no sense of a regular beat. The melodic lines are rudimentary, there are many repeated notes; the pitches tend to follow the intonations of speech. In many ways this 'recitative' is nearer speech than song, and given the more studied, musical way in which actors of past centuries declaimed speeches in a spoken drama, it may have seemed even less like music when it was first performed. The aria is very different. It is dominated by musical expression, with obvious (and usually recurring) musical ideas, with the orchestra to introduce and accompany, and with the voice singing elaborate melody. The regular rhythms of the poetry create (almost demand) regular rhythms in the music. Unless the aria is very short, it will also have an internal form of its own: the most common was a simple ternary form (schematically ABA). In eighteenth-century opera these ternary forms crystallized into what were called 'da capo' arias because they returned to the initial section after a period of musical digression or contrast; in later centuries the forms typically became more complex.

What is also obvious is a significant difference between recitative and aria in terms of the way words are treated. In the recitative, words are consumed at a great rate and hardly ever recur. In the aria, on the other hand, fragments of text are often repeated (in this example from *Don Giovanni*, almost obsessively). As we would expect, the music then responds to the sense of the words in an individual way. Don Giovanni's manic fantasy comes in the form of relentlessly driven music, an aria in which there are hardly pauses for breath. However, particularly after the first exposition of the musical material, words are repeated ad infinitum to fill out the demands of musical elaboration and then closure. In this, and in very many arias, the literary text melts away: it partly or even completely loses its meaning. Music speaks beyond the text, whose meaning has been drastically diminished.

Of course, there are many more points one could make about Don Giovanni's 'champagne' aria. In one sense (and like almost all arias), it is there partly to show off the voice, and individual singers will often add improvisations of their own: extra high notes, ornaments, frenzied laughter at the end. But even in the printed score the breakup of the text, the repetitions, the way melodic fragments obsessively return, seem excessive by any rhetorical measure. Perhaps what we're hearing is a musical–linguistic symbol for the whirling confusion Don Giovanni wants to create. There may also be a sense in which the character is *caught up* in this whirl of action, rather than (as he thinks) controlling it – a sense in which Don Giovanni is at the mercy of these obsessive musical rhythms. It's a very rare singer who doesn't, by the end of the aria, sound breathless and almost incoherent, as if the music is now driving *him*. If we know the rest of Mozart's opera, know the way in which Don Giovanni finally meets his fate, the sense of lost control that is created by the music – and its performance – is an acoustic harbinger of the protagonist's end.

EXPRESSION AND BOREDOM

The aria and its recitative were the basic building blocks out of which opera was constructed for much of its history. From the seventeenth century onwards, in Italy and elsewhere, recitative carried action and narrative, and was used overwhelmingly for conversations between characters. Recitative had a generally poor reputation as music; one contemporary of Mozart lamented the necessity of 'the recitative, which is both dull-sounding and neglected by composers and singers alike, and which no one thinks of listening to any longer. In truth its insipidity and monotony are insufferable.'[12] Once vernacular opera (*Singspiel*) began to develop in Germany in the earlier years of the eighteenth century, spoken dialogue served the analogous purpose. But operatic music involves so much more than just a distinction between various kinds of expression, between recitative and aria or other set number. Here we return to an aspect of opera that is harder to pin down and yet central to the experience: what, exactly, does music do when it becomes an aura around or beyond the action, beyond the emotions represented by the libretto, characters and situations? How might music embody the biggest things, such as an atmosphere or a worldview; how does it give life to the particular fictional world up there on the stage? These questions will have almost as many answers as there are operas; and for the best operas each answer will be elaborate.

One place to make a very small response to the most elementary version of the question is with the notion of musical signs: musical ideas that are understood within a particular opera, or even widely within a particular culture, as standing for or giving expression to an idea. Opera relies on small signs to make small points, and knowing how these work helps extrapolation to the bigger issues. One of the most familiar musical signs in Western popular culture comes from an opera: the Wedding March from Act 3 of Wagner's *Lohengrin* (1848) – known nowadays to countless millions as 'Here Comes the Bride'. In *Lohengrin* the march is played as an accompaniment to Lohengrin and Elsa's wedding, with the chorus singing along. In Victorian England, the march – sober, andante and optimistic – was quickly adopted as the processional of choice at middle-class weddings; the more ecstatic march from Mendelssohn's incidental music to *Ein Sommernachtstraum* (A Midsummer Night's Dream) became the traditional recessional. The fact that Lohengrin and Elsa's marriage turns out to be one of opera's great romantic disasters is conveniently placed to one side.

The melody from *Lohengrin*, we might say, symbolizes a wedding ceremony in our minds. Imagine for a moment, though, that something happens to that melody, something that never actually happens in Wagner's opera. Imagine that the melody is changed to the minor mode, is punctuated by solemn drumbeats, and is enwrapped in a dense chromatic accompaniment. Now we are on our guard: predictions for this marriage become quite a bit more pessimistic. There is a complicated social and musical system at work here. The melody itself is a sign that is reliant on very specific terms – music equals wedding. But the shift from major to minor – from the mode that suggests joy, optimism, contentment and triumph to the one that suggests gloom and tragedy – has changed our understanding of the music, and has conveyed, in an instant, a newly complicated message. What is important, though, is that this message is for our ears only: it is surplus to what is happening in the church, or on stage, and it is surplus to what is being said by any of the characters on stage. This very procedure was used by early accompanists in silent cinema, in full realization that a fundamentally operatic trick could now be used to say something, in music, to a cinema audience. As one such musician reported, 'Wagner's and Mendelssohn's Wedding Marches were used . . . for fights between husbands and wives, and divorce scenes: we just had them played out of tune, a treatment known in the profession as "souring up the aisle".'[13]

The combination of specific association and audible musical distortion, which enables us to appreciate 'souring up the aisle', is a two-pronged technique that composers replay in countless operatic circumstances. One could reverse the trick, say, with the 'Jealousy' theme in Giuseppe Verdi's *Otello* (1887) – a sinuous minor-key idea first sung (in Act 2) by Iago, to a line about the 'green-eyed monster'. The theme recurs instrumentally several times in the opera, always dark, and always haunted by its original verbal sidecar. You could of course dress the theme musically in ways Verdi never did, by re-harmonizing it into a sort of saccharine cadence. The new message might be that the jealousy problem is resolved. And it is a message that needs no words whatsoever.

But creating aura via a musical sign need not be so specific, or rely on decipherable associations between a theme and an idea. For instance, in a famous Act 1 trio from Mozart's *Così fan tutte* (1790) the sisters Fiordiligi and Dorabella (two sopranos), along with a sardonic philosopher called Don Alfonso (bass), bid a sad farewell to their fiancés, who have just embarked on a sea journey (the fiancés will soon return in disguise to try to seduce each other's bride; they do this because of a secret wager with Don Alfonso, who has no faith in female virtue; but that gets us ahead of the story). The text of the trio is extremely short and disarming in its simplicity:

Soave sia il vento
Tranquilla sia l'onda
Ed ogni elemento
Beningo responde
Ai nostri desir.

[Gentle be the winds / tranquil be the waves / and may every element / answer benignly / to our desire.]

During the music's first pass through these words, the string oscillations (to an eighteenth-century audience, they would have been an obvious sign for waves), the tranquil harmony and the close, slow circling of the three voices evoke a musical garden of Eden before the fall. But in a second section, as the text is repeated, Mozart creates a special effect when the characters reach the word 'desir': there is a strange harmony, a sudden, subtle loudness and odd voicing in the woodwind instruments, as if they want to be noticed; and, at this exact place, the oscillating strings, which had disappeared from the texture, return. It's like a black underline made musical, drawn under the word 'desire' to make it alien and suggest (quite rightly, as it turns out) that desires neither tranquil nor officially sanctioned may be circulating subconsciously among those present.

Emphasis of this sort is common in opera, but is not the only or even the principal way in which operatic music works as expression: we will see many others. Music can, for example, contribute an added layer to the words, illustrating them through its shape and contour. Usually called 'word painting', this type of expression was widely accepted as a theory of operatic expression through long periods of the eighteenth century. Yet at other times there were theories and practices opposed to the notion of individual emphasis. Rossini, for instance, espoused the conviction that operatic music should be in some sense ideal, self-contained within itself, not expressive of any individual word or poetic text. That exchange of texts between *Mosè* and *Moïse*, mentioned earlier, is a good illustration. Indeed, there's a sense in which the elaborate ornamental singing that predominates in Rossini's operas is radically non-symbolic: it does not express anything that can be verbalized; it does not tell you much about the character or his or her state of mind; it is simply there to be beautiful.

When today we go to see, say, a nineteenth-century French *grand opéra* or an opera from the early eighteenth century, both of which tend to be very long, we may get bored. Boredom can even overcome us at excellent performances of a canonic work. Rossini had a nice quip about Wagner, saying that he was a composer who had 'beautiful moments but bad quarters of an hour'.[14] Opera often lasts for hours and hours, and there is no operatic work, not even the greatest, without its moments of tedium. What is more, we are nowadays further encouraged to be bored by the conditions under which opera is performed: we are forced to sit in the dark, without interacting with our friends and neighbours; we are forbidden to leave the auditorium during a performance (if we do, we are barred from getting back in); rapt and above all silent attention is demanded as a courtesy to the performers and fellow attendees – and, strangely because they are almost always dead, as a courtesy *to composers*. Through most of opera's history, in most national traditions, this was not the case.

It is to Wagner, to his theatrical innovations and artistic demands, that we are traditionally thought to owe this model of complete absorption (at his home theatre of Bayreuth, attendants to this day lock the auditorium doors once the lights go down). Lighting is a good indicator. Illumination in candle-lit eighteenth-century theatres may have been dim, but it was dim both on and off the stage. In the mid nineteenth century gas lighting allowed for more intense stage illumination, but the same technology was also used in the auditoriums, meaning that spectators could see each other as vividly as they could the stage. Wagner was the first theatre producer to call for complete darkness in the auditorium; and in his writings on performance he stressed again and again that spectators should be drawn overwhelmingly into the fictional world on stage, losing their anchor in reality. The introduction of electric lighting in theatres in the last decades of the nineteenth century finally allowed this darkness to be achieved. Before then, attendance at the opera was first and foremost a social occasion; audiences interacted with each other, and with the performers and the performance, sometimes in unruly ways. Another Wagnerian innovation aiding this sense of absorption was taking the orchestra out of public view, indeed dispatching many of the noisier instruments to a 'pit' largely beneath the stage. Other composers took up Wagner's innovations enthusiastically. In the early 1870s Verdi wrote to his publisher, Giulio Ricordi, about performance conditions for his new opera, *Aida* (1871), recommending that:

> they get rid of those stage boxes, taking the curtain right to the footlights; and also make *the orchestra invisible*. This idea isn't mine, it's Wagner's: and it's excellent. It seems impossible that in this day and age people tolerate seeing tired evening dress and white ties mixed up with, for example, Egyptian, Assyrian or Druidic costumes; and, what is more, seeing the massed ranks of the orchestra, *which is part of the fictional world*, almost in the middle of the stalls, amongst the whistlers or the applauders.[15]

The sentiments are, as Verdi was the first to recognize, remarkably similar to Wagner's: above all one must preserve the special quality of opera's 'fictional world'. After the mid nineteenth century, silent attention to this world became more the norm, although Italian audiences in particular have often resisted the requirement. We now ask all operas to sustain our focused, unwavering attention, even though most operatic works were not designed to bear this burden. In the eighteenth century, few worried if there were too many arias or tedious stretches. During those artistically more generous, culturally more confident times, the audience was permitted to ignore what it found dull, and occupy its mind in other ways. We are in this sense fortunate that recordings have now made possible a non-exclusive experience of opera, one that, although belonging to a technological present, recreates in an alternative domain the freedoms enjoyed by live audiences in opera's past. Listeners can (and do) fast forward through the DVD or pre-select their tracks on a CD or iPod; they come and go as they please, dropping into the experience and keeping the lights switched on.

The question of opera and boredom also arises as a broad historical conundrum: why did the composing of opera, which for so long belonged to the present, become around the time of the Second World War a gesture to the past? Until about 1800, most operas were written for a specific season in a specific theatre (only French *tragédie lyrique* had something approaching a repertoire); some works might be repeated in other cities a year or two later, and might remain in performance or be revived a little longer than that, but they were generally expected to be supplanted by next year's crop. In the middle years of the nineteenth century, this began to change: in parallel with increasing gravitas accorded to the very idea of musical *works*, and with a new historicism that sought out and preserved past music, operatic repertories began to emerge and then harden. By 1850, it was the norm for an opera from the previous decade to be revived and performed alongside recent revivals and new, specially commissioned pieces.

This situation continued into the earlier twentieth century, with the proportions of old to new shifting inexorably towards the former; and then at a certain point – although the point is not exact, different operatic cultures negotiating the turn in different ways – the operatic repertory became primarily a matter of revivals of canonized works. One sees, in parallel to this shift, evidence of another kind of boredom: a gathering sense that the body of known works is finite and too well-known, but that refreshment is more likely to come from the past than the present. Early examples of this process emerged more than a hundred years ago now, and in more than one country almost simultaneously: the championing of Monteverdi's *Orfeo* by Paul Dukas in 1893, or Gustav Mahler's completion of Carl Maria von Weber's unfinished opera *Die drei Pintos* in 1888. The so-called 'Verdi renaissance' in 1920s Germany, the re-emergence of Mozart operas in the 1930s, the *bel canto* revival of the 1950s, the Rossini revival of the 1970s and 1980s, and the Handel revival of the past two decades are all more recent forms of this historicist passion.

There is an interesting convergence here: just as the commissioning of new operas dwindled to a trickle in the years leading up to the Second World War, the staging of canonic operas became an art in its own right. Before that time, staging had often been regarded as an important part of the operatic occasion, but one that aged along with the work in question. With staging now thrown open as an interpretative extra, as a 'reading' of a well-known text, new questions emerged about the role of directors, who seemed now to bear much of the burden for renewing works that could not be new in any other way. A classic instance is Wieland Wagner in postwar Bayreuth. Richard Wagner's grandson was given the task of purging both the Bayreuth festival and Wagner's operas of their visually embodied past, in particular the so-called realistic stagings that, although updated in the 1930s, had barely mutated since Wagner's day, and had become strongly associated with the Nazi regime. Wieland Wagner's visually stunning minimalism seemed to make the works themselves new; and this form of magic has been practised both well and badly ever since. Directors took on the responsibility for making canonic operas seem fresh or contemporary – if you will, for assuaging boredom. Staging became more assertive and visible in the experience of opera. This in turn raises questions about the role of performance in the operatic experience, and the limits (or infinite possibilities) of opera production in the twenty-first century.

Imagine you are fortunate enough to attend revivals of Verdi's *Un ballo in maschera* (1859) in London, Milan and New York. The performances are, as you might expect, all different – different casts, conductors, orchestras, staging teams – but you have expectations of both sameness and difference. You will trust the singers, despite their individual quirks, to sing a more or less identical musical text. True, a phrase here or there may be interpolated to display what used to be called the 'money notes'; and – more often than one might think – there may be a discreet transposition to ease a singer afflicted by the depredations of age or nerves; but these are matters of small detail. You will also look forward to a roughly identical literary text, although again there may be wider variation than you might think for such a classic of the repertoire. Some performances may choose to substitute aspects of an original Swedish setting, thus replacing an occasional place or character name; and there is a notorious line in the first scene (the Judge describes Ulrica as 'dell'immondo sangue de' negri' – of filthy negro blood) which is often censored. You will trust, nevertheless, that the conductor and orchestral musicians have more or less identical parts before them – although again conductors routinely adjust details to suit the theatrical space and aid audibility.

But what of the *staging* of these three productions? Your expectations of sameness in that department will, if you are a seasoned campaigner, be of the most modest imaginable, and just as well. In London there is no scenery except a naked light bulb (which swings incessantly), a crooked doll's chair and an equally crooked bed suspended halfway up a bare wall – a bed from which the soprano precariously hangs to sing her entrance aria. In Milan, eighteenth-century Stockholm has been re-created with no expense spared: real horses pull real carriages, stately ships pass in the brilliantly lit background; a many-Euroed hum is heard everywhere. And in New York the staging is what die-hards proudly call 'traditional', which means it resembles productions that took place when the people bankrolling the present show were young enough to enjoy newness: a kind of mid-twentieth-century pastiche or – more accurately – a mid twentieth century frozen in aspic.

Now imagine a different world, one in which – through some unimaginable warp in our civilization – the staging world is as fixed as the musical or literary one. In just the same way that there is a libretto and a musical score, there is now also a 'book' that instructs us about how to stage *Un ballo in maschera*: what the sets and costumes should look like, who stands where, what gestures the characters are permitted to make. As with the musical performance, tiny variations or inflections can now give pleasure or cause indignation. How expressive and daring! Riccardo was wearing *mauve* tights instead of *red* ones! I'm not sure what it *meant* exactly, but somehow it seemed to fit marvellously with that slightly off-colour door at the back of the Act 1 set. At the end of his Act 3 aria, though, Renato raised *both* hands when he turned to Riccardo's picture. That simply goes too far. He looked like he was parking an aeroplane. The text stipulates quite clearly that his other hand should be resting on his sword, and there's a very good reason why it should. These modern directors! Sharpen my quill: I must write a letter to *Opera* magazine.

This landscape, one in which 'same-staging practice' is the norm, is of course fantastic: a kind of *Groundhog Day* made opera, in which the same actions will scroll past us again and again – more like a movie rerun than live theatre. But we conjure it up because it may add a new perspective to the endless modern debates about 'contemporary' operatic staging, in particular about whether directors should be encouraged or vilified when they offer audiences a sharply modern – and often sharply contradictory – stage-reading of operatic classics. The point is this: that the *existence* of visual extravagance has almost always been a critical issue in opera, and visual splendour has sometimes been more important than either the words or the music; but the precise nature of that splendour in any individual work has always changed with changing technologies.

To return to the beginning: opera is a form of theatre in which most or all of the characters sing most or all of the time. This continuous singing is an odd state of affairs, and we should above all hang on to that idea of opera's strangeness, its special qualities. One of the most common ways in which writers have tried to make sense of opera is to domesticate it, to talk about it in ways that encourage comparisons with other art forms, ways that make it less strange. That approach can work, and in what follows we occasionally do something similar. But there will always be a lingering question about how an art form that by any other standards is almost bound to seem preposterous can inspire such intense emotions. We need to keep that question, and those emotions, before us in our journey through opera's 400-year history.

2
Opera's first centennial

Can we encapsulate the nature of opera, suggesting that at every point in its history it had enduring, immutable qualities? That is a question both about history and about us – about our ways of understanding opera today. While all opera involves the exaggerations and suspensions of disbelief we described in the last chapter, there are periods in its history that will inevitably seem more alien or artificial, and hence more distant. One great dividing line between the distant and the accessible past, or so it seemed until quite recently, was represented by Wolfgang Amadé Mozart (1756–91), in particular by his comic operas beginning with *Die Entführung aus dem Serail* (The Abduction from the Seraglio) in 1782. In opera histories during the last century, we find a story that constantly swirls around the figure of Mozart. At first he was, quite simply, an untouchable genius, the composer of the first operas whose qualities were so immediately apparent that they were canonized in Austria and Germany not long after they were written. Of course – it had to be admitted – the nineteenth century saw thin times for Mozart, particularly in places where native Italian opera set the standard. But his mature works were revived near the start of the twentieth century, and since then have never looked back. Nearer our own time, research about opera immediately before and during Mozart's life established a richer musical and cultural context for his work, but this did not alter the consensus that his operas were exceptional: indeed, the more they were put into a general historical picture, the more incalculably different they seemed. Minor works from the period that were unearthed belonged to history. Mozart's operas belonged to *us*.

OPERA'S BIRTH

To go back a further two centuries, and to talk about the origins of opera, is inevitably to refresh our preconceptions: about what we know as creatures formed by Mozart, by Verdi and Wagner, and by the other repertories and aesthetic points of reference that make up any modern-day understanding of operatic history. This is so because, in some senses, ways of recounting the birth of opera have been informed by prejudices similar to those that characterize accounts of the centrality of Mozart's operas.

It once used to be customary to think of opera history as a kind of pantechnicon, which emerged via a majestic grand tour of famous Italian cities, evolving all the while towards our present view of what makes the best kind of operatic drama.[1] It all started, we were told, in Florence, where a hotbed of Renaissance energy and invention saw various groups of scholars and musicians getting together around 1600, forming salons or 'academies' dedicated to imagining ways in which Greek musical drama might be revived. Already in the 1780s, the notion that opera had been born in Florence as a revival of the aims and effects of Greek drama was circulating widely in Europe, as evinced by Thomas Iriarte's 1783 history of music in verse form, *La musica*, which dates the invention of opera to Ancient Greece, with its modern rebirth in 1600.[2] In 1927, in Waldo Selden Pratt's *History of Music*, we get a version of the story written for US schoolchildren:

> About 1575 there began at Florence a movement that had important consequences. A wealthy and cultivated nobleman . . . drew about him a group of dilettanti in literature and art who were all inquiring after some method of dramatic expression of an intenser form than was then known. Their ambition was to restore the Greek drama in its entirety . . . the monodic style was at once applied in musical plays with plots and personages.[3]

Richard Wagner in *Oper und Drama* (Opera and Drama, 1851) described this same Italianate miracle, c. 1600, albeit with scornful velocity (and typical obfuscation) as he speeds through the seventeenth century on his way to Gluck and Mozart:

> With Aria, Dance-tune and Recitative, the whole apparatus of musical drama – unchanged in essence down to our very latest opera – was settled once for all. Further, the dramatic ground plans laid beneath this apparatus soon won a kindred stereotyped persistence. Mostly taken from an entirely misconstrued Greek mythology, they formed a theatric scaffolding from which all capability of rousing warmth of human interest was altogether absent, but which, on the other hand, possessed the merit of lending itself to the good pleasure of every composer in his turn.[4]

Not all Germans were so dismissive. One of the first nineteenth-century opera histories, Gottfried Wilhelm Fink's *Wesen und Geschichte der Oper* (The Nature and History of Opera, 1839), is more Italy-friendly in tone:

> In Florence . . . there arose a society that held regular meetings . . .; and since an affection for Greece above all had flourished for quite some time in Florence, so this society of amateurs soon hit upon the excellent idea of making the nature of Greek Tragedy the principal object of their researches . . . how many firsts have arisen in Italy, and how many inventors![5]

Already in the early nineteenth century, as Fink exclaims, the story was more or less fixed. Opera was invented in or around Florence and the first operas date from somewhere between 1598 and 1600; and high-minded ideas about Greek theatre play a significant role. Opera's first century or so was then punctuated by stopping-off points and longer stays in various picturesque Italian venues, the genre gradually spreading out over the peninsula and then beyond. Exported from Italy to France and England soon after mid-century, and to numerous central European courts, opera soon began to assume myriad local and national shapes, mutating under pressure from new political and economic conditions and from vernacular theatrical traditions in other languages and cultural domains.

Thus, according to the established historical account, was opera born and started its 400-year progress. But in the latter part of the twentieth century the picture was modified in significant details. Scholarly research gave rise to a more complex description, almost an historical anthropology of the phenomenon. Nowhere was this more evident than in accounts of opera's first decades. The story still portrayed opera flowing from an important moment of change in Italy around 1600, but the details could take us aback: for instance, the very designation 'opera' was not consistently used until as late as the nineteenth century. An impressive list of genre terms used in opera libretti or scores at various historical periods in various centres or national traditions can be reconstructed, and these differences in terminology reflect important variations in the very nature of the works. One recent history of opera in seventeenth-century Venice lists around fifteen terms that circulated in the early decades, few of which include the word 'opera' and only some of which even make reference to music. It could be *attione in musica* or a *festa teatrale*, a *dramma musicale* or a *favola regia*, a *tragedia musicale* or an *opera scenica*; the sheer proliferation speaks of a genre in the making.[6]

In this second, more modern manner of telling opera's history, the precursors and theories underpinning its emergence are now all over Italy in the sixteenth century. Opera mutated gradually out of these ancestors, most importantly out of the tradition of pastoral drama with music represented as far back as the late fifteenth century by the poet Angelo Poliziano (1454–94), whose *Orfeo* (Orpheus, 1480) had accompanying music (now lost). True, those academies of scholars and musicians trying to revive Greek drama in Florence and elsewhere were still important, but theirs was just one strand of a huge, centuries-old series of experiments devoted to combining drama, dance, song and instrumental music. One could even turn the matter on its head and ask whether, worldwide, there were many theatrical genres before 1600 that did *not* feature music in some important way. Certainly, within elite Western European traditions there were numerous forms of theatre with music before 1600: medieval liturgical plays (sung, and chanted); Renaissance pastoral plays with inserted incidental music and songs; and, immediately before 1600, so-called *intermedi* (instrumental music and songs played between the acts of spoken drama). Opera learned from them all.

In the years around 1600, the grandest of these musico-dramatic experiments were beyond extravagant. When the Medici family in 1589 wanted to celebrate a grand dynastic wedding in Florence, the festivities lasted three weeks and came to a climax with a succession of *intermedi* to a comic play called *La pellegrina*. These *intermedi* involved dance, solo song and even complicated madrigals, all played against elaborate stage pictures that insistently made visual connections between the venues of the gods, other mythological characters onstage and of the courtly audience attending. It is surely significant that their general theme was often music. The principal aim was to amaze and above all impress the audience with the profound effects of harmony (musical, poetic and scenic); the plot (such as it was – a vaguely related series of independent scenes might be more accurate) justified itself by referring explicitly to precisely that effect. These fabulous spectacles were fabulously expensive. What was their purpose? The latest technology (stage machines and magnificent painted scenery) joined hands with music and poetry to project an overwhelming sense of power that could impress supporters and put fear into the minds of opponents. Small wonder, then, that the *intermedi* were painstakingly recorded in manuscripts and printed books, allowing posterity (ourselves included) to wonder at their scope and ambition.

No single grand narrative can tie such experiments to each other or to the first operas, but they all offered a similar mix of stage action and music, and they continued through the first decades of the seventeenth century, never finding anything like a standard format. What is more, the reason why the academies and their philosophical and classicist aspirations became so important to historians probably had as much to do with later conceptions of opera, not to mention ideas about what opera should aspire to be, than it had with the messy variety of musical drama in the sixteenth and seventeenth centuries. However, establishing the minutiae of context and meticulously reconstructing the variety of genres from which the first operas grew should not change the sense that there was a minor earthquake – a moment when, quite suddenly, something new appeared and then prospered. And this earthquake did indeed occur in Florence, where a group of composers and poets loosely allied with one another began writing and publishing substantial, narrative theatrical works in which all the characters sang, and sang all the time.

The list of these works (some performed at the Florentine court, some perhaps written more as experiments in a new genre) is cited in most histories with a reverence that attends any tally of surviving 'firsts'. The poet Ottavio Rinuccini wrote a libretto called *Dafne*, set to music in 1598 by two composers, Jacopo Peri and Jacopo Corsi. Then Rinuccini's *Euridice*, twice set to music in 1600, first by Peri, then by Giulio Caccini. Caccini's version was the first to be published and thus sometimes figures officially as 'the first opera', giving us 1600 as a tidy birth date. Peri's *Euridice*, on the other hand, was also a landmark: he and Rinuccini developed in it what we now know as recitative, a kind of musical declamation (they called it, more poetically, *recitar cantando*) that followed closely the accentuation of the poetry; this was a style that enabled characters to converse in music, and would (as we saw in Chapter 1) be essential to opera for centuries to come. In the same year, Caccini and others composed music for a libretto called *Il rapimento di Cefalo* by the poet Gabriello Chiabrera. And then, seven years later in 1607, came a work that almost everyone agrees offered an entirely different order of artistic achievement: *L'Orfeo*, subtitled as a *favola in musica* or 'musical fable', written for the Gonzaga court in Mantua by Claudio Monteverdi (1567–1643). It makes sense that this particular *Orfeo* is so special. Peri, Caccini and company were musicians of local standing. Monteverdi was already a famous composer by the time he came to opera. He had written much religious music and an innovative series of madrigals in which he had experimented with what he called a 'second practice' (*seconda pratica*) of music writing, a style that distanced itself from the usual sixteenth-century contrapuntal manner. He had, in other words, a great deal of musical experience to bring to the new genre.

In strictly operatic terms, Monteverdi nevertheless learned from Peri and the others: his 'musical fable' is sung throughout, and thus has a fair amount of *recitar cantando* (perhaps too much for modern taste). But, like the *intermedi*, it also contained an anarchic mix of dances, madrigals, solo songs and purely instrumental interludes or 'sinfonias'. Again like many of the *intermedi*, it featured the idea of music's power as an important element of the plot. We may be surprised, though, that initially there were few obvious concerns about verisimilitude. The first debates about the illogicality of conversing in song, or the surreal aspect of characters who conduct their business and express their feelings in music, came only later, around 1650, after opera had been around for a half-century. These debates will mark a critical moment in opera aesthetics, one to which we will need to return. Another disquieting surprise is that, while we now celebrate Monteverdi's *Orfeo* as the earliest great opera, it remained almost completely unknown for the first 300 or so years of its existence. True, it was published in 1609, and again in 1615 but after a few revivals it passed into obscurity and was not performed again (or even much discussed) until the late nineteenth century. Its elevation soon after that, as *the* Ur-opera, the best from the Florentine crucible, tells us much about changing opera aesthetics over historical time.

Corsi, Peri, Caccini, Monteverdi. Why so many similar works all at once? One radical (and now very much out-of-fashion) explanation was offered by our opening chorus of historians: that opera was cobbled together out of odds and ends that included notions about classic Greek theatre, evolving Italian musical styles (most importantly, the idea of *recitar cantando*) and sheer inventive tenacity. This is a bizarre historical supposition: basically that opera emerged out of an intellectual conviction that such a thing *should* exist. Accounts along these lines point out that the philosophical grounds for the experiment followed on from debates that began as early as the 1550s in Florence, among academies (or looser groupings, without official statutes) peopled by aristocrats, intellectuals and musicians.[7] The group always cited in this pre-history (although not officially an academy) was called the Camerata (1573–87), whose central figure and convener was Count Giovanni de' Bardi (1534–1612). In the preface to his *Euridice*, Caccini cited the Camerata, and its association with the 'birth of opera' originated from that citation. Those connected with Bardi included the music theorist Vincenzo Galilei, whose work included acoustics, and whose famous son, Galileo Galilei, inherited his father's fascination with the physics of sound transmission. Bardi, a polymath and classicist, wrote speculations about the nature of music in Greek tragedy, many examples of which he had translated into Italian, and channelled ideas that had circulated in earlier Florentine academies, including the Umidi – associated with the theorist Girolamo Mei, another passionate classicist. Debates about the nature of ancient song were also central to an academy known as the Alterati, founded in the 1560s.

In all these groups, working poets and musicians – the librettist Rinuccini, or Caccini, Corsi and Peri – were involved on the edges; and recent research has stressed that these edges were where theory turned into practice. As scholars over the last twenty or so years have delved further into the details of early opera creation, they again and again reveal that poets and musicians, being practical people, turned to concrete musical and literary materials, rather than to philosophy or theory, for the basis of their experiments. In light of all this research, we can now see that earlier accounts of the birth of opera lent excessive weight to philosophy and theory. But that in itself is significant. The fact that historians a hundred and more years ago returned to this particular strand says something about an idealization of opera – as a noble, prelapsarian form of expression – that has characterized so many accounts of it for so many centuries.

Why Greek tragedy or 'ancient song'? The Florentine academicians invoked Aristotle, and specifically a passage in the *Poetics* about the emotions evoked by tragedy. The spectators, Aristotle tells us, feel for the characters to the point that they experience an intense emotion that he called 'catharsis' – a kind of purification brought on by understanding what the characters undergo. Count Bardi in particular was convinced that poetry alone could not have produced this powerful reaction, and his conviction led him to a leap of imagination: classical tragedy had achieved its effect because the words were sung, not spoken; music constituted a second continuum within the drama, one that created miraculous results. (This theory has often been challenged, but today's scholars of Greek theatre seem to think that choruses may indeed have been intoned in musical fashion, and that perhaps even speeches were chanted.) Bardi and his circle then speculated about what would happen if they created a form of theatre that used words and music simultaneously. This would not be music between the acts, or songs or dances or madrigals thrown in as a diversion. It would have words, and a scenic backdrop and costumes; but it would make music carry the essential burden of the drama.

However, when they arrived at this point, the theorists reached an impasse. How could they attempt a modern re-creation of what they thought had been Greek musical drama? This was a blank slate: no music seemed to exist that could possibly bear the burden thus imagined. At the same time, though, the practising musicians who were privy to this philosophizing were experimenting with their own ideas. They had plenty of experience with existing musical forms: those songs and dances and madrigals that had featured in the *intermedi*. But the kernel of this new theatrical form – the miracle music, the second continuum, the bearer of the drama – was something different and initially very simple: it would be musical recitation, *recitar cantando*. The accompaniment would be rudimentary, as nothing should distract from tones whose sole aim was to heighten the emotional flux of the poetry. Play texts invented for this purpose came at first mostly from the tradition of pastoral; they were stories about nymphs, shepherds and half-gods, living in marvellous gardens or fantastic country paradises, characters so exceptional that they might plausibly be imagined to converse in music. As we can see from the titles of those Florentine 'firsts' around 1600, it was clear from the start that one particular plot would dominate: the plot of Orpheus and Eurydice.

ORPHEUS AS OPERA COMPOSER

It is certainly significant that Orpheus became the first (and most often-recurring) early operatic hero. Orpheus, son of Apollo and one of the legendary poets of antiquity, was a demigod whose magical powers of singing could even drown out the deadly music of the Sirens. On the death of his wife Eurydice, Orpheus' songs were so sad that the nymphs and Gods allowed him to descend into Hell to rescue her, commanding only that he must not look back as he leads her out of the underworld. He descends with his lyre, moves Persephone and Hades by his singing, is reunited with Eurydice and starts to lead her back. But then, in anguish at her laments, he disobeys the Gods and looks back. Eurydice is lost for ever. Orpheus, desolated, forsakes the love of women, and because of this is murdered by the Maenads (frenzied female devotees of Dionysus) in a Bacchic orgy. He is dismembered, his head and lyre left to float down the river Hebrus. But even after death his voice continues, his dismembered head singing on, causing the stones, trees and rivers to resonate. From that time forth, and in a remarkable pre-technological presentiment about how musical sound can be amplified and transmitted, all nature sings in his place.

For the early makers of opera, the most important scene in this myth was a moment of performance: Orpheus appears before the rulers of the underworld in order to persuade them to release Eurydice, and he does so by singing. This moment clearly appealed because it was an allegorical representation: Orpheus' power over the dark rulers, his ability to sway them through song, resonated with opera's power over its audience; operatic music was meant to induce in listeners extremes of emotion, so much so that they would be lost, cast into a state in which reason gave way to the miraculous. For a composer, successful representation of this scene would be the ultimate challenge and the ultimate justification of the new art form.

What is significant, 400 years later, is that the scenes of actual music making in Monteverdi's *Orfeo* – whether the shepherds' pastoral songs or Orfeo's improvisation of elaborate coloratura to impress the Gods – almost outweigh scenes in which music functions as a direct expression of the soul, the sort of thing fundamental to what was new in opera. As we pointed out in Chapter 1, music-within-the-opera (music required by the plot) often provides both temporary relief from the ever-impinging unreality of the medium, and can be the composer's way of encouraging a particular reaction to his efforts: he can put on stage both a musical statement *and* the kind of listener-response he hopes for. But music-within-the-opera is not opera's basic mode. In one sense it's no different from music-within-the-play in spoken drama – the mad Ophelia singing about flowers, or Ariel singing his hymn to freedom. What we recognize as necessary for opera is not these self-conscious songs and dances, but passion given voice as singing. This second kind of singing thus becomes a more potent form of utterance, being music that exists outside or beyond the limits of the fiction.

Where does this mode appear in *Orfeo*? One classic instance is the long *recitar cantando* scene in Act 2, in which a Messenger (soprano) brings news to Orfeo (tenor) of Euridice's death, and in which Orfeo then laments her fate and vows to descend to Hell to bring her back. This is essentially an elaborate recitative, accompanied by various instruments sustaining the harmonies. The words are sung in free, speech-based rhythm, and there is little obvious melody, little sense of periodic structure in the voice part. The vocal line in part traces the intonation of the words – as a kind of natural pitch – but also, and more significantly, it traces the symbolic meaning of certain words or the images they convey. There is very little music to spare: we are immersed in a rarefied world in which each small melodic and harmonic gesture stands out, earnestly soliciting a high degree of attentiveness and absorption. At the precise moment the Messenger recalls Euridice's sudden pallor, there is an harmonic schism: alternating E-major and B-major chords are followed by an anomalous G minor; in harmonic terms we shift somewhere else entirely. Another example is the description of nymphs rushing around and of attempts to revive Euridice, which are paced much faster than any other text – the words pour out in a panicked tumble. The only time a word is repeated is when the Messenger imitates Euridice's dying cry of 'Orfeo, Orfeo', higher the second time;

and then there is a scripted silence following the evocation of her death, 'spirò fra queste braccia' (she expired in these arms). When Orfeo responds to the Messenger's tale, his dismay causes him to repeat words as if he can't understand them: 'You are dead? dead? . . . you have left me? left me, and I remain here?' At the end of his lament, following his decision to descend 'into the abyss' (his voice goes down to the lowest note in his vocal part), he bids farewell to earth, sky and sun in an ascending melodic line that traces the very upward arc he describes.

These are all moments in which we hear obvious musical translations of poetic content. They are like the tricks that classical rhetoric prescribed for skilled orators: repetition for emphasis; dropping the voice and raising it; changing the tempo of one's words. But other moments in *Orfeo* are uniquely musical. One of the most magical is born from the way Monteverdi fashioned an acoustic image of the dying Euridice's cry. We do not hear the original sound, but (he implies) it must have been terrible and it refuses to die. It re-resonates. First, there is the Messenger's imitation and repetition of the cry. Then Orfeo repeats it in disguised forms, for instance in his repeated 'No, No', also rising in pitch. Again, as in oratorical effects, the reasons for such moments may be didactic. This is, after all, a depiction of a vocal sound that goes forth to touch those who hear; it is an encrypted image of opera's power to move its listeners.

When this culminating achievement of opera's brief first period of existence was unveiled in Mantua, the spectacle – both as an event and in its circumstances – bore little resemblance to what opera would become through most of its subsequent history. *Orfeo* was first seen not in a theatre but in a private room (and not a very spacious one) in the Duke of Mantua's palace. The main part was probably sung by a tenor called Francesco Rasi, who was himself a composer; most or perhaps all of the female roles were taken by castrati, the most famous of them being Giovanni Gualberto Magli, a court singer who was on loan from the Grand Duke of Tuscany. It was enacted in front of a small audience placed very near the singers, and there was certainly no proscenium or mystic gulf between performers and spectators. According to a contemporary account, it was given again a week later. Even though the Duke had attended many rehearsals and the premiere, he ordered another showing for an audience including 'all the ladies resident in the city'; Magli in particular had apparently 'given immense pleasure to all who had have heard him sing, especially My Lady'.[8] The intimacy of the venue provided an ideal opportunity for demonstrating opera's capacity to wield music's power over its audience: a restricted space, a small group of people, an architectural space and an acoustic that allowed every word to be understood, with listeners so close that they could not fail to notice each minute expression on the singers' faces, each variation in their vocal delivery. The earliest operas flowed in part from lofty notions of theatrical catharsis and emotional directness, and in this case the venue greatly facilitated intensity of experience. To appreciate some of its message 400 years later – in, say, the 3800-seater Metropolitan Opera in New York – requires a prodigious leap of imagination and necessarily compromises some of the opera's original mission.

It is no accident that many of the ideals we have underlined both in theories about early opera and in *Orfeo* would be rediscovered at later periods, in particular by poets or theorists who feared that the essentials of opera had in the interim been corrupted by musical excess or frivolity. One of these ideals was the symbiosis of music and poetry, which the Messenger's narrative in *Orfeo* exemplifies with its extraordinary spare beauty. In surprisingly formulaic and repetitious ways, calls for the reunification of melody and word recur in several later reform polemics: it is the ground-note of writers as diverse as Jean-Jacques Rousseau, who, amongst even greater achievements, was one of the philosophers of the so-called *Querelle des Bouffons* (War of the Comedians), a mid-eighteenth-century French vs Italian opera polemic, and Richard Wagner (in his treatise *Oper und Drama* – Opera and Drama – of 1851). What Rousseau and Wagner shared was an abhorrence of music for its own sake, music lacking what they called an 'organic' connection to poetry and drama. More specifically they shared a distaste, often couched in terms of lost morality, for virtuosic singing: those flights of ornament and detonations of high notes in which the words fade away.

These complaints convinced many sober judges. But theorizing away audience tastes for beautiful singing, a listener's fascination with vocalism and the flights it can take, has proved futile many times over in operatic history. One cautionary tale is the divergence between philosophical accounts of what is noblest in *Orfeo* and the persistent attractions of those episodes that involve virtuoso display. Obvious cases are Orfeo's aria 'Possente spirto' in Act 3, in which the hero tries to influence the underworld Gods, or the final Orfeo–Apollo duet, which is also notable for its prolonged warbling. In so many accounts of early opera, we read that Orfeo tries unsuccessfully to impress the Gods with coloratura but only succeeds in winning a passage to the underworld when he resorts to more heartfelt singing, in which the words are clearly audible. But this description of the scene falters in several respects. One is that it misrepresents the plot, in the process saying much about the strength of the anti-virtuosity view. Orfeo doesn't 'charm' Charon (bass) into ferrying him across the river Styx; far from it. His singing does nothing more heroic than bore Charon to sleep, thus offering a combination of comedy and high-mythic gravitas that can still seem alien today. More seriously, though: by what authority can we claim that the virtuosic parts of the aria are less moving or enticing than the simpler singing at the end? For which audience, at which performance, in which historical era?

The persuasive power of pure singing had a great deal to do with the evolution of opera. Around 1650 the genre bears so distant a resemblance to those first, post-Renaissance operas that some scholars have even argued for stripping the *Dafnes*, *Euridices* and *Orfeos* of the very name opera. The turn from noble *recitar cantando* to agile vocalism has much to do with that argument. But equally important to those who want to draw a new starting line were economic and social considerations: the earliest operas, with their strong links to pastoral and myth, were also the product of court environments and private commissions. Once public theatres began to commission and perform opera, the pressures of audience taste and business practice interacted to re-form operatic style. This time, Venice was the centre.

VENICE AND THE ASCENT OF SINGING

In 1637 Venice's Teatro San Cassiano opened its doors to the public during the carnival season, for a performance of an opera called *Andromeda*. The libretto was written by Benedetto Ferrari (1603/4–81), who was part of a travelling company of musicians plying their trade in the city, and who also figured in the production as impresario and continuo player. The music, not mentioned on the title page of the libretto, was by Francesco Manelli (1595/7–1667). Within four years, three more Venetian theatres had opened. By mid-century over fifty operas had been performed in the city; twenty-five years later the total was 150. New works were constantly required, and were often fashioned to resemble previous hits and so make them more immediately understandable to the regular paying public (just like popular films or novels today). Monteverdi spanned the two worlds: in venerable old age he produced several operas for Venice, only two of which now survive (*Il ritorno d'Ulisse in patria* – The Return of Ulysses, 1640 – and *L'incoronazione di Poppea* – The Coronation of Poppea, 1643). A wave of opera composers working for Venetian theatres were formed by the new style. Francesco Cavalli (1602–76) and Antonio Cesti (1623–69) stand out in this new order: both were popular, prolific and – the new acid test – commanded the highest fees for new works (Cavalli was also significant for his sojourn, in 1660–62, at the court of Louis XIV, where he played a role in the export of Italian opera to France). In the opera theatres of Venice, though, composers were by no means the most important people employed in the new industry. Impresarios, engaged by theatre owners and usually bearing some of the financial risk, were responsible for arranging the season: hiring a roster of singers and a small army of scene painters, machinists and musicians; trying (sometimes vainly) to make the books balance at the end of a run. In 1681, Cristoforo Ivanovich – whose writings on opera in Venice are a fabulous cornucopia of practical detail – described the finances of opera production, saying that 'the first and foremost considerable [expense] is that of remunerating the men and women who sing, their pretensions having become excessive'.[9] Something quite a lot closer to opera as we know it had arrived. Why did this happen in Venice? What was special about the city that caused this remarkable flowering of a new genre?

After centuries of literary and then cinematic mythmaking, even people who have never set foot in Venice can understand the city's uniqueness; and its attractions as a modern-day tourist centre, a kind of city-wide heritage site, were part of what made it such fertile ground for the emergence of opera. Almost all the operas that sprang up in the decades after 1637 were performed in the carnival season, from 26 December until Shrove Tuesday. During that period the city became a magnet for tourists and, in their wake, visiting theatrical troupes. Venice's population of about 50,000 could double in carnival, guaranteeing an audience for those first operatic impresarios. Just as important, though, was the city's political structure. Venice was, at least in theory, a republic: a place where a relatively large number of noble families had influence over the election of their ruler, and where wealth was more than usually well-distributed. Despite its decline as an international power during the seventeenth century, the greatest of these noble families were anxious to compete in patronage of the arts, and one result was a proliferation of theatres. However, many of these noble families had elevated themselves through trade and other entrepreneurial activity, and were not willing to lay down money simply to impress others. The new genre of opera thus became a business, something that could be run by impresarios and could attract a paying public who might even lease a box for the entire season, consuming the product again and again. In other words, opera became such a successful public genre in Venice in part because it could boast a balance sheet.

These circumstances fostered a new brand of operatic entertainment, one very different from Monteverdi's *favola in musica*. True, there were resemblances to previous court spectacles such as those in Florence by Peri, Caccini and others. Sometimes (certainly more often than they would have liked) the noble families who owned the theatres had to bail out the impresario and subsidize the season, making the enterprise closer to the economic model of court entertainment. There were also artistic continuities. These new Venetian musical dramas continued to use the idea of *recitar cantando*, as always interspersed with songs, instrumental interludes and dance; and there was still an emphasis on shock-and-awe scenic spectacle (although, for financial reasons, never quite on the scale of those Medici *intermedi*). But the whole genre now needed to please a more diverse and in some ways more demanding audience; in response it took on some of the spirit of Venice's carnival – of the excess, pageantry and bad behaviour that carnival celebrates.

This freewheeling stance is evident in new types of operatic plot. At least by 1650, many aspects of libretto writing had established routines. A standard genre designation began to be used: an opera now tended to be called a *dramma per musica* (drama for or through music; a theatre piece written for the addition of music). A three-act format with prologue also became the norm. Although ancient mythology still featured in the plots (prologues often involved deities discoursing about human foibles), both historical romances and political events from classical antiquity – stories in which human characters predominate – edged out gods, goddesses, shepherds and nymphs. What's more, the range of plots expanded. Now we find stories in which, as well as lovers lamenting against pastoral backdrops, servants can make fun of their masters; in which virtue will not necessarily be rewarded as the plot unravels; in which, to be brief, the whole messy business of human fallibility is explored. Although exclusively comic opera did not begin until later in the century, injections of comedy became an important means by which opera expanded its tone. As with the scene between Orfeo and Charon in Monteverdi's *Orfeo*, it is the contrasting registers – boredom and myth, suicide and farce, existential crisis and buffoonery – that perpetually startle us in early Italian opera. Only at the beginning of the eighteenth century did there emerge a more rigid division between the antic and the tragic.

It soon became clear that a major attraction in this new, staged version of carnival excess would be vocal virtuosity, the singing voice in full flood. The account books make this plain. The opera industry may have been fuelled by librettists and composers, and it may have been decorated by scene painters and scenic engineers; but the top wages went to (and have remained with) the star vocal soloists, the performers who don't just impersonate a god or goddess, but who for a brief time become one through sheer force of vocal virtuosity. In 1658 Cavalli, a conspicuously high-earning composer, got 400 ducats for writing his new opera, *Antioco*; but the leading soprano ('Signora Girolama') was paid 750 ducats for singing in it. And singers' wages continued to spiral: in 1685 a top singer (Margherita Salicola) could command an individual fee that fifty years earlier would have financed an entire production.[10] These virtuoso singers, trained to perform at a level of difficulty unprecedented in musical history, also began to have power and influence over the events in which they starred. Opera began to feature more elaborate arias, with music whose formal design became the scaffold for their crowning glory.

Vocal virtuosity is not just a matter of pure voice appealing directly to pure emotion, there is an aspect of magic that comes into play. Once singers are trained to overcome the limits of what was thought possible – in terms of pitch, speed, agility, power, endurance – they pass beyond what the audience can plausibly imagine itself capable of doing, to the point where listeners cannot connect ordinary human effort to what they hear. A tale repeated about Farinelli, one of the most famous and gifted of eighteenth-century singers, was that he kept a mechanical whistle or flute in his pocket and that his most sustained long notes were produced by this instrument. No one could believe that a human being could have so much breath in him.[11] The moral of the story is clear: the appeal of singers was, at its extreme, not unlike the appeal of circus performers, magicians, professional athletes, indeed of all performers who seem to be going beyond the physical capabilities of real humans or beyond the physical limitations of reality.

Who were these singers, and how did they make a living? The two most popular types at this early stage, and for some time to come, were both high voices: one was female; the other was a surgically altered male, a castrato such as Farinelli. Much horrified fascination and breathless mythmaking has collected and continues to collect around the phenomenon of the castrato. Briefly (we go further into the subject in the next chapter) the practice of castrating young boys with promising voices before they reached puberty, thus preserving their high voices into adulthood, was almost exclusive to Italy. It was primarily done in order to provide high voices for church, where women were forbidden to sing; it flourished in opera only secondarily, and became unacceptable there in the early nineteenth century whereas the church variety, the so-called 'sacred capons', continued into the early twentieth century. The acceptance of castrati in Venetian opera – often as the virile male lead, but sometimes cross-dressed as the female principal – is certainly another example of 'carnival misrule', but seventeenth-century audiences were far less concerned about realism in our modern sense. Cross-dressing was readily accepted in serious as well as comic situations; often women would alternate with castrati in playing the leading male roles.

Given the newness of the genre, opera singing as a sole occupation was not yet possible: in spite of high wages for the most sought-after performers, no one in Venice could hope to make a living from it. So singers had alternative employment. The castrati could find work in the multitude of church choirs in the city and elsewhere, and often both they and the women relied on a noble protector – a sponsor who would provide them with residence and employment as 'court singer' in an aristocratic household. A good case in point are the Manelli family, who in 1637 were largely responsible for that inaugural production of *Andromeda* at the Teatro San Cassiano. Francesco Manelli, the composer,

also sang two roles; his wife Maddalena, a Roman, sang tw
After *Andromeda*, they and their troupe embarked on other
ventures, but at the same time they held other positions. Franc
started life as a church singer, and in 1638 became a bass at
most famous church, the San Marco; Maddalena held a series of court positions (notably with the Orsini family in Rome). Some years after *Andromeda*, although still involved in occasional operas, the Manellis moved to Parma. Francesco and his son (also a singer) were employed in a church choir, Maddalena was a performer at the ducal court.[12] As the market for opera increased, there could be tension between these various occupations (some the product of a nearly modern market economy, others ancient and intimately involved with aristocratic or ecclesiastical privilege). Such conflicts of interest could result in undisguised threats. When in 1667 the Duke of Savoy summoned back two of his singers who had decamped to perform opera in the Venice carnival season, he threatened one of them (a castrato) with 'the effects of our rightful indignation', adding with sinister overtones that 'princes like us have long arms'.[13]

SURVIVAL OF THE FITTEST

The actual voices of these singers are impossible to re-create. What we can glean from (rare) contemporary accounts is usually so vague as to be merely frustrating. One famous early Venetian singer, Anna Renzi (c. 1620–after 1661), had an entire volume dedicated to her in 1644. Among numerous general encomiums there are passages of surprising detail, but they are couched in now-alien notions of human biology: 'She has a fluent tongue, smooth pronunciation, not affected, not rapid, a full, sonorous voice, not harsh, not hoarse, nor one that offends you with excessive subtlety; which arises from the temperament of the chest and throat, for which good voice much warmth is needed to expand the passages, and enough humidity to soften it and make it tender.'[14] More surprisingly, the music these singers performed has for the most part disappeared. Our musical knowledge of this new Venetian *dramma per musica* is limited to a few works from among the literally hundreds we know to have been performed: even those by the most famous and successful composers, such as Monteverdi, Cavalli and Cesti, are often lost.

The musical scores of this period were not regarded as precious; they were the seventeenth-century equivalent of today's film scripts, constantly changed or replaced to adapt to new circumstances. Few people imagined them as *works* in our contemporary sense, let alone thought them worth careful preservation. They were a means to an end – operatic performance, live in the theatre. Once that end had been attained, they were dispensable.

There were of course exceptions. Certain operas acquired something approaching repertory status, being revived and enjoyed in several seasons. But only two operas have established a firm place in the modern repertory, and these are the two that survive by Monteverdi. Neither is entirely typical of Venetian opera in the period, and they may initially have been revived because of their composer's fame in other genres. In 1613 Monteverdi left Mantua to become *maestro di cappella* at the San Marco, which was home to a magnificent, centuries-old musical tradition. During his long career in Venice he further confirmed his reputation, writing music in many genres and adding several more theatrical pieces, most of which are now lost. By the time 'public opera' hit Venice in the late 1630s he was in his seventies and a distinguished elder statesman of Italian music. All the more remarkable, then, that he embraced the new genre, writing three operas (one lost) for Venetian theatres. The last of these, *L'incoronazione di Poppea*, was premiered during the carnival season of 1642–3 at the Teatro SS Giovanni e Paolo, which had been built and was owned by the famous Grimani family, one of the noblest in Venice. It had been the second venue to stage opera in Venice (after the Teatro San Cassiano) and was described as the city's most magnificent, boasting seventy-seven boxes in four rows, most of them leased to wealthy patrons for the entire season. *Poppea*, like *Orfeo*, is now a repertory opera. Although buried in obscurity for centuries, revivals of the opera began in the early twentieth century and have continued to the present day.

Like many in the new Venetian genre, *Poppea*'s libretto, by Giovanni Francesco Busenello, does not deal principally with the mythological characters of the earlier court entertainments; instead, historical figures tread the stage. The setting is Rome, AD 65; Nero is Emperor. The presence of historical characters is likely to have been Monteverdi's choice, and has implications for the drama. In a letter to fellow composer Alessandro Striggio in 1616, Monteverdi made his feelings clear about what he valued in musical characterization:

> How can I imitate the speech of the winds, if they do not speak? And how can I, by such means, move the passions? . . . Orfeo moved us because he was a man, not a wind. Music can suggest, without any words, the noise of winds and the bleating of sheep, the neighing of horses and so on and so forth; but it cannot imitate the speech of winds because no such thing exists.[15]

This is remarkably modern-sounding, and makes us aware that Monteverdi wanted to write operas that, as well as amazing us with scenic splendour, make an Aristotelian attempt to 'arouse sympathy' – to persuade us, through the power of music, to feel some emotional kinship with the characters onstage.

The opera is in the Venetian norm of three acts and involves a tangled web of emotional and dynastic ties. Emperor Nerone is married to Ottavia but loves Poppea and wants to make her Empress. These three are the principals, and are all cast as sopranos (Nerone was probably a castrato role, Ottavia was first played by Anna Renzi). The plot is thickened by further love entanglements and by a disapproving moral philosopher, Seneca (bass). Eventually Nerone precipitates Seneca's suicide, exiles everyone else and crowns Poppea, allowing the two lovers to end the opera in blissful union. This strangely amoral farrago nevertheless permits a vast range of human emotions, particularly those that make the best music: love, hate, jealousy, fear and (last and by no means least) rampant sexual desire. Equally important is that the tussles of the noble principals are periodically commented upon, and often ridiculed, by a layer of lower-class comic characters. The latter are, if you will, the carnival element of the plot. As well as sleepy soldiers and cheeky pages, this satirical angle is represented by Arnalta (alto, or possibly a cross-dressed high tenor), Poppea's ancient nurse, who never fails to see the grotesque side of the amorous encounters of her betters.

The Act I scene between Nerone and Poppea is a good introduction of the opera's musical manners. There's a fair amount of Peri's *recitar cantando*. The words are commonplace and mostly unpoetic – simply two lovers who cannot bear to part company – but the dialogue is constantly interrupted by snatches of melody and instrumental interludes. What's more, the mixture of musical styles is intimately tied to the unfolding relationship between the lovers. The scene closes with a remarkable passage of *recitar cantando*. Poppea keeps repeating the teasing question 'Tornerai?' (Will you return?); Nerone seems almost desperate to reassure her. And then, at the end, comes a more rapid dialogue of verbal fragments, which ends with slow, languorous exchanges of the word 'addio', interspersed by breathless repetitions of the beloved's name: 'Nerone, Nerone', 'Poppea, Poppea'. The simple musical cadences are loaded with erotic charge and expressed with a directness that, even today, is somehow shocking.

It's entirely typical of the opera that immediately after this intimate scene comes an extended dialogue between Poppea and Arnalta, in which all this steamy wooing is mercilessly lampooned. Indeed, so relentlessly does the comic mingle with the serious that, at this distance of time, it's often hard to gauge the tone of *Poppea*. The treatment of Seneca is a case in point. Mostly he offers sententious advice, a high point coming later in Act 1, in a tremendous confrontation with Nerone. But moments before this scene Seneca has been comically caricatured by one of those cheeky pages, who even makes musical fun of the philosopher's ponderous diction. We can think of this as another example of carnival misrule, of the opera reflecting the Venetian season in which it was performed. But there are moments when we may nevertheless be confused. For example, in Seneca's death scene in Act 2 the opening recitative seems to have a comfortingly plain relationship between words and music. 'Breve angoscia è la morte' (Death is but a brief torment), the philosopher sings, and obligingly sinks to his lowest register; but then 'se ne vola all'Olimpo' (we fly to Mount Olympus), and the word 'vola' (fly) has a long flight of rising vocal ornamentation. The ensuing chorus of friends (just three of them) takes up this solemn tone in earnest. In what must have seemed at the time an old-fashioned (and perhaps for that reason particularly sombre) musical style, that of the contrapuntal madrigal, the friends intone a painful chromatic line: 'Non morir, non morir Seneca' (Don't die, don't die Seneca). A powerful sense of tragedy is, it seems, being created. But then something extraordinary happens. The middle section of the friends' chorus completely changes tone, both verbally and musically. To a nonchalant, modern-sounding musical figure, they confide to their beloved sage: '*I* certainly wouldn't want to die; life is too sweet, the sky is too clear; every bitterness, every poison, is, in the end, rather slight'. And then, after this sprightly interlude, the tragic madrigal returns, and the scene ends with more portentous recitative from Seneca. What are we to make of this chorus? Monteverdi's setting of its middle section (which is long and lovingly developed) seems like another lampoon, another sending up of the serious, another carnival gesture, this time uncomfortably inserted in the middle of the tragic. Performers and producers today must make their own decisions about how best to deliver the passage, but its difficulties are a reminder of the fact that we should never take for granted the emotional charge of music so distant from us in time.

Discussion of what we *don't* know about such an historically famous work as *Poppea* could go on and on, and small surprise: during the 1642–3 Venetian carnival season no one had any idea how permanent the new genre of opera might be. Although Monteverdi was commonly considered Italy's most famous living composer, no one thought to make a permanent record of his *Poppea* music. Had the opera not been revived in Naples in the 1650s, we might have no score at all. What's more, neither of the two manuscripts that report its music gives much sign of which instruments should play which musical lines, mostly reporting just a melody and bass. We know from various documents that Venetian theatres of the period contained numerous continuo instruments (harpsichords and large lutes in particular), and given the preponderance of *recitar cantando* in the opera such variety is certainly needed. But which instruments are supposed to play the solo lines is anyone's guess.

The most serious doubt of all hovers over the basic matter of authorship. We have so far been referring to *Poppea* as 'by' Monteverdi, but evidence that he is indeed its composer is very thin (no contemporary printed sources mention him, and the manuscript copies of the music, which do, are from a decade later).[16] The vagueness of the surviving sources tells us a great deal about the relatively lowly status of composers in the operatic economy. What is particularly in doubt is whether *Poppea*'s most famous number, the closing love duet between Poppea and Nerone, is by Monteverdi or by one of his younger contemporaries. Whoever wrote it, its presence is probably bound up with emerging operatic conventions: closing love duets became a popular way to end Venetian operas of the period, and for very practical reasons. With, as ever, economy an important factor, these operas rarely include choruses, so to end with a duet was the most obvious way to close the drama with some kind of sonic climax. The vogue for finishing with two lovers was surely to do with the sheer pleasure of hearing two high voices weave in and out of each other and end in blissful union. Lovers, particularly operatic lovers, often sing about 'melting into each other', and the closing duet in *Poppea* is a wonderful musical depiction of that ultimate loss of identity. And so, either when *Poppea* first appeared or when it was revived after the composer's death, a closing love duet became its finale. We don't know for sure who wrote it, or even whether it was intended to end this particular opera; we don't know what instruments should accompany it or how it was first staged or by whom it was first sung. What we do know is that it provides an opportunity for one of those moments that make us return to opera – an opportunity to hear the sheer sensuous beauty of mingled voices.

GENERIC OPERA

About 1650 the first serious objections to opera on the grounds of realism begin to circulate.[17] Why should characters be singing? Wasn't it ridiculous or distasteful to see such illogical goings on? In 1670 Charles de Saint-Évremond, writing about Italian operas he had seen in Paris (among them several by Cavalli), gave voice to this discomfort:

> There is another thing in Operas so contrary to Nature, that I cannot be reconciled to it; and that is the singing of the whole Piece from beginning to end, as if the Persons represented were ridiculously match'd, and had agreed to treat in Musick both the most common, and most important affairs of life. Is it to be imagin'd that a master calls upon his servant, or sends him on an errand, singing; that one friend imparts a secret to another, singing; that men deliberate in council, singing; that orders in time of battle are given, singing; and that men are melodiously killed with swords and darts?[18]

The French were particularly quick to object to Italian opera's foundational lack of realism – its continual music. But such discomfort was more widespread, and also relates to the differences between the earliest operas of Caccini, Peri and Monteverdi, and those of the Venetian and post-Venetian phases. Arias in which virtuosity triumphed over recitative-like clarity, or in which emotion was tailored to the demands of a particular genre, seem to have become an irritant that raised new aesthetic issues for opera.

What is more, the vocal writing – both its virtuosity and (soon) the greater formal complexity of the arias that showcase it – changed in response to multiple pressures, not all of them strictly musical. One point a modern operagoer tends to forget is how noisy audiences once were. In Venice, contemporary accounts repeatedly mention the rowdiness and rudeness of the public: in many theatres, boxes were fitted with shutters so that occupants could close out the opera and dally as they pleased, talking as loudly as they saw fit. One way to view the evolving formulas for opera may therefore be as a way to assert *music* against *noise*. The preference for high voices would continue in serious Italian opera until the early nineteenth century, and may have been another weapon in opera's acoustic warfare. We know, for instance, that pitting the voice against ambient noise was a factor in outdoor performances of opera and oratorio in Rome: to raise the volume, multiple singers could be assigned to an aria, all firing off together in unison. Singers also learned to perform more elaborately; arias became individual gems for the executants to polish, allowing their music to compete for attention in this loud arena.

Indeed, a key aspect of opera from 1650 to the end of its first century is the way composers, librettists, scene designers and performers negotiated (with each other, but also – crucially – with an audience that was paying at least part of the bill) a series of operatic *conventions*: standard forms of communication, some of which would then last for centuries. The most important of these is seen only fleetingly in *Poppea*: the gradual emergence of a more obvious distinction between recitative and aria – a distinction between moments in which the plot could be advanced and musical conversation occur, and those in which virtuoso singing could be enjoyed. This process had at its base the issue of verisimilitude. Monteverdi was a conservative: there are lyrical passages in *Poppea*, but they tend to flow seamlessly in and out of the old *recitar cantando*, never stopping the action for long. The next generation (Cavalli prominent among them) opened up further dramatic possibilities in which extended solo song became acceptable: there could, for instance, be solo numbers at moments that naturally called for song, such as lullabies or incantations. More significant, though, was a steady increase in soliloquies: moments in which characters might be released from dialogue to muse internally, and thus be thought able to indulge in more regular musical periods. These moments came to be placed at the ends of scenes, allowing the singer to depart after the moment of solitary reflection. In this way, that stock-in-trade of the eighteenth and early nineteenth centuries, the so-called exit aria, gradually took shape.

As might be expected, the formal shape of these arias was at first extremely varied. An early favourite was the ABB type: the last lines of text would underpin a more developed musical period in which melody could be expanded and repeated, with individual words and phrases stretched across the musical canvas. This end-based musical expansion clearly meshed well with the idea of arias as the expanded final moments of a soliloquy. But ABB slowly gave way to something with even greater possibilities of musical development: the ABA or ternary form, which would become standard in the eighteenth century. This idea – of making a musical statement, going on to something contrasting, then returning to the first idea – made eminent sense in terms of purely musical balance, and had long been used in instrumental music; but at first it did not seem suitable for operatic arias, at least in serious contexts. Comic characters, it was thought, might indulge in such obviously static musical constructions; but for those whose aim was to move the listeners, such surrender to musical elaboration was deemed too frivolous. Eventually, though, the attractions of musical expansion and repetition for singers and their audiences made ABA arias the convention, and as they became so, their lack of verisimilitude was mostly forgotten. Musical elaboration gained a further foothold on the operatic stage.

This process – in which the strangeness of continuously (and ever more elaborately) sung drama was accepted – saw the emergence of many conventions, not just aria forms. There were also scenic regulars: operatic action took place against increasingly sophisticated backdrops, and these could if necessary be recycled and become the object of renewed wonder. Elaborate perspective painting on both the wings and the backdrop presented magnificent gardens or woodlands or palaces; through the new technology of wing flats that could be rapidly interchanged, these sets could be alternated at great speed. Typical operatic interiors tended to be courtly in the manner of the old *intermedi*, flattering the audience by involving them in a world of unabashed magnificence. In one particularly lavish production (Nolfi's *Bellerofonte* – Bellerophon – Venice, 1642), the city of Venice herself was proudly displayed to the audience – patrons could see their city laid out in idealized form, made splendid and newly alluring by its representation on the operatic stage. As a contemporary reported, 'Everybody acclaimed [it] as a tour de force: the eye was deceived by the Piazza, with its public buildings imitated to the life, and it delighted increasingly in the deception, almost forgetting where it actually was thanks to that fiction.'[19]

Further conventions emerged in the forms of situations thought particularly conducive to musical and scenic elaboration. We have already mentioned the final love duet in Monteverdi's *Poppea*, a type of ending that became standard procedure, and kept a form of ensemble singing alive in Italian opera when solo singing (arias) was otherwise taking up more and more of the territory. Other stock situations included the mad scene, in which any amount of extravagant vocal effect could be accepted as true-to-life; or scenes in the underworld, which acquired a special type of poetry and a battery of unusual instruments. Underworld and magic scenes went back as far as the *intermedi*, and were of course central to all those Orpheus operas. Elaborate laments, with characters prostrated by grief, were at first done as *recitar cantando*, but shifted to aria in mid-century, gradually becoming moments at which extravagant vocalization was the norm. Once such scenes and numbers became de rigueur, librettists and composers had an easier time. Making an opera became analogous to making a movie sequel, or writing the next mystery in a series where your detective already has all his attractive quirks in place. The sequel may still be marvellous, but the content has been industrialized. It goes faster.

Cavalli's *Giasone* (Jason, 1649) – libretto by Giacinto Andrea Cicognini, based on the story of Jason and the Golden Fleece – includes a good deal of such content, and often plays a starring role in accounts of seventeenth-century Italian opera at its most extravagant.[20] Given that there are four somewhat interchangeable lovers, we get multiple love duets. Medea as a sorceress has special access to the dark arts and uses them in her incantation scene in Act 1, where an otherworldly chorus serves as her backup. There is a mad scene in Act 2 (though Isifile, the madwoman in question, is angry rather than crazy). There are sleep scenes, where dozing off provides the same opportunities for musical strangeness as do insanity or the supernatural. There is, though, one wonderful dramaturgical oddity: cameos by puppet-master Gods that are not restricted (as would be usual) to the prologue, or some deus ex machina finale. In the middle of Act 2, Giove (Jupiter) and Eolo (Aeolus) appear, meeting in the 'Cave of the Winds' to discuss whether they should interfere in the plot. This pulls the plot focus back from the doings of the human cast, making a breathing space in which the music sounds unlike any other in the opera, since Gods have a special licence to sing as they please, especially in a cave where hurricanes meet. That the Gods take an interest in the mortals comes from the source myth, and functions as always in such myths to universalize mortal travail. This very same gesture, a midway pullback from Giasone and company, is used in the 1963 film *Jason and the Argonauts*, where the analogous breathing space in Olympus shows Zeus and Hera (Niall MacGinnis and Honor Blackman) playing a game with mortal chess pieces – demonstrating that effective dramaturgy will repeat itself over the centuries.

The component parts that went into the makeup of something like *Giasone* remained robust operatic currency for many decades, their progeny even surviving into operas of the twentieth century. They remind us that artistic conventions have astonishing longevity and persistence, above all when they work for all concerned – librettists, composers, producers, singers, and audiences. And they demonstrate that the operatic passions of early Venetian audiences have something in common with our own.

POSTLUDE: THE DIASPORA

Venice, which was central in the early establishment of public opera, did not retain a unique place in its history. For one thing, public opera found another happy home in Rome (although female singers were prohibited from appearing on stage, which made for strict gender homogeneity in casting). The Barberini Palace, completed in 1639, included a performance space for opera that could hold more than 3000 spectators, which puts it on a par with the Teatro di San Carlo in Naples, also 3000 plus, and with twentieth-century barns such as the old and new Metropolitan Opera houses in New York. Opera production in Rome was inflected by the tastes of prelates and the strictures of the Church, an interesting mix that produced such notorious oddities as *Sant'Alessio* (Saint Alexis, 1632), an opera on a Catholic topic with a libretto by the future Pope Clement IX. As one eyewitness of the first performances told it, there was scandal aplenty, although not to be found anywhere within the opera's squeaky-clean plot or sedate musical aesthetic:

> The entire spectacle was recited in music with those *stili recitativi* they use in Italy, and one understood all the words as distinctly as if they had been merely spoken. All the voices were excellent, being the elite of the musicians of the Palace and of Rome. The actors who played women were beautiful, being either young pages or young castratos *di cappella*, so that muffled sighs were heard in the hall, which admiration and desire drew forth from the peacock breasts; the men of the purple, having more authority, behaved with greater freedom, so much that the Cardinals San Giorgio and Aldobrandini, with puckered lips and frequent and sonorous clucking of the tongue, invited those beardless actors to come and be kissed.[21]

Rome is here a site where ecclesiastic naughtiness and operatic decadence meet and kiss – something that would become a literary cliché. It is the basis for Honoré de Balzac's novella *Sarrasine* (1830), whose main plot is as follows: a naïve and impressionable French sculptor goes to Rome in 1758, falls in love with a beautiful (apparently) female opera singer but is warned that Cardinal Cicognara is her protector; 'she' turns out to be a castrated male who is a transvestite on and off duty; the sculptor is murdered by the jealous prelate's henchmen, general horror being conveyed at the prelate's unspeakable tastes, Rome's wicked ways and castrati as a species.

Opera was also flourishing (if less colourfully) in Naples, at the small Teatro San Bartolomeo (built in 1620), where operas deriving from Venice were taken up in local productions. In Venice itself, an economic decline in the latter part of the seventeenth century put further strain on operatic finances. As Saint-Évremond's diatribe shows, there was continuing disapproval of Venetian opera's cavalier disregard of realism, in particular its move away from the spare, elegant, intimately expressive *recitar cantando* to the extravagance of extended arias. Before the end of the seventeenth century, the disapproval would swell into a diapason of heckling and complaining, causing the first of what would turn out to be opera's periodic reforms to be set in train.

But opera was anyway on the move, carried to other Italian towns by travelling troupes, crossing borders into France and then England and further afield, finding its most famous homes in other wealthy cities. In most of these new venues, whether pushed by reform or not, opera acquired its own peculiarities and local traditions. The German-speaking lands were the least rebellious, generally welcoming Italian incursions:

Vienna established court adaptations of opera that retained the Italian language, as did Munich and other centres. In a parallel development, though, German-language opera found an audience. For a long time, the historical 'first' in this genre was said to be Heinrich Schütz's *Dafne* of 1627. Whether or not this (now lost) work is a genuine contender for the title is still a matter of dispute, and the fact that scholars argue about it illustrates how thoroughly operatic history can become intertwined with a broader sense of cultural nationalism (at stake with *Dafne* was the identity of the 'inventor' of German opera, and the fact that Schütz was an established master of severe church music made him a particularly attractive candidate).[22] But whether or not the great Schütz did indeed deserve this title, German opera's progress in the seventeenth century was always stuttering.

Much more distinctive were the various solutions found in France, in which a curiously productive love–hate relationship with Italian opera would run for centuries. In Paris the court of Louis XIV at first welcomed the exotic Italian import; Cardinal Mazarin (himself an Italian, born Mazzarini) introduced six operas between 1645 and the early 1660s. In each case they were modified somewhat to suit French taste, not least with the addition of ballet (which had long been established in France as a tragic genre) and in some cases by replacing the castrati with baritones. However, with the death of Mazarin in 1661 the fortunes of Italian opera waned. The scene was soon dominated by Jean-Baptiste Lully (1632–87), an expatriate Italian who progressed to opera through instrumental music and then ballet, in the latter via a collaboration with Molière. Lully and Molière produced a series of *comédies-ballets*: pieces that inserted singing and dancing into comic plays and were one precursor of the type of comic opera in French (and then German) that mixed musical numbers into spoken drama. In 1672 Louis granted Lully the exclusive rights to an 'Académie Royale de Musique', in effect allowing him personally to invent and patent the genre of French-language serious opera. This highly distinctive brand was called *tragédie en musique* or *tragédie lyrique* and (as those names suggest) was strongly influenced by France's powerful and prescriptive tradition of spoken drama.

One of the important ways in which French opera distinguished itself from the Italian version – apart from the integral ballets – was in matters of verisimilitude (as we shall see in the next chapter, French polemics about this topic were much more common than Italian ones, and often turned on the distinction between spoken and sung drama). The Lullian *tragédie lyrique* tended to avoid long, elaborate arias with instrumental accompaniment, generally showing a far less rigid distinction between recitative and aria, and a distrust of anything approaching Italian vocal virtuosity. It also favoured natural voices rather than those of castrati, and moved the plot forward by means of lengthy recitatives that tried hard to preserve the rhythms of spoken language (at least as that language was declaimed in classic French drama). Each act of this aria-less – or at least aria-shy – brand of opera was then enlivened by a *divertissement* (literally a 'diversion') in which plot was abandoned in favour of an elaborate ballet on a mythological subject, the dancing accompanied by scenic splendours that often rivalled the old *intermedi*. The King himself danced in these ballets on many occasions, obliging the entire court to sit through them. Another fixed feature of this emphatically court entertainment was a lengthy Prologue in which, although the subject matter was ostensibly mythological, explicit homage was made to the King. As this brief description implies, many of the developments of Venetian opera were reversed in Lully's *tragédie lyrique*, which did not have to cater to mass audience taste and could concentrate on maintaining the classical decorum suitable to glorification of the royal dynasty. Lully's works continued to be performed even after his death in 1687; they were not seriously challenged for another forty years, and remained in the repertory until as late as the 1770s.

The third country to open its doors to opera was England, but here (as in France) a strong tradition of spoken theatre ensured that entirely sung drama was slow to gain acceptance: the English retained a notably ambiguous position towards opera, in particular its more flamboyant manifestations. However, the Jacobean period (1603–25) saw a great flowering of the court masque, an *intermedio*-like extravaganza mixing song, dance and elaborate scenery, often loosely based on some allegorical subject. Many of these were granted added literary respectability by the involvement of the great playwright Ben Jonson, who in the preface to one masque, *Lovers Made Men* (1617), wrote that the masque was 'sung after the Italian manner, *stile recitativo*',[23] which suggests that developments in Italy were already having some influence. There was, though, a further aspect of the English scene, one that eventually made the capital an excellent place to foster extravagant theatrical entertainment, but that also led to its periodic downfall: the relationship between the nation and its monarchy. Many petty states in Italy had rulers who played an important part in artistic display of many kinds, and the operatic spectacles arranged by Louis XIV were legendary; but England's royal family suffered a catastrophic civil war in the middle of the seventeenth century, between supporters of the crown and rebellious subjects. At the climax of this conflict, in 1649, Charles I was beheaded and the symbolic position of his office drastically reduced. In spite of the royal Restoration, in which his son Charles II regained the throne in 1660 after a period of rule by what was nominally a republic, nothing was ever the same again in matters of kingly sway, whether cultural or otherwise.

Perhaps not surprisingly given the strength of its spoken drama tradition, the issue of operatic verisimilitude – of characters singing rather than speaking – proved particularly troublesome in England, and the preferred forms of drama with music through most of the seventeenth century were either masques or so-called 'semi-operas', in which music did not have to bear the full burden of dramatic narration, and could be reserved for special scenes such as those featuring the supernatural. William Davenant's *The Siege of Rhodes* (given during the republican period, in 1656) is usually called the first full-length English opera, and was set to music (now lost) by Henry Lawes and William Locke, two of the most famous composers of the period. But this experiment in what was called 'Recitative Musick' seems to have come into being as a way to avoid the republic's ban on theatrical entertainments, and did not have significant progeny until much later in the century. One of those progeny, indeed one of the most famous examples of English-language opera, is *Dido and Aeneas* (1689?) by Henry Purcell (1658?–95). *Dido* is very hard to categorize, as the version that has survived is one arranged for performance at a girls' boarding school in London. Although there are signs of both French and Italian influence (the former in an allegorical Prologue, whose music is now lost; the latter in the shape and style of some of the arias, particularly the famous 'Lament' that Dido sings near the end, 'When I am laid in earth'), the music is unusually simple in comparison with Purcell's other creations around the same time. Some have even suggested that *Dido* may have started life as a rather different (and more elaborate) court entertainment; but the evidence is frustratingly incomplete.

*

By the end of its first century, opera had established roots across and then outside Italy: in France, England, various parts of the German-speaking lands and central Europe, and in Spain. In most places it assumed an indigenous form to suit the new terrain. Although its development in the early days as court entertainment had been tenuous, the buoyancy and adaptability of the Venetian model, pioneered by travelling theatrical-musical troupes and exported around the country, were by now proven. Opera's historical progress would take many more turns during the next 300 years; but through most of this history it would retain some of those characteristics we have found during its first centennial. These characteristics caused courts and noble families, and later the paying public, to lay down improbable amounts of money in order to witness unprecedented vocal feats set against moments of dazzling visual splendour: to draw prestige and, lest we forget, sheer pleasure from a new form of drama, one in which a fantastic story was told through singing.

3
Opera seria

When the first public opera house opened in Venice in 1637, those who attended the new art form had few expectations. Although some of the musical styles were familiar from other genres, operatic occasions up to that point had amounted to little more than a collection of court entertainments, their shape largely dictated by the events they celebrated. Just a few decades later, and opera boasted many of the traits it would retain over much of its 400-year history. Most important, it was established as a genre – a cultural product with a set of characteristics that its consumers would expect to see repeated. By 1650, these characteristics stretched beyond the emerging alternation of 'recitative' and 'aria' to embrace stock dramatic situations: the comic aria, the sleep scene, the invocation, the mad scene. Final love duets such as that in Monteverdi's *L'incoronazione di Poppea* (1643) were a case in point. To hear two lovers singing at the end of an evening of alternating recitatives and solo arias became an expectation – something to look forward to, something that would bring a pair of principal voices together sensuously. And so such a duet closed *Poppea*: possibly written by Monteverdi, possibly by a younger composer preparing the opera for performance in far-off Naples; added, anyway, by someone who ignored the work's integrity in favour of responding creatively to audience desires.[1]

As opera expanded geographically, it almost always kept something of the public nature it had discovered in Venice. But in most places this relatively democratic aspect had to make accommodations with a prevailing court culture. In Florence the Medici family embraced the new genre but adapted it to their propagandistic purposes, using operatic performance to celebrate births and weddings in ways resembling the old *intermedi*; the Spanish viceroy in Naples did something similar; the Papal authorities in Rome were reluctant to allow public opera houses, but both comic and pastoral works were given privately in noble households. Many other places, though, contributed to the steady rise of public theatres. The later years of the seventeenth century saw larger and more diverse audiences, ones whose tastes often ran to lavishness rather than restraint. Not coincidentally, the period is also marked by the rise of professional virtuoso singers: star performers trained to beguile and amaze their auditors by singing at a level of difficulty unprecedented in previous centuries.

THE SINGING PROFESSION

The most successful of these singers consolidated the influence they had gathered in the late seventeenth century, continuing to earn more than any of the other participants, composers included. Some lamented this loud and long, but the gathering disparity in pay between singers and others was predictable. The presence of anything akin to an operatic repertory was still a long way in the future; it was not the norm for operas to be revived, and when such restagings happened (as with the Naples version of Monteverdi's *Poppea* in the 1650s) they were often adapted to suit new conditions and changing tastes. The musical part of an opera was a disposable thing, easily replaced. Librettists tended to have a little more cachet. They were, after all, men of letters – a far more respectable profession than musician – and if successful could have their creations set to music a number of times. But the great operatic venues made themselves exceptional above all through their roster of star vocalists. Small surprise, then, that the phenomenon of singers with careers exclusively in the operatic market-place began in the later seventeenth century. The existence of this new professional class had at least one important social ramification: for perhaps the first time in history, working women were paid as much as or sometimes more than men for doing an equivalent task. It was possible for women to become independent and wealthy by means of their talent.

The way was not always easy. Close professional proximity to a predominantly male world brought continual problems, particularly as regards reputation. As one Naples official put it in 1740:

> they [women singers] have never been held to be respectable, since the singing profession carries with it the harsh necessity of dealing with many men: composers, instrumentalists, poets and music-lovers; anyone who witnesses all this coming and going in and out of a woman's house readily concludes that she is immoral, whether she actually is or not.[2]

But the rewards, particularly in a mixed economy where public theatres also enjoyed noble or royal backing, could be unprecedented. In the late seventeenth century, a star singer could earn for one carnival season in Venice the equivalent of an entire year's salary in a church or ducal chapel; thirty years later, star court opera singers in Dresden could earn well over £1000 per season. This was serious wealth.[3]

The only group to come close to female soloists in terms of earning power were the castrati. The acceptance of castrati on the operatic stage was a central feature of the essential artificiality of opera in the early eighteenth century; it is also the reason why most operas of the period can never be performed today as they were performed then. The castrati have gone for ever. It is well, though, to bear in mind that relatively few of them made a living singing in opera. The principal occupation of most castrati was as singers in the Catholic church, where female voices were banned. In other words, the practice began and continued in the service of God rather than of operatic pleasure. However, and as we saw briefly in the last chapter, castrati were also a presence in opera from almost the start. A castrato sang the Prologue to Monteverdi's *Orfeo*, and castrati were cast in two of the opera's female roles. They frequently appeared in Venetian opera, playing both male and female characters. By the start of the eighteenth century they had become a flamboyant and even characteristic presence on the operatic stage, at least in serious opera, and were above all famous for playing the *primo uomo*, the heroic male lead.

The precise nature of the operation that created a castrato was for long shrouded in secrecy, but the basic process was as simple as it was brutal. Boys with promising musical abilities were operated on before their voices changed, their testicles either removed surgically or bound so tightly that they withered away from lack of blood supply. The voice thus preserved would remain high (although sometimes dropping to an alto range), and moreover could be uncommonly sustained – notes could be held for a long time through a single breath. The hormonal effects of the operation caused significant physical changes. Castrati could become abnormally tall, with expanded rib cages (hence the long held notes), spider-like fingers and other strange characteristics. As one horrified Frenchman wrote in 1739:

> Most of them grow big, and as fat as capons, their hips, rump, arms, throat and neck as round and chubby as a woman's. When you meet them at a gathering, it is astonishing when they speak, to hear a little child's voice emerging from such a colossus.[4]

Although accepted on the stage and sometimes worshipped elaborately for their vocal powers, castrati were always thought exotic, even at the height of their operatic dissemination. Myths about them, particularly concerning their supposed sexual exploits, were commonplace in the eighteenth century. Many of these stories were bound up with the fact that the castrati became symbols of the extravagance of the art form generally, a neat demonstration of its fundamental irrationality. It was frequently rumoured – whether accurately or not is difficult to know, although modern medical testimony doubts it – that castrati could still indulge in sexual intercourse, and this suspicion caused consternation, in part because their sexual pleasures could plainly be pursued without fear of causing pregnancy. An anonymous pamphlet published in 1728 in London contains an invented verse epistle from Faustina Bordoni, one of the greatest operatic sopranos of her day, to Senesino, a renowned castrato. Bordoni succinctly outlines the advantages of a castrato lover:

> Safely they give uninterrupted joys,
> Without the genial Curse of Girls and Boys.

In the same pamphlet, an imagined love duet between the soprano and castrato is portrayed as stimulating a remarkable flowering of same-sex (or even solitary-sex) activity among both the females and males of the audience:

> The Fair have wished their lovers warm as me,
> The Men themselves caress'd instead of Thee.[5]

The horrified Frenchman quoted earlier had caught on to these rumours, and used them to peddle a rather cruel joke:

> Some [castratos] are very pretty: with the fair ladies they are smug and conceited, and, if spiteful rumour is to be believed, much in demand for

> their talents, which are limitless; for they are very talented. It is even said that one of these *demivirs* presented a petition to Pope Innocent XI, asking for permission to get married on the grounds that the operation had not been entirely successful; the Pope wrote in the margin: *Che si castri meglio* [They need to castrate better].[6]

These lubricious stories suggest that the sex lives of castrati (whether imagined or real) were sometimes symbols of just the kind of hedonistic excess that opera itself seemed to represent. Those who strove to attack opera often made the connection explicit: opera's vocal excesses – its strings of wordless notes, its reliance on trills and other ornaments – were in eighteenth-century terms symbols of luxury, of vital energy going to waste. What could be more grotesquely appropriate to the genre than a stage peopled by creatures who had a sinister ability to dally with the female sex without risk of reproduction – to indulge, that is, in the most dangerous and socially disruptive form of luxury one could imagine?[7]

Perhaps not surprisingly, the historical afterlife of castrati has been extraordinarily rich. They continued in church choirs through much of the nineteenth century in some parts of Italy, and not until 1903 did the Sistine Chapel Choir in Rome finally ban them by means of a *motu proprio*. Their operatic vogue came to an end around 1830. For an era in which gender roles became increasingly differentiated, and transgression of the boundaries increasingly policed, they produced a sense of revulsion rather than excitement. We have already cited Honoré de Balzac's novella *Sarrasine* (1830), in which the hero, a young artist, falls in love with an operatic soprano called La Zambinella, only to discover to his horror that his idealized woman is in fact a castrato. Much nearer our own time is Gérard Corbiau's film *Farinelli il castrato* (1994), a fanciful biopic of the most famous castrato of all, Carlo Broschi (nicknamed 'Farinelli', 1705–82). Here cinematic opulence is combined with an unusual feat of modern sound technology to create an illusion of the castrato's lost voice, since Farinelli's singing was computer-generated by melding together a soprano and a male falsettist, a counter-tenor.

Chronologically between these two examples, in 1902 and 1904, come the extraordinary recordings of Alessandro Moreschi (1858–1922), sometimes billed as 'the last castrato', who sang in the Sistine Chapel Choir from 1883 until the early years of the twentieth century and who by a series of strange chances made a number of sound recordings.

Moreschi was only in his mid-forties at the time he was recorded. He sang not with what we imagine as eighteenth-century restraint, but in the vocal style of *his* time, which means with an attack, declamation and use of the so-called 'chest voice' that we associate more with singers of the Puccini and Mascagni era. High male voice, sacred music, *verismo*-style delivery – this is a bizarre mélange for which we have no good name. The fundamental impression for us today is of a prematurely old, quavering but still piercing, sexless, frighteningly unclassifiable voice.[8] Rational anxiety always surrounded them. Even as early as the eighteenth century, each castrato had to furnish himself with a convenient story of the youthful misfortune that had necessitated his operation. The great Farinelli sometimes allowed that he had fallen from a horse; others favoured the bite of a wild pig as the cause of their mutilation. By the mid nineteenth century such excuses had become a kind of ritual. One scholarly authority tells us, on impeccable documentary evidence, that during that period 'the surviving castrati of the Sistine Chapel had apparently all fallen victim to pigs'.[9]

OPERATIC REFORMERS

Around the time the castrati were coming to operatic prominence in the last decades of the seventeenth century, Italian opera underwent one of its periodic reforms. There were attempts to domesticate its exoticism and irrationality; in particular to bring it into greater conformity with the rules that had governed spoken drama in the later sixteenth century, and that were now being reasserted. The history of opera is punctuated by such polemics, many of which, when looked at from a distance, seem remarkably similar. Almost always the 'reform' comes about because a perception emerges (usually among men of letters) that opera has got out of hand: that its perennial extravagances have become *too* extravagant; that the sober literary and aesthetic values of spoken drama have been ignored too flagrantly; that music, and often scenic spectacle, have become too important and risk drowning out the drama; that singers have become too powerful. Such criticisms of opera have existed throughout its history, and will exist for as long as the art form flourishes. But at certain moments the polemics have taken on a peculiar force, and led to material changes – usually an ostensible return to what are declared to be 'classical' values.

These polemics have often been about a lost elitism: about fears that opera was becoming too popular. In the 1680s Cristoforo Ivanovich, whom we heard in the last chapter complaining about the fees paid to singers, was above all concerned about opera's decline into popularity, about a special, refined taste that had been invaded:

> At the beginning, two exquisite voices, a small number of delightful arias and a few scene changes sufficed to satisfy curiosity. Now we object if we hear a voice that is not up to European standards; we expect every scene to be accompanied by a change of setting and the machines to be brought in from another world.[10]

Two decades later, another critic, Giovanni Crescimbeni, went into even greater detail. Crescimbeni was a great lover of Cavalli's *Giasone* (Venice, 1648), but saw it as the beginning of a sad decline. We will hear such language and tone often in the history of opera:

> To stimulate to a greater degree with novelty the jaded taste of the spectators, equally nauseated by the vileness of comic things and the seriousness of tragic ones, the inventor of drama united them, mixing kings and heroes and other illustrious personages with buffoons and servants and the lowest men with unheard of monstrousness. This concoction of characters was the reason for the complete ruin of the rules of poetry, which went so far into disuse that not even locution was considered, which, forced to serve music, lost its purity and became filled with idiocies. The careful deployment of figures that ennoble oratory was neglected and language was restricted to terms found in common speech, which is more appropriate for music; and finally the series of those short metres, commonly called *ariette*, which with a generous hand are sprinkled over the scenes, and the overwhelming impropriety of having characters speak in song, completely removed from the compositions the power of the affections and the means of moving them in the listeners.[11]

There we have it. Opera is simply too extravagant. It won't obey the 'rules of poetry'; it is a dangerous social leveller, allowing those of all classes to mingle freely in song. Music, the cause of all these ills, is destroying a noble art form.

Before the end of the seventeenth century, Italian opera had become an important artistic export, but, as poetry or drama, it was a frail reed. Already in the 1670s, a venerated literary figure such as Charles de

Saint-Évremond was complaining that he had never seen an Italian opera 'which appear'd not to be despicable both as to the Contrivance of the subject and the Poetry'.[12] Italian poets, for whom libretto writing had become a major occupation, suffered widespread contempt for their efforts. In response to this and many other polemics, a reform did indeed take place, one over which the so-called Arcadian academy in Rome (a group formed around 1690) had much influence. The Arcadians' patron, Cardinal Pietro Ottoboni, had also tried his hand at reforming libretti, and their project was a purification and rationalization of all the arts, with opera of the anarchic Venetian kind clearly a prime target. The basic notion of sung drama was now generally accepted. So was a division between simple recitative, musically rudimentary and word-dominated, and aria, more complex musically. In arias, words were less important or even disappeared entirely underneath the weight of musical ornament. But the Arcadians wanted a rebalancing, an opera that would be more under the control of librettists than of musicians or scene designers. These men of letters also tried to insist that the subject matter should be suitable as a carrier of ideal moral statements, typically from Roman or Greek antiquity. Unsettling comic characters should disappear. A reduced number of characters should then confine themselves to endless examination of the complexities of human emotion, often through experiencing conflicts between personal feeling and public duty, in a balanced and classically poised manner. Even die-hard critics admitted that the musically luxuriant aria was here to stay; but it needed, they said, to be more controlled and carefully structured. There was, in this and all subsequent reforms, an element of compromise: everyone understood that opera's basic extravagance and lack of verisimilitude had become its crowning glory, and had to be retained; but its essential elements could, they thought, be restrained and ordered more logically.

THE NEW OPERA: *OPERA SERIA*

The judgement of history has not, at least until very recently, been generous to this new kind of opera, which is often referred to under the loose generic term *opera seria* (serious opera). True, the Arcadian reformers' sentiments and aims, particularly those that lamented and strove to restrict the influence of singers, have sometimes been applauded. But the music that came in their wake has mostly stayed in the history books, a stranger to the modern stage. Joseph Kerman's famous *Opera as Drama*, first published in 1956, went so far as to label the entire period between the passing of Monteverdi and the emergence of Mozart as 'the dark ages'.[13] It is still just possible to take such a view. Consider the operatic milieu so meticulously reconstructed in *Farinelli il castrato*. The theatre is dimly lit by candles, the spectators primarily pay attention to each other – flirting, signalling, eating – anything but attending to the drama onstage, which unfolds amid acres of musically uninteresting recitative. The only moments of relative attention are those in which a virtuoso singer comes to the footlights to beguile everyone with a beautiful aria.

Yes, by twentieth-century standards, such contempt for the art-work is benighted. Then there is the typical *opera seria* plot, a potpourri set in ancient somewhere, peopled by a small number of characters who spend much of their time trying either to murder or seduce one another (in the recitatives), and who then periodically lapse into moments of prolonged anguish (in the arias) as they bemoan the fact that their noble ideals are thus compromised. The only certainty, apart from the fact that they will express their conflicting emotions with many virtuoso roulades and trills, is that in the last scene they will all be improbably forgiven by an erstwhile despot, a figure often openly modelled on the real-life despot sponsoring and presiding over the operatic performance. And then, as if all those monstrous castrati were not enough, there is *opera seria*'s inveterate fondness for plots in which men dress up as women, or (even more frequently) women dress up as men. Almost all the principal roles were written for high voices, soprano or alto singers, female or castrato. Either a woman or a man could be cast in any given high-voiced part, regardless of the fictional character's actual gender.

Reformed *opera seria* of the early eighteenth century, though offering up cross-dressing in great profusion, nonetheless had far fewer characters, and less variety of musical forms, than *Poppea* and later Venetian opera. Minor characters had fallen away, and with them disappeared the comic aspects of the plot. The 'carnival' undercutting of the serious action, which was such a feature of Venetian opera, had been replaced by unremitting moralizing and seriousness of purpose. Comic opera, as we shall see in Chapter 5, took on a form of its own, one that eventually came to rival the serious genre. So far as music was concerned, there was yet more rationalization: the rich profusion of forms jostling in seventeenth-century Venice was reduced to two basic types of operatic communication, recitative and aria. Recitative became much simpler and more formulaic than the *recitar cantando* of early opera. Called *recitativo semplice* or *recitativo secco*, it was usually accompanied only by a string bass instrument and a harpsichord, became very close to spoken declamation and was the medium in which almost all stage action would unfold. The aria, however, became an increasingly prolonged, musically elaborate, frozen moment of reflection on the part of one of the characters. Early eighteenth-century operas unremittingly alternated recitative and aria; duets or other ensembles were rare; the chorus was often banished altogether.

The endless recitative/aria alternation may seem more formulaic, more predictable and above all less flamboyant than the variety flourishing in mid-seventeenth-century Venice. But it was nevertheless this type of opera that proved the most prestigious and durable in the eighteenth century, and that spearheaded the genre's extraordinary dissemination. Around 1690, when reform began, opera outside Italy could be seen in about twenty central European courts; a hundred years later *opera seria* was all over Europe – both in courts and in cities, from Spain and Portugal in the west to Russia in the east. Why was it so successful?

One point to bear in mind was that *opera seria*, in spite of its tendency towards restraint, showed little enthusiasm for curbing the audience's visual pleasure. An important reform librettist, Apostolo Zeno (1668–1750), admitted in a letter of 1701 that 'as for the dramatic content of opera, many years of experience have led me to appreciate that you need to be fairly heavy-handed if you are to achieve your essential goal, which is pleasure'.[14] Zeno's libretti were also notable in featuring new artistic enthusiasms such as Orientalism and exoticism, with historical architecture other than that of Greece and Rome (China, Persia and India featured among his settings). *Opera seria* had two further advantages. While the wild anarchy of Monteverdi's *Poppea* made any political meaning ambiguous at best, the new, simpler plots could deliver straightforward moral and political messages, in keeping with an age in which art was thought of as didactic and improving. What's more, those moral and political messages overwhelmingly congratulated and flattered the ruling classes, displaying their rationality and beneficence but also demonstrating that they had a human side and could experience feelings as intense as those of lesser mortals. The other advantage was that this kind of opera allowed for a more complicated musical argument. The musical glory of the drama, the solo aria, developed to a point where music bestowed greater complexity on the characters, and provided the star singers with vehicles of ever-greater elaboration to dazzle the audience.

The roster of composers during this period is largely obscure: who has heard these days of Gasparini, Pollarolo or Ziani, all of whom made 'premiere' settings of Zeno libretti? Most of the works disappeared soon after they were first performed (as did almost all operas in the seventeenth and eighteenth centuries), and hardly any have so far been granted significant modern revivals. The most famous name is Alessandro Scarlatti (1660–1725), who lived right through the period of reform and whose more than sixty operas changed with the times, in particular by an expansion in the complexity of the arias and a corresponding reduction in their number. Scarlatti was born and raised in Rome, a city in which opera always had a rather difficult time because of Papal disapproval and interference; but he made a decisive impact in Naples, which for much of this period vied with Venice as the pre-eminent Italian operatic centre. In part this came about by making typical arrangements with the ruling classes: operas were performed in public theatres, but also received special showings in the vice-regal palace of the city's Spanish rulers. Perhaps equally important, though, was the presence in Naples of a number of thriving conservatories, institutions in which operatic style soon became a staple part of the education, and which produced a steady stream of composers and star singers who made operatic Naples respected throughout the peninsula and beyond. But the composer of *opera seria* who means most to us today was not from Naples, indeed was not even Italian.

HANDEL AND LONDON

George Frideric Handel (1685–1759) was born in Halle in Germany, and at the age of eighteen moved to Hamburg, which had the only public (i.e. not court-sponsored) opera house in regular use in Germany.

From there he went on a prolonged trip to Italy, and in 1711 arrived in London, where he was based for the rest of his life. Handel, by then in his mid-twenties, had already gained some operatic experience in Germany and Italy. One of his operas (*Agrippina*) had been a great success in the Venetian carnival season of 1709–10. Handel thus came to Italian opera with a varied musical background – as well as Italian influences, he had elaborate experience of German counterpoint and instrumental forms, and his overtures tell us that he also knew something about French dance idioms. With Handel, *opera seria* became decisively international; his musical eclecticism must surely have contributed to his enormous (if precarious) success in London.

The reasons Handel arrived in London in 1711 are unclear. Although it was then the largest and richest city in Europe, London's attractions as a place for a composer to make his living with Italian opera were by no means obvious: in spite of a few attempts over the previous decade, the genre had made hardly any inroads into metropolitan life. As mentioned in the last chapter, England's rich tradition of spoken drama was an obstacle, as was the reduced position of the English crown after the mid-seventeenth-century civil war. However, not long into the eighteenth century, Italian opera at last entered London's musical scene. London theatres typically operated in a mixed economy: because they had limited support from royal and noble patrons, they needed to be financed by joint stock companies. When these enterprises ran well, the revenue they generated could compete with any on the international market: London could, and for a time did, hire the most expensive singers and scene painters, becoming the musical capital of Europe so far as performers were concerned. But producing operas in this way was extremely fragile financially: financial bubbles could be created and then burst, often with catastrophic results.

Handel's first London opera, *Rinaldo* (1711), entered directly into this world. In the first decade of the eighteenth century, the architect and playwright Sir John Vanbrugh enlisted the help of noble patrons and many stockholders to build a venue for opera, the King's Theatre in the Haymarket. This was at base a money-making proposition. By means that are unclear, Vanbrugh negotiated a deal with the government, prompting legislation that guaranteed his theatre a monopoly on operatic events. He thus gained a decisive advantage over his main rival, the theatre at Drury Lane. Although this monopoly did not last long, there were some years in which the King's Theatre flourished, helped by a series of Handel operas and a roster of star international singers.

Opera in London always had to feel its way through a dense thicket of early capitalism. William Hogarth's engraving *Masquerades and Operas (or the Bad Taste of the Town)*, dating from 1724, is a wonderfully economical depiction of the opposition some Englishmen felt towards the new genre (see Figure 6). On the left is the King's Theatre, with the impresario in an upper window inviting in the crowds. Beneath, the audience is herded in by a devil and a fool. Above them is a poster supposedly depicting a typical operatic scene: a soprano and two enormous singers are in costume (the latter are castrati, as usual caricatured as grossly oversized); to the right are three noble patrons on their knees, saying, 'Pray accept £8000' – the enormous sums that singers could earn thus being parodied. In the foreground of the main picture are a couple of 'plain men' from the country, untouched by the urban madness surrounding them, one scratching his head in confusion. There is also a forlorn figure with a wheelbarrow, carting away the pearls of the English dramatic tradition (now deemed useless and unfashionable), Shakespeare, Congreve, Dryden and Ben Jonson; the sign over the barrow says 'waste paper for shops' (shades here of Dryden's satirical poem *MacFlecknoe*: 'From dusty shops neglected authors come, / Martyrs of pies, and relics of the bum'). On the right another crowd mills around a cheap pantomime version of Dr Faustus. In the background are three aristocratic patrons, posturing and idly admiring the new cultural scene and its fancy Italian architecture. We may think of this picture as a scenic backdrop to the debates that have always raged around opera, debates made all the more intense in Handel's London by the fact that opera was so flagrantly a foreign import.

RINALDO AND THE SPARROWS

Follow the milling crowd into that building on the left and we find ourselves in the operatic world of *Rinaldo*, which premiered at the King's Theatre on 24 February 1711. For Handel's London debut, the manager of the theatre, Aaron Hill, planned something exceptional. This would be the first Italian opera especially composed for the London stage (the few previous efforts having been makeshift dramas cobbled together from the music of pre-existing works); no expense would be spared. Hill wrote a canny Preface to the printed libretto, making clear the failings of past operatic attempts in comparison with his own new production:

> As I ventur'd on an Undertaking so hazardous as the Direction of OPERA's in their present Establishment, I resolv'd to spare no Pains or Cost, that might be requisite to make those Entertainments flourish in their proper Grandeur, that so at least it might not be my Fault, if the Town should hereafter miss so noble a Diversion.
>
> The Deficiencies I found, or thought I found, in such ITALIAN OPERA'S as have hitherto been introduc'd among us were, *First*, That they had been compos'd for Tastes and Voices, different from those who were to sing and hear them on the *English* Stage; And *Secondly*, That wanting the Machines and Decorations, which bestow so great a Beauty on their Appearance, they have been heard and seen to very considerable Disadvantage.
>
> At once to remedy both these Misfortunes, I resolv'd to frame some Dramma, that, by different Incidents and Passions, might afford the Musick Scope to vary and display its Excellence, and fill the Eye with more delightful Prospects, so at once to give Two Senses equal Pleasure.[15]

Here the priorities are neatly laid out. Despite the air of operatic reform circulating in Italy, which to some extent informed the shape of Handel's opera, Hill claimed to know exactly what the public would like, and boasted of how he would cater for it. The star singers would have music written especially for them, and thus would dazzle with their virtuosity all the more completely. Their effect would be enhanced by scenic marvels to outdo anything before on the British operatic stage. This was indeed a bold vision for the future, and Hill was right to make the most of it. The published libretto contained the complete text of the opera, in both Italian and English. Given that most of the audience would have understood little Italian, such an aid was important. Audience members might buy the libretto in the streets around the theatre and then, equipped with individual candles in the dimly lit theatre, could follow it during the performance.

The main characters of *Rinaldo* form a constellation typical of opera at this period, all of them boasting that tangle of conflicting emotions and loyalties needed to stimulate multiple anguished soliloquies.

The action is set during the First Crusade in the eleventh century; the Christians are laying siege to Jerusalem and on their team are Goffredo (female contralto), the commander of the army, his brother Eustazio (alto castrato) and his daughter Almirena (soprano). Almirena is engaged to a young warrior called Rinaldo (soprano castrato). The opposition comprises Argante (bass), the king of Jerusalem, who loves a sorceress called Armida (yet another soprano). A vastly simplified account of the intricacies of the plot would be that in Act 1 everyone gets introduced and has an aria or two, laying out her or his motivations and passions. At the end of the act, Argante and Armida try to weaken the Christian cause by kidnapping Almirena. In Act 2, Rinaldo comes looking for his beloved and is captured. Here the plot thickens, because Argante falls in love with Almirena, and Armida falls in love with Rinaldo. Argante finds out about Armida's new affection and is not pleased. In fact, at this stage not a single character is happy. In Act 3 all these difficulties are rapidly resolved. Rinaldo and Almirena are released through the application of Christian magic; battle is joined and the Christians win. All ends happily. In true enlightened manner, Argante and Armida convert to Christianity and are forgiven.

Why, one might ask, is the plot so complicated? This is not just a problem for today's audiences. People at the time complained about it as well. But the plot confusions are a direct result of the larger musical structure. All the major characters must be given a series of arias spaced out across the opera, so there are between three and eight per character in *Rinaldo*. These arias must be contrasting in mood, thus giving a sense of order and balance to each character's profile but also allowing the singers an opportunity to display various emotions. By following these rules, at the end of the opera one could have a sense of what (somewhat anachronistically) might be called a 'composite' character. There was also the convention – already well-developed in later seventeenth-century Venice – that singers tended to exit after their arias, thus garnering maximum effect. These musical imperatives were the engine that manipulated the plot into its various twists and turns. It was the singers around whom the plot was constructed, not the plot around which the singers were arranged. And this situation calls into question the idea that librettists and other men of letters were the driving force in operatic reforms at the turn of the eighteenth century. Looked at from the singers' point of view, the libretto was in no sense confusing, since it furnished exactly what they required: an orderly progression of contrasting arias, spaced out across the evening's entertainment.

As soon as we examine any of these arias in detail, it becomes clear that their internal structure was also formed primarily with the singer in mind. Almost all are in 'da capo' form: an initial 'A' section outlines the basic mood; this is followed by a 'B' section, likely to be different in some way, often contrasting in musical mood; finally there is a repeat of the 'A' section, with the singer expected to improvise elaborate ornamentation the second time around. It was that surplus, the unpredictable and virtuosic addition to something already heard, that lent high drama and suspense to the event. A good example of the da capo aria at its simplest is the very first number in *Rinaldo*. The stage set shows the besieged city of Jerusalem, with soldiers about to do battle. To one side are the encampments of the Christian army. In a brief opening *recitativo* Goffredo tells his clan that they can look forward to victory, then comes the aria:

GOFFREDO
Delle nostre fatiche
Siam prossimi alla meta, o gran Rinaldo!
Là in quel campo di palme
Omai solo ne resta
Coglier l'estrema messe.
E già da' lidi eoi
Spunta più chiaro il sole,
Per illustrar co' rai d'eterna gloria
L'ultima di Sion nostra vittoria.

[aria: 'A' section]
Sovra balze scoscesi e pungenti
Il suo tempio la gloria sol ha.
['B' section]
Né fra gioie, piaceri e contenti
I bei voti ad apprender si va.
['A' section repeated]
Sovra balze, etc.

[Great Rinaldo, our efforts / mean we are close to our goal! / What remains to us / is to gather the final harvest / of palms on the battlefield. / From the shores of the east / the sun shines more brightly, / illuminating with glorious rays / our final victory over Sion.

Only on steep and jagged cliffs / does glory build its temple. / It is not with joys and pleasures / that it can be conquered.]

The recitative lays out the narrative premises and is, as always, in the Italian equivalent of 'blank verse', that mixture of seven- and eleven-syllable lines that we discussed in the opening chapter. The aria text is typical in its more regular, predictable verse metre and rhyme scheme (the lines are of ten syllables each, the rhyme scheme is abab). The sentiments are also characteristic, and can tell us something important about *opera seria*'s basic mode of operation. Like the libretto as a whole, the poetry is at base sententious and moralizing. We are informed in a highly complicated way that the road to glory is hard, but that this difficulty adds lustre to the goal. The abstract moral message is expressed in the 'A' section, in the first two lines by means of an elaborate metaphor that uses the natural world as its stage. Vivid images of the cliffs (*balze*) that are steep (*scoscesi*) and jagged (*pungenti*) lead us to the temple (*tempio*) and its glory (*gloria*). This is very direct, even naïve in its message, and the directness is echoed in the musical setting, which does everything to make the pictorial images musically manifest, thus communicating them as vividly as possible to the audience. There are sharp, jagged rhythms and melodic lines for those steep, jagged rocks; and then long held notes, stubbornly repeated pitches and elaborate passage-work for the temple and its glory – 'tempio' and 'gloria' are expanded and elongated in order to stress their importance. The text of the 'B' section provides the obligatory contrast. It stresses that pleasure won't get you to glory. Handel here changes the key for musical variation, but those jagged rhythms still echo in the orchestra, reminding us of the broad didactic purpose. Then come the reprise of 'A', and a chance to admire the singer's ornaments and enjoy again those word-painting gestures.

The orchestration of this first aria is schematic, just cello, bass and harpsichord (the so-called 'continuo' group) for the recitative, then strings and oboes for the aria. As in most Handel arias there's little sense of orchestral ingenuity, of shifting instrumental sounds furthering the musical message on a bar-by-bar basis. This is a more mechanical process, in which the strings and oboes either play together or simply alternate. There are, of course, unusual orchestral sounds in Handel's operas, but they make their effect from being exceptional. Orchestration, like the aria's formal design, is geared towards elevating the solo singer as the most important part of the fabric. Duplicating the text's poetic conceit, the aria's music strives to imitate nature, and thus control it. Handelian opera is in this way irremediably triumphalist: it reminds us again and again, in aria after aria, of man's superiority over the natural world he inhabits.

Given their fundamental similarity in form, the expressive range of the arias in *Rinaldo* is remarkable. When the other side of the cast appears (those opposing the Christian army), they are accompanied by scenic splendours, those 'machines and decorations' of which Aaron Hill was boastful:

> Argante from the City, drawn through the Gate in a Triumphal Chariot, the Horses white and led in by arm'd Blackmoors. He comes forward attended by a great Number of Horse and Foot Guards, and descending from his Chariot addresses himself to Goffredo.

A functioning chariot, complete with white horses, seems lavish indeed; but a contemporary critic mentioned that Argante actually came in on foot, so perhaps economies had been imposed.[16] Whatever the case, to accompany this splendid stage picture we get a sudden injection of musical colour: trumpets and drums appear for the first time in the opera. Again the aria text, 'Sibillar gli angui d'Aletto', is a collection of vivid images, this time the hissing of Alecto's serpents and the hungry barking of the six-headed Scylla. And again the music does its illustrative duty, the hissing translated into upwardly sweeping violin scales, the barking into the bass's angular leaping line. A further example of this scenic music comes shortly afterwards, when Armida makes her appearance. The scene description reads, 'Armida in the Air, in a Chariot drawn by two huge Dragons, out of whose Mouths issue Fire and Smoke' (the critic cited above mentioned that the fire and smoke were produced by a boy hidden inside the dragons' mouths, who could sometimes be seen by the audience).[17] Again there's obvious musical imitation in the aria 'Furie terribili': the encircling furies are depicted by an insistently repeated octave leap in the voice and the strings; a thunder machine works overtime.

These blood-and-(literally-)thunder moments are skilfully placed in the opera, and always alternate with gentler inspirations. But the central idea of musical imitation of nature is always there. After the huffing and puffing of Argante and Armida, and clearly in contrast to them, comes an aria for the Christian general's daughter, Almirena. It takes place in 'a delightful Grove in which the Birds are heard to sing, and seen flying up and down among the Trees'. We begin with familiar pastoral imagery:

Augelletti, che cantate,
Zeffiretti che spirate
Aure dolci intorno a me,
Il mio ben dite dov'è!

[Little birds that sing, / gentle breezes that waft / sweet drafts around me, / tell me where is my beloved!]

The little birds and gentle breezes all dutifully combine to help frame a simple question. They also remind us that the eighteenth century was a great age of landscape – of attempts to fashion nature into a coherent order. The delight in symmetry, with gently rolling hills, tastefully arranged sheep and murmuring streams, contains nature every bit as firmly as *Rinaldo*'s other arias with their images of roiling seas, or jagged cliffs, which have been domesticated by musical control.

Aaron Hill was not content for this aria to have a scenic backdrop of obedient fountains, purposeful paths and tidy aviaries. He decided that nature could be made theatrical in a more immediate way. Joseph Addison, in a contemporary article in *The Spectator*, takes up the tale:

As I was walking in the Streets about a Fortnight ago, I saw an ordinary Fellow carrying a Cage full of little Birds upon his Shoulder; and, as I was wondering with myself what Use he would put them to, he was met very luckily by an Acquaintance, who had the same Curiosity. Upon his asking him what he had upon his Shoulder, he told him that he had been buying Sparrows for the Opera. Sparrows for the Opera, says my Friend, licking his lips, what? are they to be roasted? No, no, says the other, they are to enter towards the end of the first Act, and to fly about the Stage.[18]

A paradise indeed, in which the outdoors would be transported into the theatre, and in which beautiful singing would vie with nature for ascendancy. Handel did his best to join in the project, and called for imitation birdsong courtesy of two flutes and piccolo. As if to emphasize the naturalness, this aria is not a 'da capo', but seems rather to obey the whims of nature. However, real birds released into the real theatre constituted a dream too far. A later commentator in *The Spectator* made all too plain that untamed nature could still have the power to disrupt the most carefully planned Arcadian fantasies:

> There have been so many Flights . . . let loose in this Opera, that it is feared the House will never get rid of them; and that in other Plays they may make their Entrance in very wrong and improper Scenes . . . besides the Inconveniences which the Heads of the Audience may sometimes suffer from them.[19]

Rinaldo was revived four times in the next six years of London seasons, and also appeared in German translation in Hamburg (1715), one of relatively few foreign outings for Handel's operas. As new London singers appeared, so Handel adapted the work to suit them. When, in a 1717 revival, the formerly bass role of Argante was given to an alto castrato, Handel duly wrote three new arias for him. When the opera came back in the early 1730s, he made further substantial revisions to suit new cast members and also reacted to newly straitened circumstances by reducing the scenic spectacle. There is, in short, no definitive version of *Rinaldo* (nor indeed of almost any opera of the period); every score was work-in-progress, awaiting new performance conditions to stimulate fresh configurations.

THE HANDELIAN AFTERLIFE

Rinaldo was a crucial moment in the history of opera in London – an event whose success changed the course of operatic life in the city for twenty years or so, and altered Handel's career with it. But the path was never easy, with financial crises endemic. To survive, opera needed the very best Italian singers. But, then as now, these stars knew their worth. Nicolini, the castrato for whom the title role in *Rinaldo* was written, was paid 800 guineas a season (not the £8000 that Hogarth suggested in his engraving, but still an astonishing sum). Patrons paid half a guinea a ticket – a steep price by the standards of the day. The heyday was in the 1720s, when the so-called Royal Academy (again, a joint-stock company, under royal charter and financed by a mix of royal patrons and stock-holders) allowed Handel to produce a steady stream of operas. His style changed little over these years. He and his audience remained faithful to the ideal of *opera seria* he had inherited; he was content to continue finding new music to clothe the basic format of the da capo aria.

Among his forty or so operas, there are peaks and valleys. *Giulio Cesare* (Julius Caesar, 1725) has been much revived and appreciated, not least because its portrayal of Cleopatra has proved popular with star sopranos. In the 1730s, Handel was freer in his choice of libretti, and produced a series of more innovative works. *Orlando* (1733), based on Ariosto's *Orlando furioso* and written for the famous castrato Senesino, has supernatural elements and a tremendous mad scene. The hero imagines an Orpheus-like journey into the underworld to rescue his lost beloved, and as he does so his musical discourse fragments, pieces of recitative and da capo aria succeed each other in an anarchic mix. In *Alcina* (1735) the supernatural has even greater play, and the usual musical forms are enlivened by a series of dances and by elaborate choral movements, clearly showing that Handel, ever the cosmopolitan, had been influenced by French models. And yet, impressive as these departures are, it would be a mistake to concentrate too much on occasional breaks with convention. Every one of Handel's operas is cast more or less as a continual succession of da capo arias, and thus of numbers in which, formally at least, he obeyed the rules – in which he *used* formal conventions rather than tried to evade them.

In London in the 1730s, making a living through operatic composition suddenly became a lot harder. Handel's theatre suffered from disastrous competition with a rival Italian company, the so-called Opera of the Nobility, based initially in a theatre in Lincoln's Inn Fields. More serious still, theatres that performed English-language musical entertainments were siphoning audiences away. In 1728 John Gay's *The Beggar's Opera* scored a huge success, in part through its Hogarth-like lampoon of the extravagances of *opera seria*. It is sad to read a contemporary account of an *Orlando* performance at which 'the Audience was very thin, so that I believe they get not enough to pay the Instruments of the Orchestra'.[20] As ever, public opera existed on the financial edge; in this case the entertainments on offer were simply too numerous for the limited patrons. By the early 1740s Handel gave up opera altogether, concentrating his prodigious energies on oratorios in English. He became in the process a national monument, but his very success in the new, more popular genre made Italian opera all the more precarious.

An intriguing question today concerns Handel's afterlife. When he stopped composing operas in the 1740s his works very soon left the stage and were plunged into dense obscurity. Although some of his oratorios (*Messiah* above all) became a permanent part of the musical universe, surviving all sorts of changes of musical fashion, the operas were rapidly judged outmoded and unacceptable. They remained unperformed (apart from a few arias that survived as recital pieces) for most of the nineteenth and the twentieth centuries: a 200-year silence. When revivals did eventually take place (first, as historical curiosities, in late nineteenth-century and early twentieth-century Germany), the revivers felt it necessary to change the works in quite fundamental ways, so strange and alienating had their dramatic language become. Baritones and basses took the castrato roles (and struggled vainly with ornamental writing that was now unknown to their voice ranges); the *recitativo semplice* was spiced up with orchestral interjections; the ubiquitous da capo arias were often shorn of their repeats (judged undramatic by generations brought up on Wagner). But such drastic musical adjustments eventually became unnecessary; audiences began to accept the works on something nearer their own terms. Now, 300 years after their first performances, the Handel operatic revival is in full flood, ever more of his operas have a place in the current repertory. They are fuelled by the new stylistic awareness of the 'historical performance' movement; by a generation of singers (male and female) who are at ease with Handelian virtuosity; and (most surprising of all) by a new generation of audiences who are no longer uncomfortable with Handelian operatic shapes and modes of expression.

It's easy to see how his operas became out of date: even to late eighteenth-century audiences the unremitting succession of solo arias seemed artificial; regular performances in the nineteenth century became impossible, in spite of Handel's continuing popularity in oratorio. What has happened to occasion his meteoric operatic ascendance over the last few decades? Partly there are practical reasons. The historical performance movement's insistence on lighter, faster interpretations of eighteenth-century music allows the drama to move more quickly; recitatives can gallop along, arias likewise; and a new generation of singers has embraced this new performing aesthetic. Also, as mentioned in Chapter 1, the virtual absence of new works joining our repertory has necessitated ever-deeper excavations of the past in search of novelty. In this sense, Handel has been a great beneficiary of the collapse of late twentieth-century opera, as were, a little earlier, Italian opera composers of the early nineteenth century such as Rossini, Donizetti and Bellini.

Perhaps as important is that directors have learned how to cope with the succession of da capo arias, with the 'portrait gallery' that is Handelian *opera seria*. Frequently they have done so by ignoring aspects of the underlying aesthetic, by injecting directorial energy that keeps the stage action moving even when the musical form is repetitive. The spectacle is made to seem hyper-alert and eventful by working *against* the music. Some have loudly lamented this practice (by no means restricted to Handel, but perhaps most commonly applied to his operas), but modern-day audiences are unlikely to prefer an 'authentic' Handel staging, in which almost the only large movements on stage would be the exits of characters as they concluded their arias. A related issue concerns casting. We are still cautious about replicating the remarkable gender indifference of Handel's *opera seria*. Although we no longer require baritones to struggle through castrato roles, we typically now use counter-tenors, the presence of their male bodies seemingly more important than the fact that their voices (however virtuosic) are unsuited to parts fashioned for castrati – particularly in the lower register, where the castrati were typically strong and where counter-tenors are typically weak.

But these performance choices are changing all the time, and as more Handel operas come into the repertory they will continue to evolve. What is more, some of Handel's contemporaries are now appearing, newly refurbished; Alessandro Scarlatti's sixty-odd operas are, admittedly, mostly waiting in the wings, but those of Antonio Vivaldi (1678–1741) are showing signs of life, and there are (according to the composer's – possibly exaggerated – count) ninety-four of them to choose from. One thing is certain: in our current operatic universe Mozart's comic operas are no longer the watershed – what we called in the last chapter the dividing line between the distant and accessible past. Handel's operas can, we now know, deliver new meanings after centuries of neglect – so long, that is, as there are singers to turn the already-heard into a daredevil feat of vocal elaboration, astonishing us with their courage.

4
Discipline

Opera is extravagant, absurd, loud and above all created by human voices. As we've already seen, it has often been thought in need of discipline, and sometimes such thoughts have turned to action. There is scarcely a decade in the eighteenth century (the golden age of the polemical pamphlet) that avoided some philosophical debate about opera's ills – often, human nature being what it is, the ills of other people's opera rather than one's own.

The year 1762 saw such an earthquake, one more powerful and long-lasting than most. It marked the premiere of yet another Italian Orpheus opera, this one performed in Vienna. After more than a century of comparatively hard times for Orpheus, an Italian poet called Ranieri de' Calzabigi (1714–96) wrote a new libretto about him; it was set to music by a German composer, Christoph Willibald Gluck (1714–87). Calzabigi and Gluck's *Orfeo ed Euridice* was widely agreed to be astonishing, revolutionary both in form and style. Gluck went on to write further highly original works in Italian and in French, including *Alceste* (1767), *Iphigénie en Aulide* (Iphigenia in Aulis, 1774) and *Iphigénie en Tauride* (Iphigenia in Tauris, 1779). The subjects were all derived from Greek mythology, and that is significant – Gluck and his librettists demonstrated that neo-classical fervour could go hand in hand with a desire to curb operatic excesses, elaborate singing above all. A generation later, and in the same way, Greek-influenced gowns and simple, natural curls modelled on images from antique amphorae would replace onstage the reeking powdered wigs and huge panniers of eighteenth-century court dress.

Gluck's new kind of opera was enormously influential: he is one of Mozart's operatic father figures, and his name was a talisman well into the nineteenth century. One need only read Berlioz's *Traité d'instrumentation* (Orchestration Treatise, 1843), or his Gluck-obsessed *Mémoires* (1870), or the polemics that swirled around his revival of *Orfeo* in Paris in 1859, or Liszt's *Orfeo* in Weimar some years earlier, to sense how the names of both composer and work continued to be influential. To assume Gluck's mantle was to make a play for opera's moral high ground, to claim a level of musical purity and abstraction that messy, quotidian theatrical practice seemed never to achieve. Staging *Orfeo* with high-minded intent and re-discovered classical restraint has always signalled a reaction against theatrical extravagance. In Germany, Greek-revival productions of the opera in the first decades of the twentieth century gave voice to exasperation with decadent expressionism in opera. Richard Strauss's Elektra may have shrieked, raved and jumped up and down in dirty rags, struggling to make herself heard over an enormous, blaring orchestra; but never mind, Gluck's Orfeo, brought back on stage to sing out his grief in sunny C major, restored much-needed restraint. How did this strange new *Orfeo* come about? What currents shaped it?

To answer these questions, we need to go back several generations. The high aspirations that created *Orfeo* in 1762 had been prepared by what some intellectuals saw as decades of offences against audiences. The sources of difficulty in Handelian *opera seria* discussed in our last chapter were obvious, and continued with the next generation of serious opera composers. According to the aesthetic attitudes that led to Gluck's new way with opera, libretto poetry had become formulaic and its emotions were made distant by endless metaphor – endless ways in which human feelings were not only likened to natural phenomena but in which those natural phenomena became the focus of the musical expression. What's more, the plots tended to revisit the same archetypes: the troubled but ultimately enlightened king, the confused hero, the spurned lover, the evil plotter; politics and public duty were endlessly set up against love and family ties; mistaken identity was facilitated by pan-soprano sounds from male as well as female characters. The plot flew by in simple *recitativo*, barely musical recitation that few seemed to care about or even listen to. The drama – the sense of suspense and release, the emotional investments that were the essential preamble to operatic pleasure – was lodged exclusively in an unyielding succession of solo arias. And each aria repeated the same formal shape (the so-called 'da capo' form), one whose *raison d'être* was realized only in performance – in the surplus brought by improvised ornamentation when the initial 'A' section was repeated. It was not just that the astonishing costumes and flat sets tended to place on stage a succession of fabulous, feathered, glittering characters; it was that the singers impersonating these characters all produced singing of such immediate and spectacular virtuosity – whether in a slow, pathetic aria or in a show-stopper with cascades of rapid notes – that all other aspects receded.

The intellectuals and men of letters grumbled about this, in particular because the singers and their audiences seemed unfailingly to know where tragedy and triumph were situated. There is a famous story about the two pre-eminent castrati of the pre-1750 period, Senesino and Farinelli, told by the great British music historian of the late eighteenth century, Charles Burney:

> Senesino and Farinelli, when in England together, being engaged at different theatres on the same night, had not an opportunity of hearing each other, till, by one of those sudden stage-revolutions which frequently happen, yet are always unexpected, they were both employed to sing on the same stage. Senesino had the part of a furious tyrant to represent, and Farinelli that of an unfortunate hero in chains: but in the course of the first song, he so softened the obdurate heart of the enraged tyrant, that Senesino, forgetting his stage-character, ran to Farinelli and embraced him in his own.[1]

Senesino's embrace of Farinelli is a wonderfully stagy (indeed, if we are to believe Burney's story, staged) demonstration of how listeners can be transfigured by a moment of live singing. It also suggests, along with many other accounts of early eighteenth-century opera in performance, that 'breaking out of character' was commonplace and not necessarily viewed as the theatrical sin it would be today, amid our darkened auditoriums and constant calls for silent absorption in the theatrical unfolding. John Rosselli, one of opera's best recent historians, retells an event in Ferrara in 1722: a cardinal is seated in a stage box (that is, he attends the opera from a seat literally on the stage, and thus in full view of most of the rest of the audience); just as a soprano sings the words 'Give alms to a poor pilgrim' he reaches out and hands her a purse of gold. As Rosselli comments, in making this gesture the cardinal 'combined two favourite baroque devices, a public show of beneficence and playing about with theatrical illusion'.[2] But the point of both this and the Farinelli/Senesino anecdote is also that some large part of the essence of *opera seria* was ephemeral and cannot now be re-created. This is, of course, true of all opera; but its extent in the early eighteenth century is exceptional. Much that was most important musically and dramatically was improvised on the spot: it couldn't be written down, still less recorded; we have no access to it. All we can do when we re-create the operas today is be aware of the loss. Now we sit in darkness; only the stage can be seen. We are isolated from each other and each other's reactions. We do not feel free to comment, and can boo or cheer only at fixed moments. Nor do we feel free to ignore the spectacle entirely if we choose; we cannot put up the shutters of our box and play cards when the recitative starts, or buy oranges in the aisles, or reach across the stage to hand a purse of gold to a singer whose words momentarily and magically give meaning to our magnanimous gesture.

As theatrical archaeologists, we might say that early eighteenth-century *opera seria* is now relatively mute, since what counterpoised for those stylized plots, that relentlessly well-behaved poetry and nothing-but-arias structure was present in performances that have now permanently vanished. What has gone are not simply the obvious items like the castrato voice, which became such an important source of fantasy. In Samuel Richardson's great epistolary novel of the 1740s, *Pamela, or Virtue Rewarded*, which appeared just as Handel's opera career was coming to an end, one character despairingly says: 'But what have I said, what can I say, of an Italian opera? – Only, little to the Purpose as it is, I wonder how I have been able to say so much: For who can describe Sound? Or what Words shall be found to embody Air?'[3] It is a lament all operatic archaeologists can echo. In the Internet age, we call the workers who produce text and ideas the 'content people'; they are not very high on the pay scale, no matter how much respect they garner as 'author'. Eighteenth-century composers knew how this felt. There's a famous and probably invented story about Handel threatening to throw the renowned prima donna Francesca Cuzzoni (1696–1778) out of the window when she refused to sing an aria from *Ottone* (Otto, 1723), one that had not been expressly written for her.[4] Endlessly repeated, this tale caters to our modern-day sense of hierarchy: composers *should* be thus manly and thus in control. But the economic and practical realities tell a different story; Handel, for all his fame, was at base a 'content person'; whatever his occasional outbursts, he was usually the one dangling out of the window, at the whim of the sopranos and castratos his music was created to showcase.

In the eighteenth century, the rumblings of revolt against this state of affairs came from both literary-critical and practical perspectives. It happened in two phases. The first concerned words, the second concerned words and music – the kind of music that singers should be encouraged or forced to favour or to avoid. A good part of the impetus for such changes, although it seemed to originate with pamphleteers and others, came from what was happening operatically elsewhere. For example, the relative decorum of state-controlled French *tragédie lyrique*, both in its libretti and its music, played a quiet role in disciplining Italian *opera seria*. With a strong tradition of high-classical spoken drama, France had theatrical rules that crossed over to and contained French libretti from their beginnings in the 1670s. And French compositional styles around the turn of the eighteenth century, in instrumental as well as vocal music, depended more on instrumentation and rich harmony – at least, so the French saw it – than on the constantly unfurling melody and unbridled coloratura of the Italian style. There has never been much point in trying to close off one operatic tradition from the alternative languages that feed it and are fed from it, whether those languages are other operatic genres or the shapes and sounds of contemporary instrumental music. There are ways in which Italian *opera seria* and French *tragédie lyrique* have sibling traits, just as there are ways in which da capo arias resemble concertos and other instrumental forms.

Exchanges were reciprocal: mid-century French musical reformers looked towards the relative simplicity and lyricism of Italian comic opera. In his *Confessions* (1770), Jean-Jacques Rousseau ascribes revelatory powers to Italian *opera buffa*. In Venice in 1744 he heard an opera called *La finta schiava* (The Feigned Slave, a so-called *pasticcio*, meaning an opera made by cobbling together arias from a string of previously existing works). The noisy, brilliant arias had little effect on him, but one simple comic tune brought him to an awakening: his 'ears and at the same time eyes' were opened. He repeatedly alludes to sleep and waking, to being brought into consciousness by the aria. Anxious to recapture the experience, he gets hold of the music, only to find that the notes on the page are not the same.[5] Describing how in 1752 he was moved to write his own comic intermezzo, *Le Devin du village* (The Village Soothsayer), Rousseau once more makes clear that Italian comic opera unlocked his spirit. After a long night talking to a friend about *opera buffa* – just talking about it – Rousseau could not sleep and the day after, 'in a kind of vaulted chamber that was at the end of the garden', scribbled down two arias and the final duet of *Le Devin du village*.[6] Whatever mythmaking is at work here – and there is no lack of it – the link was clear. *Le Devin du village* and similar operas that followed in its wake, with their Italianate manners, in turn ricocheted back to French opera; its easy musical candour lent alternative flavours both to *opéra comique* and to *tragédie lyrique* after the 1750s. And then, to complete the circle, *opéra comique* – ostensibly Italianate but nonetheless a French genre with its own set of musical conventions – re-inflected *opera seria* through Gluck.

THE METASTASIAN CODE

In the previous chapter we saw one important phase of operatic reform, stemming from the Arcadians in Rome; but even as Handel and his star singers were beguiling audiences in London, further waves of reform were washing over Italy. As ever, ancient Greece was routinely called upon: Pier Jacopo Martello's 1715 treatise *Della tragedia antica e moderna* (On Ancient and Modern Tragedy), written by a second-generation Arcadian, constructed an elaborate fantasy in which Aristotle appears before him on the road to Paris and instructs him (at length) on how to tackle the libretto problem. We have already read 'Aristotle's' advice about recitatives and arias, but there was much more. The philosopher's stream of friendly observations satirized most of opera's presumed ills: 'not too many forests, for tree trunks and leafy branches are not subjects for the theatre painters ... you should take care to choose a fabulous story composed of a mixture of gods and heroes or a true history of heroes'. Castratos must always be 'elegant, not uncouth'. 'Let the means by which the events take place lack verisimilitude', the philosopher dryly recommended, 'let there be recognitions and reversals of fortune. In recognitions let us be easily deceived by a sudden costume change, by certain objects found in the cradle of a character when he was an infant.' Poets, he concluded, are schooled by opera to 'conquer themselves and renounce their own wishes'.[7] Five years later another satirist, the opera composer Benedetto Marcello (1686–1739), wrote a fantastic, at times surreal pamphlet called *Il teatro alla moda* (Fashionable Theatre, 1720) cataloguing chapter by chapter what he considered the excesses of the Italian scene: composers and impresarios toadying before singers (and, more degrading still, before singers' mothers and other 'protectors'), absurd plots, needlessly lavish stage sets, the slave status of poets. These two reformers give us an immediate sense of the impulse to shift opera away from giddy excess, spectacular machines and even more spectacular virtuosi; and, in tandem with this, to introduce notions of restraint and balance characteristic of the greatest spoken theatre. Martello's Aristotle explicitly cites Greek tragedy as a model, as one might expect, but also evokes French classical drama, a tribute to the author's Francophilia.

Pietro Metastasio (1698–1782) was the poet who took this second wave of reformist critique most successfully to heart. He was a close friend of the castrato Farinelli (they started letters to each other with the greeting 'Caro gemello' – Dear Twin), and became easily the most famous Italian poet of the eighteenth century – his thirty-odd *opera seria* libretti were the most frequently set in all operatic history. As late as the early nineteenth century, composers still occasionally resorted to his dramas, Rossini among them. His libretti were austere and balanced enough to fill a particular cultural black hole – the absence of serious spoken-theatre works in Italian to rival the great spoken tragedies of France. As Charles de Brosses quipped in 1739, 'for tragedies in the form of opera, they [the Italians] have an excellent author still living, Metastasio, whose plays are full of wit, intrigue, dramatic turns of events, and of interest, and would no doubt work to great effect if they were played as simple spoken tragedies, leaving aside all the little arietta business and operatic devices, which would be easy to remove'.[8]

Metastasio had refined and built on Zeno's work. Complicated subjects – all those foundlings later recognized as princes, or zany subplots required to supply minor characters with aria fodder – were once again purged; the number of characters was further reduced. Crucially, he followed Zeno in the elimination of comic characters. Purity of genre – not mixing tragedy and farce – was an Aristotelian ideal and chimed well with general eighteenth-century obsessions about classification. The irony was that the outcast comic characters – all those gardeners and servant girls, bourgeois lechers, old maids, rustic lovers and tipsy functionaries – received in recompense an operatic home of their own, first in comic intermezzi and then in fully fledged *opera buffa*. In other words, the first step towards a work such as Mozart's *Le nozze di Figaro* (1786) was an act of banishment. More ironic still, the reformers' self-important adherence to codes and high ideals would eventually place *opera seria* on a large, imposing, classically styled pedestal, one that audiences, singers and opera houses over the coming decades could feel free to ignore or treat with serene indifference.

So what was the situation of Italian *opera seria* around 1750? Libretti had become stately. Metastasio, child of the rational eighteenth century, prescribed a moral code in which virtue would be eternally rewarded and sin eternally punished or, better, magnanimously forgiven after tremendous expiation. Fewer people die, and they all get up at the end to sing a chorus together. No one commits suicide, or murders his or her offspring, with exceptions always made for Medea. What is more, operatic poetry begins to engage seriously, philosophically even, with matters of political significance. One such matter is the nature of kingship, of absolute monarchs troubled by their crowns or performing sudden, desperately last-minute acts of mercy (Metastasio's *La clemenza di Tito* – The Clemency of Titus, 1734, later set by Mozart, is a classic example). *Opera seria* libretti of this kind have been seen as important social allegories, even as prescriptions for the true role of the absolute ruler. In this sense it was entirely fitting that Metastasio became court poet to the Austrian Emperor (Charles VI), as had Zeno before him. What is more, this position – in effect that of a liveried court servant – was one Metastasio fully accepted. His epistolary description of his first meeting with the Emperor gives a perfect expression of the social hierarchies his libretti endlessly celebrate:

> I spoke with a voice that I fear was not too firm, expressing these sentiments: 'I do not know whether it is my contentment or my confusion that is greater on finding myself at the feet of Your Imperial Majesty. This is a moment I have sighed for from my earliest days, and now I find myself not only before the greatest monarch on earth but here in the glorious title of his present servant.'[9]

While the spirit of these Metastasian libretti, in particular the directness of their celebration of the political status quo, was new, certain structural features stubbornly remained from earlier, more unruly libretti. The waves of reform were, in other words, primarily literary, not centrally addressed to the ways in which music is changed by alterations in poetry. To some extent, this reflected the greater prestige and longevity of the literary component of opera. Metastasio's libretti were famous throughout Europe at a time when their numerous musical settings were mostly tailored to a particular cast of singers. It was easier to commission a new setting than revive an old one when a new cast was assembled. Metastasio himself had no doubts about the relative hierarchy among opera's constituent parts. In a letter to a fellow reformer, Francesco Algarotti, he wrote:

> Those parts of opera that require only the spectators' eyes and ears to plead for them always garner more votes than the other parts, whose merits can be measured only with intelligence and ratiocination. Everyone can see, everyone can hear, but not everyone understands and not everyone reasons.[10]

But the Imperial poet's disdain for those who merely look and listen cannot hide the fact that audiences, the paying public, continued to be principally concerned with their 'eyes and ears', with the spectacle and the music. And although their prestige among intellectuals may have been low, composers of the post-Handel, Metastasio-bred generation continued to make musical adjustments, albeit ones far less trumpeted than those of their librettist companions. The most famous of them, Leonardo Vinci (1696–1730) and Johann Adolf Hasse (1699–1783), perhaps responding to the new sense of literary restraint but also reflecting broader shifts in musical taste, fashioned operas with the same basic formal outlines as the Handelian generation (strings of da capo arias), but with a less elaborate musical surface. Their melodies became simpler and more predictable rhythmically, the bass lines more functional (repeated notes in the bass, a sort of harmonic marking-time, were a commonplace of the style). They produced, in short, the beginnings of what was first called *galant* music and later became known as the Classical Style. Charles Burney (who very much approved of these modern features) praised Vinci in particular for thus simplifying music and 'disentangling it from fugue, complication, and laboured contrivance'.[11]

This *galant* style was what Gluck inherited, and it was not to everyone's taste. Some of the old guard took exception. Burney reported Handel as saying, when Gluck visited England in 1745, that 'He knows no more of contrapunto than mein cook' (the cook in question, though, was one Gustavus Waltz, who was a cellist and singer, and may have been quite capable of fugal excursions).[12] But in spite of local resistance, these musical-stylistic changes were of lasting significance, and had great impact on the instrumental forms then emerging, in particular the string quartet and the symphony. At least initially, though, Metastasian opera broke no structural rules. If we look at the corpus of his libretti, set by numerous composers (including Gluck) between 1730 and 1760, resulting in literally thousands of operatic numbers, we find little more than a festive parade of da capo arias – some exquisite, some tedious – brought to life more or less well by the singers on whom their fate mostly rested.

Pamphleteering discontent with opera's ills stems not just from asceticism – a philosophical bludgeon that can seem ludicrous when aimed at singers, scenery, orchestras and public entertainment. Operatic poetry and music, and even the singing, was at perpetual risk of being ignored by the audiences who flocked to attend the performances: in the later eighteenth century, especially in Italy, behaviour was still magnificently informal, despite reforms already undertaken. The unspoken wish inhabiting reform writings in the eighteenth century may have been a desire to see the audience absorbed and moved by art, a desire for the myth of Orpheus to come true.

In Naples, thirty years after de Brosses played chess during the recitatives, the audience remained alarmingly unruly. An English visitor, Samuel Sharp, was irritated by the chaos:

> There are some who contend, that the singers might be very well heard, if the audience were more silent, but it is so much the fashion at Naples, and indeed, through all Italy, to consider the Opera as a place of rendezvous and visiting, that they do not seem in the least to attend to the musick, but laugh and talk through the whole performance, without any restraint, and it might be imagined, that an assembly of so many hundreds conversing together so loudly, must entirely cover the voices of the singers. I was prepossessed of this custom before I left England, but had no idea it was carried to such an extreme . . . not withstanding the noisiness of the audience, during the whole performance of the Opera, the moment the dances

> begin there is a universal and dead silence, which continues as long as the dances continue.[13]

The comparatives begin to give a sense that audiences were not the same everywhere; in this case, that the English public is more absorbed in the performances than in Italy. Sharp was savaged by an Italian riposte, from Giuseppe Baretti in *An Account of the Manners and Customs of Italy* (1768), who complained about:

> your solemnity of scolding, as if we were committing murder when we are talkative in the pit, or form ourselves into card parties in the boxes. Our singers, then, though we be unwilling to listen, would be very impertinent, if they did not sing their best, since they are very well paid for what they are doing; and Cafarello was soon taught better manners when he took it into his head not to do his duty on the stage of Turin on pretense that the audience was not attentive to his singing. He was taken to jail in his Macedonian accoutrements for several nights as soon as the opera was over, and brought from jail to the stage every evening, until by repeated efforts he deserved universal acclamation.
>
> Mr Sharp wonders also that *it is not the fashion in Italy, as it is in England, to take a small wax-light to the opera, in order to read the book.* A very acute remark as usual; to which I have nothing to say, but the Italians are not so good-natured as the English, who have patience enough to run carefully over a stupid piece of nonsense while a silly eunuch is mincing a vowel into a thousand invisible particles.[14]

It was against this backdrop that the Gluckian revolution took place. In a polemical preface to a score of Gluck's *Alceste* published in 1769, Calzabigi referred to Metastasio's libretti as 'saddles for all horses', the horses in question being male and female sopranos, denounced in equal measure. According to Calzabigi, Metastasio's kings and queens may have been newly serious and newly restrained; but their passions were still frozen into too-convenient metaphors, which then too easily translated into vocal ornaments when the 'A' section of the da capo aria started up again. The singers, undefeated, were winning once more, and winning on ever more flamboyant terms. The hysteria that surrounded figures such as Farinelli was unprecedented; rhapsodies to silver trumpets, divine voices, nightingales, gods and goddesses in mortal form grew if anything more intense. Metastasio may have fluttered with pride in his position as servant to the greatest monarch on earth, but his wages in comparison with those of his 'dear twin' Farinelli were a pittance.

LYRIC TRAGEDY

It is well to recall that French tragic opera (*tragédie lyrique* or *tragédie en musique*) had seen little of these Italianate excesses. Elaborate, slow recitatives accompanied by full orchestra passed into brief formal arias; ornament was thought vulgar, at least those roulades of the extravagant, free-flowing Italian kind (there was plenty of small-scale decoration to melodic lines). Castrati were regarded with a shudder, and never got in the door. Acoustic sensuality – which is opera's fundamental note – was shared between vocal melody and instrumental sonority, the latter meaning both the sound of the accompaniment and the combinations of harmonies surrounding the singing. Orchestral playing in eighteenth-century France was the *ne plus ultra* of instrumental accomplishment. France's pre-eminence in this domain lasted into the nineteenth century, with instrumentation in French opera showing from the outset far more variety than its Italian counterparts. The operas of Jean-Philippe Rameau (1683–1764), also a renowned theorist of harmony, figured as a straw man in the *Querelle des Bouffons*, the great pamphlet battle of the early 1750s in Paris, in which *tragédie lyrique* (which had fallen on hard times) was set against the emerging Italian comic opera. Rameau's works tended to be classed, depending on allegiance, either as the ultimate in Gallic nobility and dignity or as a national burden to be suffered with groans of ennui. Some salvos in the *Querelle* took more nuanced positions: as one pamphleteer put it, Rameau as 'sacrilegious innovator' brought 'unknown harmonies' to Parisian ears, thus presaging the 'desecration' of an august institution by Italian clowns and unbearable lightness; 'the fateful event with which [Rameau] threatened us has finally come to pass'.[15] In retrospect, Rameau's music, although plainly an advance on French operatic predecessors, seems an unusual suspect for crimes such as sacrilege and iconoclasm; but words such as 'gibberish' and 'monstrosity' were flung around freely by his critics during the *Querelle*.

There is no doubt that *tragédie lyrique* was at a low ebb when Rameau began composing: the court-sustained repertoire of Lully operas had at last (after half a century) proved out of date musically, and Rameau was generally seen as offering revolutionary change. His first serious opera, a *tragédie en musique* called *Hippolyte et Aricie* (1733), is typical of what he had to offer. Although it retained the outer trappings of the Lully prototype (the five-act structure, the ballets, the obsequious Prologue, etc.), in almost every musical area it added layers of interest. The recitatives tend to increased orchestral elaboration, the harmonies are denser and more complex, and – in particular – the monologues of individual characters can become extremely elaborate. Voltaire reported Rameau putting it all in a nutshell: 'Lully needs actors but I need singers.'[16] We see this kind of opera at its best in the celebrated finale of Act 4 of *Hippolyte*, in which Phèdre (a character tellingly related to Racine's famous heroine) laments what she supposes is the death of Hippolyte (a monster has just emerged from the sea and carried him off). Phèdre's lament, couched in a highly charged recitative, is punctuated by choral laments of great poignancy – a celebration of orchestral effect, declamation and harmony that is as far as can be imagined from the endless melodic hegemony of *opera seria*.

The late twentieth century has seen the warring parties of the eighteenth-century reform movements find a peaceful co-existence. Rameau's operas began to be staged in greater numbers in the 1990s, more or less in parallel with the Handel revival, as if some French versus Italian *querelle* had been reincarnated in another age. As mentioned earlier in connection with Handel, the necessary accompaniment of this Rameau renaissance has, up to now, been that directors and choreographers will present *tragédie lyrique* as a post-modern spectacle of glorious estrangements. Although usually underpinned by historically informed musical performance, the now-unfamiliar operatic aesthetics become the basis for a stage festival of alien-looking delights and outlandish fashion statements. What is generally missing is a sense that the Italian and French genres were thought so different in the eighteenth century, their partisans as irreconcilable as Callas and Tebaldi fans in the 1950s. These differences are erased by the amiable bricolage of contemporary opera production – by the pleasurable sense of alienation postmodern directors so reliably provide. In the eighteenth century, the perceptible differences, the philosophical passion they inspired, explain why cross-fertilizations were so refreshing. What French *tragédie lyrique* infused into *opera seria* was an alternative sound: not just the pace and potential of a more thoughtful recitative, but the massed sound of choruses and ensembles and, of course, the vacations from singing that are provided by dance numbers.

A word more on vacations. At one time or another, everyone who has attended an opera feels the need for relief from singing. There is no use denying this. That is why all the gambling, eating, chatting and chess-playing endured for so long. Composers were sometimes wise enough to provide the relief, and were at other times constrained so to do by tradition and custom. In the eighteenth century, ballet interludes were a universal feature of serious opera in French, a genre that began life in Molière and Lully's *comédies-ballets*. Indeed, the tradition demanding respite through dance was a recurring refrain in French opera production as late as the late nineteenth century. In 1861, when Wagner's revised *Tannhäuser* (premiered in Dresden, 1845) appeared at the Paris Opéra, the composer was asked for a bigger and better ballet scene, and did not fully comply, merely expanding a scene in Act 1 rather than supplying the usual Act 2 blockbuster. His opera was duly howled down by members of the influential Jockey Club (lovers of traditional ballets) and withdrawn after three disrupted evenings.

In French opera danced interludes occurred within the boundaries of the drama; in Italian *opera seria* dances were entr'acte or post-opera entertainment, by and large dramatically unconnected to the opera that surrounded or preceded them. Dances also pepper *opera buffa* in the eighteenth century and beyond: sometimes, as with Mozart's *Don Giovanni*, they are worked into finales by making dancing part of the plot, with the characters whispering asides or screaming for help over the strains of an onstage orchestra. Fundamentally, though, dance in opera is almost always a 'divertissement' – a diversion and distraction. Like any elaborate visual tableaux (and like today's CGI special effects or car-chase sequences in films), they are a place to admire the view without the burden of dialogue. And dance was one of several aspects of French opera that Gluck – also an experienced ballet composer – imported with enthusiasm into his Italian reform operas.

In accordance with the French traditions, the dance scenes in *Orfeo ed Euridice* had some dramatic relevance, consisting of funereal rites for Euridice or demonic motions for the Furies in Act 2. Their choreographer, Gasparo Angiolini, was himself a reformer of dance; he claimed to have reconstructed the funereal rites from Virgil, thus adding a patina of historicity to this already self-consciously neo-classical project. To this day, Gluck's *Orfeo* attracts choreographers, now not just as wranglers for the dances but as opera directors in charge of the whole. The German choreographer Pina Bausch staged *Orfeo* at Wuppertal in 1975, with solo dancers enacting Orfeo and Euridice. The unfortunate singers were frequently relegated to moping at extreme stage right or left, singing far from the spotlight. In 2007, Mark Morris directed the Metropolitan Opera's new production, foregoing dancing doubles for the principal singing roles – thus keeping singers at the centre where they belong – while morphing the chorus, who are after all those most likely to be thrown off-kilter by having to move, into a phantasmic collective that looks down from above on the stage action. The allure of *Orfeo* for choreographers is not hard to understand, since Gluck composed brilliant dramatic music for the opera's danced portions, from the almost painfully chromatic sighs of the first act's minuet-lament to the melody-annihilating repeated scales of the Furies. It is hard to overestimate the force of this alternative soundscape in an Italian operatic realm dominated for so many generations by the monochrome tones of the single, high voice.

BETTER BEHAVIOUR

Calzabigi wrote with disciplinarian certainty – in Gluck's name – about what had gone wrong with Italian *opera seria*, and what Gluck had done to put it right:

> I decided to divest it wholly of all the abuses which, introduced either by the ill-considered vanity of the singers or by the expressive indulgence of the composers, have for so long disfigured Italian opera. . . . I thought I would restrict the music to its true function of serving the poetry in the expression and situations of the story, without chilling it with useless and superfluous ornaments. . . . I decided not to stop an actor in the heat of the dialogue, forcing him to wait out a tedious instrumental introduction, nor to stop him in mid-sentence over a favourable vowel, nor to display the agility of his fine voice with a lengthy ornamental passage, nor to let

> the orchestra give him the time to catch his breath for a cadenza. I did not feel obliged to hurry through the second part of an aria, though it was the more impassioned and significant, in order to be able to repeat four times the words of the first part, finishing the aria where the sense was left unfinished, all so the singer might have the leisure to show the many ways in which he can vary a ornamental passage at will.[17]

So much passion directed against the singers! This excerpt again comes from the preface to the score of *Alceste*, published in 1769, but it represents precepts that were also behind *Orfeo* in 1762, an opera which embodies the 'beautiful simplicity', 'clarity' and natural expression Calzabigi mentions as Gluck's goals.

Calzabigi's preface to *Alceste* both echoes and prefigures the groans of many. For example, Francesco Algarotti, in his famous *Essay on Opera* (1755):

> arias are overwhelmed and disfigured by the ornaments with which they are increasingly embellished. The ritornellos that precede them are much too long and often superfluous. In arias expressing rage, for example, verisimilitude is stretched to the breaking point: how can a man in a fit of rage wait with his hands in his belt until the aria's ritornello is concluded before venting the passion seething within his heart?[18]

Or Antonio Planelli, in *Opera* (1772):

> If any theatre music rich in pathos is examined, it will be found to contain fewer notes than even one of those deadly trills that are so fashionable today. Furthermore, it can never happen that a song made up of many notes will produce pathos in the theatre, or strengthen the emotional charge of the words.[19]

Or Rousseau, in his *Confessions* (1770):

> One day at the Teatro San Giovanni Crisostomo I fell asleep more deeply than if I had been in my own bed. The noisy and brilliant arias did not wake me up.[20]

As we shall see, serious opera in Italian would fail to live up to these austere anti-virtuosity prescriptions, either at the time or in the decades to follow. The appeal for restraint and the resentment of vocalism has an anti-Italian flavour, and few Italian composers rushed to the barricades in its wake: Rossini and his constant outpourings of vocal excess, an all-conquering European vogue, followed Gluck by no more than fifty years. However, in their project for *Orfeo*, Gluck and Calzabigi were fortunate in being able to recruit a famous singer to their cause, in some senses making *Orfeo* a genuine collaborative effort. The singer who created the role of Orfeo in 1762 was Gaetano Guadagni (1729–92), an alto castrato and much-feted virtuoso whose voice had the strong low range of many castrati. But Guadagni was said to look more normally male, something affirmed (at least in story) by his many romantic conquests of women. Although we know little about the circumstances of *Orfeo*'s composition and first performances, one enduring story is that Guadagni was willing to co-operate with Gluck because he could thereby lend his genius to a vocal idiom that was atypical for a castrato: a lyric, controlled style with, as Calzabigi/Gluck noted in their later Preface, very few opportunities for improvised ornamentation. Burney described Guadagni's gestures as 'so full of grace and propriety, that they would have been excellent studies for a statuary';[21] and tells us that he eventually fell out of favour with the British public because (uncastrato-like to a fault) he refused to bow and repeat arias, feeling that such behaviour interrupted the seriousness of the onstage drama. Guadagni had in fact been trained in theatrical gesture and expression in London, and by no less a personage than David Garrick; his bona fides as a singing actor were impeccable.[22]

Many myths were made by means of such anecdotes, with cultural uneasiness about *opera seria* and its legitimacy or frivolity added to the mix. A famous rhapsody to the historical importance of *Orfeo*, and to Guadagni's role in its success, was written by the German music theorist and critic A. B. Marx in 1863, a century after the opera's first performance. This passage, from Marx's book on Gluck's operas, is notable because it is one of the few sources for a now-popular fantasy that castrati had particularly *forceful* – as opposed to skilled or flexible – voices:

> By means of the operation performed on castrati, the development of the vocal organs – more accurately speaking, the larynx – was arrested. It is this development, beginning in puberty, that converts the discant or alto voice of a boy into a tenor or bass voice. But the further maturation of the body . . . went on as usual. The chest and lungs of the boy attained the power and flexibility that they have in men; the vocal cavity attained

> the size and resonance of the mature male. Male force resounds with utmost violence within vocal organs that have remained boyish. In comparison to a boy's voice, a superior increase of volume is obtained when this sound enters the mature vocal cavity. This is the reason for the greater power of the castrato voice, and for its violently penetrating quality. . . . No female alto is, in terms of voice quality, capable of replacing the castrato.[23]

Again, so much anxiety! So many references to men, male, manly, mature, strength, power, size, violence and penetration. But Marx could not have heard Guadagni (who died in the 1790s); like everyone of his era, he had little opportunity to experience castrati except perhaps in Italian church choirs, which were their last refuge. More importantly, this polemic had a precise point. Marx, a virulent misogynist, was protesting without saying so explicitly against the mezzo-soprano Pauline Viardot's recent, spectacular success in the title role of *Orphée* (Gluck's 1774 French version of *Orfeo*), which had been revived for her by Berlioz in Paris in 1859.

What were the musical results of the *Orfeo* experiment? For one thing, Calzabigi and Gluck's aesthetic reclaimed declamation – *recitar cantando* – as a source of expression, both in recitatives and (more radically still) in arias. In the extended third-act recitative in which Euridice finally persuades the tormented Orfeo to turn, and then falls dead to the ground, Orfeo's intense prose is vividly depicted in the orchestra (string tremolos, rapid changes of texture), while Euridice's sudden fall makes barely a dent in the musical fabric. When employed within arias, the declamatory ideal here is very far from the coloratura flights of traditional *opera seria* heroes and heroines, in which outpourings of pure vocal noise constantly threaten to rupture verbal meaning. Just as Calzabigi's libretto turned away from the metaphor-laden poetry of Metastasio in favour of more direct syntax, so Gluck aimed throughout for a more speech-like style in which individual syllables rarely receive more than a single note. The hero's two famous arias – 'Chiamo il mio ben così' (Act 1) and 'Che farò senza Euridice?' (Act 3) – both embrace this simpler idiom. These reforms did not of course occur in a vacuum. Gluck had been a jobbing opera composer for nearly twenty years before he wrote *Orfeo*, and while his earliest works were firmly in the Metastasian mould, he had also – as musical director of the French theatre in Vienna – written several *opéras comiques*, in which such simple, almost folk-like declamation was the norm. Indeed, 'Che farò' was adapted from one of Gluck's *opéras comiques*, and 'Chiamo il mio ben' was so beloved by the *opéra comique* composer Philidor that he stole it for one of his own productions in Paris.

The primal scene in *Orfeo* is a modest showpiece for the lead singer. The confrontation in Act 2 between Orfeo and the Furies who guard the entrance to the underworld is perpetually astonishing for its effect of terror – the earliest example of real uncanniness in opera. Hell's denizens dance wildly, first very slowly, then for a few bars at breakneck speed, before singing a chorus that repeatedly demands an answer to the same miserable question: what mortal dares come to this terrible place? They sing every part of this question in the same triple-metre rhythm, with three long, even strokes followed by the snap of three short ones:

Chi mai dell'Erebo
Fra le caligini
Sull'orme d'Ercole
E di Piritoo
Conduce il piè?

[Who amid the mists / of Erebus, / in the footsteps of Hercules / and Pirithous / treads here?]

After dancing again, they repeat the question. The same rhythm recurs, with added emphasis concerning Hell's unpleasant details, the wrath of the Furies, the howling of Cerberus – instrumental howls arising in concord in the orchestra, with the cellos playing loud, emphatic slurs. The message is simple. Hell is noisy. It is also repetitive, with sung speech reduced to a single rhythmic tic, as if the hopelessness of those condemned to toxic and eternal labour has been given musical shape. When Orfeo begins to sing against this noise, a second orchestra, made up of harp and plucked strings, becomes the sound of the lyre he carries. He sings his plea twice over in its entirety, then repeats lines 2–4 a third time:

Deh! placatevi con me,
Furie, larve, ombre sdegnose,
Vi renda almen pietose
Il mio barbaro dolor!

[Alas! Placate with me / furies, ghosts, / indignant shades, / at least make them feel compassion at / my cruel sorrow!]

Unlike the underworld guardians, his gift is to be able to effect change, so when the poetic text is repeated (the Furies keep yelling: 'No!') the music takes off in different directions: there is a melodic and harmonic variation on the first pass, but never its literal repetition. Gluck has composed a solo that mutates, putting into notes the idea that Orfeo is improvising, trying different flavours of the melody and, with its high-to-low sweeps, gauging which is most effective. As so often with onstage music making, the onstage audience response tells us what our reaction should be. The Furies' repeated, loud, single-pitch 'No!' finally softens into a four-part harmony 'No', voices joined in a consonant, major-mode chord that could, for an instant, be the friendly hum of a barbershop quartet. It is a first sign that the Furies will yield. Orfeo's vocal line avoids elaborate melismas – no syllable of text is allotted more than two notes. But if we consult recorded performances of the scene, we will hear that most Orfeos add some personal embellishments, at least to the final cadence in this section. It's as though, despite Calzabigi's polemics against singers, the illusion of improvisation and autonomy written into Orfeo's melody encourages free-spirited additions to the letter of the text. After this first salvo, with the Furies still not convinced, Orfeo goes on with a second poetic verse and entirely new music. After yet another refusal, there is a third: Orfeo seems to dispose of limitless imagination. What is saddest about the scene is that, even when they are finally moved by his singing, the Furies never break free of their rhythmic shackles, but are condemned to sameness. 'Let the Gate open, groaning on its black hinges!' Orfeo is allowed to pass, with this final reference to Hell's loud noise taking the form of quietness, a long fade in C minor, piano to pianissimo.

This scene was famous from the outset, and its sounds resonated through operatic and instrumental compositions for decades to follow. The orchestral beginning to 'Deh! placatevi con me' – a C-minor colour, arpeggiated triplets beginning *in medias res* on B-D-G, then C-E♭-G before moving on from there – that beginning is echoed in the tragic chorus 'O voto tremendo' in Act 3 of Mozart's *Idomeneo*. It also haunts the first number of *Don Giovanni*, when what starts unequivocally as an *opera buffa* abruptly mutates into tragedy. The Commendatore is dying, Don Giovanni and Leporello lament in shock, and we get the same minor mode and triplets, the same beginning *in medias res*. And then, via that Mozart trio, it migrates into the first movement of Beethoven's 'Moonlight' Sonata, Op. 27, No. 2, whose triplets seem to echo Mozart's number and Gluck's, and weave them (a semitone higher) into a famously atmospheric piano piece. Nor was this the only occasion on which Mozart remembered *Orfeo*. In Act 3, Euridice's fatal moment is written as an elaborate orchestral recitative, in which she berates Orfeo for his refusal to look back at her. Gluck's Euridice, passionate harridan that she is, having attracted his glance 'rises up with tremendous force, then once more sinks to the ground', saying 'io manco, io moro' (I faint, I die). In Act 1 of *Don Giovanni*, when Donna Anna discovers her dead father, the Commendatore, she faints to almost identical sounds.

Did *Orfeo* transfix people other than Mozart? Were audiences struck silent, and did this new kind of opera endure? Burney in 1772 reports Gluck lamenting how much labour had been involved in producing *Orfeo* in Vienna, how resistant the entrenched tastes and habits had been.[24] Gluck was indeed a polarizing force. One of the great musical pamphlet wars of the 1770s, Paris-based and utterly contrived, fed on a supposed rivalry between Gluck and Niccolò Piccinni (1728–1800). Yet this conflict had little to do with *Orfeo*, still less with old-style high-wire coloratura in opposition to Gluck's austerity. Piccinni had written a single comic-opera hit, *La Cecchina, ossia la buona figliuola* (Cecchina, or The Good-Natured Girl, 1760), and his preferred style was melodious and simple. It was Piccinni's acoustic lightness that formed the antithesis to Gluck's *gravitas*, to Gluck as the composer of whom the historian Marmontel would quip, 'one must admit that no one has ever made the trumpets rumble, the strings whirr, or the voices bellow as he'.[25] From what we know of audience reactions to Gluck's *Orfeo*, however, it would appear that there was indeed a significant difference between riotous, indifferent Italian spectators and audiences elsewhere. Calzabigi wrote of Italian theatregoers in 1778, 'how could one want to present a Greek tragedy in front of such a deranged audience?'[26] But in Vienna and France the situation had been different. There Gluck had accomplished a revolution in operatic form, a new way of writing opera that had the power to evoke unprecedented rapture and absorption in listeners. In the 1770s, in Paris, as evinced by weeping and solitary and silent devotion to the stage, a new 'depth and intensity' of experience 'inconceivable to earlier audiences' was being laid at Gluck's door.[27]

By the first decades of the nineteenth century, in Austria and the German states, Gluck's mature operas enjoyed a reputation for genius that Mozart's were only beginning to match. E. T. A. Hoffmann's story 'Ritter Gluck' (Chevalier Gluck, 1809) is a succinct miniature within this landscape, and gives a sense for the reverence in which Gluck was held among those most repulsed by the Italianate in opera. In Berlin, the narrator recounts, Gluck's operas are constantly being staged, and an eccentric, old-fashioned figure wanders the streets complaining about their performance:

> Once I went to hear *Iphigenia in Tauris*. As I entered the theatre, I heard the orchestra playing the overture to *Iphigenia in Aulis*. I thought, hmm, so they're playing *this Iphigenia*. But then I was astonished when the Andante and the subsequent Storm began [the first choral number from *Iphigénie en Tauride*]. A quiet ocean, then a storm, then the Greeks are washed up onto the beach – that's the opera! What! Did the composer write in the score that you could do anything you want with it, like some bagatelle for trumpet?[28]

The eccentric, in typical Hoffmannesque fashion, turns out to be the ghost of Gluck himself, condemned to wander unshriven for reasons mysteriously unexplained, since the real Gluck committed no greater sin (we are told) than overindulging in liqueurs towards the end of his life. What's interesting about the story is the way in which Gluck's reformist polemic, particularly his assertions about compositional authority *against* the pressures and exigencies of performance, are converted here into the pseudo-Gluck's fury against an opera house that mixes and matches overtures. But such mixing and matching, substituting numbers or re-arranging them, was a practical fact of operatic life (Gluck's included). Although Hoffmann didn't know it, Gluck himself had reused large stretches of his ballet music for *Semiramis* (1765) in *Iphigénie en Tauride*, and recycled other music from his ballets and *opéras comiques* in his serious operas. Mozart, too, was happy to provide substitute arias for his (and other composers') operas to please new singers at revivals. High-minded civilians and amateurs – and this includes many of the philosophers who debated about opera during the Enlightenment – have complained about what practising musicians do in realizing opera for a very long time. The same offended screams, for example, greeted Cecilia Bartoli when she sang two of Mozart's substitute arias in *Le nozze di Figaro* at the Metropolitan Opera in 1999. Critics were determined that she should be chastised for supposed sins that endured an ephemeral few minutes on stage. The spirit of Gluck, if not his actual practice, was among them.

HIGH PASSION AND EFFECT

In Act 1 of *Iphigénie en Tauride*, Iphigénie tells her assembled maidens about a terrible dream: she is back in her father Agamemnon's palace, and sees him fleeing from his murderer, who is her mother Clytemnestra. She is then impelled to kill her brother Orestes. The House of Atreus has its dreadful history summarized in a recitative that begins with an amazing sound, a repeated F♯, pianissimo in the brass and winds: a claxon going off loudly, but very far away or very long ago. As Iphigénie recounts meteorological details – 'fire burned in the air, and lightning fell on the palace in bursts, embracing and devouring it!' – the orchestra loses its musical mind; tonalities succeed one another according to their disquieting effect rather than any functional sense; with the F♯ alarm bell, now loud and clear, returning for the palace's demise.

Orchestral activity like this is typical in French tragic recitative, and forms a contrast to the held-back arias, where the very fact that there was only one character – played by a potentially wayward soloist – seemed to inspire composers to keep characters under a firm grip. Gluck unbuttoned things for duets – the railing and remorse in Orfeo's duet with Euridice, or the extraordinary scene for Oreste and his friend Pylade in *Iphigénie en Tauride*, with its funereal C minor. The two men declare their willingness to die for one another, with reproaches that speak of a 'passionate friendship' that is now, in the twenty-first century, perhaps unavoidably staged as homoeroticism (the 2003 New York City Opera production was famous for its semi-nude Oreste–Pylade duo). Passionate duets for the 'wrong' pairing are one of opera's great complications, numbers in which voice-characters declaring love via passionate music are laid on to plot-characters whom taboos must keep rigidly separate.

That last formulation sounds ultra-modern for Gluck but will (as we shall see in the next chapter) become almost routine for Mozart. It will be mostly in *opera buffa* that Mozart's propensity for such confusion reaches its height. *Opera seria*, with which Mozart was principally involved in his youth, tended to see him at his most conventional. The breakthrough came with *Idomeneo* (1781), a tale of crossed royal destinies during the Trojan Wars, in which a Trojan princess, Ilia (soprano), has been captured by Idomeneo, king of Crete (tenor), and has fallen in love with his son, Idamante (soprano castrato). There is no doubt that this opera displays Mozart's greatest debt to Gluck: numerous moments plainly adopt the principles of reform opera, with a prominent use of orchestral recitative, frequent scenic marvels, elaborate ensemble pieces (especially the famous Act 3 Quartet, 'Andrò, ramingo e solo') and a dynamic use of the chorus. This debt is so obvious that it has become something of a cliché, also carrying with it a suggestion that the composer came of age operatically with *Idomeneo* precisely because he imbibed a good dose of Gluckian discipline. There's some truth in this, but *Idomeneo* has another story to tell. The opera is also full of solo arias: numbers whose musical elaboration is unprecedented; numbers which celebrate, unashamedly so, the glories of untrammelled singing that Gluck's reforms were so eager to banish.

Given the profusion of arias, it is no surprise to learn that Mozart went to some pains to ensure that *Idomeneo* was carefully tuned to the capabilities of the first cast, whether or not the results might make ideal dramatic sense. The most obvious case is with Idomeneo himself, a part written for an ageing tenor of the old school, Anton Raff, which Mozart tailored carefully so that Raff's diminishing capabilities and old-style sensibilities would not be stretched too far. So at the centre of this reform drama stands (and sings) a relic of the past, a bewigged Metastasian presence who, in Mozart's words, 'stands around like a statue',[29] and sings like one too. This is doubly disconcerting in that many of the other arias tend in quite the opposite direction – offering a kind of musical elaboration that looks forward rather than back.

One of the best, and most complicated of these new-style arias is Ilia's 'Se il padre perdei' from Act 2, in which Ilia, with uncommon, unsettling sensuality, tells Idomeneo that he must now be her adopted father. We are lucky enough to have a Mozart letter about this aria, with instructions to be passed on to the librettist, Giovanni Battista Varesco. Mozart is extremely clear about his priorities. The original text he had been offered contained an 'aside' (a whispered comment to the audience). Mozart wants this removed. Asides, he says, are fine for dialogue (he means recitative of some kind), 'but in an aria – where the words have to be repeated – it makes for a poor effect'. Another way of saying this would be that arias are intended for *music*: verbal changes of register shouldn't intrude. What is also clear is that Mozart already had music in mind for this aria: he wants it to be 'natural and flowing', and what's more to have elaborate instrumental accompaniment, so that the piece will also be suitable for concert performance.[30] We are already some considerable distance from the musical severities of Gluck's style.

The aria itself bears this out to a remarkable degree. The words that eventually emerged would suit an old-fashioned da capo form. One can imagine a gentle, perhaps pastoral 'A' section (the first verse); some musical contrast for the 'B' section in which Ilia remembers her past problems (the second verse), and then an ornamented reprise:

Se il padre perdei,
La patria, il riposo,
Tu padre mi sei,
Soggiorno amoroso
È Creta per me.
Or più non rammento
Le angoscie, gli affanni.
Or gioia, e contento,
Compenso a miei danni
Il cielo mi dié.
Parte

[If I have lost my father, / my homeland, my rest, / you are a father to me, / an amorous sojourn / is Crete for me. / Now I no longer remember / the anguish, the pains. / Now joy, and happiness, / consolation for my injuries / Heaven gives me. / *She leaves*]

Mozart's musical realization of this conventional text adds new complications. It has, for a start, four so-called 'obbligato' wind instruments (flute, oboe, bassoon and horn), all of which require their own musical space, trilling away individually and in ensemble as the singer prepares herself. This instrumental elaboration is then grafted on to an aria that has little trace of the da capo form. Instead, the entire text is stated twice, and treated with great fluidity. For example, both musical stanzas are interrupted by a new, questioning woodwind figure just before the 'soggiorno amoroso' (amorous sojourn) line, and this new idea seems to precipitate the sudden, disconcerting dive into the minor mode and an injection of vocal sighing figures as Ilia recalls her past 'angoscie' (anguish) and 'affanni' (pains). What emerges from such sudden and unpredictable changes of mood is what we might now call emotional complexity, a sense in which the pastoral surface so simply depicted at the start can have complex undercurrents. As if to stress this further, Idomeneo's recitative that follows is launched by a shadowy, minor-mode repetition in the strings of that questioning woodwind figure, as if the aria did not, after all, completely succeed in quelling its own inner doubts.

Mozart had been in Paris at the height of the pamphlet war between Gluck's supporters and those of his mild-tempered Italian rival, Piccinni – a conflict that one venerable musicologist characterized as that between an agate and a sponge.[31] Although Gluck's influence on *Idomeneo* is unmistakable, Mozart's simultaneous embrace of expansive arias and untrammelled lyricism would ultimately place him among the Piccinnistes – a fact often overlooked by opera historians who wish to build robust, reform-led narratives peopled by strong figures. For this and other reasons it can be difficult to know where to place Gluck's operatic reform. The composer's association with an aggressively articulate and self-promoting avant-garde, Calzabigi at its head, may lead us to overlook the fact that his revolution was not much imitated. During his final decade (he died in 1787) he was a venerated figure, but one who had few immediate followers. His last Parisian opera (*Echo et Narcisse*, 1779) was a failure; he left the capital, dogged by attacks from the Piccinnistes, to finish his days in Vienna. To understand the importance of Gluck as a symbol of operatic restraint we must look to the nineteenth century and away from Italian opera, above all to Berlioz and Wagner. As we shall see in the next chapter, the crowning glory of the late-eighteenth-century opera did indeed centre on Vienna, and precisely during those years in the 1780s when Gluck was a resident elderly celebrity. But it came in a very different brand of opera, one hardly touched by Gluck's great musical manifestos.

5
Opera buffa and Mozart's line of beauty

This is how an incarcerated murderer put the case:

> I have no idea to this day what those two Italian ladies were singing about. Truth is, I don't want to know. Some things are best left unsaid. I'd like to think they were singing about something so beautiful, it can't be expressed in words, and makes your heart ache because of it. I tell you, those voices soared higher and farther than anybody in a grey place dares to dream. It was like some beautiful bird flapped into our drab little cage and made those walls dissolve away, and for the briefest of moments, every last man in Shawshank felt free.

The murderer is Ellis Boyd Redding (Morgan Freeman) the narrator of *The Shawshank Redemption* (1994), a movie about prison life based on a novella by Stephen King. Here, Ellis is heard in voiceover telling us how Andy Dufresne (Tim Robbins), a banker wrongly convicted of murder, broadcast a recorded excerpt from Mozart's comedy *Le nozze di Figaro* (The Marriage of Figaro, 1786) over the prison's loudspeaker system. Andy works in the library. He thus has access to what the Germans call *Kulturgut* – high-cultural property – and he has decided to commit this public act of defiance to ease his fellow convicts' hearts. Hearing the Mozart duet indeed transfigures a group of hardened criminals, and in a scene that might have come from Ovid, the music floats over the prison yard and the denizens of Hell stop their infernal work, pausing to listen to something beyond pain and suffering (see Figure 1).

The duet Ellis describes comes from Act 3 of *Figaro*. The 'two Italian ladies' are actually an Austrian and a Swiss, sopranos Gundula Janowitz and Edith Mathis, in the 1962 Karl Böhm recording. Or perhaps they're both Spaniards living on an aristocratic estate near Seville: the Countess

Almaviva and a servant girl called Susanna. But what *are* they singing about? In Act 3 of the opera (we'll deal with the larger plot later) Susanna and the Countess have devised a scheme to embarrass the Countess's husband, a heartless philanderer. The Countess will dress as Susanna and thus disguised will have an assignation with her spouse. By means of this ruse, she will catch him red-handed in an act of illicit dalliance. To this end, the Countess dictates an enticing letter, which Susanna copies out. The duet's text is simply the words of the letter followed by a one-line comment:

RECITATIVO
Countess: Eh, scrivi dico; e tutto
Io prendo su me stessa.
'Canzonetta sull'aria . . .'
Susanna: '. . . sull'aria'.

DUETTINO
Countess: 'Che soave zeffiretto . . .'
Susanna: 'Zeffiretto . . .'
Countess: 'Questa sera spirerà . . .'
Susanna: 'Questa sera spirerà . . .'
Countess: 'Sotto i pini del boschetto.'
Susanna: 'Sotto i pini . . .'
Countess: 'Sotto i pini del boschetto.'
Susanna: 'Sotto i pini . . . del boschetto . . .'
Countess: Ei già il resto capirà.
Susanna: Certo, certo il capirà.

[RECITATIVE *Countess*: Write what I say; I take / responsibility for everything. / 'Canzonetta sull'aria . . .' [Little Song on the Wind . . .]. *Susanna*: '. . . sull'aria'. / DUETTINO *Countess*: 'What a gentle little zephyr . . .' / *Susanna*: 'Little zephyr . . .' / *Countess*: 'Will be sighing this evening . . .' / *Susanna*: 'Will be sighing this evening . . .' / *Countess*: 'Under the pines in the little forest.' / *Susanna*: 'Under the pines . . .' / *Countess*: 'Under the pines in the little forest.' / *Susanna*: 'Under the pines . . . in the little forest . . .' / *Countess*: And the rest he'll understand. / *Susanna*: Yes, yes, he'll understand.]

This text is then repeated to accommodate additional singing. Just these few words, and they're insincere: poetic clichés about gentle breezes and pine groves in a letter meant to deceive and humiliate. But then there's the music. The Duettino joins together two sopranos in ways that make their individual voices indistinguishable. Even the melody becomes merged with echoes and re-echoes, the two lines entwining and encircling. By the end, the words have become abstract sounds; they have lost their meaning. 'Aria' means air, after all, and all those breezes, sighs and gentle currents in the text mutate, via Mozart, into sung air and vocal updrafts: very, very beautiful ones – sounds that, we now want to believe, could for a brief moment turn a motley crew of brutalized prisoners into sighing aesthetes.

What does beauty on this exalted scale have to do with comedy? That is a conundrum of Mozart's Italian comic operas. There are so many answers. Perhaps the sheer beauty of the Duettino is meant to represent women's wiles, and the joke is that we listeners, no matter how cynical, will be taken in again and again: that is, after all, the way of the operatic world. Perhaps we are encouraged, via sentimental parables like that in *The Shawshank Redemption*, to attach too much transfiguring power to opera, the joke being that Mozart was far too busy earning a living to worry about transfiguration, and tossed such numbers off casually. But one modern consensus about Mozart's comic operas has been that they involve rich sonic worlds that are beyond mere farce, just as his best libretti – the three written by Lorenzo Da Ponte – have deeply serious elements alongside silly ones.

THE DA PONTE FACTOR

Lorenzo Da Ponte was a colourful Italian who became one of the most successful *opera buffa* librettists in Vienna before emigrating to America in 1801 to escape his debts. He finished life (after a stint as a tavern owner in New Jersey) as Professor of Italian at Columbia University in New York City, and his memoirs still make entertaining reading. His contribution to Mozart's success should not be underestimated.

In Mozart's three 'Da Ponte' operas, *Figaro*, *Don Giovanni* (1787) and *Così fan tutte* (1790), there are musical moments that, for many devotees, seem as if they're worth a lifetime of waiting, moments that are now famous beyond all vagaries of operatic fashion. One comes near the end of *Figaro* Act 4 in which the Count asks forgiveness of his wife ('Contessa perdono') with a gorgeous but artful *bel canto* plea. She replies with a melody that's both mere cadence – a predictable way of marking a musical ending – and, in its simplicity, a reproach. This example of grace and promise for the future is instantly echoed in a choral crescendo sung by all the other characters. Another moment comes in the Act 2 finale of *Don Giovanni*. A supper party is visited by a ghostly stone effigy, the walking statue of a man Don Giovanni murdered in Act 1. The effigy's entrance starts a sparring between the two adversaries, one of this world, one of another. It takes place amid severe, minor-key music dominated by an obstinate rhythmic figure, along with instrumental imitations of the word 'No!' disguised as fortissimo chords that crash in suddenly.

A ghost; a philosophical discussion about redemption; forgiveness; sophisticated, sadly accepting clear-sightedness about infidelity: these are all imbued with super-charged emotional resonance by means of music. To ask how, precisely, is to pose an impossible question. Mozart's late operas, like much great art, in one sense simply *happened*, one can't account for their power simply by explaining local context and genetic lineage. There is, though, also the fact that Italian *opera buffa* as a genre was the necessary ground for these three Da Ponte works, a ground that was becoming increasingly fertile by the 1760s when Mozart started writing operas. A century earlier it had not existed; fifty years earlier it had barely begun to take shape. Some history of it is a useful starting point.

ORIGINAL SIN

As we have seen, there were comic characters mixed into seventeenth-century serious opera, but their presence within tragedy came to seem incongruous to later librettists, who disposed of them. This spoiled a lot of the fun, although it did prepare for the austerity of Gluck and his Viennese reform of *opera seria*. Almost 200 years later, Richard Strauss and his librettist Hugo von Hofmannsthal replayed this historical moment in their opera *Ariadne auf Naxos* (Ariadne on Naxos, 1912; revised version, 1916). In the Prologue, we meet a Composer who has written an *opera seria* on a classical theme, to be premiered that very evening. Immediately after this elevated entertainment, a comic troupe will improvise an *opera buffa*, the whole evening ending with a firework display. But the aristocratic patron, in order to keep to the timetable and enliven the classical austerity of the Composer's creation, proclaims at the last minute that the comic opera must be integrated into the *opera seria*. 'Simultaneously?' gasps the horrified Composer. The remainder of Strauss's opera comprises a performance of this two-in-one event, in which the 'serious opera *Ariadne auf Naxos*' and its self-important singers are interrupted, skewered and ultimately brought to a higher plane of existence by the comic troupe. 'Es gibt ein Reich, wo alles rein ist: Totenreich' (There is a realm where all is pure: The Realm of Death), sings Ariadne, only to be upstaged by a cheerful Harlequin informing her that 'Dancing and singing are so good for banishing tears!' What Hofmannsthal seemed to skewer in his early twentieth-century Vienna is the purifying aesthetic of the eighteenth century. After that time, the free mixture of despair and broad farce, of death and carefree dancing, rarely punctured operatic high-mindedness.

Ridicule was, though, a central feature in the first comic operas, which were usually in the modest form of *intermezzi*: short pieces, often for just a pair of characters, placed between the acts of an *opera seria* in centres such as Venice and Naples and Rome, the titles and their composers now mostly forgotten. Their target, not infrequently, was opera itself, the excesses, absurdities and musical habits that had taken hold by the late seventeenth century. By the early decades of the eighteenth century, Neapolitan comic operas had already established a set of conventions for characters and plot types. Much of this was inspired by the acrobatic, parodic ensemble comedy of the *commedia dell'arte*, an Italian popular theatrical tradition by then centuries old. This tradition provided the conventional plots and stock characters that populate early *opera buffa* – the miserable pedant, the scheming servant, the cuckold, the virtuous young lovers – as well as its penchant for crude, physical humour. Our word 'slapstick' refers to a baton carried by Arlecchino, or Harlequin, the scheming servant-clown; Mozart's servant Leporello in *Don Giovanni* is a direct descendant. Although *opera buffa* did not allow for the improvisation that generally characterized *commedia*, it nonetheless relied heavily on the physicality and comic pantomime of its performers. The Frenchman Charles de Brosses heard an early *opera buffa* in 1739 and remarked on the extraordinarily physical acting of its stars: 'These comedians cry, laugh boisterously, gesticulate, perform all sorts of dumb shows without ever missing a beat'.[1] Even more important was the fact that the stock *commedia* characters and plot types were set in the present day, thus granting them the potential for direct social and cultural critique that *opera seria*'s distant heroes and heroines could only claim through allegory.

Many of the earliest comic operas have not survived, a circumstance that should not surprise us, given their initially rather lowly status in the operatic world. But one that did, and – more surprising still – is still performed today, is *La serva padrona* (The Housemaid Takes Charge, 1733) by Giovanni Battista Pergolesi (1710–36). This two-scene piece was premiered in Naples as an *intermezzo* between the acts of an *opera seria* also written by Pergolesi. *La serva padrona* was enormously popular all over Europe. After it was performed in Paris in the early 1750s, it became the stimulus for prolonged polemic debate about the respective values of Italian and French opera, the *Querelle des Bouffons* – War of the Comedians – briefly discussed in Chapter 4. That war was intimately connected with the establishment of French *opéra comique*.

More significant still were developments in mid-century, ones that again placed Venice at the forefront of operatic history. By now the *intermezzi* had expanded into full-scale dramas. The key figure was the Venetian playwright Carlo Goldoni (1707–93). His libretti, which were no more than money-making offshoots of his spoken dramas, helped lead comic opera into musical territory very different from that of its serious cousin. Goldoni and his early musical collaborators, in particular another Venetian, Baldassare Galuppi (1706–85), experimented with two significant changes. First, they made important distinctions between serious and comic characters in terms of the way they express themselves operatically, adding a third type, so-called *mezzi caratteri* – mixed characters. The serious characters would continue with their ornate 'da capo' arias and high-flown sentiments; the comic characters tended towards simpler, more direct forms – arias that might even alter in tempo and metre if the mood shifted. The second critical change came through expanding the number and extent of ensembles, particularly those at act endings, which might now include action *within* fixed numbers, and which might boast a whole series of semi-independent musical movements following one another as rapidly as the action demanded.

This new type of *opera buffa* was very different from its early-eighteenth-century predecessors. It became enormously popular, soon overtaking *opera seria* as the genre of choice in all but the most elevated circles. A good example is Goldoni and Galuppi's *Il filosofo di campagna* (The Homespun Philosopher, 1754), which started life in Venice but soon spread far and wide in Europe; there were around twenty productions in its first ten years. In 1819, with the perspective of a half-century, Thomas Busby's *General History of Music* was still giving pride of place to Galuppi's *opere buffe* over Mozart's, since Galuppi's had been the rage in London years before. The Italian is praised for his 'taste, genius, and imagination', and *Il filosofo di campagna* is singled out as 'a comic opera, the musical merit of which surpassed every other *burletta* performed in England'. Busby writes that for the wedding and coronation of George III and Queen Sophie in 1761, an *opera seria* of 'circumscribed merit' was commissioned for the occasion and performed at the King's Theatre, but George III commanded that a performance of *Il filosofo di campagna* supplement it, to general rejoicing.[2]

This anecdote reminds us that *opera buffa* was increasingly being played in the same venues as *opera seria*, and could deliver an equally potent if rather different message, peopled as it was by a less monolithic collection of characters. Above all, there was the catalyst of portraying a broader social mix; although the servants tended to express themselves in forms different from those of their masters and mistresses, at base everyone spoke the same language, operated in the same lyrical sphere. There was a wider range of voice types: comic basses, seductive baritones, quavering tenor senior citizens, alto ladies of a certain age, mezzo-sopranos in pants playing boys, ingénue sopranos. What's more, in the burgeoning ensemble movements and – especially – the large-scale, multi-movement finales, servants and aristocrats could mix together musically in a way that challenged old divisions and hierarchies. Da Ponte worked directly in this tradition, adding references to Italy's glorious literary past to enrich his verse.

In another important expansion, plot types diversified, especially into 'bourgeois' or 'sentimental' genres adapted from French plays and English novels like Richardson's *Pamela* (a tale of female virtue rewarded that was reworked into opera several times in the late eighteenth century, most famously by Piccinni, to a Goldoni-reworked libretto called

La Cecchina, ossia la buona figliuola – Cecchina, or The Good-Natured Girl, Rome, 1760). In these works, the comic genre shifted away from amusing tableaux towards tears and moral education, while the contemporary plot settings ensured that the works were perceived by audiences and critics as comedy rather than tragedy. Lest we forget, the eighteenth century was an era of rigorous classification in art: high-minded critics could much better tolerate expansion and change in the lower genre (comedy) than in the higher (tragedy), where continuity and stasis could be fiercely defended. Just as did genre painting and domestic drama, comic opera became a proving ground for cultural visionaries in the second half of the century.

As its musical and dramatic purview expanded, so *opera buffa* became more international in both style and diffusion. Italian composers were usually thought the most adept, the famous Neapolitan conservatory system being a major supplier of famous names. Successful works remained active for years or even decades. An example might be Gaetano Latilla (1711–88), whose *Gismondo* was first performed in Naples in 1737. In a revised version as *La finta cameriera* (The Feigned Maid), it had travelled to fifteen other Italian cities by 1747, and had also been seen in Graz, Leipzig and Hamburg in 1745, courtesy of an itinerant Venetian troupe. Performances in London (1749) and Paris (1752) occurred soon afterwards. There was also the fact that the economic hardships of the later eighteenth century caused many courts above the Alps to shift from serious opera to comic opera, the latter almost always proving much easier on the purse. As early as 1750, *opera buffa* productions outnumbered those of *opera seria*. Not all the premieres were in Italy. *Il barbiere di Siviglia* (The Barber of Seville, 1782) by the Naples-trained Giovanni Paisiello (1740–1816), which was first seen in far-off St Petersburg, was among the most popular; the same composer's *Il re Teodoro* (King Theodore, 1784), which rivalled *Il barbiere* in popularity, premiered in Vienna. Composers of other nationalities also worked in the genre, often enriching it with features of their native musical styles. As usual, the view of Italian lightheartedness from the North was in part appreciative, in part appalled. Goethe went to see an *opera buffa* in Venice at the Teatro San Moisè in May 1786 and wrote in his *Italienische Reise* (Italian Journey, 1816–17) that it was 'not very good', but that 'the two women made an effort to act well and project themselves agreeably. That at least is something. The two have beautiful figures and good voices, and are charming, sprightly, appealing little persons.'[3] Much as we might want to resist the inevitable pro-German conclusion, *opera buffa* did sustain a bracing musical jolt when Germans and Austrians brought their experience with instrumental music – new genres like the symphony and classical concerto – to augment the charms of well-turned ankles and sweet voices. One of these composers was Mozart.

VIENNESE OPERA

Figaro, *Don Giovanni* and *Così fan tutte* seem to transport us to a new and now familiar operatic world: rapid, fluid alternations of action and reflection, emotional richness and moral complexity. Mozart's *opere buffe*, particularly *Don Giovanni*, even found a significant place in nineteenth- and twentieth-century literature and philosophy. This might seem strange. Vienna formed the unstable, constantly shifting social and political context against which all Mozart's mature operas were written. But Vienna in the eighteenth century was, at first glance, an unlikely place for moral complexity or philosophical challenge to have arisen. The centre of old Vienna, narrowly circumscribed and separated from the suburbs beyond, was a place with an unambiguous potentate – indeed, the archetypal enlightened despot, progressive and autocratic in equal measure – the Emperor Joseph II. The ruling class was composed of the ancient nobility. True, well-heeled aspirants could now buy their way into this nobility, but the price was steep and tensions between old money and new ran high. Equally true, the start of Joseph's reign, in 1780, saw a period of social reform, a further symptom of the changing views that had accompanied the rise of *opera buffa*. The power of the nobility and Church was reduced, intellectual and religious freedoms were increased, and the crippling taxes levied on the poor became less harsh, mostly at the expense of rich landowners. However, in the latter half of the 1780s, especially in the wake of disastrous military adventures and unsettling news of revolution in France, these reforms were mostly put into reverse.

Yet in this same Vienna, Mozart and Da Ponte managed to produce, and with no significant trouble from officialdom, *Le nozze di Figaro*, whose anti-aristocratic edge is very sharp. The libretto for *Figaro* is based on a play by Pierre-Augustin Caron de Beaumarchais (1732–99): *La Folle Journée, ou Le Mariage de Figaro* (The Crazy Day, or Figaro's Wedding, 1778; first performed 1784). Beaumarchais had been one of the first proponents of the bourgeois or 'sentimental' drama in France during the 1760s, but thereafter had gradually shifted from earnest didacticism to more biting social critique and moral equivocation. *La Folle Journée* was the second play in an ideologically charged trilogy about social class, one that used a recurring set of characters – the barber Figaro, his beloved Susanna, Count Almaviva and his wife Rosina, their ward Cherubino and assorted others. The first play (*Le Barbier de Séville*, 1775) was the basis for Paisiello's opera, as well as Rossini's more famous version four decades later (1816). The third – *La Mère coupable, ou L'Autre Tartuffe* (The Guilty Mother, or The Other Tartuffe, 1792) – was written many years later and is a decidedly more pessimistic *drame moral*. It too has an operatic descendant, Jules Massenet's *Chérubin* (1905), which manages to banish the play's darkness by avoiding much of its plot.

These characters, Figaro, Susanna, Cherubino, the Count and Countess, all spiralled into opera in the eighteenth century, and never quite departed. *La Mère coupable* resurfaces in John Corigliano's opera *The Ghosts of Versailles* (1991), in which Beaumarchais and Marie Antoinette meet each another in the afterlife. The playwright conjures up these operatic creatures – there's Figaro with his striped cap! there's Susanna with her apron! – in order to console the murdered Queen. By 1991, such figures represented not much more than their own quasi-mythical place in operatic history, and this of course adds considerably to the melancholy sense of nostalgia. *The Ghosts of Versailles*, for all its antic moments, is a sad opera not because Marie Antoinette is full of pathos, but because returning Figaro and Susanna to the stage can't bring back anything like Mozart's achievements.

Those achievements were founded on opportunities available in Vienna. Like other principal cities in the vast Austrian empire, Vienna housed three types of opera. Alongside *opera buffa* there was lavish *opera seria*, which had always been the bastion of old money and the ruling classes. As we saw in the previous chapter, its subject matter had not changed much since Handel's day, with mythological and ancient-world plots still preferred, and with the action likely to be an evening-long celebration of the status quo, the final curtain closing as an absolute ruler heaps boundless wisdom and mercy on his humble subjects. In formal operatic terms there was also continuity. Although the domination of solo arias was reduced, with a greater number of duets and other ensemble numbers and with the active participation of the chorus, the norm was still a statuesque notion of solo utterance. At the other end of the social spectrum, Vienna also had *Singspiel*, German-language opera, with spoken dialogue rather than recitative, and with a much more frankly popular appeal: something closer to vernacular spoken theatre, with a huge range of plots, often with fantastic or exotic settings to amuse the crowd.

Mozart had worked in all three genres before moving to Vienna. His first opera, a *Singspiel*, was *Bastien und Bastienne* (1768). *La finta giardiniera* (The Feigned Gardener), an *opera buffa* to a libretto after Goldoni, was premiered in Munich in 1775. But mostly he had been involved with *opera seria*. There is reason to think that he was always more interested in comedy, quite possibly because it gave him greater opportunities to use his skills as a composer of instrumental genres. For Mozart, unlike many Italian-born opera composers, was by no means an opera specialist, and wrote willingly in all the popular musical forms. Comedy was attractive as well because of the variety of idioms that would be available. In a letter to his father in 1783, he showed himself very definite about the kind of libretto he wanted:

> The most essential thing is that on the whole the story should be really comic: and, if possible, he [the librettist] ought to introduce two equally good female parts, one of these to be *seria*, the other *mezzo carattere*. . . . The third female *character*, however, may be entirely *buffa*, and so may all the male ones, if necessary.[4]

In short, he wanted a Goldonian *opera buffa* to the letter, albeit with an *opera seria* preference for high voices, and perhaps with a nascent imagining of how those high voices might at times contrast and at times blend seductively together, as they do in that 'Sull'aria' Duettino from *Figaro*.

Da Ponte's *Figaro* libretto boasts many hallmarks of the typical late-eighteenth-century *opera buffa*. At base, it's a story of two couples: one unhappy, one happy; one from the aristocracy, one from the servant classes. The action takes place over the course of a hectic day. The aristocratic couple is the Count (baritone) and Countess (soprano). Their marriage is unhappy because the Count has a roving eye. Very near the start of the opera it becomes clear that his eye has roved to the Countess's maid, Susanna (soprano), who is about to marry the Count's valet, Figaro (bass). Things become more complicated still via Cherubino (mezzo-soprano, a so-called 'trouser role'), the Count's excitable young page. Cherubino is new to testosterone, and is in love with Susanna, with the Countess, and with any other attractive female he encounters. There are further minor characters enacting various subplots. Over four acts, the Count makes multiple attempts at seduction, but – this is set up in 'Sull'aria' – is eventually duped by the Countess and Susanna, who switch clothes and thus expose his attempted infidelity. The happy ending is inevitable: the Count, humbled, begs forgiveness. Everyone lives happily ever after; or so we hope but somehow doubt, given the complexity of their feelings for each other. (In *La Mère coupable*, set some years after the time of *Figaro*, we learn that an older Cherubino, no longer such a little cherub, seduced the Countess and made her pregnant before going off – fatally, as it turned out – to seek glory on the battlefield.)

Even from this résumé, it is clear that one could read Da Ponte's *Figaro* through the political lens of 1780s Vienna. A typical account might see the libretto as a covert message in support of Joseph II's reform of aristocratic privilege; to put it simply, at humbling the Count's class. It is, though, hard to find historical support for such an interpretation. There is certainly no evidence that the ruling classes – who were, let's be clear, the principal patrons of comic opera – considered themselves thus threatened. An alternative reading is more likely one in which the opera might be resonant with the times, but less as a political statement than a personal and social one. *Figaro* is, according to this way of thinking, a story in which the relationships between the main characters are a commentary on the new social mobility that was such a source of tension in Vienna and elsewhere in Europe, and on the new sense of personal relationships that was emerging simultaneously. Whichever way one reads it, the opera has deep resonances with the ideals of the Enlightenment: that great, Europe-wide reforming movement during the eighteenth century, in which reason and knowledge were pitted against the absolute authority claimed by aristocracy, Church and state.[5]

'CONSTANZE!' – WEDDED BLISS

Mozart's own marriage is sometimes seen as a clue to his operatic sympathies. In that 1783 letter about his ideal libretto, we can hear Mozart's attention to female characters and voices, and the nuance and emotional plausibility of his operatic women were strikingly intense for the period. Was this artistic sympathy with the feminine grounded in real-life experience? When, in *Die Entführung aus dem Serail* (The Abduction from the Seraglio, 1782), the tenor hero sings the name 'Constanze! Constanze!' with such great longing, is there not a hint of autobiography? That, of course, is the kind of question always asked about creative artists, and in Mozart's case it's very hard to answer, in part because his biography has suffered more thoroughly than most Lives-and-Works from the romantic myths that swirled around him during the nineteenth century. Many of those myths concern his last ten years, when he forsook provincial Salzburg, and the protection of his composer-father Leopold, to swim in the wider and more uncertain world of Vienna. They have proved extraordinarily tenacious, and were injected with new life by Peter Shaffer's play *Amadeus* (1979) and by Milos Forman's 1984 film of the play. Shaffer's and Forman's veneer of shocking realism does little to disguise their reiteration of what is essentially a nineteenth-century picture of Mozart – the eternal child and musical angel who came down to us in the form of a weak and fallible man.

The basic biographical facts can easily be told. After his move from Salzburg to Vienna in 1781, the 25-year-old Mozart fashioned a lucrative career as a freelance musician. He earned money from private piano pupils, from opera commissions, from selling music to publishers and, most of all, as a composer-pianist, organizing concerts in which he starred as soloist in his own piano concertos. By 1785, with success on all fronts, he was installed in a spacious apartment in central Vienna, doing very well indeed. 1786 brought yet more prestige: he was commissioned to compose *Le nozze di Figaro* for the Court Opera. But the years that followed saw a significant decline in his fortunes. Disastrous Turkish wars caused many of his aristocratic patrons to leave Vienna, as a result of which his concert career virtually collapsed. Further opera commissions brought in considerable sums: *Don Giovanni* and *La clemenza di Tito* (an *opera seria*, 1791) for Prague; *Così fan tutte* and *Die Zauberflöte* (a *Singspiel*, 1791) for Vienna. He also obtained a modest court appointment and continued to sell his instrumental music to publishers. But his income decreased, on occasions sharply: he was obliged to move into the suburbs and, increasingly, to borrow from friends. He may have contributed to his financial woes with gambling debts. By 1790, though, his star was again in the ascendant: he was paying off debts, considering lucrative offers from impresarios in other capital cities. His fatal illness in December 1791, probably a kind of rheumatic fever, was sudden and unexpected. He was buried in a communal grave, unattended by mourners, not because he died in obscurity – far from it, his international reputation was ever growing – but in accordance with Joseph II's draconian brand of rationalism. As well as banning corsets, bell-ringing in thunderstorms and the making of honey cakes, the emperor had strictly enlightened views on how to economize on disposal of the mortal remains of Vienna's dead.

In spite of this more accurate picture of Mozart's life and times in Vienna, his persona remains something of an enigma. Compare two very different portraits (Figures 10 and 11). The first, an oil painting by Barbara Krafft, presents a severe, public figure, complete with wig and court regalia. The second, a 1789 silverpoint drawing by Dora Stock, gives a glimpse of a more private persona. Where does the real Mozart lie? His opinions gleaned from family correspondence often seem to present what a distant, cautious and deeply conservative father might want to hear, a projection of the court Mozart in the first portrait. For example, although Mozart's marriage in 1782 to Constanze Weber seems familiar in terms of what we might anachronistically call emotional equality, when describing his future bride to Leopold, Mozart painted a distinctly old-fashioned picture:

> Her whole beauty consists in two little black eyes and a pretty figure. She has no wit, but she has enough common sense to enable her to fulfil her duties as a wife and mother. It is a downright lie that she is inclined to be extravagant. . . . Tell me whether I could wish myself a better wife?[6]

Contemporary portraits of Constanze may help us. An oil painting by Joseph Lange from 1782 agrees with Mozart's less than entirely flattering picture. But a later portrait, an oil painting by Hans Hansen from 1802, a decade after Mozart's death, seems to present a different figure, and above all – the contrast is striking – a more formidable character. Which of these was Constanze? It's tempting to speculate that it was partly her husband's untimely death that allowed Constanze to grow so markedly in stature, but support for this or any other supposition is frustratingly thin.

So, in the case both of Mozart and the woman with whom he spent his Viennese years, we are left with conundrums. On the one hand, we have pictorial evidence that encourages a sense of historical distance; on the other, traces of characters who seem close to us, even if that closeness may be more hoped for than genuine. Earlier we described Mozart's operas as on the brink of a more familiar musical world. But that familiarity, which has something to do with the sense of emotional realism projected by his characters, involves alchemies that resist analysis. It is not just the by-product of Mozart's or Da Ponte's literary tastes, nor of taking existing *opera buffa* models to a higher plane, nor of Mozart's gifts as an instrumental composer, nor of his persona with all its unknowns. Adding up the parts will not account for the whole.

OPERA AS ACTION

We are on firmer ground when dealing with Mozart's comic operas directly. One aspect of *opera buffa* that adds to its enduring allure has to do with the nature of drama in comedy: it is centred far more in action, physical farce and confrontations between the characters. Monologue – static self-examination or self-presentation by noble, important beings – is still occasionally present, but is less important. This has immediate musical consequences. Comic libretti of this period engender ensembles, not just strings of solo arias; more important, the ensembles involve action, not just meditation or psychological portraiture. Mozart and Da Ponte inherited this precept from the *buffa* tradition, but their particular backgrounds were critical to what resulted. This particularly concerns the fact that Mozart was already an experienced, innovative composer of purely instrumental works such as the sonata, quartet and symphony: when these instrumental-music gifts came into contact with Da Ponte's dramaturgical ideas, the results were remarkable.

It is a truism that in Mozart's comic operas dramatic action is re-inscribed in musical guises, as the melding or clashing of harmony, thematic ideas, voice treatments and formal patterns. It has often been said that Gluck (the hero of our previous chapter) had the misfortune to bind operatic music to the words – to the rhythms of declamation and the progress of real time – just as Mozart was to liberate it.[7] While this equation is rather too simple, it holds a grain of truth. As we already saw in the case of *Idomeneo*, Mozart's love of purely musical procedures to accompany and reflect the action onstage frequently allowed a temporal and sonic expansiveness that had been banished by Gluck. In other words, Mozart often granted his music a luxurious autonomy to revel in its own procedures – those concurrently developed in instrumental music – while at the same time harnessing its ability to work in the service of drama in new ways. What is perpetually astonishing is the economy with which he did this. After *Die Entführung*, there are hardly ever numbers in which we sense that musical logic is dictating the length of a given utterance. Mozart's arias and ensembles unfurl with such impeccable musical timing that we are always left with a paradoxical feeling: we wish there could have been more, but we know that things are just right as they are.

Take, for instance, the way *Figaro* begins. The first number is a duet between Figaro and Susanna. It occurs immediately the overture has finished, without any preparatory recitative, and Da Ponte clearly derived the text from a small exchange at the start of the source text. Beaumarchais's play opens on a partly furnished room; Figaro has a measure in his hand, Susanna is at the mirror, trying on a hat decorated with flowers:

FIGARO Nineteen feet by twenty-six.
SUSANNA Look, Figaro, my bonnet. Do you like it better now?
FIGARO (*taking both her hands in his*) Infinitely better, my sweet. My, what that bunch of flowers – so pretty, so virginal, so suited to the head of my lovely girl – does to a lover on the morning of his wedding!

In an uncomplicated way we are given various pieces of information:

that Figaro and Susanna are to be married that very day, that Figaro compares his future wife to virginal flowers, that the sky is untroubled. Da Ponte embellishes the exchange:

FIGARO (*misurando*)

> Cinque... dieci... venti... trenta...
> trentasei... quarantatre.

SUSANNA (*specchiandosi*)

> Ora sì ch'io son contenta;
> Sembra fatto inver per me.
> Guarda un po', mio caro Figaro,
> Guarda adesso il mio cappello.

FIGARO

> Sì, mio core, or è più bello,
> Sembra fatto inver per te.

FIGARO and SUSANNA

> Ah, il mattino alle nozze vicino
> Quanto è dolce al mio/tuo tenero sposo
> Questo bel cappellino vezzoso
> Che Susanna ella stessa si fe'.

[FIGARO (*measuring*): Five... ten... twenty... thirty... / thirty-six... forty-three. / SUSANNA (*looking in the mirror*): Yes, I'm happy with it now; / it seems just made for me. / Just look a moment, my dear Figaro, / look now at my hat. / FIGARO: Yes, my dear, it's prettier now, / it seems just made for you. / FIGARO and SUSANNA: Ah, on the morning of our wedding / how sweet to my/your loving bridegroom / is this charming little hat, / which Susanna herself made.]

We would not have such a number in an *opera seria*, where this sort of conversation would take place in recitative, and thus be written in blank verse and inevitably followed by a solo aria for one or other character. Here the regular, rhyming poetry alerts us to the fact that, as would now be expected in an *opera buffa*, the interchange will take place within a musical number. Basically the action is the same as in Beaumarchais's play. Figaro is doing one thing; Susanna asks him to do another; Figaro obeys; they are happy. We can also see from the change in poetic metre that Da Ponte imagined the four lines of simultaneous singing at the end would have new music, and we might easily imagine a simple, two-movement musical rendition for the number as a whole: the first ('Cinque... dieci...') a playful exchange between the lovers, the second ('Ah, il mattino') perhaps a rustic duet (the verse rhythm is a typical one for 3/8 or 6/8 pastoral movements). This is exactly the musical form of a famous duet in Act 1 of *Don Giovanni*, 'Là ci darem la mano' (which we will discuss later), where the changed poetic metre in the final section produces a faster, dance-like musical setting for a passage of simultaneous singing.

When Mozart's music is added, though, matters become more complex. The orchestral introduction contains two very different themes: the first, a simple, repeated-note figure in the strings; the second a circular motif in the woodwind. When the characters start singing, it's plain that the first theme belongs to Figaro and his activities – he sings his measurements over it and its repeated notes mimic his steady pacing of the room. The second theme is equally clearly Susanna's – she sings about her hat, and the theme's circular motion invokes the circular passage of her image as it passes from her to the mirror and back. All simple enough: these are obvious musical representations of the text and the scenic actions. But the continuation of the duet is more complicated. For a start, Figaro doesn't immediately answer Susanna when she announces her theme; instead he continues with his pacing. Susanna, not surprisingly, asks him with increasing insistence to look at her. Eventually Figaro does so, passing comments on her hat while adopting her circling tune. But he sings it in a low, unconvincing register. Is he just saying the words, not really looking at her? Is he – husbands are thus accused to this day – simply not *listening*? As if to confirm that this is indeed the case, Susanna continues to ask him to look at her hat, even after he has supposedly commented on it using her theme.

Eventually, we can assume that he pays real attention, and they join together in those final four lines. But instead of supplying a new melody for this last section, Mozart ignores the change in poetic metre and has both of them, in concord, sing Susanna's theme. What, then, was a piece of dialogue in the play and libretto has become a little musical drama, one that suggests that Figaro and Susanna have not simply had a brief exchange, but have negotiated a settlement in which Susanna has triumphed, with Figaro content that she has done so. To put this another way, the audience has been offered a sentimental education in miniature, an illustration of how men and women interact freely and can – with a little insistence, with a little flexibility – resolve their differences. What's more, the education has come about by using techniques employed in contemporary instrumental music – with its play of contrasting themes – in the service of operatic drama.

There's one further level of musical communication that's important in this opening duet and in Mozart's operas generally. Susanna and Figaro are differentiated by their orchestral accompaniments. Figaro, with his plain, practical task, is accompanied mostly by the strings alone; Susanna's delight in her hat calls forth the added colour of the woodwind group. And there's another tiny detail that will be significant: a prominent horn call emerges at the end of the first orchestral introduction. We hear this call again at the end of the whole duet. You might think of it as an orchestral worm in the bud, a pun on the word 'horn' (*corno* in Italian) that turns up periodically in *Figaro*. Countless tales going back to antiquity feature the cuckold, the husband whose wife is unfaithful, and who for this reason has grown a horn on his head. A famous instance occurs in Shakespeare's *Othello*, when the jealous husband tells his wife, Desdemona, 'I have a pain upon my forehead here'. There's little doubt that prominent horn sonorities are a symbol of sexual jealousy in *Figaro*, in which infidelity both imagined and real constantly lurks just around the corner. At the end of Figaro's Act 4 aria about the wiles of women, 'Aprite un po' quegl'occhi' (Open your eyes a little), a veritable storm of horn calls signals his jealous anxieties. In Susanna's Act 4 aria, 'Deh vieni, non tardar' (Oh come, do not delay), Susanna, dressed as the Countess, sings a song to an absent lover. To Figaro, who is eavesdropping, it appears that his wife is pining for the Count. But Susanna, who knows Figaro is listening, is singing the piece both for him, her true beloved, *and* to torment him for his doubts. Her last line is 'I am going to crown you with roses', and in Mozart's setting the word 'crown' (*coronar*) is drawn out for several seconds in a cruel tease. I am going to crown you, yes, but with what? Perhaps, again, with that dreaded horn.

TRIPLE CROWN

Mozart's three Da Ponte operas have, as one might expect, many points of contact. At one famous moment in the second-act finale of *Don Giovanni*, an onstage orchestra playing at Giovanni's supper party strikes up with a famous tune from *Figaro*. Hearing the aria, Giovanni's servant Leporello makes a morose comment: 'Questo poi la conosco pur troppo' (Yes, I know this one too well). The singer playing Leporello in Prague in 1787 was the same man, Francesco Benucci, who had been Figaro in Vienna the year before. This reference was, in other words, one of those in-jokes that seem to have fuelled the Mozart–Da Ponte collaboration. We have to say 'seem' because the two men worked together in person and left regrettably few letters or other documents as clues to their chemistry. Another link between the three operas bites deeper, though, and has to do with eighteenth-century ideas of character types, with roles that demand an equivalent range because they have equivalent status within the social hierarchy. Susanna and Despina (the servant girl in *Così*) are clearly related in this way, as are Donna Elvira (*Don Giovanni*) and Fiordiligi (*Così*), two suffering, sensually aware upper-class women. Leporello and Figaro are *basso buffo* characters, comic bass servants. Even Count Almaviva and Don Giovanni, the yin and yang of the aristocrat predator, sing in comparable ways.

All these pairs could dine together without strain; they would recognize each other as social equals and it is partly for this reason that they have similar vocal physiognomies. They were, as with Benucci, sometimes premiered by the same singer. Higher-class characters on the whole sing with more elevated music: *opera seria*-derived pathos and virtuosity, or complex rhythmic designs. *Don Giovanni*, essentially the classic Don Juan story, with multiple attempted seductions and the famous descent into Hell via a vengeful stone effigy, begins with a multi-part action number, an Introduction in which these musical/social markers are made evident. The first section, in which Leporello laments his servant life, is mostly comic patter, one syllable per note, except when Leporello sings 'Voglio far il gentiluomo' (I want to act the

1. A scene from Frank Darabont's 1994 film *The Shawshank Redemption.* Prisoners in a brutal US prison fall silent and listen when one of their number commandeers the public address system and plays them 'Sull'aria', the two-soprano duet from Act 3 of Mozart's *Le nozze di Figaro*.

2. *Tristan* at the Paris Opéra, according to Billy Wilder's 1957 film *Love in the Afternoon*. Distractions abound: Audrey Hepburn has caught sight of Gary Cooper down in the expensive seats, while her colleague at the Conservatoire fussily examines the conductor and consults the score. Behind them, ordinary opera-goers are watching the actual performance.

3. A reconstruction, seen from the performer's viewpoint, of the room in the Duke of Mantua's palace where Monteverdi's *Orfeo* was first performed in 1607. Some of the seats for audience members are throne-like, but the space is comparatively intimate.

4. *Le nozze degli dei* (The Marriage of the Gods), a *favola* by Giovanni Carlo Coppola, performed in Florence on the occasion of a royal marriage in 1637, and giving an indication of the scenic marvels that could be produced in such mythological court entertainments.

5. After two centuries of almost complete neglect, the extraordinary revival of Handel opera performances over the last thirty years has often gone hand in hand with startling postmodern productions. This scene is from Graham Vick's 2010 Royal Opera House production of *Tamerlano*.

6. Many eighteenth-century Londoners felt resistance to the operatic invasion of British culture. William Hogarth's engraving *Masquerades and Operas (or the Bad Taste of the Town)* of 1724 shows the crowd flocking to entertainments featuring extravagantly paid castrati; a woman in the foreground wheels away the now discarded treasures of British literature.

7. Two famous castrati, Senesino and Gaetano Berenstadt, appear on either side of the equally famous soprano Francesca Cuzzoni, possibly in a performance of Handel's *Flavio* (1723). The tendency of castrati to be oversized and misshapen is cruelly exaggerated.

8. Rosalie Levasseur (1749–1826), one of Gluck's favourite singers, created Eurydice in the French premiere of *Orphée* (1774) and the title role in *Alceste* (1776), as well as starring in several of his other French operas.

9. Pauline Viardot (1821–1910), as Orphée in an 1859 Paris revival of Gluck's opera. Her austere costume and restrained pose suggest that the classic severity of Gluck's operatic reform had attractions even a century later.

10. The public figure. Mozart as a stiff and bewigged court functionary. This portrait by Barbara Krafft dates from 1819, nearly twenty years after the composer's death, but is based on contemporary sources.

11. The private man. Much more modern-looking than Krafft, this silver-point drawing by Doris Stock dates from 1789. It was considered by those who knew him well to be one of the best likenesses of the composer.

12 and 13. Near-contemporary images of Papageno and Sarastro in *Die Zauberflöte*. These coloured engravings from 1793 come from a set of twelve illustrations by Johann Salomon Richter (1761–1802). Papageno appears far more human than bird-like, and carries an extremely large birdcage on his back. Sarastro, with white beard, sandals, robe and solar ornaments, is a Masonic-Egyptian priest-as-wizard, reflecting the many historical sources of the *Zauberflöte* libretto.

14. Charles Edward Horn (1786–1849) as Caspar in an English-language performance of Weber's *Der Freischütz* (London, 1824), bearing a rifle, hunting horn and (somewhat superfluously) a sword. The *Musical World* (23 March 1850), recalling the event many years later, said that Horn 'had no voice, but made amends for the deficiency by gesture and attitudes'.

15. Wilhelmine Schroeder-Devrient (1804–60) as Fidelio in the second act of Beethoven's opera. Cross-dressed, tensed and ready to combat tyranny, she is one of many female symbols of early nineteenth-century 'liberty at the barricades'.

16. Caroline Ungher (1803–77), in a much more conventional engraved portrait. Born in Vienna, Ungher sang in the first performance of Beethoven's Ninth Symphony but made her greatest reputation in Italy, as one of a new, forceful, not-entirely-bel-canto breed of operatic sopranos.

17. Rossini as merchandise. The apple-shooting scene from *Guillaume Tell* (1829), the opera's most striking tableau, is captured in Sèvres porcelain.

18. Rossini as popular culture. Mickey Mouse conducts the *Guillaume Tell* overture, from *The Band Concert* (1935). The overture is continually interrupted by the popular tune 'Turkey in the Straw', just as 'Take Me Out to the Ball Game' interrupts *Il trovatore* in the Marx Brothers' *A Night at the Opera* (also 1935).

gentleman) – at which point his voice stretches for an instant to the sustained long notes and variable rhythms that would denote musically such higher status. Once Don Giovanni shows up – with an intended victim, Donna Anna (soprano), pursuing him like a fury – things get much more ornamental, as befits high-born characters. Leporello, observing from a distance, emphasizes this by commenting in patter underneath. In a third section, Anna's father, the Commendatore (bass), arrives and challenges Giovanni to mortal combat; we shift into the minor mode and tremolo strings, darker possibilities. Once the Commendatore is run through, we are uncertain where we are. If this was ever supposed to be a comedy, it certainly isn't any more. In the final, F-minor section (which, as we saw in the last chapter, has more than a hint of Gluckian restraint) the three bass voices, now undifferentiated, weave together in a lament that momentarily transcends difference and enmity, caught as they are in brief, communal reaction to the tragic events.

Don Giovanni has always been the dark sister among the Da Ponte triplets. Even its genre title is different: Da Ponte labelled it a *dramma giocoso*, a jocular drama. The protagonist, with his force-of-nature scorn for morality, has an appeal whose very ambivalence is part of his intellectual glamour. This socially anarchic force must, of course, be punished: he goes to Hell. Yet even the moral of the ending is put into question. Da Ponte, who drew on various Don Juan plays and libretti then in circulation, reacted to the anarchic central character by writing a less formally structured libretto. *Don Giovanni* is made up of vignettes, centring on the title character's attempted seductions and blasphemies, together with subplots involving Anna's mourning for her dead father and postponed engagement to Don Ottavio (the tenor), and a romance between two peasants, Zerlina and Masetto (soprano and bass). Scenes are juxtaposed without much concern for internal connection. The action takes place mostly at night. No one can see very well and characters are frequently masked.

The general lack of light and attendant bewilderment reflect a moral confusion that touches on almost every character. Anna is mysterious in her grief: for whom does she really pine? An old flame of Giovanni's, Donna Elvira (soprano), presents herself as a protector of virtue but is nonetheless seduced time and again. Leporello is happy-go-lucky, but also happy to be cruel. Zerlina succumbs to flattery. The aristocrats are prepared to kill Giovanni, and their intended victim leads them on. The libretto also seems to resurrect an antique tolerance, well-known in *commedia dell'arte*, for the contrast of extremes: murder and farce, suffering and cynical joking are freely mixed. What's more, the supernatural aspect of the story – the resurrected Commendatore as avenging effigy – guaranteed the opera's reputation for numinous gravity well into the nineteenth century, when most of Mozart's other operas had fallen on hard times. *Don Giovanni* fever produced some strange symptoms. In the 1850s, the celebrated mezzo soprano Pauline Viardot-García acquired Mozart's autograph score of the opera. She promptly commissioned a reliquary box to hold it, enshrined it in her private music room and invited her best friends to kneel in its presence. Séance-like incidents ensued over the years. In 1886 Tchaikovsky (admittedly, an unusually passionate Mozartian) wrote, 'I cannot express the feeling that overcame me when I was looking at this holy musical object – as if I had shaken the hand of Mozart himself and conversed with him.'[8]

Even the famous overture mixes things up. It begins with an ominous, minor-key section, two loud sustained chords, each framed by a silence. Those chords are meant to get our attention and get it good; it is important to remember them. They are followed by some dirge-like march rhythms in tempo largo, and sinuous up-and-down woodwind scales. But this whole tragic mode is, after only a few moments, suddenly abandoned in favour of a standard *opera buffa* Allegro. A musical question is thus posed – what does the sudden switch mean? What is the import of those two opening shouts in chord form? This is a question that remains suspended over the opera. Only much later, just before Don Giovanni exits for ever through a trap door to Hell, do we learn that those loud chords, which opened the Overture, were laden with meaning. They return in Act 2 for the stone effigy's arrival, and then sound again a few minutes later, just as Don Giovanni sings a final 'No! No!' to his unwelcome guest. The opera itself, we now understand, began with defiance, with an orchestral 'No!' that refuses the consolations of conformity. It is as well to remember, though, that this celebration of singularity is not purely heroic and is certainly no prescription for humane behaviour on earth. Many literary and critical commentaries on the opera, starting with E. T. A. Hoffmann's in 1812, ignored this sobering thought, preferring undiluted *Don Giovanni* fever.[9] Now, near the start of the twenty-first century, we may feel some distance from these recurring rhapsodies to Giovanni as the epitome of anti-bourgeois male vigour.

THE WRONG ALLIANCE

Don Giovanni performs one service unequivocally: it explores the idea of being seduced into making the wrong emotional alliance. For opera, this is a fundamental conundrum and a recurring temptation: when music overrides sense and morality, resistance flies out of the door. Mozart stated his allegiance to musical truth – above and beyond plot or character – over and over again. Writing to his father in 1781, during work on *Die Entführung*, he makes the point:

> In an opera, the poetry simply has to be the obedient daughter of the music. Why are the Italian comic operas, in spite of their miserable librettos, so successful everywhere, even in Paris, where I witnessed it myself? Because music reigns supreme, and everything else is forgotten. An opera must please all the more if the plot has been worked out well and the words have been written for music, and not stuck in to obtain some miserable rhyme here and there.[10]

Good poetry, yes, and a persuasive plot, but music's sovereign position means that if *it* is alluring, then the character who sings it will be an object of desire. Small surprise, then, that one thread which joins the Da Ponte operas is a sequence of three parallel 'seduction duets', all in the key of A major, all depicting a scene in which a male character attempts, he thinks successfully, to conquer a reluctant female's virtue. Their differences and similarities can tell us something interesting about all three operas, and also something about what we might call operatic morality and its musical undertow.

The word 'seduce' has travelled a long way over the last few centuries, adapting to shifting attitudes to property, gender difference and even to the nature of human subjectivity – of who we think we are, how individual and emotionally independent we feel ourselves to be. In these, post-sexual-revolution days, the word seems mostly used with an ironic tone and a hint of the archaic. 'Oh, the vile seducer!' As befits ideas that now seem artificial, the word has mostly taken up residence in metaphor. A real person is now less likely to seduce us than is a TV advertisement, or a gondola ride down the Grand Canal, or (for that matter) a Mozart duet about a letter, sung by two sopranos. It was not always thus. Even as late as the eighteenth century, to seduce an innocent girl was to steal her chastity, and not just from the girl in question but also from her parent or master. Another way of looking at it, during the same period, was as a dangerous crossing of boundaries. Giovanni has done this just before the curtain goes up: he has entered the Commendatore's house by clandestine means, and has then attempted a similar invasion of his daughter Anna. But often the act is a double transgression, in that the boundaries crossed will also be social, inviting contact that many in Mozart's time (particularly those in possession of old money) saw as disruptive of civil order. Again Giovanni is a good example. He is an aristocratic seducer who has little regard for social divisions, and who will – in the heat of the chase – launch himself at a peasant girl as readily as a high-born lady. As Leporello famously sings at the end of his Act 1 'catalogue' aria, 'Purché porti la gonnella, voi sapete quel che fa' (As long as she's wearing a skirt, you know what he'll do).

The seduction duet in Act 1 of *Don Giovanni* is just such an example of social boundary-crossing, and it is also the simplest and best-known of our three 'seduction' duets. 'Là ci darem la mano' (There we will join hands), sings *cavaliere* Giovanni to *contadina* (peasant girl) Zerlina, and the simplicity of the melody and accompaniment demonstrates how skilfully he can adapt to the business in hand. Nor is there much resistance, at least musically speaking, from Zerlina; just a gradual sense of increasing proximity. Giovanni leads off. Zerlina may answer his opening statement with the words 'Vorrei, e non vorrei' (I would, and I wouldn't), but her melody is just an ornamented version of his – at an important musical level the proposal has already been accepted. There is a little chromatic wavering as she thinks about her fiancé Masetto, but when Giovanni brings back his opening idea she is already closer to him, this time sharing his melody. And finally, in a rustic 6/8, the couple warble together in uncomplicated parallel thirds. This simple musical progression – first Zerlina repeats her seducer's melody, then they divide it between them, then they sing together – is an obvious musical reflection of what's happening onstage; and the naïvety of the musical picture is surely part of the game – of what is, at present, an 'innocente amor'. Later in the act, Zerlina has to draw *real* boundaries when Giovanni presses home his conquest; and she does so not with mirrored phrases but with a melodramatic offstage scream. Incidentally, the duet also shows that Don Giovanni's force of persuasion in the opera is, time and again, embodied in his singing voice. We can see this again in the trio in Act 2, when he persuades Donna Elvira once again that he adores her; or even in his brief, delicate Act 2 serenade where, standing under a balcony and strumming a mandolin, he enacts another archetype, the troubadour. For the great Danish philosopher Søren Kierkegaard, writing in 1843, 'it is this musical life of Don Giovanni, absolutely centralized in the opera, which enables it to create a power of illusion that no other [opera] is able to do, so that its life transports one into the life of the play'.[11] In other words, we as audience and listeners are completely taken in. When Otto Jahn in 1856–9 completed what would be history's first big Mozart biography, he repeated Kierkegaard's notion of the musical-erotic in *Don Giovanni*, cementing the idea that Don Giovanni gets the audience on his side without considering that such alliances may indeed be dubious.[12]

The parallel 'seduction' duet in *Figaro*, between Count Almaviva and servant girl Susanna at the start of Act 3, is more complex. The Count may think he's in control, but the spectators know that Susanna is merely acting her part in entrapping the would-be seducer. A glance at the libretto leaves no doubt about the two opposing positions. Da Ponte injects a joke, several times repeated in the musical setting, in which Susanna gets confused by the Count's ardent questioning and says 'no' when she means 'yes', and 'yes' when she means 'no'. Again, though, Mozart's music makes a potentially simple case more equivocal. The Count begins in high aristocratic tone: in a grandiose, mock pathetic minor mode ('Crudel! perché finora'), with elaborate word repetition. However, instead of high-toned resistance and outrage, Susanna meets him with bland acceptance and an artful turn to the major. Initially he maintains the pleading tone, almost as if he hasn't heard. Eventually, though, Susanna's compliance fully sinks in, and he launches into a major-mode celebration of victory ('Mi sento dal contento'). This melody is very beautiful – seductively beautiful, one might say – much more so than the severe, faux-Baroque idea of his opening. As elsewhere in *Figaro*, the Count behaves badly as a plot-character but is disturbingly likeable as a voice-character. Small wonder that, after his annunciation of this beautiful melody, Susanna becomes really flustered and starts giving the wrong answers to some of his questions. The thought may arise: which answer does she *want* to give? It may also be significant that, by the end of the duet, this socially mismatched couple seems musically almost at one, Susanna singing the Count's beautiful melody with some passion herself. Mozart's music may, in other words, be pointing out something rather subversive, namely that boundary-crossing is frighteningly easy in opera, where music is a great leveller of social pretensions. By way of her musical transformations, Susanna is revealed to have depths and human frailties that her words hardly suggest.

These two duets play out what in the end are tangential plot issues in their respective dramas. Our third example, from *Così fan tutte*, is at the very heart of its opera. The Act II duet, 'Fra gli amplessi', between Ferrando (tenor) and Fiordiligi (soprano), is one of *Così*'s grandest and most complex numbers, as befits this crucial encounter between the opera's principal characters. Fiordiligi is betrothed to Guglielmo (baritone), as her sister Dorabella (mezzo-soprano) is to Ferrando. Don Alfonso (bass), a professional cynic called in the libretto an 'old philosopher', bets the men that their respective fiancées can easily be led into infidelity. The two lovers pretend to go off to war, and then return in disguise to woo each other's bride. In one case, this proves easy: Dorabella succumbs to Guglielmo in simple recitative. But Fiordiligi's surrender is far more momentous, just as her previous protestations of constancy were more grandiose. It is typical of this, Mozart's last *opera buffa*, that while superficially the plot mechanism may seem trite and predictable, the levels of possible ambiguity are denser than ever. Unlike in *Figaro* and *Don Giovanni* there is no social barrier between the principals of this *Così* duet, which means that, dangerously for both of them, they can converse in a shared and complicated musical language.

The immediate background is important. Fiordiligi feels that the two suitors who have invaded her seaside home are more risky than she at first imagined (her immediately preceding recitative begins: 'Come tutto congiura a sedurre il mio cor' – How everything conspires to seduce my heart). She makes an abrupt decision: she will dress in her beloved Guglielmo's clothes and join him on the field of battle. She takes off her head-dress – a preparation for her cross-dressing – and begins what seems to be an heroic aria, full of masculine gestures meant to bolster her decision. She has hardly warmed to the task, though, when there's a sudden interruption: Ferrando bursts on the scene, picking up her melody and violently turning it to his own purpose. The shock is considerable. As well as a tonal and melodic shift, something more basic to operatic discourse has been violated, an aria has been invaded, turned unexpectedly into a duet. Nothing like this happened to Zerlina or Susanna, and it's no surprise that the entire number now goes into a state of flux, rapidly changing in orchestral textures and tonal directions. But gradually it winds back to the home key in which Fiordiligi began, and in that key Ferrando unleashes his final plea. This Larghetto, 'Volgi a me' (Turn to me), is, as one would expect of a tonal return, a kind of recomposition of Fiordiligi's opening, but while her melody was masculine in gesture, his is one of the gentlest, most beautiful lyrical sections of the entire opera, of the least heroic imaginable. Beauty conquers Fiordiligi, and underneath a winding oboe solo she capitulates, so ushering in a conventional closing section in which they sing together in parallel intervals. The action/music connection is inescapable: Fiordiligi has attempted to evade Ferrando by dressing as man and assuming a masculine, heroic vocal manner. In the great game of seduction, he has then vanquished her by the simplest of means – by becoming in 'Volgi a me' the essence of female lyricism and beauty.

Elaborate plays of tonality, metamorphoses of motif, fluid, witty orchestration, all these details remind us again and again that Mozart's operas were enormously enriched by their composer also being a master of instrumental music. Austro-Germans were already famous for bringing their expertise in this genre to the operatic table, and sometimes it could get them into trouble. One of the most often-repeated Mozart stories is about a comment supposedly made by Emperor Joseph II after hearing *Die Entführung*: 'Too beautiful for our ears and far too many notes, dear Mozart.'[13] The quote is usually meant to generate a feeling of smugness – it's good to think oneself culturally superior to an Emperor, after all – but Joseph's remark can also remind us that Mozart's brand of instrumental-music-influenced opera posed difficulties for contemporaries brought up on simpler Italian fare. What proved crucial in the Mozartian mix was that an alchemy took place: that the new levels of musical complexity did not simply add more detail to old forms, but transformed them into more dynamic objects, in the process allowing operatic characters to become more complex in a modern sense, more psychologically interesting.

This advance, this enrichment of the operatic fabric, is an important part of what makes Mozart so central to so many opera lovers today; but it can nevertheless be over-stressed, particularly by the academically inclined. For one thing, it sidelines the issue of musical beauty, so much a part of the Mozartian experience. What is this beauty, and how can it be defined? Is Fiordiligi, like us, or the men in Shawshank Prison, seduced by a Mozart aria on a summer evening? If so, we may have a comforting sense of closeness to these strange operatic characters who sing so beautifully but who act according to rules we now find alien and difficult to understand. At least we should question this closeness, remind ourselves of the complex codes at work, of the history of *opera buffa* that preceded (and to an extent made possible) Mozart's achievements, of the way he constantly played with well-established operatic conventions. But sometimes the experience of the operas will cause these questions to dissolve, for a few moments, while we are transported by little songs, carried on a blissful musical wind.

6

Singing and speaking before 1800

The rivalries between Italian and French opera, and then later between Italian and German opera, are age-old, but the tales told about them have a persistent appeal. In his treatise *Oper und Drama* (Opera and Drama, 1851), Richard Wagner professed to dislike all three national schools, calling the German a 'prude' with little sensuality, the Italian a 'coquette', always tormenting her besotted suitors (the audience) with flightiness and temper, and the French a 'courtesan', soulless and only in it for the money – he avoided the more explicit and at the time unprintable term he doubtless had in mind.[1] However useful it may sometimes be to draw distinctions between the three traditions, we need to bear in mind that such separations made themselves felt in different domains at different times, and that the aesthetic precepts and musical devices that flowed between the three dominant operatic traditions could often erase their differences. In the eighteenth century, composers from the German states and the Austrian empire wrote operas in Italian and French: Gluck's career is a good example. Italian composers often made their livings in foreign courts. In 1776 Giovanni Paisiello left Naples for Russia to become *maestro di cappella* at the court of Catherine II and write operas for the prestige Italian company she financed in St Petersburg. French composers and men of letters (most famously, Jean-Jacques Rousseau) often championed the cause of Italianate opera. All three national styles constantly flowed in and out of each other, just as coaches laden with performers and composers and musical materials endlessly crisscrossed the continent.

Mozart is the most famous case. From an early age, as a child prodigy and object of exhibition, he travelled often to Italy, to France, to England, to the minor German principalities. As a nine-year-old, one of his party pieces was to improvise an Italian recitative and aria, transforming into words and music whatever operatic passion might be suggested from the audience. The fact that he could do this off the cuff may amaze us (as it amazed his eighteenth-century audience); but we cannot doubt that he would already have had the necessary schooling. Everywhere he went he heard opera, in Italian, in German, in French. In Paris he sampled the repertory of *tragédie lyrique* at the Opéra (which his father Leopold disliked) as well as less austere *opéra comique*. In later life he could hear both *opera seria* and *opera buffa* in Vienna, sometimes in the same theatre. But his experience was hardly unique; even amid the nationalism and emerging states of the nineteenth century, bi- or tri-lingual opera composers were not uncommon. Almost every nineteenth-century opera composer, Wagner no exception, aspired to write a work in French for the Paris Opéra. Who, after all, would disdain this Nobel Prize of the operatic world, with the best singers and orchestra in the world, and with a budget for décor and costumes that could rise to the challenge of even Wagnerian fantasy?

However, one important difference sets apart the dominant forms of eighteenth-century French and German comic opera from Italian *opera buffa* (at least in its later and more elevated forms), and that is the presence of spoken dialogue. In France, *opéra comique* emerged over the first half of the century. Its main antecedents were comic plays, often performed in makeshift stages set up at fairs, into which were inserted pre-existing songs. Gradually this type of entertainment crossed the border from 'play with songs' to 'opera with spoken dialogue', the new genre being given various labels, most commonly *comédie mêlée d'ariettes*, something that obeyed the rules of spoken drama (the *comédie*) but would periodically break into music and, increasingly, employed musical numbers more complex than the 'little arias' that its title might suggest. After around 1750, this new form of opera became enormously popular and, like *opera buffa*, took on a broader range of subject matter, favouring sentimental or fantastic plots. In particular it became the genre of choice for French composers who supported Italian opera's simpler phrases and periodic melody.

French comic opera was, in short, typically seen as the opposite of or alternative to *tragédie lyrique*. German-language opera, on the other hand, had virtually no serious tradition; it thus came very early to comedy, and remained during the eighteenth century largely comic, even farcical. It was generally called *Singspiel*, a word that puts singing and 'play' into one (*Schauspiel*, a spoken-theatre piece, combines 'looking' and 'play'). When we talk of *Singspiel* today, we generally mean German comic opera with spoken dialogue. But the word had been used since the seventeenth century to cover a wide range of theatre with music, including German-language performances of Italian or French operas, and German plays with incidental music. Teutonic dictionary makers have had a field day with its definitions and nuances. As so often, Mozart is the pivot point, and specifically his last opera, *Die Zauberflöte* (1791), still called a *Singspiel*. This Janus-faced work, which started life as part of a rather humble tradition, was a critical force in helping turn German comic opera into the more elevated and aspirational *romantische Oper* of the nineteenth century. Thanks to its composer's gathering reputation as an instrumental composer, *Die Zauberflöte*, in spite of its origins, at last succeeded in fuelling ambitions (always thwarted in the eighteenth century) for a tradition of serious opera in German.

But to isolate eighteenth-century German comic opera as a merely local genre, a patois distinct to the lower tiers of German courts or public theatres, is to downplay its relationship to French comic opera: crossovers between the two were always common, and were obviously helped by the fact that spoken dialogue can translate much more simply than sung recitative. Some beautiful (and too little-known) examples come from Georg Benda (1722–95), who in 1750 was appointed *Kapellmeister* at the court of Friedrich III of Saxe-Gotha and who experimented with elaborate, Italian- and French-influenced *Singspiele* such as *Romeo und Julie* (after Shakespeare, 1776). What is more, the idea of rigidly distinct national schools also glosses over the schism *Singspiel* shares with *opéra comique*. This schism is the moment when talking, the everyday language of the spoken theatre, gives way to music, when characters stop speaking their thoughts and begin to sing them. It marks an acoustic and aesthetic shock that gets replayed over and over in any performance, and all operatic genres that mix spoken dialogue with singing – later there would be operettas and later still musicals – had to work with and around it. Admittedly, the shock was not equal in all genres. In some early cases, for example, the words may have been delivered in a comparatively stylized manner, and the songs delivered with comparative naturalism, thus lessening the gap between them. But the movement between one and another was nevertheless an irritant in theoretical writings, and became more pronounced in the later years of the eighteenth century. In 1775, Christoph Martin Wieland, in his *Versuch über das deutsche Singspiel* (Account of German *Singspiel*), argued for the elimination of spoken dialogue: to have music all the time was clearly superior. Parts of the French critical fraternity were also voluble on the topic. By the early nineteenth century, the shock seemed intolerable to many. E. T. A. Hoffmann wrote in 1816 that 'opera rent asunder by dialogue is a monstrous thing, and we tolerate it merely because we are used to it'.[2]

It makes sense for this reason to talk about 'dialogue opera' as a broad and unruly genre, and to keep in mind the flow between the French and German varieties, which persisted into the nineteenth century. Some time before then, the comic element of dialogue opera was fading or changing in some types, with libretti that included spoken dialogue becoming more sentimental or serious (*Romeo und Julie* is a good example). Beethoven's stately operatic experiment, *Fidelio* (whose first version was performed in 1805), has impeccably high – if notoriously simplistic – philosophical aspirations and much ecstatic music; it boasts many serious sentiments about conjugal love and political freedom; but it also has spoken dialogue. Luigi Cherubini (1760–1842), a great model for Beethoven, had attempted similar feats in the 1790s; his *Elisa, ou Le Voyage aux glaciers du Mont St-Bernard* (Elisa, or The Voyage to the Glaciers of Mont St Bernard, Paris, 1794) features star-crossed lovers, one of whom is swept away by an avalanche but miraculously survives to celebrate a happy ending. In 1875, Georges Bizet wrote an opera that ends tragically, indeed with a violent onstage murder. There may be comic, even farcical elements in *Carmen*, but Bizet called it an *opéra comique* because it has speech as well as song.

THE ACOUSTIC SHOCK

Operetta, musicals and their Hollywood progeny from the beginning of the sound era had to negotiate the border between talking and singing. They often did it via the time-honoured practice of making the musical numbers realistic in terms of the plot: we're dancing and singing because we're putting on a show right here in the barn; we're singing and dancing because we're auditioning for a role in a musical; we're dancing because the hotel orchestra is playing in the background and we're singing along because the bandleader wants us to. As historians of musicals have pointed out, the moment of transition from speech to musical number has long been recognized as dangerous – as a juncture likely to disturb audience absorption. All kinds of devices evolved to smooth it over, including the desperately literal one of having speech spill over into the sung number and then creep into song by becoming gradually more rhythmic or more intoned. Film critics sometimes call the transition from one to the other a 'suture': one mode is stitched to another in such a way that the seam is less noticeable. These speech/music sutures were mostly inherited from opera. But as we might expect – film is always burdened by its comparative realism, and opera is spectacularly *not* thus burdened – opera makers have tended to be brasher and more daring about simply letting music appear, without explanation or preparation.

A notorious example can lead the way. In Mozart's *Die Entführung aus dem Serail* (The Abduction from the Seraglio, 1782), the most exalted character is impersonated not by a singer but by an actor: Pasha Selim, an enlightened despot (albeit tending to the despotic rather than the enlightened until the opera's finale), sings never a note. This all-speaking Pasha eventually releases the heroine Konstanze (soprano), whom he has imprisoned, and after whom he has long languished, to her questing fiancé Belmonte (tenor), offering as explanation for his beneficence that he despises Western cruelties far too much ever to imitate them. But at a critical point in Act 2 he is markedly less conciliatory. Tiring of Konstanze's constant rejection of his advances, he threatens a change of tactic, a turn to something altogether more robust. He will force the issue 'not by killing you! But through torture – *torture of every conceivable kind!*' (Martern aller Arten). The actor can snarl or shout, whisper or croak this last phrase; some, perhaps ambitious for greater roles, use a combination of all four. But whatever these Pashas do, the orchestra strikes up with wind and drum, and with a six-note melodic motif that re-speaks his tag line in instrumental form, *Mar*-tern *al*-ler *Ar*-ten. So far, so good: the menace, the shock of the words, has been transformed into the shock of sudden instrumental noise: the orchestral introduction to Konstanze's aria, which she will sing in defiance of the Pasha's threat, is under way.

Incidentally, this introduction goes on and on and on, with substantial and intricate contributions from no fewer than four soloists drawn from the orchestra, flute, oboe, violin and cello. In effect we get a whole 'verse' (sixty bars) of the aria before Konstanze starts to sing. For Mozart it is likely that the long, concerto-like introduction was dramatically meaningful, a sign of the heroine's dignity and social position, as well as adding emphasis and weight to her impending defence of chastity. But in modern times this potential is drowned out by the question of what everyone on stage is supposed to do in the meantime. One can often judge the directorial style of a modern-day *Seraglio* by attending to this moment. One recent commentator on the opera describes 'Martern aller Arten' as 'show-stopping', and we can assume this is meant both ways. If the orchestral soloists and soprano do their business, then applause will stop the show when the aria ends: it's one of the most taxing in the operatic canon.[3] But 'Martern aller Arten' also quite literally stops the show (or at least its action): as far as stage business is concerned, nothing happens for an alarmingly long period. Directors these days tend to dislike such elaborate musical outpourings. They get nervous; worse still, they feel redundant. This is often bad news for the aria. In a recent Royal Opera House production,[4] constant Konstanze used the orchestral introduction to show more than a second thought for the attractions of the cruel Pasha. His attempted embrace at the start lingers meaningfully; by the time the flute, oboe, violin and cello have done their business, Konstanze is kneeling before him with a cheek lovingly pressed to his doubtless-quivering thigh. Then she sings the aria. Then we get on with the action.

As well as presenting a dilemma for stage directors, 'Martern aller Arten' illustrates the problem of speaking versus music in *Singspiel* and *opéra comique*. What motivates the presence of music? What border have we crossed when we go from the sound of speaking to the sound of music? What does the music represent? In this sense, dialogue opera continually re-poses that central operatic question about verisimilitude and levels of reality, issues about the motivation for music that were a defining theoretical and dramaturgical problem from the middle of the seventeenth century onwards. The first comic operas in French, the *comédies-ballets* of Lully and Molière in the 1670s, mostly confined music to realistic situations: someone within the fiction had to call for a song or a dance. But as audiences got used to the genre, this rigid restriction was inevitably challenged in both *Singspiele* and *opéras comiques*. Breaking into unmotivated song could and did serve as a parody of the more elevated forms of *tragédie lyrique* or *opera seria*, and such inversion was common so long as comic opera was conceived as a kind of anti-opera. The theoretical unease remained, but it was a losing battle.

Johann Wolfgang von Goethe (1749–1832) wrote a number of *Singspiel* libretti, and found the rationale for music's presence a perpetual conundrum. In a letter to the composer Philipp Christoph Kayser in 1779, written while working on his libretto *Jery und Bätely* (a text intended for Kayser), Goethe gave voice to anxieties about the motivation for music on the stage. Real music within the drama – 'songs, which one supposes the person singing has learnt by heart somewhere, and now introduces into this or that situation' – is unproblematic. But the other operatic music, either arias that express passions or 'rhythmic dialogue' in ensembles, needs a reason for being there. In arias, the music flows from the heart of the character, therefore expresses something words cannot. For Goethe, the dialogue scenes require music to give them tempo, they are 'a smooth, golden ring on which the songs and arias sit like precious stones'.[5] In other words, they are half-music, a way of speeding up or slowing down speech, and so not far from plain, Italian, *recitativo*.

The debate about dramatic reasons for music in *Singspiel*, and how music should be classified according to its rationale for existing, constituted a minor thought-experiment among eighteenth-century German essayists such as Goethe. But after about 1780 the debate took place in the abstract, since the day-to-day practice of *Singspiel* was going its own way, in particular becoming more Italianate. And the theorizing mostly took place in north and central Germany. *Singspiel* in Vienna, the type Mozart inherited, was produced in an environment that, judging from his correspondence, was less burdened by intellectual manias. Mozart wrote many detailed letters while composing *Die Entführung*, but none of them has a hint that he anguished over the issues that preoccupied Goethe or any other *Singspiel* warrior. And as if to demonstrate his lack in concern, unmotivated music is everywhere in Mozart – even in his very first German opera, *Bastien und Bastienne* (written when he was twelve, in 1768). Operatic music in the Italian sense – *opera seria* with its never-ending cascades of anti-verisimilar music – had been common in German-speaking lands since near the start of the eighteenth century. But, as if in stubborn refusal, the idea of real song remained critical to *Singspiel* and *opéra comique*, and was a model for a particular aria form, the strophic song in imitation of folk or simple singing; the parallel for ensemble singing was a 'vaudeville' (a lovely example ends *Die Entführung*), in which each character sings a simple verse rounded off by a group refrain.

As it happens, the second scene in Act 1 of *Die Entführung* blends the three potential registers of dialogue opera – operatic music, song-in-the-play and spoken text – into a single, overflowing number. The harem guard Osmin (bass) appears at the wall of the seraglio and sings a strophic song about the frailties of women and the need to protect them from amorous young men; Belmonte, who is lurking below, shouts up spoken questions in the pauses between verses, questions that Osmin ignores. In the end, Belmonte gets Osmin's attention by stealing the melody, and singing it back at him: 'Verwünscht seist du samt deinem Liede!' (A curse on you and your song!). At this point realistic singing is over: the two characters exchange further insults in music and suddenly we're in opera in the more modern sense, in a duet that ends with simultaneous singing for the two male voices. But the brilliant, subtle way in which the passing from one register to the other is made seamless bears witness both to the continued force exerted by the gap between them, and of course to the poet's and composer's thoughtfulness about how to bridge it.

One can even see how the problem of acoustic shock shaped plots in German *Singspiel*. Most accounts in the latter part of the eighteenth century stress its literary differences from *opera buffa*, in particular its taste for Oriental or exotic characters confronting Europeans, or its fairy tale and folk tale plots. To some extent, *opéra comique* shared these fictional preferences (as in André Ernest Modeste Grétry's fairy tale piece *Zémire et Azor*, 1771), while also embracing sentimental fables (Pierre-Alexandre Monsigny's *Le Roi et le fermier* – The King and the Farmer, 1762 – has a monarch in the obligatory enlightened despot role). In *Singspiel*, though, libretti involving magical or farcical musical instruments were in some places – Mozart's Vienna for one – almost the norm. *Die Zauberflöte* was, in its early years, just one in a long tradition that included works such as Karl Ditters von Dittersdorf's *Die Liebe im Narrenhause* (Love in the Madhouse, 1787), in which a madman, believing himself to be Orpheus, carries around a violin and plays magical music on it.

Such libretti furnished numerous possibilities for motivated music making. Exotic people tend to have exotic instruments and can be represented by the strange sounds they make: particular favourites were 'Turkish' instruments such as piccolo, triangle, cymbals and bass drum. Nor did rustics lose any of their utility as creatures who are naturally tuneful or prone to break into song. Finally, magical stage instruments can introduce tuned sound into the musical silence that otherwise reigns during spoken dialogue, or can even be played over spoken text. In *Die Zauberflöte*, we hear enigmatic brass fanfares offstage during especially solemn moments in the dialogue, and the hero Tamino is several times directed to play on his flute.

COMIC VOICES

As we have seen, comic opera evolved in the eighteenth century as a pendant – often an overtly ironic pendant – to serious opera: a less expensive and simpler form whose production involved fewer demands. *Singspiel*, for instance, particularly in the north German provinces, was often produced in public theatres by actor-impresarios. In Paris, the acting talents of the singers were as important as their vocal talent. And, as in Italian *opera buffa*, there were no castrati. Their training made them too expensive to waste on comedy and they were anyway indelibly associated with the fundamental artificiality of *opera seria*. The roster of voice types we now tend to imagine as standard in opera – soprano heroine, tenor hero, with lower male and female voices parcelled out to the supporting cast – arose in French and German dialogue opera, and was normal by the time Mozart wrote *Die Entführung*. Osmin, the comic buffoon, has a low bass voice that is played against the high soprano of Blonde, the English servant girl who scorns his affections. But the singers at the premiere were hardly simple, natural talents. Blonde ascends to high E in her aria, and Konstanze's part, as we have seen, demands virtuosity every bit as strenuous as that in *opera seria*.

Die Entführung was commissioned by Emperor Joseph II, who had established a court National-Singspiel in 1778 to encourage the composition of new German operas – a project that struggled to find a sufficient roster of works and more or less collapsed in 1783, when an *opera buffa* company took its place. Mozart's singers were thus court performers trained in the Italian repertory, and included Catarina Cavalieri, for whom Mozart wrote Konstanze. While working on the opera, he admitted to his father that he had 'sacrificed' some of his own ideas for the first aria – 'Ach, ich liebte' – to Cavalieri's 'flexible throat', an anatomical phrase with undertones.[6] Being able to draw on singers of this rank had a profound effect on the music of *Die Entführung*, which, like all Mozart's later operas, is not tied to any one operatic type but presents a disorientating mélange. There are the long, elaborate ensembles of *opera buffa*; the extended set-piece arias of *opera seria*; simple, folk-song-like ditties; blissful Orientalist nonsense such as 'Vivat Bacchus', a drinking song with Janissary orchestration; and arias that are serious in mood but have none of the elaborate virtuosity and archness of the *seria* types – moments whose emotional candour trumps Gluck even at his most passionate.

Konstanze's second aria, 'Traurigkeit' (Sadness), a minor-key essay in pathos with the orchestral sound darkened by basset horns (low clarinets), is a wonderful example of this last type. It plays with the libretto cliché of the wind that carries the lover's sighs by inverting the image in the second verse:

Selbst der Luft darf ich nicht sagen
Meiner Seele bittern Schmerz,
Denn, unwillig ihn zu tragen,
Haucht sie alle meine Klagen
Wieder in mein armes Herz.

[I cannot even speak to the air / the bitter pain of my soul, / because, unwilling to endure it / the air blows all my laments / back to my poor heart.]

This is about not being able to speak: about a woman who, if she confides to the wind, will have the breath with which she spoke, along with the pain she expresses, simply pushed back into her throat. There are strange silences built into the musical setting, tokens of muteness, and these pauses are always followed by a single, low woodwind blast, a blast of wind sending voices back where they came from. Yet Konstanze's most searing vocal line comes after these woodwind tones, and accompanies the very line that describes her muteness, how the wind 'blows all my laments' back into her heart.

We stressed the importance of the voice types for dialogue opera in part because Mozart's two great *Singspiele* – *Die Entführung* and *Die Zauberflöte* – involve elaborate acoustic symbolism across the range of natural voice types. This is especially true in *Die Zauberflöte*, whose libretto has firm ideas about good and evil, light and dark, day and night, and whose ranks of characters Mozart organizes – with the exception of the central pair of lovers, Tamino and Pamina – according to voice registers. The Queen of the Night is introduced to us as a kind and sorrowing monarch whose daughter Pamina has been abducted by a wicked magician called Sarastro. Tamino, a questing prince, is sent to rescue her by the Queen and her three attendant Ladies; he is accompanied by Papageno, half bird, half man, a natural-magical creature of small intellect but large appetite. Midway through Act 1, though, Tamino discovers that he has been deluded. Sarastro is in fact the benign ruler of a Temple of Wisdom, and has merely been protecting Pamina from the Queen, who seeks the downfall of the Temple. A minor character, Monostatos the moor, defects from Sarastro to the Queen and is promised Pamina for his treachery. In the end, goodness prevails. The lovers are united, and the Queen, her Ladies and Monostatos are banished to the depths. In Mozart's palette for the opera, high voices become the sign of decadence and fury. The Queen's Ladies, who pose as sirens in the first scene, when they are wooing Tamino to the Queen's cause, are by Act 2 merely pecking, chattering and hooting. Monostatos has a high, quavering tenor, an unflattering parody, perhaps, of a castrato past his prime. The Queen of the Night, famously, has the highest notes in the operatic repertory, reaching the F above high C in both her virtuoso arias. Sarastro is her polar opposite, a deep, reassuring bass.

Among this small army of theatrical eccentrics, what does a simple, unschooled voice in a normal human pitch range come to mean? Papageno's part was written for Mozart's librettist, Emmanuel Schikaneder, an actor-impresario of a type familiar in the history of eighteenth-century dialogue opera, for whom, like the actors in *opéra comique,* delivering spoken text was important and whose singing (he was a baritone) was distinctly on the sub-virtuoso level. But this simplicity, which was always of course artful, was now not just a consequence of economics or audience preference, and no longer just a by-product of

Singspiel's distant origins in rustic improvised comedy. Simplicity had become another convention to be manipulated to dramatic ends.

REAL SONG

By the later eighteenth century, conventions for what we earlier called 'real song' in *opéra comique* and *Singspiel* had been long established. Real song is announced and prepared by spoken dialogue and/or the dramatic situation, often involves a prop instrument and is invariably strophic. The same (or very similar) music repeats for each stanza of text – in the simplest cases the number can be written out with several stanzas under a single musical verse, as in a hymnal or folk song collection. Precisely because the notion is so straightforward, the potential for elaboration – for song to spill out with implications beyond its border – is significant. One famous instance of overflow is the *romance*, 'Une fièvre brûlante' (A burning fever) from Grétry's *Richard Cœur-de-Lion* (1784). In Act 2, the troubadour Blondel (baritone) wanders into the vicinity of the tower where Richard the Lionheart (tenor) has been imprisoned. Accompanying himself on his violin, he sings a song that Richard had long ago composed for his beloved Marguerite. Richard, recognizing both the song and the performer, joins in; Blondel discovers his lost master by means of locating his voice. The overflow in question involves elaborate anticipations of this music in Act 1. Blondel, in conversation with Marguerite (soprano), plays the *romance* on his instrument in between lines of their spoken dialogue, Marguerite exclaiming, 'O heavens! What do I hear? Good sir, where can you have learned the melody you are playing so well on your violin?'

Grétry lingered on this pivotal theme in his *Mémoires* (1797), demonstrating in the process his own peculiar preoccupations about speech and song:

> Never was a subject better suited to music, it has been said, than that of *Richard Cœur-de-Lion*. I share that opinion with regard to the main situation of the play, I mean that in which Blondel sings the *romance* 'Une fièvre brûlante', but one must admit that the subject as a whole does not call for music more than any other. I will go further: the drama ought really to be spoken; for, since the *romance* needs by its very nature to be sung,

> nothing else should be except that number, for then it would produce an even greater effect. I remember I was tempted not to let it be preceded by any other music in the second act, solely for that reason; but reflecting that in every situation during the first act there had been singing, I gave up my first idea, never doubting besides that the spectators, through the power of illusion, would listen to the *romance* as if it were the only piece of music in the whole work.[7]

Grétry goes on to explain that he also took pains to make 'Une fièvre' musically distinctive, writing it in an 'old style, so it would stand out from the rest': again experimenting with the boundaries between song and 'real song'. But whatever his hesitations, music is a critical element in the fiction, having been ascribed powers both of reviving memory and of salvation. As Grétry proudly proclaims, it turns up no fewer than nine times in the opera, each varied slightly to suit the dramatic situation. And if all this sounds uncannily proto-Wagnerian, we might recall that Grétry advocated a concealed orchestra and a theatre that was largely devoid of decoration (a kind of Bayreuth-in-the-making). As with Wagner, the very simplicity of the outer trappings was meant to encourage a new seriousness of purpose, and a new sense of absorption in the emotional and moral truths depicted in the drama.

'Une fièvre brûlante' is deliberately simple, both rhythmically and melodically. As Grétry knew well, it needed to be immediately recognizable to play its role in the drama, to absorb the weight of reminiscence ascribed to it. That simplicity is not a prerequisite of real song. At the other end of the scale is Mozart's *romanze* for Pedrillo in Act 3 of *Die Entführung* ('Im Mohrenland'), which is one of the most mysterious and musically disorientating pieces he ever composed. The tale it tells – of a pretty, white-skinned maiden who is imprisoned in Moorish lands and rescued by a gallant young knight – clearly retells in miniature the plot of the opera, but its reassuring strophic form is set askew harmonically and melodically: so much so that it seems to begin in the middle and trail off at the end without closure, its fleeting, exotic harmonies acting as trapdoors for our assumptions about Mozart's so-called 'classical' style. Again, there is a dramatic explanation. Pedrillo's *romanze* is mysterious because it is shrouded in nocturnal uncertainty; the young men are anxiously waiting for the coast to clear so that they can rescue their beloveds from the harem. The moment is, then, as full of anxiety as is the music; eventually it fizzles out as Pedrillo sees Konstanze's window opening and knows they can proceed.

The strophic arias written for Papageno in *Die Zauberflöte* take us nearer conventional territory, indeed they have always been thought the epitome of straightforwardness, and are often said to be direct expressions of a kind of Rousseauvian noble savage. This may be particularly true of the first of them, 'Der Vogelfänger bin ich ja' (I'm the bird-catcher), which happens early in Act 1. It is punctuated by pan-pipes and the violins double the voice throughout. But Papageno's second-act aria, 'Ein Mädchen oder Weibchen' (A sweetheart or a little wife), may carry a more complicated message: with its accompanying magical Glockenspiel there are hints (found elsewhere in the opera) of frozen mechanism and unnerving, obsessive repetition. And when Sarastro, the noble character, is given simple strophic arias to sing, the convention has clearly transcended its origin. While it may be possible to read too much into Sarastro's musical humility – the leap from Sarastro singing in strophic form to universal enfranchisement, the French Revolution and principles of human equality has often been too short and too easy – there is nonetheless something striking about Mozart's decision to give him such simple music, not least because it mimics Masonic hymns whose overt sentiments were in tune with such lofty sentiments.

This simplicity is certainly evident in his second aria, 'In diesen heil'gen Hallen' (In these sacred halls), sung in Act 2 to comfort Pamina after she has seen her mother's true colours. But taken as a whole, the aria is nevertheless extraordinary. The text of the first verse makes the kind of vague, sententious statements that are characteristic of the opera:

In diesen heil'gen Hallen
Kennt man die Rache nicht.
Und ist ein Mensch gefallen,
Führt Liebe ihn zur Pflicht.
Dann wandelt er an Freundes Hand
Vergnügt und froh ins bess're Land.

[In these sacred halls / one knows not revenge. / And should a person fall, / love will guide him to duty. / Then he travels, hand in hand with a friend, / cheerful and happy into a better land.]

The musical setting seems at first merely to support this tone, with simple, chordal accompaniment, each phrase rounded off by a flourish in the woodwind, and no obvious word-painting. But when Sarastro gets to the final two lines, with their image of the repentant sinner who travels to a better land, the musical shapes and the accompaniment enter into a more complicated relationship with the words. These two lines are repeated three times by Sarastro, each time differently. In the first statement, the 'travel' is clearly expressed in the chugging inner strings and the purposeful rise of Sarastro's line. However, in a very strange orchestral texture, he is shadowed by the first violins a full two octaves higher; and when he reaches the top of his register and gracefully descends with a flourish, the violins continue ever upward, as if their ascent has taken over the burden of the word-painting, as if they themselves are the traveller, looking for that better land and giving a sigh figure as they reach the peak. The second and third repetitions then perform a remarkable exchange. In the second, Sarastro sings the melody, now again simpler, but with echoes of those 'travelling' violins; then in the third he assumes the role of accompanist (or rather, of bass part) while the melody is taken by violins and solo flute. By the time the aria comes to a close, there is thus some considerable doubt about who is in charge musically, even a sense in which the orchestra, and particularly the violins and flute, have taken over. To use terms introduced long ago in this book, 'voice-Sarastro' has in some way disappeared into the background, with a speaking orchestra taking his place.

MELODRAMATIC IMAGINATION

Perhaps in that aria for Sarastro, and certainly elsewhere in *Die Zauberflöte*, Mozart reveals the influence of a bolder, more complex form of spoken opera, one that came to prominence in the later eighteenth century. In its pure manifestation, this form was bolder in that it proposed a *combination* of spoken dialogue and instrumental music as the basis for an entire theatrical work. This new kind of music theatre was given a cavalcade of names, as was usual in the genre-obsessed eighteenth century; but eventually it became known as *mélodrame* in France and *Melodram* in German-speaking areas (terms not to be confused with the Italian *melodramma*, which is simply another word for opera, or the English word melodrama, which describes a sensational form of spoken theatre that flourished in the nineteenth century). *Mélodrame* is usually said to have started in France with Jean-Jacques Rousseau's *Pygmalion* (words written by him in 1762, set to music by various composers) and then to have spread all over Europe in the following decades. Rousseau described his aim as ensuring that 'the spoken phrases are in some way announced and prepared by the musical phrases',[8] and the genre became particularly popular in German-speaking lands, where such 'speaking' instrumental music was in vogue.

The master of the form was acknowledged to be Georg Benda, whom we met earlier as the composer of *Romeo und Julie*, and whose most famous examples of *Melodram* were *Ariadne auf Naxos* and *Medea*, both 1775 and both composed for a German theatre troupe at the court of Gotha. These two works were commissioned as vehicles for the flamboyant, emotionally explicit acting styles of two leading German actors, Charlotte Brandes (the first Ariadne) and Sophie Seyler (Medea). As in Rousseau's *Pygmalion*, not a note was sung. Consisting largely of dramatic monologues in a Shakespearean style, the texts provided ample opportunities for Brandes and Seyler to chew the scenery and die violently; meanwhile, the orchestral music rendered even more vivid the text images, as well as underpinning the actors' physical gestures and changing emotional states. Musical ideas rarely last more than a few seconds before breaking off for the next verbal interjection, changing when required to paint a sigh, or a sunset, or a bolt of lightning, or a shift from hope to despair. With continuity thus challenged, Benda resorted in *Medea* to methods of creating purely musical coherence. He attached melodic ideas to characters or concepts, and modified them according to developments in the drama. Rousseau's ambition in creating the genre was thus preserved: nowhere, not even in the old *recitar cantando* of the very first opera composers, was music more intimately connected to the representation of a character's inner life and particular mode of expression.

Despite Benda's achievement, and perhaps not surprisingly, the genre had its own problems of verisimilitude. Music generally ebbs and flows at a much slower pace than spoken words; the time required to present even a small melodic fragment is significant in terms of the time that reigns in spoken drama. This is one of the reasons why pantomime became so important. As in that Royal Opera House production of *Die Entführung*, having the actors gesture meaningfully overcame the dramatic lull resulting from musical development. Critics of the genre, though, felt that the *Melodram* music replaced formal exposition and thematic development with mere accumulation and sequence. Faced with such challenges, composers after Benda resorted either to stretches of simultaneous music and text or to the familiar operatic trick of introducing 'stage music' to allow lengthier musical sequences while remaining within the rhythms of spoken drama. Offstage military bands became virtually a necessity. And as *Melodram* turned more operatic, so composers of opera took notice of its dramatic potential by replacing *recitativo secco* – increasingly felt to be opera's great tedium – with orchestrally accompanied recitative (so-called *accompagnato*) and, just as important, by bridging the gap (the acoustic shock) between spoken words and aria in *opéra comique* and *Singspiel*.

These last developments will be the topic of the next chapter. Whatever the attractions of *Melodram* in the eighteenth century (and in its purest form it was relatively short-lived), the genre has proved difficult to revive as live theatre in recent times: the loud, rhythmicized elocution required to intone lines over the noise of instrumental accompaniment is often unpalatable to modern ears – it can seem merely pompous and contrived, accustomed as we are today to actors' less self-consciously melodious speech and to nuance conveyed sotto voce. There are a few famous twentieth-century examples (Prokofiev's *Peter and the Wolf*, Stravinsky's *L'Histoire du soldat* come to mind), but in each case the fact that the spoken voice is that of a narrator rather than a character seems important, as the spoken voice is then immediately distanced from the musical narrative. A primary reason for our current unease is surely that *Melodram*'s present-day technological form – background music on a film soundtrack, where modern technology can ensure that a whisper is heard over a brass band in full flood – has now become standard. Modern *Melodram* is, in other words, now so completely normal that its original form is proportionately exotic.

One brief admirer of *Melodram* was the youthful Mozart. Significantly, though, and despite the fact that he tried a few examples of characters speaking over orchestral commentary, his encounter with Benda's *Medea* caused him immediately to make an imaginative leap into operatic practice. As he wrote in 1778, after hearing Benda: 'I think most operatic recitatives should be treated in this way – and only sung occasionally, when the words *can be perfectly expressed by the music*'.[9] In the world of *opera buffa* or *opera seria*, this aspiration was utopian – to do away with *secco recitativo* would have been to break with a tradition that was now a century and more old, and also to risk revitalizing those verisimilitude problems that had dogged opera from its beginnings. But of course in *spoken* opera there was no such barrier: the normal words could be spoken, and then – for special effect – a new, more musically substantial recitative could emerge, one that rivalled *Melodram* in its passionate resonance between verbal and musical gesture.

The clearest Mozartian example of this new style comes in an episode of speech and elaborate orchestral accompaniment in Act 1 of his unfinished *Singspiel* called *Zaide* (1780), in which the harmonic experiments are among the strangest of his entire career. But his most daring adaptation of the technique comes at the crux of *Die Zauberflöte*, the moment in which Tamino sees the light – when he realizes that his quest to rescue Pamina has led him not to an evil tyrant, but to a Temple of Wisdom. This critical scene is set as elaborate, orchestrally accompanied recitative, quite unlike the usual *opera seria* type. Tamino attempts to enter the Temple and is repulsed at two gates; but at the third, the Gate of Wisdom, he encounters an Old Priest, usually these days called the Speaker (bass), who informs him of Sarastro's true nature. The scene starts simply, with routine orchestral interjections, but as it develops it takes on a startling variety of musical moods, orchestral sounds and tonal excursions. The tempo fluctuates wildly: Allegro and Allegro assai as Tamino tries the gates; Adagio for a solemn moment as the Speaker appears; Andante and then Adagio for their lengthy dialogue; finally Andante again as Tamino is sent on his way. Most surprising is the way musical motifs in the orchestra so minutely follow the progress of the words. Sometimes this is obvious, as with the two-note idea that both accompanies and mimics rhythmically the command 'Zurück!' (Go back) when Tamino is turned away from the first two gates; but other moments, such as the delicate, syncopated figure in the violins that begins to lure Tamino into changing his mind (it first occurs after Tamino's despairing 'So ist denn alles Heuchelei!' – So everything is false!), may suggest that, as in Sarastro's aria discussed above, the orchestra is the primary 'speaking' voice, and that its music leads the conversation onwards.

At the end of this extraordinary scene the Speaker departs, leaving Tamino to his new quest with a solemn couplet:

So bald dich fürht der Freundschaft Hand
In's Heiligum zum ew'gen Band.

[As soon as friendship's hand has led you / into the shrine of everlasting union.]

The tonality settles to a portentous minor; regularly phrased melody, with prominent dotted rhythms, takes over in the bass. It is as though the musical spirit of Sarastro (whom we have not yet seen in the opera) is already in the air. Tamino briefly injects more recitative, asking, 'When will my eyes find the light?'; offstage priests reply, 'Soon, soon, young man, or never!', with that same bass melody plodding along underneath, repeated yet again as the voices tell Tamino that Pamina is indeed alive. This melodic stability proves lasting: Tamino celebrates his release by playing a melody on his flute; soon the tune is picked up by Papageno's pan-pipes and leads into his duet with Pamina; and then we are plunged into the first-act finale, with its continuous music. It is as if, with the gradual turn-around in Tamino's quest, the gradual emergence of Tamino's enlightenment, Mozart has also plotted the emergence of music: from speech, to *Melodram*-like accompanied recitative, and then to fully fledged song. But this particular progression from speech to music doesn't create the usual problem. Instead, Mozart has wrapped the transition around the turning point of the plot (Tamino's realization of his true quest) and also tied it to the governing metaphor of the entire opera, that of enlightenment, of finding illumination on the true path. The problem of music's voice in a spoken world has suddenly been put to remarkable, unprecedented operatic use.

It is in this context no surprise that the Speaker scene has been one of the most elaborately praised passages in *Die Zauberflöte*, indeed in all operatic Mozart. Put simply, the unusual fluidity with which music and words combine has often been called a glance into the future, a hint of the kind of 'musical prose' that will finally be consecrated (no less) by Richard Wagner and will lay to rest the whole gaudy edifice of arias and vocal display that had sustained opera for so long. Those who single out the Speaker scene for special praise have, in other words, a distinctly forward-looking agenda, and would be likely to profess dismay at Konstanze standing there with the Pasha listening to an immense orchestral ritornello and then warbling through the hundreds of bars of 'Martern aller Arten'. On the other hand, an eighteenth-century opera advocate might suggest that the Speaker scene, although it has moments of great effect, also has moments that are, frankly, rather dull – passages in which Mozart's enthusiasm for the novelty of an abstract concept obliged him to resort to the old clichés of recitative, of simply declaimed text with basic accompaniment, but which then placed these clichés in a musical context that encouraged or even necessitated ponderous delivery. Forward-looking, proto-Wagnerian this scene may be; but – as is often said of Wagner – few have wished it longer.

There are, what is more, moments in *Die Zauberflöte* when this basic sense of music aspiring to Rousseau's idea (music announcing and preparing for the words) are managed differently. One of them again involves Tamino, and occurs in his first aria, 'Dies Bildnis ist bezaubernd schön' (This picture is enchantingly beautiful), which he sings in wonder at the portrait of Pamina that the Queen's perfidious Three Ladies have presented to him. The text is itself a kind of object lesson in Enlightenment rational progress:

Dies Bildnis ist bezaubernd schön,
Wie noch kein Auge je geseh'n!
Ich fühl' es, wie dies Götterbild
Mein Herz mit neuer Regung füllt.
Dies' etwas kann ich zwar nicht nennen,
Doch fühl' ich's hier wie Feuer brennen.
Soll die Empfindung Liebe sein?
Ja, ja, die Liebe ist's allein.
O, wenn ich sie nur finden könnte!
O, wenn sie doch schon vor mir stände!
Ich würde, würde, warm und rein,
Was würde ich?
Ich würde sie voll Entzücken
An diesen heissen Busen drücken
Und ewig wäre sie dann mein.

[This picture is enchantingly beautiful, / as no eye has ever beheld! / I feel it, how this heavenly picture / fills my heart with new emotion. / This something can I indeed not name, / yet I feel it here like fire burning. / Can the feeling be love? / Yes, yes, love it is alone. / Oh, if only I could find her. / Oh, if only she were standing before me! / I would, would, warmly and chastely, / what would I do? / I would full of rapture press her / against this warm bosom / and then she would be mine for ever.]

There's a steady, patient logic by which plot-Tamino makes sense of his feelings. First come the facts, then the analysis, then the conclusion: this picture is beautiful (lines 1–2); it makes me feel something new (3–4); I don't know what this feeling is, but it's very strong (5–6); could it be love? (7); yes it could (8); if I could find her (9–10); what would I do? (10–11); I'd press her to me and make her mine for ever (12–14). Enraptured though he is, plot-Tamino knows the rules of logic and follows them impeccably.

The musical setting of 'Dies Bildnis' is as radical as that of the Speaker scene, but this time the argument is firmly embedded within an aria. It is, though, an aria in which strange voices compete. We get a hint at the very beginning, in which the 'acoustic shock' of moving from spoken words to song is managed through the orchestra. The strings surge forward in two gestures that then seem to erupt into Tamino's first utterance, as if the instruments in some way represent his inchoate emotions, his feelings before they receive verbal and vocal substance. This is explored more teasingly when those feelings are forensically examined. Tamino sings the words 'ich fühl' es' (I feel it) to a distinctive three-note musical shape, but the rhythm of this shape has sounded in the orchestra twice already, and is then teasingly echoed by the strings in dialogue with the voice. Other moments continue this process: Tamino's fifth line, 'Dies' etwas', introduces a new stage in his argument, and the change is formally introduced, as it were, by a new key and a new orchestral melody played by two clarinets, almost as if another character has entered the scene. Later still, Tamino discovers that the emotion he feels is indeed love, 'die Liebe', and to make the connection musically explicit the three syllables of 'die Liebe' are sung to a return of that three-note figure, now inverted to become a statement rather than a question, and again teasingly placed in dialogue with the orchestra.

Moments such as this – moments in which the play of musical motifs between voice and orchestra is constantly changing as Tamino's argument progresses – continue throughout the aria. Most radically of all, there is an entire bar of silence after his final question, 'Was würde ich?' (What would I do?). So strange and musically disorientating is this silent bar that hardly any performance dares observe it to the full: the tension of silence (in the end, *the* most disruptive gesture any composer can make) is just too great, the conductor is compelled to forgo his rhythmic sense and bring the orchestra in with premature sound. Of even greater reach is what we might call the aria's afterlife, the way that resonant fragments of it disperse across the opera. One tiny example occurs in the very next aria. The Queen of the Night is in full flood, persuading Tamino with alarming flights of coloratura that he must rescue Pamina from evil Sarastro. And the last line of her aria is a subtle echo of Tamino's aria. He sang 'Und ewig wäre sie dann mein' (And then she would be mine for ever); the Queen now promises 'So sei sie dann auf ewig dein' (May she then be for ever yours). And just before she sings the line, in the second phrase of her final peroration, Tamino's 'die Liebe' motif sounds repeatedly in the violins. A ghostly (or is it magic?) echo, the speech of the orchestra offers him a reminder; his courage is bolstered by hallucinatory reminiscences of past emotions.

There is, as always, so much more to say about *Die Zauberflöte*, Mozart's last opera. It will be clear already that, although it is written in an overtly popular genre, its experiments with how orchestral music, vocal music and words might interact are very different from those in the Italian operas, where a greater weight of tradition meant that the relationships between these mediums remained relatively stable. In this sense, and in many others – its use of motifs, its periodic solemnity, its moments of extended musical prose, and so on – it had a profound effect on nineteenth-century German culture. Beethoven thought it was Mozart's greatest opera and wrote some delightful variations for cello and piano on the Papageno–Pamina duet; we shall see some more direct examples of *Zauberflöte*'s operatic effects on him in the next chapter. At the other end of the century, Freud mentioned it in *The Interpretation of Dreams* and, although he was not sure about the music, found the lyrics profound (unfortunately he didn't go into detail). In between come innumerable acts of homage and imitation. Goethe, as we have seen no stranger to more modest forms of *Singspiel*, even wrote a libretto sequel. But he should have guessed – no composer would take it on, the comparisons would have been too cruel. And so *Die Zauberflöte* stands alone, the greatest instance of what could be achieved in a century and more of experiments with speaking and singing.

7
The German problem

According to a later composer of the greatest conceivable eminence, it was a seventeen-year-old girl wielding a pistol who secured Ludwig van Beethoven (1770–1827) his place in operatic history. The girl in question was Wilhelmine Schroeder-Devrient, who in 1822 made her debut in a Vienna production of Beethoven's *Fidelio*. The opera's signature moment is a quartet in which the heroine, Leonore (soprano), disguised as a young man called Fidelio, confronts the prison governor, Don Pizarro (bass), who has made a special visit to the dungeons in order to murder her unjustly incarcerated husband, Florestan (tenor). When Pizarro threatens Florestan with death, Leonore shields his body with her own, singing, 'First you will have to kill his wife!' Pizarro and his reluctant accomplice, the wrinkled old retainer, Rocco (bass), shout back,'His *wife*?' A bit later, she pulls the gun on them, but the fact that they are now staring down the wrong end of a loaded pistol seems as nothing compared to their shock at realizing that Fidelio, whom they had employed as a trusty prison-worker, is a transvestite. A famous contemporary engraving shows Schroeder-Devrient in doublet, pantaloons and tights (we are spared the codpiece); her legs are tensed as if ready to pounce; she points her gun with scary intent (see Figure 15). This became an iconic image of its day. Maria Malibran, one of the greatest Leonores of the 1830s and a famous rival of Schroeder-Devrient, upped the ante by drawing *two* pistols.[1]

The Schroeder-Devrient engraving has been reproduced time and again in accounts of *Fidelio* and of opera in the Napoleonic era. It even turns up in biographies of Richard Wagner (the eminent source of the story above), whose admiration for the singer was, he said, profound. In Wagner's 'A Pilgrimage to Beethoven' (1840), the narrator describes his experience:

> A very young maiden played the role of Leonore; but youthful as she was, this singer seemed already wedded to Beethoven's genius. With what a glow, what poetry, what depth of effect, did she portray this extraordinary woman! She was called Wilhelmine Schröder. Hers is the great distinction of having set this work of Beethoven before the German public; that evening I saw the superficial Viennese themselves aroused to the strongest enthusiasm. For my own part, the heavens were opened to me; I was transported, and adored the genius who had led me – like Florestan – from night and fetters into light and freedom.[2]

As Wagner reminds us, *Fidelio*'s success depends enormously on the singer playing Leonore, a role generally taken by sopranos who otherwise feature in Wagner and as the weightier Strauss heroines. Schroeder-Devrient would go on to become a famous Agathe in Carl Maria von Weber's *Der Freischütz* (1821) and the first Senta in Wagner's *Der fliegende Holländer* (1843) – the latter another part that specializes in female exaltation and drive, even obsession. Leonore was, in short, the first important dramatic soprano in German opera, and as such bore many daughters.

Fidelio doesn't have this effect on all listeners. It has indeed been worshipfully regarded by many; but others have judged it a lurching paradox, written by a composer who needed more operatic practice. Even the worshippers grant that *Fidelio* is a work in which single moments have a tendency to trump continuity. It opens as farce. Little Marzelline (soprano), Rocco's gamine daughter, is in love with Fidelio and hopes to marry him. The fact that Fidelio is uninterested and oddly preoccupied seems to concern her very little. Marzelline is one of those head-tossing minxes familiar from eighteenth-century comic opera, and she and her despairing boyfriend Jaquino (tenor) at first seem important. Oddly, though, they virtually disappear after the first forty minutes or so, returning only to lend anonymous vocal heft to the finales. This anomaly is usually blamed on *Fidelio*'s libretto, which was adapted from a French *opéra comique* by Jean-Nicolas Bouilly, *Léonore, ou l'Amour conjugal* (Leonore, or Married Bliss, 1798). *Léonore* has the combined registers that typified opera with spoken dialogue by around

1800: mortal action and philosophical hauteur freely mixed with flouncing soubrettes and mistaken identity. But whereas Mozart's *Magic Flute* (1791) seemed to negotiate these registers with no apparent effort, Beethoven, arch-serious heroic composer, managed best with the elevated moments, and even then in no more than fits and starts. What's more, he kept changing his mind. There are three quite different versions of the opera (1805, 1806 and 1814) and no fewer than four overtures. In the follow-up to that pistol-waving moment in the Act 2 quartet, an offstage trumpet call signals that salvation has arrived: beneficent Don Fernando (bass), a 'minister and Spanish nobleman', is heralded from afar. He makes a majestic, chorus-assisted entrance, releases Florestan, arrests Pizarro and generally sets the world to rights. Beethoven wove this trumpet call into the intricate symphonic music of his three rejected overtures, but omitted it from the final one, attached to the 1814 version. By then, the merely comic characters had gradually been cut back and Beethoven had also worked in some music from earlier choral pieces, showing once again that – in opera as in all lyric genres – the same music can, when pressed into service, suit disconcertingly different texts.

To add to the confusion, the long-standard 1814 *Fidelio* is now threatened by historically aware resurrections of its two earlier shades, both of which (usually called by the opera's alternative title, *Leonore*) have their passionate advocates. Even before these versions were revived, there were alternative ways of performing the 1814 *Fidelio*. Although now it's usually frowned on – in our austere times, any addition or change not explicitly sanctioned by the composer tends to be automatically excoriated – producers of yesteryear, anxious to pack every last ounce of Beethovenian seriousness into *Fidelio*, would sometimes interpolate a complete performance of one or other of the three rejected overtures – often the sublime *Leonore Overture No. 3* – into Act 2. Sometimes it happened like this. After the quartet, Pizarro and Rocco depart to officiate at Don Fernando's arrival, leaving Leonore and Florestan to sing an ecstatic duet, 'O namenlose Freude!' (Oh nameless joy!) Their voices echo in powerful arpeggios and short, almost breathless melodic snaps, by any standards a ferociously hard sing. What more natural, then, that after finishing the duet, newly reunited man and wife become sleepy and lie down for a nap in the dungeon; and what more fitting that the resulting pause is filled by *Leonore Overture No. 3*, performed by an orchestra deemed to have taken up residence in the vicinity. At the overture's conclusion, the lovers awaken refreshed; the plot of *Fidelio* can continue its course, although with an added boost of instrumental music to remind us of Beethoven's greatest glory.

All this confusion of registers and versions and production habits accounts for *Fidelio*'s reputation as a work of erratic genius, an opera with wonderful individual passages and less than wonderful overall sense. And then, there is the pervasive oddness of the vocal lines, which at times resemble brass instruments blaring primary notes in triadic fanfares rather than human voices raised in lyrical melodic arcs. But *Fidelio* nevertheless stands as a craggy monument to the confused state of German opera at a moment of transition. Why that swift move from the knock-about antics of *Singspiel* in the eighteenth century to the tragic German operas of the nineteenth? Why, in short, did opera in German quite suddenly become so *serious*?

A NEW ANTAGONISM

The term 'German Romantic Opera' covers much of this serious repertory, and Romanticism is an amorphous, geographically diffuse phenomenon. In German culture, as in all others, it did not arrive punctually in 1800. Virginia Woolf's *Orlando* has a wonderful Gothic description of midnight on 31 December 1799:

> The clock struck midnight, clouds covered the sky from the north, a cold wind blew, the light of a thousand golden candles was extinguished, and, suddenly, those who had been dressed in diamonds and white silk hose and silver lace and peach satin wrapped themselves in gloomy velvets and jet bead ornaments. The nineteenth century had arrived.

This image of instant meteorological and sartorial transformation places in a perfect literary conceit the upheavals of several decades. Europe changed radically between 1789 (the start of the French Revolution) and 1814–15, when the Congress of Vienna orchestrated by Prince Metternich determined the future map of Europe as the Napoleonic adventure was coming to its last bloody end at the battle of Waterloo. The terrifying aftermath of the French Revolution; Napoleon's ascension to the Imperial throne and his subsequent European conquests, defeats and exile; all this came in between. During this time, there were also huge changes in musical culture, including a marked acceleration in the slow-motion death of aristocratic patronage as a source of support for operatic entertainment, and a redefinition of composers as artists rather than employees. This is why the 'starving artist' became such an alluring accessory in Romantic lore. Left to support themselves by publishing enduring masterpieces, and/or by becoming migrant labourers, writing operas on commission for impresarios hither and thither, composers could now get seriously rich; but they could also remain spectacularly poor. Copyright laws had hardly taken force, and anyway differed from state to state. France, progressively, led the way with respect to royalties, but ideas of 'intellectual property' were mostly in the future. In the early part of the century, a composer often ceded his operatic score to the theatre that first performed it. Piracy was as rife in the theatre as it was on the high seas, and skirmishes concerning who owned what continued throughout the century.

Beethoven became the defining musical figure of this period in the German-speaking sphere. His position between the Enlightenment and Romanticism in some ways parallels that of Gioachino Rossini (1792–1868) in the Italian world, even though Rossini was a generation younger than Beethoven. But generally these two great men have been seen as opposites, with Rossini, the operatic conqueror, supposedly showing little aptitude for instrumental music or the heroic gesture, and Beethoven, the presiding genius of the symphony and string quartet, showing equally little aptitude for opera. Rossini wrote operas at huge speed, sometimes on close to automatic pilot, and he could do so because he was a professional, knew the tricks of the trade. Beethoven was different and admitted it, in later life even offering faint praise to his upstart young rival. In a grumpy letter to a composer colleague, he wrote that Rossini's music was

> the translation of the frivolous spirit that characterizes our times; but Rossini is a man of talent and an exceptional melodist. He writes with such ease that for the composition of an opera he takes as many weeks as a German would take years.[3]

And Beethoven, in spite of all those years of labour on *Fidelio*, made amateur mistakes: forgetting about Marzelline and Jaquino; not giving his villain Pizarro nearly enough to sing; bestowing on beneficent Don

Fernando, who turns up only for the last scene and thus cannot be taken by a principal singer, some of the most magnificent music of the evening. All these mistakes were probably born of moral sincerity: Marzelline and Jaquino belong to the *opéra comique* world that the opera begins with but then rejects; dark-voiced, attractively lyrical villains were, Beethoven felt, ethically wrong, and the fact that they were one of opera's great pleasures concerned him not a jot; and although Don Fernando is indeed desperately late to arrive, he nevertheless makes sense of everything, perhaps even musical sense.

As it happens, or at least as it was told, Beethoven and Rossini exchanged words in 1822, when Rossini came to Vienna for a performance of his opera *Zelmira*. In a period that later became dubbed 'the age of Beethoven and Rossini',[4] this meeting has taken on the status of a mythological clash of titans. We have no real idea what went on, since Rossini seems to have told the story only in 1860, during an encounter with none other than Richard Wagner. The later discussion was reported (with what accuracy we can only guess) by Edmond Michotte, a Belgian friend of Rossini's who had introduced the two. To beat a path back to what Rossini and Beethoven might have said or gestured to each another in 1822, by way of the recorded reminiscences of a senior citizen playfully sparring with Wagner in 1860, is of course impossible. Could Beethoven really have communicated, in Italian (as told by Rossini to Wagner via self-styled note-taker Michotte), 'Ah! Rossini, you are the author of *Il barbiere di Siviglia*? Congratulations; it's an excellent *opera buffa*. I have read it with pleasure and I enjoyed myself. So long as there is Italian opera, it will be performed'? Atmospheric details about the rain that could pour in through gaps in Beethoven's ceiling, or Rossini's comments on Beethoven's appearance, have the ring of genuine fiction:

> What no etcher's needle could express was the indefinable sadness spread over his features, while from under heavy eyebrows his eyes shone as from out of caverns, and, though small, seemed to pierce one through and through.[5]

The mythic meeting is cast even further in doubt by other Rossini anecdotes that circulated freely after the composer's death. According to one source, Rossini was asked if he had met Beethoven in Vienna. '"No," replied Rossini; "he was a very bad character, he refused to receive me; he detested my music. Which does not," he added with a smile, "prevent him from being the greatest composer in the world."'[6] An important background to Michotte's account is that, by 1860, German and Italian music had taken on fixed and opposing identities, identities that were even then easy to parody as grave, important and world-historical on the one (German) side, and light, melodic and pleasurable on the other (Italian). Moving back from 1860, the same distinction appears in Wagner's treatise *Oper und Drama* (Opera and Drama, 1851) and in Italian revolutionary Giuseppe Mazzini's *Filosofia della musica* (Philosophy of Music, 1836); even Madame de Staël's *De l'Allemagne* (On Germany and the Germans, 1810) aired the problem. If debates about Italian versus French style were the defining aesthetic conundrum of eighteenth-century opera, after 1800 the story inexorably becomes one about Italians versus Germans.

What had German composers done to make this happen? The interregnum between Mozart's death in 1791 and the 1820s was a critical time for German opera. Partly this was the result of social change. The old aristocratic guard, who had for so long controlled opera, were mostly cosmopolitan in outlook, an international fraternity that thought little of national boundaries. But the increasing emergence of the bourgeoisie as a social and political force saw the onset of a more fervent nationalism about German operatic art, and also a new cultural xenophobia that arose in literature and from there fed into opera libretti. By the 1810s, rumours began to circulate that Mozart had not died a natural death, but had been poisoned by a rival, the Italian opera composer Antonio Salieri (1750–1825). This scurrilous invention was dignified by Alexander Pushkin, who turned it into a play in 1831. The successful but ultimately mediocre Italian perfidiously destroys the Austrian whose genius he envies: paranoia about rivals across the Alps could not be clearer.

It would be too simple and neat to see Mozart's death as marking the end of a tradition in which Austro-German composers moved fluently in and out of the world of Italian or French opera. Beethoven's operatic career is an excellent case in point. When he began to think about possible operatic subjects, he enrolled on a course of instruction about Italian word-setting – and chose as his tutor none other than Vienna's respected Hofkapellmeister Salieri, both men as yet blissfully unaware of Salieri's future in music history's hall of shame. Beethoven dutifully produced homework assignments, including a duet for soprano and tenor, 'Ne' giorni tuoi felici', to an antediluvian text by, of all people, Pietro Metastasio. His foray into Italian territory eventually proved something of a dead end, but at almost the same time his ear was caught by an important new operatic style coming from France, one proving enormously popular in Vienna. This new style, which seemed to emerge directly out of the major political event of the past decade, once more brings French opera into view.

FAITS HISTORIQUES

The revolutionary turmoil of the 1790s had stimulated French operatic activity in a way that later revolutions would not, at least overtly. This sudden politicization of opera partly reflected the theatrical nature of the revolution itself, in particular the fact that so-called *faits historiques* – vast open-air allegorical stagings of revolutionary deeds – were a primary means of state propaganda in the first years after 1789. Equally important was a daring gesture made by the Constituent Assembly in January 1791. After decades of strict control over theatrical privilege (*tragédie lyrique* only at the Opéra, comic works at the Opéra-Comique, and so on), the Assembly, radically iconoclastic in culture as in so many other spheres, proclaimed that any genre of opera could be performed in any type of theatre. This revolutionary pronouncement did not last long. The first decade of the nineteenth century, the years of the Consulate (1799–1804) and then the Empire (1804–14/15), saw a backing-away from the Constituent Assembly's position and in 1807 Emperor Napoleon restored many of the old theatrical privileges. Despite this retrenchment, a new type of opera had been born in the interim. The 1790s saw a mass of overtly propagandistic operas in a proliferation of genres, from *opéra comique* to vaudeville to pantomime. Republican tales, in which the heroic deeds of the Revolution were allegorized, crowded on to Parisian stages, often in the form of so-called 'rescue' operas, in which beleaguered heroes and heroines were miraculously saved from mortal danger in the final moments of the plot.

The surge of innovation in *opéra comique* during the 1790s and after, one that made the great tradition of *tragédie lyrique* at the Opéra seem somehow less exciting, produced several composers who influenced

Beethoven. One was Étienne-Nicolas Méhul (1763–1817), who had made his name in the 1790s as both an opera composer and a contributor to revolutionary *faits*. Befriended by none other than Napoleon, Méhul continued to create successful works during the Empire, among them *opéras comiques* that derived some of their character from Italian composers such as Paisiello. But Méhul was also a committed innovator, and modern scholars have been more interested in his Ossian cult opera *Uthal* (1806), which tapped into a vein of early Romanticism that was to prove prophetic. This was not simply a case of subject matter: *Uthal* omitted violins from the orchestra in an attempt to give a darker, more Romantic flavour.

Most important, though, was the Italian-born Luigi Cherubini (1760–1842), who had made a considerable reputation in the 1790s with hybrid works such as *Lodoïska* (1791) and *Médée* (1797), both performed at Paris's Théâtre Feydeau (which merged with the Opéra-Comique in 1801). Cherubini's greatest popular success was with *Les Deux Journées* (The Two Days, 1800), a *comédie lyrique* in three acts, also with a libretto by Bouilly, which Beethoven studied in some detail while preparing to write *Fidelio*. The opera's first Paris production enjoyed more than 200 performances, and it also became popular in German-speaking lands, still being revived there in the 1840s. No less a luminary than Goethe praised its libretto. Just like Bouilly's *Léonore* libretto (hence, like *Fidelio*), it tells a story of rescue and humanitarian triumph. Although set in the seventeenth century, the plot was clearly meant to resonate with the revolutionary tastes of the audience, featuring characters with strongly defined abstract virtues. It tells of a Savoyard water-carrier who hides a parliamentarian and his wife from Cardinal Mazarin. In common with many such 'rescue' operas, the parliamentarian is finally pardoned: the opera ends by reminding everyone that 'le premier charme de la vie c'est de servir l'humanité' (the principal pleasure of life is to serve humanity).

In many ways *Les Deux Journées* is a typical *opéra comique* of the period. It makes full and dramatic use of its various modes of delivery, from spoken dialogue to *mélodrame* (a genre featuring words spoken over musical accompaniment, as discussed in the previous chapter), to accompanied recitative, to aria and then ensemble. But there is an imbalance between these last two: the opera's only arias are its first two numbers after the overture (out of a total of fifteen), and both of them are simple, strophic, 'characteristic' pieces – a narrative ballad and a prayer – which recur at key moments in the plot. The rest of the work is made up of choruses and ensembles, the most ambitious of the latter being multi-tempo and multi-key, not unlike a Mozartian *opera buffa* finale. Cherubini's opera, and indeed all those other French-language works that celebrated the impact of the French revolution, are little seen today, but their impact on nineteenth-century opera was long-lasting and intense, particularly in the German lands. Felix Mendelssohn (1809–47), often ambivalent about opera, saw *Les Deux Journées* in Düsseldorf in 1834 and wrote to his father, 'it was the most pleasurable evening I have had in the theatre in a long time, for I took part in the performance as a spectator, smiling and clapping along, and shouting bravos'.[7] His enthusiasm, which was coupled with continuing worries about the state of his own national opera, was symptomatic. The oratorio-like manner and grand symphonic gestures of Don Fernando's final scene in *Fidelio*, which may now seem so utterly Beethovenian and Germanic, are cousins of the French-Revolution-inspired choral hymns to liberty that were a commonplace of Cherubini's opera.

THE GERMAN RESPONSE

Even as *Fidelio* was going through its agonized, multi-national genesis, new, narrower ideas of what 'German' might mean were beginning to circulate. In this increasingly xenophobic world, anyone who passed effortlessly from his native culture to a foreign one was liable to be seen as dubious and deceitful. To be bilingual became immediately suspect. One need look no further, for instance, than Wagner's sustained polemic against Giacomo (Jakob) Meyerbeer, a rival German composer who wrote Italian and French operas, and whose great successes in Paris in the 1830s and 1840s we will consider in a later chapter. What lay behind Wagner's anti-Meyerbeer polemic was largely anti-Semitism, but German xenophobia in the early nineteenth century also had roots elsewhere. It was nurtured in the trauma of the Napoleonic invasions and occupations of the German states, and in the subsequent imposition of the Napoleonic code, which enfranchised various residents considered alien, including the Jews. The spectre of invasion, the fear that a protected homeland would be violated, became a dominating theme in German

Romantic literature after 1800. Its cultural results in the nineteenth century were often glorious; its repercussions in the twentieth century were unprecedentedly violent and tragic.

An important player in the German opera saga was *Die Zauberflöte* (1791), which became hugely popular in the decade following Mozart's death and was often cast as the originating work in a new genre: serious opera in German that, despite the *Singspiel* remnant of spoken dialogue, aspired to grandiose, even transcendental status. Mozart became a cult figure very soon after his death, with *Die Zauberflöte* regarded as something far distant from *Singspiel*, in fact as high art. One important moment in this elevation, briefly mentioned at the end of the last chapter, came in 1794, when Goethe planned a sequel libretto, *Die Zauberflöte zweiter Teil* (The Magic Flute Part Two). Goethe wrote this curious piece, together with various essays praising *Die Zauberflöte* and *Don Giovanni*, for a particular purpose: to show that these operas' magical and supernatural themes could be seen as a meeting place between the human and the transcendent or numinous. He argued, in other words, that Mozart's works elevated the use of supernatural and magical plots, taking them out of the realm of farce and making them elevated and serious. Although there were, understandably, no composers willing to take on Goethe's sequel, German librettists in the early decades of the nineteenth century had new volumes of magical stories to draw upon, including the Grimm brothers' first collections of German *Kinder- und Hausmärchen* (Children's and Domestic Fairy Tales, 1812–14) and its companion work, *Deutsche Sagen* (German Sagas, 1816–18).

The Grimms were relative latecomers in the vogue for collecting and inventing fairy tales, which had begun in seventeenth-century France and moved to Germany a little later. Such tales had already been the basis for many opera libretti with spoken dialogue in French, German and English. But what was different now was the tragic gravitas attached to magic. Take the case of E. T. A. Hoffmann (1776–1822), already heard as a trenchant music critic, whose opera *Undine* (1816) is based on a literary fairy tale by Friedrich de la Motte Fouqué. Hoffmann the writer was a famous bard of the uncanny, whose stories about the clash between human and non-human worlds typify the disquieting and pessimistic aspects of early German Romantic literature. Undine (soprano) is a beautiful water spirit adopted in infancy by a human couple. She falls in love with Huldbrand (baritone), and they are betrothed even though Undine warns Huldbrand that if he is unfaithful, she must return to her natural element and will become a danger to him. The obligatory sinister-bass tempter appears in the form of Kühleborn, a powerful water spirit who represents the lure of the unseen realm. Sure enough, through Kühleborn's machinations Huldbrand is tricked into proposing to another girl and Undine sinks back into her watery realm. But she emerges from a fountain at the betrothal celebration and drags Huldbrand down into the waters.

DER FREISCHÜTZ: THE BOOK OF GHOSTS

Undine represents the archetype for German Romantic operas with supernatural plots. The setting is normal – a self-contained human society with its small emotions and tightly knit family structures – but the visitors from outside, the violent invaders of this safe space, are not. A seductive female spirit entoils a virtuous man; the nastier male variety seeks converts or brides or victims (sometimes bride and victim are the same thing), seducing mortal targets. Human order is invariably restored at the end, but often after considerable sacrifice. And although comic versions of magical plots continued, along with so-called 'Turkish operas' in which (as we saw in Mozart's *Die Entführung aus dem Serail*, 1782, discussed in the previous chapter) clever Westerners outwit scheming Easterners, the serious and semi-serious supernatural libretti represent the ground note. The most famous opera of this new genre was Weber's *Der Freischütz* (1821), an operatic cornucopia in which the fairy-tale genre crashes against social anxiety and parochialism. Even the title is so local as to be impossible to translate sensibly. 'Freikügeln' are literally 'free bullets', and 'Freischütz' is 'free marksman', but the word 'frei' has here the sense of magic or enchantment; a 'Freischütz' is a 'hunter who has bargained his soul away for magically infallible bullets', but that's too long for a title. Not just for this reason, it is now rather rare to find productions of *Der Freischütz* outside Germany, and those that occur are almost invariably estranging and critical, the folkishness and the phobia about aliens are otherwise too problematic. But Weber's opera was a global success in the early nineteenth century, a success that depended on its reputation for being authentically quaint and German. As mentioned in Chapter 1, when *Der Freischütz* was revived in Paris in the 1840s, Wagner felt he had to write an explanatory note for innocent French opera-goers who might not understand its German seriousness; yet the opera's easy dissemination – it played Cape Town, Rio and Sydney, all before 1850 – suggests that Wagner's note reflected little more than a secret contempt for the French character.

Gespensterbuch, 'the Book of Ghosts', was the collection Weber's librettist, Johann Friedrich Kind, mined for the *Freischütz* story. The protagonist is Max (tenor), a huntsman and sharpshooter whose bullets have, of late, gone all awry. As the opera opens he is in despair: if he doesn't win the shooting contest to be held the following day, he can't marry his beloved Agathe (soprano). Caspar (bass), another huntsman, suggests a rash remedy: Max should come with him that night to the 'Wolf's Glen', where a demonic Black Huntsman called Samiel (speaking role) will help them forge magic bullets that never miss the target. After two acts and many tuneful numbers for Agathe, her feisty cousin Aennchen (mezzo-soprano), Max and assorted others (Samiel sometimes appearing silently on the edges of things), Max meets Caspar in the Wolf's Glen, where Samiel speaks for the first and only time in the opera. Caspar, we discover along the way, has sold his soul to Samiel and now intends to trade in Max as his replacement. The bullets are duly cast amid much thunder. In Act 3 the shooting contest is held; Samiel directs Max's seventh bullet towards Agathe, but she is saved by a miracle and Caspar is killed instead. Max is forgiven and all ends well.

Even from this description it will be clear that *Der Freischütz*'s dramaturgy is as creaky as a first-night scene change, and the pantomime-level spoken dialogue has the added problem that talk of shooting matches and bagging sixteen-point male stags lays a minefield of doubles-entendres. One glances randomly at the libretto to find 'Leid oder Wonne, beides ruht in deinem Rohr' (roughly: Sorrow or joy, both reside in your barrel). But there are more troubling aspects underneath. What, for example, is at stake in a libretto so saturated with anxieties about things that lurk in the woods, and with fiendish people (the Caspars of this world) who might be infiltrating our society while seeming to be part of it? This second phobia – about the apparently native speaker who is really something else – was both a general cliché and a specifically anti-Semitic worry. Once German Jews assimilated and became middle- and upper-class secular citizens, there was perilously little to mark them as different; the special cunning of these foreigners and aliens within was to be indistinguishable in voice or appearance from true Germans. There have been numerous sociological and psychological explanations for this new obsession with the uncanny on the part of the German Romantics. Freud, famously, psychoanalysed Hoffmann and his confrères retrospectively, discovering a whole range of mental pathologies in their preferences for terrifying *Doppelgänger* (self-doubles), dark figures who keep coming back and feet that dance by themselves. But the stories – especially when music is wrapped around them – are not always so black and white. In Heinrich Marschner's *Der Vampyr* (The Vampire, 1828), the titular un-dead person, a quasi-Byronic figure called Lord Ruthven (baritone), gets many of the best tunes. Wagner's *Der fliegende Holländer* was indebted musically to Marschner's score, and in Wagner the sinister supernatural insurgent became a romantic anti-hero and tragic matinée idol, to be pitied, adored and of course given great music to sing.

Der Freischütz was called a *romantische Oper* on its title page, but its *Singspiel* and *opéra comique* legacy can be heard everywhere, first of all in that perilous spoken dialogue. When it was put on at the Paris Opéra, Hector Berlioz was enlisted to turn the dialogue into interminable recitatives, lengthening the performance time significantly and, in Wagner's opinion, adding inappropriate frills: 'When you replace a naïve and often humorous dialogue by a recitative which always dawdles in the singer's mouth, don't you think you will efface the stamp of robust heartiness that marks the scenes of the Bohemian rustics?'[8] But that was the rule. When Bizet's *Carmen* was done at the Opéra in 1883, it too was bolstered with added recitatives (as it had been in many other respected venues, where speech would just not do). However, *Der Freischütz* also has links, not entirely happy ones, with the comic tradition. These are particularly prominent in the soubrette character Aennchen, another head-tossing minx, who in a duet with Agathe in Act 2 describes her outlook on life as follows: 'Pessimism is not my style! To dance through life with a light heart, that is what suits me best. You need to banish cares and woes!' This lightness of being tells us that she is definitely *not* the leading lady; yet Agathe's moody counterpoint to Aennchen comes off as unrelieved solemnity, which Aennchen in Act 3 skewers when she sings a mock-Gothic ballad number.

If the libretti for these German Romantic operas seem quintessentially local – in the sense that their anxieties and (usually) their literary sources are Germanic – the same is hardly true of the music. German opera composers of the early nineteenth century often argued vociferously about the superiority of the local product; Weber referred in 1816 to Rossini as 'the sirocco wind blowing from the South, whose heat will soon be cooled'.[9] But like his contemporaries Hoffmann and Louis Spohr, Weber had greedy ears for what was going on elsewhere, especially in Italy; like it or not, cosmopolitan musical habits emerged. In Act 2 of *Der Freischütz*, Agathe sings a famous aria, 'Leise, leise, fromme Weise' (Softly, softly, pious song). It begins with a slow verse whose opening melody is recapitulated at the end. Then there's a break, a recitative-like transition in which Agathe observes the landscape outside her window and, finally, sees Max approaching in the distance. 'O heavens! O newly won happiness', she sings – and we're off into a rapturous, virtuosic, fast final movement. In other words, the whole number is a slow–fast, multi-movement aria, very close to the Italian manner established by the despised Rossini. It's not, of course, that every aria beginning slowly and ending fast is automatically Rossinian: two-part arias of this sort had been around since the eighteenth century; Mozart has several famous examples. But the style of Agathe's aria, as well as its form, strongly suggests that Weber had his own sirocco moments.

Strophic songs in German Romantic opera, on the other hand, typically represented reassuring folk idioms, as they had in *Singspiel* going back to the mid eighteenth century. But we know from examples in *Die Zauberflöte* that the strophic form was also beginning to assume more complex meanings: far from merely asserting rustic simplicity, the repeating stanzas could now represent reassuring order, a musical antithesis to chaos or unpredictability. In Act 3 of *Der Freischütz*, the hunters in a local tavern sing a strophic song ('Was gleicht wohl auf Erden des Jägers Vergnügen') accompanied by onstage hunting horns, about the pleasures of their profession: 'What pleasure on earth can compare to the joys of the hunter? For whom is life's cup so fizzy and full?' The strong, close harmony of the male voices and the thunder of the horns make for an astonishing acoustic picture; a moment in which the safe, homely setting of the tavern and its male camaraderie seem to spill out as sheer sound, as a snapshot of the collective Voice of the People. But these days the scene is extremely difficult to stage (or watch) with a straight face. It's hard not to think of Gaston, the boorish hunter in Disney's *Beauty and the Beast* (1991), who sings with similar exuberance, 'I use antlers in all of my decorating!' Exhilarating though the sound may be, we've heard too many tight-blazered, all-male glee clubs doing this sort of thing – their style, indeed, derived from the male *Gesangsvereine* (singing clubs) that were popular in Germany in Weber's time and beyond. As successful as *Der Freischütz* was, it was also, from the outset, ripe for parody and mockery.

Strophic song, however, was transcending its folk origins, and not just in the German tradition. By the 1820s, a particular kind of strophic ballad number was becoming ubiquitous in operas with supernatural plots. A character is urged or volunteers to tell a story in the form of a song. The story is about a supernatural figure who haunts human terrain; and the fairy-tale ballad turns out to enact in microcosm the plot of the opera itself. We have seen predecessors of this in the previous chapter: in Mozart's *Die Entführung*, Pedrillo's serenade in Act 3 narrates a story about rescuing girls from a harem, which is exactly what Pedrillo is doing. And there are also august followers, not just in the German tradition. In Verdi's *La forza del destino* (The Force of Destiny, 1862), by some distance the composer's most Gothic opera, the vengeful baritone Don Carlo's Ballata in Act 2 ('Son Pereda, son ricco d'onore') is nothing more than a mock-comic re-enactment of the opera's plot so far; small wonder that when *La forza* became a cult opera in 1920s Germany, a suitably translated, heavily northern version of this aria was a particular favourite.

Back in the 1820s, the cultural and literary complications within Gothic plots came to the fore in both the poetry and music of such ballad numbers. Take the case of *La Dame blanche* (The White Lady, 1825), an *opéra comique* by Adrien Boieldieu (1775–1834). As *Die weisse Dame*, the opera became hugely popular in Germany in the 1830s and beyond. The text was by Eugène Scribe, the most important French librettist of the early nineteenth century, and it was drawn, like so many other Romantic libretti, from the historical novels of Sir Walter Scott. In the course of Act 1, a minor character called Jenny sings a strophic song ('D'ici voyez ce beau domaine') about the legend of the White Lady, a benign ghost who watches over the Avenel family, and who once saved them from importunate enemies. Sure enough, the same thing happens in the opera (although the White Lady turns out to be a real girl: the Avenel's helpful ward, Anna, craftily disguised in a white sheet). Marschner also included a striking ballad number in *Der Vampyr*: one of Ruthven's future victims warns her audience, in song, about unfortunate girls who met the very fate that is about to overtake *her*. In all such numbers, there is a fundamental tension at work. The musical and poetic pattern, being strophic, is ordered to the highest degree, repetitive and predictable. But the content of the story describes a disruption of human life and order brought about by all those supernatural insurgents. In this sense, it's as if the music refuses to recognize the narrative. By remaining so closed and simple, it distances itself; a dangerous vision is kept at bay or, better, is heard through a protective filter. Marschner's ballad, in the strange key of E♭ minor, has an ensemble refrain at the end of each verse whose music seems to come from a lost past, a strange slow gavotte sung by a mesmerized circle of listeners.

DER FREISCHÜTZ: SCENIC MUSIC

Weber's opera is also revolutionary in its advanced taste for 'scenic music', music (either solely instrumental or sung) expressly written to accompany some occurrence onstage, whether a mundane procession or an epic disaster. As we saw in Chapter 4, this habit had roots in the eighteenth century, in particular inspired by the French operatic taste for visual spectacle. Rare indeed was a *tragédie lyrique* that did not feature a storm, whether at sea or on land, with accompanying musical effects. One given of scenic music in opera is that it can be much messier, far less formally predictable, than would be the case in a purely instrumental piece. After all, the music has an added responsibility: it has to convey disruptions of nature, or match the pageantry of people coming and going, and if incongruous things take place visually, then incongruous or surprising things also happen musically. One need only compare the storm scenes in Rossini's *Il barbiere di Siviglia* (1816) or *La Cenerentola* (1817) with the equivalent, and musically much better behaved, passages in Beethoven's *Pastoral* Symphony (1808) to hear the difference.

Scenic music established an aesthetic of visual–musical collaboration that would shoulder a considerable burden of operatic meaning in the next hundred or so years, particularly in German opera. Again, Weber was a leader. One of opera's most spectacular storms – indeed, one of opera's greatest instances of scenic music – comes in the finale to Act 2 of *Der Freischütz*, the bullet-casting scene in the Wolf's Glen. It became a benchmark for visual–musical extravaganza, and one of the first proto-cinematic moments in opera. The finale is best described as a fascinating musical pile-up. It mixes spoken dialogue with *Melodram* (speaking over orchestral music, discussed in the previous chapter), singing and instrumental scenic music into a multi-section number that includes instructions for marvellous and, in 1821, more or less unrealizable special effects. We are deep in the woods at midnight; Samiel – an otherwise mute character – is now firmly in his element and thus able to speak. But he never sings. A hierarchy is strictly maintained: when interacting with Samiel (who is very bad), Caspar (half bad) sings while Samiel speaks; once Max (mostly good) arrives and starts singing, Caspar reverts to speech. But after Max has carried out the bullet-casting ceremony he too can no longer sing. Of course, and to keep the opera going, both Caspar and Max recover their capacity for melody during the interval that follows the Wolf's Glen scene: they are needed in Act 3.

What happens in this finale? The curtain opens to a scene described in the libretto in extraordinary detail, with a veritable roll-call of German Romanticism's visual markers:

> A terrible woodland glen largely planted with pines and surrounded by high mountains. A waterfall rushes down from one of them. The full moon shines wanly. Two thunderstorms are brewing from opposite directions. Nearer to us a tree struck by lightning and withered, decayed inside so that it seems to glow. On a gnarled branch at the other side sits a huge owl with fiery, circling eyes. Crows and other wood birds on other trees. Caspar, without hat or coat, but with hunting bag and knife, is busy with black boulders, laying out a circle in the middle of which a skull lies: a few paces away are a pair of eagle's wings, a casting-ladle and a bullet mould.

A ghostly chorus (F♯ minor Sostenuto, with occasional shrieks) sings about moon-milk and murdered brides; a clock in the distance strikes midnight; Caspar plunges his hunting knife into the skull, raises it up, turns round three times and summons Samiel; Samiel appears and demands to know Caspar's purpose; Caspar sings a monologue (C minor,

Agitato and sensuous, a strong moment for the bass) asking for a revised contract if he can give Max to Samiel in exchange; Samiel agrees but alludes to the seventh bullet and Agathe before disappearing; Caspar frets about Max (*Melodram*, with the orchestra reacting nervously). The music moves to the major mode for the first time (E♭ major) and a silvery blast from a quartet of horns announces Max's arrival – he is first seen on a rocky peak above a waterfall, peering down into the glen; he climbs hesitantly down, pausing frequently and voicing his reluctance; Caspar yells encouragement; various visions appear in the air, including the ghost of Max's mother warning him away and finally, courtesy of Samiel, Agathe dressed as a madwoman ('hair strangely adorned with leaves and straw') and poised to commit suicide (minor mode and *molto agitato*); Max finally reaches Caspar. There's a brief pause, after which Caspar describes the ingredients needed for the bullets (ground glass from a church window, the left eye of a lynx, and so forth) and blesses the brew.

Caspar begins to cast the bullets. 'The mixture in the mortar begins to foment and bubble and gives out a greeny-white glow. A cloud passes over the moon, so that the surroundings are lit only by the fire, the owl's eyes and the rotten stump of the tree.' As Caspar counts the bullets into the mould, strange things begin to happen. First ('One!') the woodbirds act oddly, to orchestral murmurs and rushing; at 'Two!' a black boar rushes about to the accompaniment of some bizarre, trombone-like slides in the cellos, basses and bassoons; at 'Three!' a storm begins and trees wave in the wind (string runs up and down, discordant); at 'Four!' ghostly, fire-rimmed wheels roll on- and offstage, to more of the same. At 'Five!' we have to use our imaginations because no staging can make it happen: a horde of dead huntsmen ride across in the night sky with spectral hounds baying; they sing sinister rhymes while blowing on their mistuned horns (marked in the score as *sempre tutto fortissimo possible*); at 'Six!' comes thunder and lightning as the storms meet, trees crashing, a huge, C-minor tempest, with strings, wind, brass, timpani and conductor all on overdrive, Presto and fortissimo. Then Caspar, unable to manage the seventh bullet, cries out 'Samiel! Help!' and his words echo back to him – at which point ('Seven!') Samiel, who is the worst disturbance that can possibly happen, much worse than the thunderstorms, returns and reaches for Max's hand, an appearance that generates a musically outlandish modulation from C minor to F♯ minor: polar opposite keys that don't belong anywhere near each other. Max makes the sign of the cross and falls to the ground. The offstage clock strikes one, but little more than fifteen minutes of performance time have passed and we're done.

Music carries a large part of the burden of conviction when the scene is staged, of course. At the 1821 premiere, in Berlin's Schauspielhaus, the visual effects were conjured up partly with magic lanterns: projections of coloured transparent images, which in German were called *Phantasmagoria*. Nowadays, the Wolf's Glen is always a director's 'signature scene'. Some try to match nineteenth-century surround sound with twenty-first-century IMAX-quality visual effects. In an English National Opera production from the late 1990s by David Pountney, the magic bullets were concocted with much violence in the mouth of a sleepwalking (or imagined) Agathe, and then extracted from her with spasms and groans of sexual release; in the background various period scenes were enacted, among them a naked female dancer chased around by some very nasty-looking supernumeraries. The whole episode was finished off by a chorus of First World War soldiers with full trench accoutrements – given the volume of coloured smoke enveloping the stage, they may have needed their gas masks. This may sound impressively modern, but other directors question more fundamentally an audience's taste for overwhelming Gothic illusion. In one recent Hamburg production, the finale ended with emergency lighting going on in the theatre, flashing red lights from (apparent) ambulances parked just outside. The audience (as captured on the DVD) were left in a state of indecision, half afraid that a fire had broken out or that someone had died, half suspecting that this was all part of the plan and smiling broadly. That Weber's music can accommodate both these imaginings is a tribute to its sheer unruliness and visionary energy.

Weber's daredevil finale, the sense that he simply let everything fly at once, is a remarkable moment in the history of opera. The fact that the performers can never hope to get through it with neatness or precision – as some conductors say, you just close your eyes and pray – is integral to the scene's effect, to all its intimations of disorder and inhuman forces. There is a famous special effect built into the music, one whose implications are much the same. If you look at the keys that are central to several sections in the finale – F♯ minor at the beginning and end, C minor in Caspar's monologue and the storm sequence, A minor for the

Agathe manifestation and E♭ major for Max's entrance – you see that Weber has played a trick. Earlier in the opera, he has punctuated references to Samiel and his underworld menace with a particular harmonic sonority, a so-called 'diminished chord' made up of stacked minor thirds. This idea of attaching musical ideas to prominent elements of the drama, and then recalling them at critical moments, has been seen before, notably in French operas such as Grétry's *Richard Cœur-de-Lion* (discussed in the previous chapter). It had, via the French examples, become popular in German opera: Weber may have been particularly influenced by Spohr's *Faust*, which he helped to stage in 1816 and which he praised for its use of 'a few melodies, felicitously and aptly devised, [which] weave like delicate threads through the whole, and hold it together artistically'.[10] But in the Wolf's Glen scene he took the process a stage further. The pitches that make up Samiel's diminished-chord motif (F♯, A, C, E♭) have been spread out in time and buried deep into the music: they become the pitch foundations on which the finale's harmonic journey is composed. This device has attained some notoriety. It is a subliminal symbol of Samiel's domination, and Weber's sketches for the opera show that it was carefully planned and worked out, almost in the manner of a symphonic movement. Yet again, as we saw with Mozart in Chapter 5, German composers were bringing to opera some harmonic and orchestrational techniques from the instrumental genres in which they were increasingly regarded as the masters. It would be a gateway to many further experiments. But the French origins of the reminiscence motif, and for that matter of Weber's scenic music spectacular, demonstrate that the German Problem was also a matter of symbiosis, of Beethoven's and Weber's cosmopolitanism and of greedy ears and profitable exchanges both ways across the Rhine.

8
Rossini and transition

No one was more certain than the French novelist Stendhal (1783–1842), who in 1824 wrote an entire book about his passion for the operas of Gioachino Rossini (1792–1868): 'Napoleon is dead; but a new conqueror has already shown himself to the world: and from Moscow to Naples, from London to Vienna, from Paris to Calcutta, his name is constantly on every tongue.'[1] According to Stendhal's endlessly quoted comment, Rossini was a revolutionary, changing the face of Italian opera as he had inherited it from the late eighteenth century, an opera exemplified by such composers as Domenico Cimarosa (1749–1801) and Giovanni Paisiello. Nearly 200 years on from Stendhal, these sentiments might seem odd, if not alienating. Rossini as *revolutionary*? Possessing the power and conviction of a *Napoleon*? Stendhal's statement seems so hyperbolic that we are inclined to wonder not just about Rossini but also about the personal passions and obsessions that could inspire such critical excess.

The ways in which Rossini was of his time is itself a difficult question. Stendhal's idea of the composer as a new Napoleon at least has some chronological force: the defeat of Napoleon, and the various edicts of the Congress of Vienna that accompanied it, coincided almost exactly with Rossini's rise to European fame in the years around 1813–15. These political upheavals ushered in a period commonly called the 'Restoration', which is usually seen as a misguided (or at least unsuccessful) attempt to quash the threat of renewed revolution by reinstating the eighteenth-century political status quo, in particular by restoring to power a small army of monarchs and other absolute rulers whose rights had been compromised or swept away by the French Revolution and its Napoleonic aftermath. In the context of this large, top-down restructuring of the political map, a question arises: was anything *operatic* restored in the Restoration? Was there, for example, a turning back of the operatic clock to match the counter-revolutionary edicts of the Congress of Vienna? Rossini was without doubt the operatic standard bearer of the period, and there might at first blush seem an obvious connection between operatic and political history. Move back into the Napoleonic era, and we find the unambiguous political message of an opera such as Beethoven's *Fidelio*: a work born in Napoleon's shadow, and one whose revolutionary commitment is perfectly expressed by its violent, unmediated mixing of an old-fashioned comic-opera language and a new music of libertarian commitment. Viewed in such a way, *Fidelio* has revolution writ large not only over its plot but also over its musical surface; what is more, Beethoven's complex relationship with revolutionary ideals and with Napoleon, who was the original dedicatee of his *Eroica* symphony, is very well-known. Compare this with Rossini, the man of the Restoration, whose lack of political radicalism is mirrored both by his notorious willingness to reuse comic music in serious plots and vice versa – a practice that we like to think would have been unthinkable for Beethoven – and by his inveterate tendency to drench every vocal line (never mind the sentiments it was meant to express) in hedonistic vocal ornamentation.

Whatever the force of such caricatures, there is no doubt, both for us and for audiences of the time, that the operatic Restoration period was inescapably characterized by Rossini. One of his Italian contemporaries, Giovanni Pacini, ruefully mentioned in his memoirs that, during the Rossinian heyday, everyone had to become an imitator: there was simply no other way to earn a living.[2] Rossini was born in Pesaro, on the Adriatic coast, into a family of musicians, and – after counterpoint studies in Bologna – entered at a comparatively young age into a thriving operatic tradition in northern Italy, writing mostly comic operas and farces for theatres in Milan, Rome, Bologna and, most frequently, Venice. Rossini's breakthrough to national and then international prominence came in 1813 with a comic opera, *L'italiana in Algeri* (The Italian Girl in Algiers), and a serious one, *Tancredi*, both first performed in Venice. In 1815 he moved to Naples, and there produced a sequence of serious operas including *Otello* (1816) and *La donna del lago* (The Lady of the Lake, 1819). Comic works also continued to appear, notably *Il barbiere di Siviglia* (1816) and *La*

Cenerentola (Cinderella, 1817). In terms of later reception, though, there was a crucial difference between comic and serious works. Some (not all) of the serious operas were at first popular, and were to some extent influential on the next generation. But the vogue for *Il barbiere* and *La Cenerentola* was of an altogether different order: they became and have remained stalwarts of the repertory, fixed presences in the world's opera houses ever since their first performances.

Rossini, then, was the first essential element in the gradual formation during the nineteenth century of what we now call the operatic repertory, a body of works that have been revived countless times in countless different venues. Admittedly, repertory operas of a kind had existed in previous centuries. As we have seen, some of Lully's and Rameau's operas achieved that position in seventeenth- and eighteenth-century France, as had some of Gluck's and Mozart's in several countries during the Restoration period. But, with the partial exception of Mozart's *Don Giovanni*, these works failed to maintain their currency in the nineteenth century, and were then the objects of revival in the twentieth. A crucial change, the gradual emergence of the repertory, began around the second and third decades of the nineteenth century, and its first exhibits were Rossini's comic operas, whose permanent position around the operatic globe was then equalled by a favoured few works by Bellini, Donizetti and early Verdi. By the 1840s the term 'repertory opera' was in common use in Italy and rapidly spread elsewhere; the political disruptions of 1848–9 put many theatres into such financial difficulties that they were obliged to rely increasingly on revivals of past works; the international successes of Verdi's middle-period operas, and a little later of Meyerbeer, solidified the process.

Rossini's serious operas were repertory casualties: they gradually fell away and by the end of the nineteenth century had been almost completely forgotten. In 1892, George Bernard Shaw, who might have known better, celebrated the Rossini centenary by pronouncing him 'one of the greatest masters of claptrap that ever lived',[3] and there was plenty more where that came from. So much so that, not long ago, the most common caricature of Rossini would have been of a mannered, thoroughly professional composer who, despite heroic specialist effort, was prized not for the operas that made his name in Stendhal's time but for decidedly lighter fare. Most famous of all was *Il barbiere* and its virtuoso bass aria 'Largo al factotum', which has had a rich afterlife in twentieth-century popular culture. The buffoon barber Nicki Papaloopas, mugging it in *Broadway Melody of 1938*, is one iconic example. In *The Rabbit of Seville* (1950), Chuck Jones's cartoon version, Bugs Bunny performs the aria with considerable flair. Other notable moments in Rossini's twentieth-century reception might include use of the *Barbiere* overture (which often represents a morbid but comic *italianità*, as in the Mafia movie *Prizzi's Honor*, 1985), and of course the *Guillaume Tell* (William Tell) overture, known to millions as the theme music for *The Lone Ranger* TV series of the 1950s. It is hard for those of a certain age and a certain upbringing, even if now well-educated music professionals, to hear the fast finale of that overture without a vision of the masked rider of the plains shouting 'Hi-yo, Silver!' More than this, *Il barbiere* and several other Rossini comic operas remain genuinely popular on stage. Regional producers may find themselves at odds with financial boards and audiences when they propose *Tancredi*, but *Il barbiere* has never needed special pleading.

During the later twentieth century the Rossini image became more complicated. Consider one symptom of an extraordinary revival. The Metropolitan Opera in New York performed *Semiramide* (1823), Rossini's last Italian serious opera, for three seasons in 1892–5 (Adelina Patti and then Nellie Melba sang the title role). Almost a hundred years went by before it was done again, in 1990, and its reappearance testifies to a modern Rossini industry brought into being by complex changes in operatic culture. Such works have found a place in opera houses partly because repertory spaces are now freely available. Very few new operas in the later twentieth century have awakened much lasting enthusiasm, which has encouraged delving into the past in order to refresh and expand the repertory. Rossini's serious operas have been one of the prime beneficiaries of such excavations. What is it in his brand of musical drama that was once so unacceptable and now again seems so attractive?

There are external reasons that have aided his renaissance. Rossini was entirely of his time in tailoring his music carefully to the skills of the virtuoso singers who would create any given role. In this sense, the creator of the title role in *Semiramide*, the Spanish soprano Isabella Colbran (1785–1845), who became Rossini's wife in 1822 and for whom he wrote no fewer than ten major roles, is a prime example. Colbran was notable for the power of her voice in its lower register, and also for her stage presence. Stendhal described a remarkable transformation, from the ordinary to the classically, regally poised. She had:

> noble features which, on stage, radiated majesty; an eye like that of a Circassian maiden, darting fire; and to crown it all, a true and deep instinct for tragedy. Off-stage, she possessed about as much dignity as the average milliner's assistant; but the moment she stepped on to the boards, her brow encircled with a royal diadem, she inspired involuntary respect, even among those who, a minute or two earlier, had been chattering intimately with her in the foyer of the theatre.[4]

The Rossini revival has likewise been helped by virtuoso artists interested in fresh repertory. Why did the Met in 1990 choose *Semiramide*? One strong reason was undoubtedly that they saw the opera as an excellent vehicle for one of their star singers, Marilyn Horne, whose powerful low register and formidable stage presence had by that time proved its worth in several Rossini roles. Since the 1990s, the cause of Rossini has been further enhanced by a new generation of light, agile tenors – musicians such as Juan Diego Flórez, who have not had the elasticity of their vocal cords stretched and compromised by heavier roles. And behind all such revivals lie the musicological labours that are producing a Rossini complete edition, and the large-scale business concern of a major Rossini summer festival in Pesaro, which among other things launches these editions into the world. But, to repeat, these practical endeavours would hardly suffice were there not something newly attractive for performers and audiences in the ways of Rossinian opera.

Recall for a moment that idea of Rossini as a *revolutionary*. Stendhal cast him in this role because he thought that Rossini had changed Italian music decisively. But another near contemporary put things rather differently. The Italian political activist Giuseppe Mazzini wrote a famous treatise called *Filosofia della musica* (Philosophy of Music, 1836), which claimed that:

> Rossini did not overstep the boundaries of the era that we now proclaim is dead or about to expire. The mission of his genius was to comprehend and sum up, not to initiate. He neither destroyed nor transformed the characteristics of the old Italian school, he re-consecrated them. He intro-

duced no new element to cancel or even greatly modify the old: he brought it to its highest degree of development.[5]

These two attitudes, Stendhal's and Mazzini's, sum up the dominant reactions to Rossini even today. Some, like Stendhal, see his music as injecting a whole new vitality into a tired formula, of awakening a sleeping people; others, like Mazzini, may appreciate the beauty and balance, but also hear formula, the endless repetition of predictable (albeit beguiling) conventions. A little later in his *Filosofia* Mazzini described Rossini's music as 'without shadow, without mystery, without twilight'.[6]

Can we join Mazzini in seeing Rossini as faux-Romantic, a late-late-classical composer, bringing with him a faded air of knee britches and perukes? How is Rossini's face turned towards the eighteenth century? Some of his libretti certainly look backwards, their subjects drawn from antiquity. *Semiramide* is one of them, the Oedipal story of a Babylonian queen who usurps her dead husband's throne and falls in love with her (unrecognized) adult son. Metastasio did a version of this story in the 1740s, and Gluck set it as an *opera seria*; the topic goes back to the seventeenth century, being one of the most popular libretto plots in opera's first 150 years. And yet there is also *La donna del lago*, which was derived from Walter Scott's *The Lady of the Lake* – a libretto from a Romantic novel, leading the way to *Lucia di Lammermoor* (from Scott's *The Bride of Lammermoor*), set by Donizetti two decades later.

The clearest, least ambiguous token of Rossini's bond with the eighteenth century is in the vocal range of his tragic heroes. They often have high voices. Rossini inherited this acoustic template for the male lead from the conventions of *opera seria*, and from a sound-world in which castrati impersonated princes, kings and warriors. In this sense, the year 1800 was no dividing line in Italian opera, and the preference for the high, sweet sound of a burly warrior or passionate lover did not die all at once in the era when the castrati – increasingly pitied and loathed – began at last to wane. On the contrary, things happened gradually. Up to the 1820s and 1830s composers still wrote male parts for castrati; Giovanni Battista Velluti (1780–1861), the most famous soprano castrato of the nineteenth century, was singing away into the 1820s. He figured in operas such as Rossini's *Aureliano in Palmira* (1813), and in those by now little-remembered composers such as Simon Mayr

(1763–1845), Stefano Pavesi (1779–1850) and Giuseppe Nicolini (1762–1842), all of whom bridged the eighteenth and nineteenth centuries. Giacomo Meyerbeer (1791–1864), the kingpin of French *grand opéra* for several decades from the 1830s and the subject of a later chapter, wrote a male soprano part for Velluti in his Italian opera *Il crociato in Egitto* (The Crusade in Egypt, 1824). But after the 1830s, all these gender ambiguities would be eclipsed by heroic tenors, whose high notes became ever more vociferous, and by a new fixity of voice and character types in Italian opera.

THE ROSSINIAN CODE

The names of Rossini's forgotten Italian contemporaries put the question of innovation versus regression in another light. Because opera history has so often been written as a progressive march of mutating musical forms, talking about Rossini necessarily means reviewing his use of the fixed and conventional types he shared with contemporaries and bequeathed to his followers. As discussed earlier in this book, the early eighteenth century's rigid alternation of recitative (involving dialogue and stage action) and single-movement aria (involving monologue and reflection) had already been challenged in the later decades of the century; but around the time of Rossini came the emergence of the multi-movement 'number' as the expected formal unit. The unit tended to be most predictable in Italian operas, but it formed the backbone of many works in other languages too. The number contained within it both static movements, in which the stage action stood still and characters examined their emotional states, and kinetic ones, in which new events precipitate new moods. During the early decades (longer in comic opera), continuo-accompanied recitative or spoken dialogue alternated with these numbers; but the recitative gradually became orchestrally accompanied, thus absorbed stylistically into the kinetic sections of the number.

It was probably one of the keys to Rossini's success, one reason he dominated the emerging repertory of the 1820s, that his multi-movement numbers were generally less adventurous than those of older Italians such as Mayr. Although he wasn't the inventor of such forms, in Rossini's hands a matrix of recurring formal patterns – a kind of

Rossinian code – emerged, one that would be influential through the next several decades in Italy. The standard number was the solo aria, typically made up of introductory recitative followed by three movements: a lyrical first movement, usually slow in tempo and often called the cantabile; a connecting kinetic passage stimulated by some stage event and called the *tempo di mezzo*; and a concluding cabaletta, usually faster than the first movement and usually requiring agility on the part of the singer. The grand duet and large ensemble numbers were identically shaped, although with an opening movement before the cantabile, often employing rapid, dialogue-like exchanges between the characters. The entire opera would be fashioned out of such numbers, with an occasional chorus, ensemble or single-movement aria to add variety.

The scheme as described here was not slavishly followed. Rossini's operatic solutions often differ, especially in the ensemble movements of the later Italian operas, where he was more likely to experiment. Sometimes, as in Act 2 of *Semiramide*, he would expand the range of a number by means of an 'additive' technique, making a sequence of single-movement numbers responding more immediately to the particularities of the dramatic situation. More radical still is the final act of *Otello*, a bold attempt to transpose what was then thought the Romantic subject matter of Shakespearean drama into Italian operatic terms. Fixed forms all but disappear in favour of brief atmospheric numbers, sudden contrasts and injections of local colour. But *Otello* was an extreme: more often Rossini would retain the multi-movement number but expand or inflect it. A classic case is the so-called 'terzettone' (Rossini's own term, meaning a huge *terzetto* or trio) from Act 1 of *Maometto II* (1820), in which an entire scene, with elaborate stage action, is enclosed within the usual multi-movement form.

Despite frequent manipulations, the fixed forms aided theatrical communication in two important ways. First, it gave the principal singers an elaborate, varied canvas on which to showcase their art, and thus to claim audience identification; second, it assured a level of audience expectation that could then be harnessed to dramatic effect. The same could be said of some signature Rossinian devices that make his music instantly recognizable: the energetic rhythms of his orchestral themes, typically with dotted rhythms and unexpected accents; or his delicately sentimental, finely balanced lyrical melodies. These often appear together in his overtures, with a sentimental melody in the slow introduction and a distinctive rhythmic idea as the first main melody. The overture is also a prime site for the most famous Rossinian device of all, the 'Rossini crescendo', in which a section of eight or sixteen bars will be repeated again and again, each time with increased orchestration and dynamic level. In these crescendi, repetition was clearly part of the pleasure: the fact that everyone knew at the start how a crescendo would develop enhanced anticipation and visceral effect rather than dampened it.

TANCREDI

This talk of form and characteristic devices can explain only an element of Rossini's unprecedented success: it's entirely typical of the age in which he was writing that Stendhal hardly mentions form in his preposterously lengthy and exhaustive book on the composer. To go deeper, we need to look closely at some music, and a good place to start is in northern Italy in 1813, the year of Rossini's first great serious opera, *Tancredi*, premiered at Venice's Teatro La Fenice. Based on a play by Voltaire written in 1760, *Tancredi* is set in the eleventh century, the time of the crusades. The hero, Tancredi, has the usual anguished relationship with the heroine, Amenaide (he believes her unfaithful but in fact she is being forced into a political marriage). Rossini revised the opera for performances in Ferrara just weeks after the Venetian premiere. Near the end of Act 2 of the revised version, Tancredi confronts Amenaide and tells her to go to the camp of his rival:

AMENAIDE Ecco amici Tancredi.
ARGIRIO Tancredi . . .
TANCREDI Il nome mio . . .
Tu qui? Perfida! e vai
Di Solamiro al campo?

AMENAIDE Oh! mio Tancredi, esci d'errore omai . . .

TANCREDI Taci, è vano quel pianto, orror mi fai.
(ai cavalieri)

Sì, con voi pugnerò, con voi; la patria
Salverò col mio sangue. Il mio destino
Si compia allor.
(ad Amenaide)
T'invola!
Penai, piansi per te, lo sai, lo vedi:
Vanne, infedele, morto è per te Tancredi.

[AMENAIDE: Here, friends, is Tancredi. ARGIRIO: Tancredi . . . TANCREDI: My name . . . You, here? Betrayer! And you go to Salamiro's camp? AMENAIDE: Oh! my Tancredi, be in error no longer . . . TANCREDI: Silence, your tears are in vain, you disgust me. *(to the cavaliers)* Yes, I will fight with you, with you; I will save the fatherland with my blood. My destiny is now completed. *(to Amenaide)* Be gone! I suffered, I wept for you; you know it, you see it: go, unfaithful one, Tancredi is dead to you.]

From this brief excerpt we can recognize the recitative verse typical of the previous century and earlier: a free mixture of seven- and eleven-syllable lines, some of them split between the characters. The music of this recitative is orchestrally accompanied, but for the most part is similar to the old, eighteenth-century, continuo-accompanied variety. It has a few rhythmic gestures to round off verbal statements, one sustained chord to add pathos to Amenaide's lamenting 'Oh! mio Tancredi', and some martial arpeggios when Tancredi addresses the *cavalieri*. The vocal lines are entirely formulaic except for one flourish from Tancredi near the end. This section is, in other words, almost entirely preparatory. In the minimum of musical time and space, it explains the emotional and physical motivations of the principals, the performers who are about to drench us in song.

The set piece that follows begins with a solo for Tancredi; it is called a Rondò (a name that suggests a complicated and highly ornamented end-piece). As we've now come to expect, the text becomes more rhythmically measured and predictable, and also more poetically high-flown:

TANCREDI
Perché turbar la calma
Di questo cor, perché?

Non sai che questa calma
È figlia del dolor!

[Why disturb the calm / of this heart, why? / Do you not know that this calm / is the child of sorrow!]

This first musical section is in two parts, in both of which there is a complete statement of the text, with internal repetitions. In the first part, as is common with Rossini, the words are clearly declaimed, with a simple orchestral accompaniment and relatively little vocal ornamentation except at the close of phrases. The second part begins with a notable change: it is dominated by chugging accompaniment rhythms and by the insistent repetition of a little descending figure in the orchestra, one whose ending 'sigh' figure is perhaps intended as an illustration of the supplication in the text's question. But then the chugging and the 'sigh' figure stop and ornamented declamation resumes. Look at the text one more time: 'Do you not know that this calm is the child of sorrow?' Tancredi's formulation encapsulates the idea that deep emotion is hidden beneath a serene surface – a poetic formula that might be taken as almost a summary of the Rossinian musical aesthetic.

We might stand back and ask our own questions about this perfect melodiousness. What it lacks – despite its tremendous beauty – is any heroic quality in the modern sense, any feeling that the voice-character is afflicted by an unbearable sorrow that, in an act of self-control, is being kept under the very musical wraps that give it expression. Instead, there is something more like a state of musical dissociation, in which the voice-character has retreated from distress to a calm that has, despite the poetic metaphor, no musical implications of harnessing sorrow or despair. A passage like this is far more disquieting than the musically cheery cabaletta that closes the Act 3 'mad scene' in *Lucia di Lammermoor*, where we have insanity to explain the space between what the libretto asserts and what the music does with that assertion. Many a sceptical Rossinian (particularly those of a forward-looking stamp) echoed this sense of dissociation, even when the operas were in vogue. Mazzini again: 'The music expresses decided passions, energetically felt – anger, sorrow, love, vengeance, joy, desperation – and all are defined in such a manner that the soul who hears them is entirely passive'.[7]

Tancredi's Rondò has, though, further revelations, demonstrating that vocal flourishes can attain added meaning in dramatic circumstances. The poised first section comes to a gentle close, and then, quite suddenly, Tancredi becomes angry with Amenaide, driving her to tears. But he also falls prey to doubt: is she the traitor he thought? Doubt leads to remorse, but then there is more action as the chorus enters to remind Tancredi that he is supposed to be on his way to war. Now he's completely confused: 'Ove son io?' (Where am I?) he laments. He is torn between two ideas, between articulating his pain and charging into battle with the chorus.

> Traditrice, io t'abbandono
> Al rimorso, al tuo rossore;
> Vendicar saprà l'amore
> La tua nera infedeltà.
> Ma tu piangi . . . gemi . . . piangi . . .
> Forse? . . . oh! dio! tu . . .
>
> CHORUS Vieni al campo.
> TANCREDI Ove son io!

[Betrayer I leave you / to remorse, to your shame; / love will know now to avenge / your black infidelity. / But you are weeping . . . shuddering . . . weeping . . . / Why? . . . oh God! You! . . . CHORUS: Come to the battlefield. TANCREDI: Where am I!]

This incursion of the chorus stimulates a change of tempo (from Andantino to Allegro), a sudden modulation, a musical transition. The orchestra gains motive force, repeating some of those martial arpeggios we located in the opening recitative. Tancredi moves back to simpler declamation, with few ornaments. But as he sees Amenaide's tears another modulation – and another, more lyrically expressive orchestral melody – intervenes. The martial chorus then closes the section by again taking over the musical action. The contrast between 'Perché turbar la calma' and this new passage is enormous. The first four lines, which were about pain, represented passivity but are subject to ever-increasing ornamental flights. In the music that starts at 'Traditrice', it is as if the pull of pure song is warring with the pull of pure action. Ornament has become a symptom, betraying the degree to which action is making its claim.

It is clearly possible to describe Tancredi's Rondò in these terms – as a form being invented in response to textual prompts and a particular dramatic impasse. But this description would conceal something important about the formula at work – the slow lyric verses of 'Perché turbar la calma', the dramatic turn that pulls the character away from self-pity, and the more agitated and repeated peroration of 'Traditrice, io t'abbandono'. A particular formula is being codified and (in Mazzini's word) re-consecrated. In terms of the patterns mentioned earlier, the music so far would constitute the first two movements of a multi-movement aria, with 'Perché turbar la calma' the reflective cantabile and 'Traditrice' the kinetic *tempo di mezzo*, the traditional call to action in which stage action and orchestrally dominated textures are the norm.

To complete the formula, the final movement is a cabaletta:

Non sa comprendere
Il mio dolor
Chi in petto accendersi
Non sa d'amor.
Sì: la patria si difenda;
Io vi guido a trionfar.

[No one can know / my sorrow / who kindling in their breast / does not know love. / Yes: we must defend the homeland; / I lead you to triumph.]

As usual, the cabaletta is in two musical stanzas. The first sets the opening four lines of text and is remarkably simple and untroubled, dissolving into rapid figuration towards the end. The final two lines then underpin another martial interlude as Tancredi revives his warlike intentions. Then the first four lines are repeated for the second stanza, this time with the addition of the chorus and with (one assumes) ornamentation invented by the singer. A rousing coda brings the entire number to an end. As mentioned earlier, the power of such recurring formal schemes (they might also be called recurring rhetorical patterns) will be clear over at least two further generations of Italian opera composers; the three-movement pattern of lyrical cantabile, action-injected, orchestrally dominated *tempo di mezzo* and florid two-verse cabaletta will be summoned as the model for the majority of operatic numbers. But the essential point is not that this is a presumption against which every number should dutifully be measured. Rather, it is that such predictable shapes could and should be forgotten; they became commonplace and thus unremarkable, allowing the artifice of opera to communicate through singing.

More interesting for us today is this number's aesthetic strangeness, the 'virginal artlessness' (Stendhal's famous phrase, 'candeur virginale')[8] or what Mazzini called 'without shadow'. For today's audiences, the image of a suffering human character bathed in untroubled melodic perfection, controlled and represented by the fine art of singing, may seem exceedingly mannered. And while the intense control required of the performer in Tancredi's cantabile and cabaletta – the soft singing, the orchestra whispering that allows every ornamental turn to be heard in the cantabile, the streams of semiquavers in the cabaletta – could be read as symbolic, reflecting Tancredi's own command of himself, it now also engenders a sense of estrangement between the fictional character and his musical representation. Rossini so seldom wrote vocal moments in which, according to our present aesthetic, real musical pathos and desperate emotion break through, so much so that the few passages which attempt this register risk standing out as alien and disquieting.

Such alien pathos is certainly present in the last moments of this, the Ferrara version of the *Tancredi* finale. While the original finale had an improbable happy ending, now the hero dies in Amenaide's arms to a final, recitative-like passage whose free-flowing shape and unbridled agony could have been part of Gluckian reform opera. What stands out is the degree to which these last, tragic bars are not reliant on the pleasures of virtuoso display – Tancredi's vocal line is in one sense child's play to sing, its range no more than an octave in the low to middle part of the voice. Given the restraint, it is no surprise that this version has found great favour with modern commentators (and is usually preferred in performance). At the time when Rossini wrote it, though, matters were more contested. One contemporary critic reported that 'The new scene and aria for Malanotte [this is Tancredi's Rondò] were much appreciated, but not the death of Tancredi, there introduced, to which the Public is unwilling to adapt itself.'[9] As if echoing this rejection, there were no further performances of the Ferrara finale until very recently. Audiences continued to enjoy the original, Venice version, or further revisions that Rossini made, one of which had a spectacular florid aria for Tancredi and a spectacular florid duet for Tancredi and Amenaide.

Early nineteenth-century audiences can come off badly in this tale of rejected tragedy – particularly so when their excesses in praise of the two female singers are included. At the original, emphatically *non*-tragic Venice performances, for example, a critic reported on the final night of the run:

> Although poetic tributes are often nothing but the children of individual enthusiasts, the profusion and variety offered on many consecutive evenings to the distinguished singers Malanotte [Tancredi] and Manfredini [Amenaide] – accompanied by the usual throwing of pigeons and canaries, and, on this last evening, a garland of flowers descending from on high escorted by two artificial pigeons – showed how impatient the audience was to demonstrate, with these and other means, the general feeling of rapture.[10]

Such an account may encourage some to feel superior about the past, taking pride in the fact that the tragic Ferrara version has rediscovered Voltaire in all its simplicity and spare emotional appeal. The original Venice version was, after all, celebrated by bouquets of flowers lowered from the ceiling on the backs of fake pigeons. But the sheer extravagance of those artificial birds could tell another and more positive story about the enthusiasms of this particular celebration, of an audience whose sense of wonder in the face of vocal virtuosity is something that we can no longer retrieve in the same flamboyant and creative manner.

So perhaps there is a moral here, and a moral that doesn't congratulate so automatically our contemporary preference for spare tragedy. Perhaps Rossini's audiences – ostentatiously favouring the more vocally resplendent, non-tragic end to *Tancredi* – celebrated something valuable to them and invisible to us: that, rather than being dissociated or bizarre, it is extraordinarily sensual, even erotic, when passion is kept at a distance and sublimated in melody. Allowing fictional high emotions to mesh seamlessly with their musical representation – as in the tragic finale, which was both avant-garde and retrospective – means losses as well as gains.

AUDIENCES, ORNAMENTS

The differing reactions to *Tancredi*'s finales might lead us to ask why and how audiences attended opera in Italy and elsewhere during the Restoration. Think of all those composers, in countless small towns up and down the peninsula, turning out operas very like Rossini's in terms of libretto subjects and musical forms; or recall Pacini's statement earlier, that this was the only way to earn a living. Or consider all those operas, performed repeatedly during a given season, with audience members – particularly the wealthy and aristocratic – owning or renting boxes and using them primarily as social spaces. Stendhal was adamant that devotees could watch a Rossini opera countless times without becoming bored, and other reports confirm that the experience, particularly of famous singers repeating famous arias, could be soothingly ritualistic. When you attend the same work time after time the piece per se, if it was ever in the foreground of your consciousness, begins to recede. What you notice is the performance: the way a singer negotiates a particular difficulty or does things differently, renewing or failing to renew some improvised ornaments. Under these conditions, can the more modern theatrical ideal of total operatic fusion possibly exist? Can the singer become the character, and the music become a seamless flow from a fictional soul to an enraptured audience? For its early viewers, the most stirring aspect of Tancredi's aria may have been that a favourite singer was singing it, one whose presence was enjoyed night after night. One way to understand Rossini's aesthetic is that it simply prepares the ground for this situation and ensures that nothing interferes with the endlessly ornamented melodiousness emerging from vocal display.

We could go further and insist that the experience of Rossini's (or anyone else's) operas has never been uniform. To proclaim with moral certainty that one musical solution to a particular plot situation is dramatically superior to another, regardless of performance, is hazardous. In Honoré de Balzac's story *Massimilla Doni* (1839), a performance of Rossini's *Mosè in Egitto* (Moses in Egypt, 1818) figures in the plot. The scene is set at La Fenice in Venice, in a box where an Italian duchess (the protagonist Massimilla Doni) and a prince – the two are secretly in love – have been joined by a French physician. The characters give vivid expression to the ways in which Rossini could be experienced, and loved or hated. The duchess, an articulate partisan, praises every note in a blow-by-blow commentary delivered to her companions during the performance:

> But the lovers are suddenly interrupted by the exultant voice of the Hebrew people in the distance. . . . 'What a delightful and inspiriting *allegro* is the

> theme of this march, as the Israelites set out for the desert! No one but Rossini can make wind instruments and trumpets say so much. And is not the art that can express in two phrases all that is meant by the "native land" certainly nearer to heaven than the others? This clarion-call always moves me so deeply that I cannot find words to tell you how cruel it is to an enslaved people to see those who are free march away!' The duchess's eyes filled with tears as she listened to the grand movement, which in fact crowns the opera.

This tells us that even the most rapt nineteenth-century listener felt inclined to talk, albeit quietly, during the music. But the duchess's rhapsody is interrupted by an onstage contretemps:

> 'But what is the matter? The pit is dissatisfied!' 'Genovese is braying like an ass,' replied the prince.
>
> In point of fact, this first duet with la Tinti was spoilt by Genovese's utter breakdown. His excellent method, recalling that of Crescentini and Velluti, seemed to desert him completely. A *sostenuto* in the wrong place, an embellishment carried to excess, spoilt the effect; or again a loud climax with no due *crescendo*, an outburst of sound like water tumbling through a suddenly opened sluice, showed complete and wilful neglect of the laws of good taste. The pit was in the greatest excitement. The Venetian public believed there was a deliberate plot between Genovese and his friends. La Tinti was recalled and applauded with frenzy while Genovese had a hint or two warning him of the hostile feeling of the audience.

Audiences become unruly and even louder when voices fail: even the duchess cannot sustain her absorption in Rossini's genius under these circumstances. This interruption gives the French doctor, already accused of rationalism and lack of soul, his chance to criticize the music:

> During this scene, highly amusing to a Frenchman, while la Tinti was recalled eleven times to receive alone the frantic acclamations of the house – Genovese, who was all but hissed, not daring to offer her his hand – the doctor made a remark to the duchess about the *stretto* [i.e. the cabaletta] of the duet. 'In this place,' said he, 'Rossini ought to have expressed the deepest grief, and I find on the contrary an airy movement, a tone of ill-timed cheerfulness.' 'You are right,' said she. 'This mistake is the result of

> a tyrannous custom which composers are expected to obey. He was thinking more of his prima donna than of Elcia [the character] when he wrote that *stretto*. But this evening, even if la Tinti had not been more brilliant than ever, I could throw myself so completely into the situation, that the passage, lively as it is, is to me full of sadness.'
>
> The physician looked attentively from the prince to the duchess, but could not guess the reason that held them apart, and that made this duet seem to them so heartrending.

Balzac's French doctor has couched his critique of a Rossinian cabaletta in terms almost identical to ours, and even a fanatical partisan like the duchess not only agrees, but identifies the convention as driven by the virtuosi. Most telling of all, her ability to 'throw herself in the situation' – despite the music's 'cheerfulness' – is in the end dictated by a social situation utterly divorced from Rossini's work or its performance: the proximity of her lover, the prince.

Balzac's description also reminds us about the role that ornament and general vocal decoration played in Rossini performances. Singers in the eighteenth century had been expected to improvise ornaments freely, and this practice continued (albeit gradually diminishing) into the middle of the nineteenth century and beyond. There's an old story, often repeated, about how Rossini heard his music treated to liberal ornament by a singer of the old, eighteenth-century school (as it happened, a castrato) and vowed from that moment on always to write out in full all his vocal decorations. This neat tale has now been discredited: although the earliest Rossini operas have fewer written-out decorations, there was no sudden shift in style. There's no doubt, though, that Rossini's tendency to notate vocal ornamentation in such detail was a significant sign of the times. It showed how important he thought this aspect of vocal performance was; but it also illustrates how performers gradually lost their creative rights in the nineteenth century. Notation became ever more detailed, and singers were increasingly expected merely to obey the (all-powerful) composer's instructions. We will hear more about this development as the century progresses.

Rossini's written-out ornaments are born not merely from a desire to control performers in a much-loved activity. Behind all the magnificent flowing forth of vocal sound is a kind of aesthetic constant, the fact that Rossini continued stubbornly to believe in the singing voice as the means whereby beauty and expressiveness are finally linked. The fact that so many of his melodies are festooned with so many notes is a trait that can seem, particularly if our operatic centre of gravity is located elsewhere, mechanical and even superficial. But for Rossini and his adoring public this florid writing, the endless gruppetti, trills and roulades, were not *ornament* in the modern sense, not decorations of a basic melody lying underneath. Rather, they were the very means by which beautiful melody could communicate its special message. Those long, lovingly crafted strings of wordless notes *were* expression. Stendhal summed this up near the end of his book on the composer. Rossini's music, he admitted, was 'perpetually slithering over the brink into the echoing abyss of concert-platform virtuosity'; but it also 'brings us every day nearer to a state of mind in which, eventually, we may deserve to hear the accents of *genuine passion*'.[11]

AFTER *TANCREDI*

After *Tancredi*, Rossini's success was assured. He went on to write around thirty more operas, both serious and comic, the Italian phase of his career culminating with *Semiramide*. He then moved to Paris, the Mecca of so many successful Italian composers, and switched to writing operas in French. The last of his French-language works, the grand opera *Guillaume Tell* (1829), is a piece Stendhal couldn't know when he published his biography in 1824. It's extraordinary, quite unlike the Italian operas – so much so that we will defer discussion to a later chapter. But after *Guillaume Tell* the 37-year-old Rossini stopped composing operas; he lived on for almost forty years, in Bologna, then Florence, then Paris, a noted raconteur and gourmand (there is a famous recipe named for him, 'tournedos Rossini', an extravagantly rich dish involving filet mignon, foie gras and black truffles). Why did he give up? Certainly he had achieved financial security and was released from continually writing new works. But it was also significant that the years around 1829 saw the emergence of new, more forthright modes of Italian opera, modes he had no wish to emulate.

So Rossini simply called a halt to writing operas. In later life he wrote some exquisite religious pieces such as the *Stabat mater* (1831) and the *Petite messe solennelle* (1864), and he entertained his Parisian salon with instrumental and vocal miniatures playfully called *Péchés de vieillesse* (Sins of Old Age). Among the most poignant of the latter are multiple settings for voice and piano of an ancient text by Metastasio, 'Mi lagnerò tacendo della mia sorte amara' (I lament in silence my bitter fate), surely a coded commentary on his long silence, delicately poised, as always, between the ironic and the sentimental. His choice of Metastasio for these 'confessional' statements makes more pressing a question posed earlier: which way was Rossini's face turned? To the eighteenth century with its Arcadian coolness, or to the vaguer but emotionally more explicit Romantic future? In later life, while composing his *Péchés*, he sometimes lamented modern operatic taste, saying that the rot had set in with the departure of the castrati, singers whose bodies were mutilated in the search for some ideal of vocal purity. There are other obvious points of continuity with the eighteenth century in Rossini's music: the farcical action ensembles in the comic operas; the similarity to Mozartian practice in his orchestral taste. One of the chief ways in which the next generation of Italian composers distinguished themselves from him (and were duly criticized for so doing) was in their 'noisy' orchestration, although some earlier critics had accused Rossini of the same sin. Rossini kept a bust of Mozart on top of his bedroom clock in later life, and routinely mentioned him in adulatory terms, often as the genius who had overcome the Italian–German opposition. He was reported as saying that 'we Southerners have been beaten on our own ground, for [Mozart] rises above both nations: he combines the whole magic of Italy's cantilena with German's profound heartfelt inwardness'; but the reporter of this was a German composer (Emil Naumann, 1827–88), and that 'profound heartfelt inwardness' may have been his own gloss.[12] On the other hand, the Mozartian influence in his compositional maturity is mostly superficial – there may be an aesthetic similarity in the way melodic inspiration was born, but not in how that inspiration was subsequently developed. Rossini by temperament always avoided the degree of harmonic and orchestral elaboration to which Mozart was forever drawn.

The difference between Mozart and Rossini is worth pursuing. Mozart's Italian operas were occasionally revived in Italy during the first half of the nineteenth century, and were generally thought extraordinarily difficult – both melancholy and bewilderingly dense, too full of harmonic, contrapuntal and orchestral detail. As we saw in the previous chapter, his and certain other works (Weber's *Der Freischütz* in particular) fuelled endless debates about German vs Italian opera. For the Italians (and Rossini was emphatically on their side, although he made an exception for Mozart) German opera composers were unpleasantly dominated by harmony and complex orchestration: their theatrical works might have been for orchestra alone with optional voices. An important early writer on Rossini, Giuseppe Carpani, shared the composer's taste, and put it this way in 1824:

> If, then, the composer has the most beautiful poetic text to set to music, he must not treat it in so servile a way that he loses sight of his chief duty, which is to offer *musical* delight. Expression should therefore be his second objective, and he should always treat musical thought, or the *cantilena*, as his primary aim, as the *sine qua non* of his science. I challenge the most ardent supporter of *Gluck* to argue differently. . . .
>
> Music that is not allied to, but is a slave to, the word; music of bumps, of clashes, of caprices which, dragged along by the varying progress of the passions, scarcely permits you the hint of a tight-laced and foreshortened song, whose ups and downs seem like the sea in a storm: song that is not song, but the uninterrupted wish for song – in a word, something like *Fidelio* by Beethoven . . . orchestral declamation, scattered here and there with fine points of light, but never an opera, because song wishes to be where music lays its claim.[13]

There could be no better summing-up of the Rossinian code, a code in which words must always be subservient to music, and in which wordless aesthetic pleasure is the goal. In a similar manner, Weber's symbolic orchestral effects, the notion that the orchestra might 'speak', was ridiculed by Stendhal: why, he asked, should you need the orchestra to tell you what the singing voice should convey? Stendhal even had a theory about the origins of these national differences: 'the German, who is indebted to the icy climate of the North for a coarser physical fibre, will require his music to be *noisier*; and further, this same cold . . . conspired with the absence of wine to deprive him of a singing voice'.[14] These polemics, set in increased motion by the Rossinian vogue, would circulate around opera throughout the nineteenth century, although elevated opinion shifted decisively to the German camp as the decades rolled on.

Rossini's serious Italian operas, which were the purest example of the vocal ideal, became casualties in the long march of progress.

But his comic operas survived and even prospered. What is it about Rossini that allowed him to stamp his comic vision so permanently on the operatic firmament? Probably the work closest to Mozart, both musically and in spirit, was also among the most successful. *La Cenerentola* has, like *Il barbiere*, maintained a hold on the public imagination ever since the period of its first performance, with only a slight hiatus in the earlier twentieth century when its mezzo-soprano heroine proved difficult to cast. It was first performed in Rome in 1817, following the premiere of *Il barbiere* in that city the year before. Its retelling of the Cinderella story is immediately striking and significant. There are none of the magic elements that characterize Charles Perrault's famous version of the tale (no fairy godmother, no pumpkin and mice turned into coach and horses, no glass slipper). In *La Cenerentola*, the neglected heroine is persecuted by her sisters and step*father* (a down-at-heel aristocrat, ironically named Don Magnifico, *buffo* bass), who is primarily driven by financial need; her transformation into the bride of a handsome young prince (Don Ramiro, tenor) is effected by the prince's tutor, a rationalist philosopher called Alidoro (bass). There are the usual comic-opera extras, a servant much savvier than his master, etc.; but the dominant tone – and here the connection to Mozart is strongest – is of sentimental comedy or, perhaps more apt, of comedy with an edge.

Strangely, given the opera's popularity and his enthusiasm for most things Rossinian, Stendhal voiced persistent doubts about *La Cenerentola*, which he aired at length and with a gusto bordering on the *méchant*. With a fine display of liberal leaning, for example, he suggested that a likely explanation for the opera's defects was to be found in the venue of its première: written expressly for the citizens of Rome, it catered to those 'from whose manners every trace of dignity and refinement has been banished by three centuries of Papal government'.[15] His central objection – to a lack of *idealism* in the score, a certain coldness and absence of heart – was less fanciful. As he summed it up, 'I doubt whether there are really ten bars on end that wholly escape the taint of the sordid little backrooms in the rue Saint Denis or the fat financier intoxicated with gold and banal ideas.'[16] What had gone wrong, one wonders: from 'candeur virginale' to the squalor of the rue Saint Denis in the four years that separate *Tancredi* and *La Cenerentola*?

One aspect of *La Cenerentola* is a heroine who, unusually for Rossini, alters markedly in vocal character as her dramatic situation changes. At the start, treated as a simple scullery maid by her sisters and stepfather, she sings a wistful, minor-key melody, 'Una volta c'era un re' (Once upon a time, there was a king). There is no trace of vocal ornamentation in this sad fantasy: it has a directness of melodic appeal that recalls folk music, and is notably un-Rossinian in its simplicity. The theme, which recurs several times as a symbol of Cenerentola's desolation, was clearly part of Stendhal's problem. He found it moving, but in a completely predictable manner: 'the song of Cinderella . . . contains a few "touching" passages, but they are to be classed with those similar "touching" scenes that form so indispensable a part of our good old middle-class melodrama, where the audience is driven to weep hot tears by the very commonplaceness of the misfortunes'.[17] When Cenerentola meets her prince for the first time, she assumes a more conventional vocal persona in the love-at-first-sight duet 'Io vorrei saper perché', but the novelty of the situation still keeps her vocal line unusually simple by Rossinian standards. Again Stendhal was unimpressed, judging that 'the pretty impertinence of the music is still somewhat reminiscent of some little milliner from the rue Vivienne'.[18] By the time of the heroine's final aria ('Nacqui all'affanno'), however, she is fully in command of the stage, and carries all before her in a torrent of vocal ornamentation. Only now does Stendhal admit that, for him, there is 'a flash of sincerity and real emotion'.[19]

One could see this accumulation of vocal virtuosity, which occurs as Cenerentola is transformed into a princess, in very simple terms: of a character growing up musically as she does so emotionally. But another way, perhaps nearer the spirit of Rossinian drama, is to see her emergence as marked by a gradual release from the word and a simultaneous embrace of the musical. The clear emotional message and sense of character of her opening, folk-like melody has, by the end of the opera, been overturned – transformed into something far less personal, far more a celebration of music itself. In line with this reading is the curious silence of the other characters at the end of the opera. We expect, of all things, a comedy to end with reconciliation, a tying of loose ends. But just before Cenerentola's virtuosic conclusion in 'Nacqui all'affanno' there is a curiously blank exchange between her and her father. Seeing her now-elevated state, Don Magnifico attempts rapprochement of a kind (or at least to ingratiate himself with a newly powerful figure) by abjectly falling on his knees before her. This could have engendered a transforming musical gesture, one to recall the Count kneeling before the Countess at the end of Mozart's *Figaro*. But the moment virtually disappears. Cenerentola answers her father in simple recitative:

DON MAGNIFICO	Altezza... a voi si prostra...
CENERENTOLA	Né mai udrò chiamar la figlia vostra?

[DON MAGNIFICO: Your highness... I bow before you...
CENERENTOLA: Will I never hear you call me your daughter?]

And then there is silence; Don Magnifico does not reply. The recitative continues on its stately progress towards Cenerentola's closing aria. Even the handsome prince Don Ramiro has no closure, no moment marking his partnership with the new, elaborately singing character to whom he is now joined. True, everyone sings together in the closing ensemble, but their contributions are merely those of an undifferentiated chorus. Modern producers, who like visual and verbal closure, are often unhappy or uneasy with these final moments. What are the other characters supposed to *do*? The answer is simple, and ignores the niceties of dramatic motivation. These theatrical supernumeraries are, at base, merely supposed to listen – to admire an abstract ideal of musical beauty, vocal beauty, as it unfolds before them in Cenerentola's voice.

Another revealing episode, similar in its combination of loss of communication followed by elaborate musical celebration, occurs in Act I. Alidoro arrives at Don Magnifico's house to invite all marriageable females to the prince's castle for selection. His list says that there are three daughters here, but Don Magnifico corrects him:

ALIDORO

Qui nel mio codice
Delle zitelle,
Con Don Magnifico
Stan tre sorelle.
Or che va il Principe

La sposa a scegliere
La terza fliglia
Io vi domando.

DON MAGNIFICO

Che terza figlia
Mi vai figliando?

ALIDORO

Terza sorella

DON MAGNIFICO

Ella morì.

ALIDORO

Eppur nel codice
Non è così.

CENERENTOLA

(Ah, di me parlano!)
(Ponendosi in mezzo, con ingenuità)
Non, non morì.

DON MAGNIFICO

Sta zitto lì.
Guardate qui.
(Balzandola in un cantone)

RAMIRO, DANDINI

Dunque, morì?

DON MAGNIFICO

(dopo un momento di silenzio)
Altezza, sì.

[ALIDORO: In my list / of unmarried women, / with Don Magnifico / there live three sisters. / Now that the Prince / is going to choose a bride, / I ask you for your third daughter. DON MAGNIFICO: What third daughter / do you want to put on me? ALIDORO: The third sister. DON MAGNIFICO:

She died. ALIDORO: Yet it doesn't say that / on the list. CENERENTOLA: (Ah! They're talking about me!) (*Placing herself between them, and ingenuously*) No, she didn't die. DON MAGNIFICO: Be quiet there. / Look here. (*Pushing her into a corner*) RAMIRO, DANDINI: So then, she died? DON MAGNIFICO *(after a moment of silence):* Your Highness, yes.]

In the libretto, with its rapid rhymes and pit-a-pat lines, one could easily imagine this exchange flying by as passable comedy, and Rossini's setting up to the last line is indeed in this vein, with simple, triadic melodic lines and one of his trademark incisive orchestral melodies. The tone is maintained even for Cenerentola's 'ingenuous' contradiction of her own death. But then, quite unexpectedly, Don Magnifico's last line sees a striking change of orchestral rhythm, with sinister death figures (an imitation of funeral drums) in the strings, a precipitate turn to the minor mode, a slowly descending chromatic line and a solemn close. What are we to make of this? What are the characters supposed to be feeling as this solemn orchestral moment sounds out? Are they emotionally implicated in this doleful music and sudden change of tone, or is it meant purely for the listener? None of these questions is answered by what follows. There is a long pause, which prepares for yet another favourite Rossinian device, a quintet of mutual confusion. Another enigma is created by an excess of Rossinian music, a deluge of sound that seems to overwhelm the characters.

So once again the question, why the vogue for Rossini now? Why are there today more of his operas in the repertory than ever before? As we said, there are practical reasons: the international festival at Pesaro; the presence, there and elsewhere, of major singers who feel suited to the demands of the roles. However, and particularly with those strange moments from *La Cenerentola* in mind, a cynic might find no surprises in Rossini as a perfect composer for the second half of the twentieth century, just as he was for the Restoration period. What must it have felt like for Italians in 1815? A decade earlier they had emerged bewigged from an eighteenth century in which they had been governed by despots (Enlightened or otherwise) worthy of Metastasio, to find themselves, suddenly and by force of arms, in the bright light of a Napoleonic dawn. Their laws, their world views and certainties were shattered. But then, in 1815, Napoleon was defeated and back came the despots, their costumes a little shabbier, their authority and grip on power more fragile, but in charge again. Was it possible to reverse the clock, to put Pandora back in the box? With these kinds of questions in the air, and with a prevailing uncertainty about even such basic beliefs as the existence of one's nation, it may suddenly seem apt that the characteristic musical voice of the age was owned by Gioachino Rossini, with his ambiguous emotions and his Janus face, at once turned back to the past and forward to the future. But now, nearly two centuries on? One reason might be that we have freed ourselves, or at least established some distance from, the later nineteenth century's operatic ways, with its 'music of bumps, of clashes, of caprices'. With the help of that distance, we can once again take pleasure in mellifluous, well-behaved tragedy; and, more important, we can relish anew the ambiguities and manic escapism, the energy and ornament and sheer musical allure that Rossini so unfailingly brought to operatic drama.

9
The tenor comes of age

In May 1911, at the bottom of the world, a party of Antarctic explorers must devise a way to wake the Watch in the dead of night. They were men sent out on a mission to Cape Adare by Robert Falcon Scott, whose bid for the South Pole was to end in disaster in March 1912. The Cape Adare group had forgotten their alarm clock, and a reward was offered to the man who could invent a substitute that was both shocking and sure. The winner constructed a device called the Carusophone:

> At midnight, the latest member of the party turned in, and before doing so lighted the candle on the 'Carusophone'. This then burnt steadily for two hours while all hands slept the sleep of the just, until at two o'clock . . . the thread which passed through the wick was burnt through. Then the bamboo spring, released by the breaking of the thread, sprang back and pulled the starting-lever of the gramophone. The plate and record then commenced to revolve, increasing in speed little by little to the accompaniment of a noise which bordered on the infernal, and was at first calculated to wake the whole party. . . . The record which performed this honourable duty every night [was] the 'Flower Song' from *Carmen*, sung by Signor Caruso, not, I am afraid, because of our classical taste in music, but because it was the loudest we possessed.[1]

This anecdote, besides documenting the ingeniousness of the British navy, gives voice to several operatic truths. Enrico Caruso (1873–1921) was *the* great operatic star of early sound recording, famous for a clear, piercing tone that cut through any and all acoustic undergrowth. The voice type Caruso possessed, that of the Italian heroic tenor, was loud in ways that transcend sheer decibels – somehow it has more volume than all the dance tunes, sentimental songs and military favourites otherwise preferred by Antarctic explorers. When this kind of tenor hits a high note – generally defined as anything higher than the A above middle C – and hits it in chest voice (that is, without a hint of falsetto), the resulting acoustic explosion is a force of nature that would come to represent overwhelming male passion. This voice type is now regarded as quintessential, the prerequisite for phenomena like the Three Tenors and Andrea Bocelli, for the caricature of Italian opera as a tussle between sopranos and tenors competing on the high wire, and for so many more givens of the genre in legend and song. But we have to remember that this heroic tenor voice did not exist until the nineteenth century. The coming of that voice, and the special ground prepared for it within new operas of the 1830s and 1840s, were one of those seismic events that pepper operatic history.

An emerging new tenor voice coincided with Gioachino Rossini's farewell to operatic composition in 1829, not yet in his forties and at the height of his European fame. Rossini, we should recall, wrote only a single part for a heroic tenor, and that was in a French grand opera, *Guillaume Tell*. The roster of operas at Milan's La Scala in 1829, however, demonstrates that both his serious and his comic operas still dominated the repertory. The Carnival season, which started on 26 December 1828, opened as always with a serious opera – his *L'assedio di Corinto* (The Siege of Corinth, first performed, as *Le Siège de Corinthe*, in Paris in 1826, although itself a remake of an earlier Italian opera, *Maometto II*); the very next opera to appear was his *Zelmira* (Naples, 1822); his early *Demetrio e Polibio* (Rome, 1812) was also part of the season. Later in the year, three of his comic operas, *Il barbiere di Siviglia* (1816), *La pietra del paragone* (The Touchstone, Milan, 1812) and *La gazza ladra* (The Thieving Magpie, Milan, 1817) were also revived. No other composer came remotely close to his total of six operas in the year. What is more, this dominance could be repeated almost everywhere that opera was performed. There was continuing Rossini fever in the major capitals of Europe, such as London, Paris and Vienna; and, increasingly, in parts of South America and elsewhere around the globe. By the mid-1830s, Italian opera had been performed in New York and several other US towns, in Buenos Aires, Valparaíso and Rio de Janeiro, in Calcutta and many other far-flung places that intrepid travelling troupes could reach. In almost every place, Rossini was the staple fare.

The reasons Rossini decided to retire at this particular moment, when his star was so much in the ascendant, were complex. He may initially have stopped writing for personal reasons such as illness and depression. But it was also significant that important changes were happening in serious Italian opera at just that time, changes certainly not to Rossini's taste. What is more, once he was becalmed the operatic horizon altered so swiftly about him that any thought of matching his style to the demands of shifting taste must quickly have become daunting in the extreme.

One of the changes that occurred quite suddenly, however, was a new array of voice types in Italian serious opera: a shift in vocal register felt over much of Europe. By 1830, the castrati, already in decline during the later eighteenth century, had all but disappeared from *opera seria*. Their last days were gloomy indeed – a far cry from the time a century earlier when theatres could celebrate their vocal feats with shouts of 'Evviva il coltello!' (Long live the knife!). As early as the 1790s, rumours were circulating of strange physical reversals. One persistent story was of a man who had been born without testicles, and who in adult life had made his living by singing as a castrato. But then disaster struck: during an act of impassioned singing, his hidden body spontaneously emerged. A late-eighteenth-century version described the event thus:

> This man was born without any visible signs of those parts which are taken out on castration . . . . One day, he exerted himself so uncommonly in singing an arietta, that all of a sudden those parts, which had so long been concealed by nature, dropped into their proper place. The singer at this very instant lost his voice, which became even perceptible in the same performance, and with it he lost every prospect of a future subsistence.[2]

This fantastic tale is arresting because it depicts as a (literally) dramatic physical event something that happened gradually to an entire culture: condensed into a single moment are the years during which the castrato fell away, to be replaced by the male singing voices we know today.

The way this actually happened was inevitably less spectacular, but its suddenness is still surprising. The principal castrato of these twilight years was Giovanni Battista Velluti, who managed to enjoy international renown into the 1820s, singing roles created for him by, among others, Rossini. In the mid-1820s he signed a contract with a London theatre, and was at first a success. But in the last years of the decade audiences turned on him, his concerts were drowned out by howls of derision (amateur falsettists in the galleries had a field day), his very person became a source of horror and disgust. When the young Mendelssohn heard him in London in 1829, the experience was literally the stuff of nightmares: 'his voice so excited my loathing that it pursued me into my dreams that night'.[3] A British critic of the same period described Velluti's singing as 'the spectral moan of an unearthly being'.[4] Unable to bear such demotion to the underworld, Velluti fled back to Italy, but even there his career was soon over. He retired, preserving what dignity he could muster, spending his last years in pastoral seclusion.

The heroic roles with which castrati once thrilled audiences had by this time migrated. At first, in the hands of Rossini, they often became the province of so-called 'trouser roles' (cross-dressed sopranos or contraltos), so preserving the eighteenth-century love of high voices, and also something of that age's laissez-faire attitude to gender representation on the operatic stage. But around the time of Rossini's retirement the cross-dressed soprano herself became an implausible and even vilified figure, at least in heroic roles. She would resurface occasionally during the later nineteenth century in various new guises, but tended to be on the periphery and comic in nature – a winsome page or other stock type. A trousered or helmeted soprano would no longer suffice to impersonate the romantic lead, the ardent troubadour or gallant knight. As a critic expressed it in 1833:

> We always see the woman who dresses as a man on stage . . . as a female in male garb, as if for a joke or a masquerade. Never does she take on the character and the appearance [of a man]. . . . How shall we ever deceive ourselves, seeing a Conquistador, a fearsome warrior, being represented by these figures through the whole performance?[5]

This critic, by the way, was an ex-tenor (Nicola Tacchinardi). He thus had a professional stake in the matter. To impersonate the 'fearsome warrior' with heaving chest and ready sword, a significantly more manly presence was now thought necessary. The romantic tenor came of age.

Tenors had been on stage since the start of Italian opera, but they were rarely among the first rank of characters. In eighteenth-century *opera seria* they mostly appeared as the senior citizens of the metropolis, perhaps of noble extraction, but unlikely to be enmeshed in the central emotional tangles. As we saw in Chapter 4, Mozart's Idomeneo, a role written specially for an elderly tenor of the fading Metastasian school, fits the bill perfectly. Even in *opera buffa*, which favoured natural voices, tenors tended to have the whiff of redundancy about them, albeit often with compensatory lyric charm. Again there is a classic Mozartian example: the ineffectual Don Ottavio of *Don Giovanni* is a character as long on beautiful cantilena as he is short on decisive action. In Rossini's Italian operas, the lead tenor came into his own in the comic genre. But in serious operas, and with the exception of certain works written for Naples, where female heroes were in short supply, sword-waving women held their ground. *Otello* is the most obvious Neapolitan counter-example: it has no fewer than three leading tenor roles and, partly for that reason, remained in the repertory much longer than most of Rossini's serious operas.

The arrival of the manly tenor is itself sometimes turned into a primal scene, enacted by the famous French singer Gilbert-Louis Duprez (1806–96) in a 1837 revival of Rossini's *Guillaume Tell* (1829) at the Paris Opéra. Duprez recollected later that his appreciation of the 'manly accents' in Arnold's Act 4 aria 'Suivez-moi' caused him to attack the high Cs of that number (which would traditionally have been produced in a mixed voice, with elements of falsetto) in an all-out chest voice.[6] Rossini was horrified by this extreme vocal machismo; he tried to unman Duprez's innovation by describing it as 'the squawk of a capon with its throat cut' (telling shades of the castrato in that reference to the 'capon').[7] But a Rubicon had been crossed. After Duprez's Arnold, or so the story goes, nothing was the same; like it or not, the road to Caruso and those Three Tenors was paved and signposted.

As might be guessed, this simple tale of yet another momentous staged event in vocal history is far too neat. Tenors (Duprez included, as we shall see) had for some time been experimenting with darker, more forceful vocal production, and with higher chest notes. What's more, the voice's gentler, 'floated' high notes by no means disappeared overnight: as any devotee of old recordings will know, such notes remained an important part of all but the most unrelentingly robust tenorial armoury well into the twentieth century. But the years around 1830–40 still marked an important aesthetic shift. A type of vocal sound that to earlier generations would have seemed extreme, even animal (witness the capon), became uniquely exciting. Italian composers who moved to the front rank as Rossini retired, above all Donizetti, but also Bellini and Saverio Mercadante, were quick to exploit its potential.

The rise of the heroic tenor was closely related to other alterations in the Italian operatic universe around 1830. An obvious parallel was the emergence of the dramatic baritone, who became the tenor's classic antagonist ('I am her brother/father/uncle; so long as I breathe she shall *never* be yours'), or even – although rarely until around 1850 – the all-out protagonist. Both these new male voices had one aspect in common: they sacrificed flexibility for sheer power. The typical Rossinian bass or tenor could and would ornament his aria with as much dexterity and showy virtuosity as his female counterpart; indeed, in the entire history of opera up to and including Rossini, the vocal skills required of men and women had differed only marginally. But around 1830 that began to change. Some sopranos and mezzos followed the tenors and baritones, specializing in a darker, more forceful delivery. But most did not. Florid vocal writing gradually became the exclusive domain of female singers. Instead of the charged beauty that Rossini and his audiences wished to hear in all operatic characters, vocally florid music became feminized, akin to the corsetry and crinoline that now surrounded, constricted and adorned the female body. Male singers, on the other hand, increasingly adopted the vocal equivalent of stovepipe hats and dark suits, fast becoming the obligatory masculine uniform in society. This is not to say that their actual costumes changed much – in sartorial terms males on stage still remained largely wedded to tights and jerkins, often accessorized with – for us – an alarming quantity of paste jewellery. No, the new operatic garb was acoustic in nature. Duprez's 'manly accents' were *de rigueur*; real men no longer trilled or sketched roulades, they sang the words plainly, so the words could be understood; and as a default they sang them loud. Gender difference, long ignored or deliberately confused on the operatic stage, had arrived with a vengeance.

These alterations in operatic voice types were not confined to Italian serious opera, even if felt most acutely there. They can be linked to larger changes in society, most obviously to new ways in which men felt the need to differentiate themselves from women, as evinced in visible form by the new fashions. But there are also more narrowly theatrical explanations. These years saw an inexorable amplification of operatic orchestras. Technological developments in instrument making, married to aesthetic preferences deriving from instrumental genres, saw the wind and brass instruments of the orchestra increase in volume, a development that in turn required string sections to expand their numbers; what is more, and in tandem with a new extravagance of operatic plot subject, the centre of gravity of the Italian opera orchestra became lower, with new importance granted to the lower brass (trombones in particular). This was not so great a problem for sopranos, whose voices could ride above this darker, heavier orchestral sound; but for male voices, obliged to make themselves heard in the same range as these newly powerful instruments, the acoustic competition was severe. They reacted in the only way possible, by darkening their voices, in the process making them more powerful but also less flexible. Another explanation might connect the move from heroic sopranos and altos to heroic tenors and (later) baritones to new perceptions of operatic realism. Opera came closer to the manners of spoken drama when singing voices were differentiated in ways similar to those of spoken voices in a stage play. This desire for a new realism was, in its turn, fuelled by technology. Gas lighting appeared in theatres around 1820. As well as being (a little) safer than previous, naked-flame expedients, which routinely resulted in fires that burned theatres to the ground, gas also allowed for more sophistication of stage illusion.

AMOR VIOLENTO

What did the first examples of this new serious opera sound like? The best come from among the approximately seventy operas produced by Gaetano Donizetti (1797–1848), one of a pair of post-Rossinian Italian composers (the other is Vincenzo Bellini) whose most famous works have remained in the repertory to this day. Donizetti spent the first decade of his career – the 1820s – writing operas (both comic and serious) that are for the most part unabashedly Rossinian in manner. His maturity is sometimes said to emerge with *Anna Bolena* (1830), an opera that brought him new national and then international prestige. In formal terms *Anna* does indeed show a gathering freedom from the Rossinian code, in particular by investing greater emotional significance in heightened recitative. But the opera's basic vocal manner remained old-fashioned, in particular in its continued use of Rossinian ornamentation for all characters.

Departure of a more radical kind comes in a slightly later and less well-known opera, *Parisina*, first performed in Florence in 1833. The libretto was written by Felice Romani (1788–1865), commonly thought the most talented stage poet of the day, but someone who, because of this, regularly became over-committed. In spite of frequent complaints and pleading, the last sections of the *Parisina* libretto arrived on Donizetti's desk little more than a month before the scheduled premiere. In terms of its plot, and small wonder given the time pressures, *Parisina* is highly conventional: set in the standard-issue Middle Ages, it relies on the conventional love triangle of soprano, tenor and baritone. But by Rossinian standards the story – taken from a long poem by Byron – is unusually violent and bleak. Aristocratic, grizzled Azzo (baritone) is married to young Parisina (soprano); but she nurses a secret passion, ardently reciprocated, for Ugo (tenor). Azzo sniffs out the passion but then discovers that Ugo is his son by a previous wife. This complicates things, but not for long: consumed by jealousy, Azzo has Ugo murdered. In the final scene, he presents Parisina with her lover's cadaver, at which sight she falls lifeless to the ground. This gruesome tale was parcelled into a sequence of musical numbers that conforms to the standards of the day: multi-movement entrance arias for each of the principals, a series of duets to place them in confrontation, and a grand central finale.

Given the predictable exterior, reviews of the premiere make curious reading. *Parisina* was generally a success with the public, but the critics were divided. Even the positive ones had caveats. The music, one warned, was 'extremely austere, and tiring both for the singers and instrumentalists'.[8] There was praise for the poetry, although some found the story morally repellent. The most intense criticism, though, came in reaction to a new type of vocal delivery. The first-act finale was 'more noisy and irritating to the ear than instructive and delightful to the soul'; some other scenes were 'too intense and prolonged'; it seemed to some that the opera was being 'shouted rather than sung'. One critic reported open discussion in the theatre:

> A shout thundered from the stage. 'Good!' was proclaimed from some sides. 'Bad!' was murmured from others. The first group said: 'In certain terrible situations, a shout can be singing raised to the sublime'. The second replied: 'A shout is always a shout, and never singing'. 'But', added the first, 'in nature, when the soul is tormented, men shout'.

Attending to *Parisina* today, we may find these comments puzzling. Donizetti's operas are, after all, now thought the essence of *bel canto*, of beautiful singing, but it's clear that for those in 1833 who were listening with Rossinian ears, attuned to the operatic past, something was amiss.

This conundrum can in part be explained by looking at the singers who created *Parisina*'s major roles. Donizetti, like all good opera composers of the time, carefully tailored his music to the skills of his first performers, and for very good reason – if they were successful, then his opera would be successful too. And the performers engaged for this 1833 Florence season were extraordinary. Caroline Ungher (Parisina) was an Austrian mezzo who had come to Italy in the mid-1820s. Famous above all as a singing actress, her voice was not conventionally beautiful, especially in its somewhat forced upper register. Bellini, definitely of the old school vocally, said that 'every sound she utters is like the stab of a stiletto';[9] Rossini, only a little kinder, said she had 'the ardour of the south, the energy of the north, and brazen lungs'.[10] Domenico Cosselli (Azzo) had started life as a Rossinian bass but now, halfway through his brief career, specialized in higher, more forceful roles, becoming one of a group of singers who created the new baritone voice type. The Ugo was Duprez, whose voice was at this point in transition. He had started life in Paris as a light, Rossinian tenor, but in these Italian years his voice had darkened and become more powerful. In his memoirs he mentions *Parisina* as the dividing point, the crucial move into a different kind of vocal production, one that – as we have seen – would lead him to become the iconic 'manly tenor' of the late 1830s.

Looking at *Parisina* from the perspective of these singers – as Donizetti's attempt to create a new style of music drama out of performers with new expressive means – we find an opera that, although conventional in its outer trappings, is radical in its treatment of the major roles. A good example comes in Act 2, when Azzo steals into Parisina's bedchamber and overhears her murmur Ugo's name in a dream. He awakens her and confronts her; she admits her love and the duet ends with furious imprecations from him and desperate, suicidal asides from her. All this is standard operatic fare for the 1830s. What is extraordinary is how much the scene relies on declamation rather than well-tuned melody, with no hint of a conventional slow movement of lyrical repose. The tenor part is if anything more unusual still. Donizetti tailored for Duprez a role that freely mixes his old and new styles of singing. In his second-act aria, for example, the slow section has a great deal of florid writing reminiscent of the Rossinian past (Duprez's debut, in 1825, was in *Il barbiere di Siviglia*). The tessitura is set very high, with high Cs in abundance and even a high D in the cabaletta. But the musical context and markings in the score make clear that Donizetti intended many of these high notes to be declaimed forcefully rather than floated in a falsetto-tinged voice. At the same time, then, as Duprez was in transition, so too was the very language of serious Italian opera. Fresh demands were emerging in the alchemy between performers, composers and audiences.

Parisina is today only on the fringes of the repertory, but its new style was certainly a popular success, both in Italy and on the ever-expanding international operatic stage. A sure mark of Donizetti's popularity in this new manner was the fact that operas of his in a similar vein opened the Carnival season at La Scala no fewer than three years running in the mid-1830s (*Fausta* in 1832, *Lucrezia Borgia* in 1833 and *Gemma di Vergy* in 1834). But *Parisina* is doubly radical – and different from those other three operas – in that it attempts this new, darker vocal style for the soprano as well as the tenor. As mentioned earlier, forceful sopranos of the Ungher type were relatively rare; for the most part Donizetti was encouraged by his principal female performers to retain the old, gentler, more ornamental style.

The classic case comes in Donizetti's most enduringly popular opera, *Lucia di Lammermoor* (1835), a work that has remained in the repertory through nearly two centuries of changing fashion. *Lucia* again centres on the classic vocal triangle. Edgardo, the heroic tenor, is in love with and loved by Lucia, the tragic soprano. Their union is implacably opposed by Enrico, the nasty baritone, who is Lucia's brother and for reasons of finance and ancient family rivalry wants her to marry a husband of his own choosing, the mild-mannered Arturo (tenor). There are the usual entanglements and tragic misunderstandings. Lucia, thinking Edgardo has deserted her, ends up engaged to Arturo and is publicly denounced by Edgardo when he shows up out of the blue just as she is signing the nuptial contract. This event spawns the famous *Lucia* Sextet, a great frozen moment (Italians called it the *concertato*) in which all the principals, backed by a chorus of shocked onlookers, face one another and together sing out their pain, anger and confusion. In the last act

Lucia murders her new husband in their wedding bed, falls into an elaborate vocal madness and dies. In the final scene Edgardo is told of her death. Bidding her spirit a passionate farewell, he stabs himself onstage and then expires, singing to the last. Donizetti succinctly defined his taste in libretti: 'Voglio amor, e amor violento'[11] (I want love, and violent love); *Lucia di Lammermoor* supplied it in full.

Edgardo was written for Duprez, now well settled into his second, more robust vocal manner. The final scene, at night amid the tombs of Edgardo's ancestors, is thus a good place to spot the new heroic tenor in his natural habitat. Like almost all solos and duets in the opera, the scene is in the standard multi-movement form: orchestrally accompanied recitative leads to a slow movement (in which Edgardo, thinking he has been spurned by Lucia, resolves to kill himself); a change of pace heralds the *tempo di mezzo*, in which the chorus brings news of Lucia's death; this leads to the cabaletta, during which the hero commits suicide. The slow movement, 'Fra poco a me ricovero' (Soon to give me refuge), shows how far we have moved from Rossinian vocal ornament. The opening strains are more like recitative; only later does Edgardo expand into lyrical melody and a few perfunctory melismas; at the end he again retreats into declamation, repeating the spare motto of the opening. What substitutes for the lack of vocal flourish is quite simple: Edgardo's part is studded with vehement high notes – moments in which he pauses to shout forth his feelings of loss and despair.

The announcement of Lucia's death is marked by an incursion of operatic funeral clichés: a sudden turn to the minor mode in a slow march, punctuated by solemn orchestral drum beats. But as the chorus launches into its narrative of Lucia's last moments, there is a stunning about-face. The music turns to sunny major and to light-voiced close harmony, as though adopting the language of the heroine whose death is being described. The contrast with Edgardo's anguished reaction couldn't be more obvious. His cabaletta, 'Tu che a Dio spiegasti l'ali' (You who have spread your wings to God), in which he imagines joining his beloved in heaven, seems at first to take on some of the chorus's delicacy; but soon, as he repeats the words 'bell'alma innamorata' (beautiful, beloved soul), Edgardo returns to the upper reaches of his voice. In between the two stanzas of the cabaletta, he deals himself the fatal blow, and in the second stanza his melody is seconded by a lachrymose solo cello. But what breath he has left is saved yet again for impassioned high notes. By the end, ornament has disappeared, even lyrical, periodic melody has become fragmented. The tenor is down to his essentials, the high notes sung to a long, drawn-out 'Ah!', the desperate cry of the new, manly man.

Lucia's famous mad scene, which precedes this finale, is in exactly the same multi-movement form (orchestrally accompanied recitative, slow movement, *tempo di mezzo* and cabaletta), but its vocal style couldn't be more different. In the recitative, the deranged heroine is assailed by orchestral themes. Some of them are reminiscences of earlier numbers, but in her disordered state she is unable to respond to them adequately. The slow movement, 'Ardon gl'incensi' (The incense burns), seems at first to repeat this pattern, with the melody held by the orchestra and Lucia responding in fragments of declamation. But at 'Alfin son tua' (At last I am yours), in which she retreats into fantasies of a happy wedding to Edgardo, Lucia's utterances become progressively more florid until, by the end, she seems little more than an instrument herself, a mechanical producer of vocal noise, released from the constraints of the word. The cabaletta, 'Spargi d'amaro pianto' (Sprinkle with bitter tears), repeats this trajectory: the final cadences are also marked by disintegration into a world close to pure vocal sound.

A small industry has grown up around Lucia's madness, with producers and other arbiters of operatic fashion all seeking to tell us precisely what such vocal extravagance might mean. Some remind us that both real-world and operatic madness in the nineteenth century was typically a 'female malady': Lucia's manic vocalism is thus a sign of her imprisonment in a cruel male world. She is trapped in beautiful, ornamental singing just as she is trapped by society at large.[12] Others, finding this reading too depressing, stand it on its head. According to them, Lucia's flights of vocal fancy are a feminist victory, a proud refusal to obey the rules of convention. Her extravagant vocal finale now marks a triumphant *release* from male authority.[13] The fact that both interpretations use as evidence exactly the same music suggests that both attempt too precise a relationship between the notes and their cultural meaning. The message of the *Lucia* mad scene is probably best seen as more basic. Once upon a time in opera, elaborate vocal ornament was the province of all opera characters; now, in opera's Romantic age, florid singing was, like colourful costume, becoming a marker of the feminine. Small wonder, then, that those who contract the 'female malady' display as a prime symptom an uncontrollable excess of singing.

The *Lucia* mad scene has had a fascinating afterlife on stage as well as among academic interpreters. Scholars studying Donizetti's autograph score (the manuscript that contains his hand-written draft of the entire opera) discovered that the slow movement, 'Ardon gl'incensi', was originally conceived with the accompaniment of a glass harmonica, something that would have added an exotic and uncanny timbre to the scene. But it seems that the resident glass harmonica virtuoso in Naples got into a contractual argument with the theatre, and Donizetti (as ever, pragmatic about such matters) crossed out the part and substituted a solo flute. Modern performances sometimes reinstate the glass harmonica, which is one way of refreshing a passage now very well-known. But a more important variation to the scene occurred some thirty years after Donizetti's death. Around 1880, the Australian soprano Nellie Melba began to perform an extended cadenza with solo flute at the end of the slow movement, a nearly incredible high-wire act in which the soprano enters into an 'anything-you-can-play-I-can-sing-higher' competition with the flute. This crazy cadenza became the most famous moment in the opera, and is to this day faithfully reproduced by most sopranos, even though it obviously reflects a conception of soprano vocalism much later than Donizetti's.[14] What are we to make of such accretions to the opera's text? Purists might automatically welcome the 'authentic' glass harmonica and automatically denounce the later cadenza-with-flute. But the fact that sopranos continue to test themselves (and each other) against the cadenza's extreme difficulty could also be something to celebrate – if nothing else, as another demonstration that, in opera at least, the living performer can still exert power over the dead composer.

In part by means of additions and alterations such as the mad-scene cadenza, *Lucia di Lammermoor* survived momentous changes in fashion, changes that might in other circumstances have caused the entire opera gradually to seem ridiculous. An early indication that its violent contrasts were becoming dated is captured in one of the most famous novelistic scenes to take place in an opera house. In Flaubert's *Madame Bovary* (1857), the adulterous heroine, Emma Bovary, and her dull husband, Charles, go to see a performance of *Lucia di Lammermoor* (or rather its French version, *Lucie de Lammermoor*) in provincial Rouen. Much is made of the artificiality of the acting and dramatic premises – Flaubert, at the forefront of modern developments in literary realism, clearly disapproved of such old-fashioned behaviour. The Act 2 Sextet is described with all the novelist's famous precision of language and eye for telling detail:

> The instruments and the singers began the sextet. Edgar, flashing with fury, dominated all the others with his clearer voice; Ashton hurled homicidal provocations at him in deep notes; Lucie uttered her shrill plaint, Arthur at one side, his modulated tones in the middle register, and the bass of the minister pealed forth like an organ, while the voices of the women repeating his words took them up in chorus delightfully. They were all in a row gesticulating, and anger, vengeance, jealousy, terror and stupefaction breathed forth at once from their half-opened mouths. The outraged lover brandished his naked sword; his guipure ruffle rose with jerks to the movements of his chest, and he walked from right to left with long strides, clanking against the boards the silver-gilt spurs of his soft boots, widening out at the ankles.

But then, quite suddenly, the ridiculous physical exertions of the singers become unimportant as Emma is drawn into the operatic spectacle, in particular into the orbit of the tenor hero:

> He, she thought, must have an inexhaustible love to lavish it upon the crowd with such effusion. All her small fault-findings faded before the poetry of the part that absorbed her; and, drawn towards this man by the illusion of the character, she tried to imagine to herself his life – that life resonant, extraordinary, splendid, and that might have been hers if fate had willed it. They would have known one another, loved one another. With him, through all the kingdoms of Europe she would have travelled from capital to capital, sharing his fatigues and his pride, picking up the flowers thrown to him, herself embroidering his costumes. Then each evening, at the back of a box, behind the golden trellis-work she would have drunk in eagerly the expansions of this soul that would have sung for her alone; from the stage, even as he acted, he would have looked at her. But the mad idea seized her that he was looking at her; it was certain. She longed to run to his arms, to take refuge in his strength, as in the incarnation of love itself, and to say to him, to cry out, 'Take me away! carry me with you! let us go! Thine, thine! all my ardour and all my dreams!'[15]

The trajectory is revealing: the tawdry dramatic details are cast aside, they fade 'before the poetry of the part'; then, 'drawn towards this man by the illusion of the character', Emma constructs an elaborate fantasy about an alternative life she might lead – not with the operatic hero, but with the tenor who impersonates him. Previously in this book we have seen a castrato or soprano having the same effect; but this time the repercussions are more insidious. Those 'manly accents', we can guess, worked on Emma Bovary in what were for her unpredictable ways. The mood generated in her that evening leads to decisions that change her life disastrously and for ever.

Lucia successfully entered the operatic repertory, but most of Donizetti's seventy or so operas were forgotten until the closing decades of the twentieth century, when they began to be revived in a 'Donizetti Renaissance' that followed on from, and then rivalled, the contemporary explosion in Rossini performances. This renaissance has made available several extraordinary works, particularly from his final creative phase in the early 1840s, when Paris was his base of operations. There and in Vienna, where from 1842 he took up a court position, he produced a string of innovative works in a startling array of genres, from full-scale *grand opéra*, to *opéra comique*, to both comic and serious Italian opera. One in the last of these genres, *Maria di Rohan* (1843), is influenced by French *mélodrame*, to the extent that it condenses the usual Italian forms and focuses on moments of intense theatrical tension in which the music is sometimes little more than atmospheric. On the other hand, *Linda di Chamounix* (1842) engages with the tradition of *opera semiseria*, in which liberal injections of local colour enrich a plot that wavers between the tragic, the sentimental and the downright comic.

A third opera, *Don Pasquale* (1843), is that *rara avis*, an *opera buffa* from the mid nineteenth century that has thrived and endured. Why so rare? Recall that for the greater part of its history, serious Italian opera had been partnered by, often lampooned by, its comic twin. Composers tended to write in both genres, and by the time of Rossini there was sometimes little to distinguish between the musical style of one and the other. Around 1830, though, this too had begun to change. Composers increasingly specialized in one genre or the other (both Bellini and Verdi kept by and large to serious works), and although *opere buffe* continued to be composed, after 1840 they rarely had the cachet or prestige of *opera seria*. Again the repertoire at La Scala bears this out. Until around 1830, comic operas hugely outnumbered serious ones, even though an *opera seria* always inaugurated the new Carnival season (the most prestigious event of the year). But in the 1840s the number of comic works drastically declined: in 1842 only two *opere buffe* were staged in the entire year, and both were elderly classics – Rossini's *Il barbiere* and Donizetti's own *Le convenienze ed inconvenienze teatrali* (1827), a comic work that explicitly lampooned serious opera. Partly as a result of this fall in esteem, comic opera became stylistically somewhat stagnant – as late as the 1850s, new works in the genre might still repeat old Rossinian clichés, orchestral crescendos and all.

Donizetti was the last major Italian composer to ignore this trend. He continued to write comic operas as readily as serious ones, and excelled in both genres even at the end of his career, when such versatility went against prevailing trends. Part of the reason he did so was because in his hands comic opera was itself mutating, becoming more consistently coloured by a sentimental vein – a tone that had emerged in earlier decades only occasionally. This new atmosphere is present as early as his *L'elisir d'amore* (The Elixir of Love, 1832), another enduring success. But in *Don Pasquale* the innovations go further. The plot could hardly be more traditionally farcical: basically it parades the *commedia dell'arte* standby of a rich old man (Don Pasquale, bass) duped by a pair of young lovers (Norina, soprano, and Ernesto, tenor) with the help of a wise old friend (Dr Malatesta, baritone). But the *music* of *Don Pasquale* is anything but old-fashioned; indeed, so imbued is it with sentimental and even serious touches that it periodically calls into question its very identity as a comedy. In this respect it is revealing that Donizetti tried to insist that at the Parisian premiere (given at the Théâtre Italien) the main characters dress in contemporary costume, something on which he was overruled by most of the singers and the librettist, who insisted on 'perukes and velvet habits'.[16]

The new departures are signalled musically as soon as the curtain goes up. Most obviously, there is no opening chorus, no larger social world from which the main characters can emerge. The concentration, here and throughout the opera, will be on individuals, immediately increasing the possibility of the kind of audience identification usually reserved for serious subjects. At the heart of this opening Introduzione, embedded in its *opera buffa* exterior, lies a cantabile aria, Malatesta's 'Bella siccome un angelo' (Beautiful as an angel), that has few concessions to the comic style. Ernesto's cantabile, 'Sogno soave e casto' (Sweet and chaste dream), follows in the same vein. There is no dissolve into *buffo* patter, simply because the melody will accommodate little interruption or deflation. Instead the phrases build powerfully towards a lyrical release, almost in the manner of middle-period Verdi. As Donizetti's music oscillates between the comic and the sentimental, it encourages us to believe in the emotional capacity of the cast: their comic antics onstage become merely a surface, as if the *characters* (rather than the actors) are acting out their roles. And this is surely why the opera survived (indeed thrived) despite its clichéd plot. The comic superstructure is really only a pretext, making the road forward to Verdi's *Falstaff* (1893) clearer than the road back to Rossini's *Il barbiere*.

According to this reading of Donizetti's last comic opera, it is fitting that that most celebrated passage of the score is Ernesto's Act 2 aria, 'Cercherò lontana terra' (I will seek a distant land). The orchestral prelude features a long, beautifully poignant trumpet solo. Whatever its contemporary associations, the strange effect of this gentle, sorrowful melody enunciated on the most unlikely of instruments can for us stand as a symbol of the ambiguity of the opera as a whole. Small wonder that the passage provided so transparent a model for the greatest modern master of musical ambiguity. In Act 2 of Stravinsky's *The Rake's Progress* (1951), a haunting re-composition of Donizetti's prelude sounds as Anne Trulove arrives at Tom Rakewell's house. She raises her hand to knock on the door, but hesitates:

> How strange! although the heart for love dare everything,
> The hand draws back and finds
> No spring of courage. London! Alone! seems all that it can say.

The hesitation is there in the music, in Stravinsky's shuddering opening dissonances and – most of all – in the delicate conceit that allows the trumpet, Donizetti's trumpet, to peal forth a song of isolation and loneliness.

The desolate trumpet solo in *Don Pasquale* might supply an apt soundtrack for Donizetti's last years, which were tragic indeed – locked away in an asylum and increasingly paralysed by syphilis contracted many years earlier. As befitted the time, his infirmity was wrapped in layers of romantic narrative by contemporary men of letters. The French publisher Léon Escudier left a memoir informing the world that

Donizetti had been driven insane by an imperious prima donna at the Paris Opéra, who had forced him to make compositional adjustments to his final *grand opéra*. The story has scant basis in fact but is repeated to the present day, so well does it chime with a strain of operatic criticism that sees singers as the constant potential enemies of composers.[17] As Donizetti languished in the asylum, friends occasionally came to visit, one even trying some strains of the mad scene from *Lucia*, vainly hoping the music might awaken the stricken musician to reason.[18] Heinrich Heine reported a surreal picture of the composer ever in attendance:

> While his melodies cheer the world with their merry playfulness, while they are sung and hummed everywhere, he himself, a terrible image of imbecility, sits in a sanatorium near Paris. With regard to his appearance alone he has, until lately, retained some childish consciousness, and had to be carefully attired every day in complete evening dress, his coat adorned with all his decorations; and would thus sit without moving, from early morning until late at night.[19]

Heine's fantasy cunningly recycles two German stereotypes about Italian opera during this period: its essential lack of seriousness, its 'merry playfulness', and the readiness of its composers to please at all costs, to be endlessly in waiting, for a new commission or for audience applause to call them onstage. But Donizetti's career and his music tell a different story. True, he seemed to write un-selfconsciously and made it his business to suit his inspirations both to his performers' abilities and his audiences' tastes. Yet for these very reasons, his greatest works articulate with passion and precision a moment of tumultuous change in Italian opera.

TO DIE THROUGH SINGING

Vincenzo Bellini (1801–35) suffered his own tragic fate by dying young. Bellini's earliest operas, like Donizetti's, show an inevitable Rossinian influence, despite the fact that his teachers in Naples took an old-fashioned line against Rossini. For them, Rossini was too artificial and elaborate, even too 'German', in his orchestral writing. But *Il pirata* (The Pirate, 1827) and *La straniera* (The Stranger, 1829) signalled that

Bellini had something different to offer, something often called 'romantic' or even 'philosophical' by contemporary critics. These appellations had little to do with the plots. Though both operas were influenced, as were several of Donizetti's, by the fashion for the Gothic, it was Bellini's highly individual writing for the solo voice that was heard as 'romantic'. His gift was to imagine melody, extended arcs and lines that could poise human voices to break hearts on the turn of the smallest phrase. This was his unique marker, recognized as the source of his creative force, and it made him immediately distinguishable from Donizetti.

An important strand of Bellini's originality sprang from his close relationship with the librettist of all but the last of his mature works, that same Felice Romani who had sent a frantic Donizetti the *Parisina* libretto just weeks before its premiere. But Bellini wrote much more slowly than Donizetti – he produced an average of just one opera a year during his short career – and would not have tolerated such last-minute scrambles. His preferred method was to involve himself extensively in the making of the libretto, frequently insisting on revisions and ensuring that the text was precisely what his music needed. Given his slower rate of production, he could not possibly match the overall popularity and reach of Donizetti; but several of his operas became instant classics, remaining in the repertory to this day.

Il pirata was the first opera Bellini wrote with Romani, and his first great success. Set in thirteenth-century Sicily, the plot centres again on a classic love triangle. Ernesto (bad, jealous, baritone) and Gualtiero (good, heroic, tenor) are rivals for the hand of Imogene (gentle, frail, soprano), who of course loves Gualtiero but is blackmailed into marrying Ernesto after Gualtiero has been exiled and has taken to piracy. Gualtiero appears (post-shipwreck) at Ernesto's castle and kills him in a duel. Imogene goes mad. Because of the individual singers Bellini wrote for and also because of his particular sensibility, which always tended towards the gently sentimental, he tended to avoid the new, more robust tenor voice that Donizetti employed to such great effect. In *Il pirata* both the baritone and the tenor are granted a fair degree of ornamentation, particularly in the slow movements. Gualtiero was written for one of the most famous singers of the day, Giovanni Battista Rubini (1794–1854), who started life as a Rossinian tenor and never made the transition that Duprez underwent, instead retaining his extreme flexibility and ability to sing in the stratosphere with a mixed, falsetto-tinged voice. The part is so carefully tailored to Rubini's particular abilities that it is very difficult to cast today.

But if the principal voices remain Rossinian in one sense, *Il pirata*'s novelty lies in the extent to which their music responds to individual nuances in the words, both in recitative and in formal arias. This extreme attention produced a fragmented surface, one in which the musical mood can change at any moment. For Donizetti such an approach was an exceptional effect – it features, for example, in Lucia's mad scene, as she is assailed by music from the past. But in Bellini the sense of fragmentation is closer to a continual state. In the recitatives, orchestral interjections – often mimetic of characters' movements or feelings – are an almost constant presence. In arias, instead of the symmetrical melodic patterns of Rossini, Bellini announced his difference with long, somewhat sprawling melodies in which the line is often broken by tiny, expressive pauses, and by isolating brief musical motifs in order that key phrases of the text, or even single words, are communicated in a far more direct manner than Rossini would have thought pleasing. Imogene's mad scene, which makes up the finale of the opera, is a good example. It begins with elaborate orchestral preparation, music choreographing the heroine's faltering steps around the stage and punctuating her opening recitative. Even in her closing cabaletta, 'O, sole! ti vela di tenebre oscure' (O sun, hide yourself with dark shadows), the ornamentation is periodically interrupted with leaps into the lowest register (for the 'dark shadows') and passages of slower, more syllabic declamation.

While *La straniera* continued the innovations of *Il pirata*, the next two operas, *I Capuleti e i Montecchi* (The Capulets and the Montagues, 1830, a version of the Romeo and Juliet story) and *La sonnambula* (The Sleepwalker, 1831), seem to return to the Rossinian mode both in plot type and in increased vocal ornamentation, although Bellini's tendency to linger expressively over particular verbal/vocal moments is again in evidence. His fame assured, he could now write exclusively for the finest singers of the day. The most important of these was the soprano Giuditta Pasta (1797–1865), who created the title roles in *La sonnambula* and in his next two operas, *Norma* (1831) and *Beatrice di Tenda* (1833). *Norma* was one of the best-loved and most influential operas of this period. Set in Gaul during Roman times, its version of the love triangle is slightly unusual. Norma (soprano) is a druid priestess leading a rebellion against the Romans, but she also loves Pollione (tenor), the Roman pro-consul, and has secretly borne him two children. He once loved her in turn, but now pines for Adalgisa (soprano). The opera ends with Pollione captured by the Gauls and sentenced to death; Norma decides to sacrifice herself with him.

The single most famous aria in *Norma*, a piece endlessly recycled in arrangements during the nineteenth century, is the heroine's 'Casta diva' from Act I in which Norma invokes the goddess of the moon. We can imagine through it something of Pasta's incomparable abilities and the adulation she could excite, as well as the particular alchemy at work between her voice and the composer's musical invention. One of Pasta's greatest and most verbose contemporary fans, Stendhal, pointed out that she was 'extremely reserved in her use of *fioritura*, she resorts to it only when it has a direct contribution to make to the dramatic expressiveness of the music'.[20] The description would be equally apt for 'Casta diva' itself. Although Bellini initially made his mark by differentiating his melodic style from that of Rossini, by the time of *Norma* he could again deploy Rossinian vocal gestures; however – and just as Stendhal thought of Pasta – he would use such gestures sparingly, forever interrupting the line with the expressive, declamatory lingering and pauses that had become his trademark.

The opening of 'Casta diva' is a demonstration of the best that Bellini could achieve in this vein. It has often been celebrated as a classic example of what Verdi, much later, would praise as Bellini's 'long, long, long melodies such as no one had done before him';[21] but the peculiar qualities of the aria, its sense of slow development, are dictated by the dramatic situation, as a priestly incantation. Romani's words are set in telling poetic shapes, but they are also unusually direct:

Casta Diva, che inargenti
Queste sacre antiche piante,
A noi volgi il bel sembiante,
Senza nube e senza vel!

[Chaste goddess, who makes silver / these ancient sacred trees, / turn your beautiful face to us, / unveiled and unclouded!]

True to the pattern established as early as *Il pirata*, Bellini freely repeats individual words and phrases, but this repetition is far from mechanical, not merely to fill out the musical phrases. If isolated from their music, the words would indeed be a repetitious gabble: 'Casta diva, casta diva, che inargenti, queste sacre, queste sacre, queste sacre antiche piante'; but when attached to the musical phrases each of the verbal repetitions contributes to the intensity. The first syllables of '*ca*sta diva' and '*que*ste sacre' are stretched out and then ornamented, so much so that their literal meaning is obscured; but the urgent repetitions then make certain that the essential sentiment is communicated. In spite of the fragmentation – the momentary pauses that articulate each tiny musical phrase – this 'long, long, long' melody progresses towards a remarkable climax on 'sembiante', one whose climactic upper notes (A to B♭) repeat an octave higher the opening two notes of the entire melody.

Verdi's comment about the length of Bellini's melodies is often quoted, but its continuation, less well-known, is also worth bearing in mind: 'And what truth and power of declamation, as for example in the duet between Pollione and Norma'.[22] He refers here to a duet near the end of the opera ('In mia man alfin tu sei'; At last you are in my hands) in which Norma tries one final time to prise Pollione away from Adalgisa and, when she fails, calls down destruction on herself and him. Rossini also praised this duet, saying that 'The words are so enmeshed in the notes and the notes in the words that together they form a complete and perfect whole'.[23] It is a prime example of the fact that Bellini had a great deal more than simply a melodic gift. He could, as in 'Casta diva', use melody to articulate dramatic situations, and do so in a way that had an undeniable influence on the next generation.

The start of 'In mia man', which develops through many moods and movements, is the most remarkable. Like many of those 'long, long' solo arias it is preceded by a leisurely instrumental introduction. The vocal line then unfolds in three statements of the main melody, an inspiration that – again like 'Casta diva' – is made up of fragments of melody that rise gradually to a melodic climax and then more swiftly descend to the starting register. In the first statement Norma establishes her dominance in a series of fragmentary utterances: 'At last . . . you are in my hands; . . . no one can break . . . your bonds. I can do it'. That final statement, the four syllables of 'Io lo posso', is timed with the moment of melodic climax, and its detonation stimulates dialogue: the remainder of the melody is articulated through a hurried exchange between Norma and Pollione. The second statement is all Norma's, as she lays out her bargain: 'For your Gods, . . . for your children, . . . you must swear that from now on . . . Adalgisa . . . will see you no more'. Those four syllables of the hated rival's name, 'A-dal-gi-sa', are now at the melodic climax, and her name seems to derail and extend the melody, which spins off into motivic and verbal repetitions. The first phrase of the third statement is uttered by Pollione, 'No: sì vil non sono' (No: I am not so cowardly), but his refusal is ignored by Norma, who 'with repressed fury' replies 'Swear, swear!' More rapid dialogue ensues, and the melody, whose shapes have so far controlled their exchange, is broken; modulations and new melodic ideas crowd in.

Verdi admired 'the truth and power of declamation' of this remarkable passage. It is articulated by means of a beautiful melody, but it is also a *dialogue*: every individual phrase is intimately wedded to its words, and those words have an immediate effect on an interlocutor. This is, in this sense, musical drama which could be traced back to the earliest operas (works certainly unknown to Bellini), and which is unusual in the generally extrovert early nineteenth-century Italian context. Another composer and enthusiast over Bellini, one generally contemptuous of Italian opera's shortcomings, had this to say: 'Among all Bellini's creations [*Norma* is] the richest in the profoundly realistic way in which true melody is united with intimate passion'.[24] This was Richard Wagner, who conducted the opera in his apprentice years in Riga in the late 1830s, wrote extensively and enthusiastically about Bellini at the time, and (more surprisingly) preserved his appreciation even into old age. His praise was a potent illustration of the fact that Bellini's individuality, especially his extreme concentration on minute details of word–music relationships, allowed his operas to cross national borders – borders that would become increasingly well-policed as the nineteenth century progressed.

Bellini's final opera, *I puritani* (The Puritans, 1835), like *Don Pasquale* first performed at the Théâtre Italien in Paris, was a further sign that the French capital had become a Mecca for Italian opera composers with international aspirations. He had by then fallen out with Romani, whose tardiness severely compromised *Beatrice di Tenda*; for *I puritani* he was thus obliged to work with a theatrical beginner, the exiled revolutionary Count Carlo Pepoli. To our great good fortune, this meant that he had to put down on paper, in the form of letters to his librettist, some basic facts about the nature of opera. Donizetti, as we have seen, insisted on 'amor violento'. Bellini's prescription sounds even more drastic:

> Carve into your head in adamantine letters: *Opera must make people weep, feel horrified, die through singing.* It's wrong to want to write all the numbers in the same way, but they must all be somehow shaped so as to make the music intelligible through their clarity of expression, at once concise and striking.[25]

The second sentence is clear enough, and hints at what Bellini was trying to achieve in *Norma*; it also signals that, although he needed variety in his dramatic forms, he was – like Donizetti – no formal revolutionary: he constantly called for poetry that would shape itself neatly (and thus intelligibly for the audience) into the standard Rossinian patterns. But what are we to make of that opening, 'adamantine' statement? Their violence offers a conception of musical drama at odds with the image of Bellini we now tend to preserve, of a sentimental genius of vocal nuance. It is a salutary reminder of this new, post-Rossinian operatic world, and – yet again – of Bellini's creative energy and sensitivity within it.

I puritani also contains a famous mad scene: its heroine, Elvira (soprano), believes herself deserted by her lover, Arturo (tenor), and gives way to elaborate desolation. The passage is often compared to the mad scene in *Lucia*, and its popularity is another indication that the rise of the 'manly' tenor coincided with an intensification of other types of gender difference, one of which was to make madness, at least of the theatrical kind, into a female malady that could be elaborately marked by the singing voice. There are many aspects in common between the two scenes, not least that Elvira, like Lucia, ends by falling into ever more elaborate ornaments, a release from the word into vocal excess that clearly signifies her loss of reason. Also Lucia-like is the fact that she is assailed by past music from the opera, these reminiscences seeming to spring from her disordered mind. But at the start of the scene there comes another of Bellini's 'long, long' melodies, again with his characteristic tendency to melodic fragmentation, telling pauses and word repetition.

> Qui la voce sua soave
> Mi chiamava, e poi sparì;
> Qui giurava esser fedele
> E poi crudele, ei mi fuggì.

> [Here his gentle voice / called me, and then disappeared; / here he swore to be faithful / and then, cruelly, he deserted me.]

The sentiments are again direct, and the first two lines are simply declaimed, closely following the words: a continuous melody for the first line, then two anxious fragments for the second. But in lines 3 and 4 that directness is lost, the words begin to be repeated and the melody loses direction, sinking chromatically as Elvira searches for meaning. As with the Pollione–Norma duet, the melodic utterance is so intimately linked to the character that, as her reason wavers, so her basic means of communication also seems to slip away.

Very soon after *I puritani*, Bellini died in tragic circumstances: he was just thirty-five, at the height of his fame, and succumbed to disease (in all likelihood amoebiasis) in a suburb of Paris. As it happens, Heine was again on call to add a half-romantic, half-ironic gloss. His story 'Florentine Nights' contains an extended, highly coloured portrait of Bellini as a childlike genius:

> His hair was dressed in such a romantically wistful fashion; his clothes fitted his frail body so languorously, and he carried his little malacca cane in such an idyllic manner, that he always reminded me of the young shepherds in our pastoral plays mincing about with beribboned crooks, in pastel jackets and breeches. And his gait was so maidenly, so elegiac, so ethereal. The creature altogether looked like a sigh in dancing pumps.[26]

Heine, the self-declared 'young German', makes it clear that Italians are not, in the end, to be treated entirely seriously; and love of opera is a symptom of their condition. Elsewhere in the story he writes that 'the whole life of the beautiful Italians shows itself to us when we see them in the opera': a prominent strand of nineteenth-century Teutonic thinking was that natural, sunny, laughing Italians are different from dark, serious, masculine practitioners of German art. In the chapters that follow, we will hear plenty more about this antithesis.

It is doubly ironic that Bellini proved the one nineteenth-century Italian composer after Rossini who was influential on broader European musical culture – a culture that increasingly valued instrumental music over opera, at least in theory (in practice, at the box office, opera maintained its prestige in spite of all the solemn words). But Bellini's melodies were ever potent. Their impact on Chopin is obvious and much talked about. Some of the most prominent German composers continued Heine's ambivalent attitude, the most notable and voluble among them being, as we have seen, Richard Wagner. As late as August 1872, with most of his mature operas behind him, Wagner was described by his wife, Cosima, as singing 'a cantilena from *I puritani*'; he remarked that 'Bellini wrote melodies lovelier than one's dreams'.[27]

Given the influence that great singers had on Bellini's musical inspirations, it is entirely fitting that the revival of his fortunes in the middle of the twentieth century was encouraged by a new generation of star performers. The most famous was the Greek-American soprano Maria Callas (1923–77). Operas such as *Norma* had never entirely disappeared from the repertoire, but when Callas appeared in the title role in the early 1950s, she made the opera newly popular, and inspired excavations of Bellini's lesser-known works. We will never know what Giuditta Pasta sounded like in 'Casta diva', but exactly what Callas managed to do with the aria during those early years of her fame is well-preserved on recordings. Revisiting them today, Callas's Bellini-like awareness of detail remains extraordinary. She pays minute attention to the subtle turns of the melody, varying her vibrato and mode of attack to make the succession of notes speak volumes. Such is Bellini's fortune: that singers mined his long, long lines, over the centuries, for the purest of operatic gold.

10
Young Verdi

By the mid-1840s Bellini had been dead for a decade and Donizetti was forced by illness into premature retirement. As we saw in the last chapter, both had made important changes to the Rossinian 'code' that spread throughout Italy (and then the rest of Europe) in the 1820s; but – although conservative contemporaries often had reservations – neither has been seen as a revolutionary. For one thing, neither challenged the formal outlines that had solidified during the Rossinian period. Their individuality came in different ways, mostly by altering forms from within – changing the way sentiments were uttered but leaving the exterior largely intact. By the 1840s, this meant that Italian opera had begun to seem conservative. As opera in other countries became ever more adventurous, and as instrumental genres acquired greater importance in the musical universe, the Italians stubbornly continued in the old ways, widening the gap between themselves and composers elsewhere (operatic or otherwise). This conservatism did little to damage their popular appeal, but it caused Italian opera gradually to lose aesthetic prestige, the pedigree of progressiveness. By the 1860s, and for the first time in operatic history, the hegemony of the Italian manner of doing things with opera was being called into question.

It is a paradox that this loss of prestige coincided with the career of Giuseppe Verdi (1813–1901). The paradox is so glaring that Verdi is often cast as perpetually struggling to overcome his legacy, to shake off the restraints of the Italian tradition and emerge blinking into the freedoms of the later nineteenth century. Standard accounts tell us that Rossini set up that continual succession of multi-movement forms, ending with the eternal cabaletta, its showy virtuosity demanded by the eternally imperious prima donna. Donizetti and Bellini, albeit sporadically, had tried to escape this tyranny, but they were gentle and willowy Romantics, and so remained under its spell. The breakthrough came with Verdi, the full-bearded revolutionary. Equipped with powerful implements and firm resolve, he managed to fight free from the formal shackles, forswearing cabalettas and other singer-pleasing, applause-seeking clichés.[1]

There is some truth in this story. Opera in all languages and national traditions became less predictable during the nineteenth century, and Verdi's operas are no exception. The replacement of solo arias with duets and other types of musical dialogue, something that had been in train since at least the middle of the eighteenth century, gathered pace; and these dialogue episodes became less likely to fit pre-established patterns such as the Rossinian multi-movement duet. But, despite all this, there remains the unfortunate fact that, in the broad European context of such formal innovation, Verdi's early operas were reactionary rather than revolutionary. In one sense, the idea of revolution sits even more uncomfortably when applied to him than it did when Stendhal, famously, attached it to Rossini. Verdi was, it is true, fond of grand epistolary gestures to the contrary. To the librettist of *Il trovatore* (1853) he confided that: 'If in the opera there were no cavatinas, duets, trios, choruses, finales, etc., and if the whole work consisted ... of a single number, I should find it all the more right and proper.'[2] These are fine words, and are often quoted. But *Il trovatore* turned out to be among Verdi's most conventional operas – in some senses a triumphant *celebration* of the old forms – and is none the worse for it. For the most part, and in spite of hortatory statements to the contrary, Verdi held faith with the Rossinian code. More than anyone, he was responsible for keeping Italian opera distinct from the styles emerging in other countries. When, in mid- and late career, he followed everyone else by loosening these forms, he was rebelling against constraints to which he himself had given a new lease of life.

THE PAGES OPENED

With its clear-cut multi-movement arias and duets, Verdi's first great success, the biblical drama *Nabucco* (Nebuchadnezzar, 1842), is in many ways closer to Rossini than are the late works of Donizetti or Bellini. The reason is not hard to find: tinkering with the Rossinian code, blurring the distinction between recitative and aria, was not at this stage as important to him as a more basic kind of dramatic immediacy. When instructing a later conductor about how *Nabucco* should go, he was unequivocal: 'as for the tempi', he said, 'they should not be too broad. They should all move.'[3] While that was an exaggeration (there are obvious moments of lyrical relaxation in *Nabucco*), Verdi showed from the very start a directness of vocal utterance that made his operas unmistakable. Yes, he sometimes wrote passages of ornamentation reminiscent of his predecessors, but these were the exception. More typically, Verdi reined in any suggestion of vocal elaboration, constraining his singers to communicate within a tight sequence of symmetrical phrases. We hardly ever get movements such as the mad scene in Donizetti's *Lucia*, in which the musical progress seems to stall during massive floods of ornament. Verdi wanted above all to sculpt the progress of musical time. He wanted his auditors to be aware of his controlling presence, as a composer.

The chorus of Hebrew slaves in Act 3 of *Nabucco*, 'Va pensiero', the most famous melody in the opera, indeed one of the most famous in all opera, is a case in point, even though it is choral and even though it moves at a stately pace. The poetry supplied by the librettist Temistocle Solera for these slaves, captive in Babylonia and looking nostalgically towards their homeland, is full of naïve nature-painting and echoes of the 137th Psalm:

Va pensiero sull'ali dorate,
Va ti posa sui clivi, sui colli,
Ove olezzano libere e molli
L'aure dolci del suolo natal!
Del Giordano le rive saluta,
Di Sïonne le torri atterrate . . .
Oh mia patria sì bella e perduta!
Oh membranza sì cara e fatal!

[Go thoughts on golden wings, / go rest upon the slopes, the hills, / where, soft and mild, the sweet breezes / of our homeland smell so sweet! / Greet the banks of the Jordan, / the ruined towers of Zion . . . / Oh, my homeland so beautiful and lost! / Oh remembrance so dear and fateful!]

This invitation to sentimentality and antique word-painting is taken up in the orchestral introduction. But when the chorus enters, the filigree comes to a halt. The melody is simple, disarmingly so, a series of symmetrical phrases, with no rhythmic or harmonic surprises, just a steady alternation of dotted rhythms and triplets over a rocking accompaniment. More surprising still is that the chorus sing mostly in unison, as if they have one collective voice (Rossini called the piece 'a grand aria sung by sopranos, contraltos, tenors and basses'[4]). When they break into harmony, they do so in the simple parallel thirds typical of Italian folk music.

This new, hyper-direct voice, its brand of radical simplicity, took the Italian opera world by storm. Within a few years, *Nabucco* had been performed all over Italy and in many far-flung places around the world. A few years more and Verdi had overtaken all his rivals and predecessors, becoming (and remaining to this day) Italy's most famous and popular opera composer. There are many reasons for this fame, but it is important to start with the essentials. Verdi was, like all the greatest opera composers, fundamentally a musical dramatist. He was content to write in the standard musical parlance of the day, in idioms that he knew could communicate readily to his audiences; but through these predictable shapes he channelled an acute sense of dramatic time and – his means to this end – an undeviating sense of musical direction.

Like so many nineteenth-century composers, Verdi also proved an able manipulator of his life story. In a Sketch of his early life, published several decades after the events they describe, he headlined 'Va pensiero' as nothing less than the keystone of his entire career, saying that a first, miraculous glance at the words had dragged him back from the abyss, saved him for posterity. The Sketch had up to that point often been gloomy, as befitted a struggling Romantic artist. Verdi had suffered an embarrassing fiasco with his previous opera, a clumpy Rossinian comic work called *Un giorno di regno* (King for a Day, 1840), and this together with personal tragedy had, he tells us, made him resolve never to compose again. His decision held firm until a chance meeting with an impresario forced on him the *Nabucco* libretto. Reluctantly, he carried it away:

> Along the way I felt a kind of vague uneasiness, a supreme sadness, an anguish that swelled in the heart!... I went home and, with a violent gesture, threw the manuscript on the table and stood before it. As it fell,

> the sheaf of pages opened on its own; without knowing how, my eyes stared at the page that lay before me, and this line appeared to me:
>
> 'Va, pensiero, sull'ali dorate. . .'
>
> I glanced over the following lines and received a deep impression from them. . . . I read one passage, I read two: then, steadfast in my intention of not composing, I made an effort of will, forced myself to close the script, and went off to bed! . . . No good. . . . *Nabucco* was trotting about in my head! . . . I got up and read the libretto, not once, but two, three times, so often that in the morning you could say that I knew Solera's entire libretto by heart.[5]

The most remarkable aspect of this Sketch was not that people believed it at the time. It was first published in 1879, when Italy was a very new nation and anxious to shore itself up with national myths. The age was generally prone to 'anecdotal' biographies and autobiographies, flowery artistic justifications and confessions as generous in narrative flair as they were meagre in documentary back-up. What is astonishing is that modern scholars have continued to quote Verdi's account, treating it as a reliable record of an historical event. They have done so even though, elsewhere in the Sketch, Verdi is known to have made gross manipulations. He changed by years the death dates of his two young children, having them and his young wife expire within months of each other in order to intensify the pathetic reach of his story. Such lapses seemed not to matter, however, as soon as 'Va pensiero' became Verdi's topic. The numinous moment, the miraculous appearance of the 'right' text, was too perfect: 'As it fell, the sheaf of pages opened on its own; without knowing how, my eyes stared at the page that lay before me'.

What was, what is going on here? The answer is that Verdi's early music became, and to a degree remains, entangled in an alluring tale about opera and politics, a neat tying together of the two. According to this story, 'Va pensiero' and other Verdi choruses from subsequent operas, such as *I Lombardi alla prima crociata* (The Lombards at the First Crusade, 1843), *Ernani* (1844) and *Attila* (1846), were a rallying cry in what came to be called the Risorgimento (literally, resurgence). Their new manner – aided by suggestions in the text ('la mia patria sì bella e perduta') that were easily understood by audiences as referring to their present situation – is supposed to have energized an emerging

Italian nation, encouraged the masses to the barricades in the revolutions of 1848 and generally acted as a soundtrack to the formation of the nation state in the 1860s. As far as the 1840s are concerned, hardly any historical evidence supports this story. Operatic performances in Italy were occasionally the site of public demonstrations during the immediate run-up to the 1848 revolutions, but Verdi's music was not particularly prone to arouse such demonstrations. Several other composers, in particular gentle, Romantic Bellini, had proven more significant as theatre-based incendiaries. The aftermath of the 1848 revolutions, which failed miserably, makes clear a different and more prosaic story. In the case of Milan (the hub of Verdi's activities during this period) the Austrian authorities, who had been driven from the city in March 1848, were soon back in power, and in the next couple of operatic seasons at La Scala (Carnival 1849 and Carnival 1850) they approved revivals of several of Verdi's greatest hits, *Nabucco, Ernani* and *Attila* included. It is inconceivable in the circumstances that any of these works were associated with the failed revolution.

So why did the connection between Verdi and political upheaval become so strong? Links between operatic history and political history have emerged a few times already in this book, but the nineteenth century is their fulcrum. Such obvious political watersheds as 1814–15 and the collapse of the Napoleonic empire, or the Europe-wide revolutions of 1848, have also been claimed as important moments in operatic history (we do so ourselves in the next chapter). And it's certainly true that, in the largest sense, the 1848 revolutions started a process that shook the opera industry to the core. They posed a dire threat to many of those petty principalities and places of absolute rule that had been such great oilers of the operatic wheel. But in the shorter term these historical events seem to have interrupted the steady production and consumption of operatic pleasure in no more than superficial ways. True, the theatre was an important meeting place for the urban bourgeoisie – in some places, and apart from the church, virtually the only meeting place. Occasionally performances became caught up in the century's great bourgeois revolutions. But it was more often a place where, as had been standard throughout opera's history, the ruling classes could rely on stability and an opportunity to display magnificence and power. As the century progressed and revolutionary movements embraced a wider socio-economic spectrum, an ever larger element of the putative revolutionary population was excluded from all but the humblest of operatic events. Even in Italy, nineteenth-century operatic performances were never 'popular' in a twentieth-century sense. The art form remained a relatively elite entertainment, from which most of the population was barred through simple lack of economic means. Thus any revolutions being depicted on stage, or allegorized in music, were essentially for show, their entertainment value being equivalent to all those other operatic staples, female madness or pathological male jealousy.

However, by the 1860s and 1870s, when Italy had achieved statehood and was searching anxiously for national monuments to symbolize the new order, Verdi's early music lay conveniently by and (with anecdotal help from the great man himself) was found eminently fit for purpose. It seems likely that his image as a bard of political protest was first articulated, almost accidentally, with the brief vogue for the acrostic VIVA V.E.R.D.I. (which stood for VIVA Vittorio Emanuele Re D'Italia, i.e. to acclaim the Piedmontese monarch, who would become united Italy's first king) in late 1858 and 1859. That image then received more stimulus during Verdi's (reluctant) service in the first Italian parliament in the early 1860s. From these and other shards arose the myth of 'Va pensiero' and a few other Verdi choruses, a myth that has remained in stubborn currency ever since. The chorus has served as background accompaniment for countless groups wishing to assert a simple sense of 'Italianness', from the most benign to the most destructive. An instance of the latter comes in Mussolini's regime, which was a great propagator of the patriotic Verdi, for obvious nationalistic reasons. In 1941, in spite of serious military distractions, it financed extensive commemorations of the fortieth anniversary of Verdi's death. One of the most impressive publications marking 1941 was an iconography of Verdi's life and times, which featured on its final page a picture of the Duce enjoying his Verdi, seated among the audience but placed on a specially raised platform.[6] Political appropriations of 'Va pensiero' go backwards and forwards from this grim moment, backwards to Verdi's attempts to boost its significance in his own life story, forwards to its recent appearance as the 'Padanian hymn' (*l'inno della Padania*) of the north Italian separatist group, the Lega Nord.

None of this is to deny that opera in the early nineteenth century was in many ways intimately bound up with the idea of nation and national representation; nor that much operatic music in the lead-up to 1848,

Verdi's included, sometimes traced in its contours a new mood, glorifying public energy and the possibility of action, albeit with the aim to entertain and beguile rather than to engender actual political engagement. We will see potent examples of this mood later in this chapter, and in those that follow. Nor does it deny that 'Va pensiero' is an extraordinary piece of choral music: it would not have been elevated to its position both present and past without that potent mixture of melodic single-mindedness and popular appeal. But political events and operatic events are very different, their relationship is often complex and subterranean. In this case, Verdi's reputation as 'bard of the Italian Risorgimento' was real enough, but it was for the most part constructed in the latter half of the nineteenth century, when a young, newly consolidated, fragile Italy required cultural monuments to cement a sense of national identity, and in which 'Va pensiero' supplied an intoxicating recollection of simpler times past.

SOPHIE LOEWE, TENOR SOPRANO

The explosive effect of Verdi's presence on the Italian operatic scene was at first mostly restricted to the northern half of the peninsula, but by the mid-1840s he was making an impact even in the south, and had also established a reputation (at first strongly contested) in the German lands, France and Britain. His distinctive new voice was part of the reason his later fame as a 'revolutionary' took shape. And although this voice speaks out clearly in the powerful simplicity of 'Va pensiero', it was at least as obvious to contemporary audiences in his music for solo singers, then and always at the centre of operatic communication. Although the young Verdi did little to challenge the formal devices of his predecessors, his way with vocalists went decisively beyond them. For example his fifth opera, *Ernani*, shows important variations in something as basic as the classic 'vocal triangle'. The manly tenor was now a fixed feature. While Donizetti only flirted with this new type of romantic hero, Verdi was virtually unwavering in his allegiance. To balance the tenor came darker-voiced, often more psychologically complex antagonists: the Verdian baritone, whose uppermost vocal reaches Verdi remorselessly pushed; and the booming Verdian bass, the voice of the patriarch, the symbol of political or religious power.

These new vocal allegiances were controversial. Although Verdi's popularity in the north of Italy soon swept all before it, that was not the case in the south; still less was it so abroad, where national and other sensibilities were often at stake. One of the most vociferous anti-Verdians was the long-time critic of *The Times* of London, James William Davison. Performances of *Nabucco* in 1850 stimulated one of his very many jeremiads:

> Never was a writer of operas so destitute of real invention, so destitute in power or so wanting in the musician's skill. His sole art consists in weaving ballad tunes – we never find any tune in his songs – into choruses which, sung in unison, make an immense noise; or in working up a finale by means of a tremendous crash of the brass instruments, drum and cymbals and voices screaming at the top of their register.[7]

The three main reasons critics found Verdi troublesome are neatly laid before us here: he was too popular (the 'ballad tunes') at a time when the divisions between 'elite' and 'popular' music were just beginning to form; he made too much noise, both chorally and in his orchestra, which habitually used the loudest new instruments (the brass in particular); and he misused the voices cruelly, obliging singers to scream rather than sing.

Although Davison didn't mention it, one of the young Verdi's most startling innovations, present in both *Nabucco* and *Ernani*, involved the soprano voice. His operas of the 1840s feature women of two distinct types. The first are heroines of the conventional feminine sort, with much fluttering and fainting amid showers of vocal ornament. Verdi could manage this when his sopranos proved incapable of anything more roburst; he did so, however, by resorting to a rather old-fashioned musical language. He was more at home with an opposite and almost wholly new type – sopranos who sacrificed beauty of tone and ornament at the altar of sheer forcefulness. This new species adopted what became Verdian trademarks: liberal use of the low, chest register; preference for short, intense utterances rather than long lyrical lines; and ornamental writing that, far from embellishing the line, was bound in with it and rigorously restrained. Music like this, requiring both force and agility, proved extremely hard to sing, and virtually impossible to sing beautifully; it aimed for dramatic effect at the expense of vocal poise.

The plot of *Ernani*, based on a drama by the arch-Romantic Frenchman Victor Hugo (1802–85), has plausibly been retold in abstract, new-Verdian vocal terms as the story of a soprano besieged by three male voices.[8] The higher the male voice, the more youthful and more romantically successful its possessor; but, as so often in opera, life expectancy diminishes alarmingly as one ascends the vocal ladder. On the top male rung is the tenor, Ernani, a nobleman turned bandit, who is loved by the soprano, Elvira; next down is the suave baritone, Don Carlo, the King of Spain, whom Elvira treats with cautious respect; growling away at the bottom is the bass, Silva, old, noble, vengeful and nasty, whom Elvira hates but to whom she is betrothed. There is a further twist. Although plot-Elvira is a classic passive female, around whom all these lovers circulate while casting heavy curses on each other, voice-Elvira is as far from passive as can be imagined; in fact she is the most forceful musical presence in the opera. Such is the alchemy that operatic music can perform on gender stereotypes.

The opening two multi-movement arias of *Ernani* illustrate the new vocal regime perfectly. In libretto terms, a scene for forceful, dynamic, tragic Ernani is followed by one for passive, love-lorn, tragic Elvira. But the music turns this on its head. Ernani has his share of high notes and lively syncopation, but Elvira's aria is on an entirely different level of musical energy – is indeed a classic example of the new Verdian voice. Far from dissolving into vocal virtuosity in the manner of Verdi's Italian predecessors, both movements of her aria continue to harness the ornamentation within periodic phrases. The energy so typical of Verdi's early operas is thus created – through a tightening of form coupled with an intensification of expressive content. The fact that the contrast between tenor and soprano is so noticeable also chimed with the changing vocal qualities of a new generation of female performers: Verdi, like his predecessors, was careful to tailor his vocal writing to the skills of his first vocal interpreters, as were all operatic composers. In this case, Elvira was created by the formidable Sophie Loewe (1812–66), a German soprano whose directness of vocal utterance was undoubtedly an influence on Verdi's 'new vocal woman'.

In the final trio in Act 4 of *Ernani*, this new intensity of vocal utterance becomes extraordinary. Elvira and Ernani are about to be married, the problem of Don Carlo's interest in Elvira having disappeared, reasonably enough, when he is elected Holy Roman Emperor in Act 3.

But old Silva is still lurking out there somewhere – Ernani struck a fateful pact with him, as a result of which his life is now forfeit whenever Silva decides to claim it. Wedding preparations are cut short by the sound of a distant horn, Silva's sign that he is calling in his pact. Silva's appearance then precipitates the final trio, 'Ferma, crudel, estinguere' (Stop, cruel one, extinguish). As in 'Va pensiero', a simple alternation of triplets and dotted figures creates a concentration on crucial pitches and melodic shapes – and hardly any ornamentation or other possibility of conventionally beautiful singing. The trio thus becomes a remorseless exploration of vocal desperation, with the orchestra precipitating the voices forward through the drive of its accompaniment patterns. The soprano and her two male antagonists are strikingly similar as voices, with no hint of the gender distinctions Donizetti's operas had emphasized. On the contrary, Elvira yields nothing to Ernani in vehemence of declamation, and the bass matches them both in fierceness. In the *Ernani* final trio, *everyone* sings like the new, manly tenor.

FELICE VARESI, UGLY BARITONE

In the decade after *Ernani*, Verdi produced a steady succession of operas (roughly one a year), his worldwide fame ever greater. His basic musical personality changed little (always that forcefulness and dynamism), but almost every work breaks new ground. *Ernani* had made effective use of a recurring motif, a solemn melody associated with the pact between Ernani and Silva; in his next opera, *I due Foscari* (The Two Foscari, 1844), Verdi experimented with a larger system of recurring motifs, all the major characters being given a melodic tag that is restated each time they enter.

As we saw in earlier chapters, reminiscence themes had long been used in French and German opera, and they could be effective if saved for special moments – interruptions of normal operatic procedure. The problem in *I due Foscari* is that the recurring themes are more numerous but don't develop as the characters move through the opera: they simply get restated, as a kind of musical 'calling card' presented on each entrance. The themes quickly begin to sound redundant: the music simply replicates what our eyes have already taken in, and who needs a calling card on the *second* visit? They are also constricting, the characters seeming forever trapped within the musical gestures of their themes. The experiment taught Verdi a valuable lesson. His later treatment of recurring themes would never again be so systematic, and he found other ways of injecting musical connections into his operas. But *I due Foscari* raises a question that nevertheless becomes acute in the later nineteenth century: how much musical connection should an opera strive for? As the prestige of instrumental music, with its connective musical tissue such as themes subjected to elaborate development and periodic return, became ever greater, so the pressure intensified for operatic composers to display symphonic wares.

After *I due Foscari*, Verdi continued to experiment, sometimes returning to the grand choral style first heard in *Nabucco*, sometimes trying out more intimate subjects with greater literary sophistication. The most ambitious was *Macbeth* (1847). Fuelled by a longstanding interest in Shakespeare, Verdi took special pains over the opera, and later discouraged it featuring as an 'opera di ripiego' (a stop-gap work used to fill up the repertory if other, more important productions failed). Most revealing, though, is a comment he made as late as 1875, at a time when – much to his annoyance – he was being bombarded by questions about Richard Wagner. An interviewer in Vienna steered round to the inevitable topic, and Verdi is reported as commenting in a most surprising manner:

> When our conversation turned to Wagner, Verdi remarked that this great genius had done opera an incalculable service, because he had had the courage to free himself from the tradition of the aria-opera; 'I too attempted to blend music and drama, in my *Macbeth*', he added, 'but unlike Wagner I was not able to write my own libretti'.[9]

What might Verdi have meant? The most important experiment in *Macbeth* is the new way musical moods define two strands of the opera's world, giving them what Verdi later called *tinte* or identifying colours. The first strand belongs to the witches, and is largely confined to the opening scenes of the first and third acts, which in Verdi's words had to be 'trivial but in an extravagant and original way'.[10] Both scenes move from the minor to the major mode, and both employ similar musical means to depict the witches: sudden changes of rhythm and texture; rapid, Mendelssohnian passages in thirds for the strings; dark woodwind sonorities. The second strand of *tinta* is associated with Macbeth (baritone) and Lady Macbeth (soprano) and is more widespread. Here there is a prominent recurring motif: a simple alternation of middle C with the note a semitone above, which accompanies Macbeth's words 'Tutto è finito!' (All is finished) as he returns from murdering King Duncan, immediately before his Act 1 duet with Lady Macbeth. This device was very different from the calling cards of *I due Foscari*; the 'tutto è finito' idea is simple enough to perform its purpose without ostentation, and flexible enough to function in subterranean ways, in particular disappearing into accompanying figures.

But *Macbeth* offers more than just an added sense of musical coherence. In order to do justice to the excess – in particular the free mixing of the comic and serious – that the nineteenth century found in Shakespeare, Verdi was even more uncompromising about the vocal urgency of his dramatic message. A hint of this comes in a letter by Emanuele Muzio, Verdi's composition pupil and general dogsbody, who could be relied on to repeat uncritically his master's opinions. Writing to a mutual friend, Muzio stressed *Macbeth*'s novel use of the baritone protagonist, whom they hoped would be sung by Felice Varesi (1813–89), one of the great singer-actors of the day (he later created both Rigoletto and Germont *père* in *La traviata*):

> Now everything depends on an answer from Varesi; if Varesi agrees to sing in Florence . . . then [Verdi] will write *Macbeth*, in which there are only two principals: [Lady Macbeth] and Macbeth – Loewe and Varesi. The others are secondary roles. No actor in Italy can do Macbeth better than Varesi: because of his way of singing, because of his intelligence and even because he's small and ugly. Perhaps you'll say that he sings out of tune, but it doesn't matter at all because the part would be almost completely declaimed, and he's very good at that.[11]

Verdi's own letters to Varesi were more circumspect, but their sentiments were the same. It is also significant that Verdi imagined Loewe, so forceful a presence in *Ernani*, for the part of Lady Macbeth. In the end she was not available, but Verdi was adamant that he must have someone who was a fitting partner for the unprepossessing but uniquely dramatic Varesi. When one of the greatest sopranos of the period, Eugenia Tadolini, was suggested as Lady Macbeth, Verdi rejected her with great explicitness:

> Tadolini's qualities are far too good for this role. . . . Tadolini has a beautiful and attractive appearance, and I would like Lady Macbeth to be ugly and evil. Tadolini's voice has an angelic quality; and I would like the Lady's voice to have something of the diabolical! The two principal numbers in the opera are . . . the duet between Lady and her husband and the sleepwalking scene. If these numbers fail, then the opera is ruined. And these pieces must not be sung: they must be acted out and declaimed with a very hollow and veiled voice; otherwise they won't be able to make any effect.[12]

This was an astonishing reversal of the values that had sustained Italian opera through the eighteenth century and up to Rossini, in which beauty of vocal delivery had conquered all in the expression of drama. Vocal beauty, the quality that had portrayed saints and sinners alike for so long, quite suddenly became insufficient. Voice must now suit character.

The kind of music Verdi wrote for these extraordinary performers is well illustrated by the Act 1 'Gran Scena e Duetto', which he mentioned as one of the opera's 'principal numbers'. Its outer shell, as so often in early Verdi, follows the old Rossinian four-movement model; but internally there are sea changes. Not least is that the duet is introduced by a remarkable accompanied recitative, 'Mi si affaccia un pugnal?!' (Is this a dagger I see before me?), as Macbeth steels himself to murder Duncan. This passage is unusually rich in musical invention, as sliding chromatic figures jostle with distorted, mock-religious harmonies and fugitive reminiscences of the witches' music. It sets in motion a fluid musical argument that doesn't so much *introduce* the formal movements of the duet as set their tone; the recitative language becomes, in other words, a vocal model for what follows. The first fixed-tempo movement begins as Macbeth returns, having murdered the king, to meet Lady Macbeth. As mentioned, Macbeth's first utterance, 'Tutto è finito!', then presents in its simplest form a recurring motif that becomes critical to the fabric of the duet. As if to demonstrate this, its distinctive musical contours immediately migrate into the accompaniment material. A crucial reversal thus takes place. On the surface the first movement involves a rapid exchange between the characters, with an emphasis on recitative-like declamation over orchestral underpinning; but the orchestral contribution is impregnated with the 'Tutto è finito' motif. The orchestra doesn't just communicate a standard sense of agitation, but has precise semantic associations. In other words, it performs a narrative role.

Even though this duet is conventional in being cast in multi-movement form, it is unconventional in making few distinctions in vocal behaviour between one movement and the next. Both characters express themselves mostly in stifled phrases. In the first two movements, Macbeth makes sporadic attempts to introduce more traditionally lyrical ideas (in the first movement he recalls Duncan's sleeping attendants, in the second with 'Com'angeli d'ira' – Like angels of anger); but on both occasions he is countered, silenced even, by brittle ornamental explosions from Lady Macbeth, who derides his doubts as 'follie' (madness). The fact that her crazed coloratura recurs in three of the four movements is itself unusual, contributing to the sense that the entire duet is a single musical argument. Equally important, though, is that Verdi uses her vocal virtuosity to unorthodox ends. What had traditionally been decorative and ornamental here marks hysteria, or at the least forced, unconvincing gaiety. In other words, in this heavily charged, declamatory world, vocal ornament becomes jarring, laden with negative meaning. The final movement of the duet, traditionally the place in which ornament spills forth no matter what, makes this clearer still: it is stifled and subdued throughout, ending with isolated staccato exclamations low in the singers' registers.

It was a further mark of *Macbeth*'s significance that Verdi agreed to add ballet music to a revival planned for Paris's Théâtre Lyrique in 1865; he also decided to make substantial changes to some sections that were, as he called them, 'either weak or lacking in character'.[13] These included a new aria for Lady Macbeth in Act 2 ('La luce langue'; The light weakens) and the replacement of Macbeth's death scene with a final, French-sounding 'Inno di vittoria' (Hymn of victory). The Paris version is what we usually hear today, in spite of the stylistic dissonances Verdi's revisions create. 'La luce langue' makes no attempt to adapt to the surrounding musical atmosphere, indeed is one of the most radical stretches of music (both orchestrally and harmonically) that Verdi had written even by the mid-1860s. Another example is the 'Inno di vittoria'. The 1847 death scene it replaced was faithful to Macbeth's vocal personality, being almost entirely declaimed, and returning chillingly to the tonality and motivic ambience of the Act 1 duet with Lady Macbeth. The 'Inno', on the other hand, is a jaunty chorus of celebration, with a virtual quotation of 'La Marseillaise' at the end (something guaranteed to get the French up and saluting). These revisions again raise the question often asked in this book, and critical in the nineteenth century and beyond: how much musical coherence does an opera need? In 1847, Verdi invested parts of *Macbeth* with much connective musical tissue (recurring orchestral combinations, motifs that appear periodically in different context, etc.); in 1865 he sacrificed some of this to bring his opera up to date and make it more amenable to Parisian taste. Today we have access to both versions; we can (at least on recordings) mix-and-match, perhaps including 'La luce langue' but retaining the old death scene. And the choices may well be invigorating, reminding us that operatic texts from the past need not be sacred objects, even in today's museum culture.

LAUGHING VILLAIN, WEEPING JESTER

In 1847, the year of *Macbeth*, Verdi transferred to Paris and remained there for most of the next two years. It was an important move, most of his subsequent operas betraying obvious Parisian manners, including French-style arias and a greater refinement of orchestral writing. Much of this came from exposure to Meyerbeer and other *grand opéra* composers; but Verdi also attended more humble theatrical events. In his *Stiffelio* (1850) the final scene is influenced by spoken melodrama, then hugely popular in the Parisian boulevard theatres. In some scenes, intense personal confrontation is mimed or declaimed over a spare, atmospheric orchestral background, in a manner very similar to what was happening in spoken theatre. It was a style Verdi would use to even greater effect in the operas of the early 1850s, in particular *Rigoletto* (1851), which marked another stage in his long musical development.

Verdi's early letters about the setting of Victor Hugo's play *Le Roi s'amuse* (The King Amuses Himself, 1832, another Romantic drama in the vein of *Hernani*) brim over with enthusiasm. 'There's a character in it who is one of the greatest creations that the theatre of all countries and all times can boast';[14] '[Rigoletto] is a creation worthy of Shakespeare!'[15] The elevated comparison should alert us. Like Hugo, whose Preface to *Le Roi s'amuse* he had surely read, Verdi found in his new protagonist a tragic divide that posed new musical challenges. Even the greatest of his past operatic characters had tended to be one-dimensional. Like their eighteenth-century forebears, they may be cruelly torn by conflicting emotions (romantic love and filial duty, or personal and public responsibilities); but these trials are visited on them by the plot mechanism, not by faults within themselves. Their behaviour under duress is always resolutely predictable. Rigoletto was to be different. The seeds of his destruction are embedded deep in his own psyche. Outwardly he is deformed, a hunchbacked jester who encourages a debauched and unscrupulous ruler. Secretly, though, he nurtures a beloved daughter who is innocent of the evil that surrounds her. As Hugo put it with uncharacteristic economy: 'Triboulet [Hugo's name for what became the Rigoletto character] has two pupils, the king whom he instructs in vice, his daughter whom he rears in virtue. One will destroy the other.'[16]

The plot is easily told. Rigoletto (baritone) is court jester to the Duke of Mantua (tenor), a notorious philanderer. The Duke's latest enthusiasm is a young woman called Gilda (soprano); he ardently woos her after illicitly entering the walled garden in which she is enclosed. His courtiers discover that she is under the protection of Rigoletto (they assume she is a mistress) and, in the finale of Act 1, they abduct her. In Act 2 Rigoletto tries to rescue Gilda, but finds that she has been seduced by the Duke; he swears revenge. In the final act, Rigoletto hires an assassin, Sparafucile (bass), to murder the Duke, but Gilda hears of the plan and – having fallen in love with her seducer – allows herself to be killed in his place. Rigoletto takes delivery of what he thinks is the Duke's body in a sack, but then hears the still-libidinous aristocrat singing of love from afar; he opens the sack to find his daughter on the brink of death.

Verdi saw his complex baritone protagonist as another operatic experiment, one whose influence could spread to all the major characters. In part this was, as with *Ernani* and *Macbeth*, a continuing play with voice-characters. Rigoletto was again tailored for and created by Felice Varesi, whose smallness and ugliness made him highly desirable for the role, and whose melodramatic exterior as the wrong character (deformed, and thus – according to the melodramatic codes of the day – evil), could then be contradicted by his dramatic presence and ability to move audiences. But there were further changes. Gilda starts the opera as an old-fashioned soprano: her Act 1 entrance aria, 'Caro nome' (Dear name), is a famous virtuoso display piece. But as events overtake her, and particularly after she is seduced, she changes vocally, adopting a more direct style – in Act 3 even matching the declamatory mode of her father. The most surprising innovation is in the tenor role. For the most part, the philandering Duke's musical idiom is close to comic opera: voice-Duke is, in other words, charming and persuasive, and is fitted out with almost all the opera's famous melodies. But plot-Duke is unrelievedly negative. Just as Lady Macbeth's vocal virtuosity acquired a new, sinister meaning, so here the entire façade of easy, lyrical singing is called into question: it is placed at the command of a libertine, a man whose outer charm is grotesquely ill matched to his inner cynicism.

There is one further important aspect of *Rigoletto*'s innovation in vocal personae. Previous Verdi characters had been vividly differentiated by voice type and mode of singing, but they had all expressed themselves through largely identical vehicles – the multi-movement arias, duets and ensembles that, somewhat against international trends, remained the building blocks of Verdian opera. But, in *Rigoletto*, Verdi for the first time distinguished between the main characters through their engagement with these forms. Rigoletto is the emotional centre of the drama but has no multi-movement arias. He typically sings in a free, declamatory style, one that allows the tragic division in his character to be made musically manifest in an immediate way. On the other hand, the Duke perpetually inhabits stock formal numbers, both his charm and his superficiality thus projected through this sense of conventional predictability, just as his mellifluous tenor seems to have emigrated from some *bel canto* paradise lost. Caught between the two, forever responding to one and then the other, is Gilda, who moves from extreme conventionality to extreme fragmentation as she grows up, painfully, during the drama.

In this sense it is fitting that *Rigoletto*'s most celebrated number is the Act 3 Quartet 'Bella figlia dell'amore' (Beautiful child of love). Rigoletto has brought Gilda to a remote inn to show her the man she loves continuing in his philandering ways. The Quartet has all the principals sing together, but they remain crucially divided: Rigoletto and Gilda stand outside the inn, peering in on the Duke, who is courting his latest flame, Maddalena (contralto). Verdi conducted a radical experiment, making the Quartet's most distinctive feature its vocal difference. The Duke (who carries the main melodic thread) is ardent, lyrical and wholly conventional, advancing his amorous suit with a rhythmic predictability that teeters on the banal, punctuated by staccato woodwind chords after each phrase and by Maddalena's chatter. Rigoletto, at the opposite pole, is stubbornly *un*lyrical, his line made up of declamatory outbursts, often on a single note. And Gilda is as ever caught between these two, expressing herself in fragmented, 'sobbing' figures. One early commentator described her contribution to the Quartet as 'canto spezzato'[17] – a broken song for a broken, divided heart.

These musical innovations in the *Rigoletto* Quartet have often been extolled – the number is iconic in histories of Italian opera. Less often mentioned is that Verdi followed Hugo in placing the Quartet within an innovative scenic picture:

> Divided stage. Deserted bank of the Mincio. To the left is a two-storey house, half-ruined, whose front, facing the audience, reveals through a large arch the inside of a rustic inn on the ground floor. A rough ladder leads to the loft, within which, from a balcony without shutters, is visible a cot. On the side of the building which faces the street is a door that opens towards the inside: the wall, furthermore, is so full of cracks that from the outside one can easily see what is happening within.

As many contemporary illustrations of the scene demonstrate – it was a favourite among engravers and appeared on the frontispieces of many libretti and vocal scores – the characters of the Quartet are further separated by this divided stage. The Duke and Maddalena flirt in a warmly lit interior; Rigoletto and Gilda peer through cracks in the wall from the dark outside. There could be no more telling representation of the harshness of the divide, the gulf between characters, the impossible rifts that fuel their march towards destiny.

What exactly is the nature of this rift? Just as those conflicts made the title character so stimulating to Verdi, so these fractures play out a mid-nineteenth-century version of the divide between outside and inside, between the public and the private world. Rigoletto is the public figure, the court jester who hides within himself an intense private world – the world of Gilda, locked away from view. It is when, near the end of the first act, these two worlds collide, when the Duke slips into Gilda's garden to pursue his adventures, and then when his courtiers abduct her, that the tragedy is set in motion. In Act 2 Rigoletto appears in the ducal palace, searching for his lost daughter, still acting out his public persona as jester. But he soon realizes that, just beyond the public space bounded by the stage set, on the other side of a door to the side, his daughter is alone with the Duke – that something he would call seduction and we would call rape is taking place. 'Cortigiani, vil razza dannata' he rails (Courtiers, you vile, damned creatures). The outburst is nothing like an aria in the conventional sense, more a fragmented series of emotions that ends in a plea. Laying bare his hidden, private emotions, he begs to have access to the hidden space in which the true action of the opera is taking place.

'The time is out of joint', says Hamlet after seeing his father, who belongs in another world, standing before him on the battlements. The phrase could be a motto for *Rigoletto*. Public and private are disturbingly intertwined. The feigned emotions and posturing of the public world can penetrate and damage irreparably the private places where true feelings are harboured. No wonder Verdi called his protagonist 'worthy of Shakespeare', and no wonder that *Rigoletto* marked an important new stage in his operatic career.

Verdi's early operas are in many ways predictable. Like Donizetti and Bellini, he preferred to follow the old forms and change operatic manners from within, in his case by single-mindedly raising the emotional temperature, forcing the voices into new, more declamatory modes. But after *Rigoletto* this early manner never returned. From then on the old certainties – of character, of venue, of musical conventions that could align characters in predictable patterns – were never again to be trusted. Verdi did sometimes return to the old Rossinian code, and use it to great effect. But the choice was by no means automatic. Operatic forms, like operatic space and operatic characters, had quite suddenly become more unpredictable.

11
Grand Opera

In 1946, the American publisher Simon & Schuster brought out a musical anthology called *A Treasury of Grand Opera*. Designed for opera lovers who might also be aspiring musicians, the book includes excerpts from seven operas, all in simplified vocal score, with English translations under the vocal lines for immediate access. The original languages are given only in italics below the English, and all arias entailing professional-calibre high notes are transposed comfortably down, sometimes by drastic intervals. Each opera has its own chapter, the musical excerpts preceded by a synopsis illustrated with charcoal and pastel drawings (see Figure 26). This post-war collection marked the end point of a long historical tradition of adapting and publishing opera for amateur performance at home. Such arrangements go back at least to the eighteenth century and usually involved voice and/or keyboard, or accommodations for other instruments. When Wagner was living in Paris in the late 1830s, he earned part of his meagre living by adapting popular French operas for various combinations – by no means the only fledgling composer to rely on such hack work. By the later nineteenth century, at the height of music-at-home, popular operas would emerge in literally dozens of instrumental formats. One patient bibliographer has unearthed over 400 separate publications that serve up excerpts of *La traviata* for amateur consumption. There's even a version of the entire opera for solo clarinet, a daunting prospect for that slow Sunday evening in the parlour.[1] Most of this homespun activity took place before the advent of the gramophone and radio, in those halcyon days when the way to take opera home was in a form you could play or sing yourself. Amid all this book's talk of theatres and premieres, there's an important point here: taking opera home has always been part of its pleasure. Almost as long as there have been live performances, a passion for repeating the experience in some form – on demand, away from the theatre and its professionals – has remained compelling.

What was meant by Grand Opera back in 1946? *Don Giovanni*, *Lohengrin*, *La traviata*, *Faust*, *Aida*, *Carmen* and *Pagliacci*. These works were hugely popular in Britain and America in the years before the Second World War. They were staples at elite theatres such as Covent Garden and the Metropolitan, but were also served up (and sometimes boiled down) in innumerable more modest venues. Often they were tweaked to fit the mould better: *Lohengrin* might be given in Italian, still opera's default language, not to mention its default repertory; *Carmen* and *Faust* were usually equipped with recitatives rather than spoken dialogue. But one point the anthology insistently makes is that Grand Opera had few limitations. It could be written by French, Italian or German composers, and although it was mostly a matter of nineteenth-century tragic works, an exception could always be made for Mozart. Nor did Grand Opera always condemn us to hour after hour and act after act: *Pagliacci* detains its audience for no more than seventy-five minutes. Nor does it necessarily require virtuosic performance: *Carmen* makes no such demands. It may parade massed choruses and dazzling visual spectacle (the Triumphal Scene from *Aida* is biggest and best here); but not always, since apart from a few party scenes *La traviata* and *Don Giovanni* are chamber pieces by comparison. Judging by the *Treasury,* Grand Opera in 1946 was not so much a genre as something you associate with a long-deceased great aunt, fondly recalled for the ropes of pearls, the mink and the whiff of mothballs. It's a repertory, an attitude and a mark of status all rolled into one, and wrapped up in conventions for staging and costumes whose sentimental realism is captured so perfectly by those charcoal illustrations.

Grand Opera does not, then, simply mean general operatic grandeur or glamour. We have already seen a great deal of that in emphatically pre-*Treasury* repertoires. Seventeenth-century opera at Versailles gave us Lully's five-act spectaculars, with their fantastic décor and outrageous flattery of the monarch; as did eighteenth-century *opera seria*, with its kings and emperors, its warriors and flying machines, with the stateliness of their comings and goings. But even if Grand Opera was as broad as the *Treasury* made out, most of its repertoire (Mozart was the big exception) nevertheless owed some debt to a very specific and limited genre. This second, restricted sense of the term started in France, and is best given its French designation, *grand opéra*, a term describing certain works written for the Paris Opéra between the late 1820s and the late 1860s. It's important to remember that in French the word 'grand' also means 'big', so that *grand opéra* is both magnificent opera and, quite simply, opera that is seldom over much before midnight. Grand Opera in the broader, *Treasury*-endorsed sense is mostly a phenomenon of the later nineteenth and twentieth centuries; but, as we shall see later in this book, it was largely formed out of the diffusion of the effects and conventions of the French form, of *grand opéra*.

LUMBERING TORTOISES

The middle years of the nineteenth century in Paris were extraordinary, creating an operatic microclimate that had never occurred before and that allowed *grand opéra* to emerge. It was permitted by state subsidies that were unprecedented by nineteenth-century standards. The *directeur-entrepreneur* of the theatre in the late 1830s and 1840s generally received around 600,000 francs per annum, in addition to free use of the theatre.[2] In spite of this, very few *directeurs* made any money. The costs of putting on a new production were astronomical. The bill for Giacomo Meyerbeer's *Les Huguenots* came to over 100,000 francs just for scenery, costumes and props. Then there was the problem of ever-rising star singer salaries (the best of them, such as the tenor Adolphe Nourrit or the soprano Julie Dorus-Gras, were getting 25,000 francs a year, with 'appearance fees' on top). The eighty chorus members, eighty-piece orchestra and thirty ballet dancers were also a constant drain, even though the poorest among them were paid a pittance. In 1836, the year of *Les Huguenots*, the triangle player, one Dauverné junior, received an annual salary of 300 francs (the orchestra's leader, François-Antoine Haberneck, was on 8,000 francs); some of the female *corps de ballet* were paid so little that they could not afford food and lodging and turned to prostitution.[3]

All this money went to create an international operatic event whose scenic, vocal and orchestral splendour was unprecedented. So much so that the behind-the-scenes complexity became notorious. One dyspeptic onlooker, whose composer partner was more used to the last-minute, budget-strapped Italian scene, but who was trying to make a financial killing with a *grand opéra* in Paris, complained about the 'tortoises of the Opéra'.[4] She was referring to the various people entrusted with details of staging, who would – she said – argue for twenty-four hours about whether a singer's gesture required merely a finger or the entire hand. Staging and movement were no longer left to chance or to singers' whims, as they had been for much of opera's history. It was as if the maxims of choreography were flowing over from the ballets that had for long been integral to French serious opera, spilling out into the management of sung scenes. The obsession with creating a picture, the idea of meticulously managed scenic tableaux, was new and significant. The effect on audiences was undeniable. When it worked (which was by no means all the time) this species of opera so captured the imagination that its impact was felt throughout Europe. Foreigners were perpetually amazed at the lavishness on show. As one wide-eyed American put it in 1838:

> They call this French opera, the 'Académie Royale de Musique', . . . the 'Grand Opera'; this latter name because it has a greater quantity of thunder and lightning, of pasteboard seas, of paper snow storms, and dragons that spit fire; also a gorgeousness of wardrobe and scenery not equalled upon any theatre of Europe. It is certain its 'corps de ballet' can outdance all the world put together. Mercy! How deficient we are in our country in these elegant accomplishments.[5]

Librettists, composers and scene designers from Catania to Stockholm, from Lisbon to Moscow, also felt its power and tried to emulate it. Hardly anyone succeeded. The sad fact was that, outside Paris and its state subsidies, no one found a way to pay the bills.

What were the essential ingredients of *grand opéra*? Our culinary metaphor, the idea of a recipe, is deliberate. No less than Handelian *opera seria* or Rossinian comedy, *grand opéra* had its prerequisites, designed to match a set of audience expectations that seemed largely unchanged over several decades. To merit the name *grand opéra*, you had to concoct something large-scale, serious, French and almost always in five acts. History of a monumental brand furnished plot material, often the history of religious conflict: Jews or Muslims against Christians, perhaps, or Protestants against Catholics. While tragic opera often involved clashing tribes of some kind, librettists writing for the Opéra defined those tribes as whole nations or faiths, not just Montagues and Capulets. You needed

19. Operatic spectators on and off the stage. Natalie Dessay as Donizetti's Lucia at the Metropolitan Opera in 2007, directed by Mary Zimmerman. In her famous mad scene, Lucia appears before the assembled company having stabbed her husband Arturo on their wedding night. The stark contrast of white gown and bloody hands retains its power to shock.

20. A caricature by Gustave Doré from the 1860s in which the grotesque facial and physical contortions of the singers emphasize the strain and exertion that had become typical in operatic performance where vocal heroics trump finesse.

21. *Un bal de l'Opéra* (A Ball at the Opéra), coloured lithograph from the middle of the nineteenth century by Eugène Charles François Guérard (1821–66). From 1821 to 1873 the Paris Opéra ball was held at the Salle Le Peletier, where masked participants were more than happy to shed their inhibitions.

22. The famous divided-stage scene from Act 3 of *Rigoletto* (1851), as illustrated in a card advertising Liebig meat bouillon. Liebig opera cards were issued in German, French and several other languages from 1872 until well into the twentieth century. The bouillon company has taken liberties with the plot, since Rigoletto is shown with the assassin Sparafucile rather than his beloved daughter Gilda.

23. Verdi's funeral procession in Milan, 1901; 300,000 people reportedly attended, more than half the total population of the city. Although his early operas of the 1840s were, at best, only sporadically regarded as political, their composer became a potent symbol of Italian nationhood in the later nineteenth century.

24. Act 3 of Meyerbeer's *L'Africaine* (1865) at the Paris Opéra. The scenic splendour demanded at this theatre is obvious, as is the prevailing taste for operatic sets that seem precariously balanced and far from the *juste milieu* with which the Parisian mid-century is often associated.

25. *Tannhäuser*'s Song Contest in the Wartburg, as staged by the Metropolitan Opera in 2004. This lavish production, designed by Günther Schneider-Siemssen, quotes and re-creates the luminous richness of nineteenth-century German Romantic paintings, conjuring up an idealized and long-lost Middle Ages.

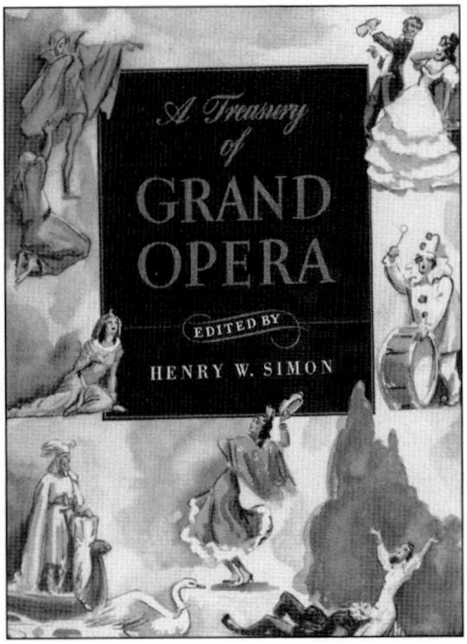

26. The cover of *A Treasury of Grand Opera* (1946), with a montage of scenes from famous works which are featured inside in easy piano arrangements, transposed for amateur voices. Note the central position of opera's most famous gypsy.

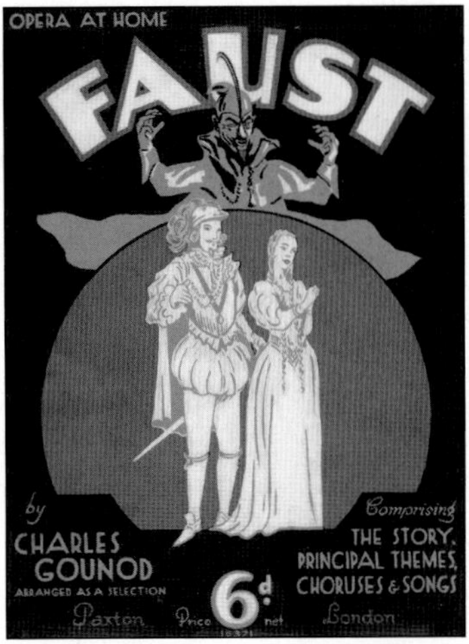

27. Gounod's *Faust* (1859) was one of the most popular operas of the early twentieth century. Here, in 1931, it is arranged and much condensed for solo piano, with libretto text in English helpfully written above the musical staff.

28. Risë Stevens, a famous Carmen, in an advertisement from the 1950s. The endorsement – Stevens prefers Chesterfields because she is 'careful' about her voice – is yet further testament to a bygone age.

29. Sophia Loren as the heroine in Clemente Fracassi's 1953 film spectacular of Verdi's *Aida*. Loren lip-synched and mimed the lead role, which was sung by Renata Tebaldi.

30. Emma Calvé (1858–1942) as Carmen, one of her most famous roles. Calvé was reported to have researched the deep background of the part, touring Spain and even its gypsy camps. George Bernard Shaw said she had 'divested Carmen of the last rag of romance and respectability'.

31. Two robber accomplices in an 1857 London revival of Auber's *Fra Diavolo* (1830). One critic remarked that they were 'the very incarnations of that mixture of the terrible and the ludicrous which go to make perfect specimens of the grotesque'. Another felt that 'their make-up was irresistible'.

32. Jacques Offenbach in a caricature by André Gill, garlanded, astride his cello with baton in hand and surrounded by images of his famous works. In the sketch of *La Belle Hélène* (upper right), Offenbach's head is grafted on to Hélène's body.

33. The Wagnerian anti-hero: the American bass Carl Cochems (1877–1954) as Hagen in *Götterdämmerung*, *c.* 1910. This atmospheric photograph is in striking contrast to the bluff, heroic portraits of contemporary Wagner singers in roles such as Siegfried, Brünnhilde or Wotan.

34. 'Verdi, the Latin Wagner', a caricature by Carl von Stur published in 1887. This was a familiar view of the ageing Verdi. He still has his big drum and barrel organ, and screaming Aida is in the background; but the beret and angry-looking swan (presumably let loose from *Lohengrin*) mark Wagner's inescapable influence.

a long ballet, one that you were obliged, often with desperate ingenuity, to weave into the plot. Charlemagne (or some other grand historical personage) broods on the eve of an important battle? In that case, what could be more fitting than the sudden appearance of a troupe of ballerinas, impersonating nearby gypsies, to beguile his melancholy with dance? To attempt *grand opéra*, you also had to deploy large choral forces in several acts. Your libretto would be set in a decently remote historical period, ideally the Middle Ages or a little later. And you would of course write for the Paris Opéra, an institution that survived the French Revolution and whose changes of name over the course of the nineteenth century track the nation's tumultuous political history: the Académie Royale de Musique (during the Bourbon restoration), the Académie Impériale de Musique (when various Napoleons were in charge) and the Académie Nationale de Musique (during republican times).

Any list of its most successful composers immediately reveals that, although *grand opéra* was always sung in French and almost always first produced in Paris, it was in many senses an international genre, with Italian, French and German composers mixing and matching modes, all of them important in the stylistic miscellany. What's more, the master practitioners made a point of being musically international, as adept at German harmonic exploration and orchestral nuance as they were at French declamation and delicate programmatic touches, or at Italianate vocal lyricism and ornamental extravagance (although this last mode was typically reserved for the lead soprano and no one else). All these styles would be required during the long evening's entertainment. One influential contemporary critic, Joseph d'Ortigue, went even further, announcing that an early *grand opéra*, Meyerbeer's *Robert le diable* (Robert the Devil, 1831), had inaugurated a new, eminently French genre that fused Rossinian *bel canto* with Beethovenian symphonism.[6] Such a formulation, yet another example of that emerging Italian/German opposition we have discussed in earlier chapters, was surely exaggerated: neither of d'Ortigue's musical extremes would have been suitable to the delicate balance of *grand opéra* at its best. But his sentiments, and the height of the ambition he claimed, were typical. What's more, the genre's vaunted internationalism was often enriching rather than merely bewildering. The sheer variety of modes and tones in *grand opéra* make comparisons with the historical novel, that dominant literary genre of the nineteenth century, hard to avoid.

There was, as always with new artistic departures, resistance to *grand opéra*, especially from those who felt that the entire business was too grandiose, and that audience delight in scenic spectacle overpowered all other aspects. Heinrich Heine, whose condescending caricatures of Donizetti and Bellini we met in Chapter 9, suggested that 'nothing exceeds the luxury of the grand opera, which is now become a paradise for the hard of hearing'.[7] Wagner put it more bluntly when he talked, in the context of an attack on Meyerbeer, about 'effects without causes'.[8] But there was no going back. *Grand opéra* raised the stakes, with a richer, denser sonic landscape, louder instruments and more complex orchestration, and voices that could hold their own against such increased sonic competition. These requirements would over subsequent decades become prerequisites for composing serious opera in any language, with the shift to heavier voices especially significant. From the late eighteenth century to the 1840s, the sound of operatic singing would change radically in several ways. We've already seen how, in Italian opera, heroic tenors supplanted altos and sopranos (whether castrati or female) in starring male roles after the 1820s. Though the light, supple voices that had dominated operatic singing did not change overnight into clarion Brünnhildes or red-faced Manricos, the diffusion of *grand opéra* increased a sense, already felt in the Italy of Donizetti and Verdi, that force, with or without agility, would be the new fashion.

The late 1820s in Paris were, then, a significant juncture in the history of operatic voices. Just as important, they saw the beginnings of a new visual regime. A crucial change was the formation of a staging committee at the Opéra, the so-called *Comité de mise-en-scène*, which included those in charge of scene painting, props and general stage management. This made manifest a newfound seriousness about staging practices (what the French call *mise-en-scène*); when wedded to elaborate scenic pictures and machinery it made Paris the centre of all things visual so far as opera was concerned. A key to these scenic developments was the idea that the expanding bourgeoisie of Paris, the new audience that flocked to the Opéra, needed a novel and more sophisticated form of theatrical representation, one in which the old, rough-and-ready historical clichés would no longer be acceptable. As Jean Moynet, an Opéra scene-painter, put it:

> Under the influence of Romanticism, the study of local colour became a necessity. One no longer contented oneself with the 'approximate' or old

> devices which had served until then .... The theatre was asked to make its characters live in the actual environment in which they had lived.[9]

What is more, the variety of styles and effect that was so important to the music of *grand opéra* also became critical in the visual domain. The doyen of scene design in the early days was Pierre-Luc-Charles Cicéri (1782–1868), a landscape painter whose concern for realism took him on a visit to the Swiss Alps in preparation for his sets for Rossini's *Guillaume Tell* (William Tell, 1829). By the extravagant 1830s, each act of an opera tended to have its own particular scenic character, and was farmed out to specialist *ateliers*, ones dealing with the intricacy of architecture and interiors, or with effects of light on water, or with Romantic contrast.[10]

STAY PERFECTLY STILL

As if on cue, *grand opéra* found its first long-lasting repertory works at precisely this time: in *La Muette de Portici* (The Dumb Girl of Portici, 1828), music by Daniel Auber (1782–1871) to a libretto by Eugène Scribe (1791–1861); and, the very next year, in Rossini's *Guillaume Tell*. It's worth pausing over *Tell*, which was Rossini's last opera. The difference from his earlier, Italian manner has much to do with the power local Parisian conditions could exert over composers. The libretto was not particularly French and certainly not Italianate: it was based on a play by the German poet and dramatist Friedrich Schiller (1759–1805), who was a friend of Goethe and a writer revered by the Romantics. Schiller's plays turned out to be a major resource for opera in the nineteenth century, although not in German – as with Goethe, German librettists shied away from turning national literary monuments into fodder for sopranos. Neither Schiller's play nor Rossini's libretto is tragic, but rather a serious political drama set in Switzerland in the thirteenth century. The Austrians have occupied Switzerland and are oppressing the people; this sets the stage for a classic love-versus-duty conflict that duly arises when Arnold (tenor), an ardent Swiss patriot, falls in love with Mathilde (soprano), an Austrian princess. The villain of the piece is Gesler (bass), a local Austrian enforcer who murders Arnold's father (in revivals of Schiller's play, Gesler is the plum role and always goes to the alpha-male actor). William Tell (baritone), an equally ardent Swiss patriot and expert crossbowman, rescues a friend who has killed an Austrian soldier attempting to rape his daughter. This gets Tell into trouble and, in the opera's most famous scene (Act 3, scene 2), Gesler sadistically tests Tell's nerve by forcing him to shoot an apple from his son Jemmy's head. Tell succeeds to general rejoicing, but Gesler nonetheless arrests him as a traitor. In the closing scenes Arnold, Tell and the Swiss populace rise up in rebellion. Tell shoots Gesler, freeing the canton from Austrian rule.

The apple-shooting scene became a classic. Wagner, who otherwise had little good to say about Rossini, spared nothing in praising it. *Guillaume Tell* even seems to have haunted his sleep: in a diary entry from the later 1850s, he recounts a dream in which he is surrounded by singing antagonists and remembers Gesler.[11] What accounts for the scene's power? Tell's nerve and bowmanship are only one part of a multi-section finale in which Rossini uses free, declamatory music. Anyone used to the flights, ornaments and regular phrases of his Italian operas will find the style almost unrecognizable. Singing itself has been damped down. Tell's solo address to his son, 'Sois immobile' (Be still), is introduced by a solo cello whose melody and timbre anticipate the vocal line, as if to say that heroic voices such as Tell's are descendants of the orchestra, communal and not individual. The message is plain: the stakes are too momentous for anything remotely frivolous or narcissistic in the vocal department. It is in this sense significant that 'Sois immobile' makes a cameo entrance in the famous encounter between Wagner and Rossini in 1860 (discussed in Chapter 7). The two composers have been sparring about melodic style in opera. Wagner is, as one might expect, in favour of the flexible and the declamatory; Rossini sees this, again predictably, as 'a funeral oration for melody'. But Wagner persists, citing Rossini's own 'Sois immobile' as an example of what he means. A cunning move, one might think. But Rossini, nimbler than he looks in those photographic portraits in old age, counters with a barbed joke: 'So I made Music of the Future without knowing it'.[12] Whether Wagner was deflated by the barb is not known; somehow one doubts it.

There is, though, more to the scene's power than its musical innovations. In one sense, William Tell becomes a hero not because he risks his son's life, but because he displays physical prowess in a single moment of intense concentration and sang-froid. This is, in other words, an iconic act. The child, the apple, the bow and arrow are caught in a frozen moment; the opera springs back to life only when the bowstring is finally released. There is almost no music when Tell lifts his bow for the shot, only a single pitch from the tremolo strings, and that is significant. This almost-silence and almost-stasis is the epitome of tense anticipation, allowing the audience to concentrate on what they see rather than what they hear. The freeze frame, compressing the idea of heroic rebellion into one image, becomes the symbolic inspiration for a mass political uprising, and this process of part representing whole – what grammarians call *synecdoche* – turns out to be an important technique for the entire genre. French *grand opéra* was famous for its attraction to iconic visual moments, frozen stage pictures or tableaux that, captured in lithograph and distributed widely through Paris's print media, could represent or recall the massive sound and slow, sonorous time that bracketed the scene in actual performance.

Guillaume Tell and its predecessor, *La Muette de Portici*, another grand 'tableau' opera, have significant similarities, not least in their use of colourful geographical locations (in French, *couleur locale*) and of The People as a new dynamic force – a force quite different from those routine, scene-setting choruses of previous decades. But they also have notable individual traits, again suggesting the stylistic variety that *grand opéra* could accommodate. *La Muette* ends with an extravagant disaster scene in which the heroine flings herself into the lava of an erupting Vesuvius, and the simplicity of the music at this climactic moment (nothing more than a sequence of mechanically repeated scales) is like the spare tremolo in Tell's apple-shooting scene. An absence of musical interest underlines the fact that the visual element is meant to carry all before it. On the other hand, and unlike *La Muette*, Rossini's musical ambitions and past glories ensured that *Tell* had much more. Its greatest moment of pure visual splendour – the revelation of a magnificent Alpine landscape in the last finale – is accompanied by music that aspires to translate the sublime scenic effect into sound, its grand musical gestures seeming to slow down the very passing of time as man contemplates nature.

THE ARCHAEOLOGY OF GRANDEUR

In the 1830s and 1840s a small number of similar works joined *La Muette de Portici* and *Guillaume Tell*, with them dominating the repertory at the Paris Opéra for several decades. Three of these blockbusters were written by Meyerbeer, a German expatriate with an Italianized first name (he was born Jakob Liebmann Meyer). The international aspirations of *grand opéra* are summed up in Meyerbeer's career. After a conventional musical apprenticeship in Germany he went on a prolonged sojourn in Italy; there, inevitably, he became a follower of Rossini, but his last Italian opera, *Il crociato in Egitto* (The Crusade in Egypt, 1824), already shows an emancipation from Rossinian style in its tendency to more complex orchestration. He then moved to Paris, where he remained until his death in 1864. Meyerbeer's first French opera, *Robert le diable*, was begun as early as 1827 but did not reach the stage of the Opéra until four years later. Over this period, with *La Muette* and *Tell* showing the way, Meyerbeer turned his score from a three-act *opéra comique* into an authentic five-act *grand opéra*. In its latter guise it was enormously successful and, as we have seen from d'Ortigue's comment about its fusion of Rossini and Beethoven, was recognized as an important milestone. By 1835, *Robert* had been exported to ten other countries, enjoying a vogue that rivalled even Rossini. Over the next decades, Meyerbeer would define classic *grand opéra*. His next works in the genre, *Les Huguenots* (1836) and *Le Prophète* (1849), achieved a repertory status matched only by Jacques Fromental Halévy's *La Juive* (The Jewess, 1835) and Gaetano Donizetti's *La Favorite* (The Favourite, 1840). For Chopin, of all people, *Robert* was 'a masterpiece of the new school, where the devils sing through speaking-trumpets and the dead rise from their graves', a work that had made Meyerbeer 'immortal'.[13] Into the 1850s he was routinely hailed, Verdi notwithstanding, as the greatest living opera composer.

There is a temptation to see the rise and fall of *grand opéra* in France as a matter of social barometers. Contemporary documents remind us again and again that what defined *grand opéra* was not just the shape of the works, but the shape of the audiences – their needs and fantasies. Louis Véron, who was appointed *directeur* of the Opéra in 1831, and who ran the place as a private venture (albeit with the state subsidy and its attendant controls still in place), was unequivocal about his social mission in the wake of the 1830 revolution: 'The July Revolution is the triumph of the bourgeoisie: this victorious bourgeoisie will be fond of lording it, of having a good time; the Opéra will become its Versailles.'[14] According to Véron, the image of this ruling class in their modern court also had a diplomatic function, announcing to the world that the image of France as a font of violent revolution had at last come to rest: 'Successful performances of musical masterpieces need to attract foreigners to the Opéra, where they must see loges occupied by an elegant and carefree society. The Opéra's successes and receipts need to give the lie to the riots.'[15] To see and be seen, to display one's social status on a public stage, was critically important for this aspirant audience. Small wonder that one of the central features of the newly spacious public spaces in the Opéra were large mirrors in which the public could see themselves and others reflected in all their finery.

If *grand opéra* was a barometer, by what means did it read the pressures of its time and the tastes of its audience? What were its chief characteristics, and what value does it have for us now, at the start of the twenty-first century? Almost all the most successful *grands opéras* had at least one overwhelming scenic tableau or iconic visual moment, designed to elicit wonder and noisy acclaim. One of the most talked-about was the great Imperial procession in Act 1 of *La Juive*. Before the Emperor appears, we have seen guards on horseback, buglers, standard-bearers, twenty crossbowmen, cardinals, bishops, guildsmen, abbots, twenty pages, 100 soldiers, and so on and on. Newspaper critics dutifully listed all these extras, one of them quipping that 'if we're not careful, the Opéra will become a power capable of throwing its armies into the balance of Europe'.[16] This remark displays a nice turn of French irony, but it also gives voice to a peculiar process: you experience the performance with awe because it overwhelms the senses, but when it's over, you sober up and see something overdone – faintly ridiculous and absurdly expensive. The during-versus-after effect is characteristic of *grand opéra*'s reception today. Perhaps, though, we are now spoiled by cinema, which can do things (again very expensively, but with an unprecedented mass of spectators) that Meyerbeer could not even dream about.

One element that differentiated *grand opéra* from even the most elaborate Italian serious works was decoration in a very broad sense, not just the vocal decoration that had long graced Italian opera, but a much larger array of effects that could enliven and intensify experience. There were of course lavish props and trudging supernumeraries, but just as important were musical numbers that existed merely for colour, not as vehicles for the plot or direct expressions of emotion. The most obvious of these decorative objects were the elaborate ballets precariously embedded in the centre of the plot. They were at base eye candy for the gentlemen of the audience, the most privileged of whom (the season-ticket holders) were granted access to backstage areas and, in particular, the so-called *foyer de la danse*, where they could meet the (female) dancers and aspire to take their visual and other pleasures further. But in most *grands opéras* there are also choruses and even solo arias that do little more than act as extensions of the scenery.

Many opera historians have disapproved of opera when it gets easy on the eye; they worry that if music drops too far out of the frame, prestige will be lost.[17] It is as well, then, to remind ourselves periodically that whenever opera becomes more visually orientated, when singing diminishes or is turned over to a colourful choral mass, the chance to feed the eye is also a chance for the ear to relax. This can be tremendously important, and composers (both French and others) have rarely been blind to its advantages. We've already mentioned that the conventions of *grand opéra* resurfaced in its international diaspora in many subsequent decades, with episodes like the Triumphal Scene in *Aida* right out of the Meyerbeer playbook. Such scenes are not so much ballet as a choral, processional, marching-band extravaganza: a twenty-minute *tour de force* whose comforting qualities should be evident even to the most austere critic.

In *grand opéra*, most bountifully in Meyerbeer, we also find links between visual and symbolic musical gestures on the small scale, links that were later thought characteristic of Wagner. In *Robert le diable* a narrative ballad ('Jadis regnait en Normandie', There once reigned in Normandy) simultaneously establishes plot background by describing a villain and his son (the opera's anti-hero, Robert) and links the story to certain musical motifs. The motifs introduced in the ballad will recur not only to accompany verbal allusions to the characters, but also to announce these characters' appearance on stage. This is one primal form of what became known as the leitmotif – that all-important link between a musical fragment and a visual or verbal manifestation. And while certainly present in earlier composers such as Weber, leitmotif was manipulated and organized by Meyerbeer in ways that prefigure early Wagnerian habits. Senta's ballad in Wagner's *Der fliegende Holländer* (1843), whose melody also recurs over the course of the opera, is unthinkable without the model of *Robert*. What is more, in using small, visual-musical recurring units, Meyerbeer escaped the boundaries of single numbers, a formally radical step which had, as we have seen, been anticipated in French opera going back to the eighteenth century, but which Wagner in *Oper und Drama* (1851) identified as an innovation of the 1840s – and one that, as those who know his literary style might expect, he claimed as his own.

Concentration on great political events will have an inevitable acoustic consequence: because in the past making history was unambiguously the province of men, *grand opéra* often involved multiple starring roles for low male voices. Ensembles involving four or more male singers, none of whom could manage a high A, are an acoustic flavour special to *grand opéra*, and one of its enduring pleasures. In *Les Huguenots* the Act 4 blockbuster is a conspiracy scene in which the Count of Saint-Bris, starring bass and arch-Catholic, whips his supporters into a murderous frenzy. It opens after elaborate orchestral recitative with a sextet of sensual male voices led by Saint-Bris in a manly, foursquare theme, 'Pour cette cause sainte' (For this sacred cause). Throughout the scene, which lasts a good fifteen minutes, this male ensemble splits apart and comes together into duets or solos, rejoining in close harmony (without orchestra) for the scene's iconic moment: the daggers that will massacre the Protestants are raised up and consecrated, 'pious blades, be blessed by God!' Even the arch-radical Berlioz loved this number, and conducted it several times in Paris concerts. Its avant-garde aspects include stretches of through-composed, free-flowing music in which individual subsections cede to one another; but it also has a reprise of the opening melody ('Pour cette cause sainte') at the end, with absolutely everyone on stage joining in (by now there are scores of conspirators), accompanied by trombones and ophicleide. In this formal aspect the number is no less radical than such famously advanced Wagnerian episodes as the 'Rome Narrative' in Act 3 of *Tannhäuser* (1845).

After consecrating the daggers and after the crowd has trailed off the stage, the benighted lovers Raoul (tenor, Protestant) and Valentine (soprano, Catholic) spring from the hiding place where they have overheard all and sing a desperate duet. The passage tears both a character and music itself in two, as Raoul, hearing the massacre that is taking place outside, becomes frantic to rush to the defence of his religious comrades, and sings ever more loudly against the sounds he hears. It inspired even Heine – like Meyerbeer an expatriate German – to ambiguous praise:

> Meyerbeer did not accomplish this through artistic means, but through natural ones, inasmuch as the famous duet speaks of a series of feelings that have perhaps never before been introduced into opera – not at least with such verisimilitude. But they are, for those Sprits of our age, fiercely sympathetic feelings.[18]

Act 4 of *Les Huguenots* exemplifies *grand opéra*'s teeming variety, as a mass in which musical and dramatic styles are hefted and cantilevered into ungainly wholes. This ungainliness was part of its visual character as well, and explains, perhaps, the designers' prevailing taste for imposing asymmetrical sets. Look at any of the classic Meyerbeerian stage pictures. Alarming foliage will threaten to engulf an outdoor scene (*Les Huguenots*, Act 2), or a huge ship will lurch sideways as if about to topple over (*L'Africaine*, Act 3; see Figure 24). In visual terms this is emphatically *not* the world of the so-called *juste milieu*, not a world classical symmetry in which everything balances and the status quo is unproblematic. At the level of plot, this sense of imbalance plays out chiefly in all those tales about how warring political factions put such strain on private emotions and relationships. Stage spectacle is typically a presentation of public life in all its grandeur, a show of power and consensus; but *grand opéra* libretti undermine this potential stability by including the affective presence of troublesome individuals and their problems. Within the kaleidoscope of characteristic scenes, amid the high-calorie orchestral effects and massive choral numbers, comes music for these soloists, intimate encounters and Italianate duets that unfold the private sphere and its interior emotions.

The glory days of *grand opéra* continued into the 1840s, but the revolutions of 1848 were a serious impediment. This was not so much in the financial sense, since the Paris Opéra continued to function more or less as before in terms of expenditure. Rather, by the 1850s and 1860s, the spirit and culture that had given impulse to works like *Guillaume Tell* were past. There were, inevitably, complex reasons for its decline. One is certainly the new strain of more virulent nationalism that emerged after 1848: an atmosphere in which the cosmopolitan virtues of *grand opéra* no longer held sway. The great line of foreign composers who had contributed to *grand opéra* (Rossini, Meyerbeer, Donizetti, Verdi) petered out in the second half of the century – Verdi's *Don Carlos* (1867) was the last nineteenth-century premiere at the theatre not written by a Frenchman. What's more, Paris's claim to represent the operatic avant-garde, strong in the decades before 1850, was severely weakened by Verdi's middle-period works and, later, by Wagner.

But such explanations only tell part of the story. Another might emerge from looking again at *Guillaume Tell*, the work that helped form and define the genre in its heyday. Its famous Overture is, like many at the time, a potpourri type; but instead of quoting vocal numbers from the opera, it uses some of the opera's iconic moments, music associated with landscapes or tableaux. In the first, slow section a solo cello is set against four other cellos and the double basses, prefiguring Tell's 'Sois immobile' and with timpani rolls that stop everything dead and anticipate the frozen moment before Tell pierces the apple. The second section, a furious musical storm, is openly descriptive and is concluded by a pastoral in which local colour is supplied by a *ranz des vaches*, cow-herding pipes that signify Switzerland but also create a sense of real space, of sound that exists in a landscape and for a purpose. Then comes the famous closing section, the fanfares of trumpets and horns calling the populace to arms and the gradual crescendo of excitement. The music in this finale is visceral – it tells us to get up and move, a summons that can hardly be ignored – and with it the marvellous energy of early nineteenth-century idealism appears in almost pure form. As so often in *grand opéra*, the idea of political action, that one should not just listen but should *do* something, is transformed into a musical effect. That idea could not endure. Once the revolutions of 1848 had petered out into inaction, this illusion of the will to action seemed to belong to the past. It was a past that was actively nurtured by the audiences, indeed *Tell* and the other *grand opéra* standards of the 1830s were repeated endlessly through to the end of the century. But new operas in the same vein increasingly seemed irrelevant or emptily grandiose – effects whose causes had long passed into history.

LOST DECADE AND FOUND OBJECTS

In the 1850s, then, the Opéra looked increasingly to the past. With repeat performances of Meyerbeer's warhorses mounting into the hundreds, repertory fatigue set in. Even Meyerbeer's *Le Prophète*, although it entered the lists in 1849 and might have been the last hurrah of the old regime, was not a runaway success. Its scenic marvels included a ballet on skates, as well as the first use of electric lighting in the theatre – an arc light used to depict a sunrise. We are so accustomed today to miracles of lighting technology that it's hard to imagine how stunning electric light might have seemed when first witnessed. But that sense of 'effects without causes' – of the absent sublime – became more insistent. The Opéra administrators in the 1850s tried hard to discover a *Guillaume Tell 2* or a *Young Huguenots*, and duly commissioned elephantine works such as Halévy's *Le Juif errant* (The Wandering Jew, 1852) and Charles Gounod's *La Nonne sanglante* (The Bleeding Nun, 1854). Both satisfaction and success were elusive, and desperation took hold. Even a work specifically written for the Opéra by Giuseppe Verdi (*Les Vêpres siciliennes* – The Sicilian Vespers – 1855) did only moderately well. Verdi's partner, Giuseppina Strepponi, the dyspeptic onlooker we mentioned earlier, blamed it on the Opéra's petrified ways. When the theatre decided to import Wagner's *Tannhäuser* (1845) in 1861, it was not just because *Tannhäuser* looked, tasted and sounded like *grand opéra*, but because it had demonstrated box office success over much of Europe in the 1850s.

Talk of such success leads, albeit uncomfortably, to the operatic career of Hector Berlioz (1803–69), a composer who would dearly have loved those epithets lavished on *Tannhäuser*. Part of the problem, then as now, is that his music so stubbornly defies categorization. Though Berlioz was a self-confessed admirer of Gluck, Spontini and Beethoven, his copious and entertaining operatic criticism is often dismissive of *grand opéra*, not to mention the products of the new Italian school. Even so, he was (at least in early life) an enthusiastic admirer of Meyerbeer, in particular of his skill in orchestration. It is possible to see much of Berlioz's music during this early period as the strivings of an opera composer *manqué*. In spite of misgivings and reluctance, he agreed to help in converting Weber's *Der Freischütz* into a work suitable for the Opéra in 1841. As he wrote to the theatre's director, Léon Pillet, 'I do not think one ought to add to *Freischütz* the recitatives you ask me for; however, since without that condition it can't be put on at the Opéra, and if I didn't write them you would entrust their composition to someone less familiar with Weber than I am and certainly less dedicated to the glorification of his masterpiece, I accept your offer on one condition: *Freischütz* will be performed exactly as it is.' Berlioz stood firm on this condition even when Pillet – ever searching for variety – suggested that the ball scene from Berlioz's *Symphonie fantastique* (1830) might make a good addition.[19] Berlioz's only original work for the Opéra was *Benvenuto Cellini* (1838), which fared badly with the public in spite of its innovative, Meyerbeer-influenced orchestration and rhythmic energy.

There is, though, no doubt that his operatic masterpiece, *Les Troyens* (The Trojans, composed 1856–8), was intended for the Opéra and was for this reason equipped with all its prerequisites – and more – in terms of size and scenic ambition: the opera was inspired by Virgil's *Aeneid* and laid out in five mighty acts. But *Les Troyens* was not thought a safe enough financial prospect by the Opéra management (Berlioz was primarily known as a conductor and composer of instrumental music). Although the last three acts, which take place in Carthage, and have Dido and Aeneas as their protagonists, were first given at the Théâtre Lyrique in 1863, the entire opera (with its first two acts set in Troy and featuring Cassandra) was not performed during the composer's lifetime, and only found general recognition in the Berlioz renaissance of the 1960s and 1970s. In spite of the fact that modern-day revivals of *Les Troyens* are routinely trumpeted as special events, impossible to compare with other, more commonplace operatic experiences, the work has much that will remind us of classic Meyerbeerian practice, and not just in its ostentatious show of unusual orchestral effects. There is also the standard collection of reminiscence motifs (such as the 'Trojans' March' in Acts 1, 3 and 5), innumerable choruses both on and off the stage, and plenty of conventional operatic numbers, even though some of Berlioz's most impressive moments are so-called 'monologues' that blur the manner of recitative and aria.

One crucial *grand opéra* element lacking in *Les Troyens*, however, is the 'frozen moment', which had been so important a part of the genre's early attraction. The first two acts have little to do with the last three in conventional narrative terms, and are primarily bound together not by developing characters and their tussles with public/political forces, but by a more abstract sense of destiny constantly in the wings. Perhaps for this reason, more conventional operatic numbers such as the Act 4 love duet between Dido and Aeneas, in which the focus is on the characters' interaction, tend to fall back on earlier models. 'Nuit d'ivresse et d'extase infinie!' (Night of rapture and boundless ecstasy!) sing the two lovers in caressing parallel intervals over a pulsating orchestra. The number is self-consciously beautiful and aspires to a kind of simplicity of effect reminiscent of Berlioz's beloved Gluck, even down to the rather antique, unusually purposeful modulations to closely related keys. But characteristically Berliozian traits also intrude in the form of piquant additional harmonies and bursts of elaborate, attention-seeking orchestration.

More successful – indeed, Berlioz at his operatic best – is the start of Act 4. A 'ballet-pantomime' called the 'Royal Hunt and Storm' is staged, in which water nymphs are frightened away by hunters, who are then themselves dispersed by a violent storm that forces Dido and Aeneas to take shelter in a cave. The whole passage is best seen as an elaborate symphonic interlude in which some of the most conventional operatic/orchestral clichés (the hunt, the storm) are imbued with a new level of detail, the whole episode coming to a tremendous climax with offstage choral cries of 'Italy!' to mark the fact that Aeneas must soon depart on new conquests. Here Berlioz comfortably meets *grand opéra* traditions on his own orchestral terms, ones in which the characters become puppets in an instrumental drama. The finest vocal moments do something similar, with the characteristic Berlioz monologue format best seen as a dialogue between the character and the orchestra. Dido's final 'monologue and air', 'Je vais mourir' (I am going to die) in Act 5, is a wonderful example in which there is a productive tension between the character's individuality and more abstract forces of fate represented by the orchestra.

Because of its difficulty and idiosyncrasy, *Les Troyens* had virtually no impact on operatic history until its revivals in the 1960s. Since that time is has often been cast as an antidote to Wagner (Greek vs Teutonic myth). In historical terms, though, the unexpected success of another French work of that period was far more influential, and far more indicative of the way the old *grand opéra* mould was decaying. This was Gounod's *Faust*, first seen at the Théâtre Lyrique in 1859. Gounod had tried and failed at the Opéra with *La Nonne sanglante* in 1854, but in *Faust* he created an opera that was to be enshrined a century later in Simon & Schuster's *Treasury*, and that remained until recently one of the most often performed works in the international repertory. Gounod's unfortunate past Opéra experience was no doubt important as *Faust* took shape. The opera is, for example, distinctly undersized by the usual standards of the genre. Although in five acts and with four star singers, it uses spoken dialogue rather than recitative (at least in its original version), has no half-hour choral numbers and no world-historical event with political conflicts or war-and-peace stakes as a background to the central romantic entanglement; nor does it feature orchestral depictions of bad weather or natural catastrophe. Indeed, history is almost entirely absent. We are instead plunged again into the *Freischütz* world of German Romanticism, with supernatural insurgency given form in the person of Mephistopheles.

What strikes the ear in listening to *Faust* against the background of earlier *grand opéra* is the concision of its numbers. One of the most famous moments, the final trio for Faust (tenor), Marguerite (soprano) and Mephistopheles (bass), actually seems too short. We are in a dungeon. Faust, with Mephistopheles' help, has arrived to rescue Marguerite from execution. But again and again she refuses to leave, trusting in God as her saviour. The trio's recurring refrain, 'Anges purs, anges radieux' (Pure angels, radiant angels), in 6/8 metre with woodwind pulses enforcing the beat, has the air of a transfigured march in which Marguerite's adamant voice will lead to heaven, come what may. Each time the refrain recurs it is sung a half-step higher, raising the stakes both in the drama – Faust's pleas become more urgent – and in the performance, as the tenor and soprano climb progressively up the register. The sense that *grand opéra*'s leisurely musical forms have been radically curtailed links nicely with the devil's best number, 'Le veau d'or' (The golden calf), which can even be heard as a mockery of big opera per se. Mephistopheles sings his strophic song to a festive chorus that ebulliently echoes his refrain: gold, wealth, dancing and splendour, these are all Satan's snares! The grotesque, thumping low brass that accompanies this devilish ditty is exactly the kind of odd, trombone-and-ophicleide-heavy instrumentation that Meyerbeer loved, and used without irony in every one of his French works. In Gounod's hands, though, this classic *grand opéra* effect is lampooned as lively but moribund, as *danse macabre*.

By the 1860s, the Opéra was at a crossroads: forever trying to find new big opera to add to its fading repertory; nervously looking abroad at disturbing signs of the musical future; increasingly aware of the new tastes represented by younger Frenchmen such as Gounod and, a little later, Camille Saint-Saëns and Georges Bizet, a generation who would seldom encounter those remembering the eighteenth century. Meyerbeer's final opera, *L'Africaine*, was produced posthumously in 1865. He had been working on it, on and off, for nearly thirty years. Some thought it a great monument, but it struggled to achieve the success of his earlier operas. Above all, it seemed belated. Another sign that the end was near occurred in 1869, when the Opéra sought to capitalize on *Faust*'s success by treating it to a prestigious and expanded revival. Gounod had already added recitatives, and now included the obligatory ballet and other bulk items. In essence, though, it was the same old *Faust*. Embarrassingly, it outstripped nearly all the Opéra-reared products: by the time Gounod died in 1893, *Faust* had been played more than a thousand times at the Opéra. Even in France, *grand opéra* had now entered its afterlife, sustained as a lingering taste for precious objects and dancing girls in the serious, Oriental-themed operas that swept through Paris in its wake. One of the first of these, Saint-Saëns' *Samson et Dalila* (1877), was in fact commissioned by the Archducal Theatre in Weimar under Franz Liszt, a circumstance that demonstrates how fully the internationalism of the original genre was taking new forms in its descendants.

WITHOUT THE SLIGHTEST ATTENTION

Those new forms were at their most potent as products of the troubled relationships that the two greatest nineteenth-century opera composers struck up with *grand opéra*. Neither Wagner nor Verdi was immune to Meyerbeer-envy: there was a time, and not in their earliest years, when Meyerbeer was the most envied musician on the planet. What's more, every aspiring opera composer dreamt of a commission from the Opéra, of commanding all those lavish musical and scenic resources, not to mention the high fees and royalties a Parisian success would bring.

Not surprisingly, *grands opéras* were sometimes produced without commission by aspirant composers. Wagner graduated to first maturity with a classic instance, a five-act, historical, heavily orchestrated curio called *Rienzi, der Letzte der Tribunen* (Rienzi, the Last of the Tribunes, 1842). He brought his partially completed score with him to Paris in 1839 and asked Meyerbeer to intercede in its favour at the Opéra. In spite of Meyerbeer's attempts at advocacy (he wrote numerous letters on the younger man's behalf),[20] Wagner's Parisian ambitions went nowhere, apart from helping to engender a lifelong animosity towards his hapless helper, an attitude fuelled – in the words of one modern commentator – by a heady mix of 'personal envy . . . persecution mania, exaggerated aesthetic convictions and racial bigotry'.[21] When opera historians identify Wagner's *grand opéra* lineage, it is almost always *Rienzi* that serves as the exemplary case. One can hear why even from the overture, heavy on foursquare brass themes that have some of the wonderful, loud vigour of 'Pour cette cause sainte'. But, as we shall see, to lean too heavily on *Rienzi* is to hide the fact that Wagner's French side is evident in almost every opera he wrote. When in 1861 he finally brought a work to the Opéra – the revised *Tannhäuser*, with a token ballet – it had numbers that were hailed as virtually home-grown.

First among them was the all-male septet in Act 1, scene 4. Although it would be a simplification to explain (away) Wagner's genius by saying that he simply did French opera better than anyone else, sometimes the claim is just. The septet in *Tannhäuser* takes the idea of big, joyous, onstage noise to stratospheric levels. The basic drama is of a prodigal's return. Tannhäuser (tenor), prostrate in the Thuringian woods, is discovered by six former companions, virtuous knights led by Landgrave Herrmann (bass). They recognize him as a long-absent associate and urge him to rejoin their number. Tannhäuser, suffering from something like a moral hangover (he has been expelled from the underworld by the Goddess Venus, soprano), refuses until his friend Wolfram (baritone) reveals that Princess Elisabeth (soprano) still loves him and pines for him. He agrees to accompany the knights, a decision that provokes general rejoicing. Throughout a long, free-form introduction, the male voices blend and separate, coming together over a brief, gorgeous melody ('Gegrüsst sei uns, du kühner Sänger' – Be welcome, you valiant singer) that seems to emerge and then dissolve within seconds. Then begins a solo for Wolfram, who will consistently sing the most sensual music in the opera, a number designed to foreground a voice type that is unusual in Wagner, a true baritone. Wolfram's melody is taken up by all the other men, and when Tannhäuser finally gives in there's a final stretta in which the voices, taking turns to show off their high notes, are joined by fanfares from onstage hunting horns. In most performances, the entire stage seems to be vibrating with sound by this point: the horns, the voices, the pit orchestra, even the rumbling tread of those rushing in just before the curtain falls, all contribute their part. The septet conveys a kind of lyric optimism, a surfeit of hope and energy, that is a characteristic flavour in Romantic opera before 1848, before the disillusion of so many foiled revolutions set in.

Tannhäuser was booed off the Opéra stage in 1861 after only three performances. The token ballet, added as a curtain raiser in the Venusberg scene, was in the wrong place. It was customary for large factions of the Opéra audience to arrive late, usually during Act 2, and that was why the ballet numbers were invariably placed mid-way through an opera. Such traditions should again remind us that opera, until a very late historical point, was on many occasions little more than an addendum to social interaction. One reason audiences found the hours and hours of *grand opéra* so palatable was that many of them didn't show up for the whole thing. They strolled in for the good bits and (as we have seen) even then did not always pay attention. In Alexandre Dumas's novel *Le Comte de Monte-Cristo* (The Count of Monte Cristo, 1844), several scenes set at the Paris Opéra in the 1830s record this custom in detail. In Chapter 88, the Count arrives for *Guillaume Tell* at the beginning of Act 2. In between scene changes, and even while the opera is being performed, there is a great deal of talking and even a challenge to a duel, delivered in the Count's box. Unbothered, the Count stays put: 'according to his usual custom, until Duprez had sung his famous "Suivez-moi", then he rose and went out'. An earlier chapter (53) is set at a performance of *Robert le diable* and spells out local habits in no uncertain terms:

> The curtain rose, as usual, to an almost empty house, it being one of the absurdities of Parisian fashion never to appear at the opera until after the beginning of the performance, so that the first act is generally played without the slightest attention being paid to it, that part of the audience already assembled being too much occupied in observing the fresh arrivals, while nothing is heard but the noise of opening and shutting doors, and the buzz of conversation.

Chapter 53 makes clear that the stage is also widely ignored during Act 2 ('The second act passed away during one continued buzz of voices'), and although Act 3 seems to catch the audience's attention, once again the Count goes early, this time before Act 4 begins. One character comments acidly that the Count does nothing like other men: he walks out before the big number everyone else has been waiting for. But for us today, reading Dumas's novel might above all encourage heretical thoughts. Perhaps Meyerbeer's work is lost to us because it cannot survive the attentiveness that modern audiences have felt obliged to bring to all opera. Perhaps a truly enterprising, twenty-first-century general manager will bring back Meyerbeer performances as social events, with all the grandeur intact but with listeners nonetheless free to come and go, to ignore Act 1 and dine after Act 3.

The erratic behaviour of audiences did nothing to interrupt the allure of *grand opéra* for composers of many nations during its golden years before 1848. A generation of Italians found the operatic journey to Paris an essential career move – a way of escaping what was seen both inside and outside the peninsula as an increasingly parochial and insular national muse. As we have seen in earlier chapters, during the 1830s Bellini and Donizetti both staged works successfully at Paris's Théâtre Italien (which was dedicated to Italian-language opera); and Rossini and Donizetti went further, creating *grands opéras* (*Guillaume Tell* and *La Favorite* respectively) that proved among the most successful and long-lived examples of that risky, failure-prone genre. Part of their success was that, unlike Berlioz, they tended to be less than idealistic when adapting themselves to local taste. Here is Donizetti in 1839, writing about his conversion of an Italian opera (*Poliuto*, which the previous year had been banned by the censors in Naples) into a *grand opéra* called *Les Martyrs* (1840). It was to be:

> expanded into four acts, instead of three, and translated and adjusted for the French Theatre by Scribe. This means that I've had to re-do completely all the recitatives, make a new finale for Act I, add arias, trios and a ballet such as they use here, so that the public won't complain (rightly) that the shape is Italian. French music and poetry for the theatre have a *cachet* all their own, to which every composer must adapt himself . . . . There can be no [Rossinian] crescendi, and none of the usual cadential repetitions *felicità, felicità, felicità*; and between the two verses of a cabaletta there's always poetry which moves the action forward, without the usual repetition of lines that our poets do.[22]

Here is a true treasury, a native informant's take on the differences between *grand opéra* and Italian serious opera. The French variety needed to be longer, with an internal ballet, more frequent finales and different kinds of lyrical pieces, etc. But equally important was that French audiences were more impatient than their Italian cousins about 'musical architecture': they wanted the action to move forward more quickly in set pieces, and were less tolerant of elaborate, repetitious vocal warbling as numbers come to a close – what Donizetti charmingly calls 'repetitions *felicità, felicità, felicità*', using as his descriptor a word endlessly repeated at the close of many an exuberant Italian cabaletta.

What's missing from Donizetti's account is any suggestion that writing a *grand opéra* entailed profound musical rethinking of his earlier *modus operandi*. True, the shape and sometimes the manner of an Italian opera had to change; but in many ways Italian opera was already influenced by its grander French cousin, and of course vice-versa. The notion is strengthened by looking at Verdi's first attempt at a French-language work for the Opéra, his *Jérusalem* (1847). Like Donizetti before him, Verdi made this, his debut at the Opéra, by revising an existing Italian work, *I Lombardi alla prima crociata* (The Lombards at the First Crusade, 1843). The changes were again largely on the surface. To Donizetti's list of alterations, Verdi added denser, Meyerbeer-like orchestration, an increased sense of local colour, and – probably related – some experiments with a wandering kind of chromatic harmony, rarely essayed in his Italian operas. In the end he produced an opera judged barely worthy of the occasion; it was soon dropped from the Opéra's repertory.

'JE DORMIRAI DANS MON MANTEAU ROYAL'

During the next two decades, Verdi's encounters with Paris, in particular with the shadows cast by French *grand opéra* and opera production, were frequent. He spent a two-year period in Paris (1854–5) during which he completed *Les Vêpres siciliennes*. In a letter to his librettist, the inevitable Scribe, he made clear that he had Meyerbeer firmly in his sights when he asked for:

> a grandiose, impassioned original subject, calling for an impressive, overwhelming production. Ever before my eyes I have the many, many

> magnificent scenes to be found in your librettos; among others, the Coronation Scene of *Le Prophète*! No other composer could have done with that scene what Meyerbeer did: but with that spectacle, and above all with a situation so original, grandiose and at the same time so impassioned, no composer, however little feeling he had, would have failed to produce a great effect.[23]

A desire to compete with the most imposing Parisian successes of the 1830s and 1840s is obvious (note how Verdi uses the word 'grandiose' twice in the space of three sentences). Probably because he was writing to Scribe, Verdi is politely deferential to Meyerbeer; his partner Giuseppina Strepponi put the matter more crudely a few years later, calling *Les Vêpres* an attempt to 'make the Jew die of an attack of publicity'.[24] On another level, though, this insistence on spectacle and effect is curious because since the later 1840s Verdi had tended to more intimate, private subjects. It might also have been against the Parisian times: as we have seen, the later 1840s and 1850s saw hardly any successful attempts to re-create the great spectacular successes of the 1830s.

The picture becomes even more confusing during the later 1850s and 1860s, when Verdi's correspondence is routinely punctuated by diatribes against the French, in particular for their *blague*, their insolent *politesse* and their contempt for all things foreign.[25] The grandest diatribe of all came in a much-quoted letter from the late 1860s:

> Everyone wants to express an opinion, to voice a doubt; and the composer who lives in that atmosphere of doubt for any length of time cannot help but be somewhat shaken in his convictions and end up revising, adjusting or, to put it more precisely, ruining his work. In this way, one ultimately finds in one's hands not a unified opera but a *mosaic*; and, beautiful as it may be, it is still a *mosaic*. You will argue that the Opéra has produced a string of masterpieces in this manner. You may call them masterpieces all you want, but permit me to say that they would be much more perfect if the *patchwork* and the adjustments were not felt all the time.[26]

The letter places the blame squarely on staging conditions in Paris, in particular on the inevitably collaborative nature of the enterprise. But the problem was also internal, within the very nature of modern opera; the works were threatening to become too complex to be under any single person's exclusive jurisdiction.

The confusion arises because, just before the time of this letter, Verdi had spent another two years in Paris and had created *Don Carlos* (1867), his third and last *grand opéra*, and a work now generally thought the one durable masterpiece of the genre (Rossini's *Tell* would be its nearest rival). In many ways it has all the classic ingredients. There are five long acts; an imposing historical backdrop; royal dynasties in France and Spain in the mid sixteenth century; with the Inquisition to boot; freedom fighters for the Protestant Netherlands; and a sexy temptress providing local colour. There are elaborate love-versus-duty conflicts – Carlos (tenor), heir to the Spanish throne, falls in love with French noblewoman Elisabeth de Valois (soprano), but then his father, Philip II of Spain (bass), decides to marry her himself; and that's just in Act 1. And there is, of course, also a magnificent iconic-moment tableau in Act 3, out-Meyerbeering Meyerbeer with a public clash between Carlos and his father in a large square in front of Valladolid Cathedral, and then, at the curtain, victims of the Inquisition writhing on the stake accompanied by a Voice from Heaven assuring them of future bliss. Perhaps small wonder, with Verdi at close to the peak of his international fame, that the Opéra's vast resources ground into motion, producing a spectacle that rivalled Meyerbeer in expense and luxury. One mind-boggling statistic is that the opera required no fewer than 535 costumes: 177 recycled gratefully from the Opéra's store cupboard; 118 altered to suit the occasion; and 240 brand-new.[27]

However, and in spite of all these competitive moves, it's significant that when Verdi was first approached about the subject, which is again taken from Schiller, he immediately singled out two relatively intimate vocal confrontations (one a clash between the Grand Inquisitor and King Philip) as catching his imagination. The significance is that, while Verdi's first insistence for *Les Vêpres siciliennes* was that it must have grandiose scenes, in *Don Carlos* his focus was from the start on *individuals*. While *Don Carlos* might seem identical to the classic Meyerbeer model on the outside, it is actually best seen as a *grand opéra* inside out. In Meyerbeer one senses that the public world is always threatening to overwhelm private emotions (the Act 4 love duet in *Les Huguenots* is typical); in *Don Carlos* it's the other way around, with individual expression constantly threatening to overwhelm public display. A good instance comes in Act 1, in which Carlos falls in love with Elisabeth only to lose her almost immediately. At the close of the act, Verdi sets in extreme musical contrast two opposing emotions, Carlos and Elisabeth's private despair versus the public celebrations of the crowd announcing Elisabeth's marriage to Philip. All seems set for a noisy finale à la Meyerbeer; but then, at the very end, the chorus carries Elisabeth away and Carlos is left alone onstage. His line disintegrates, becoming breathless and fragmentary; the musical certainties of the chorus disappear, and the act ends with a close focus on a moment of individual despair.

Time and again this trajectory recurs in *Don Carlos*. Individuals, the opera tells us insistently, matter more than crowds. Another instance is at the start of Act 4, where we are shown the tragedy of Philip. The act begins with his famous aria, 'Elle me n'aime pas' (She doesn't love me), which takes place near dawn, the king leaning wearily on a table overflowing with official papers, the nearly spent candles marking the end of a long night wrestling with duties of state. The stage seems set for a contemplation of the melancholy verities of public life, but Philip begins instead with a simple, tragic statement about his marriage to Elisabeth: 'She doesn't love me', a bare utterance clothed musically in the simplest of means – made, that is, into an iconic moment in which restrained accompaniment, simple declamation and one melodic outburst serve to etch the emotion into our minds. Philip's subsequent historical reveries in this aria, in particular his dreams of wielding a royal power he so obviously lacks in the private sphere, employ martial rhythms and themes from past public moments in the opera; but they lead nowhere. They sound as if heard at a distance, already foregone. At the end, Philip closes where he began – he can do no more than repeat his impassioned outburst of personal loss, 'She doesn't love me!', a retreat from the public ambitions that have deluded him, a descent into the labyrinth of the soul.

In spite of all this concentration on the individual, or perhaps because of it, *Don Carlos* did not succeed at the Opéra. Verdi, not for the last time and to his profound irritation, was accused of Wagnerism, which in this case was an easy shorthand for 'not like his earlier, Italian self'. Sometime later he cut the opera down to manageable Italian length, jettisoning almost the entire first act in the process (performing, if you want, the kind of surgery less painfully achieved by Dumas's Count). In terms of Simon & Schuster's *Treasury*, this turned his *grand opéra* into simply a Grand Opera. It was practical too: *Don Carlos* mostly trod the twentieth-century boards in its reduced form. Current attempts to recapture the original French version, sometimes even adding sections that Verdi cut during those interminable rehearsals at the Opéra, have proved musically revelatory; but, as with so many *grands opéras*, there will always be an embarrassing surplus of music. To experience such resurrections we must arrive at 6 p.m. and depart after 11 p.m.: modern life is against such profligacy. We will do this for *Don Carlos*; we will also – when we get the chance – do it for Berlioz's *Les Troyens*; at least for the time being, though, we will not do it for *Les Huguenots*.

The difference between Verdi's and Meyerbeer's modern fortunes may partly be a matter of simple quality. *Don Carlos* captivates us precisely because individuals are at its centre: Verdi had the ability not only to amaze and impress, but also to engage us with his characters. But we should be cautious of such conclusions, which too easily congratulate our present-day taste at the expense of countless musicians and others who in 1850 thought Meyerbeer had brought opera to some kind of pinnacle. The caution might be increased by recalling that it is eternally difficult to separate the quality of operatic music from the quality of the performance it receives. *Les Huguenots* was, for example, dubbed 'the night of the seven stars', because that is how many top-flight, highly paid singers are needed to perform it convincingly. If such a constellation could be assembled today, it would surely be enough to raise any self-respecting opera lover's heart rate. But when Meyerbeer is performed nowadays, cautious impresarios are reluctant to spend lavishly enough to cast all seven parts with superstars, and this becomes a self-defeating economy, one often repeated by stage designers and procession-planners. Before a note is heard, the opera has been gravely disabled.

So: we can if we wish retreat into vague statements about musical values to explain the demise of almost all *grand opéra*, and thus feel reassured that our present musical world is more discerning. But, at least as historians, it is better to think instead about the sheer cosmopolitan variety that characterizes the genre, a trait so suited to the times in which it flourished but so much less in tune with the newly nationalist and increasingly racist atmosphere of the later nineteenth and twentieth centuries. After 1848, Meyerbeer's fall was hastened by anti-Semitic abuse from Wagner and many others, and his reputation in the twentieth century reached a low point from which it has barely emerged since. When the notion of the 'cosmopolitan' became a threat rather than something to be proud of, it is easy to see how the idea of Meyerbeer – a Jewish composer born in Germany, trained in Italy, master of Paris – would become distasteful. Once the break had been made, the overwhelming difficulty of staging his works, and their unfamiliarity to singers, then formed an effective barrier, ensuring that they would remain in the wilderness. By such means is the operatic canon made and unmade; by such means did the greatest operatic composer in the world in 1850 fall from grace.

12
Young Wagner

In 1849, Richard Wagner (1813–83) was accused of treason for his participation in the Dresden Revolution of 1848–9, and a warrant was issued for his arrest. Notices reporting Wagner as a wanted man appeared in several newspapers. One was issued as late as 11 July 1853 (Wagner being still at large), in a publication called *Eberhardt's Allgemeiner Polizei-Anzeiger* (Eberhardt's General Police Gazette). It includes an unflattering lithograph portrait of the composer – his lower jaw appears to have grown to vast size – captioned 'ehemal. Capellmeister und politischer Flüchtling aus Dresden' (former court conductor and political fugitive from Dresden). The notice reports that Wagner 'allegedly intends to travel to Germany from Zurich, where he currently resides. In order to aid in his capture, a portrait is included here; if discovered and caught he is to be arrested and turned over to the Royal Municipal Court in Dresden.'[1] An original notice from 16 May 1849 was more laconic: 'All police departments are to be on the lookout, and are requested to arrest Wagner if he is discovered and caught. . . . Wagner is 37–38 years old, of medium height, has brown hair and wears glasses.'[2] Like celebrities ever since, Wagner always removed the glasses when being photographed or sitting for his portrait. Only a few candid shots – amateur sketches drawn by those observing him in rehearsals – have ever revealed that his eyesight was less than perfect.

We begin here, with Wagner on the run, because it can sometimes seem as if he has been wanted ever since. As the most controversial, most politically dubious musician in the history of Western music. As 'Hitler's favourite composer'. As an unrepentant anti-Semite whose tendency to publish any and every thought that came into his head has left us with ample traces of his most unpalatable ideas. As a habitual debtor, who was unfaithful to his wife (admittedly, he had many composer rivals where that sin was concerned) and who bamboozled King Ludwig II of Bavaria out of immense sums, which he spent not only on grandiose operatic ventures but also to nurse an abiding passion for silk dressing gowns. As a sinister magician whose purpose was to rob audiences of their capacity for rational thought, imprisoning them in a dark theatre filled with sounds and sights that seemed to flow directly from his imagination, with little homage to artistic achievements of the past.

Wagner is wanted for so many reasons. Although it was not clear until the later 1850s, he rewrote the opera rulebook. Before Wagner, operas (no matter what language they were written in) were united in their use of certain musical forms, and in a shared sense for the proper relationship between the voice and the orchestra. After Wagner, those forms and that relationship could never again communicate in quite the same way.

What's more, Wagner's revolution in musical thinking, in notions of operatic time and musical rhetoric, and his radical ideas about theatrical production and architecture, engendered works whose impact was far from merely operatic. We can easily compile a list of composers who, although they never thought to write an opera or were never principally opera composers, nonetheless absorbed basic precepts from Wagner's musical language: Anton Bruckner, Claude Debussy, Gustav Mahler, Nikolai Rimsky-Korsakov, Arnold Schoenberg, Hugo Wolf. Wagner was, in other words, a prime mover of musical modernism, an imposing, often stifling father figure who loomed impossibly large over the later nineteenth century and beyond. His music and theories also caught the imagination of artists outside the sphere of professional composition, and in a way unprecedented among mere opera composers. In France, he was the poet Charles Baudelaire's principal inspiration, as Baudelaire himself acknowledged in a famous letter of 1860, written to Wagner, never sent, but then published as a piece of journalism. Baudelaire's idolatry was self-consciously exclusive: 'I want to be distinguished from all those jackasses'. But it was also close to self-annihilating: 'At first it seemed to me that I knew your music already, and later, in thinking it over, I understood what had caused this illusion. It seemed to me that this music was *my own*'.[3] Confronted with Wagner, such a heady combination of pride and abasement was not unusual. The most famous acolyte of all was the philosopher Friedrich Nietzsche, whose encounter with Wagner's 1859 opera *Tristan und Isolde* was so devastating and violent that it resulted in Nietzsche's first great philosophical essay, *Die Geburt der Tragödie aus dem Geiste der Musik* (The Birth of Tragedy out of the Spirit of Music), in 1872. His later repudiation of the composer (he defiantly announced a preference for Bizet, of all composers), articulated at length in *Der Fall Wagner* (The Case of Wagner, 1888), was no less traumatic.

It is always naïve to imagine that the history of opera can be outlined simply by rewinding to the time when this or that work was written, by pretending to discuss the work's historical context as if it only included the period immediately surrounding its composition. The intervening past, the time between this or that opera and ourselves, can never be so easily willed away. Wagner is the trump card when this matter is debated, the unassailable test case. The impossibility of forgetting Wagner, of rewinding and capturing a time before Wagner's music and writings burned a path through the nineteenth century, is clear to us all. This is even the case, albeit on a more modest scale, when trying to deal with his earlier operas – those written before 1849 – in comparison with the later, more revolutionary works. One cannot hear the young Wagner's operas without reflecting on how they prefigure his innovations after 1849. And it is typical of the way Wagner's works were generally received that this inability – this sense of the unassailable prestige of the later works, the way that all music preceding them seems inevitably filtered through their lens – was fostered by the composer himself, if not actually engendered by him. Wagner was hyper-loquacious, both in the print media and viva voce. Catulle Mendès reported after a visit to Wagner in Lucerne in 1869 that he 'talked, talked, talked, it was an unending flood'.[4] He was also, when not creating opera, prone to writing long letters and even longer essays about himself, and about culture and politics generally. His collected writings in the most complete edition run to sixteen volumes. One has the impression of someone who produced sound – whether verbal or musical – perpetually and fluently. As if to demonstrate this, many of Wagner's best and worst writings come from a fallow period in his life as a composer, the five years that followed his abortive involvement in the Dresden Revolution. This period saw his exile from German lands and his literary preparation for the gradual explosion of the later works.

He was born, the youngest of nine children, into a family of theatrical hangers-on and art-smitten amateurs. One relative (the adopted daughter of his brother Albert), Johanna Wagner, became a celebrated opera singer who was for years the more famous musician in the family.

Wagner had no formal training as a composer. In his teens he wrote a number of derivative works in the standard instrumental genres (sonatas, string quartets, overtures) and toyed with various theatrical and operatic projects, using as models the German cultural high-ground of Goethe and Schiller. He eased into the world of opera as a largely self-taught conductor who drifted through minor positions at small provincial theatres: Würzburg, Magdeburg and then a longer stint in Riga, where from 1837 to 1839 he conducted many operatic repertory works. In 1839 he fled his wretched credit history by moving to Paris, hoping – brashly, it would seem – to be commissioned by the Opéra. All that time he continued writing operas and other occasional works, minor and trivial pieces. But the way in which he placed the early works in later life is significant. One still-repeated cliché, again deriving from his own writings, tells us that his first three operas, *Die Feen* (The Fairies, 1833), *Das Liebesverbot* (The Ban on Love, 1835) and *Rienzi, der Letzte der Tribunen* (1842), represent an early, naïve and soon-to-be-overcome fascination with, in neat succession, German (*Die Feen*), Italian (*Das Liebesverbot*) and then French (*Rienzi*) operatic traditions. There is some truth in this formulation. *Die Feen*'s supernatural subject matter can certainly be related to previous trends in German opera (it has substantially the same plot as E. T. A. Hoffmann's *Undine* of 1814) and its musical forms owe much to Weber. Obvious too is the fact that *Rienzi* was planned as an assault on the *grand opéra* tradition and specifically in emulation of the works of Giacomo Meyerbeer: a five-act grand opera in the most inflated French tradition, based on the novel by Edward Bulwer-Lytton, intended to storm the Opéra but failing to find a performance there. However, *Das Liebesverbot* has very little that can be laid at the door of contemporary Italian opera, again relying on a rude mixture of French and German models. As we shall see, the Italian model of *bel canto*, much as he liked to denigrate it in later life, would not so easily be laid aside.

The likely reason behind Wagner's dissemination of this idea of a brisk, youthful tour through the main European operatic styles was to encourage people to hear the post-*Rienzi* works as a kind of *synthesis* of these national idioms. The intended rivalry with Meyerbeer, whose early career had indeed involved prolonged exposure to German, Italian and then French opera, was obvious. In an obsequious letter to Meyerbeer, written before he reached Paris, Wagner stated as much: 'in you

I behold the perfect embodiment of the task that confronts the German artist, a task you have solved by dint of having mastered the merits of the Italian and French schools in order to give *universal* validity to the products of that genius. This, then, is what more or less set me on my present course'.[5] He returned to these sentiments in a long and equally laudatory essay about Meyerbeer's *Les Huguenots*, probably written in Paris: 'Meyerbeer wrote world history, a history of hearts and feelings: he destroyed the shackles of national prejudice and the constraining boundaries of linguistic idioms: he wrote deeds of music.'[6]

While in Paris, Wagner finished another opera that he hoped might be performed in the capital, although this time in an entirely different genre: it was a short German Romantic opera, initially drafted in a single act, called *Der fliegende Holländer* (The Flying Dutchman, 1843). He also wrote literary essays and journalistic criticism, learned French badly and put bread on the table by making piano reductions of operas for vocal scores, or arrangements of numbers for various instrumental ensembles. Two of these opera arrangements, vocal scores of *grands opéras* by Donizetti (*La Favorite*, 1840) and Halévy (*La Reine de Chypre*, 1841), have recently been published, with elaborate scholarly apparatus, in a state-funded new critical edition of Wagner's collected works – just one indication of how far his reputation has continued to expand from these desperate beginnings. At the time, though, the lack of recognition was galling, and accounts for some (not all) of his later, jaundiced views of the capital. Success eventually came from elsewhere. In 1843, Wagner gained an important post, and did so on the strength of the thinnest of résumés. He had sent the score of *Rienzi* to the Royal Saxon Opera in Dresden; bolstered by a recommendation from Meyerbeer to the director of the theatre, it was performed there and proved a wild success; on the basis of this, and despite the fact that *Der fliegende Holländer*, also premiered in Dresden, made a lesser impact, Wagner was invited to become the court conductor.

THE ORIGIN OF A SPECIES

Wagner left us dramatic, artfully embellished accounts of most of these events in his autobiography, *Mein Leben* (My Life), which he published in four volumes between 1870 and 1880. Much earlier, though, in 1851 while in exile in Switzerland, he wrote an important essay on his artistic development during these early years, a self-analysis of his first four big operas, *Rienzi* and *Der fliegende Holländer*, having by then been joined by *Tannhäuser* (1845) and *Lohengrin* (1848). This essay, which is called 'A Communication to My Friends', is a cornerstone for conventional histories of Wagner as composer. We can go straight to the critical part, a description of what Wagner saw as a small but radical element in *Der fliegende Holländer*. The opera's story, of a ghostly voyager condemned to sail the seas perpetually until the love of a woman can redeem him, clearly anticipates one of the main themes of Wagner's post-1850 works. What's more, the work (particularly in its original, single-act version) strives for an unusual consistency of tone and atmosphere, occasionally even a blurring of the distinction between recitative and aria – something that had previously been rare in German opera. These points notwithstanding, *Der fliegende Holländer* is – in both its one-act and three-act versions – at base still a conventional number opera, with arias, duets, choruses and the like. However, and ignoring these formal matters, Wagner picked on a particular moment in the opera, a passage that – he said – presaged the earthquake he was to unleash on the operatic world in 1851:

> I remember, before I set about the actual working-out of *Der fliegende Holländer*, drafting first the ballad of Senta in the second act, and completed both its verse and melody. In this piece, I unconsciously laid the thematic germ of the whole music of the opera: it was the picture *in petto* of the whole drama. . . . In the eventual composition of the music, the thematic picture, thus evoked, spread itself out quite instinctively over the whole drama, as one continuous tissue; I had only, without further initiative, to take the various thematic germs included in the Ballad and develop them to their legitimate conclusions.[7]

Near the middle of the opera (Act 2 in the three-act version), there is indeed a Ballad sung by the heroine, Senta (soprano). This number, like ballads we have seen previously in early nineteenth-century opera, tells a story in miniature – about a supernatural mariner and his search for a true beloved – that is gradually revealed as the plot of the opera itself, with Senta as the true beloved and the Dutchman (baritone) as the tall dark stranger looking for a human bride. Wagner enthused in particular about one aspect of the Ballad, how its main theme occurred not just within the piece itself but was repeated as a musical motif here and there through the entire opera, whenever dramatically apposite. What Wagner was describing became called, much later, 'leitmotif technique', and what he stresses is that repeating symbolic musical ideas (or, as they became called, 'leitmotifs') has the potential to transcend the borders of single numbers, drawing what would otherwise be a collection of separate musical movements – the beads on the string – into a whole.

To point out what is narcissistic about Wagner's account may seem obvious, but so much mythology has grown up around the leitmotif that the task is still necessary. First of all: Wagner didn't invent either the leitmotif or the process by which themes from an allegorical ballad are spun out during an opera. We have already seen instances of such recurring themes, going back to French opera in the late eighteenth century. In the previous chapter, we saw the young Verdi at almost exactly the same time experimenting with similar devices in his opera *I due Foscari* (1844). Wagner could not have known Verdi's opera, but direct models for what happens in Senta's Ballad in *Der fliegende Holländer* were much closer at hand: the idea was probably derived from 'Jadis régnait en Normandie' (There once reigned in Normandy), the Ballad in Meyerbeer's *Robert le Diable* (1831), which was a work Wagner had, so to speak, ordered by mail in plain brown wrappers long before. But it was not merely a leap in degree to go from the occasional symbolic theme that recurs here and there in a number opera (the *Fliegende Holländer* or *Due Foscari* model) to what Wagner was imagining in the early 1850s. He was by that time busy conceiving opera devoid of conventional numbers, which meant devoid of conventional structures of operatic time. To a significant extent he was imagining opera created *ex nihilo*, a manifestation of real compositional freethinking.

Be that as it may, Wagner's way of historicizing his earlier operas – seeing them as way-stations towards the post-1850 pieces – was copied in most subsequent discussions, with the inevitable result that these first works were found wanting. He quickly realized this himself and, even as he was establishing his terms of reference, tried to lessen their negative impact. In the 'Communication to My Friends' essay, he mentions his 'views on the nature of Art that I have proclaimed from a standpoint it took me years of evolution step-by-step to gain', and lamented the fact that critics would 'point them back to those very compositions from which I started on the natural path of evolution that led me to this standpoint'.[8] But the 'natural path of evolution' was too powerful a symbol, particularly in the evolution-obsessed second half of the nineteenth century. Not only did such language colour perceptions of Wagner's pre-1850 operas, it also informed more general ways of seeing opera in the nineteenth century. Not for nothing did Verdi become incensed that a few scattered recurring themes in *Don Carlos* (1867) and *Aida* (1871) were enough to make critics call him an Italian Wagner, and a late-arriving one at that. Had these critics known *I due Foscari*, they might have been given pause; but by then *Foscari* had faded from the repertory. As we shall see in later chapters, Verdi was far from alone in being subjected to such unwelcome comparisons.

However, when it comes to Wagner's earlier operas, there is a more important distortion in the other direction: to see works such as *Tannhäuser* and *Lohengrin* in this way is to overlook their greatness, which mostly resides in another realm, and has little to do with what might be prophetic of the later Wagner. The reason is simple: it is because the strongest music in Wagner's earlier operas is the most conventional. Their glory, why we return to them, stems from the inspiration he poured into well-worn shapes. One gets from them the clearest idea of Wagner's greedy ear, the fact that he had listened closely to and, judging by his musical love-letters, been swept away by Italian *bel canto* opera, by French *opéra comique* and by *grand opéra*. Wagner the essayist was, with a few notable early exceptions in which his real musical enthusiasms overflow, generally dismissive of French and Italian opera, and grudgingly praised the Germans only so far as they led up to him. But Wagner the composer was different altogether. As a maker of music he frequently wrote out his ardour for Romance-language operas, and wrote it out in musical sound.

WAGNER THE ITALIAN

The classic cases are *Tannhäuser* and *Lohengrin*, which are twins in the sense of being similar in scope and dramatic sources. Both are set in the vague middle ages, in Thuringia and Brabant respectively, and both draw on stories that Wagner derived from contemporary German Romantic updates: stock knights-and-damsels material. *Tannhäuser* deals with the legend of the 'Song Contest on the Wartburg', in which the hero Tannhäuser (tenor), who has secretly dallied in Act 1 with the Goddess Venus (mezzo-soprano), offends the Thuringian court in Act 2 by expatiating on her erotic charms in his contribution to a song contest. He is ordered to go to Rome to seek pardon from the Pope. In Act 3, returning unpardoned, he seems to be back on the road to perdition until the heroine, Princess Elisabeth (soprano), sacrifices herself for him, at which point he can die a happy man. In *Lohengrin*, the heroine, Elsa (soprano), has been falsely accused by two malicious schemers, the knight Telramund (baritone) and his wife Ortrud (mezzo-soprano). Elsa is in danger of being condemned for the murder of her brother; but a mysterious white knight (Lohengrin, tenor) appears on a boat drawn by a swan and offers himself as her defender. Lohengrin has a condition, though: that she must never ask his name, nor where he comes from. Assurances on this having been received, he defeats Telramund in combat and thus proves her innocence. Over the course of a long evening's drama, Elsa's inevitable curiosity about the identity of her knight gets the better of her and eventually she asks the fatal question. This prompts Lohengrin's departure (the departure boat is this time drawn by a dove, making all those jokes about 'by the next available swan' rather unfair) but at the same time sees the return of Elsa's brother, who was not dead, as it turned out, but en-swanned by an evil spell that is now broken.

We can see Wagner's *bel canto* roots most clearly in the beautiful, big-curve melodies that emerge within the conventional numbers in both operas. But before exploring this, it's worth savouring Wagner's affection for Vincenzo Bellini, whom he would continue to the end of his life to call 'the gentle Sicilian'.[9] In the 1830s and 1840s, Wagner could pay tribute to Bellini as standard-bearer for *bel canto* aesthetics not just in borrowing from his melodic language but also in his prose. In 'Bellini, a Word in Season' – written in 1837 as a memorial piece (Bellini had died in 1835) – Wagner exhorts his countrymen to be honest with themselves about their passions:

> How little we are convinced by our pack of rules and prejudices. How often must it have happened that, after being transported by a French or Italian opera at the theatre, upon coming out we have scouted our emotion with a pitying jest ... let us drop for once the jest, let us spare ourselves for once the sermon, and ponder what it was that so enchanted us; we

> then shall find, especially with Bellini, that it was the limpid Melody, the simple, noble, beauteous song. To confess this, and believe in it, is surely not a sin. It would be no sin, perchance, if before we fell asleep, we breathed a prayer that heaven would one day give German composers such melodies and such a way of handling song.[10]

And he tried. In the duet between Elsa and Ortrud in Act 2 of *Lohengrin*, it is only the libretto that tells us we are listening to an innocent and a schemer: two women having an earnest discussion about loyalty and forgiveness. Take the words away and, particularly towards the end, we are treated to something resembling a love duet from Bellini's *I Capuleti e i Montecchi* (1830, a Romeo and Juliet story), with soprano and mezzo-soprano twining in and out of one another, an effect that survives the occasionally dense chromatic harmony reminding us of the composer's German origins. If one looks at the score of this duet, one is struck by how many times Wagner puts the notation for a vocal turn (the sideways 'S') over the high points of the vocal lines: a graceful embellishment that refers to the lightness, the *leggerezza*, of Italianate vocal writing. *I Capuleti* was in fact a critical text in Wagner's accounts of his artistic evolution. Judging by the number of times he mentions it and the passion attached to reminiscences of the event, Bellini's opera entered his consciousness for good when he saw Wilhelmine Schroeder-Devrient; as Romeo in Leipzig in 1834, and again in Magdeburg in 1835. Schroeder-Devrient; the part of Romeo; Bellini's opera; all make up a theme that returns unrepressed in Wagner's writings throughout his life, even if the emotions became more mixed as time went by.

On the other hand, the form of the *Lohengrin* duet, and many effects within it, are far from the Italian gold standard. For one thing, the number splits in two. The first part involves Ortrud singing upwards to Elsa, who is safe on a balcony high above her (Romeo and Juliet come subversively to mind). Ortrud begins (in recitative) by twice calling Elsa's name, two syllables 'El-sa', almost like a whispered hunting horn call, accompanied by oboes and muted horns. Muting the instruments creates a near-for-far effect, as if loud sounds are being heard at a great distance. The second 'El-sa' is sung to non-muted horns and flutes, as if an Ortrud very far away had instantly teleported nearer: a sign of her magical nature. They converse. After Ortrud (throwing in a few vocal ornaments and turns) convinces her victim to come down to the door, she is left alone for a few moments and uses the time to sing a revenge monologue – a conventional outburst with loud tremolo strings. When Elsa joins her and the two occupy the same space another duet begins, this time more convoluted. Ortrud drops her Italianate style: now her aim is to plant suspicions about Lohengrin in Elsa's mind. The more emphatic and incisive Ortrud's vocal idiom becomes – when she reverts, as it were, to prose – the more flowery and ornamental are Elsa's ingénue responses.

But the best Italianate operatic moment comes with the return to conventional form: the end of the duet, when they sing together. Elsa's lines are naïve: 'Laß mich dich lehren, wie süß die Wonne reinster Treue' (Let me teach you, how sweet the bliss of pure faithfulness). Ortrud's are snarls: 'Ha! Dieser Stoltz, er soll mich lehren, wie ich bekämpfe ihre Treu'' (Ha! This pride will teach me, how I can defeat her faithfulness). But her specific words are, in performance, incomprehensible because the simultaneous singing cancels them out. This is where the voices start twining around one another, sometimes with echoes of one line in another, sometimes in parallel intervals. Just as Ortrud's musical prose dominated earlier, now Elsa's blissful mood dictates the musical mood – and because it does, the beautiful remnants of an Italian love duet come back out from the wings.

Compared to the old-fashioned operatic aesthetic given expression in this duet, the one famous leitmotif in *Lohengrin* – the so-called 'Question Motif' – is insignificant indeed: something which was obviously meant to be sinister, but which turned into a major miscalculation. This 'Question Motif' is an absolutely straightforward symbolic theme: as Claude Debussy, that most uncertain of Wagnerians, later said of such musical recollections,'It's rather like those silly people who hand you their visiting cards and then lyrically recite what is printed on them'.[11] It is sung by Lohengrin in Act 1, when he tells Elsa of the prohibition she must obey: 'Nie sollst du mich befragen, noch Wissens Sorge tragen, woher ich kam der Fahrt, noch wie mein Nam' und Art' (Never should you ask me, nor should you concern yourself to know, whence I have come from, and what is my name and nature). It recurs whenever Elsa is wondering about Lohengrin – one can almost see her furrow her brow and look tempted on cue – and whenever scheming Ortrud tries to sow doubt and lead Elsa astray. For instance, it is blared out at the end of Act 2, after a scene in which Ortrud has confronted Elsa on the way to her wedding, and hinted that Lohengrin might not be all he seems. In traditional stagings of *Lohengrin*, the mezzo playing Ortrud is often required to sneer knowingly to trombone accompaniment as the curtain falls. And then, predictably, Elsa also gets to sing a breathless version of the motif when she finally asks the question in Act 3.

It is instructive to look for a moment at the twentieth-century career of the 'Question Motif' in film music. Music from *Lohengrin* tended to be used a great deal by composers in the classic sound-film era: in part because it was a popular opera in the 1930s and 1940s; in part because the 'Wedding March' from Act 3, via inherited Victorian ceremonial habits, had become a clichéd musical accompaniment to matrimony. But the 'Question Motif' is often used ironically, for humorous effect. For instance, in Michael Powell's *The Life and Death of Colonel Blimp* (1943), when a British war hero sends his best friend in London a postcard from Berlin, a close-up of said postcard triggers the 'Question Motif'. In the opera the motif is too obviously a portent of bad things, too musically isolated from the contexts in which it recurs, too likely to be a mere 'visiting card'. Again, the comparison with Verdi's *I due Foscari* comes to mind, if only because that is another opera in which the intellectual lure of recurring motifs led the composer away from his best operatic instincts.

This is not the only way in which *Lohengrin* sometimes falters when it most obviously looks forward to the avant-garde works of Wagner's maturity. Another instance is found in the experimental stretches of unstructured dialogue, which can become heavy going. The long, elaborate discussion between Elsa and Lohengrin in Act 3, in which they sort things out on their wedding night, is an instance of Wagner looking for the free-flowing exchanges that he would later call musical prose – his rejection of the profiles and limits of predictable melody and fixed forms. But it doesn't work. In short, Wagner appears to have experienced a crisis with melody in *Lohengrin*, something hinted at in his prose writings from the time.

As in *Tannhäuser*, his mastery of overwhelming musical effects and small uncanny details experienced no crisis whatsoever. An example of the first: stage directors from time immemorial have struggled with the Act 1 *deus ex machina*, Lohengrin's arrival on the swan boat. In its way, the apparition is as old as the hills: Zeus or Apollo arriving from heaven, against flat painted clouds, in a golden carriage dropped from the catwalks, circa 1650. Wagner wants no such artifice. We have to be convinced that this is a miracle in truth, and not a charming allegory wrapped up in stage machinery. His solution is to overwhelm us in the acoustic realm. The people of Brabant are assembled on stage to witness Elsa's trial – she is brought on to repudiate Telramund's accusation that she murdered her brother. Elsa has a vision that a knight from afar will defend her honour, and a herald blows his trumpet in summons. Two times, there is silence. But after the third summons and a plea from Elsa and her ladies, the swan appears in the distance and a magnificent pandemonium ensues. The orchestra begins with a near-for-far fanfare, distant-sounding trumpets and horns, a metallic miniature that will keep getting louder until it becomes a brass leviathan assailing our ears. But the most profound shock is in the chorus, up to this point a well-disciplined, somewhat tedious collective whose style runs to simple hymn-like harmonies. Now they are too amazed to be prim, and individual voices or groups of voices burst out with exclamations: Look! A swan! A miracle! These calls and cries are so rhythmically unpredictable that they sound like absolute astonishment, as if the chorus were improvising this stretch on their own, not following a script. Here we get a sense for Wagner's special verve in creating the illusion of the un-composed, the spontaneous or the unmediated.

As for the uncanny moments, they are seldom associated with a repeating motif, and often slip in with a minimum of fanfare. Most of Act 2 (several scenes' worth in the score) is taken up by an immense finale entailing much slow choral singing and snail's pace processing, punctuated by the occasional spark when Ortrud and Telramund show up to cause trouble. This is a musical passage where doughty virtue glazes the eye and the villains provide welcome relief. But something odd happens with Telramund, who up to this point has a particular musical and vocal presence: bold, forthright and not completely unattractive in his obsessions with honour, transparency and protocol. Near the end, under the cover of choral sermonizing from the blameless, he approaches Elsa (who is now seriously worried about Lohengrin's identity) and whispers a strange thing to her: 'Vertraue mir! Laß dir ein Mittel heißen, das dir Gewissheit schaft. Laß mich das kleinste Glied ihm nur entreißen, des Fingers Spitze, und ich schwöre dir, was er dir hehlt, sollst frei du vor dir seh'n!' (Trust me! Know that there is a way to be certain. Let me but rip the tiniest member from his body, the tip of his finger, and what he is concealing will be revealed to you!) Even stranger is the change in his voice, as if he has become a different being, from sonorous chest voice and ringing tones to fast, almost hysterical patter, sung so high in the baritone register as to verge on falsetto. For a moment, something from an unsettling Wagnerian future makes an unexpected appearance here, the feminized bloodlust of the dwarf Mime (in *Der Ring des Nibelungen*, 1876) or the shrieks of Klingsor, the castrated sorcerer in Wagner's last opera, *Parsifal* (1882). Such dramatis personae are not far from representing Wagnerian caricatures of Jews, as even a cursory reading of his infamous anti-Semitic pamphlet, *Das Judentum in der Musik* (On Judaism in Music, 1850), would suggest.

Perhaps this disquieting moment from *Lohengrin* shows us one way to understand the difference in flavour between *Der fliegende Holländer* or *Tannhäuser* on the one hand and *Lohengrin* on the other: that Wagner's turn to ugliness marks an attitude that spoils his confident operatic touch. Up to *Tannhäuser*, Wagner was an optimist, still young, barely into his thirties. His optimism rhymes with the philosophies that engrossed him up to that point, in particular the 'Young Germany' movement with its energy and faith in future betterment. His writings about the theatre, about opera, literature and history have an idealistic tenor at this time, and naïve energy. In the exuberant finale to one of his fictions, 'A Happy Evening' (1841), the protagonist and his friend 'R' have just attended a concert:

> 'And tonight' – my friend broke in, in full enthusiasm – 'it is joy I taste, the happiness, the presage of a higher destiny, won from the wondrous revelations in which Mozart and Beethoven have spoken to us on this glorious spring evening. So here's to happiness, here's to courage, that enheartens us in the fight with our fate! Here's to victory, gained by our higher sense, over the worthlessness of the vulgar. To love, which crowns our courage, to friendship, that keeps firm our faith! To hope, which weds itself to our foreboding! To the day, to the night! A cheer for the sun, a cheer for the stars!'[12]

It is worth noting that the two individuals in this story have just consumed a considerable amount of punch, which may account for some of the exalted mood. But the artist-friends, strolling arm in arm and laughing at the Philistines, could just as well be members of Robert Schumann's fictional *Davidsbund* from 1834, the Davids fighting the Goliaths without any sense that they might ever suffer defeat.

These were the currents of air that lofted *Tannhäuser* to great heights in musical terms. Like Bizet's *Carmen*, it is a near-perfect opera. That has in part to do with the energy and verve in its conventional numbers, which are ideals of their types. In part it has to do with instances of what we see in *Lohengrin*'s Act 1 Swan Chorus – creating the illusion of music that has flown beyond a composer's control over musical form and melodic choice, to become something seemingly more spontaneous and unguarded, the voice of the People or of Nature itself.

WAGNER'S *CARMEN*

Tannhäuser was by far the most popular of Wagner's operas throughout the entire nineteenth century and well into the twentieth, with glowing reviews that evidently softened impresarios and theatre directors worldwide. Between its premiere in 1845 and the first Paris production in 1861 it was produced hundreds of times; Ernest Newman's four-volume Wagner biography devotes an entire chapter to the phenomenon. It was the first Wagner opera played in America, being staged in New York in 1859. After the premiere, an article in the *New York Musical Review and Gazette* discussed its formidable reputation:

> If there really is no melody, no truth, no beauty in this work, how is it possible that it has taken such a hold upon the Germans for the last eight or ten years? We saw this opera about six years ago, in Leipzig, when it was performed for the thirtieth time. *The house was crowded.* Since then it has been given repeatedly in small and great cities of Germany, and the statistics of all the performances of last year in that country prove that this one opera was given oftener than any other single work of the popular Meyerbeer or Verdi. And let us also say, if this opera was really in principle and treatment so exceedingly original and new, as friends and foes with different views have claimed it to be, this great success would not have accompanied it.[13]

Quaint sociological evidence of *Tannhäuser*'s predominance is everywhere in the historical record. The *Aeolian Quarterly*, a trade publication devoted to Aeolian piano roll products and the player-piano industry, reported in 1897 that:

> it is a significant fact, as showing the class of music-lovers to whom the Aeolian appeals, that of all the thousands of pieces cut for that instrument, no other has had so large a sale as the 'Tannhäuser' Overture. Some years ago, the audience at a Crystal Palace concert, in London, were allowed to vote for the most popular overture. The 'Tannhäuser' came out ahead, with 317 votes; the 'Midsummer Night's Dream' by Mendelssohn coming next with 253.[14]

In 1861 in London, 'Neville Temple' and 'Edward Trevor' published their hundred-page epic *Tannhäuser, or the Battle of the Bards*, based on and in tribute to Wagner.[15] Its literary merit is small. Tannhäuser is described as having 'a sinuous frame, compact of pliant power'; Wolfram is 'like an orphan child in charity / whose loss came early, and is gently borne, / too deep for tears, too constant for complaint', which shows who wears the trousers in this particular poem. In 1917, the *Victrola Book of the Opera* gauges *Tannhäuser*'s popularity by several barometers:

> There are a great many people who like to go to the opera, but who do not care for Wagner's Ring Operas, with their Teutonic myths and legends, and their long and sometimes undeniably tedious scenes. But *Tannhäuser*, with its poetry, romance, and passion, and above all its characters who are real human beings and not mysterious mythological gods, goddesses, and heroes, appeals strongly to everyone. To show the wonderful vogue of this work, it is estimated that there are more than one thousand performances of the opera that take place annually throughout the world; and in Germany during the decade of 1901–1910 it was given 3,243 times.[16]

When the number is so specific, one feels the author has had access to a reliable pre-war statistical record.

The 1859 reviewer in the *New York Musical Review*, like the Victrola summary, identifies a significant truth: *Tannhäuser* is not music of the future. Unlike *Lohengrin*, there is nothing unconventional in its libretto. We know from the original composition draft and score that it was originally conceived as a number opera. It was then revised several times, a complicated story, with the most significant revision being for another assault on the French capital – also disastrous – in 1861. But in its first,

1845 form, and up to the Paris revisions, there are no long meandering discussions between characters. Yet again there are obvious elements relating to earlier German opera, particularly in the old-German local colour and its attendant choral episodes. And, as discussed in the previous chapter, many of the opera's most glorious inspirations are clearly written in homage to French *grand opéra*, particularly in the big ensemble scenes and their love of sheer noise. The French delight in operatic shows was persistent and crossed the boundaries of time and taste. When the 24-year-old Marcel Proust saw *Tannhäuser* in Paris in 1895, he was left unmoved by the female characters or the love duets, gravitating instead towards avant-garde moments where music combined with stage images to make a kind of resonant picture:

> I was extremely bored with *Tannhäuser* up to the solo. And in spite of the general cries of admiration, Elisabeth's languishing prayer [in Act 3] left me cold. But how beautiful the whole last part is . . . the more legendary Wagner is, the more human I find him, and in him the most magnificent artifice of the imagination strikes me only as the compelling symbolic expression of moral truths.[17]

Proust is referring to *Tannhäuser*'s famous narrative solo in Act 3, in which an account of the journey to Rome is accompanied by music that gives expression to the scenes described, their sounds and colours. And while one disagrees with Proust but rarely, the most avant-garde (least artificial) passage in the opera is in fact the site of an evident truth, this very Act 3 narrative. Here, in a prefiguring of Wagner's post-1850 style, the orchestral contribution is of greater importance, bringing with it a web of motivic connections to enrich the through-composed progress of the hero's narration. Everything that follows the narrative, to the end of the opera, involves scenic wonders: Proust's affinity for music that accompanies visual magic is evident. But such scenes are not ubiquitous. Generally, if two people in *Tannhäuser* have something to say to one another – as do the hero and Elisabeth during their happy reunion in Act 2 – they say it in the form of recitative and then a big duet.

Elisabeth's entrance aria in Act 2 of *Tannhäuser*, 'Dich, teure Halle, grüß ich wieder' (Cherished hall, I salute you again), is a good case in point. There is a bare minimum of prosaic utterances. When Elisabeth finishes her first, fanfare-like lines and thinks back to less happy moments in the Hall of Song, her voice becomes appropriately melancholy, and the musical volume is turned down: she no longer sings finished melody, but rather some gestures accompanied by rhythmically free chord progressions, with pauses between and a plaintive melodic fragment in the oboe. But this interruption is very brief. 'Wie jetzt' (But now) she reminds herself: joy will return, and the opening music of the aria duly comes back in a traditional formal gesture towards balance and completion. The best part is at the very end, in which the music ignores the words because the text is now irrelevant, being just a repetition of the same motto, 'Sei mir gegrüßt, sei mir gegrüßt, du teure Halle, sei mir gegrüßt' (I salute you, cherished hall). Wagner sets the four syllables to ascending three-note arpeggios (the last note repeated), higher each time, building up sequentially to an arched bow at the top of the soprano's range: as perfectly formed and as moving as, say, Amonasro's 'Pensa che un popolo, vinto, straziato, per te soltanto risorger può', the spectacular melodic peroration in his duet with Aida in Act 3 of Verdi's opera.

Tannhäuser is an opera about singing, indeed about who is the best singer, and its Act 2 song contest is the central dramatic event. In this sense there is a clear expectation that beautiful melody will take centre stage. Honours in this respect are shared between Elisabeth – a role created by Wagner's niece Johanna – and Wolfram (baritone), a knight who, unlike Tannhäuser, has no sensual blots on his résumé. Both are given big solo pieces in which melody dominates the compositional palette. Their particularly melodic music is absent from the opera's potpourri Overture, a lacuna that one early commentator read as symbolic of their lesser power: 'The gentle love of Elisabeth, the faithful friendship of Wolfran [sic], are alone absent from the overture; but the one is really as much drowned in religion as the other is absorbed by the complete uselessness of Wolfran's fidelity and the ultimate triumph of Tannhäuser.'[18] True, in comparison to Tannhäuser's obvious susceptibility to sins of the flesh, Wolfram's saintliness might seem uninteresting; nor does he get the girl. But he is by far the more captivating singer. In Chapter 1, we mentioned that his contributions in the song contest, in terms of vocal line and harmonic gesture, are musically sensual in a way that the hero's never are. Wolfram is one of the most Italianate of Wagner's roles: as if to emphasize this, the part is written for a high, light baritone – very rare in Wagner. He has an aria in Act 3 that, as a reward for its sheer singability, became a parlour staple in the Victorian and Edwardian eras, 'O du, mein holder Abendstern', the 'Song to the

Evening Star'. A marvellous review from 1882 homes in on the truth of Wolfram's charm, referring to 'the most melodious and juicy baritone part hitherto written by Wagner' with Wolfram's song in the Act 2 contest and the 'Evening Star' number deemed the 'chief bits of fat in the whole opera – the nearest things in it to real, coherent, recollectable songs', which afford 'ample opportunities for the display of a mellow and eminently sympathetic [vocal] organ'.[19]

There is one single place in the opera where all-conquering song – singing that overwhelms and convinces – actually accomplishes something on stage in front of us. This comes in the final septet in Act 1, in the section where Wolfram convinces Tannhäuser, who has just extricated himself from Venusberg, to return to the Thuringian court. This septet, as we have seen, was beloved by French audiences. Much urgent discussion (Will Tannhäuser return? No, I cannot, my destiny lies elsewhere!) gets cut off by a dramatic intervention as Wolfram invokes the name of Princess Elisabeth to the sound of celestial harps. The *coup de théâtre* invites a pause for slow, lyric excess, and Wolfram is given sole responsibility: he describes to Tannhäuser how much Elisabeth has missed him, and he begs the hero to return.

In a curious way, the effect is of Wolfram pausing to take up a mandolin and sing a real song, since this lyric subsection is so self-contained, so formally simple (ABA, no less) and so well-framed by an orchestral lead-in. It's even scored as if to profile pure voice, with the baritone sounding out against quiet woodwind and strings. The contrasting verse ('Denn, ach! als du uns stolz verlassen, verschloß ihr Herz sich uns'rem Lied' – Ah, but when you left in injured pride, her heart was closed to our singing) swerves appropriately into the minor and melancholy. And this second verse ends with a fabulous cadence, a little piece of musical pathos. The voice skips up through an interval, then retraces it downwards while filling in the missing notes of a major scale that is revealed at the end as an ornamental colour, just a step above the true minor centre. When the opening melody returns immediately afterwards – slyly, to the text 'O kehr' zurück' (Oh, come back) – it seems doubly marvellous in the way it has been reintroduced. This is a classic instance of an operatic moment that seems to ask the listeners to sing along *with* the character, so strong is the melody's pull: it is one of those passages in Wagner that again makes sense of his affection for Bellini, an affection that was to wane once there could be only one unassailably perfect opera composer in all history – Wagner himself. Returning in 1871 to the experience of Schroeder-Devrient and Romeo, Wagner's view has become harsh:

> No matter how absurd or trivial its shape, one could not deny to Opera a power unrivalled even in the most ideal sense. . . . We need but instance the impersonation, surely unforgettable by many yet alive, once given by Frau Schröder-Devrient of 'Romeo' in Bellini's opera. Every fibre of the musician rebels against allowing the least artistic merit to the sickly, utterly threadbare music here hung upon an opera-poem of indigent grotesqueness; but ask anyone who witnessed it, what impression he received from the 'Romeo' of Frau Schröder-Devrient as compared with the Romeo of our very best play-actor in even the great Briton's piece?[20]

Alas, the Wagner who snarls at Bellini is a much-diminished soul.

NOISE

When Wagner finally managed to convince the Paris Opéra to put on one of his works, *Tannhäuser* was chosen; but that was as late as 1861. The choice has sometimes been read as evidence that the French public would have been unable to deal with the most recent Wagner, an idea that hardly bears serious scrutiny. For one thing, by 1860 Wagner had only just finished his most radical piece, *Tristan und Isolde*; for another, the only other post-1850 works – the first two episodes of the four-opera *Der Ring des Nibelungen* – were operas that Wagner would not allow to be performed separately. Perhaps the explanation for choosing *Tannhäuser* was simpler: that it was a wonderful *grand opéra* in the finest Parisian tradition. The opera also shows how spectacular the formal conventions of *grand opéra* could become when invigorated by a young composer. And at the time this youthfulness expressed itself not just in new thinking about instrumental sound (more of this later) or in impatience with the status quo of the operatic world, but in the kinetic energy and optimism of the big numbers, those stalwarts of so many operas past.

New instrumental sounds abound in *Tannhäuser* and *Lohengrin*, and there are different ways of reading their significance. The critic and philosopher Theodor Adorno, for instance, read Wagner's near-for-far instrumental effects as a form of acoustic deception, a phantasmagoria that aimed to confuse by concealing the material basis for sound. This, he argued, was a way to detach the listener from an awareness of history or time, of his or her responsibility and presence in the real world – hypnotized dreamers are unlikely to man the barricades or agitate for social revolution. On the other hand, one could also see such spatial effects as an experiment in acoustic realism, of Wagner being hyper-aware of how sound is perceived in terms of distance, volume and architectural surroundings. He was a happy master of onstage (or just barely offstage) sounds: trumpets, horns, shepherd's pipes and bells, unseen voices and lonely calls from the rigging. It was a talent that once more reveals his *grand opéra* tastes, even as it shows how in his hands the model mutated into unpredictable and almost unrecognizable forms.

The *pièce de résistance* in this regard is Act 1, scene 3 of *Tannhäuser*, in which Tannhäuser has been transported instantaneously from Venus's underground lair to his old haunts in Thuringia, and lies unconscious next to a rustic Marian shrine. For almost ten minutes, every sound comes from the fictional world on- or offstage; nothing is heard from the orchestra pit. A young shepherd seems to improvise a song to spring, and accompanies himself with a random-sounding, wandering tune on his pipe (offstage cor anglais). Unseen livestock are wearing bells, which clang from somewhere in the distance. Pilgrims approach, far away at first, then coming nearer: their singing goes from almost inaudible to right there in front of us as they cross the stage. It is all completely, uncompromisingly realistic, and attempts to create the impression that no one composed this scene, it just *is*. The purism ends when the pit orchestra returns – unnoticed at first – as the shepherd calls farewell, 'Glück auf! Nach Rom! Betet für meine arme Seele' (Godspeed! To Rome! Pray for my poor soul). This wakes up Tannhäuser and the full orchestra comes roaring to life at maximum volume; the fading reprise of the Pilgrims' Chorus gets instrumental support as Tannhäuser echoes their melody.

No description can capture the radical acoustic imagination behind this scene, the utter newness. It has to be heard to be believed. Not for nothing was it greeted with laughter and hoots of disdain in Paris in 1861, for even though sixteen years had passed since it had been composed, it seemed incomprehensible. It remains a triumph of sheer daring, and predicts the best of the Wagnerian future, passages such as the opening of Act 3 of *Tristan und Isolde*, or what we hear before the curtain goes up in *Die Meistersinger*, Act 3, scene 2.

LIBRETTO RULES

Wagner's twenties and thirties were the period when he was most attracted to reform and revolution, to liberationist ideals that were half formed and naïve in a way that is (in a non-pejorative sense) young or youthful. His most obviously reformist writings come from the late 1840s, when his political activities were also at their height: one need only cite titles such as *Die Kunst und die Revolution* (Art and Revolution) and *Das Kunstwerk der Zukunft* (The Artwork of the Future; both 1849) to get the flavour of the enterprise. In the context, it is hardly by chance that this was also the period during which he was closest to Franz Liszt (1811–86), who was also a renegade both musically and socially. Liszt had been an extremist as a concert pianist and composer, pushing the limits of technical virtuosity in his playing and attempting to capture improvisation – which necessarily means fanciful messiness – in his musical compositions. In the late 1840s he, like Wagner, experienced a turning point, renouncing his life as a virtuoso to become Kapellmeister in Weimar (a city famous even then for its association with Goethe), devoting himself to self-consciously serious, determinedly avant-garde composition. Not surprisingly in these circumstances – and also because Liszt became an important enabler of grandiose Wagnerian projects – Wagner found the reformed virtuoso a sympathetic interlocutor.

Adorno thought that Wagner was a would-be revolutionary who secretly craved security, comfort and wealth, his self-identification as a revolutionary mere self-aggrandizement.[21] One might also question the degree to which Wagner's hobby of political philosophizing had much impact on his musical thinking. But we do need to remember that as an opera composer, right from the start in his early twenties with his first fledgling pieces, he was 'revolutionary' in one technical but critical point: he wrote his own libretti. For almost the first time in the history of opera, a composer did not depend on a professional poet to put this or that drama into shape, as words for operatic music. What did this mean in practical terms? Wagner, with his usual poetic licence, said that he often conceived actions and situations at the same time as musical ideas, and that the two were implicated in one another's genesis. In practice, though, he was much more conventional, following the traditions of opera composers in other countries and other centuries. He always wrote the libretto first and got to the music once the words were finished, polished and sometimes even published. Of course the fact that he wrote his own libretti also meant that if he wanted a scene that dispensed with traditional numbers in favour of free dialogue, he had no need to cajole some painting-by-numbers professional into writing something out of the ordinary. Quite simply, there was no friction to overcome in rethinking the formal terms in which opera had always been written. This aspect became hugely important in the post-1850 operas. If there was going to be an opera composer who changed the fundamental ways in which operatic music communicated, it was almost bound to be someone who wrote his own words.

Here, with the question of the how and the how-to of a libretto, we come to the surprisingly practical origins of the earthquake Wagner was about to unleash. While working on *Lohengrin*, he was already looking ahead to the next libretto. He decided to use the story of Siegfried at the court of the Gibichungs, a classic tragedy with a famous source in Middle High German poetry, the *Nibelungenlied*, and in earlier Norse sagas. He wrote the libretto – calling it *Siegfrieds Tod* (Siegfried's Death) – in 1848, a year in which he also finished an essay dabbling in grand speculations about the connections between Norse myth, Friedrich Barbarossa (the twelfth-century Holy Roman Emperor) and, of all things, the Holy Grail. Then his revolutionary contretemps with the Dresden police intervened, the 'Wanted Poster' was issued and he fled into exile without even managing to hear the premiere of *Lohengrin*, which Liszt staged at the Weimar Court Theatre in 1850.

The libretto of *Siegfrieds Tod*, which went with Wagner to Switzerland, was in technical terms bizarre to a fault. First of all, Wagner decided to imitate medieval German poetic style by writing it in alliterative rather than rhyming poetry – that is, the verse lines (and often many words within) had matching initial consonants rather than rhyming vowel sounds at the line ends. This may not sound like much of an innovation, but the decision has serious consequences for the rhythmic and melodic design of any vocal inspiration. The stresses in alliterative poetry are unpredictable and constantly redistributed; there is no inevitable sing-song effect to the sung line. In other words, there is no way to predict, as all previous operatic libretti had allowed, that a four-bar phrase which happens to fit well for line 1 will be at all useable for line 2, where three bars or five may be needed. By his choice of this eccentric style of poetry, Wagner preordained an unprecedented degree of melodic discursiveness and rhythmic freedom in any forthcoming music. The second radical aspect of the libretto was that it extended Wagner's nascent leanings towards dialogue and interchange. While there are still many *grand opéra* hallmarks in *Siegfrieds Tod* – notably a big trio at the end of Act 2, with the anti-Siegfried conspirators joining their voices in condemnation – these are surrounded by solo or conversational marathons. There is an immense, wandering monologue for Siegfried's doomed beloved, Brünnhilde, just before she casts herself on his funeral pyre at the end of the opera; and Act 1 contains an extremely long, three-way conversation among denizens of the Gibichung court, in which they complain about their lassitude and speculate on the (not-yet-arrived) hero Siegfried. Unlike any operatic trio that had preceded it, this last libretto section has no simultaneous singing anywhere in sight, not even at the end.

These two formal points – the unconventional, alliterative prosody and the decision to write long discursive scenes with no formal verses for operatic numbers – were extraordinarily radical, so much so that they seem to have paralysed Wagner musically for almost five years. He began the music of *Siegfrieds Tod* in 1850, but broke off after getting part-way into Act 1, scene 2. One explanation is that his musical capacities had not yet caught up with the implications of his libretto, and that he was experienced enough to know not to go on. His own stated reason for laying down the pen was more elaborate, but does refer to the approaching earthquake; it is probably true in part, and also makes excellent legend-fodder. As Wagner saw it, the problem was not with prosody or structure, but with the fact that the opera's first scene was a narrative: three Norns (Fates) explain to the audience the pre-history of what we are about to see. We need to know that a magic ring was forged and cursed; that Siegfried won the ring in mortal combat; and that the curse spells disaster for Siegfried, Brünnhilde and various Gods (who happen also to be Brünnhilde's and Siegfried's immediate relatives). What is more, we need to know how these Gods are related, and what their investment is in one another. So the Norns have to tell us. The problem, Wagner wrote, was in the corresponding *musical* telling. How can the music of the Norns refer to a past that doesn't itself exist in musical form?

Wagner concluded that he must bring that past into being as music, by enacting the events the Norns will describe. So he drafted another libretto that concerned the events before *Siegfrieds Tod* (called *Der junge Siegfried* – Young Siegfried, 1851) and showed how his hero got the magic ring; and then yet another libretto about Brünnhilde, who befriended and tried to protect Siegfried's parents from the wrath of the Gods (*Die Walküre* – The Valkyrie, also 1851); and finally a last libretto about Brünnhilde's parents and how the magic ring was forged by a dwarf and cursed in the first place (*Das Rheingold* – The Rhine Gold, written 1852). And as a prelude to writing these three extra libretti that explain everything leading up to the death of Siegfried, he also felt he needed to work out his personal place in the history of opera and, in theory, how to write the music for these increasingly radical new libretti. And so, endlessly loquacious, he wrote his largest theoretical work, the dense treatise *Oper und Drama*, in 1850–51.

Perhaps because these four linked libretti delve into notions of racial purity, inherited power, the despoliation of nature by thieving, dark, half-people, and the natural superiority of German heroes, Wagner around the same time wrote *On Judaism in Music*, a disquisition on the inferiority of Jewish artists and the dangers inherent in their continued existence. It is a tract extreme even among anti-Semitic literature of the time. His diminishment was now well in hand, a circumstance that makes the knot represented by his work in the fallow years 1848–53 – the adjective is now revealed as purely ironic – even less easy to untwist.

13
Opéra comique, the crucible

Opéra comique, comic opera in French, in the nineteenth century: what comes to mind? If talking about the earlier decades, it's mostly a now-forgotten repertory – light, operetta-style works with lively set pieces, some sentimental moments, lots of spoken dialogue. Daniel Auber's *Fra Diavolo* (1830) might, if time were short, stand in for the entire genre. The laughing bandit, Fra Diavolo (tenor), is a dashing though murderous highwayman who gets to sing a bravura aria about the life enjoyed by robber chiefs; he poses as a marquis but is eventually foiled by a young officer called Lorenzo (tenor), who of course is in love with and loved by the soprano lead Zerline, who is actually the daughter of ... And so on. Supporting characters include further brigands, a pair of eccentric English aristocrats and two choruses – soldiers on one side of the law, bandits on the other. Another signature work, Ferdinand Hérold's *Zampa* (1831), helps show the pattern. The dashing though dissolute pirate Zampa (tenor) is, unbeknownst to all, actually a disgraced nobleman in disguise. He tries to romance the ingénue Camille, and gets to sing a passionate aria about how much he loves her, but is foiled when the statue of a woman he once seduced and abandoned squeezes him to death as Mount Etna erupts in a fiery explosion. There are also some noisy – very noisy, and very wonderful – pirate choruses. The overture to *Zampa* is one of the nineteenth century's finest and was thumped out in piano-duet arrangements for more than a century in living rooms around the world. It was also a favourite orchestral showpiece of Arturo Toscanini (who recorded it in 1952) as well as providing the soundtrack for a famous Mickey Mouse cartoon, 'The Band Concert' (1935), in which the strains of two overtures being played on a bandstand (*Zampa* and *Guillaume Tell*) uncannily manifest themselves in nature as earthquakes, storms and tornados. The *Zampa* overture fell into almost total obscurity after the 1950s, but made a late twentieth-century reappearance on the soundtrack of the comedy *To Wong Foo Thanks for Everything, Julie Newmar* (1995). This is not as random as it might seem. The film is about three drag queens (one named 'Vida Boheme') driving cross-country to Hollywood, and chronicles their derring-do along the way. In such a large-hearted rhapsody to disguises, to silliness and courage, the spirit of *opéra comique* is not so far away.

Lest the impression is forming that *opéra comique* actually *requires* the presence of alluring criminals and their associates, we should recall that the most popular example of the genre to emerge from the 1830s – performed thousands of times in Paris and elsewhere up to the early twentieth century – was Auber's *Le Domino noir* (The Black Domino, 1837). This is a Spanish-intrigue drama, with a masked ball and at least one tenor of uncertain reputation and dubious morality; but in this case the rowdy males are merely tipsy Iberian aristocrats celebrating at a local inn. Entire books could be written about *opéra comique* and the inn: about taverns as sites of chance encounter between the disparate classes of humanity; as a kind of stage-within-a-stage where a visitor's willingness to sing, dance or tell stories is encouraged and imitated. Ambroise Thomas's *Mignon* (1866) starts with a virtuosic inn scene, moves in Act 2 to a theatrical dressing room and then to a park where a performance of Shakespeare is happening just offstage, in a nearby conservatory. All Thomas's scenes are, in other words, almost-theatrical. It's as if the place of *real* performance – the professional stage with its footlights, painted backdrops and painted singers – is too central and intimidating to be shown. But on the other hand the professional stage and the liberties allowed there are so attractive that it's seldom far away from the action – it's just offstage, or through the nearest door, or replaced by an inn.

This short tour of semi-forgotten works reminds us of the setting of the nineteenth century's most famous *opéra comique*: carefree soldiers and alluring smugglers, both groups ready to break into song at a harp's flourish; a gypsy who seduces through vocal performance and dancing; several other gypsies; roadside inns, dubious innkeepers and the exotic and alien realm of Spain – a place of alluring alternative colours and sounds for the city-bound Parisian public. The genealogy of Georges

Bizet's *Carmen* (1875), one of the nineteenth century's greatest operas, becomes clear. And *Carmen* is great not because it also, famously, has a tragic register that engenders passionate music – music that contrasts nobly with the close harmony of those trivial, carolling soldiers and smugglers. Far from it, what makes *Carmen* exceptional is its never-incongruous mesh between these registers, above all its sense that each register has equal value. The trivial and the decorative can sit there alongside the sentimental and tragic, all of them co-existing, without fuss, making way for each other when required.

Early nineteenth-century *opéra comique*, so obviously the crucible for *Carmen*, was a protean force in other ways. Its popularity in German theatres encouraged the delightful spill-over of its libretto conventions and musical styles into German Romantic opera. We have seen this already amid the supernatural aura of Weber's *Der Freischütz*. More surprising, and certainly not something the composer would have enjoyed recalling in later life, *opéra comique* also smiles out from those nautical choruses and happy spinning-maidens in Wagner's *Der fliegende Holländer*. Later still, Verdi mined the genre when he felt that his Italian operas were becoming too gloomy and monochromatic, when they needed an injection of trivial energy. In *Un ballo in maschera* (1859), a cheeky page called Oscar (soprano) skips on from time to time to rattle out arpeggios and flirt both with the doomed, tragic hero (tenor, and with a hint of the pirate in his carefree personality) and with the muttering villains (basses, of course) who are plotting murder.

There were also spill-overs in the opposite direction, into even-more-comic opera. *Opéra comique* was the main progenitor of French, German and English traditions of operetta, and hence of what would become the twentieth-century musical. Jacques Offenbach (1819–80), a critical figure in this transition from comic opera to operetta, started as a cellist in the orchestra of the Opéra-Comique (the Paris theatre that was first home to most of these pieces); his analytical attention to the genre is evident in his 1856 manifesto on the subject, made in connection with a competition he arranged for young opera composers.[1] It is tempting to think that what Offenbach encountered, listening as he did from the orchestra pit, mutated into his idiosyncratic brand of ironic compositional wit, with *opéra comique* becoming not just *operette* or *opéra bouffe* but mutating into bizarre genres such as 'bouffonnerie musicale' (*Les Deux Aveugles* – The Two Blind Men, 1855) or even 'anthropophagie musicale' (*Oyayaye, ou La Reine des îles* – Oyayaye, or The Queen of the Islands, 1855). A composer who could come up with genre designations such as these had thoroughly absorbed *opéra comique*'s genius for the ridiculous.

LAWS AND LOCALITY

The names of French operatic genres always raise questions about geography, since in Paris during much of the nineteenth century the shape of an operatic work was dictated by the venue for which it was written. Offenbach wrote many of his so-called *opéras bouffes* of the 1850s to 1880s for the Théâtre des Bouffes-Parisiennes. *Opéra comique* is, similarly, both the name of a genre and the name of the theatre that housed it. Around 1830, Paris offered its public three distinct, indeed rigidly defined and policed, types of operatic entertainment, enacted in three distinct spaces. These distinctions had been laid down (or rather reinstated) by Napoleon in 1807, and they remained in force until the 1860s: theatres had *by law* to perform a certain type of opera. At the Opéra (at various venues, but from 1821 to the 1870s at the Salle Le Peletier on the rue Le Peletier), you could attend – if you had the cash and the right cut of trouser – the largest and most prestigious of these types, the *grand opéra* which was just emerging as a genre and which we discussed two chapters ago: huge works, set on the largest of world-historical stages, costing unprecedented sums. The Théâtre Italien (from 1841 at the Salle Ventadour, on what is now the rue Méhul), catering to a no less elevated clientele, was reserved for Italian-language opera, and delivered it in such style, and with such high-calibre singers, that Italian composers saw premieres there as close to the pinnacle of their careers. Rossini was Director of the Théâtre Italien for a period in the 1820s, and remained its *éminence grise* for some time after; Bellini and Donizetti enjoyed high-profile premieres there in the mid-1830s. Paris's third main venue was the Opéra-Comique (mostly at the Salle Favart, on what is now the place Boieldieu), the home of *opéra comique* and thus the place that presided over a continuation of the eighteenth-century tradition of using spoken dialogue rather than recitative. This genre was no less popular with the public, and certain works dominated the repertoire for decades, as did their serious siblings at the Opéra. The 1830s were also a high-water mark in *opéra comique*'s international success, with the injection of a new, more Italian-influenced manner making the product more exportable than it had been previously.

Boieldieu's *La Dame blanche* (1825), with its tale of supernatural derring-do in exotic eighteenth-century Scotland, pushed the genre as close as it could go (at least this early in the century) towards the territory of Romantic drama. But it was Eugène Scribe and Daniel Auber, the pre-eminent *grand opéra* librettist–composer team in its formative period, who dominated the *opéra comique* repertory in the 1830s and 1840s. In spite of competition from hits such as Adolphe Adam's *Le Postillon de Lonjumeau* (1836), Hérold's *Zampa* and Donizetti's *La Fille du régiment* (The Daughter of the Regiment, 1840), Scribe and Auber successfully managed to match their style to the changing times, in the process amassing numerous successful *opéras comiques* to their names. They were responsible for both *Le Domino noir* and *Fra Diavolo*.

The sheer longevity of the best of these works was remarkable even by the standards of the most popular *grands opéras*. *Fra Diavolo* received nearly a thousand performances at the Opéra-Comique alone in the nineteenth century: by the 1850s it had been seen as far afield as New York, Buenos Aires, Sydney and Calcutta. The plot even proved malleable enough to serve as the basis of one of Laurel and Hardy's movies of the 1930s: directed by Hal Roach, it is known in the US as *The Devil's Brother* (1933) and is worth searching out. Scribe offered his composer a three-act drama, set in southern Italy during Napoleonic times. Added variety and local colour are supplied by the exotic English aristocrats (Lord and Lady 'Cokbourg') and by Fra Diavolo's two bumbling companions in crime (in *The Devil's Brother* this pair become, of course, 'Stanlio' and 'Ollio'). Auber's music is simple and direct: the pace may slacken occasionally, but the dominant tempo is that of the quick march, with dotted rhythms ever prominent. It's certainly no coincidence that this dotted-rhythm march is also characteristic of the 'Marseillaise' – distant, comedy-refracted strains of the French Revolution are never far from the surface. An excellent example comes at the opening of Act 3, in which Fra Diavolo indulges in a (rare) solo aria outlining his philosophy, 'Je vois marcher sous ma bannière' (I see marching under my banner), which has brief moments of pathos but is dominated by the inevitable march tunes and (as this is a solo) a distinctly Rossinian vocal style in bravura sections.

It was certainly fun. These are works that were played hundreds, even thousands of times in the nineteenth century, occasionally to high praise. In 1844, Heinrich Heine reported satirically on the situation:

> While the Academy of Music [the Opéra] was dragging along so wretchedly, and the Italians limping along as miserably behind it, the third lyric stage, or the Opéra Comique, rose to its joyous height. Here one success followed another, and there was cheerful ringing in the money-chest; in fact, there was a much larger crop of money than laurels, which was, however, no misfortune for the management. . . . Tremendous approbation has been awarded to Scribe's new opera, *The Siren*, for which Auber composed the music. The author and musician are perfectly matched; they have the most admirable perception or sense of the interesting; they know how to entertain us agreeably; they enrapture and dazzle us by the brilliance of their wit; they both have a certain *filigrane* talent for welding together all kinds of charming trifles, and they make us forget there is such a thing as poetry.[2]

But they are at present little more than names in the history books. What happened? Why are pieces like *Fra Diavolo* and *La Sirène* (1844) now essentially forgotten works? Why did *opéra comique*'s gaudy troupe of drum majorettes, pleasure-seeking nuns, carefree bandits, singing coachmen, accident-prone foreigners and laughing corsairs become passé? As early as 1839, an English-language guide to Paris was complaining that the 'light agreeable character of the music, which formerly distinguished the *opéra comique* in France, has given place of late years to a more elaborate style, more scientific perhaps, but certainly less popular'.[3] It seems that a sense of mechanical repetition, of *vieux jeu*, eventually set in. Just as we saw with *grand opéra*, classic *opéra comique* gradually disappeared from the purview of contemporary composers, and by the early twentieth century had mostly fallen away from the international repertory But if one sticks to another, broader definition, then *opéra comique* can, just like *grand opéra*, also refer to works that mutated from those limited origins into wilder and more varied forms. And in that sense there was no decline. As with the emblematic case of *Carmen*, some of these sibling works have never once disappeared into obscurity.

Opéra comique can thus be a serious matter in two senses. First, in the simple sense that, over the course of the nineteenth century, the clichés of the genre gradually became precious sentimental remnants of a lost comic world, remnants that survived within operatic works whose plots were concerned with sadness and mortality, even tragedy. Those carolling sailors in Wagner's *Holländer* and that flirtatious page in Verdi's *Ballo* are resonant particles from a French tradition of tongue-in-cheek local colour. Or, to choose examples closer to the genre's origins, both Ambroise Thomas's *Mignon* (of which more below) and Bizet's *Carmen* are called *opéra comique* even though they have loftier ambitions. They bear the title literally because they have spoken dialogue and were written for the theatre of that name; but they also bear it spiritually because they have choruses of strolling players, or smugglers, or some other insouciant collective with a predisposition for close harmony.

This transformation was also mapped on to the architecture of its capital city. Paris's Opéra-Comique – although the oldest and most venerable counterweight to the Opéra – could not indefinitely remain the *only* French operatic venue whose repertory ran to spoken dialogue and less-elevated plots. If nothing else, Paris continued inexorably to expand in the nineteenth century: more people required more operatic venues. In 1847 the Opéra National opened, a theatre that fostered a French repertory running to sleek, semi-serious libretti, with speaking rather than recitative, and with a brisker musical apparatus than anything found in *grand opéra*. Renamed the Théâtre Lyrique in 1852 (it changed venue several times), it often became the Parisian theatre of choice for younger composers frustrated with or preparing to conquer the Opéra and its regime of obligatory musical weight and scenic bulk.

But there is a second sense in which we should value *opéra comique*, even aside from the descendent works that were performed at these alternative venues. What is the serious worth of the purely trivial? This large question hovers over all forms of comic opera, but is most complicated in the case of the obviously frivolous: not Mozart's humane comedies but the lowest and most farcical works, the *opéras bouffes*, the forgotten trifles that Offenbach, Alexandre Charles Lecocq or Edmond Audran were pouring forth with wicked prodigality at a time when latter-day Romantics such as Hector Berlioz were summoning up Shakespeare and the Greeks, and agonizing creatively over such generously inflated magnum opuses as *Les Troyens*.

AESTHETIC SCORN

Even during its days of greatest popular success, classic *opéra comique* had a hard time with the critics. Foreigners like Heine tended to be mystified and – especially if they came from parts of Europe lacking a Mediterranean coast – suspected that they were up against yet another manifestation of brazen Parisian immorality. Mendelssohn thought *opéra comique* 'as degenerate and bad as only a few of the German theatres are', and feared that, if he agreed to write something so unworthy, the Paris 'label' would – *quelle horreur* – cause it to be imported into his beloved homeland.[4] It should come as no surprise that serious-minded Berlioz, whose *Benvenuto Cellini* (1838) was turned down at the Opéra-Comique before being accepted and then failing miserably at the Opéra, inclined towards the caustic. In one of his longest essays, he identified a problem which didn't seem to concern audiences of the day, but which he connected to the genre's hoped-for future demise: *opéra comique* had, he said, a fatal oscillation of styles.[5] Berlioz, uncompromising purist that he was, could never accept the notion that it was precisely this free juxtaposition that would be the genre's greatest glory.

According to Berlioz's analysis, part of this dangerous oscillation was between national modes. By the 1830s, French composers knew plenty of German Romantic operas: *Der Freischütz*, disguised as *Robin des bois*, was a great favourite, perhaps not surprisingly given that its polyglot style was so indebted to French models. *Opéra comique* composers, as Berlioz saw them, had the same greedy ears, borrowing freely from the Germanic specialties of orchestral elaboration and charged harmonic language, and – worse by far – from Rossinian vocal excess. In the 1820s Rossini's operas were the rage of the Théâtre Italien, and guilty memories of many an elaborately warbled duet travelled thence into *opéra comique*. But rigid Parisian divisions between the various genres meant that, when such influences reached the Opéra-Comique, they had to be grafted on to the old, spoken dialogue convention. While German *Singspiel* managed to morph into *romantische Oper* – shedding spoken dialogue and most of the comedy along the way – the *opéra comique* tradition was chained more firmly to its designated theatrical space. For Berlioz, though, the genre's most problematic oscillation was one of artistic ambition. The repertoire of the Opéra-Comique was, as he put it, 'forever drifting between the high and low regions of thought',[6] catering at one moment for those who wanted no more than simple vaudeville entertainment (comic plays with some tunes thrown in), at the next for those aspiring to the greater musical heights. Eventually, as he saw it, the strain of pleasing both audiences would become too much. Classic *opéra comique*, he thought, risked obsolescence precisely because it had begun to drift away from pure farce.

In some ways Berlioz had a point. If you approach opera expecting classical balance or purity of genre, you will start to feel critical when that balance is not maintained. A good illustration is the way in which all *opéras comiques* had to deal with the perpetual problem that *Singspiel* and other dialogue opera wrestled with in the eighteenth century – the problem of how to negotiate that moment when spoken words turned to song. This issue became particularly fraught in the nineteenth century, as expectations for musical continuity and elaboration grew more demanding. It's thus no surprise to see in the typical roll-call of *opéra comique* numbers all those elaborate stratagems that made the leap seem less extreme: arias that aren't *really* arias, because the character would sing a song at this point in a spoken drama; choruses that are performed by uncomplicated rustic types who are assumed to sing because they're simple and pleasure-loving; ensembles that tend towards the action variety, and thus with lots of singing dialogue maintained. In a rapidly changing operatic world, these were hard limits to maintain, but the rule of the Opéra-Comique, the insistence on spoken dialogue, was inexorable.

Berlioz is, however, a notorious fountain of aesthetic hauteur, a rather too dominant source of Romantic Era opinion. Who, sitting there in the Opéra-Comique in the middle of the nineteenth century, saw spoken dialogue or mixing things up as a particular problem? Whose expectations were not being met, where and when? There is a similar danger of seeing the whole issue through equally dominant Wagnerian eyes. By the time Wagner emerged as a popular force, in Dresden with *Rienzi* in 1842 and *Der fliegende Holländer* in 1843, it was clear that a new, astonishing kind of German opera was in the wings, elaborate in its instrumentation, tragic in plot and intent, with lots of notes, no speaking whatsoever, and edging towards a continuity of tone that would (ideally at least) exclude mongrel oscillations. This is another symptom of the prejudice about mixing genres. That rich array of musical registers in *Holländer*, mentioned at the start of this chapter, has often been seen as a flaw that Wagner rightly expunged from his later works. And in Paris, too, there were audiences – an elite of opera-goers nurtured on those elephantine works booming forth from the Opéra, or an elite of refined amateurs who followed the critiques of a Berlioz or a Heine – who were dissatisfied with hybrid forms. For certain composers, for certain audiences, the gap between speech and song – a gap that could stand for all the many forms of operatic incongruity – threatened to turn into an unbridgeable gulf. We are heirs to this way of thinking. Audiences of today, conditioned to continuous music in the opera house, may need new attitudes to performance or staging, new ways of hearing its 'oscillation of styles', before classic *opéra comique* once again becomes something to be savoured.

Even Offenbach responded to the pressure of aesthetic hauteur in his final work, *Les Contes d'Hoffmann* (The Tales of Hoffmann, 1881), which he called an 'opéra' and left unfinished at his death in 1880. It is impossible to establish any kind of definitive text for *Hoffmann*, which has left it gloriously open to rewritings and musical interventions in ways unprecedented for a major repertory opera. In 1992, the Lyon Opera did it as *Des Contes d'Hoffmann* (A Few Tales of Hoffmann), mixing and omitting and adding (dialogue, new music, high concepts) in ways that left some customers apoplectic. For others, though, *Hoffmann* commands special respect as a work because, alone among Offenbach's operas, it aspired to real seriousness. For the libretto, Offenbach returned to his natal roots, using three German Romantic stories by E. T. A. Hoffmann. For the music, he mined lyric veins remembered from works such as Gounod's *Faust*. Yet he also put his deep familiarity with the musical grotesque to serious purpose, in order to give body to the uncanny and disturbing aspects of his source stories, tales about automata that can sing and mirrors that steal your soul. No less a luminary than Gustav Mahler championed the work in Vienna, mounting a new production in 1901, and thereby putting the composer of *La Grande-Duchesse de Gérolstein* only a half-degree away from the high-German avant-garde.

THE TRAUMA OF SADNESS, THE SURVIVAL OF BLISS

In his 1856 manifesto on *opéra comique*, Offenbach shows a delicious capacity to savour incongruity; his alternative views can thus make a colourful foil to Berlioz's dismay. The two decades from 1855 to 1875 were, in retrospect, an extraordinary time for *opéra comique* in the broadest sense. Offenbach's farces can be seen as mirrors on society, with politics and social undertows satirized and negotiated within their libretti. And Paris was to undergo a great political trauma in 1870–71, at the end of a decade that had seen the decimation of a fabled older generation of operatic composers (Halévy in 1862, Meyerbeer in 1864, Rossini in 1868, Berlioz in 1869). By 1870 hardly any were left of that phalanx who had placed a new kind of French opera on the map in the 1830s. In July 1870 France embarked on a disastrous war with Prussia, one that saw the downfall of Napoleon III, the formation of a French Republic and a five-month period during which Paris was besieged by Prussian troops; for some months in 1871 a workers' uprising took control of Paris (the period of the so-called Commune), only to be bloodily suppressed by Republican troops.

Auber, who survived until 1871, was one of the last of the old generation to die and, as many pointed out at the time, there was a palpable sense that he had simply overstayed his welcome. Born in 1782, just after the 25-year-old Mozart had moved to Vienna, his first theatrical work was written as early as 1805 and he carved out a sporadic career through to the early 1820s. As we have seen, his collaboration with Scribe, both in making *grands opéras* and *opéras comiques*, then put him in the forefront of operatic events in Paris in the late 1820s and 1830s. But he lived on and on: through the 1848 revolutions and the formation of Napoleon III's Second Empire that came in their wake, he doggedly continued to compose comic operas in the vein of *Fra Diavolo*, although occasionally dabbling in newer trends such as exoticism. By 1870, in his late eighties, he was a remarkable relic of a past age, perhaps even a last link to the eighteenth century. He still exercised his beloved horses, aptly named Almaviva and Figaro, in the Bois de Boulogne and was a regular at the Opéra and the Opéra-Comique, insisting that Paris was the only place worth living in. He refused to leave his beloved city during the siege, but suffered cruelly when Almaviva was requisitioned and eaten by the city's starving inhabitants (Figaro was hidden in a piano-maker's shop and so escaped the dinner table). The ageing, grieving composer finally gave up the ghost during the desperate days of the Commune. In spite of his advanced age, journalists were quick to load the event with melancholy significance; as one obituarist put it: 'The Prussians dealt him the first blow but it was the Frenchmen of the Commune who finished him off'.[7]

The sad tale of Auber's death cried out – as the journalists understood – for end-of-era platitudes. Yet the antics of Fra Diavolo and his like continued to please the public for several decades more. As with serious opera, *opéra comique* became a revived repertory as well as a living compositional genre. After the Siege and the Commune, the revivals may have been seen as remnants of a past age; but *opéra comique*, both in the sense of opera with spoken dialogue and in the sense of farcical opera, continued to flourish in Paris, the former within works such as Gounod's *Faust* and *Carmen*, the latter as the operettas of Offenbach and his peers. The restrictions on what kind of opera could legally be produced in which theatre were officially lifted in 1864, but they had for some time been thought anachronistic and unenforceable: the Opéra-Comique and the Théâtre Lyrique had already begun producing a very different kind of drama, one more suited to the changing European times.

Take the case of Thomas's *Mignon*, premiered in 1866. *Mignon* was one of the most popular operas of the nineteenth and early twentieth centuries. An immediate hit on opening night, it would be performed a thousand times at the Opéra-Comique alone between 1866 and 1894. Nor was its popularity limited to France. The 1915 edition of *The Victrola Book of the Opera* (published by the recording company to promote its wares) reports an astonishing statistic: 'Thomas's opera is among the most popular of all operas in Germany, and during the decade of 1901–1910 was given nearly three thousand presentations'.[8] There was even an American silent movie version in 1915 (directed by William Nigh), joining an elite club of silent-film operas that included Cecil B. DeMille's *Carmen* (also 1915). But during the next hundred years *Mignon* gradually disappeared from the stage. In 2005–10 it was performed only eight times worldwide, half of those at a 2010 production at the Opéra-Comique, putting *Mignon* one performance behind *Fra Diavolo* for that five-year period.[9]

Mignon started with high aspirations. The libretto was by Jules Barbier and Michel Carré, a pre-eminent Parisian writing team of the later nineteenth century (other credits include *Faust* and *Les Contes d'Hoffmann*). The source was Goethe's novel *Wilhelm Meisters Lehrjahre* (Wilhelm Meister's Apprenticeship, 1795), an intimidating Romantic classic, and the choice reflected elevated literary aspirations that were becoming common in *opéra comique*. Barbier and Carré transformed the Mignon episode in Goethe's novel from tragedy into a strange mélange of themes and incidents that included a happy ending. Mignon (mezzo-soprano) is a girl who, kidnapped aged six by gypsies, has grown up cruelly mistreated and forced to perform for crowds. In the courtyard of an inn (Act 1) she is liberated from the gypsy impresario by Wilhelm (tenor), an Austrian student wandering the world in search of life experiences. She falls in love with her rescuer, but as she is a boyish waif – and he is smitten by the glittering actress Philine (soprano) – he cannot return her love. An important supporting role is played by a mysterious, half-crazed harpist (Lothario, bass), who regularly consoles Mignon and who (it turns out) is actually Marquis Cipriani, an Italian aristocrat driven mad long ago when his daughter Sperata (aged six) was believed drowned. By the end of Act 3, everything is sorted out via a recognition scene between Mignon/Sperata and Lothario/Cipriani, and via Wilhelm discovering that it is indeed Mignon he loves.

In Goethe's novel Mignon is a pathetic figure. She is also a character who sings songs, printed in the novel as inserted poems and soon among Goethe's most famous lyrics: 'Nur wer die Sehnsucht kennt' (Only he who knows what longing is) and 'Kennst du das Land, wo die Zitronen blühn?' (Do you know the land where the lemon trees bloom?). Via Schubert's and many other settings, Mignon's songs soon took on a new life in the domestic musical circles of the nineteenth century. But the Mignon of the novel, after being wounded at Wilhelm's side by highwaymen, fades from the narrative, reappearing only on her deathbed (after which, Wilhelm gets happily married). The Mignon of the libretto is far more modern in the sense that her strange psychological wounds seem not at all softened by her antique setting. In a scene played out as a trio in Act 2, she tries to put her despair over Wilhelm's and Philine's love at a safe distance by willing herself to fall asleep. This number uses an old trick: the lovers sing a duet, oblivious to anything else; but underneath this first level, Mignon's whisperings to herself establish a separate musical strand that calls their bliss into question. Just afterwards, Mignon decides to make herself more feminine, recasting her appearance at Philine's dressing table and putting on a borrowed dress. It's an uncomfortable moment, but precisely why is hard to say. Since Mignon is a woman, why shouldn't she get rid of her trousers? When Wilhelm sees Mignon in the dress, he realizes that he can't possibly take this girl with him on the road as he had planned. But he knew already that she was a girl; it was never a secret. The scene ends with Philine making fun of Mignon for her incompetence with makeup and petticoats. At the end of the act, Mignon is trapped in a burning building, one that she herself has in effect torched, since when she hopes out loud that Philine's performance space be struck by lightning and flames, crazy Lothario takes it into his head to grant her wish.

The scenario is by this stage far outside anything traditional: how many other popular operas of the nineteenth century feature the starring diva as an anguished tomboy whose romantic passions are so long unrequited? The music Mignon sings, however – including the impossible-to-avoid 'Kennst du das Land?' (here 'Connais-tu le pays?') – shows why star mezzo-sopranos coveted the part, starting with Célestine Galli-Marié (1840–1905), who created the role in 1866 and who went on to be the first Carmen in 1875. Geraldine Farrar (1882–1967), a genuine high soprano known for Massenet's Manon, Marguerite in *Faust* and Cio-cio-san in *Madama Butterfly*, lowered herself for Mignon because the part was so good. Little of Mignon's singing, however, has the exhibitionist verve of Carmen. Her biggest number is a duet with Lothario in Act 1, 'Légères hirondelles' (Gentle swallows), an unusual instance of a mezzo–bass duet, owing something, perhaps, to the soprano–baritone duets that Verdi (*Rigoletto*, *La traviata*, *Simon Boccanegra*) had been doing to such great effect. 'Légères hirondelles' is a song-within-the-opera (Mignon is accompanying on the harp) sung by two bereft characters. Their topic is an alien and unimaginably beautiful country – Italy certainly, but Italy as a site of memory, a place to which one can never return in reality. Although the text refers to birds, there will be no vocal trilling or hooting. *Opéra comique*'s great liking for numbers involving the geography of elsewhere, numbers that conjure up distinctive musical colour, leads in this case to a moment in which the voices twining around one another are not the usual two sopranos. The pairing of lower-register voices can't possibly be heard as acoustic substitutes for the swallows mentioned in the poem. But if the characters describe unattainable things, their melodic lines are so beautiful that singing becomes an object of desire, a place where we want to linger. As if to underscore the point, the duet ends with an extremely intricate double cadenza, one of the few places where Mignon's singing voice is put on display. The number begins like a journey begins. Harmonic patterning sends the melody onwards rather than keeping it trammelled within little birdsong circles. The first four-bar phrase is in D major but is then elaborated a step higher in the minor, a shift suggesting that, just for a moment, the fantasy could travel anywhere. Yes, the duet is still recognizable as a genre number. But just like the unsettling smugglers' chorus in Act 3 of *Carmen* – obligatory bandits whisper admonitions to 'listen, listen' and, falling into odd chromatic slips and slides, 'beware of a false step!' – this duet from *Mignon* transcends its origins in *opéra comique*.

The same could be said for the one number from *Mignon* that survived the opera's obsolescence, Philine's bravura aria in Act 2, 'Je suis Titania la blonde' (I am blonde Titania), sung just after she has finished that evening's performance of *A Midsummer Night's Dream*. To this day, the aria is a regular audition piece for Francophone coloratura sopranos, rivalling Olympia's song in *Les Contes d'Hoffmann*. The aria was present at the dawn of opera recording, when Luisa Tetrazzini (1871–1940) did it as 'Io son Titania' in 1907 for HMV. In the Hollywood comedy *Seven Sweethearts* (1942), Kathryn Grayson – who has spent much of the movie dressed as a boy à la Mignon – proves her femininity by performing the aria, à la Philine. Julie Andrews, aged twelve, sang it in her professional debut at the London Hippodrome in 1947. When Beverly Sills was invited on to *The Dick Cavett Show* on 23 June 1969, 'Je suis Titania' was her entrance number. Closer to our own time, Natalie Dessay has recorded the aria and sung it frequently in concert recitals, but – given the virtual absence of contemporary *Mignon* productions – has never taken the part on stage. 'Je suis Titania' is, for all this, actually based not on a vocal genre but on a dance, a polonaise that happens to be sung. When transposed into the Overture, the tune is completely at home among the instruments.

We mentioned earlier that *opéra comique* of the 1860s and 1870s, in becoming broader in its ambitions, was in step with the changing social and political landscape of those decades. That is, of course, a familiar, almost clichéd assumption. Opera duly reflects the society of its time. But while the idea remains obvious, the mechanism for how such reflection happens is ever elusive. The matter is more complicated in this case because one way in which Parisian *opéra comique* and operetta responded to the political crises of those years was by providing distraction. This is a familiar role for the arts, and for opera in particular, and would become an important function of film in the twentieth century. Human beings have routinely sought to counteract the miseries of their existence by constructing a parallel life of the imagination, and in the nineteenth century musical theatre served this purpose on an unprecedented level. But there is also a more sinister way of seeing the phenomenon: the musical arts may respond to politics by sleight of hand, by leading the eye away from trouble. What often happens is a middle ground between these two functions. For example, Offenbach's libretti are well-known for their satires of contemporary political topics and figures, but we can also see ways in which the music that clothed these satires was capable of assuaging any anxieties that arose.

Consider *Orphée aux enfers* (Orpheus in Hell), a farcical version of the myth with a libretto by Ludovic Halévy and Hector-Jonathan Crémieux. The operetta premiered in October 1858 at the Théâtre des Bouffes-Parisiennes, and audiences were duly delighted and outraged. Six weeks later, in an incident now so famous that no Offenbach biographer can omit a reference, it was pilloried by Jules Janin, the all-powerful cultural critic of the *Journal des débats*. Janin saw a disgusting parody of noble antiquity. Orpheus does indeed go to the underworld to rescue Eurydice. But on Olympus the Gods roll in, yawning from all-night prowls chasing other people's spouses. Jupiter proposes that everyone head down to hell with Orpheus to check out its goings-on, where Eurydice, guarded by the comedian John Styx, is bored and annoyed. Pluto flatters Jupiter with fulsome courtier praise (for his speech, the librettists parroted an old essay by none other than Janin). It all ends up in Act 4 with a huge party in Hell. Everyone cheers when Jupiter tricks poor Orpheus into looking back at Eurydice on the way out, so that she can rejoin the festivities.

After Janin's article appeared, box office receipts soared. But

Siegfried Kracauer, in his marvellous 1937 biography of Offenbach, points out that parodies of Greek antiquity were widespread in France at the time, suggesting that the outrage, whether Janin's or others', may well have had some other source:

> This is what it was: Offenbach's operetta, though in play, laid bare the foundations of contemporary society and gave the bourgeoisie an opportunity of seeing themselves as they really were. . . . No less drastic was the exposure of the shifty expedients by which the apparatus of power was kept intact. In order to escape punishment for the rape of Eurydice, Pluto incited the Gods against Jupiter, and Jupiter himself did not shrink from the meanest and most dishonest devices in order to maintain himself in power or attain some private end. His reign corrupts Olympus, just as that of their dictator [i.e. Napoléon III] did the bourgeoisie [i.e. in Second Empire France]. No sooner did Jupiter propose taking the Gods with him to the underworld than they forget their rancour against him and start singing his praises, forgetting everything except their own amusement and distraction.[10]

There's a single couplet in the libretto that asks the audience to squint through its delusions and distractions, 'Abattons cette tyrannie, / Ce régime est fastidieux' (Let's combat this tyranny / This regime is sickening), and it's set to the 'Marseillaise'. In Second Empire France, this was music that meant revolution, so if the libretto is a contemporary political allegory, the message is just on the edge of treasonous. But of course it's all within a joke, which is what took it in beyond the censor's purview. However, although Offenbach's *Orphée* music distracts with giddy delights – the acoustic frenzy of Act 4 includes a danced 'Galop infernal' that would for ever after be known as the 'Can-can' – there is one extended sober moment, John Styx's lament 'Quand j'étais roi de Béotie (When I was king of Boeotia). The lament is an extraordinary mélange, its simplicity of tone unlike anything else in the opera, mixing the trauma of sadness with allusions to a bliss that survives only in memory. John Styx was played not by an opera singer but by an actor from the Comédie Française, Alexandre Debruille-Bache. Thus the lament, in the original performances, was an acoustic island apart. But not a note of the opera's music is mean-spirited. As Kracauer put it, 'A kind of inverted magician, [Offenbach] took it as his mission to unmask the hollow phantoms that tyrannize over mankind; but he gave his blessing to every genuine human emotion he met on the way'.[11]

THE PROMISE OF INFINITE POSSIBILITIES

As political allegory goes, *Carmen* is a similarly complicated case. It could be argued that the opera's smugglers, and perhaps even Carmen herself, are meant to warn of the dangers of a rebellious underclass, representing them to a public whose first glimpse of such an underclass in power (during the Commune) had proved traumatic in the extreme. But the fact that these smugglers are consistently depicted as easy-going, freedom-loving rogues, and that their gypsy muse's attractions are so determinedly sexual rather than political, surely blunted the disquiet of the post-Commune bourgeoisie, or at the least pleasingly beguiled them. These matters are made more difficult still by the fact that the *Carmen* libretto was understood at the time to march under the general banner of realism, a problematic and protean word whose meanings for opera will be explored in more detail in a later chapter. How did Georges Bizet (1838–75) whose earlier operatic libretti were so much more exotic and/or conventional end up with this frank story and its down-to-earth heroine?

To answer that question, some background will be useful. Bizet had lived for three years in Italy from 1857 to 1860 as the Prix de Rome winner (a prize given yearly by the Paris Conservatory to its most promising composition student), and had spent those years casting about for an identity as an opera composer. In both completed and unrealized projects up to the 1870s, one can see him shape-shifting through various nineteenth-century operatic genres. In Italy, he flirted with the local opera, both serious and comic, on the model of Donizetti (he toyed with a new version of *Parisina*, then completed a comic work called *Don Procopio*). He took on *grand opéra* with plans for a *Hunchback of Notre-Dame* that was never written and an *Ivan IV* (1865) that was only performed posthumously. His commissions tended towards Orientalist *opéras comiques* (the lost work *La Guzla de l'émir* – The Guzla Player and the Emir, 1862; *Les Pêcheurs de perles* – The Pearl Fishers, 1863; and *Djamileh*, 1872).

Bizet's *grands opéras* were scorned by the Opéra, and his relatively brief career unfolded largely at the Théâtre Lyrique and the Opéra-Comique; it was the directors of the latter who offered him the commission for a new *opéra comique* in 1872, with a libretto to be a subject of Bizet's choosing and written by a seasoned team, Henri Meilhac and Ludovic Halévy. Bizet chose Prosper Merimée's novella *Carmen* (1845), which made for a libretto distinctly unsuited to a family theatre, with low-class individuals, a promiscuous heroine and women who fight with knives. The plot is simple. Set in Seville, it is the story of a gypsy smuggler, Carmen (mezzo-soprano), who seduces a poor corporal, Don José (tenor), and convinces him to turn to crime. José abandons his army career and his sweet fiancée from back home, Micaëla (soprano), to follow Carmen and her gang of smugglers. But the couple are hopelessly mismatched. In the novel, the inevitability of their estrangement is articulated by Carmen, 'Chien et loup ne font pas longtemps bon ménage' (Dog and wolf don't live together happily for very long). She soon grows tired of José, rejecting him in favour of a flamboyant toreador, Escamillo (bass-baritone). Supporting characters include Carmen's backing group, Mercédès (mezzo-soprano) and Frasquita (soprano), as well as various army officers and smugglers. In the final act, outside the bullring in which Escamillo is performing, José confronts Carmen and realizes that his case is hopeless. 'Tu ne m'aimes donc plus?' (So you don't love me any more?), he says almost unbelievingly, and then stabs her when she refuses to return to him. This was, notoriously, the onstage murder that changed for ever the shape of what could be called *opéra comique*. Carmen, whose antecedents were comic, became a tragic heroine, one among a long line of singing women who in the final act are strangled, crushed, shot, stabbed and put in sacks (Gilda's fate in *Rigoletto*), drowned, poisoned or cast into a vat of boiling oil (Rachel's in *La Juive*, 1835).

Carmen was a troubled project. Bizet fought with one of the directors of the Opéra-Comique, Adolphe de Leuven, who wanted the heroine to survive at the end. After de Leuven resigned and the score was finished, Bizet had to battle with the musicians (particularly the Opéra-Comique chorus, who were not accustomed to screaming and fighting for a living). The remaining director, Camille Du Locle (a great supporter of Verdi and his operas), continued to regard the libretto as vulgar and brutal, its heroine antipathetic and immoral. In the end Bizet fought with more or less everyone except the singer cast as Carmen, Célestine Galli-Marié, who showed intense faith in the work and its main character. Galli-Marié's versatility as a singing actress is demonstrated by the fact that she was brilliant both as Bizet's promiscuous gypsy and as Thomas's Mignon, the innocent tomboy of nine years earlier. One of the earliest reviewers summarized the impression she made in *Carmen*: 'To see her, rocking her hips like a filly on a stud farm in Cordova: quelle vérité, mais quel scandale (what realism, but what scandal)'.[12]

Then there is the story, told over and over, concerning an alleged supernatural event at *Carmen*'s thirty-third performance, on 2 June 1875. Galli-Marié had reached the Act 3 tarot card scene, in which Carmen predicts her own death with fatalistic resignation, 'Recommence vingt fois, la carte impitoyable répétera: la mort!' (You can start again twenty times, but the merciless card will be repeated: death!) At this moment, Galli-Marié was apparently overcome with foreboding. Some reports have her experiencing a pain in her side. She fainted and left the stage but managed to return and continue the performance to the end, after which she burst into tears and could not be comforted.[13] News arrived later that Bizet had died that night.

Whether Galli-Marié had a premonition or not, and whether – if she did – it happened so appropriately during the card scene, we can be sure that Bizet, by dying on 2 June 1875, did not survive long enough to learn that *Carmen* would become one of the most beloved musical works ever written, performed thousands of times by the end of the century. It was Queen Victoria's, Otto Bismarck's and James Joyce's favourite opera; it was worked into novels by Thomas Mann and even by tone-deaf Vladimir Nabokov; its story was retold countless times in films, where arrangements of Bizet's music lurk like a phantom in the background; Cecil B. DeMille's in 1915 – being silent – called for gramophones or pianos and singers, armed with vocal scores, on duty during showings. Friedrich Nietzsche, a passionate Wagner acolyte who turned against his idol after the 1870s, ended his life praising *Carmen*:

> Yesterday I heard – would you believe it – Bizet's masterpiece, for the twentieth time. . . . This music seems perfect to me. It approaches lightly, supplely, politely. It is pleasant, it does not *sweat*. 'What is good is light, whatever is divine moves on tender feet': the first principle of my aesthetics. This music is evil, subtly fatalistic: at the same time it remains popular – its subtlety belongs to a race, not to an individual. It is rich. It is precise. It builds, organizes, finishes: thus it constitutes the opposite of the polyp in music, the 'infinite melody'. Have more painful, tragic accents ever been

heard on stage? And how are they achieved? Without grimaces. Without counterfeit. Without the *lie* of the grand style![14]

Richard Strauss, modernist opera composer and terrific German chauvinist, held up Bizet's orchestration in *Carmen* as a model of ingenuity and timbral imagination. And what's more, his ire over Nazi-era musical censorship was roused over one particular outrage, as described in 1934 to Julius Kopsch: 'I hear that the paragraph concerning Aryans is to be tightened up, and *Carmen* banned! In any event, as a creative artist, I do not wish to take an active part in any further foolishness of this kind.'[15]

All this love was bestowed on a mere *opéra comique*, and one much tinkered with by Bizet during rehearsals. There are conflicting editions, no definitive text and even a posthumous 1875 *grand opéra* version with recitatives by a composer called Ernest Guiraud. But all this, which might in other cases have cemented a distinctly non-canonic status, was unimportant. The music that sounds as the curtain goes up on Act 1 of *Carmen*, a pyramid that slowly swirls out and gets louder over a quasi-folk drone bass, is the promise of infinite possibilities and one of the best musical daybreaks ever. The opera never goes back on that opening promise.

What makes *Carmen* so brilliant, adaptable, so protean, so patient of interpretation? It has the advantage of an unmannered story in which the anti-heroine is both unfailingly brave and blithely unconcerned about conventional social roles. In this sense, and in terms of her tremendous musical energy, Carmen is a female version of Don Giovanni. The plot divides the world, as does Carmen herself, into wolves and others. Yet the tame, domestic types – especially Micaëla, who makes two appearances as a messenger from home and is a point of stability in José's crumbling world – are no less sympathetic than the wolf characters, Carmen and Escamillo. Bizet's greatest gift was to imagine the music for every element of the plot with equal seriousness: the trivial, ornamental characters, the tragic proletarian soldier, the smugglers singing in close harmony, the swaggering exhibitionist, the generic supporting roles; he pays close attention to each and every one. As was usual by the 1870s, any opera that had recurring motifs – there are a few in *Carmen*, and also some longer musical stretches that return – was thought Wagnerian. But there is nothing radical about *Carmen*'s set pieces in terms of form. It is an opera created from the cloth of convention, with well-behaved arias, duets and ensembles, duly separated by stretches of dialogue (or by recitatives in the posthumous *grand opéra* version, which is often anathematized by the purists but which has its own grandeur and effect, and has now acquired a particular antique charm).

What *is* unusual is that a very large proportion of the music is realistic in the sense of being real singing within the stage world. The opera is full of songs, dances, military fanfares, outdoor choruses and parades. The preponderance of such occasions allowed Bizet to experiment with exotic sounds, and since the story is set in Spain among gypsies, a lot of these sounds refer to Spanish or Moorish rhythms and modes, or at least to what a French composer in the 1870s understood these to be. The episodes of real performance are particularly centred on Carmen: music making is part of her persona. She likes to sing and dance, and she exploits singing and dancing to convince and to seduce – or simply as a means to express herself. When José first sees her and is instantly smitten, she is performing for the crowd. This is significant: Carmen and José are most profoundly mismatched not because one is a gypsy and the other a petit-bourgeois soldier, but because one is an extravagant, uninhibited performer and the other is an intense, shy spectator.

Carmen is herself susceptible to the lure of bold, exhibitionist singing. Her susceptibility is staged in Act 2, when she becomes part of the audience for Escamillo as he performs for patrons of an inn. The toreador's two-verse song, 'Votre toast, je peux vous le rendre' (I can return your toast), which narrates a typical bout in the bullring, belongs to the then-ancient operatic tradition of presenting a story in the form of a strophic song with choral refrain. The minor-key music of the verses has Spanish cadences and snapped-back Flamenco rhythms; it's obviously a confection, an elaborate, over-the-top fantasy of Spanish music, but at the same time it's so gleeful that we struggle not to be carried along. The refrain – 'Toréador, en garde!' – is set to a major-key melody that long ago escaped from the stage to become a kind of universal signifier for opera. It's important, though, not to forget that, banal and over-familiar as it may now sound, this refrain comes back later in much changed circumstances. Carmen hears it in Act 4, sounding offstage as the unseen chorus, who are spectators celebrating Escamillo in the bullring, once more salute his prowess. In this reminiscence, the tune is musically deracinated. It no longer has that thumping orchestral accompaniment, but is underpinned by an alarming cello counterpoint, a sign that the atmosphere has changed and that something tremendous is about to happen. The musical sounds attract Carmen, draw her towards the bull-ring gate and past José's waiting arm – a fatal attraction, as it turns out.

Music's fatal attraction is, in a sense, felt throughout *Carmen*. In Act 1, Carmen is arrested for brawling and is forbidden to talk by José, her custodian. She declares that she will sing instead, and during the course of the song manages to reel in her catch. By the end of the second verse, José has agreed to free her, be arrested for her sake and join her when he is released. On the other hand, the music that is *not* presented as part of the stage world, the 'non-wolf' music – numbers like Micaëla's duet with José in Act 1 and her aria in Act 3 – seems removed: beautiful, but at a distance, referring to (or coming from) a past that can no longer be regained. This strand of the music is about an ideal world, one that probably never existed and that certainly didn't exist in 1875.

Poised between these two styles is José's music, in particular his Flower Song in Act 2, one of the opera's most celebrated moments, but also one of its most conflicted. It tells a simple story, with Carmen this time as the audience. When he was in prison, José kept the flower that Carmen had dismissively thrown to him in Act 1: its perfume transported him, creating a dream world. Whenever he thought of reproaching her, the dream world would intervene. The aria is introduced by a ghostly orchestral reminiscence of the moment when the flower was thrown, the remembered tune played by the cor anglais, as if to mark that instrument already as a restrained but potent force in the aria, a kind of sonorous worm in the bud. José begins his narrative against a simple but luminous accompaniment (flute, clarinet, cello), but when he mentions the 'sweet smell' of his faded, desiccated flower, the cor anglais reappears to mark the word 'odeur', underlining the dangerous forces that José has been keeping alive. 'Then, I accused myself of blasphemy, and felt inside me a single desire, a single hope: to see you again, Carmen. You had but to appear, but to cast a glance at me, to steal my entire being.' The musical setting of this long line begins conventionally enough, but soon the harmony clouds, exotic cadences intervene and we enter an unreal world in which passion threatens to lose itself. The end of the aria is in one way a settling of this tension, but in another keeps it extraordinarily in play. At the words 'Et j'étais une chose à toi' (And I was a thing of yours), marked by Bizet *pp rall. e dim.*

(very quiet, slowing down and getting quieter), José ascends to high B♭, the highest note in the aria, and remains there in eerie quietness on a long held note.

It's a moment that strongly resembles the end of 'Celeste Aida' in Verdi's opera (to be discussed in the next chapter), and surely has a similar meaning. The tenor may earlier have been forceful and passionate, but here he has become absorbed into another realm. José's obsession with Carmen is so great that he is drawn into her musical milieu, a place in which he loses all sense of tenor force. And just as at the end of 'Celeste Aida', most tenors can't bear this kind of realism: they ignore the composer's marking and sing the high note with full force. There's some sense in this (particularly if you're a baritonal tenor with a burnished high B♭, one of the most exciting notes in all opera); but it's not Bizet's kind of sense, at least not here. As if to underline what has been put in question by that *pianissimo* B♭, José's final words in the aria, 'Carmen, je t'aime' (Carmen, I love you), involve another wonderfully expressive instrumental effect. José sustains 't'aime', and underneath we hear that woodwind sonority which started his aria (flute, clarinet and now also the cor anglais) playing three strange chromatic chords. These chords pose an unanswerable question. Is there, can there be, a true or right harmony for José's love or does this tonal wandering call into question the reality of the emotion? And then, as a balance to the orchestral prelude, there's a gentle orchestral close, reprising José's opening phrase. But on the very last chord, as tonal stability is finally achieved, the cor anglais sounds again, strangely insistent, the erotic colour that won't go away and that will eventually destroy both the singer and the woman he addresses.

Carmen reacts to the beautiful, terrible indecision of this aria with brutal realism. 'Non, tu ne m'aime pas' (No, you don't love me), she sings, and on the last word, she spins the music out of José's anguished tonal orbit and back into her own. It's as if she hasn't been listening, hasn't heard a thing. But that's the problem with wolves, their deafness to the meek. The same inability to listen plays out in more obvious musical ways in José and Carmen's final duet. This is their only extended passage of singing together, and its musical trajectory is ever downwards. José keeps proposing a beautifully shaped melody, a tune from another realm; Carmen responds by refusing to echo him, instead supplying musically unrelated ripostes. The single time they sing simultaneously is when he repeats his beautiful, insistent phrase, 'Carmen, il est temps encore' (Carmen, there is still time) and she adds an aggressive counterpoint, a completely different melodic line, 'Pourquoi t'occuper encore d'un cœur qui n'est plus à toi?' (Why do you still concern yourself with a heart that isn't yours any more?) Soon after that, with José still determinedly, insanely lyrical, she funnels down to monotones, single notes, rising only to try to make an end – with spectacular high cadences – at her most definitive 'no': 'Jamais Carmen ne cédera! libre elle est née et libre elle mourra' (Carmen will never yield! she was born free and will die free). Gradually the singing breaks down until the two are essentially half speaking, half shouting in sung form at one another. At the opera's end, Bizet thus plays out an aesthetic of realism with very high stakes: he lets singing itself, its form and line, degrade under the pressure of impending disaster.

THE VALUE OF FRIVOLITY

Once the age of recording had arrived, Carmen's death could instantly be turned around, since one had only to go back to Side 1 and start over again. And, of course, *Carmen* is hardly a tragedy from the point of view of the impresarios who have profited from it, the baritones who have twirled Escamillo's cape while singing 'Toréador, en garde', the tenors and sopranos, the flute soloists who get a star turn playing the customary entre'acte music to Act 3 (music which actually comes from one of Bizet's *L'Arlesienne* suites and over many years of performance practice has been pasted into *Carmen*; but that hardly matters), and the mezzo-sopranos who get to impersonate a force of nature. French mezzo Emma Calvé (1858–1942), a famous Carmen, described her experience of singing the opera at the Metropolitan in New York in 1893–4:

> We gave it again and again, to packed houses. The box office receipts were astounding. In the succeeding seasons its popularity never waned. There were no further questions as to how it should be sung. What unforgettable casts, what glorious evenings! Jean de Reszke, Melba, Plançon and myself! The public was wildly enthusiastic. After each performance we would be recalled a thousand times. It was said that *Carmen* became epidemic, a joyful contagion.[16]

Underneath Calvé's clichés is an arresting sense that the *experience* was glorious, a source of happiness for the audience but also for the singers. This is of course the paradox of operatic performance. The piece itself can be tragic, but the experience of its embodiment, as singing and as spectacle, can be joyful. In *opéra comique* and *opéra bouffe*, as we have said, the works themselves can be unstable: what the composer intended is often not clear. Yet since they occupy an aesthetic register that is between serious and farcical, because they allow these antagonists a peaceful coexistence, they are particularly good at producing joy.

This can happen, for instance, in performances of Offenbach. Like many early *opéra comique* composers, Offenbach was a master of using dance forms as a basis for vocal numbers, a trick that requires almost non-vocal melodic writing, presenting a particular challenge for singers. His soprano roles can be as difficult as Donizetti's in their way. This trick appears in brilliant form in *La Grande-Duchesse de Gérolstein* (The Grand Duchess of Gerolstein, 1867). The eponymous Grand Duchess, coming herself from a military family, is enamoured of soldiers in general, and expresses herself in quasi-marches that quickly veer off into galops, quadrilles and other frivolous dance pieces, as in her Act 1 couplets, 'Ah, que j'aime les militaires' (Ah, how I love a uniform). In this aria's fast, virtuosic refrain, there is an incongruous pairing: the military-march idea with obligatory cymbal clashes joins Parisian ballroom dance, with opportunities for coy slowdowns and hesitations at upbeats. The character being impersonated – the rapacious Grand Duchess – is neither ideal nor idealized. But her number allows a singer to convey unfettered glee: the pure bliss of singing when there is nothing serious at stake, the joy of *opéra comique*.

14
Old Wagner

The bare bones of Wagner's progress after finishing *Lohengrin* in 1848 have already been sketched. He wrote a libretto based on Norse mythology, called *Siegfried's Tod* (Siegfried's Death), but put it aside during his involvement with the Dresden uprising and flight into exile. In 1850, he decided that this libretto needed a predecessor, and produced one called *Der junge Siegfried* (Young Siegfried). He then felt he needed to go still earlier in the tale, and wrote a libretto that might have been called *Siegfried's Parents* since it tells their story: it ended up as *Die Walküre* (The Valkyrie, 1851), named after its most important character, who is the immortal half-sister of those parents and called Brünnhilde. Finally he decided that this trilogy needed a prologue, *Das Rheingold* (The Rhine Gold, 1852), which would deal with the prehistory of the family drama: how magic gold was fashioned into an accursed ring; how the Gods won and lost it; and how Wotan, their ruler, must scheme to get it back. The four libretti were bundled together and published in 1853 as *Der Ring des Nibelungen* (The Ring of the Nibelung).

The music for the first three parts of the story – up to and including *Der junge Siegfried*, Act 2 – was finished between 1853 and 1857, at which point Wagner broke off. He had (as so often) severe money problems, and his attention was captured by a new project: an opera called *Tristan und Isolde*, which he told his publishers Breitkopf & Härtel – with insane, probably debt-driven optimism – presented 'almost no difficulties in terms of the scenery and the chorus. Practically the only demanding task will be to find a good pair of singers for the main parts.'[1] He wrote this libretto in the summer of 1857, and by 1859 the music was also complete; *Tristan* was not performed, though, until

1865. In 1860 he was again in Paris, to oversee and compose some new music for a revival of *Tannhäuser* at the Opéra (which occurred in March 1861). And then, having at last been granted an amnesty and allowed to return to Germany, he shifted his base to Munich, where, supported by subventions from the Bavarian king, Ludwig II, who was a passionate devotee, he wrote *Die Meistersinger von Nürnberg* (The Master Singers of Nuremberg, 1865–7; first performed 1868), his only mature comedy and an anomaly in his oeuvre. After *Die Meistersinger* he returned to *Siegfried* (by now, the title had been shortened) and finished Act 3 in 1869.

Along the way Wagner was widowed: his first wife, Minna, died in 1866, the couple having lived separately for years. Well before Minna's death, he had acquired a new partner, Cosima von Bülow, the daughter of Franz Liszt and, when they met, the wife of Wagner's (until then) good friend Hans von Bülow. Children were born. *Siegfried's Tod* was renamed *Götterdämmerung* (The Twilight of the Gods) and its music completed by 1874. In these last years, Wagner was constantly distracted by the labour of conducting, which he did to raise funds for building a new theatre he planned in Bayreuth (a small town in northern Bavaria) and then for productions of his works to be mounted there. The complete *Ring des Nibelungen* was premiered in Bayreuth in 1876, inaugurating a Wagner summer festival that continues to this day, currently under the direction of Wagner's great-granddaughters Eva Wagner-Pasquier and Katharina Wagner. For his final work, *Parsifal*, Wagner returned to a project first conceived in the 1840s. He called it a *Bühnenweihfestspiel* (A Festival Play for the Consecration of the Stage). Its libretto was written in the late 1870s, the music completed in 1882; the premiere was in Bayreuth that same year. In February 1883 Wagner died in Venice.

Thus briefly told, the tale only emphasizes the accomplishments. The most striking part has always been the interruption of the *Ring*. Wagner broke off a project of epic proportions, one whose size was unprecedented in the history of opera. He then resumed after more than a decade (a decade in which he had written two quite different but equally revolutionary new works, *Tristan* and *Die Meistersinger*), and did so without apparent anguish or lack of fluency. Indeed, he seemed to make the differences between his musical voice in 1857 and in 1869 part of the dramatic effect. Another startling achievement was the composition of

Tristan und Isolde, the most influential opera – probably the most influential piece of music – in the second half of the nineteenth century. This *magnum opus* took a mere two years of effort, from writing the libretto to scoring the final B-major triad.

These tremendous creative feats would not have been possible without a circle of self-sacrificing women, open-minded male friends, generous benefactors and devoted musicians. That Wagner tended to betray the women and the friends, exploit the benefactors and crush the musicians was his particular pathology. That he relied on such a support structure, though, is unremarkable: composers in the nineteenth century seldom got much done without a similar collective of publishers and acolytes. Verdi, as so often, offers a convenient comparison: the way in which his career ran in mutually sustaining parallel with that of his publisher, Ricordi, was a sign of the times (the nineteenth century saw an inexorable rise in the power and prestige of music publishers, just as the twentieth century saw their decline); and Verdi's long-term partner, Giuseppina Strepponi, offers in many ways a classic exemplar of the trials and tribulations that could attend those who elected to serve at the altar of nineteenth-century genius.

In Wagner's case, though, the women seem to have been an even more powerful force than usual. This aspect of his biography may well have influenced his higher intellectual detractors – Friedrich Nietzsche and Theodor Adorno are the most famous – in their views about his unpleasantly feminine side, his uncontrolled outbursts of anger, his racial panics and his penchant for silk. The silk issue, by the way, was serious, as one sees in Wagner's correspondence with Judith Gautier, the Paris friend (and perhaps lover) charged with exporting fabrics for him. He wrote to her in December 1877:

> Cancel the pink satin entirely: there would be too much of it and it would be good for nothing. Can I expect the two remnants which I mentioned in my last letter? The brocade can be reserved. I'm inclined to order 30 metres, but perhaps the colours can be changed to flatter my taste even better; in other words, the fawn-striped material would be silver-grey, and blue, *my* pink, very pale and delicate.[2]

Yes, that was *thirty* metres, no misprint. But to argue that emotional outbursts and strong opinions about furnishings are universally and eternally the proper domain of the female, ergo repugnant in males – or indeed that they are ills to be combated – is hardly philosophical wisdom. Wagner was indeed fascinated by the feminine as an abstraction, pronouncing frequently on its meaning; one of his favourite ideas was of 'feminine' music submitting to the dictates of 'masculine' poetry, a metaphor whose potential for twentieth- and twenty-first-century irritation he could not have anticipated in 1850. This notion of creative duality became the centrepiece of an argument about musical form in his treatise *Oper und Drama* in 1851. Taking matters even further, the last prose essay he worked on, a fragment called 'On the Feminine Element in the Human' (1883), makes the case for reconciliation of masculine and feminine, and even suggests that nirvana would be the erasure of their differences.[3]

Wagner, whose literary writings are famous for their changes of mind and even frank contradictions, wavers in this last essay between, on the one hand, putting men and women on a similar footing and, on the other, arguing that masculinity and femininity might be eliminated as distinct conditions. These alternatives nevertheless converge in *Tristan und Isolde*, which was based on Gottfried von Strassburg's medieval epic, a classic of the Middle High German canon. Gottfried's poem centres on the life of Tristan, beginning with the tragic death of his mother and father, his adoption by his uncle King Marke of Cornwall and Tristan's various heroic deeds, in particular his slaying of an Irish usurper called Morold. Tristan sustains a wound in the battle with Morold and goes back to Ireland (in disguise) to be cured. There he encounters Princess Isolde, Morold's fiancée, who heals him but in the process discovers his identity. Trouble ensues, but after some shuttle diplomacy between Cornwall and Ireland, Tristan escorts Isolde to Cornwall to wed his uncle. While on board the ship, however, Tristan makes the mistake of sharing with Isolde a love potion, which has the usual results. Duty prevails on disembarkation; Isolde marries King Marke. The poem then becomes an account of the undying erotic passion between Tristan and Isolde. He is eventually separated from her, wounded a second time and dies waiting for her to return to him over the sea. For his three-act opera, Wagner radically simplified the action. In Act 1, Tristan (tenor) and Isolde (soprano) are sailing from Ireland to Cornwall and drink what they believe to be deadly poison, but in fact is the love potion. Act 2 is set in Cornwall: the lovers meet at night and sing about love, only to be discovered in flagrante at dawn by King Marke (bass) and his entourage, one of whom wounds Tristan. In Act 3, having returned to Brittany, Tristan languishes in sickness and hallucinations; he dies at the very moment Isolde arrives over the sea to heal him, whereupon she too expires.

We will consider the opera in more detail later, but for the moment we can concentrate on one aspect of the libretto. It is strikingly modern in placing the two lovers on an equal plane rather than assigning them female and male behaviour along the nineteenth century's usual social or indeed operatic lines (imagine for a moment *Otello e Desdemona,* or *Carmen et Don José*, or *Lohengrin und Elsa*). Isolde is Tristan's rival both as verbal sparring partner and as musician. In Gottfried's account she is portrayed as musically superior, and Wagner was happy to write music that reflected this superiority. We can see this at the end of Act 2, when Tristan sings a formal verse in a relatively stable minor key, inviting his beloved to follow him on a journey:

Dem Land, das Tristan meint,
der Sonne Licht nicht scheint:
es ist das dunkel
nächt'ge Land
daraus die Mutter
mich entsandt.

[To the land that Tristan imagines, / where no sun ever shines: / it is the dark, / nocturnal land / from which my mother / sent me forth.]

Isolde replies with a parallel verse:

Nun führst du in dein Eigen,
dein Erbe mir zu zeigen;
wie flöh' ich wohl das Land
das alle Welt umspannt?

[Now you are leading the way to your domain, / to show me your heritage; / how could I escape a place / that spans the entire world?]

Musically she starts by re-voicing his first two lines, but then she detours into stranger harmonic and melodic terrain. And rather than following the music of his last three lines, she takes another tack entirely, redoing what she has just sung in yet another way, the orchestration twice as rich. Her version is, in other words, meant to sound independent and more inventive. Such examples of gender equipoise and rebalancing are repeated many times elsewhere. For instance, Tristan throughout the opera is an unusually and wonderfully un-masculine male, constantly suffering from what were regarded in the nineteenth century as feminine maladies such as nervous melancholy; and in this sense he is a match for Isolde, who has her own surfeit of wildness and despair. In Act 3, just before Isolde arrives, he is given music in 5/4, the most off-balance metre Wagner could have chosen, to express his descent into self-annihilation: 'with blood flowing from my wounds, once I fought Morold. With blood flowing from my wounds, let me now hunt Isolde' – this is one of the craziest lines in all opera, and the hunting image recalls, from the medieval source, that Tristan was an expert at dismembering stags.

Quintuple metre is extraordinarily rare in European classical music before the twentieth century (at least outside Eastern European music, where it tends to reference national song types), and it suggests here that time is out of joint. The passage distorts music from Act 2, where the same theme appears as a sleepy interlude in the love duet, setting the lines 'lausch' Geliebter! / Lass' mich sterben!' (Listen, beloved! / Let me die!). In Act 2, this is a berceuse or lullaby in 3/4 and the single most peaceful stretch in the act. Hearing this same music distorted into 5/4 in Act 3, in the chaos and roar of the moment, it is extremely hard to tell exactly why music that *seems* like it should be in 3/4, and *was* in 3/4, and seems just on the border of being metrically stable, now sounds so profoundly wrong. The confused souls in the audience – made so by a strange metre – momentarily share an experience of instability with the man onstage.

The relative equality of Wagner's couple is also exemplified in the most famous subsection of the long Act 2 love duet, music that returns at the end of Act 3 and is known there, colloquially, as the 'Liebestod' (death-from-love):

So starben wir,
um ungetrennt,
ewig einig,
ohne End',

ohn' Erwachen,
ohn' Erbangen,
namenlos
in Lieb' umfangen,
ganz uns selbst gegeben,
der Liebe nur zu leben!

[So we would die, / and thus inseparable, / for ever, as one, / without end, / without awakening, / without fear, / nameless / encircled by love, / be given only to ourselves, / living only love!]

Tristan leads with these lines and Isolde echoes them, following suit by repeating more or less verbatim, as is appropriate both to immemorial operatic gender roles and to the order in which they will die – first him, then her. But even to early audiences, the personae in this duet were nonetheless interchangeable. Wagner travelled to London in 1877 to conduct excerpts from his later works as part of a 'Wagner Festival', and most of the Act 2 *Tristan* duet was featured on the final day, 26 May. James William Davison, the critic of *The Times* and generally no lover of Wagner, wrote that 'the lovers echo one another, phrase after phrase, as if what one said was precisely what the other would have said if their positions had been reversed'.[4]

Then in Act 3, as Isolde is kneeling over Tristan's corpse, this same music is played quietly in the orchestra, representing an acoustic hallucination that she will give a name to, a few moments later, in her final monologue: 'How gently and quietly he smiles. How delicately his eyes are opening. Do you see it, my friends? Don't you see? . . . Don't you see how his lips are parting, and his breath drifts out? Am I the only one who hears this melody . . . that resounds from him, and resonates in me?' All this is sung to the music of 'So starben wir, um ungetrennt' from Act 2, but Isolde, now a soloist, takes it far afield. It is as if she remembers Tristan's musical leads and then improvises a spectacular variation around them. She says that she hears music emanating from his corpse, but the music *we* can hear, its immense sonic plenitude, is coming from the singer who is impersonating *her*. Such feats of musical daring were hard, very hard, to emulate. Fifty years later, Richard Strauss set his sights on a libretto in which the dying heroine, Elektra, says to her sister, Chrysothemis, 'How could I not hear the music? The music comes from me' – and that was as close as he was ever willing to get to *Tristan*.

There are famously prim responses to *Tristan*, including several from Nietzsche in the years after he had turned away from his initial Wagner passion: 'Who dares say the word, the actual word for the ardours of the *Tristan* music – I put on gloves when I read the score of *Tristan*'.[5] And armoured matrons like Clara Schumann were predictably offended: in an oft-quoted remark she pronounced the opera 'the most disgusting thing I have heard or seen in my entire life'.[6] But we may be too quick to attribute the vitriol to dislike of onstage adultery, or the idea of sex, or strange music. The fact that male and female weigh evenly on the scales, that a female character is sometimes even allowed mastery, may have been more disturbing to Nietzsche or Clara Schumann than kissing or infidelity or unresolved harmonic dissonances.

Later in life, when Wagner came around to arguing not merely for the erasure of sexual inequalities but of sexuality entirely, an essential misogyny would re-emerge, perhaps one not much different from that found in his earlier operas. In his last writings, women are distinct from The Feminine: they figure as aliens, as temptresses luring the upright masculine figures into a slide towards barbarism. One wonders whether this sort of thing was qualitatively much different from the thinking that produced the more ordinary clichés of the works pre-1850. There, woman's proper role was to sacrifice herself to redeem men, as do Senta in *Der fliegende Holländer* and Elisabeth in *Tannhäuser*. And if such a role is not played with complete conviction, with never a doubting moment, then you become Elsa in *Lohengrin*: a failure, and a dead one at that.

It is unlikely that Wagner's intellectual convictions and fictions about ideal women had no effect on his real-life interactions with them, and some of his encounters with women were indeed strange beyond fiction. One instance was his long, intense relationship with Mathilde Wesendonck. She was the wife of the Swiss banker Otto Wesendonck, who was one of Wagner's greatest supporters and patrons. Wagner first met the Wesendoncks in Zurich in 1854; they provided him and his wife Minna with a cottage on their estate (called 'Asyl', sanctuary) from 1856 to 1858, the place where the larger part of *Tristan und Isolde* was written. Mathilde was Wagner's muse in these Zurich years and, inevitably in the circumstances, became enmeshed in a great deal of domestic tension. The nature of the relationship between her and Wagner is not known, but her devotion to him was at one point extreme. For example, she traced Wagner's pencil copy of the *Tristan* libretto in ink, so that he might have a slightly clearer manuscript to work from. This willingness to undertake tasks of crushing tedium and near pointlessness makes the rather sphinx-like Mathilde – her portraits show a Botticelli bourgeoise in Victorian silks – even more inscrutable. The letters Wagner wrote to her fill an entire printed volume, revealing significant details about his working habits and musical thinking during the composition of the *Ring* and *Tristan*. At the same time, they offer a generous sampling menu of Wagnerian flirtatiousness, as in this letter from 21 May 1857, written right as the composer was about to abandon *Siegfried* and start on *Tristan*:

> The Muse is beginning to visit me: does this betoken the certainty of *your* visit? The first thing I found was a melody that I didn't at all know what to do with, until of a sudden the words from the last scene of *Siegfried* came into my head. A good omen. Yesterday I also hit on the commencement of Act 2 – as Fafner's Rest, which has an element of humour in it. But you shall hear all about it, if the little swallow comes to inspect her edifice to-morrow.[7]

However, it matters not whether Wagner is writing to Mathilde about the secret of musical form in *Tristan* or about plans for a picnic outing; what he says in both cases utterly fails to illuminate *her*.

Given Wagner's close alliances with the women in his life, and his concern for the feminine and the masculine in theory, it might seem odd that, with the exception of *Tristan und Isolde*, he became increasingly clumsy at depicting romantic passion in opera. But this is probably where his essential misogyny left its mark. The classic illustration of the problem is Wagner's last opera, *Parsifal* (1882), with its questing stranger (Parsifal, tenor), chaste knights, Grail ritual, self-castrated evil sorcerer (Klingsor, baritone) and single female character, the self-annihilating Kundry (soprano). Kundry serves the Grail knights wearing muddy sackcloth in Acts 1 and 3. They refer to her as a 'wild animal' and are accustomed to scorn her. But in Act 2 she shape-shifts under the control of Klingsor and appears (cleaned up nicely, indeed at the head of a whole bevy of Flower Maidens) as a temptress in Klingsor's magic garden. The ensuing scene – Kundry attempts to lead Parsifal astray, and at a turning point in the drama bestows on him a languishing kiss – is terribly contrived, even deliberately so. She is putting on an act, and the music is obviously artificial and cloying. But one gets the sense that Wagner did not mean it to be quite so unconvincing, just that he couldn't by that stage imagine what real seductiveness sounded like. For a near-contemporaneous musical representation of the latter, all too human sensation, listen to 'Mon cœur s'ouvre à ta voix', Delila's hymn to wilting Samson in Act 2 of Saint-Saëns' *Samson et Dalila* (1877).

IN PRAISE OF THE PERIPHERY

This is not a small matter. Romantic passion, whether ingénue or mature, had been for much of operatic history the single necessary ingredient of serious opera, and of much comic opera as well. True, operatic couples were often paper-doll figures, and libretto love might well be expressed in formulaic ways. But romantic love had been such an operatic mainstay; it comes as a shock to realize that many central nineteenth-century repertory pieces effectively pass it by. Yet again Verdi offers a case in point. One might imagine that passionate love duets are of course the crowning glory of Verdi's greatest works, but in the second half of his career they are actually rather meagre. They do exist: in *La traviata* Act 1, *Un ballo in maschera* Act 2 and *Otello* Act 1, to name three famous examples: but even among these it's only in *Un ballo* (often thought of as Verdi's *Tristan* moment, and premiered in 1859, the very year Wagner finished his grand love-opera) that the soprano–tenor effusions are placed firmly at the centre of the drama. In most other cases, Verdi preferred his high-voiced principals to be pitted in grand confrontations against an Older Man, usually one singing in a baritone register. A possible reason is that, as Verdi himself grew older, heroic young tenors became less attractive to him, and were banished to the operatic sidelines.

This was also the case with Wagner, and above all with Wagner after the divide around 1850. *Tristan* aside – and that is of course a big aside – his ability to put a soprano together with a tenor and make it seem like love was largely over after *Die Walküre* in 1856. His interests both as librettist and composer veered perpetually towards other realms: sometimes, as with Verdi, to clashes between passionate young men and mature, world-weary antagonists; but more often to larger, less domestic issues, a path that partially explains why his works became so intriguing to ensuing generations of philosophers and academics.

In *Die Meistersinger*, for example, the philosophical point involves a debate about traditionalism and innovation in art. The opera is set in sixteenth-century Nuremberg. Three men vie for the love of a goldsmith's daughter, Eva (soprano), in a picture-postcard late-medieval city complete with guilds, professions and bourgeois order. Eva is an allegorical figure, a golden 'prize' to be won by the greatest citizen-composer, the man who can triumph in a song contest sponsored by the city guild. The opera's three male stars – the tenor Walther and the bass-baritones Sixtus Beckmesser and Hans Sachs – schematically represent untutored creative innovation (Walther), stolid, unthinking conservatism (Beckmesser) and self-effacing mediation (Sachs). Wagner tries hard to give them corresponding music: fiery and innovative for Walther; studious and ungainly for Beckmesser; reassuringly stable, although occasionally tinged with melancholy and transcendence, for Sachs. But there is one terrible misfire: Walther's Prize Song, the composition that will win him Eva in the teeth of opposition from Beckmesser after Sachs yields the battle to the younger man. Walther conceives his song in an inspired dream, Sachs helps him work out a satisfactory structure and Walther then sings it in the Act 3 contest. It should be the crowning glory of the opera, a demonstration that all is well creatively in this enclosed society and that innovation can enrich age-old traditions. Unfortunately it can't remotely fulfil these obligations, turning out to be one of Wagner's dullest and most predictable inspirations.

Instead, the most moving, beautiful and sensuous music in the opera is sung by a minor character, David (tenor), Hans Sachs's young apprentice. In Act 1, David explains the rules of the Master Singers' guild to Walther, who aspires to be admitted to their society. At some length, David describes the modes and melodies, the formal dictates for constructing verses and the elaborate customs surrounding creativity. As a demonstration of vocal virtuosity, and of the range and command of a great musician and performer, there is nothing else like it in the opera. The singer must master every style, every mode and melodic type contained within David's catalogue of the art. It's as if an actor were required to deliver dozens of lines, one after another, each in a different language and demanding exquisite variations in expression, as a native speaker for each one, and make it all seem easy. Although the plot presents David as a beginner, and although his is a secondary role, such singing can only be done by a top-quality tenor.

His penultimate verse in the disquisition about Master Singers involves a very beautiful melodic turn:

Der Dichter, der aus eignem Fleiße,
zu Wort und Reimen, die er erfand,
aus Tönen auch fügt eine neue Weise:
der wird als 'Meistersinger' erkannt.

[The poet, who through his own endeavour, / for the words and rhymes he has invented, / also creates, from sounds, a new melody / – he will be recognized as a 'Master Singer'.]

The line 'creates . . . a new melody' has the expressive marking *äusserst zart*, which means 'with extraordinary sweetness and softness'. In Italian it would be *dolcissimo*, and it is an expressive direction rarely found in Wagner. David's melody starts in the major but then drifts down in a delicate sequence on minor-key steps. There is a pause, an intake of breath before the triumphant punch line (with brass fanfare): '*he* will be recognized as a Master Singer'. This *dolcissimo* music for David turns out to have an ancestry and development in the opera that is far from trivial. In the next scene, when Walther appears before the singers' guild and is asked about his teacher, he names a legendary Middle High German poet, Walther von der Vogelweide (the name literally means Walther of the Meadow of Birds), someone clearly meant to symbolize natural inspiration and compositional grace. But if you listen closely, you hear that when Walther sings the name, the music echoes David's *dolcissimo* inspiration, now marred by Walther's louder, brasher way with it. The same motif will later turn up as part of Walther's Prize Song, similarly mistreated.

Wagner's failure with the Prize Song points once again to a fundamental operatic truth: when operas must, for plot reasons, invest any particular song with overwhelming power and transfigured loveliness, the actual music is invariably insufficient to deliver on the debt. This is why the composers of all those early Orpheus operas were sensible enough not to attempt the actual miraculous song (the performance in front of Pluto himself) and stuck with preliminary pleas to gatekeepers such as Charon or the Furies. In the case of *Die Meistersinger*, Walther's song puts in peril much dramatically important music in the final act, since motifs from the song are endlessly repeated, quoted, recalled and anticipated. With one exception – the beginning of Act 3, which features a moving orchestral prologue, another solo for David ('Am Jordan Sankt Johannes stand') and a world-weary monologue for Hans Sachs ('Wahn! Wahn! Überall Wahn!') – it is the incidental music in *Meistersinger*, the music for minor characters, or for activities unburdened by central themes, that attains the glory Walther strives for in vain. In the festive music for Act 3, scene 2, set in an open field where Nuremberg's trade guilds – cobblers, bakers and tailors – march in to the sound of drums, flutes and trumpet calls, and ordinary people spontaneously dance, the ear is drawn to the margins, where the absence of allegorical gravitas and compositional over-attentiveness lets a less encumbered musical voice emerge. Looking back to the youthful Wagner's cosmopolitan musical influences, one might hazard that this peripheral voice recalls his early fascination with *opéra comique*, while the central tread of the Prize Song marks the fact that his affection for Mediterranean lightness had mostly faded.

MOTIFS IN THE DARK

Matters both schematic and philosophical dominate much of Wagner's longest work, *Der Ring des Nibelungen*, whose action over the four operas is so complex as to defy easy synopsis. However, so strong are the links between musical development and epic detail that it's impossible to understand singing, sound, motif or harmony in the *Ring* without knowing the plot. In the first opera, *Das Rheingold*, the dwarf Alberich (bass) steals gold from under the Rhine, snatching it from its guardians, the Rhine Maidens (two sopranos and a mezzo). He returns underground and forges from it a magic ring that gives him great power. A phalanx of Nordic Gods hear about this: their leader, Wotan (bass), is urged by his scheming henchman Loge (tenor) to steal Alberich's wealth in order to meet the construction costs of their new fortress, Valhalla, built by two giants, Fafner and Fasolt (basses). These busy workers were originally promised the goddess Freia (soprano) as payment, but have reluctantly agreed to take gold in lieu. Wotan and Loge visit Alberich and his cringing brother Mime (tenor), kidnap Alberich and force him to deliver up his wealth. Wotan also seizes the ring, and Alberich lays a curse on it. Above ground, the giants demand the entire hoard, including the ring. Wotan hesitates, but the earth goddess, Erda (contralto), rises from the depths to warn him of the ring's dangers. Wotan hands the ring to Fasolt, who is immediately murdered by Fafner, a first example of the ring's curse in action. The Gods (except for Loge) cross a rainbow bridge to Valhalla, but the Rhine Maidens, singing unseen from below, accuse them of falseness and cowardice.

This takes us only to the end of the first opera, but the remainder can be compressed into genealogical high points. For *Die Walküre* we move forward untold eons. Wotan has sired two half-human twins, Siegmund (tenor) and Sieglinde (soprano), as well as some all-magical daughters, the Valkyries, whose number includes Brünnhilde (soprano), Erda's daughter. His aim is to breed a great hero who can extract the ring from Fafner. Siegmund and Sieglinde, separated in childhood, meet as adults and fall in love. A single, highly illicit night engenders their son, the future hero Siegfried. But Siegmund is killed battling Sieglinde's husband, and Brünnhilde, who has incurred Wotan's anger by trying to defend Siegmund, is punished by being put into a magic sleep on a mountaintop.

Forward one generation for *Siegfried*. Sieglinde died giving birth and her child, Siegfried (tenor), has been raised in a forest by Mime. Siegfried is uneducated and brutal and knows no fear. From Mime, he learns about his ancestry and about Fafner (who has turned himself into a dragon and guards the ring and his hoard of gold). Siegfried finds the dragon, kills him, gets the ring, hears about sleeping Brünnhilde, finds her, wakes her up and weds her with a kiss.

Forward one night for *Götterdämmerung*. The next morning, Siegfried gives the ring to Brünnhilde and leaves the mountaintop seeking adventure. At a nearby court he encounters Gunther (baritone), his sister Gutrune (soprano) and their half-brother Hagen (bass), who is Alberich's son, although no one but Hagen and Alberich are privy to that information. Hagen is also after the ring. At this point complications escalate alarmingly. Siegfried is given a forgetfulness potion, and loses all memory of Brünnhilde. He promptly falls in love with Gutrune.

To demonstrate his worthiness and loyalty to Gunther, he goes back to Brünnhilde magically disguised as Gunther, and claims her as (the latter's) wife. He seizes the ring as symbol of a union that he will not, being a proxy, actually consummate, although he does demand to sleep next to her for the night, with a sword between them. Next morning, he brings Brünnhilde to the court for a double wedding. But seeing the ring on Siegfried's finger rather than Gunther's (Siegfried has taken off the Gunther disguise but has kept the ring) she cries betrayal. Hagen convinces Brünnhilde and Gunther that Siegfried is false and must be killed. The next day, the men go off to hunt. Siegfried stumbles on the Rhine Maidens and they ask him for the ring, warning him of the curse, but he laughs at them. Rejoining the others, he is slipped a remembering potion by Hagen, which leads him to blurt out intimate details about awakening Brünnhilde with a kiss and what ensued. Since no one is keeping track of exactly which night(s) are at issue here, this revelation suggests gross insult and treason against Gunther. Hagen skewers Siegfried with his spear and Siegfried dies. His corpse is brought back to the court, but as Gunther and Hagen squabble over the ring, Siegfried's dead hand rises to ward off its theft. At that moment Brünnhilde appears. She has consulted the Rhine Maidens and they have explained all. She pockets the ring, orders a funeral pyre for Siegfried and, announcing that she will return the ring to the Rhine, immolates herself. The Rhine overflows. Hagen jumps in to snatch the ring and is drowned by the Rhine Maidens. The flames reach Valhalla and the Gods. The world ends.

A mythic farrago, especially when thus briefly narrated, the *Ring*'s plot is also serious, at times disturbing, at times engrossing in the way that myth can be, and provides endless material for interpretation and reinterpretation. Most of all, though, it is the narrative scaffold for an enormous acoustic tapestry, one which can be mistaken for no other, and which represents a singular and ambivalent fictional world. The *Ring* involves more than sixteen hours of continuous music performed over four nights, broken only by the ends of acts, and drawn together by scores of recurring musical motifs and sonorities. Wagner began it with one of the most famous *creatio ex nihilo* effects in all music history. The prelude to *Das Rheingold* starts from a single, subterranean E♭ in the double basses – the players have to tune their lowest string down – which then becomes a chord, a rising call in the horns, with more instruments, gradually most of the orchestra added in, building to cascades and waves of E♭ major. This goes on for several minutes – E♭ everywhere and nothing but E♭ – before the curtain goes up. More than a century and a half later, this prelude is still astonishing.

In 1876, when the *Ring* was about to be performed for the first time at Bayreuth, one of Wagner's disciples, Hans von Wolzogen, published a musical guide to the four operas. Wolzogen enumerated all the many recurring motifs. He called them *Leitfaden* or 'guiding threads', but they later became known as leitmotifs or 'guiding motifs'. Each motif was equipped with a small music example and a name such as 'Renunciation', 'Curse' or 'Ring'. In the later twentieth century it became fashionable to refine and correct Wolzogen's guide and also to deplore the fact that Wagner's music could thus be reduced to what Claude Debussy famously disparaged as 'calling cards'. In 1882, a foreign correspondent for *The Theater* reviewing the *Ring* at Bayreuth mentions the guide, and makes an unusual observation, one that links Wagner's penchant for music-with-labels to another special Bayreuth phenomenon, that of darkness in the auditorium:

> Physically incapacitated from reading the libretto during the performance, and infrequently able to follow the words by ear, owing to the general predominance of orchestral sound over vocal utterance, the Bayreuth audience was mainly dependent upon the Leit-Motiven for its guidance through the bewildering maze of the Nibelungen story and psychological phenomena. It is Wagner's wish that this should always be the case; and, should the auditorium of Her Majesty's Theatre be veiled in Cimmerian darkness during a coming performance of the Trilogy, those who propose to attend a 'Cyclus' will do wisely to master beforehand Herr von Wolzogen's notes on the Leit-Motiven, and to commit these latter to memory.[8]

Press this review a little harder and the implications are stunning. At an extreme, it could mean that when Wagner began composing the *Ring* in the 1850s, he invented a radically new operatic music not because he had interesting ideas about continuity, or about musico-poetic synthesis, or because he wanted to avoid conventional numbers, but rather because he was seeking an operatic music that would be perfect for the dark. Blind Cimmerian night would not actually occur in any operatic theatre until 1876 at Bayreuth – so it would have been an imagined darkness. But did its sensory deprivations inspire a musical revolution, circa 1854?

Whatever their original motivation, the numerous motivic recurrences – the symbolism of returning sonorities – are critical in the *Ring* and constitute a large measure of its effect. Being sceptical about the leitmotif phenomenon does not mean that it loses its fascination or its relevance. One way to understand Wagner's technique in the *Ring* is to realize that these leitmotifs, whether melodies, orchestral sonorities, particular harmonies or other recurring musical ideas, usually appear first in simple forms and then in transformation, and that the transformations – the way the music is changed – have symbolic heft. This process of association and then change has been called the 'semanticization' of music, the motifs' gradual saturation with meanings.[9]

A single example must stand for hundreds. The *Rheingold* prelude, as noted, grows from a rising E♭ major arpeggio. The curtain goes up. We are under the Rhine and the Rhine Maidens are swimming joyously; but they are about to be visited by Alberich. The musical wave appears over and over again in many keys other than E♭, but always in the major, always going up, cascades of sound washing up again and again on to the shore. Once Alberich disturbs the scene, however, the wave retreats: it represented unspoiled nature, music in its most basic form; Alberich's presence sullies the scene, causing the motif's immediate departure. Much later, in the fourth and final scene of *Das Rheingold*, Erda, the prophetic earth goddess, rises slowly out of the ground surrounded by an eerie bluish light, a mysterious and utterly unexpected visitation. As she appears, that musical wave from the prelude and scene 1 returns, but in a minor key and much slower, as if the water has turned glacial. Like the Rhine Maidens, Erda represents the primordial; but she does so in a more pessimistic form. The sapphire sibyl warns Wotan of impending doom: 'Alles was ist, endet. Ein düst'rer Tag dämmert den Göttern' (Everything that exists will end. A dark day will dawn for the Gods). Her first two lines are set to iterations of the rising wave, first in the minor, then ('endet') in the major. But when that major-key arpeggio reaches its crest ('ein düst'rer Tag') Wagner turns it around. For the first time in the opera, the wave goes downward, inverted, back to its origins. The symbolism is clear: the world's upward arc will collapse into ruin. But because of the orchestration, the voicing and the particular harmonies involved, this passage sounds deeply uncanny and disquieting. The music prefigured here returns, sparingly, over the entire *Ring*, always in predictions and visions of the world's end.

EROS AND CARITAS

We suggested earlier that the older Wagner lost touch with romance, which may seem odd in the case of the *Ring*, where love affairs routinely muddy the mythic waters. But despite these episodes, hunger for power and the nature of greed are the predominant themes, so much so that the sexual couplings seem contrived largely for dynastic purposes. The low point here is a character who never appears, Hagen's mother Grimhilde (we are told she spent a night with Alberich in exchange for payment). The love between Gutrune and Siegfried in *Götterdämmerung* represents what Wagner may have thought the perverse truth about Eros. Siegfried becomes enraptured shortly after catching sight of Gutrune in Act 1, and falls truly, deeply in love with her after imbibing the forgetfulness potion. But after Hagen delivers the antidote in Act 3, Siegfried recalls that he is truly, deeply in love with Brünnhilde. Is there any strong musical difference between the genuine and the drug-induced state? Certainly, the plot works hard to tell us that his real love is Brünnhilde, but love in the *Ring* – as in much of Wagner – can be portrayed as madly ardent in the instant while remaining artificial when viewed from any other perspective. Passion can, in other words, occur on demand, pharmaceutical in both its origins and its demise.

The crowning romantic liaison in the *Ring*, between Siegfried and Brünnhilde, turns out to be among the least convincing. It is, at least minus the music, one of the most patently prescribed and dramatically forced soprano–tenor pairings in all opera. When Siegfried awakens Brünnhilde from her enchanted sleep, in Act 3 of *Siegfried*, she seems her old self at first – the headstrong girl who defied her father in *Die Walküre*. But once the libretto calls for her to stop patronizing the juvenile enthusiast, and to fall in love with him instead, it is as if she too has been slipped a potion. The liaison is required by the source legend for the libretto, and its misfire in the opera has been attributed to the composer's miscalculation of Siegfried as an operatic character. Wagner chose to make the hero jejune – young, brash, unchangeable, incorrigible – for schematic reasons, since Siegfried is conceived as Youth defeating Age (the rule breaker and World Hero). But as a character on stage Siegfried seldom fulfils the promise invested in this abstract idea. In the Prologue of *Götterdämmerung*, after a single night and a rousing duet with Brünnhilde, he takes off in pursuit of further adventures, leaving her on the top of her mountain with a ring for company – a classic operatic case in which only the music, which by this time in the *Ring* is invariably elaborate and disquieting, can possibly save the situation from comedy.

The programmed quality to Siegfried and Brünnhilde's passion may also account for peculiarities in the music they sing, in particular their farewell love duet in the Prologue of *Götterdämmerung*. Towards the end, Wagner detours into a curiously antique musical mode: he uses harmonic sequences, procedures characteristic of eighteenth-century music, rolling them out in particular for the overlapping salutes that end the duet: 'Heil dir, Brünnhilde, prangender Stern. / Heil dir, Siegfried, siegendes Licht' (Hail, Brünnhilde, radiant star. Hail, Siegfried, victorious light). These old-fashioned sequential repetitions are not genuine antiques and their effect is hard to pin down. It is as if music – genuinely moving music – from a benign past has found its way into a present that is soon to end catastrophically. So the peroration of the love duet and the lovers' simultaneous singing sounds jubilant; but it does so in the way that whistling in the dark can sound both jubilant and futile at the same time.

This particular passage in the *Ring* is laden with implications. One other reason the music sounds curiously old-fashioned – even though it was written relatively late in Wagner's life, in 1872 – is that it sets one of the oldest passages in the *Ring* libretto. The idea for this duet was present in the original poetic draft for *Siegfried's Tod* in 1848. Back then, Wagner could still imagine love duets involving separate solo statements: soprano first and then tenor, or vice versa, capped off by simultaneous singing, almost in the manner of Donizetti's *Lucia di Lammermoor*. By the time he wrote the *Walküre* libretto a few years later, he was more self-consciously radical as a poet. In the first act of *Die Walküre*, Siegmund and Sieglinde's affectionate expressions never once involve their voices in parallel verses, let alone being placed over one another or heard together. For this reason, these two, unlike Siegfried and Brünnhilde, sound less allied to the operatic past. They are very new and very daring, quite apart from the fact that they commit incest without hesitation or qualm. And this is a musical phenomenon that meshes beautifully with their role in the plot as 'bourgeois terrorists'. That last phrase belongs to Theodor Adorno, who used it to describe Rienzi, Wagner's first operatic anti-hero. One of Adorno's – many – anti-Wagnerian ideas was that 'In Wagner the bourgeoisie dreams of its own destruction, conceiving it as the only road to salvation, even though all it ever sees of the salvation is the destruction'.[10]

Siegmund and Sieglinde jolted Wagner to a higher plane in his thinking about motifs in the dark, those intricate musical transformations that depict the twins' increasing passion in Act 1 of *Die Walküre*. Some alterations engage with the very nature of recognition, since for most of the act Siegmund and Sieglinde do not realize they are brother and sister: their family connection dawns on them just before the curtain drops, seeming if anything to ignite them further. In the lead-up to this revelation, Sieglinde has drugged her loathed husband, Hunding (bass), and as the lovers prepare to flee, the wind blows the hut door open and moonlight streams in. This shock is the scenic prelude to a lyric effusion from Siegmund, who reacts with an allegorical poem about Love, a brother, who finds his sister, the Spring; it is a rare late-Wagner quasi-aria, one that tenors sometimes even perform in concert. Indeed, one of the most famous Wagnerian singers of the twentieth century, Lauritz Melchior, sings it on screen in the ocean-cruise film *Luxury Liner* of 1948. The allegory in the poem seems absolutely clear; but as so often in opera, a revelation staring the audience in the face remains obscure to the dramatis personae. The music, in other words, is much more prescient than the characters, with Wagner's melodic writing and his inventiveness with musical symbolism achieving peak colour.

One detail must again stand for many. In this Spring Song, Siegmund sings his first line, 'Winterstürme wichen dem Wonnemond' (Winter storms yield to the rapturous moon), and 'Wonnemond' is set to a three-note descending scale, E♭-D-C. A few lines later, he enthuses about the spring's power, 'seinem warmen Blut entblühen wonnige Blumen' (from his warm blood bloom rapturous flowers). On 'wonnige Blumen', his voice returns to the three-note scale of 'Wonnemond', but ornamented by two extra notes, F-E♭-B♮-D-C. Still later, in a contrasting verse, he gets to the brother-and-sister allegory: 'Zu seiner Schwester schwang er sich her' (He [the Spring] to his sister did rush). On 'Schwester schwang' the motif returns, but the kaleidoscope has been tapped again, and the five notes coalesce into four, F-E♮-B♭-D.

What Wagner has done here is to create a precise musical analogy for dawning consciousness, as something long forgotten becomes clear to the mind. The final, four-note form is actually something we have heard a great deal in Act 1. In the first scene, for example, where Siegmund stumbles into Sieglinde's hut and is revived by her, it sounds in the orchestra to accompany much mute gazing and blushing. In guides to the *Ring* this collection of notes is therefore often called the Love Motif—a label whose invention required minimal imagination. When the motif re-emerges in the Spring Song, its melodic face is already familiar. The difference is that now we have been treated to its pre-history, its musical evolution: a featureless three-note bundle first gets ornamented, and then morphs into a symbolically charged and recognizable motif. It is a perfect way to express in music the distant impression that something or someone is familiar; then becomes a charge on memory; and then a revelation of identity.

The same thematic inventiveness takes flight in later parts of the *Ring*, as Wagner's taste in harmonies and sonorities grew stranger and more complex in the 1860s and 1870s. So those old-fashioned operatic numbers hiding in the *Götterdämmerung* libretto preordain a peculiar past-in-the-future sound. The story's younger generation, Siegfried and Brünnhilde, end up sounding older than their parents in one way (in their formal cut, the manner in which their music unfolds) and far more advanced in another (in harmony and orchestral combination). But the mix is perverse. Brünnhilde and Siegfried singing together inhabit a peculiar sound-world, where a past in which outcomes were not yet disasters becomes tangled up in an apocalyptic present whose nihilism they have yet to discover.

That effect reaches its peak in the music Siegfried sings just before he dies, 'Brünnhilde, heilige Braut' (Brünnhilde, exalted bride) – addressed not to Brünnhilde herself but to a hallucination of her. The passage opens with an alarming sound: a single, loud minor chord scored for high-register brass, preceded by a long silence, and followed by contrasting low-register arpeggios that start soft and stay soft, lofting up from the bass to end in the high stratosphere of the violins and upper woodwind. The arpeggios per se have a distinct pedigree. They are derived from the waves we hear at the opening of *Das Rheingold*, during the prologue and the first scene under the Rhine; and from those same arpeggios as they migrated into the minor mode when Erda appeared. However, this alarm-plus-arpeggio idea is heard on only three special occasions in the entire *Ring*. The first is when Brünnhilde awakens in *Siegfried* Act 3, singing 'Heil dir, Sonne. Heil dir, Licht!' (Hail, sun, Hail, light!). The second is at the very beginning of *Götterdämmerung*, where the low-lying arpeggios seem to turn into a terrestrial mist swirling around the feet of the three Norns (Fates), who will review past, present and future in scene 1 after the curtain rises.

The third and last time is for Siegfried's ante-mortem hallucination. One way of understanding this last recurrence is via the poetic text. Siegfried imagines that he is seeing Brünnhilde asleep again, and wonders why she does not wake. Logical, then, that music from his first encounter with her sleeping figure (in the last scene of *Siegfried*) would come back. But press a little harder and the logic wavers. Why bring back music for *her* salute to the sun? Why music we last heard in the prologue to Act 1 of this opera, ushering in the shapeless Norns? The very questions define the limits of Wagnerian musical symbolism. Those labels that Wolzogen first broadcast certainly have their uses. But time and again in the *Ring* any expectation that leitmotifs should work with semantic consistency will bind the operas to rules they were never intended to obey. Wagner himself had something to say about this, though contemplating his statement may make things even less clear. In the late essay entitled 'Über die Anwendung der Musik auf das Drama' (On the Application of Music to Drama, 1879), he complained that 'one of my younger friends ... has devoted some attention to the characteristics of "leitmotifs", as he calls them, but has treated them more from the point of view of dramatic import and effect than as elements of the musical structure'.[11]

It seems as though Wagner is issuing a warning: over-attention to the semantic side risks obscuring larger aesthetic or formal designs. To put this another way, musical recurrences in the *Ring* are, as one might expect in such a sprawling, symbol-rich plot, quite plentiful; but sometimes they happen primarily because the effect is good. What's more, in Wagner's other post-1850 operas – in *Tristan*, *Die Meistersinger* and *Parsifal* – the whole business is on another footing altogether. In these operas there are indeed themes, sonorities, melodic ideas and motivic particles that recur, but very seldom do they do so with the elaborate dramatic associations Wagner likes so much in the *Ring*. You can make your way quite satisfactorily through these three operas without knowing a single leitmotivic association.

For Wagner, 'effect' is a charged word. In his writings, he accuses other composers, or stage actors, or conductors or assorted lesser artists of being lured into 'effects' that he judges unmotivated (in German,

Effekt means an empty effect, rather than *Wirkung*, an effect resulting from a cause and in turn causing something beyond mere astonishment). This is the gist of his objection to Meyerbeer's music, already mentioned in Chapter 11:

> In fact, Meyerbeerian music produces – on those who are able to edify themselves thereby – effects without causes. This miracle was only possible for the most exaggerated music, that is, music aspiring to a power that, in opera, had from the first sought to make itself more and more independent of anything worth expressing, and had finally proclaimed its complete independence by reducing to a moral and artistic nullity the object of expression.[12]

In an 1871 essay, 'Über die Bestimmung der Oper' (On the Destiny of Opera), he connected this error to both a style of performance, and – a common *bête noire* – to the ills of Italian opera:

> As everything written for and acted in the theatre is nowadays inspired by nothing but this tendency to 'effect', so that whatever ignores it is promptly condemned to neglect, we need feel no surprise at seeing it systematically applied to the performance of pieces by Goethe and Schiller. . . . The need of poetic pathos made our poets deliberately adopt a *rhetorical mode of diction*, with the aim of working on the feelings; and, as it was impossible for our un-poetic actors either to understand or carry out the ideal aim, this diction led to that intrinsically senseless, but melodramatically telling style of declamation whose practical object was just the 'effect', i.e. a stunning of the spectator's senses, to be documented by the outburst of applause. This applause and its unfailing provoker, the 'exit-tirade', became the soul of every tendency in our modern theatre: the 'brilliant exits' in the roles of our classical plays have been counted up and numbered – exactly as with an Italian operatic part.[13]

Yet the alarm-plus-arpeggio music in the *Ring* is a 'stunning' effect,with enigmatic self-containment as the heart of its power. The music jolts the audience from their seats. Then, having sounded this warning, it veers off into waveforms recalling primordial life. Far too strange to be signalling an upcoming romance, it becomes the audible advance notice of something bleak, the intimation of far-off disaster even as the plot seems to have reached a fairy-tale high point where Sleeping Beauty awakes.

And disaster is not far off. Wagner turned out to be very good at musical apocalypse. Perhaps, as in so many other ways, he took his lead here from the final theatrical shocks of so many French *grands opéras*. The hallowed routine – collapsing scenery plus orchestral thunder – rounds out *Götterdämmerung*, *grand* as well in being Wagner's longest single opera. Composing it took him several years, and this comes as no surprise when we consider the opera's facts and figures: Act 1 alone lasts about two and a half hours, making it longer than *Das Rheingold* in its entirety. There are noisier operas and there are operas whose orchestras are as large (Richard Strauss's *Elektra* figures in both respects), but for sheer, terrifying acoustic mayhem there is nothing that rivals *Götterdämmerung* Act 2, scene 2, in which Hagen blows a steer horn and summons a male chorus. It illustrates the brutal side of nineteenth-century German art, and is good for frightening children. Those who imagine dissonance to be merely unpleasant, or who think close harmony by male singers makes for sure-fire merriment, cannot have heard it.

Much of the male-chorus music returns for the revenge trio at the end of *Götterdämmerung* Act 2, in which Hagen, Gunther and Brünnhilde vow to sacrifice Siegfried. Wagner's musical sketches for this trio survive, and show that he wrote some of the final section, which includes simultaneous singing, without words under the voice parts, also going so far as to use the old Italian-opera trick of repeating some of Hagen's lines to fill out the evolving vocal line.[14] This may seem like a small issue, until we recall that for decades Wagner had proclaimed this sort of thing as an ancient and execrable operatic flaw. The trio also draws on another old-style 'number', Siegfried's and Gunther's oath of blood brotherhood in Act 1, scene 2, a passage involving a tenor–baritone singing competition and momentous onstage drinking. But old operatic conventions are colliding with the eerie acoustic flavour of Wagnerian harmony circa 1870, and the benign forms of leitmotifs heard in the earlier operas have been subjected to progressive distortion. Thus were the old, grand opera ways changed out of all recognition.

TRISTAN'S OTHER WORLD

Around the time Wagner was completing the *Ring*, Friedrich Nietzsche was finishing his first book, *The Birth of Tragedy out of the Spirit of Music*, which is among other things about Wagner. Nietzsche is famous for having begun with a passion for Wagner but ending up loathing him. In 1886, when he republished *The Birth of Tragedy*, he wrote a new preface calling the book 'embarrassing' and 'effeminate' because of its Wagnerian enthusiasms.[15] Yet in both the initial enthusiasm and later disillusionment Nietzsche's insights about Wagner's music were very often to the point, even though they had been preformed by philosophical dogma. This, for example, is a passage about *Tristan und Isolde*:

> I must appeal only to those who, immediately related to music, have in it, as it were, their motherly womb, and are related to things almost exclusively through unconscious musical relations. To these genuine musicians I direct the question whether they can imagine a human being who would be able to perceive the third act of *Tristan und Isolde*, without any aid of word and image, purely as a tremendous symphonic movement, without expiring in a spasmodic un-harnessing of all the wings of the soul? . . . How could he endure to perceive the echo of innumerable shouts of pleasure and woe in the 'wide space of the world night', enclosed in the wretched glass capsule of the human individual, without inexorably fleeing towards his primordial home, as he hears this shepherd's dance of metaphysics?[16]

When it comes to expiring, the exertions of *Tristan* have in fact claimed several. Famously, the tenor who created the role in 1865, Ludwig Schnorr von Carolsfeld (1836–65), only managed three performances before he caught a chill, which turned to rheumatic problems, which turned to apoplexy, which turned to an early grave. And at least two famous conductors have died while leading the opera: Felix Mottl (Munich, heart attack, 1911) and Joseph Keilberth (Munich, heart attack, 1968). All this is talked about as if it is hardly surprising. Nietzsche was by no means the only critic to write in such hyperbolic terms about the opera – his comments exemplify a common tone among devotees. Even a more measured observer, writing from Bayreuth in 1891, was struck by the opera's effect on the audience:

> Yesterday the opera was *Tristan and Isolde*. I have seen all sorts of audiences – at theatres, operas, concerts, lectures, sermons, funerals – but none which was twin to the Wagner audience of Bayreuth for fixed and reverential attention. Absolute attention and petrified retention to the end of an act of the attitude assumed at the beginning of it. . . . This opera of

> *Tristan and Isolde* last night broke the hearts of all witnesses who were of the faith, and I know of some who have heard of many who could not sleep after it, but cried the night away. I feel strongly out of place here. Sometimes I feel like the sane person in a community of the mad; sometimes I feel like the one blind man where all others see; the one groping savage in the college of the learned, and always, during service, I feel like a heretic in heaven.[17]

That was Mark Twain. Whether people actually *did* cry the night away (Twain's 'I know of some who have heard of many' doesn't strike a rigorous documentary tone) is irrelevant: what's important is that people talked about the opera in these terms – terms that were granted to no other.

Tristan is also the only mature Wagner opera to escape the stigmas that were attached in the twentieth century to his other works: stigmas concerning their German hyper-nationalism, racist fantasizing, distasteful political allegory, xenophobia and misogyny. That *Tristan* eluded taint is in part a consequence of the fact that it was seldom in the repertory of Nazi-era Germany, being too neurotic and somehow French for the Reichskulturkammer.[18] Another thermometer gives a similar reading. Like *Die Meistersinger* and *Der Ring*, the music of *Tristan* has had a resonant afterlife in film soundtracks, but unlike them, never as propaganda. The Liebestod – the orchestral excerpt based on Isolde's final monologue – has served inevitable duty as an accompaniment to doomed love, as in *Humoresque* (1946), where Joan Crawford, devastated by rejection, drowns herself to a piano-concerto version; or *Escape* (1943), where Conrad Veidt, personifying decadence and neurasthenic passion, plays the Liebestod from memory, again on the piano. But in what is probably the most complex case – a film noir, *The Blue Gardenia* (1953, directed by Fritz Lang) – the *Tristan* Prelude escapes all typecasting, even though there is doomed love aplenty in the plot. The director and his sound designer, through direct quotations from the Prelude, elaborate instead an idea that is easy to spot in *Tristan* once you are not focused on intimations of adultery and midnight trysts. It is the idea of caritas, of humane love and pity. This is what Kurwenal gives voice to when he comforts the dying Tristan in Act 3, 'The ship, yes, it will arrive today. It can't be delayed much longer.' It is also expressed in a melody played by unison cellos as Isolde in Act 1 recounts how she spared Tristan's life, even after discovering his identity as the knight who killed her betrothed: 'his suffering moved me. I let the sword fall'. Almost sixty years after *The Blue Gardenia*, in Lars von Trier's film *Melancholia* (2011), that cello melody from the Prelude serves the same purpose it had in the earlier film. We hear it on the soundtrack when a mother, her sister and her young son – theirs being the only love left at the end of the world – clasp hands.

It is indeed hard to draw much political edge from the *Tristan* plot, which is relentless in its focus on love in all its forms. As outlined earlier, Wagner followed the broad lines of Gottfried's medieval tale, but radically simplified the action. Little happens; much is said. The music is orchestrated in such a way as to trick the ear about the instruments being heard, sometimes within a complicated, plush sound and sometimes – although this might seem impossible – when only a few instruments are playing. The libretto is a mélange. Gottfried's plot is cut down, but additional poetic images and metaphors are supplied by *Hymnen an die Nacht* (Hymns to the Night, 1800) by the German Romantic poet Novalis. Wagner also threaded in some unsettling nihilism, ideas about death and transcendence that he had absorbed from the philosopher Arthur Schopenhauer's *Die Welt als Wille und Vorstellung* (The World as Will and Representation, 1818), which he read in 1854. There was, finally, a minor contribution from Wagner's own dabbling in Buddhism in the mid-1850s.

There is also that oddly modern quality in the human interactions, despite the contrived poetry through which the characters express themselves, the faux medievalism of their milieu and the extensive philosophizing that Tristan and Isolde manage to pack into their protestations of undying love. For instance, in Act 1 Isolde is furious with Tristan for having tricked her when they were in Ireland and then running away, returning only to fetch her as a bride for his uncle. Tristan, on the other hand, seems indifferent: he ignores Isolde and remains distant. During their great confrontation in Act 1, scene 5, her hurled accusations and his cool responses are played out in flawless style, Isolde using the familiar form of address ('du'), perhaps as an insult yet also to suggest emotional proximity, while Tristan keeps to the antique, aristocratic form ('Ihr'), which is unfriendly, albeit in a polite way. But Tristan becomes tired and morose, and finally says: 'if Morold meant so much to you, then take the sword again, and strike sure and true this time, so it doesn't slip from your grasp'; and at that moment he switches to the familiar form ('war Morold *dir* so wert, / nun wieder *nimm'* das Schwert') for the first time. Suddenly, through the alchemy of grammar, there is an entire unexplained past in the room, an intimacy that happened long ago and instantly rekindles. It is well to remember that at this point the starring beverage, the love potion, is nowhere in sight.

We know that the later two acts of *Tristan* were written without Wagner having access to what he had written earlier, at least in full score. In part to pay off his ever-spiralling debts, he sent off the manuscript act by act to his publisher in Leipzig. Just as a feat of memory, this is astonishing. Wagner did of course have his preliminary drafts for consultation, but the circumstances of the opera's creation dictated that to a great extent each act is musically independent, in particular inhabiting a different orchestral sound-world. Prominent aspects of these sound-worlds are then anticipated in the preludes to each act. Of these, the Act 1 Prelude is by far the longest and most famous, and is often played as an orchestral excerpt in concert. It starts with a four-note melody played by the cellos. On the last note the cello is joined by other instruments, forming perhaps the most famous chord ever: starting from the bottom, F, B, D♯ and G♯, scored for oboes, clarinets, cor anglais, cellos and bassoons. Ever since 1865 this collection of notes in this particular order and spacing has become instantly recognizable, peculiar and inimitable, notorious in its instability. It is dissonant and unstable, demanding resolution; but it resolves to yet another unstable chord – a more conventional dominant seventh – as if a question has been answered by another question. The so-called *Tristan* Chord is, though, merely the first instance of an unsettled harmony that stretches over the entire Prelude: melodies end by beginning other melodies, harmonic resolutions are constantly delayed or obfuscated or never arrive or are there only for an instant. Conductors today have the habit of performing the Prelude at a snail's pace, which it hardly needs since the music, by never seeming satisfied, produces languor at any speed. In Richard Strauss's recording, the piece is played lightly enough for the waltz rhythm hidden within Wagner's notes to break through now and then.

The music of this Prelude turns up now and then in the opera, most spectacularly near the end of Act 1. After drinking the love potion (they think it is a death potion, but Isolde's panicky maid Brangäne has substituted an alternative), Tristan and Isolde fall silent for several long moments, waiting to die. As they wait, the orchestra rewinds almost literally to bar 1 of the prelude, and a recapitulation of the opening accompanies their pantomime as it dawns on them what has happened. Since it has been made abundantly clear that they fell in love when in Ireland, it is uncertain what the potion has to contribute here, except perhaps a pretext.

Even the most rigid, scientific approaches to musical analysis – which may barely mention text or drama, treating the opera as if it were some kind of elephantine string quartet – can be read as over-compensation for the devastating impression the music of *Tristan* leaves. Because it is wondrously complicated, full of sheer musical verve and tricks of construction, *Tristan* has held perpetual fascinations for musical theorists (analyses of the *Tristan* Chord, showing precisely how it might be explained in terms of conventional harmonic syntax, go back well into the nineteenth century). One of Wagner's technical tricks runs as follows: the Act 1 Prelude begins with the cellos playing the opening melody, which leaps from A to F, then goes down via E to D♯ (D♯ then forming one pitch in the *Tristan* Chord). The same melody is then repeated twice more, moved up to jump from B to G♯, and then from D to B. The first statement is thus very slightly different from the other two in that its opening leap is a half-step shorter, in technical terms a minor sixth rather than a major sixth. Is the very first note, then, the A♮, in some sense a wrong note substituting for an absent A♭ that would lengthen the jump to a major sixth? And could a there-yet-not-there A♭ represent some Schopenhauerian salute to mystery and transcendence, a beyond that cannot precipitate into the material world and yet haunts it?

This may seem a dispute over minutiae, but the tension or ambiguity about A♮ versus A♭ turns up again and again, in big ways and small, throughout the opera. An important recurring theme is built around it when in Act 1 Isolde (catching sight of Tristan through the rigging) mutters an imprecation:

> Mir erkoren,
> mir verloren,
> hehr und heil,
> kühn und feig!
> Todgeweihtes Haupt!
> Todgeweihtes Herz!

[Chosen for me, / lost to me, / sublime and unhurt, / courageous and cowardly! / Head consecrated to Death! / Heart consecrated to Death!]

At 'Todgeweihtes Haupt!' the orchestra plays two chords: A♭ major (loud, woodwind), then A major (soft, trumpets and trombones). And there is more. When the ship is about to reach land, Tristan and Isolde are interrupted by the voices of unseen sailors, 'Auf das Tau! Anker los!' (Haul up! Anchor away!), set to rolling waves and fast runs in the strings. The chords alternating here are G♯ major (which is A♭ major re-spelt) and A major. And there is more still. This enigma of two competing notes and the chords formed on them stretches far into the opera. Recall the parallel verses for Tristan and Isolde in Act 2, discussed in the opening of this chapter: he invites her to follow him into night ('To the land that Tristan names') in A♭ minor; she takes up his music and makes it more interesting in her reply. One way she does so is that, while he sticks to A♭ minor, she makes a strange modulation to A minor for her last two lines.

We use the word 'enigma' to indicate the degree of assimilation between the music and poetry in the opera. The technical devices can be described. But to do so without saying that the music is so strange and otherworldly, in the final case so moving, would be to allow attempts at rationalization to falsify the description. As a libretto, *Tristan und Isolde* tries to evoke the transcendent – what is beyond life, the material world, sex and intellectual thought, past explanation, eluding representation. The music has so many transfixing moments, passages like the song the invisible Brangäne sings from her watchtower in Act 2, twice warning Tristan and Isolde that dawn is near, a real song – a song demanded by the fiction – amid the lovers' philosophical-operatic wanderings. Brangäne's song ('Einsam wachend in der Nacht') performs magic in many ways, not least because her melody begins and ends on the same note (D♭/C♯), but the music departs from and returns to this note in a way precisely calculated to create the illusion that beginning and end are very far away from one another, not the same note at all. These moments are, in the larger sense, often themselves enigmas or questions. To turn Wagner's disparaging term back on to him one last time, they are effects without causes. This does not mean they are separate from the drama, in fact quite the opposite: a mystery, as proposed by the drama, is given expression without being answered or contained.

THE RAINBOW BRIDGE

No matter how hard he tried, slogging around Europe to raise funds to build his theatre-cum-shrine at Bayreuth, Wagner could not dictate his own afterlife. At Bayreuth, the dictum that all must remain true to the composer's intentions, indeed to his every whim, continued in some shape or form until the Second World War. After the war, Wagner's grandchildren and then great-grandchildren realized that the Festival needed to establish some distance from the past, particularly the immediate past, in which Bayreuth's links to Hitler had been very strong and very visible. Production values had to be shaken up, and that shaking up had to involve scenic and directorial freedoms. In 1994, on the occasion of a new *Ring* production in Bayreuth, the twelfth since 1876, a conference was held at which Wolfgang Wagner, the composer's grandson, presided. 'Mythos oder Gesellschaftskritik?' (Myth or Social Critique?) was the conference title, which attempted to put names to the principles by which staging should be judged. The title's opposition is a very blunt instrument, and raises a good question: can we stage opera in a way that eludes easy qualification as one or another? Might there be an opera staging that is neither Myth (fairy tale prettiness, fashion runway, archetypes, historical kitsch), nor Social Critique (expose political subtext, reveal ideology, disenchant), nor some amalgam of the two?

In the case of Wagner, the question of how to interpret and understand and therefore stage his operas must engage with an afterlife that is more fraught, more repugnant and richer, than that of any other opera composer. As we shall see in later chapters, at the end of the nineteenth century, French symbolist writers – not to mention Claude Debussy, French symbolist composer – fought the attraction even while pulled into the undertow. Debussy made jokes about Wagner – he ruminated about 'the ghost of old Klingsor' appearing in his musical sketches, he even parodied the opening of the *Tristan* Prelude in his piano piece 'The Golliwog's Cakewalk' (marking the passage to be played *avec une grande émotion*) to prove his irreverence. The ambivalence represented by these gestures turns up in many other guises. There are critics who profess to loathe Wagner and his works yet devote numerous books to explaining him. There are directors who are deeply suspicious of Wagner yet relish the opportunity to stage his work.

We end with a paradox: Wagner's operas were largely conceived as forms of complete artistic control over an audience. They are routinely imagined to be the first theatre pieces in the modern era to enforce absorption, to attempt to erase both the social function of opera-going and the impulse to interpret opera in concrete social or cultural terms. In media theorist Friedrich Kittler's formulation, their mythic libretti and narcotic music are the 'amplifiers [that] put philosophy out of commission'.[19] And yet the history of their performances and staging through the twentieth and twenty-first centuries has proven this to be nonsense. Wagner's works were among the first in the repertory to be subject to irony, challenge and socio-political probing through critical staging. In other words, they have engendered immense interpretative freedom. How is one to account for this phenomenon? Perhaps by the fact that, in such a monumental *oeuvre*, inherent unruliness is to be expected.

Thus Wagner's operatic music can be outdone. This happens, for example, at one moment in the Metropolitan Opera's *Ring* staging of 2010, directed by Robert Lepage, a production generally faithful to the old French grand opera precept that visual effects should astonish. The usual argument about the scenic wonders required by the *Ring* is that staging can only suggest them, since theatre scenery and lighting are bound by material rules and physical limitations. Music will create the awe when, say, the set at the end of *Götterdämmerung* collapses, or Brünnhilde is surrounded by fire at the end of *Die Walküre*. And we must never forget that music will also cover the noise made by the technology when these things happen, as every French grand opera composer knew full well. The end of *Das Rheingold* asks for a Rainbow Bridge, over which the Gods ascend to Valhalla (see Figure 50). For this moment at the end of the opera, Wagner's music is indeed wonderful. Yet when, as at the Met, you see Gods walking *vertically* up the face of a cliff, easily and effortlessly, surrounded by three-dimensional prismatic colour, the primary frisson of wonderment has actually come from something not under Wagner's command. His music was merely an inspiration.

15
Verdi – older still

We left Verdi in his *Rigoletto* years, the early 1850s. From 1842 to 1851 he had written fourteen operas, a burst of activity that would culminate in adding two more, huge successes in their turn: *Il trovatore* (The Troubador) and *La traviata* (The Fallen Woman; both 1853). By then he was near the height of his fame, but the culture of Italian opera production was about to undergo some serious tectonic rearrangements. The 1850s would see the Italian repertory, for the first time in history, begin a slow and inexorable drift towards curatorial revivals. La Scala Milan in these years tells the tale. While a decade before, in the early 1840s, there had been a healthy sprinkling of composers with new operas, the Milan repertory by the 1850s was dominated by revivals of a relatively small number of works, almost all by Rossini, Donizetti, Bellini or Verdi (and with Verdi by far the most popular). In 1850 revivals of Verdi's *Attila*, *Ernani* and *Nabucco* were followed with Bellini's *La sonnambula* and *Norma*, and Rossini's by now hallowed *Il barbiere di Siviglia*. Vincenzo Capecelatro's new opera that year, *David Riccio*, was an unmitigated disaster. One reviewer commented: 'it lacks situations, grandeur, oppositions, contrast and feeling; and ultimately it has no originality, no lyrical, elegiac or tragic power'.[1] And that was just the libretto. Amid competition from increasingly revered masterpieces, writing new operas became ever more perilous.

Aged forty in 1853, Verdi was to have four more decades of professional activity. But during those forty years, just eight operas appeared. Even Wagner managed seven in his (shorter) post-1853 career, and given the size of them he easily comes out ahead of Verdi in sheer opera-hours. What stemmed the flow?

The comparison between Verdi and Rossini, who retired in 1829 at a similar age, would seem inevitable. Increasing financial security was certainly involved in both cases. But with Verdi there was the added distraction of finding himself transformed into a national monument. He was being sculpted into a prominent cultural symbol in Italy's new nation state, which came into being in the early 1860s. Even after the heyday of the 1850s, when most of his pre-*Rigoletto* operas fell out of fashion, their most popular tunes graced recital programmes and enlivened domestic and *al fresco* (often brass-band) entertainment. Some were reinvented in the form of revolutionary symbols. As we saw in Chapter 10, this applied especially to 'Va pensiero', the chorus of Hebrew slaves from Act 3 of *Nabucco*. The piece's gentle nostalgia made it an ideal vehicle for conjuring up a now distant time when progress towards national unity had seemed uncomplicated. That period of communal struggle now became an alluring lost world, one preferable to the present uncertain mood, the strife of Italy's early years as a nation.

Verdi was not averse to furthering this image of himself, supplying 'anecdotal' evidence to the small army of biographers, journalists and other quote-seekers who now crowded around his rustic retreat near Parma. But collaborating in one's own mythmaking and celebrity has its price. Rossini also suffered from celebrity, of course. A more arresting similarity between him and Verdi, however, was shared despondency over a musical world that was changing too fast, and along paths they had no desire to follow. In Rossini's case, unwelcome modernity came with the new, Romantic expressiveness of Donizetti and Bellini. That expressiveness had sounded the death knell for Rossini's own brand of impersonal vocal beauty. For Verdi, the cultural enemy was even more threatening, as it came from outside Italy's new frontier. Fulminate as he might, he could do little to diminish a new Italian fascination for other European operatic styles (first the French, then – worse – the German) that invaded the birthplace of opera just as it achieved nationhood. Gounod's *Faust* reached La Scala in 1862 and was revived many times thereafter. Meyerbeer's *Gli Ugonotti* (*Les Huguenots*) arrived in 1864, Halévy's *L'ebrea* (*La Juive*) came the year after and also became a repertory stalwart. Time and again, from behind the walls of his villa and farmlands, Verdi trumpeted forth his distress at these foreign imports. The French had their *blague* and superciliousness, their over-inflated *grand opéra* – he liked to call the Paris Opéra 'la grand boutique'. The

Germans were worse still: their barbarity and symphonic obsessions theatened to influence and thus destroy native talent. As Verdi grew older and richer, and as he turned towards the political right, his grumpy nationalist conservatism became ever more extreme. When asked what kind of curriculum should govern Italy's new state conservatories, he prescribed the musical equivalent of bread and water, dispensed specifically to blunt the enthusiasms of the nation's impressionable youth. Students, he said, 'must attend *few performances* of modern operas and avoid becoming fascinated either by their many beauties of harmony and orchestration or by the *diminished seventh* chord'. Instead, they should 'practise Fugue constantly, tenaciously, until they are satiated'.[2] In a pedagogic nutshell, here was the old man's eternal lament. Turn back the clock, life isn't what it used to be.

But there was a critical difference between Rossini's and Verdi's later careers. Rossini's operatic retirement was permanent. His last forty years produced not a single new theatrical work. With Verdi the flame refused to go out. Although he constantly threatened Rossini-like farewells to the stage, and although the gaps between each new work grew steadily greater, he kept composing. Even in advanced old age, when his public pronouncements about the sins of modernity were ever more uncompromising, the dramatist and the musician in him kept thinking about how to adjust to changing times. And so, slowly and painfully, those eight new operas came into being. Several of them were misunderstood by their first audiences, and some were temporarily forgotten; but nearly all have now become important planets in our operatic solar system. The compelling vitality that was such a feature of Verdi's early operas migrated underground in the second half of his life. The energy now fed inner compulsions: compulsions to reinvent himself as a symbol of the new nation, certainly; but also to create musical drama that could move audiences whose allegiance was given to a world of changed values.

The sheer variety of the post-*Rigoletto* works remains astonishing. There is no 'older Verdi' style, either in shape or in tone. By comparison, even Wagner's later works are monochrome in their technical means and dramatic exteriors. The most obvious connecting thread is that each opera engages in a dialogue with the past, specifically with the glories of Italy's operatic legacy. Increasingly seen as provincial and uninspiring by the intellectual elite, both within and outside Italy, this legacy – to which the young Verdi had contributed so much – managed to sustain him in maturity and old age. But only just. Operas of the kind Verdi wanted to write – grandiose tragic works of the highest aspirations – became harder and harder to produce as the nineteenth century wore on.

WALTZES AND A WEEPING FATHER

Given the ageing Verdi's regular diatribes against foreign modernity, *La traviata* (1853) harbours ironies aplenty. Principal among them is that it enthusiastically adopts the very latest scandalous foreign fashion. The work on which it was based is Alexandre Dumas *fils*'s play *La Dame aux camélias* (The Lady of the Camellias), first performed in Paris in 1852 only months before the opera itself premiered. The play was immediately seen as an important new moment in French drama. The novelty of Dumas's work (which in turn derived from his 1848 novel of the same name) was not so much its rebellion against Victor Hugo's brand of French Romanticism, a literary movement already moribund by 1850. No, the rebellion hit closer to home. Dumas was jousting with Eugène Scribe, with a bourgeois theatrical tradition made famous by France's most prolific creator of *grand opéra* and *opéra comique* libretti. In flamboyant defiance of Scribean orthodoxy, Dumas rejected a dénouement in which morality triumphs. More than that, he chose contemporary subject matter. His play was set in the present and involved modern-day problems. It was much criticized, and much praised, as an early example of realism.

In gravitating to Dumas's play, Verdi was clearly seeking the means to challenge Italian opera's traditional ground. Romantic plots of heroism and love, set in a remote historical past, were waved aside. This story tackled a social issue urgently debated at the time, that of prostitution and the spread of disease in the ever more crowded nineteenth-century city. At the opera's premiere, the Venetian censors insisted that it be staged in an early eighteenth-century milieu, putting its social critique at a comfortable remove. Verdi, however, wanted *La traviata* set in the time and place of Dumas's novel and play, wanted it to evoke the modern metropolis, the ambivalent symbol of a 'progress' whose blessings were mixed.

35. The travails of modern opera. Janáček's *Jenůfa* was written between 1894 and 1902 and first performed in Brno in 1904. The sheer difficulty of his task, and his multiple changes of mind, are graphically illustrated on this page of his sketches for the opera.

36. Enrico Caruso (1873–1921) as Cavaradossi in Puccini's *Tosca* (1900). For many at the time Caruso defined the idea of the heroic tenor. He was one of the first and most astute of a generation of singers who exploited new gramophone technology to enhance their fame.

37. Geraldine Farrar (1882–1967) as Suor Angelica, a role she created in Puccini's 1918 opera. Farrar, one of the most popular sopranos of her day (her followers in New York were called 'Gerry-flappers'), recorded widely and even starred in a 1915 silent film of *Carmen*, directed by Cecil B. De Mille.

38. Lauritz Melchior (1890–1973) as 'world famous Danish tenor Olstrom' in the movie *Two Sisters from Boston* (1946), recording the Prize Song from Wagner's *Die Meistersinger*. The film is set in the early 1900s, this scene re-creating the recording processes of the time.

39. Costume for Mélisande by Erté (Romain de Tirtoff, 1892–1990), the Russian-born French artist and designer. This art deco design for the Metropolitan Opera in 1927 captures the darker undertones of Debussy's opera: light beams as icicles threaten impalement, and the heroine's rope-like hair is as much a noose as an adornment.

40. Hugo von Hofmannstahl with Strauss in a 1914 silhouette by Willi Bithorn. By this time, the two had collaborated on *Elektra* (1909), *Der Rosenkavalier* (1911) and the first version of *Ariadne auf Naxos* (1912).

41. Nadja Michael as Salome and Duncan Meadows as the Executioner in David McVicar's 2007/8 production of Strauss's opera at London's Royal Opera House, by which time the opera had been giving trouble in London for nearly a century. When Thomas Beecham attempted to get it staged in 1910, Jokanaan's severed head had to be replaced by a bloody sword. When that proved too messy, a tray (sans head) was substituted.

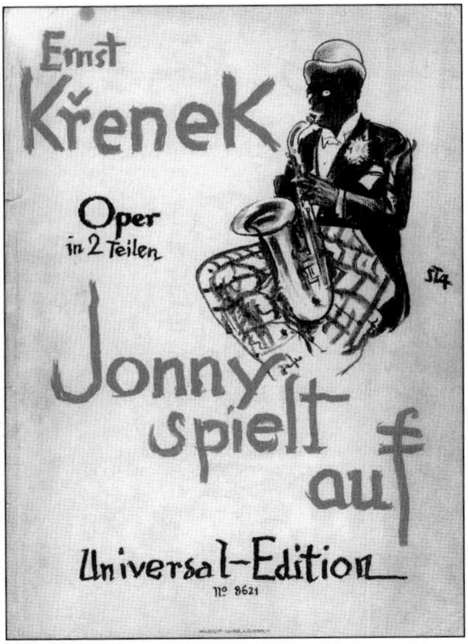

42. The vocal score of Ernst Krenek's *Jonny spielt auf* (1927). Unsurprisingly, given its jazz-influenced subject, the opera was banned in Germany six years later.

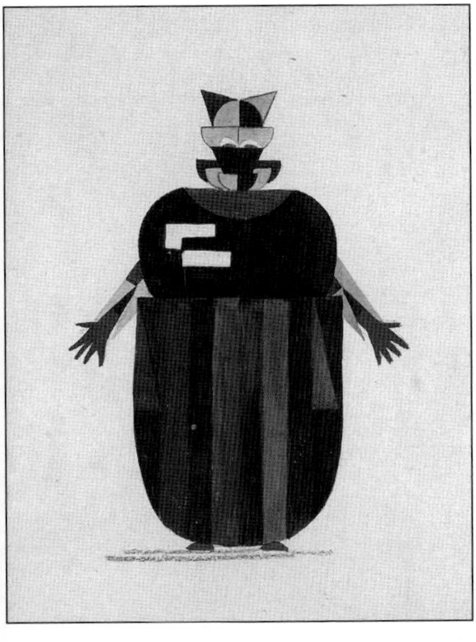

43 and 44. Costume designs by Eduard Milén for the first production of Janáček's *The Cunning Little Vixen* (Brno, 1924).

We are alone, O angel mine!

45. In René Clair's musical comedy, *Le Million* (1931), an opera called *Les Bohémiens* is staged. The tenor's opening vocal salvo, 'We are alone, O angel mine!', is received with bewilderment by the nearby brigands. *Le Million* pays tribute to opera's enchanting absurdity as well as its transformative force.

46. One of the Hamburg opera houses in 1945, lying in ruins after an Allied bombing raid. It was not rebuilt until 1955.

47. John Adams's *Nixon in China* (1987), at its Metropolitan Opera premiere (2011), directed by Peter Sellars. This scene illustrates the opera's epic treatment of an episode (and a notably vilified protagonist) from recent history.

48. The tenor Neil Shicoff as Peter Grimes in Willy Decker's production of Britten's opera at Turin's Teatro Regio (2009/10). One of the last operas to become a firm part of the operatic repertory, *Grimes* has proved itself readily adaptable to a variety of staging fashions.

49. Leaving the opera. In this lithograph from the early 1880s, the audience (and possibly some costumed characters) depart after an evening at the Paris Opéra 'in the year 2000'. Open-top aerial transport (goggles optional) was the order of the imagined future.

50. A final glance. The Gods walk vertically up the rainbow bridge in Robert Lepage's 2010 staging of Wagner's *Das Rheingold* at New York's Metropolitan Opera. Froh looks back. Whether this is in allusion to Orpheus, or a gesture of nostalgia and loss, or merely to check the position of the other body doubles, is poignantly uncertain.

La traviata was thus Italian opera's first brush with urban modernity. Act 1 introduces Violetta Valéry (soprano), a pleasure-loving courtesan afflicted with tuberculosis, a disease commonly thought to be consequent upon loose metropolitan morals. During a no-holds-barred party, she flirts with young Alfredo Germont (tenor), who has fallen in love with her. Act 2 takes place some months later; Alfredo and Violetta have set up house together in the country. Life and love are idyllic until Germont senior (baritone) appears. In a fraught interview, he demands that Violetta renounce Alfredo in order to protect the Germont family reputation. She tearfully agrees and returns to Paris. Alfredo (believing she has deserted him for another lover) pursues her there and publicly insults her. More months have passed by the time of Act 3. Violetta is now desperately ill. She is finally reconciled with Alfredo, who has discovered the true reason she left him; but in the final moments of the opera she falls dead at his feet.

Although we know from Verdi's letters that the subject's contemporaneity had attracted him, the basic musical shapes in *La traviata* hardly respond to its radical subject matter. Not very different in its formal types from the operas that preceded it, *La traviata* has its share of lyrical adagios, exuberant cabalettas, long, multi-movement duets and grand ensembles. But this outward conformity masks two ways in which it breaks new ground. The first is in what the French called *couleur locale* (local colour), the rich musical colouration that conjures up a particular geographical location. In *La traviata*, Verdi found a new sense of dramatic potential in these colours. *Rigoletto*, which premiered only a couple of years earlier, was eventually set in sixteenth-century Mantua, even though Verdi wrote the music thinking it would be in eighteenth-century France. He complained about the shift in locale, which was demanded by government censors fearing revolutionary parallels; but in the end no great harm was done. Hardly any of the music jars in its new surroundings, quite simply because it is geographically and temporally neutral, making no gestures towards a specific time or a certain place. *La traviata* is different. The opera's setting in the Parisian demimonde is obsessively highlighted by the simplest of musical means, by continual reference to the quintessential symbol of nineteenth-century social velocity and uncertainty, the waltz.

Here's how one American, breathless and – one might guess – a little flushed, observed a Parisian ball in 1847. It was a court event, and so probably more decorous than Violetta's Act 1 party, but even so the sheer visceral excitement leaps off the page:

> To see so many persons, elegant and richly attired, at once entangled in the dance; crossing, pursuing and overtaking each other; now at rest, now in movement; and seeming to have no other movement than that communicated by the music; and to see a hundred couples twirling around in the waltz, with airy feet that seem scarcely to kiss the slippery boards; first flushed and palpitating; then wearying by degrees, and retiring, to the last pair, to the last one – she the most healthful, graceful and beautiful of the choir, her partner's arm sustaining her taper waist, foot against foot, knee against knee, in simultaneous movement, turns and turns, till nature at length overcome, she languishes, she faints, she dies![3]

Such a description could almost be of the opening scene of *La traviata*, in which the constant, driving waltz rhythms propel a similar sense of excess, with life in the big city moving dangerously fast. More important, though, this opening sequence is not an isolated section, not merely the scene-setting preliminary common in earlier Italian opera. Far from it, Violetta's entire musical personality is conceived in waltz rhythms. Not only does *La traviata*'s special ambience saturate the music but – crucially – this ambience is absorbed by the opera's heroine, fusing her with her setting.

In this sense, Violetta is unlike the other main characters of this or any other opera of the period. Take for example the obsessive trills that become a prime symbol of both of the salon and of Violetta's fanatical gaiety in Act 1, from the first bars of the opening scene through to the heroine's frantic celebrations in the closing cabaletta, 'Sempre libera' (Forever free). More subtle, but equally marked, is Violetta's famous Act 3 aria, 'Addio, del passato' (Farewell, of the past), which continues in the same vein, even if with telling musical refractions to suit her weakened state. The waltz rhythms are still there in the accompaniment, but now they are hesitant and fragmentary, accompanied by a doleful cor anglais that completes her phrases as her strength fails.

This is a devastating aria. But Verdi was shifting his attention from exquisite solo expression, towards ensemble clashes and confrontation. Confontations give rise to battles between opposing vocal forces, and the imperative to give musical expression to antagonism would in time break several old formal moulds. In *La traviata* the great hostile encounter comes in Act 2 between Violetta and Germont senior. In it, Verdi turns his back on his former ways and means for personifying women and men on the operatic stage. The younger Verdi was at his most characteristic when he minimized differences between the sexes, in particular by creating a new, more forceful idiom for his soprano heroines. *La traviata*, though, addresses the question from another angle. Its plot, after all, confronts some of the most vexed issues surrounding sexuality, not least whether women had the right to choose their own destinies. These were matters that preoccupied people at the time, but had never before been raised so overtly on the operatic stage.

Where Verdi the man stood concerning such moral issues is not easy to fathom. There are hints in his correspondence he occasionally frequented prostitutes, notably a 'Sior Toni' in Venice. His partner, Giuseppina Strepponi, had had three illegitimate children during her career as an operatic soprano, and thus certainly knew what it was to be on the wrong side of a perceived moral divide. Simple equations between biography and musical/cultural attitudes are, then, fairly easy to make, and *La traviata* has been a favourite spot for those wanting to do so. But the supposed resonances are, as always, dulled by the way in which emotions are packaged into conventional formal units in Italian opera. One point is clear. The misogyny of Dumas's novel, which is told throughout from a male point of view, is inevitably softened in the play, where Violetta appears as a character onstage; and it is softened even further in the opera. To use a distinction we've made several times already in this book, Verdi's version of the story makes 'voice-Violetta' the unambiguous centre of attention. The composer was evidently more interested in her than in the male principals, who are wooden and one-dimensional by comparison.

Does Violetta nevertheless suffer from *musical* misogyny? In terms that recall those debates about Lucia's mad scene mentioned in Chapter 9, it is possible to argue that she does. In the first act, for example, she may be prominent but she lacks musical agency, even musical independence. The famous *brindisi* (toast) that enlivens her Act 1 party is launched by Alfredo, Violetta merely repeating it after him; and in the ensuing love duet the tenor is again granted the musical power of invention – he states the main themes and then looks on admiringly as Violetta releases a shower of ornament around them. Even in her act-ending aria, Alfredo's voice again intrudes, insistently reminding us of his musical presence. Such arguments are in many ways attractive. They offer a powerful way of understanding the opera within today's cultural context, and modern stage directors frequently echo them. But is there a sense in which this reading seriously underplays voice-Violetta? At the least, an opposite interpretation of the passages is possible. The *brindisi* may be sung first by Alfredo, but it is more suited to Violetta's vocal capabilities – in performance, her verse almost invariably sounds more convincing. And in the love duet, Alfredo may introduce the melodies, but Violetta makes them *alive* by decorating them and altering them to suit her character. Similarly, at the end of Act 1 the hero's melody is heard only in the distance, while Violetta's reactions are immediate and impressive; she, after all, is centre stage; and – to be prosaic – she gets the bulk of the applause when the scene finishes. And so the argument could go on, each negative interpretation countered by a positive twin. As so often, we need something better than these simple equations between music and meaning.

All of which can bring us to that central, confrontational duet between Violetta and Germont in Act 2. In conventional feminist terms this is where plot-Violetta is crushed by patriarchal authority. The voice of the father requires her sacrifice on the altar of conventional morality: she obeys, and is rewarded by flamboyant insults from her lover (later in Act 2) and by poverty and a painful death (Act 3). Told in these terms the opera fully endorses dominant mid-nineteenth-century attitudes to female sexuality and freedom: one might even say it *celebrates* them – makes them into an object of aesthetic pleasure, to be enjoyed in the theatre. But what does Verdi, Verdi the composer of music, have to do with this?

When the Violetta–Germont duet starts, the music seems to be articulating gender stereotypes. The first few minutes stage an emotional dialogue, with contrasting sections dominated in turn by one character and then the other. The musical difference is clear. Germont's opening melody, 'Pura siccome un angelo' (Pure like an angel), describes his immaculate daughter, and is the very essence of stability and self-assurance – a patriarchal voice made musical. The regular tread of the accompaniment, the predictability of the phrases, the way in which the wind instruments support the voice to round off phrases; all this gestures in one direction, painting a picture of rationality and above all conventionality. Violetta's answer, 'Non sapete quale affetto' (You don't know what feelings), is in obvious contrast. It is a succession of brief, hurried vocal phrases, full of sighing figures that draw attention to the body uttering them, with unpredictable leaps and dynamic shifts underpinned by a hesitant, off-beat accompaniment.

This contrasting musical conversation continues through the first part of the duet, as Germont wears down Violetta's resistance. But at the moment of Violetta's capitulation, as she agrees to renounce Alfredo, there is a marvellous reversal. Violetta sings 'Dite alla giovine' (Tell the young girl), asking Germont to let his daughter know of her sacrifice. And, schooled by the duet so far, we are ready to hear her vocal differences maintained and heightened. Instead, the musical roles are inverted. Violetta's line is marked *piangendo* (weeping) in the score, but it is stable and predictable, with a conventional accompaniment. What's more, the melody develops over a long arc through several phrases, having far more emotional force than Germont was granted earlier. By contrast, Germont's answer, 'Piangi, piangi' (Weep, weep), is in short, sobbing phrases that graphically mimic the bodily gesture of weeping. His words may say that he is magnanimously allowing her to cry ('piangi, o misera' – weep, unhappy woman), but the music tells us that Germont is gasping out in feminine tears, while Violetta serenely rewrites herself and her destiny.

The power of this musical reversal, the force of her long melody and of Germont's incoherent sobs, are hard to dismiss. 'Dite alla giovine' has a calm beauty that makes it the still point in this scene, indeed in the entire opera; and from within that still point we hear Violetta, solemnly addressing an unknown woman. If we agree that this moment is the crux of the opera, the moment around which the action hinges, then one-dimensional answers to *La traviata*'s questions about gender will be unsatisfactory. Verdi's setting tells us that, at least in this fictional world articulated through music, every relationship of power is fragile. It is a message that all operas can potentially articulate, and contributes to the art form's remarkable ability to communicate across cultural and chronological divides.

Given the forward-looking nature of *La traviata*, one might imagine that subsequent years would see something of a retrenchment. But circumstances, together with Verdi's mid-life creative verve, dictated constant experimentation. First he tried a Parisian *grand opéra*, *Les Vêpres siciliennes* (The Sicilian Vespers, 1855). The next opera, *Simon Boccanegra* (1857), makes yet another departure, both from *Les Vêpres* and from the earlier Italian works. There are few traces of the Gallic mode in this rhapsody to the dour side of Italian opera. Only glance at the cast list, and gloom is evident – there are no secondary female roles, and a small army of low male voices. The sombre mood becomes more obvious still in the extreme economy of the vocal writing, with declamation more prominent than ever before. Next came yet another volte face: if *Simon Boccanegra* is single-minded and monochromatic, then *Un ballo in maschera* (A Masked Ball, 1859) is a potpourri masterpiece. After his experiment in *Vêpres* – a largely unadulterated version of French *grand opéra* – Verdi here gestured to the lighter side of French opera, in particular the *opéra comique* of Auber and his contemporaries. The juxtaposition of this style with a newly intense, interior version of Italian serious opera is extremely bold and, as we saw in Chapter 13, offers further evidence that it was not only the grandest French genre that was influential on European opera in the later century.

Like *Ballo*, *La forza del destino* (The Force of Destiny, 1862, revised 1869) quilts many styles and modes together. An episodic plot and extended geographical and temporal span are matched by an astonishing range of operatic manners: post-Rossinian *opera buffa* from the comic priest Fra Melitone (baritone); *opéra comique* from the camp-follower Preziosilla (mezzo-soprano); Meyerbeerian scenes of religious grandeur; and at the centre a classic soprano–tenor–baritone love-triangle in the best Italian manner. The opera is Verdi's most daring attempt at what he would later call 'mosaic' drama.[4] Its disparate parts hang together, as much through an abstract idea – the 'fate' (*destino*) of the title – as by the progress of individual characters. After *Forza* came a further attempt to scale the citadel of Paris's home of *grand opéra*. The result this time was *Don Carlo*s, not notably more successful with the Parisian public and critics. With *Don Carlos* Verdi, stood accused of Wagnerism, but in the later twentieth century the work came to be seen as the greatest *grand opéra* of them all.

EXOTIC IMMOBILITY

After all these wildly experimental operas, *Aida* (1870) may seem like Verdi's vacation from eclecticism. Judged against the narrative diffusions of a *Don Carlos* or a *Forza del destino*, the libretto is plain and simple, even though the spectacular scenic world of *grand opéra* is obvious in its genealogy. *Aida*, whose scenario was dreamed up by a French Egyptologist, was commissioned for the opening of the Cairo Opera House. It is set in Memphis and Thebes 'during the reign of the Pharaohs'. Verdi refused to attend the premiere, joking that he was afraid of mummification;[5] and his opera, for all its magnificence, does indeed have an immobilized quality. A state of war exists between civilized Egypt and savage Ethiopia. Radames (tenor), an Egyptian captain, is loved by Princess Amneris (mezzo-soprano) but is in love with the captured Ethiopian slave Aida (soprano), who is later revealed as the daughter of the Ethiopian king, Amonasro (baritone). In other words, we have a reiteration of the old love vs duty plot. Radames is lured by Aida into giving away a military secret and for this crime is sentenced to be entombed beneath the temple. The final scene requires a split stage, the temple above, the tomb below. When Radames enters the tomb he finds Aida there, determined to die with him. The lovers end the opera singing gently together of love and death; Amneris hovers above, murmuring a requiem.

Aida used to be Verdi's most popular late opera, performed far more often than *Don Carlos* or *La forza del destino*, whose sprawling plots and uncommon length caused them to be dubbed 'problem' pieces. For the first half of the twentieth century it was something like the epitome of Grand Opera: the Act 2 triumphal scene (Radames, the victorious warrior, brings back Amonasro in chains), with its exotic dancers, massed ranks of spear carriers, opportunities for elephant extras, and famous march and trumpet tune, were enjoyed by audiences who found Wagner or even Mozart forbiddingly elite. A late mark of this fame was a 1953 screen version, directed by the aptly named Clemente Fracassi (*fracasso* means 'loud noise' in Italian), in which the opera is given a filmic makeover. We see nothing of the singers who provide the soundtrack (a stellar cast led by Renata Tebaldi as Aida); instead, film icons of the day gesture their way through the plot, often hardly attempting to suggest that singing is heavy work, requiring open mouth and heaving chest. Sophia Loren blacks up decorously as Aida (and if that sounds implausible, Gina Lollobrigida was considered for the role). Such a film would be impossible now: it's a relic of the *Treasury of Grand Opera* days, a time when epic cinema was so close to Grand Opera that the transposition could be tolerated. Viewers who enjoyed *Ben Hur* could be easily drawn into a film world in which sounds produced by Renata Tebaldi came from the mouth of Sophia Loren.

But if the 1950s marked the height of *Aida*'s popularity, recently it has been in decline. This is a matter of sheer expense, of course, but the opera is also out of season because now we are uncomfortable with the subject matter, all those slaves and Pharaohs and general Egyptian kitsch. The case was made eloquently by the cultural critic Edward Said, who in a famous essay argued that *Aida* was implicated in nineteenth-century colonial expansion. For him the opera was an example of Orientalism, the means by which Western colonial powers have, over the last centuries, differentiated themselves from, and so managed to think themselves superior to, non-Western cultures. For Said, '*Aida* can be enjoyed and interpreted as a kind of curatorial art, whose rigour and unbending frame recall, with relentless mortuary logic, a precise historical moment and a specifically dated aesthetic form, an imperial spectacle designed to alienate and impress an almost exclusively European audience'.[6]

The accusation of exoticism could of course be directed at many works of art from many periods, and can raise intense passions, these days particularly among those who feel that they derive from such works something like pure aesthetic pleasure, a pleasure that risks being damaged by what they call 'political' readings. We have met exotic operatic locales in earlier chapters – the Turkish ambience of Mozart's *Die Entführung aus dem Serail* (The Abduction from the Seraglio, 1782) is an obvious example – but during the later nineteenth century, as Europe's global adventures became more wide-ranging, such settings were popular in art of many kinds. What's more, a precise sense of geographical locale became increasingly important to opera at just the same time, with Verdi's works again no exception. In short, *Aida* obsesses about its exotic ambience. What is more, its genesis not only intersects with but was dependent on colonialism. What's disputable, though, is whether the opera should be held accountable for the circumstances of its birth; and also – more important – whether Verdi's musical treatment of the exotic ambience is so easily co-opted into Said's Orientalist reading.

The matter emerges at the very start of Act 1, in the opera's most famous aria. Radames sings 'Celeste Aida' in reaction to news that he will lead the Egyptian army against the invading Ethiopians. Although excited by the prospect of military conflict, his thoughts turn to a fantastic vision of Aida as a goddess:

Celeste Aida, forma divina,
Mistico raggio, di luce e fior,
Del mio pensiero, tu sei regina,
Tu di mia vita sei lo splendor.
Il tuo bel cielo vorrei ridarti,
Le dolci brezze del patrio suol;
Un regal serto sul crin posarti
Ergerti un trono vicino al sol!

[Celestial Aida, divine form, / mystic ray of light and flower, / you are the queen / of my thoughts, / you are the splendour of my life. / I want to give back to you your beautiful skies, / the sweet breezes of your homeland; / place a regal garland on your head, / erect a throne for you next to the sun.]

The multi-movement entrance arias of Verdi's early operas are now a thing of the past. Audiences, composers and critics all agreed that it was now artificial to stand alone onstage and sing through a sequence of musical forms, each with its own beginning, middle and end. Instead, Radames has a one-movement aria, here called a Romance. Although the poetry is in two four-line stanzas, Verdi brings back the first stanza at the end, thus making the piece an ABA form, something resembling the international norm for operatic solos.

The main melody, 'Celeste Aida, forma divina', uses singsong half-rhymes and internal repetition to echo a rising melodic shape, one that mimics the idea of putting Aida on a mystic pedestal. What rescues this from banality is its orchestration. A flute in its lowest register doubles the voice, contributing barely heard atmospheric colour; very high violin tremolos (just two soloists) round off each phrase. The combination of these unconventional instrumental effects spelt 'exotic' in the vocabulary of the day. Unexciting melodic material is thus locked in a slow dance with novel orchestral colour, and it would be easy – too easy – to reach for Said and interpret this as an Orientalist move. The colonized Aida is reduced to primitive status (the simple melody), which then allows pleasure to be drawn in the colourful exterior (those low flutes and high violins) in which she is wrapped. Too simple a reading, yes: but nowhere else in Verdi is the slow dance between substance and colour enacted quite like this.

After a short 'B' section, the 'Celeste Aida' music returns to round off the ternary form. But at the end of the aria Verdi adds another statement of the 'B' section and then a coda. The latter is extraordinary: the stratospheric solo violins and low flutes reappear, and Radames' closing image, of a throne near the sun for his beloved, takes him with obvious word-painting to a final, high B♭. In the score this note is marked *pp morendo* (very quiet, dying away): Radames is instructed, in other words, to *disappear* into the orchestral ambience that has been so important to the aria. (The effect is very close to the end of José's Act 2 Flower Song in *Carmen*, discussed in Chapter 13.) From very early in the history of *Aida* performances, those singing Radames, one of Verdi's most strenuous tenor roles, have hated this *pp morendo*. Most of them simply ignore the instruction, singing the note in full voice with bulging neck and reddening face, thereby drowning out the delicate orchestral effects. It's worth wondering why they choose to do this. Of course, the opportunity to trumpet out a high B♭ – if you have the ability – is not to be ignored lightly; but many tenors over the years have, in other musical contexts, demonstrated just how effective *pianissimo* high notes can also be. (John McCormack, one of the greatest star tenors of the inter-war years, made a splendid career specializing in just that.) Here, though, something makes the moment highly charged. It's as if a quiet, floated B♭ would suggest that Radames, in spite of his military ambitions and the trumpets that blare around him, is not fully in control of his fantasy about Aida. Just like those gender reversals in *La traviata*, the music can pose difficult questions, in this case – perhaps – questions as basic as who is enslaving whom. True, the message may still be Orientalist, but certainly not in the crude manner of *Aida*'s plot.

That earlier quotation from Said used a strange adjective, mentioning *Aida*'s 'mortuary logic'. The idea that the 'reign of the Pharaohs' was impossibly removed from modern concerns surely accounts for the opera's static splendour, its sense of being somehow buried and inert, despite its new orchestral technologies and moments of grand passion. This feeling is at its strongest in the final scene, in which the two lovers sing out their last moments incarcerated beneath the temple. Their duet offers an end-piece to match 'Celeste Aida', this time with both principals heading towards the bright sun:

O terra addio, addio valle di pianti . . .
Sogno di gaudio che in dolor svanì.
A noi schiude il ciel e l'alme erranti,
Volano al raggio dell'eterno dì.

[Farewell, earth, farewell valley of tears . . . / Dream of joy that disappeared in sorrow. / Heaven closes on us and the errant souls / fly to the ray of eternal day.]

As with Radames' first aria, there is a disarming simplicity here. In earlier, brasher days, Verdi might have inserted a showy final cabaletta, and in some ways this piece is cabaletta-like in its progress: the same tune is sung first by Aida, then by Radames, then by both in unison. What's more, the vocal writing is extremely simple, just a two-bar melody that seems to be repeated endlessly. But the emotional exuberance for which cabalettas are famous is nowhere to be found. The tempo is slow; the delicate orchestra is *pp* almost throughout; and, most unusual, the two-bar melody is extremely angular, with an exceptional stretch at the start and a difficult, augmented fourth interval in the middle.

This ending is unlike any other Verdian finale. On the one hand, it extends the message of 'Celeste Aida' by making the characters disappear into the ambience. Far from closing with a grand gesture, they fade away, caught in endless, mysterious repetition and thus in the grip of another cliché through which the West has imagined other cultures. However, there may be a further angle to this 'mortuary' feeling, one closer to home. The words tell us that this is a farewell to life, but the music and the biographical context suggest another kind of leavetaking. Verdi had been threatening to retire from the rapidly changing, technology-fuelled world of international opera for more than a decade; he had even described his career before 1860 as 'years in the galley',[7] his compositions those of a mere slave to the opera industry. Something always brought him back during the 1860s; but after *Aida* he acted on his threat. At the age of fifty-eight, in his prime as a composer, he stopped writing operas. 'O terra addio' – farewell, familiar ground. And then there are all those oblique references to the glory days of Italian opera, when cabaletta-rich *Il trovatore* could be seen, as Verdi himself said, 'in the heart of Africa or the Indies'.[8] *Aida*'s final duet could thus have been a very personal leavetaking, of an operatic world for ever changed.

OTELLO, FALSTAFF AND THE INTANGIBLE DIVIDE

Verdi's retirement after *Aida* was, as it turned out, merely a prolonged sabbatical. In the 1880s the operatic spark again ignited. In spite of the chronological gap, his last two operas (*Otello* in 1887 and *Falstaff* in 1893, both based on Shakespearean subjects) perhaps self-consciously recapture old habits and wiles. Although he was now an international celebrity who could – and did – dictate his terms, Verdi continued to compose in the antique manner, in the sense of paying attention to the singers at his disposal, being willing to adjust passages to accommodate them. He even used shards of old operatic forms from time to time. But such continuities can be deceptive. Between *Aida* in 1871 and *Otello* in 1887 opera in every country was moving inexorably away from previous comfort zones. At some moment between the two operas, we can guess that Verdi, like so many other composers, crossed an intangible divide.

What marked the crossing? Throughout its history, opera had articulated drama by an alternation between action (musically less complex, reliant on some form of declamation) and reflection (the moments in which music could expand). Now, and although there always remained vestiges of the division, opera became a matter of continuous motion, as musical activity matched activity in other realms: passing time, antagonism and confrontation, or the unspooling of emotions. Wagner and his followers sometimes labelled this new style as 'unendliche Melodie' (infinite melody), and in some ways that term suits late Verdi equally well. In *Otello*, the long Act 2 duet between Otello (tenor) and Iago (baritone) is a good example of how the new disposition worked. The duet, in which Otello gradually becomes convinced that his wife Desdemona (soprano) has committed adultery, cannot easily be parcelled out as an old-fashioned set piece in contrasting movements. It darts around too fluidly. There are indeed set pieces in this act of *Otello* – a 'Racconto' (Narrative) for Iago, a Homage Chorus to Desdemona and a Quartet – but these numbers are embedded in moving waves, and they are interruptions rather than places of repose.

The changes in Verdi's style were inevitably linked to Wagner, even though Verdi's nationalist convictions made him wary of Wagnerism and loud in rejecting its lure. However, he would be involuntarily caught up in recent European trends by means of an extraordinary relationship with his last librettist, Arrigo Boito (1842–1918). The partnership had started as early as 1862, when the two men worked amicably together on an *Inno delle nazioni* for the second Great Exhibition in London. But considering the generational gap, a more predictable exchange occurred a year later. Boito, a leading figure among Italian bohemians, the so-called *scapigliatura*, improvised an Ode 'To Italian Art' that described its 'altar' as 'defiled like the wall of a brothel'.[9] Verdi took this personally; nor was he further disposed towards the young firebrand by some cool journalistic reviews that Boito published about Verdian revivals.

That rocky start holds a key, in that a significant aspect of the Boito–Verdi collaboration was that they came from different generations. Verdi had grown up in an environment hardly affected by foreign influences, in which new Italian works were the staple of every opera house, and in which there was much formal similarity between individual works. In the 1870s and 1880s that world finally disappeared. As the Italian state fell into parlous economic and (he felt) artistic decline, Verdi's skin became thinner, his temper shorter; and his production of new operas ceased altogether. Boito's generation was precisely the problem, powerfully influenced as they were by French *grand opéra* and later by Wagner. As the 'brothel' episode indicates, Boito and his bohemian friends tended to think of Italian music of the first half of the nineteenth century – with Verdi the inevitable figurehead – as embarrassingly provincial, a world of dusty velvet swags and distasteful financial Realpolitik.

Their collaboration on *Otello* reflects the fact that Boito had mellowed by the late 1870s. His magnum opus, the opera *Mefistofele*, failed disastrously at La Scala in 1868. When he restaged it seven years later he had toned down many of its most radical aspects, replacing them with more palatable operatic solutions. But there was still that generational gap. Early work on *Otello* was punctuated by sharp differences of opinion. A recurring problem was the end of Act 3, in which Otello, now in a jealous fury, confronts Desdemona publicly in a scene that had all the trappings of an old-fashioned *concertato finale*. In his first letter to Boito about the project, commenting on Boito's draft libretto, Verdi suggested that the 'dramatic element' was missing. After a traditional set piece ensemble in which all on stage react to Otello's striking of Desdemona, he suggested a radical departure from Shakespeare:

> Suddenly distant drums, trumpets, cannon-fire, etc., etc. . . . 'The Turks! The Turks!!' . . . Otello shakes himself like a lion and draws himself erect; he brandishes his sword and, addressing Lodovico, says: 'Come on! I will lead you to victory again.' . . . They all leave the stage except Desdemona . . . isolated and motionless, her eyes turned to Heaven, [she] prays for Otello.[10]

True to the theatrical conventions of his past, Verdi sketched here an external event that would lead the musical action onwards, provide some impetus to break the musical spell he would weave around the great communal reaction to Otello's violence.

Boito, for whom *Otello* was above all a modern, claustrophobic, psychological drama, was horrified:

> Otello is like a man moving in circles beneath an incubus . . . if we invent something that must necessarily rouse Otello and distract him from this incubus . . . we destroy all the sinister fascination created by Shakespeare. . . . That attack of the Turks is like a fist breaking the window of a room where two people are dying of asphyxiation.[11]

The decadent imagery, of Otello 'moving beneath an incubus', and especially of that couple expiring (more *Tristan*-like than *Aida*-like) in a sealed room, says it all. For Boito the drama took place essentially within the psyche, in the realm of what Wagnerians liked to call the 'inner drama'. But what is most arresting about the disagreement is that Verdi – who had earlier been a veritable tyrant in dealings with librettists – gave way to Boito, trusting his perception of modern drama. What is more, this trust obliged him to do nothing less than reinvent his operatic language, find a newly flexible, rapidly changing mode of musical expression. With many anxious glances backwards, Verdi cautiously made his way across the intangible divide.

In Boito and Verdi's struggle to establish common ground, there was one binding point of contact. For Boito, true to his modern heritage (and again Wagner's influence comes to mind), operatic characters were above all abstract symbols. 'Jago è l'Invidia', he wrote in a published description of the characters: 'Iago is Envy';[12] Desdemona wasn't a mere woman, she was also a symbol of female purity. Nothing might seem further from Verdi's practical conception of theatre than this abstract, self-consciously meaningful attitude. But then, in a late letter about the opera, the composer offered his own remarkable gloss on his three main characters:

> Desdemona is a part in which the thread, the melodic line never ceases from the first note to the last. Just as Jago has only to declaim and *ricaner*, and just as Otello, now the warrior, now the passionate lover, now crushed to the point of baseness, now ferocious like a savage, must sing and shout, so Desdemona must always, always sing.[13]

The letter is fascinating because it suggests that Verdi had channelled Boito's tendency towards the symbolic and the interior to his own ends, in this case fashioning the violent conflict between the characters into a parable about the violent upheavals of Italian *fin-de-siècle* musical drama. The opera's principals musically embody the conflicting demands of the lyrical and the declamatory. Iago, the modern man, is constantly declamatory: when he sings beautifully, it is merely to deceive. Desdemona, on the other hand, is a symbol of that lost time when *bel canto* was at the centre of theatrical communication. Otello, like Verdi himself, is caught agonizingly between the new and the old. But, despite or even because of this, the ageing composer managed to renew himself, symbolically imagining his creative struggle in the opera's clash of personalities.

Whatever Verdi's intentions, it was of course inevitable that *Otello* and then *Falstaff*, his last opera, and his only comic work since *Un giorno di regno* (King for a Day, 1840, a youthful failure), were judged by comparison with Wagner. Verdi was yesterday's man, Wagner was the model for the future. Some went against the tide and bravely proclaimed a Verdian challenge to Wagnerian mists and Teutonism. The French critic Camille Bellaigue called *Falstaff* 'a masterpiece of *Latin*, classical genius'.[14] Boito proudly displayed his awareness of contemporary German philosophy by alluding to Nietzsche's critique of Wagner: 'the human spirit must be "Mediterraneanized"; only there is true progress'.[15] But the majority, finding the operas so unlike Verdi's earlier music, concluded that he had succumbed. The famous musicologist Hugo Riemann, writing in 1901, was one of them: 'A significant change of style separates "late" Verdi from the works of his middle period. This, quite frankly, is to be traced to the influence of Richard Wagner.'[16] Verdi was by now used to this kind of opinion – accusations of Wagnerism had beset him as early as the Parisian premiere of *Don Carlos* in 1867 – but they never ceased to enrage. As he once said, to work in the theatre for forty years and still be called an *imitator* was galling indeed.[17]

But what *was* Verdi's attitude to Wagner? Amid the polemics flying back and forth, it is difficult – even after more than a century – to arrive at a balanced view. Consider this famous letter from Verdi to his publisher, Giulio Ricordi. It is dated 14 February 1883, the day after Wagner had died in Venice:

> Sad. Sad. Sad!
>
> Wagner is dead!
>
> Reading the news yesterday, I was, I don't know, struck with terror. Let's not talk about it. – A great individual has disappeared! A name that has left a most powerful mark on the history of art![18]

This letter, on the surface quite simple, is in several ways rather odd. Its melodramatic opening ('Triste. Triste. Triste! Wagner è morto!'), with its ghostly echoes of the title of Wagner's most famous opera, reads like the opening lines of a grand lamenting aria; later, its uncertain searching for words suggests genuine involvement mixed with genuine confusion (he feels 'terror' rather than the conventional 'regret' or 'sorrow'). But the most significant moment is at the close. The handwritten original shows us that Verdi first wrote 'has left a powerful [*potente*] mark', but then crossed out 'powerful' and wrote over the top '*most* powerful' (*potentissima*). Just how important *was* Wagner? Verdi was revealingly unsure of where to pitch his rhetoric.

As the 1880s rolled on, and as Wagner*ism* took hold ever more powerfully, Verdi's attitude hardened. Time and again he inveighed against the Wagnerian style that was now pan-European, and had turned the heads of young Italian composers. A typical jeremiad, from the late 1880s:

> Our young Italian composers are not good patriots. If the Germans, starting out with Bach, have arrived at Wagner, they're acting like good Germans, and do the right thing. But we descendants of Palestrina, if we imitate Wagner then we commit a musical sin, and our labours are useless, even damaging.[19]

There was plenty more in that vein. During the last thirty years of his life, Verdi's letters and public pronouncements constantly lament the influence of Wagnerism on young Italians, the dangers of harmonic and orchestral complexity, in particular the errors of composers (Puccini among them) who had been lured by the 'symphonic' style. They should return to the national roots, learn counterpoint, revere Palestrina and the great choral traditions of Italy's musical past.

This is the atmosphere in which *Otello* and *Falstaff* were born, and the circumstances left traces. *Falstaff* begins and ends, for example, with ironic glosses on two grand pillars of 'academic' musical form. The first minutes of the opera are in a kind of mock symphonic sonata form, and as each new section begins, Falstaff (bass-baritone) offers laconic comment: 'Ecco la mia risposta' (Here is my reply) as the 'second subject' begins; 'Non è finita!' (It's not finished!) at the start of the development; there's even an 'Amen' at the coda. In light of Verdi's concern at the 'symphonism' (i.e. Wagnerism) of young Italian opera composers, these asides assume a rich irony. More obvious still is the opera's closing fugue (which Verdi's letters tell us was his first musical inspiration for the opera). 'Tutto nel mondo è burla' (All the world's a joke) might be thought a fitting end to Verdi's long career, but it is also a pointed reminder to the younger generation – counterpoint is our Italian heritage, return to Palestrina and find salvation. Other connections are more fragile. *Falstaff*, for example, is more highly chromatic than any other Verdi opera, but is also obsessed by cadence, forever punctuated by unequivocal gestures of closure. Related to this is the contrast between the work's looseness of form and its frequent gestures of closure – huge orchestral climaxes that seem to overwhelm what they ostensibly close off. Was this also a reminder? Just after finishing *Falstaff* Verdi wrote to a friend, making fun of the 'modern' (again, read Wagnerian) school for their melodic style: 'a modern melody [is] one of those beautiful ones that has neither beginning nor end, and remains suspended in the air like Mohammed's tomb'.[20] Again, those emphatic, triumphant cadences are making a point about the state of the operatic world.

Perhaps, though, these music-and-politics equivalents are too simple. Germanophiles see *Otello* and *Falstaff* as influenced by Wagner; their opponents see them as pillars set against the Wagnerian tide. Do we need to continue such ancient polemics? There is, after all, an important distinction between Wagner's work and Wagner*ism* – between the operas and the critical message they were dragooned into undertaking. Verdi certainly feared and set himself against the latter, especially the exaggerated claims about 'symphonic' operatic structures. One of his most famous letters, again to Ricordi, offers admonitions to his most famous Italian successor:

> I've heard good things about the musician Puccini. . . . He follows modern tendencies, and that's natural, but he keeps contact with melody, which is neither modern nor ancient. It seems, though, that the symphonic element predominates in him. He needs to go cautiously here. Opera is opera; symphonies are symphonies; and I don't think that in an opera it's fine to have a symphonic element, merely for the pleasure of making the orchestra dance.[21]

But the letters about Wagner have become different in tone, suggesting a shared project and genuine (if troubled) admiration and understanding. Does this conciliatory stance also show traces in the last operas?

Some have found resonances between the Act 1 finales of *Falstaff* and *Die Meistersinger*,[22] but more immediately audible is Verdi's use of that pillar of Wagnerian technique, the recurring theme. Such themes had appeared in many of his earlier operas, but typically they were used in a very un-Wagnerian manner. Ideas like the 'curse' theme in *Rigoletto* stand in isolation from their context, communicating translatable meaning precisely because they are infrequent. But in *Falstaff* we find a different technique. Ford (baritone) has a tremendous monologue in the first part of Act 2 ('È sogno? o realtà'; Is it a dream? or reality?) where the musical fabric is largely constructed out of confused fragments of previous themes. The soloist's psychological state is as much evident in the orchestra as in what he sings. Another moment comes at the start of Act 3, where Falstaff has an extraordinary monologue in which he reaches the depths of despair and then gradually reconstitutes himself (with a little vinous assistance) and prepares for life ahead. At the lowest ebb, he looks at himself with brutal honesty: 'M'aiuti il ciel! Impinguo troppo. Ho dei peli grigi' (Heaven help me! I'm getting too fat. My hair is greying). This unhappy litany is sung in a bare, exhausted recitative, punctuated orchestrally only by a sinister chromatic figure in the bass – one that wanders without tonality, just as Falstaff has, for a moment, found himself bereft of energy and direction. This little figure is an obvious quotation, more or less identical to one of Klingsor's motifs from

Wagner's last opera, *Parsifal*. What can it mean, set here in the middle of *Falstaff*? There's no obvious reference in the libretto. Perhaps it is merely one of those fortuitous resemblances that music sends forth from time to time, to our bewilderment or delight. Or perhaps it is indeed a cryptograph to be unravelled and understood, a musical way for Verdi to repeat: 'Triste. Triste. Triste! Wagner è morto!'

We know something of the final years of Verdi's life through photographs – the white beard, the wise grin, the battered hat. This period is often thought of as his Indian summer. Although the operatic world had changed, the aged composer persisted with some of his ancient creative habits until the last. One was in finding a source of creative energy in the vocal characteristics of singers. At a late stage in the composition of *Falstaff* he auditioned a possible Mistress Quickly, Giuseppina Pasqua (1855–1930), and liked her voice so much that he created for Quickly – and Pasqua – a tiny aria in Act 2 ('Giunta all'Albergo'). More important still, there is plenty of evidence that the roles of Iago and Falstaff would not have been as they are – in their sudden changes of mood, their disarming flashes of lyricism and above all their sometimes uncanny imitations of other characters – without the remarkable histrionic talents of their creator, bass-baritone Victor Maurel (1848–1923).[23] Maurel's recordings of 'Era la notte' (*Otello*, Act 2) and 'Quand'ero paggio' (*Falstaff*, Act 2) are now available, and display his extraordinary diction and abilities in vocal mimicry. His sinister enunciation of 'Desdemona soave' in the former is still chilling, more than a hundred years after it was recorded.

After *Falstaff* in 1893, and in spite of some beautiful late religious pieces (collected as the *Quattro pezzi sacri*), Verdi's world inevitably narrowed. His partner of some fifty years, Giuseppina Strepponi, died in November 1897, carried off by pneumonia after long and painful illness; in her will she hoped to be reunited with Verdi in Heaven. There are some very sad final letters to another soprano, Teresa Stolz, with whom he had been much involved, perhaps romantically, in the dark, opera-less years of the 1870s. In one of the last, he is eighty-seven and she is sixty-six:

> We had some delightful hours, but they were too short. And who knows when even ones as short as those will come again! Oh an old man's life is

> truly unhappy! Even without real illness, life is a burden and I feel that vitality and strength are diminishing, each day more than the one before. I feel this within myself and don't have the courage and power to keep busy with anything. Love me well and always, and believe in my love, which is great, very, very great, and very true.[24]

Verdi laments the loss of vitality and strength, courage and power – those qualities that he gave so generously in the service of musical and dramatic expression. There is also, at the last, a tender expression of love and loyalty. Most striking of all, though, is an uncompromising honesty, a willingness to stare full in the face what a changing world offers.

16
Realism and clamour

La traviata and *Carmen*: both are realistic in their fashion. Under the influence of the latter, realism became an operatic buzzword in the late nineteenth century – and in several countries almost simultaneously. But the large differences between the types of opera that sailed under a realist flag should make us wary of taking the term too literally. As we wrote in the very first chapter, opera is in a basic sense not realistic – operatic characters go about their business singing rather than speaking. To compound matters, the idea of realism in the arts is famously problematic even when applied to literature and fine art, in spite of its extensive history and obvious purchase in those forms. Linda Nochlin starts her classic survey of nineteenth-century artistic realism by identifying 'a basic cause of confusion bedevilling the notion' in the movement's 'ambiguous relationship to the highly problematic concept of reality'.[1] In opera – in any genre that involves music – these problems become more confusing still. But realism keeps emerging as a slogan in the history of opera, usually as a means to attack yesterday's operatic practice, an agent in those continual attempts to reform opera, discipline it, rein it in, purge it of the excesses yesterday is deemed to have committed. The late nineteenth century was no exception; indeed, realism was summoned to the cause as never before. One reason was that late nineteenth-century operatic rebels needed all the slogans they could muster to distance themselves from the immediate past. The 'yesterday' they were confronting loomed before them, imposing as never before, in the form of three shadows cast by three puissant giants: Giacomo Meyerbeer, Giuseppe Verdi and – largest and darkest of all – Richard Wagner.

The idea of operatic realism is, then, historically important, but is always a relative term, potentially meaning many things. It could involve realism of acting, of a singer entering into the character rather than simply performing in costume. Both Wagner and Verdi fought strenuously for reforms in this direction. Singers, they argued, should lose themselves in their roles, should *become* the figures they impersonate, allowing the audience to absorb the illusion that the world on stage exists and matters. Again, though, we need caveats: calls for – or elaborate praise of – engaging operatic acting predate the later nineteenth century. They can be found, for instance, in critiques of the singing actresses who populated French *tragédie lyrique* during the eighteenth century.

There were other forms of realism through which the fundamental strangeness of opera came under challenge. One of these involves time – specifically the suspended time of operatic numbers or parts of numbers, in which nothing aside from singing is happening. In most opera before the later nineteenth century there are places in which action or discussion is set aside, in which all energies are devoted to sheer music. The performance keeps unfolding, but time in the stage world stops. During these freeze-frames, one might imagine a kind of psychological truth at work – at moments when bliss or shock is extreme, the world may seem to pause for an instant. Operatic numbers can take hold of that instant, making space for a large musical object that will occupy several minutes. Wagner was most radical in breaking this down. He had the insight that characters' bliss or shock could be extended almost endlessly, meaning that one didn't necessarily have to pause fictional time. *Tristan und Isolde* stages a continual unfolding of intense emotional states: as its composer famously said, it stages the art of transition.[2]

Wagner was not alone in attempting to reorganize operatic time by favouring continual dialogue and stage action, by reducing the libretto's pauses for poetic roughage consumed by soloists or multiple characters simultaneously. To a greater or lesser extent, all late nineteenth-century composers felt this pull towards continuity. In the last chapter, we discussed how Verdi's final operas, *Otello* and *Falstaff*, crossed an intangible divide, realigning the relationship between 'set piece' and 'dialogue', making the first an interruption of the second rather than an inevitable end-point. The change particularly called into question solo arias, which had been the staple of opera for two centuries and more but which now became exceptional events. Grand duets and larger ensembles, numbers in which a looser idea of musical conversation could occur, inexorably replaced them. And the shift from arias to duets, from opera as soliloquy to opera as dialogue, often went hand in hand with the gradual acceptance of prose as opposed to verse libretti. Wagner was yet again enterprising in this regard, especially in his four-opera extravaganza *Der Ring des Nibelungen* (1876). With its marching army of arrogant Gods, sword-brandishing heroes, cavorting water nixies and sweaty dwarves, the *Ring* could hardly be thought realistic in terms of its story. It is, though, far more realistic than, say, the human tragedy of Verdi's *Rigoletto* (first performed in 1851, around the time Wagner started working on the music of the *Ring*) in letting time in the stage world flow relatively unimpeded within each scene. These innovations profoundly affected the musical shape of opera, changing the relationship between musical time and fictional time, bringing them into a more continual alignment.

Wagner was also a musical realist in his love of noise or, as he would have preferred to put it, of natural sound. Scenic music, music to accompany stage effects or stage pictures, had existed in opera for quite some time. But such music typically acquired conventions that assured it a readily understood relationship to the world depicted. Rossini's pastoral music in *Guillaume Tell* (1829) draws on imitations of real sounds (the Swiss cowherd's horn) to create local colour; but mostly such descriptive music works by behaving correctly as a musical code that resonates with emotions traditionally associated with pastoral scenes – peace, a sense of simplicity and timelessness, benign lassitude. Wagner often worked in the same way, by what we might call 'mediation'. The orchestral interlude (known as Siegfried's Rhine Journey) between scenes 1 and 2 of the first act of *Götterdämmerung* (1874) is understandable as geographical progress through a landscape mostly because its leitmotifs – Siegfried's horn call, the 'Fire' motif connected to Brünnhilde's place of exile, the Rhine music – were close to traditional musical representations of hunting scenes, fire and water.

However, there was also a more direct way to represent the locations inhabited by operatic characters, and that was by imitating natural sounds and adding almost nothing. This is the unruly music, at minimal distance from the thing it represents, that we saw in the Pilgrims' Scene in Act 1 of Wagner's *Tannhäuser*. Another example is from his *Der fliegende Holländer* (1843), in which musical storms are elemental as well as symbolic: they contain not just the conventional minor-key tremolos, but the pure shrilling of wind in rigging (flutes and piccolos) or claps of thunder (timpani with hard sticks). Verdi was equally adept. In *Rigoletto*, the storm scene in the final act uses distant human voices, singing with closed mouths, to create an uncanny effect of unruly wind; in *Aida*, Act 3, he invokes a kind of noisy silence (a starlit night on the banks of the Nile) by means of muted strings playing a single note in many octaves, pizzicato, tremolo and with harmonics. When it came to the human voice, Wagner was sometimes even more direct: he sometimes instructed his singers to scream – not to sing a scream written into the score as notes, but to scream out for real, to break the musical shell. This was as radical as any of his more famous innovations. Noise can reorder the balance of power in opera, changing both singing and the way operatic music is written.

BORIS AND DIVOS OF THE DEEPS

Sheer noise and a resistance to frozen moments are, then, the advance guard of operatic realism: before libretti shifted to prose, or adopted the urban poor as favoured subjects, natural sounds and continuous dialogue were signalling a more fundamental change. *Boris Godunov* (1869, revised 1874) by the Russian composer Modest Musorgsky (1839–81) is in this sense one of the first and most radical late-nineteenth-century realist experiments. Musorgsky's formative background was the period between 1830 and 1850, which saw the establishment of a number of self-consciously national operatic traditions, in particular those in Russia, Poland and various parts of the Habsburg empire, notably Hungary. All these areas had seen vernacular opera during the eighteenth century, but the emergence of a 'national opera' was, as in Italy and Germany, intimately bound up with the process of cultural nation-building undertaken by the expanding middle classes. In several cases one can identify key operas that managed, more by dint of multiple performances or association with political events than by their occasional use of folk materials, to collect around them a miscellany of musical and literary motifs that could function as symbols of a nation.

The process here is important, and is often misunderstood: rather than appropriating an already existing fund of national musical material, these operas typically tended to *construct* that material – becoming (as Verdi's would in Italy) 'national works' through the cumulative acts of national reception they underwent.

A good case in point, and the earliest of these national operatic figures in Russia, is Mikhail Ivanovich Glinka (1804–57). His *A Life for the Czar* (1836), which describes itself rather grandly as a 'patriotic heroic-tragic opera', is in some ways a 'rescue' opera in the style of Cherubini's *Les Deux Journées* (1800), and also shows more than a hint of Rossinian influence, doubtless deriving from Glinka's Italian travels in the 1830s. Set around the seventeenth-century figure of Ivan Susanin, a peasant fighting against Polish invasion, the score makes one or two gestures towards folk material, but most of its Russianness derives from an urban tradition of salon music. The newness in Glinka's work, however, comes through the way in which this material, which had been used often enough in earlier works as 'local colour', inhabits the core of the drama, in particular during climactic moments. The novelty and importance of *A Life for the Czar* was very quickly appreciated, and the opera is to this day regarded as a watershed in the development of Russian music. Glinka's second opera, *Ruslan and Lyudmila* (1842), has never been as successful, although it was much imitated by later Russian composers, who developed its fairy-tale and Orientalist themes.

Against this background, Musorgsky will sound more radical than ever. The second scene of *Boris* begins with bells: not real bells but a fearless imitation, an alternation of functionally unrelated chords (based on a non-tonal collection of notes called the octatonic scale, a favourite device of advanced twentieth-century composers such as Bartók and Stravinsky). These dissonant masses seem extraordinarily alien for 1869; they make little sense within the musical grammar of the time. The sense they *do* make is by reference to the real sounds they imitate: those deep bells that peal forth on solemn ceremonial occasions, and which, more pertinently, create discordant overlapping pitches and overtones – Musorgsky does nothing to prettify the sound. Soon afterwards, *real* bells also peal forth, the point thus being made explicit. Those opening, octatonic bell-chords, with their shadowy kind of musical sense, are on the cusp between music and the bells one would hear in the everyday world. Musorgsky's bells are, in other words, a portent of *fin-de-siècle* things to come. Wagner – without knowing a then-obscure Russian opera – made his own version of atonal bell noise in Act 3 of *Parsifal*: the cruel voices of the grail knights reproach Amfortas in tolling, dissonant waves that turn bell sounds into an uncanny form of communal song.

In *Boris*, the clamour of the bell music is one of many blunt moments that testify to Musorgsky's drive towards frankness, his displeasure with opera's fabulous and frivolous aspects. Although his choice of subject matter and – occasionally – musical idiom has reminiscences of Glinka, his attitudes to such material were very different. Rather than hammering some literary source into a proper libretto, with well-behaved poetry and ample opportunities for frozen moments, Musorgsky carved words directly from an earlier play by the poet Alexander Pushkin, itself based on events from Russian history. The explicit intention of both poet and composer was didactic – to instruct and educate by issuing warnings from the past. The setting is the late sixteenth century, and in that bell-resonant second scene Boris Godunov (bass) is about to be crowned Tsar. But he harbours a guilty secret – he has committed murder on the road to power. At the end of the drama, wracked by guilt, fearful for his young son and threatened by a Pretender to the throne, he succumbs to a terrible seizure.

The libretto in the original, 1869 version of *Boris* allows for only a few traditional operatic situations; there are instead many long conversations and some monologues, all cast as musical prose that ebbs and flows with the words. For the revised version, staged at St Petersburg's Mariinsky Theatre in 1874 (the 1869 version was rejected by the authorities and not performed until the Soviet era), Musorgsky was encouraged to bulk the piece up with more conventional operatic fare, and did so with some enthusiasm. Along with other, more piecemeal changes, he added an entire act set in Poland. It has a mazurka-style aria for the heroine Marina (soprano), a brilliant formal Polonaise and a lengthy love-duet finale between Marina and the Pretender Dimitry (tenor), complete with harps and interlocking voices. In such passages, *Boris* sounds like *grand opéra* in its Russian incarnation. Sometimes the influence came via predecessors such as Glinka and his *A Life for the Tsar*, but at other times it is more general and direct: the historical/political subject matter, the determined variety of musical styles, or the

Coronation Scene with massed tableau and scenic glitter. There is, though, one sense in which *Boris* (in whatever version) makes a deep commitment to an eternal operatic truth, and that is in its celebration of the alpha singer. Musorgsky manipulated Pushkin's *Boris* in order to make his opera a showpiece for a star bass, a landmark in the repertoire of that rare creature, the divo of the deeps. The work's performance history has been punctuated by a magnificent procession of these prodigies, from Feodor Chaliapin to Alexander Kipnis, from Boris Christoff to René Pape. Recalling its attractions for the star singer can caution against overemphasizing the radical aspects of *Boris*, a move that often goes hand in hand with exoticizing Russian music generally – keeping it separate by extolling its palpable difference from the Western European mainstream.

We could underline that caveat by noticing that *Boris* mixes up past traditions without reserve, putting experiments that were *sui generis* next to a splendid variety of opera-as-usual. For this reason, the work eludes easy categorization according to historical position or genre, but probably fits better in the *fin de siècle* than it does as an appendix to *grand opéra*. Partly this is because of a further aspect of Musorgsky's style which could, like those bell chords, attract the realist label, and which could also be thought a Musorgskian lance into the operatic future. During the creation of *Boris*, its composer described his operatic aesthetic thus: 'my characters speak onstage as living people speak, but so that the character and force of their intonation, supported by the orchestra, which is the musical background for their speech, hit the target head-on; that is, my music must be an artistic reproduction of human speech in all its most subtle windings'.[3] Tracing the literary origins of this credo can uncover an interesting journey, one that (although Musorgsky cannot have known it) can lead back via a circuitous route to the ideals of those sixteenth-century Italians whose theories helped create the first operas.[4] They too had insisted on fidelity to the flow of emotions and the rhythms of speech, and they dubbed the new style *recitar cantando* – singing recitation. But that had been three centuries ago, three centuries during which, despite various attempts to stem the tide, the *cantando* part of the operatic equation or, more broadly, the musical aspect taken as a whole, had been in almost continual ascendancy. The political, didactic aspirations of Musorgsky and some of his Russian contemporaries (a group of reformers who were dubbed the 'Kuchka' – literally the 'little heap' or 'little group') caused them to strive for a new kind of declamatory realism, one in which the rhythms and cadences of Russian speech would be etched on to their operatic style. Although these attempts had little immediate influence, their later reverberations were powerful and would reflect the operatic attitudes of many of the greatest late nineteenth- and twentieth-century composers.

Boris's death scene, which ends the 1869 version and became the penultimate scene in 1874, is to be sure not *just* a musical version of speech. It is better thought of as a virtuoso demonstration of the powers that can be invested in realistic sound, where little of what we hear seems to involve musical artifice or clear formal construction. The first section of the monologue, as Boris addresses his son, Fyodor (mezzo-soprano), draws on all the lyric authority of the bass voice, in the form of short, individual melodic waves for virtually each line of the text. When Boris appeals to God for mercy, his almost Schubertian lyricism gives way and the voice climbs to its highest register – to near-whispers with high tremolo strings. But the strange bell chords from the Coronation Scene return and, from that point until shortly before the end, the music is nearly all meant to be audible to the characters onstage, including the bells and an offstage chorus of mourners. Boris starts singing *with them*, winding his voice through them and around them.

Whenever this happens in opera – whenever characters respond musically to sounds around them – there's a sense in which borders have been erased and reinvented. It's not just that the characters can hear music being produced nearby: that, after all, is true in all those let's-sing-a-song-in-the-inn situations. But Boris responds to his ambient music by improvising a sung counterpoint. In one sense we are very far from realism. What human being, at a moment of extreme emotion, would hear a hymn in the background and respond by singing his words in loose concord? This part of the death monologue nevertheless marks an important aesthetic turn for opera, one in which an old certainty – that operatic characters don't know they are singing – dissolves, giving rise to a fruitful confusion. And this basic compositional device – using background music or background sound as the anchor, with characters singing freely and conversationally around it – becomes a widespread technique in *fin-de-siècle* opera. It's a kind of musical curtain against which sung conversations or monologues can be held, with the naturalness and only-half-sung quality of the vocal lines anchored the richer music in the (apparent) distance. Act 2 of Puccini's *Tosca* proceeds in this way for a long stretch, when Tosca – who is offstage – sings a cantata for the Queen while Scarpia and Cavaradossi exchange rhythmically free insults and information in the foreground. There was one significant earlier model for the trick that all these composers would have known: Mozart's comedies, in particular *Don Giovanni*, where in both finales dances or aria arrangements are played on stage while characters eat, whisper, conspire, joke and converse in singing over the musical background.

The quirks and habits that have arisen over more than a century of *Boris* performances reflect a continuing sense of the opera's peculiar brand of truthfulness, its reality factor. As anyone who has seen the work will know, it has become *de rigueur* for the principal bass to give his spectacular all and (in excess of the stage directions) cause the stricken Tsar to keel over in front of his throne. Those massive bodies crashing to the floor, the very sound of it, the fearlessness of the gesture, is a perpetual shock. As the great Russian director Stanislavski advised his Boris in 1928, 'do not tear at the collar of your shirt to show you are suffocating. That is what all the other singers in this part do and it is just a stale cliché. Lean forward and fall as an ox does when he is butchered.'[5] So now they all do it, and gasps are always heard. But there is another performance tradition which, though less overtly shocking, reflects this fearlessness in another way. For his 1874 revision, Musorgsky added a local colour number right out of *opéra comique*, a rustic song for the blowsy Innkeeper (mezzo-soprano) in Act 1, scene 2. The Innkeeper's role has become a favoured destination for great divas in their twilight years, and is often sung by genuinely ravaged voices, with a roughness appropriate to the character's identity. Martha Mödl (1912–2001), for instance, whose roles at Bayreuth in the 1950s included Kundry, Isolde and Brünnhilde, appeared as a half-comic, half-tragic Innkeeper in performances of *Boris* in Munich in the 1970s and 1980s. Musorgsky's unreserved attitudes towards realistic singing seem, in other words, to call up fearlessness in performers as well, attitudes that cause the aesthetic world of *bel canto* to seem an exceedingly distant memory.

ONEGIN: SALON OPERA

It is in some ways fitting that the old woman with the ravaged voice, sung by those not afraid to demonstrate the toll taken by years of service in large theatres, will recur frequently in twentieth-century opera. Clytemnestra in Richard Strauss's *Elektra* (1909), opera's Queen of Decadence, is also played by ex-Brünnhildes whose range and beauty of tone have disappeared for ever. Astrid Varnay (1918–2006), a star Wagnerian soprano of the 1950s and 1960s, can be seen and heard stealing the show as Clytemnestra in the 1984 German television version directed by Götz Friedrich. Two decades before Strauss, Pyotr Ilyich Tchaikovsky (1840–93) created a similar role in his penultimate opera, *The Queen of Spades* (1890). The plot, based on an 1833 novella by Pushkin, is full of phantoms, phantasms and other inexplicable phenomena. An obsessive hero, Hermann (tenor), is in love with Liza (soprano), the aristocrat granddaughter of a haughty old Countess (mezzo-soprano) who is a decayed remnant in paint and patches. Hermann believes that the Countess has a supernatural gift and knows a secret combination of three cards that will always recoup a gambler's fortunes should he bet on them. He invades the Countess's bedroom at night and frightens her into a fatal heart attack before she can reveal the secret; nevertheless, she later appears to him as a ghost and names three cards. But her final card is wrong, as Hermann discovers in a disastrous game that ends with his suicide. The Countess, a grotesque character with no redeeming virtues, is invariably performed either by a brave ex-diva or by a young mezzo pretending to have no voice left. The ugly sounds the singer makes are meant to be an indication not just of the Countess's age, but of her rotten soul. Mödl first sang the Countess at the Nice opera in 1989, at the age of seventy-seven. Varnay, who added the Countess to her repertory in 1984 at the age of sixty-six, referred to this and other post-Brünnhilde character roles as 'silencing the heavy artillery'.[6]

Tchaikovsky was never associated with the Kuchka, and had – unlike them – benefited from a thorough professional training and thus greater acquaintance with the music of Western Europe. He is rarely a point-blank composer, and showed little interest in brash representations of noise. But despite the aesthetic gap, we can trace *Boris*-like flavours in Tchaikovsky's operas, flavours that involve the many alternative senses of realism and the paradoxes that could arise from their musical manifestations. In Act 2 of *The Queen of Spades*, for example, there is an extended ballroom scene whose music is largely presented as taking place onstage. Besides the obligatory dancing, the guests also assemble for a complete performance of a small pastoral opera called *The Faithful Shepherdess*, written in the style of Mozart. Tchaikovsky's music-within-music involves disorientating chronological displacements. Mozart-like music would be the proper contemporary style for Hermann's actual era, since the libretto, by Tchaikovsky's brother Modest, shifts Pushkin's novella to the eighteenth century. But Tchaikovsky doesn't write imitation Mozart. Instead he creates something that sounds like Mozart through the filter of lost time, music that may have been performed long ago but somehow is heard only now, after a hundred years. The dramatic situation is clear. This is a ball and *The Faithful Shepherdess* is a divertissement being played for real, right there on stage. The characters hear the dance and operatic numbers just as the audience does. But the strangely refracted music tells another story, suggesting that the experience of this real performance is a dream or hallucination. It is a wonderful trick, in its way just as radical as Musorgsky's dissonant bell chords.

Tchaikovsky's other great opera, *Yevgeny Onegin* (Eugene Onegin, 1879), was also based on Pushkin and was consciously written against the grain of Kuchka ideology, with no overt nationalism and not a hint of grand historical scenes, tsars, battles or marches. *Onegin* is essentially a chamber opera and tends to creak under the pressure of lavish production values or the starry, larger-than-life singers that typically inhabit *Boris*. This much can be seen from Tchaikovsky's diffident promotion of the opera: it was first performed by students of the Moscow Conservatory; even when it reached the professional stage at Moscow's Bolshoy Theatre in 1881, the composer continued to insist on modest forces and discreet gestures – above all nothing too theatrical. The plot is at heart a drama of sentiment. An impressionable girl, Tatyana (soprano), becomes infatuated with a world-weary older man, Onegin (baritone). One night, alone in her bedroom, she impulsively writes him a love letter; he rejects her with gentleness but more than a hint of condescension. Some years later, with Tatyana now married to elderly, doting Prince Gremin (bass), Onegin reappears and declares to Tatyana that he is hopelessly in love with her. But Tatyana will not desert her husband and Onegin ends the opera in pathetic despair. There is a subplot in which Onegin needlessly provokes a duel with his friend Lensky (tenor) during a ball scene, and then kills him in a dawn duel; and there are various interpolated choruses, including a group of peasants in the first scene who sketch in a rare moment of folkishness. Elsewhere, especially in the two ballroom scenes, the tone is determinedly urban and urbane.

The realist aspects of *Onegin* certainly include the restraint of Tchaikovsky's subject matter – its intimacy and domesticity – and the fact that the music is written for singers of relatively modest skills. At the time, these could be seen as defects of realism. As one critic had it:

> it seems to be the custom nowadays to contend that the modern domestic or social element is best suited for the requirements of an operatic libretto . . . to associate music with colloquialisms and the conversation of the nineteenth century appears to us the height of the ridiculous.[7]

But the opera's best claim to the realist label is the way in which its musical ideas and forms are embedded in everyday language. In *La traviata*, as we saw in Chapter 15, waltz rhythms continually underpin Violetta and her progress through the opera. In *Onegin*, Tchaikovsky does something similar (it was in this sense fitting that the first Bolshoy production recycled old *La traviata* sets in its final scene): he constructs his most intimate scenes from refractions and repetitions of the light, salon music of his day. It is as if salon music, with its predictable phrases and periodic repetitions, is sounding somewhere nearby, with the characters singing against its background, with it or around it. This is in one sense like the device in Boris's death scene, the difference being that the background in *Onegin* is not music played within the stage world. It is instead music that sounds as if it *could* be from the stage world, a background inaudible to the characters on stage but nevertheless influencing profoundly the way they sing.

Tatyana's famous Letter Scene, one of opera's great monologues and Tchaikovsky's first inspiration for *Onegin*, is a slightly different case. During the scene, in which Tatyana gradually convinces herself to write her declaration of love to Onegin, the heroine's emotional journey takes the form of four loosely defined sections. Each is related in its melodic shapes, yet each could be musically self-sufficient and almost function as an independent orchestral number, a concert piece. Tatyana's vocal delivery is mostly conversational; because of the orchestral background she is free to linger over thoughts and indulge in sudden hesitations, to weave through the sound in a quasi-natural rhythm or to become lyrical in tandem. Significantly, each of the sections carries strong reminiscences of the public music elsewhere in the opera, music that was actually performed and heard in the stage world. So radical was this innovation that the first reviewers missed it completely, accusing the scene of being recitative throughout. Later audiences learned to hear the unusual musical flow differently.

THE FRENCH CONNECTION

The forms of operatic realism in the later nineteenth and early twentieth centuries often transcend local operatic languages, and – as Musorgsky and Tchaikovsky show – were not necessarily devised at the Western European centre, to travel by osmosis to outlying places. Nor was writing for voices against a heard or presumed stage-musical background the sole province of Russian composers. Indeed, if anywhere would seem the natural home of realist opera it would be France, origin of the earlier realist innovations in the other arts such as the novels of Gustave Flaubert and the paintings of Gustave Courbet. Whatever realism these two achieved was by no means confined to subject matter. One of the outcomes of Flaubert's notorious lack of empathy, disgust even, with the characters he created in his most famous novel, *Madame Bovary* (1857), was to abandon grand rhetorical gestures in treating their vicissitudes; a related technique can be seen in Courbet's avoidance of conventional ways of making his chosen scenes picturesque. Together with later developments in the novels of Emile Zola (who even tried his hand at libretto writing), and of course the enormous impression made by *Carmen*, the French background might seem as rich as anywhere.

But so far as opera was concerned there were two large obstacles. One was the continuing influence of chorus-rich *grand opéra* at its most inflated. Camille Saint-Saëns' *Samson et Dalila* (1877) is one of the strangest stylistic concoctions along these lines to emerge from the period. Much of the first act betrays all too clearly the work's origins in oratorio: there's even a Handelian fugue for the Hebrews. The Philistines, as one might expect, seem to be having more musical fun, although their quasi-exotic inspirations in Act 3, which are deliberately trivial, risk sounding *merely* trivial. The saving grace of the opera is the love music of Act 2, in particular Delila's famous 'Mon cœur s'ouvre à ta voix' (My heart opens at your voice), which remains one of the stalwarts of the mezzo-soprano's recital repertory. Much of the rest of the act wallows quite enjoyably in the other large obstacle, which was (again) the influence of Wagner; in this case the seemingly irresistible attraction of those distinctive harmonies that characterize the steamiest moments of *Tristan*.

A revealing illustration of the difficulties faced by French composers of the post-*Carmen* era can be gleaned from listing the manners and modes tried out by its most successful composer, Jules Massenet (1842–1912). Massenet himself seems to have sampled almost every libretto tradition available: Goethe adaptation (*Werther*, 1892), *grand opéra* historical extravaganza (*Le Cid*, 1885), femme fatale from the exotic East (*Thaïs*, 1894), comedy in powdered wigs (*Chérubin*, 1905), high-minded sentimental fable (*Grisélidis*, 1891) and even a Wagnerian amalgam with magic swords, an eroticized knight and teleportation (*Esclarmonde*, 1889). The cornucopia can on occasions seem rather desperate and perhaps resonates with Massenet's notoriously chameleon-like personality, his penchant for pranks and for pretending to be a dog or a monkey at fashionable parties.[8] Among them, *Chérubin* is an object lesson in the fact that libretti owing nothing to Wagner's plot models could nonetheless become places where Wagnerian acoustic shadows were all too obvious. While the libretto is a sequel to Beaumarchais's Figaro plays, the music is a flood of free, melodious dialogue, standard procedure for post-Wagnerian opera around 1900.

To say that Massenet's operas were merely a litany of types is, though, to underestimate the appeal of his music, which in its time was understood to have a distinctly feminine genius in its celebration of the soprano voice. French *grand opéra* began in the 1830s with its eye fixed on men and male voices, with the great all-male ensembles of Meyerbeer as the classic examples. But by the end of the century, and especially in the hands of Massenet, vocal preference moves to the opposite pole. In *Esclarmonde*, the hero (Roland, tenor) is overwhelmed by the sound of Esclarmonde's voice calling to him in cascades of soprano coloratura. The battle lines are clearly drawn: just as Roland is about to yield, Catholic priests come thundering in with 'In the name of the Father, Son and Holy Spirit'. This patriarchal task-force obviously fights fire with fire, making enough sound to blow the trilling heroine clean away. Such victories were, perhaps, all the more impressive when the heroine in question was a difficult customer. Massenet wrote the part of Esclarmonde for the famous American soprano Sibyl Sanderson, a 'fair Californian' with whom, one correspondent reports in 1894, the composer was enraptured. 'Some had seen Massenet dining in a restaurant in the Rue Daunou with an American girl, accompanied by a lady who . . . was probably her mother', reports the observer; Massenet was heard to enthuse at the same restaurant, 'this girl has an extraordinary voice, from the G below treble clef to the G in the fourth line above'. That G – a whole step above the Queen of the Night's high F – was dubbed 'the Eiffel Tower note' by Parisians of the time.[9]

Massenet made so many stylistic experiments that 'realism' was bound to be among them. *Manon*, first performed at the Opéra-Comique in 1884, is loosely based on episodes from an eighteenth-century novel by the Abbé Prévost, and so might seem – on setting alone – an unlikely candidate for the realist label. Fifteen-year-old Manon (soprano) is destined for a convent, but en route is spirited away by handsome young Des Grieux (tenor), thus evading both her venal cousin Lescaut (baritone) and a lecherous old aristocrat called Guillot (tenor). They enjoy a blissful if impoverished life in Paris before Des Grieux is abducted by his anxious father and Manon becomes the mistress of a richer man. The lovers get back together in the church of St Sulpice, with Des Grieux about to take holy orders. Des Grieux then gambles recklessly in order to keep Manon in luxury. He is accused of cheating by Guillot, and he and Manon are arrested. The final scene takes place on the road to Le Havre. Manon is to be deported; Des Grieux fails to save her, and she dies of exhaustion. As the reviewer of *The Musical Times* put it in 1884, 'the story is painful and its atmosphere unwholesome', unwholesomeness having by then become a code word for realism amongst the disapproving.[10]

Manon had stock-in-trade *opéra comique* scenic favourites such as drama in church and drama in a gambling house, not to mention an eighteenth-century setting with attendant chances to write pastiche and so evade for a time the lure of Wagnerian sounds. However, and although *Manon* has a standard poetic text, Massenet's self-confessed mode of composition – to memorize the words and repeat them endlessly until the perfect melodies emerged from the individual rhythm of each phrase – meant that his opera sounds very much as if it were mined directly from a prose libretto. One need only sample the soprano heroine's first number, the famous 'Je suis encore tout étourdie' (I am still completely overcome), to hear the freedom of word-setting. Some lines, such as the first, are sung with breathless or lingering pauses ('Je suis . . . en-core . . . tout é-tour-*di* . . . e'), others are rushed through as fast as possible, others furnish occasions for long-held high notes. When this unpredictable rhythmic surface is matched by a form that seems improvised on the spot – by sudden, seemingly unprepared repetitions and by harmonic progressions that often unfold in metrically unexpected ways – the overall effect is very close to musical prose. Such qualities may have been what inspired Thomas Beecham's most famous provocation, 'I would give the whole of Bach's Brandenburg Concertos for Massenet's *Manon* and . . . think I had vastly profited by the exchange'.[11]

The overtly realist declamation might possibly gesture towards Wagner (in form if not in manner), but less ambiguous Wagnerian signs are also present. The hesitant melody of 'Je suis encore' is repeated twice during the aria (to give it some graspable form), and then reappears later, played by the orchestra and underpinning other vocal sentiments, suggesting that it is a subterranean voice with a message. Indeed, the entire opera is somewhat weighed down with leitmotifs, melodic ideas that recur out of duty rather than of necessity. Perhaps this is just another illustration of the extent to which French opera at the time had become enmeshed in Wagnerian fantasy.

Act 2 of *Manon*, which shows the lovers living together in Paris, contains two of Massenet's most famous arias, moments in which he emerged from the shade of any looming influence to produce tiny gems of musical sentiment. In the first, Manon knows of the plot to take Des Grieux away from her, and also knows there are other, wealthier lovers waiting; left alone, she bids their room a wistful farewell in the aria 'Adieu, notre petite table' (Farewell, our little table). As in her earlier 'Je suis encore', there are repetitions of the opening phrase (in the middle and at the close); but these are not placed as formal markers (at the start of new verses) but give the impression of loose, almost unintentional returns to past expressions – repetitions that are, if you will, conversational rather than rhetorical.

This mood is then matched by Des Grieux, who summons up a

dream-like evocation of their life together, 'En fermant les yeux' (On closing my eyes). Although this is one of the most famous arias in the tenor repertory, it is again restrained in its poetic language:

En fermant les yeux je vois
Là-bas une humble retraite,
Une maisonette
Toute blanche au fond des bois!

[On closing my eyes I see / down there a simple retreat, / A little house / all white in the depths of the wood!]

The aria is marked by an almost constant accompaniment figure, high oscillations in the muted violins, to which Massenet adds, for further brightness, flute and oboe. Unlike those over-determined leitmotifs discussed earlier, this figure is vague in specific meaning. It resonates with the simplicity of the house 'Toute blanche au fond des bois', and later in the aria with babbling streams and joyous birdsong. But part of the oscillating figure's effect is that it resists firm assignment to a visual image. There are virtually no bass notes in the entire aria, and the tenor melody is also restrained, as if the number might float off into space at any moment. The sense of evanescence comes via harmonic means. The accompaniment constantly swings between two chords, and the vocal melody – strangely repetitive, almost narcotic – also sketches harmonic gestures; but the two rarely combine, which again gives the aria its airborne feel. All this is Massenet at his most persuasive; and also – not coincidentally – his least Wagnerian. 'En fermant les yeux' probably resembles most closely those local colour invocations so popular in the final acts of Meyerbeerian *grand opéra* – in the end a far less threatening past tradition. But in its minute depiction of small detail and its lingering over simple, evocative images, it bears the epithet 'realist' more plausibly than most. Over the years it has, as have all great operatic inspirations, proved itself remarkably adaptable. In 1904, Enrico Caruso recorded it as 'Chiudo gli occhi', with piano accompaniment, ringing high notes and even a sob or two; in 1929, Julius Patzak's recorded version, sung in German as 'Ich schloss die Augen' but still sounding nothing like Wagner, is orchestrally accompanied, much slower, and extraordinarily moving in its restrained vocal intensity.

VERISMO

Late nineteenth-century Italy is conventionally seen as the true home of operatic realism. The Italian term, *verismo*, had been applied to literature since at least the 1870s, being connected with a taste for scientific objectivity in low-life situations, notable in the works of the Sicilian writer Giovanni Verga. But in the 1890s *verismo* became associated with a new kind of Italian opera, and the term has stuck. The starting point is usually said to be *Cavalleria rusticana* (Rustic Chivalry, 1890), a one-act opera by Pietro Mascagni (1863–1945) based on a short story (and then play) by Verga: a lurid tale of infidelity and murder among Sicilian peasants. A companion piece emerged two years later in the form of *Pagliacci* (Clowns, 1892) by Ruggiero Leoncavallo (1857–1919), a story that involves the same elements as *Cavalleria*, but is set among a troupe of travelling players, and thus with an added spice that the violence – a jealous husband kills his unfaithful wife – is staged as a play-within-a-play. Both operas offered something new, in particular a directness of melodic and orchestral effect, not to mention a liking for lurid dramatic shock, and both made great headway internationally, particularly in Germany, where they were a welcome antidote to Wagnerian domination.

Many found them distasteful. An American essayist writing in the 1890s sums it up thus:

> Simple means shake the spectator. The march of events rasps his nerves. Dramatic touches are really blows in their directness . . . phrases are short. The rhythm frets. Dissonances scream. There is feverish unrest. . . . Examine the librettos of *Cavalleria rusticana*, *Pagliacci*, *A Santa Lucia*, *Mala vita*, *A Basso Porto*, *La martire*. You will find them to be tragic episodes in low life. The characters are peasants, mountebanks, stevedores, drunkards, punks. The tragedy is the outcome of illicit sexual relationships. Animal passions rage and cry out. The elements are squalor, lust, and blood. The life depicted is short, brutal, and nasty.[12]

Before we imagine this as mere Puritan prejudice, we should recall that many of the old school in Italy also found this repertory boorish and offensive. The aging Verdi, for example, was dismissive, saying that it was far better to be like Shakespeare and 'invent the truth';[13] but what he disliked most was the raw immediacy. The plots of both *Cavalleria* and *Pagliacci* owed something to literary *verismo*; and so the term began to be applied to them and to other, similar operas. But several early critics were sceptical of the *verismo* label. Partly this was because any realistic elements in the source texts tended to get submerged in the stubbornly old-fashioned, high-flown libretto language. But a more basic reason concerned prevailing Italian ideas about music aesthetics: the view that music was in essence abstract, and thus simply incapable of realism in the sense of truthfully representing human situations. Yet again there is the sense of an impasse: the sense that the term realism (or *verismo*) will always be problematic when applied to opera.

Stranger still, at least at first glance, is that *verismo* might refer – as it sometimes does in the history books – to the works of Giacomo Puccini (1858–1924), Italy's greatest opera composer of the post-Verdi generation. Certainly Puccini's first international success was as far from gritty realism as could be imagined. This was *Manon Lescaut* (1893), another setting of the Prévost novel that Massenet had used, and so an opera taking place in a distant, bewigged eighteenth century. In homage to its historical setting, Puccini indulged in lovingly fashioned, antique-style madrigals and gavottes at the opening of Act 2 – as with *The Queen of Spades*, the rococo setting seemed to cry out for pastiche. What's more, both *Manon* operas anticipate a twentieth-century vogue for the exotic eighteenth century, and for nostalgic allusions to its simpler, more self-contained music, as in Strauss's *Der Rosenkavalier* (1911) and *Ariadne auf Naxos* (1912/16). As an example of *verismo* – in the literary sense of urban blight or muddy peasants – *Manon Lescaut* is, then, bizarrely inappropriate. Puccini's opera is nevertheless a powerful example of what the composer would bring to post-Verdian musical theatre, in particular of his almost infallible instinct for devastating and concise emotion, a talent that would make him for decades the most successful living operatic composer in Europe and far beyond.

Late nineteenth-century Italian operas tended to experience tortuous births, and *Manon* was no exception. Puccini declared himself inspired by Prévost's novel, and was in all likelihood equally enthused by the success of Massenet's opera. In the end, though, the libretto took three years and at least three librettists to complete. The result, as with so many libretti of the time, looked far less conventionally poetic, and far more like prose, than had those earlier in the century. What's more, Puccini continued to tinker with the opera for decades after the premiere: there is no definitive *Manon Lescaut*, performers simply making a choice from among the variants (far from minor) chaotically on offer in competing versions of the vocal and orchestral score. In this uncertainty Puccini was very much of his time, betraying a difficulty especially severe in Italy, which had boasted the most imposing operatic lineage. In the first half of the century, composers such as Bellini, Donizetti and the young Verdi had worked within this centuries-old tradition. They could kick against the formal conventions, the showy cabalettas, dispiriting *cori d'introduzione* and elephantine *concertati*, but the fixed forms were nevertheless there to fall back on when inspiration flagged. By the 1880s, however, the joint onslaught of French and German influences, and the vogue for Meyerbeer, Bizet and the theories of Wagner, had virtually destroyed this predictability. Each opera had to create its own formal world, define its musical and dramatic terms uniquely. An aria, far from merely freezing the action and taking on a well-tried form, was – ideally at least – expected to assume an individual shape, intimately suited to the particular situation; orchestral timbre and even harmonic language should likewise be governed by the dramatic ambience. The rate of Italian operatic production slowed as composers picked over subjects, searching for a plan that would be at once effective and – the new watchword – original. Puccini offers a vivid illustration of such creative struggle. His maturity is marked by repeated periods of stagnation, compositional blocks in mid-opera and obsessive searches for new subjects. But, uniquely among his rivals, he produced an unprecedented number of operas that have survived to the present day. His most famous contemporaries, Mascagni and Leoncavallo, managed no more than one each; Puccini wrote at least seven. What accounted for his success?

We might start with a seemingly negative point. The most initially striking aspect of *Manon Lescaut*, particularly in comparison with Massenet, is its blatant discontinuity. Act 1 ends as young Des Grieux (tenor) has persuaded Manon (soprano) to escape with him to Paris, under the noses of her venal brother (baritone) and a raddled old roué called Geronte (bass). Act 2, though, opens with Manon in Geronte's household, already bored by her pampered existence. A few sketchy narratives tell us that life with Des Grieux had been wonderful but penniless, and that Geronte's money lured her away. Similarly, Act 3 ends with Des Grieux and Manon once more reunited, this time boarding a ship deporting her to America (on quitting Geronte at the end of Act 2, she tried to take her new jewellery with her: a bad mistake). But the start of Act 4 reveals the lovers staggering about in a vast desert outside New Orleans (geography becomes approximate in exotic locales). Puccini routinely drove his librettists, anxious as they were about their literary reputations, to despair. But he bullied and overrode them because he knew instinctively that modern opera didn't rely on such trivial narrative coherence. What mattered was that each of *Manon*'s four acts had its own powerful individuality and dramatic shape.

Equally remarkable about *Manon Lescaut* is how easily it lays to rest those looming shadows that so much troubled others of the period. Admittedly, Wagner's presence is powerful during the Act 2 love duet between Manon and Des Grieux, especially when the hero finally succumbs to Manon's pleas for reconciliation. The falling sevenths that end vocal phrases, the progressions by chromatic sequence, the liberal use of interrupted cadences, the frequent appearance of the *Tristan* chord, the general orchestral colour: all conjure up a distinctly Wagnerian world. This atmosphere then comes to an apotheosis during the instrumental Intermezzo between Acts 2 and 3, in which the aspiring string melody and concluding cadences sail very close to plagiarizing the end of *Tristan*, Act 3. On the other hand there are moments in which Puccini showed that he could appropriate rather than be submerged by Wagnerian musical language. Most significant is the 'love theme' in the Act 2 duet, first sung to Des Grieux's words 'Nell'occhio tuo profondo' (Deep in your eyes). The Wagnerian ancestry is clear, but now it points to the heroic Siegfried of *Götterdämmerung*. Wagner's rhythmically robust melodic idiom serves here as a triumphant affirmation of love, a clearing of the air after the earlier, *Tristan*-like murkiness.

Just as telling in terms of the dominant trends in late-nineteenth-century opera, Puccini skilfully avoids the stock-in-trade of the old Italian school. There is just one gesture towards the classic Verdian way of doing things: the Act 3 embarkation scene, in which Manon and other female prisoners are called forth and consigned to their convict ship. This scene centres on an ensemble that recalls obliquely a *concertato*, the imposing centrepiece of Verdian drama. According to convention, the *concertato* was the greatest of all freeze-frame moments: it would begin with an extended solo by one of the principals; other soloists would join in, to comment or offer conflicting views; finally the chorus would add weight in a grandiose climax. The Act 2 finale of *Lucia di Lammermoor* or the Act 3 finale of *Otello* are two fine examples separated by half a century. In *Manon Lescaut*, though, the suspension of time is abolished. Instead of a principal's lamentation, the opening is given to a minor character (the Sergeant, bass), who begins a slow roll-call; bystanders offer desultory comments as the prisoners move slowly, one by one, across the stage; Lescaut then mixes with the crowd, trying to instigate a riot. Only later do Manon and Des Grieux make their emotions heard and, in spite of an impressive climax, they return to muteness at the quiet close of the ensemble. The roll-call has continued throughout: there has been no 'frozen moment' in which the passing of stage time is halted.

Puccini's avoidance of leisurely musical unfolding goes further in his solo arias, which tend to be fleeting ghosts of the formal Italianate model, arising seamlessly out of the surrounding texture and then disappearing back into it, with all the more emotional power for their brevity and lack of ostentatious beginning and ending. Beautiful nodes of musical attraction – more musically formal than the flow of dialogue around them – tend to coalesce gradually, as with the roll-call in *Manon Lescaut*, making us realize we're in a set piece without knowing exactly how we got there. A famous example occurs in Act 2 of *Tosca* (1900), in which a trio emerges from nowhere when Spoletta (tenor), henchman of the evil tyrant Scarpia (bass-baritone), bursts in to announce Napoleon's victory at Marengo. Given that Spoletta's audience – Scarpia, Cavaradossi (tenor, who has just been brutally tortured) and Tosca (soprano, his lover, trying to save him) – are at the apex of a private and traumatic impasse, this political reportage might seem beside the point. But Cavaradossi, being a staunch republican, draws vocal inspiration from the news. Shouting 'Vittoria! Vittoria!', he launches into music of martial exultation, around which Tosca adds injunctions to prudence and Scarpia gloats ferociously. A very old operatic gesture – shocking news elicits ensemble reaction – is being replayed, but only for a moment; the trio passes away almost as soon as it has begun. A second example comes towards the end of Act 1 of Puccini's last opera, *Turandot* (1926). Prince Calaf (tenor) decides to wager his life in a Riddle Contest for the hand of Princess Turandot (soprano). Timur (bass),

Calaf's aged father, and Timur's servant, Liù (soprano), attempt to dissuade him. Calaf has declared his passion in a circling, minor-key phrase that suddenly becomes the scaffold around which Liù adds *her* voice, and then come Timur's grieving exclamations. As if by magic, the three voices are together, and the circling phrase starts to sound like a collective dirge. It is over almost too soon, leaving a sense of amazement that something so swift could be so devastating.

Lacking elements of literary *verismo* but toying with realist devices in other domains: *Manon Lescaut* has long stretches of stage music, including most of the first half of Act 2, before the love duet, done as an eighteenth-century pastiche. And it maintains stage action in large ensembles. Puccini's next and most famous opera, *La bohème* (1896), is different. Its setting is bohemian Paris, and the main characters are far from aristocratic. The heroine, Mimì (soprano), is a simple seamstress who gazes out over the roofs and is afflicted by tuberculosis; the hero, Rodolfo (tenor), is a poetic dreamer, trying to write grandiose plays but scraping a living as a journalist. Poverty, disease, hunger and cold are constant companions, even though these trials are seen through a sentimental lens that makes the tone very different from that in *Cavalleria* or *Pagliacci*.

But *La bohème* has another aspect that became important to *fin-de-siècle* operas and can certainly be related to realism: its extended soundscapes, crowd scenes depicting Parisian street life that sample many varieties of ambient noise without caring in particular about musical coherence. The start of Act 2 is knit from the cries of street vendors, conflicting choruses of citizens and children who traipse in and out singing or just shouting. Against this babble, the conversations of the principals emerge from time to time but can at any moment be barged aside by the crowd's urgent noise. There are frequent changes in tempo, metre, dynamics and texture, as if the music were eavesdropping freely at this or that location in the crowd. Puccini may have learned this technique from Massenet (*Manon* has some good examples), and such scenes also became something of a French speciality. Another French opera that persistently received the realist label was *Louise* (1900) by Gustave Charpentier (1860–1956), which has two soundscape scenes. At the beginning of Act 2, there is an urban aubade in which the cascading musical cries of street vendors and workers at dawn do not just hawk wares but consider existential questions about life and the future. And the end of Act 3 sees a chaotic parade featuring the King of Fools, that stalwart of Parisian bohemianism who goes all the way back to François Villon. The reign of the King of Fools is the reign of carnival, and the anything-can-happen licence that prevails seems to liberate the music to choose whatever sounds it wants to, no matter how brief or extended, or disconnected to what was heard just before.

La bohème seems almost completely free from Wagnerism, something that – as we shall see in the next chapter – could be said of very few operas of the 1890s. This partly has to do with the subject matter: as Puccini said, *La bohème* was an opera of 'small things',[14] of tiny objects delicately sketched. (One thinks of Massenet's Manon and the farewell she bids to her 'petite table'; *La bohème* is much more influenced by Massenet than is *Manon Lescaut*, in which the shared subject matter probably discouraged any fleeting reference.) Whereas the *Ring* deals in spears, swords and mighty ash trees, *La bohème* presents hand-warming muffs, bonnets and an unreliable, smoky stove. Each of these objects is delicately attached to a musical motif, but Puccini's treatment of recurring themes is again distant from the Wagnerian norm. The very first motif in the opera is an energetic idea identified with the Bohemians, and derived from a student composition of Puccini's entitled *Capriccio sinfonico*. The original title is apt, as the motif dominates the drama's exposition (the first part of Act 1) and is caught up in a quasi-symphonic process of tonal tension and release. But there's an important difference from Wagnerian usage: the motif's shape is unchanging and is rarely heard in connection with other themes. Rather than functioning primarily as a semantic marker, as something attached to an *object*, it is fundamentally connected to *gesture*; it's not the 'bohemians' theme' but an accompaniment to moments when their energy dominates the stage; it returns only when that kind of energy is (however briefly) repeated.

The same could be said, in an even more remarkable way, of the very last chords of the opera, which have presented many academic commentators (though few listeners) with a famous motivic problem. Earlier in the act, one of the minor bohemians, the philosopher Colline (bass), decides he must pawn his overcoat in order to buy a cordial for the dying Mimì. In a gesture typical of the opera's 'small things', he then addresses a tiny farewell aria to his overcoat, a solo that ends with solemn orchestral chords in parallel motion. This aria is important in its context: it acts as a brief moment of stasis, of lyrical contemplation, before Mimì's death scene begins. But what are we to make of the fact that these solemn chords then return to close the entire opera, underpinning the final, desolate tableau with Mimì faded away and Rodolfo shouting in despair? Efforts to connect the two citations by means of semantic identification risk deflating the pathos. It can hardly deepen the impact of Rodolfo's mourning to connect it with Colline's distress at losing his overcoat. On the gestural level, though – the sense in which this motif announces the final tragedy and then marks its conclusion – no such strain occurs. Indeed, it may be the *absence* of semantic connection that makes the recurrence so telling. Puccini allows a space to emerge between words and music, a space in which musical drama could reside.

The famous arias in *La bohème* again involve a technique mentioned earlier: the ghost number, in which a musically substantial statement is summoned forth out of ambient threads and textures. When Puccini's arias are performed in concert, they always seem short compared to the set pieces of earlier generations, and often require retrofitted musical frames to help them stand alone – a new introduction that is not a transition, or a new ending that really is an ending, and not the beginning of what happens next. Mimì's autobiographical aria near the end of Act 1, 'Mi chiamano Mimì' (They call me Mimì), is an immortal example. Puccini's word-setting means that the formal poetry hardly survives from a rhythmic point of view; more surprising is that, until nearly the end, the language is disarmingly prosaic. Rodolfo has, in the moments before, outlined his poetic aspirations in grandiose terms. Mimì lowers the temperature in her answering narrative, which starts in the most basic of ways. 'Yes, they call me Mimì, but my name's Lucia.' Puccini sets this as a kind of question-and-answer. 'They call me Mimì' is harmonically and melodically unstable, left hanging in the air suggestively, like a continuation, not a beginning. This is then countered by the cadences and melodic closure of 'but my name's Lucia', which is an ending, not an intermediate phase. It's as if Mimì has two characters as well as two names, one that is 'poetic' and potentially tragic, another that is determinedly ordinary.

This alternation between the poetic and the prosaic characterizes the aria as a whole: not just because the 'Mi chiamano Mimì' motif turns up twice more but because the entire piece is taken up with such alternations. The grandest occurs towards the end. First there are further details of her simple life: 'I make dinner for myself, alone. I don't always go to mass, but I pray often to the Lord. I live alone, all alone, there in a little white room; and I look over the roofs and into the sky.' All this is set to predictable rhythms and simple harmonies, with frequent uncomplicated cadences. Then something different emerges. 'But when the thaw comes, the first sun is mine, the first kiss of April is mine!' The words become conventionally poetic, and the music floods into one of Puccini's great lyrical inspirations. Strings and woodwind double the melodic line and a rising sequence takes shape: 'ma quando vien lo sgelo' (first phrase); 'il primo sole è mio' (repeated, higher); and the third statement explodes into the wonderful melodic climax of 'il primo bacio dell'aprile è mio!' A lesser composer might have capped this with repetition, a bang on the drum and solicitations for applause. But Puccini gradually leads us back to the humble 'Lucia' music once more. By the end, Mimì is again expressing herself in simple recitative, as unassuming as when she started. 'Mi chiamano Mimì' is what Puccini was wont to call a *pezzo forte* – something he knew would make an effect. It's also *La bohème* in a lyrical nutshell. The constant oscillation between the ordinary and the sentimental is what makes the opera as a whole so effective.

Tosca, which followed *La bohème*, took Puccini four years to write and is very different from its predecessor. The libretto was based on a recent Grand Guignol play by the Frenchman Victorien Sardou and is set in 1800 during the Napoleonic Wars. It features passion, blackmail and murder among Rome's political and artistic elite. Baron Scarpia, one of the great Bad Boys of opera, is the despotic head of a repressive regime and uses his position to feed two great intertwined enthusiasms: sadism and lechery. At the end of Act 1 this demon gets caught up in a grand religious ceremony, creating a scene that would remain the most radical of Puccini's many operatic soundscapes. While chasing a runaway convict, Scarpia guesses that the tenor hero Cavaradossi has something to do with the escape; Scarpia is in the church of Sant'Andrea della Valle and has just interrogated Tosca, Cavaradossi's lover and the present object of the baron's carnal ambitions. As two bells toll slowly in the background ('in the distance, but audible', marks Puccini in his score), a religious procession starts up. Various choral collectives sing Latin texts in quasi-liturgical monotones.

One extraordinary feature of this scene is its obsessive harmonic repetition, the bells providing two low pitches, B♭ and F, which alternate for long minutes. From offstage, cannon blasts timed to the beat of the music are heard, signalling the prisoner's escape. Puccini devises harmonies that wind around the bells' fundamental tones but cannot depart from them. The Latin chanting fits around them too, as does an orchestral melody – necessarily a circular one – that in turn will join and underpin the soliloquy Scarpia delivers over all this rising clamour. Once again there is a sonic background, with a sung peroration in front of it, but here the background grows louder all the time and the explosions from the cannon, like the anvils in Wagner's *Rheingold*, break the boundaries that limit operatic noise to nature's murmurs and bring it into a sterner age. The baritone singing Scarpia has to put all his power into delivering the soliloquy, in which he imagines converting Tosca's jealous fire into the passion of a willing lover. Finally, coming out of his lascivious reverie and recalling that he is in a church, he shouts out, 'Tosca, mi fai dimenticare Iddio!' (Tosca, you make me forget God!). As if in response to an unheard blasphemy, the choir bursts forth with a unison statement of an authentic Te Deum melody, Scarpia joining in. Just when you imagine things couldn't get any louder, the full orchestra then blares forth Scarpia's leitmotif (full of evil tritones, rasping brass and cymbals). When the curtain comes down, you almost expect the stage fabric to fall with a crash.

Surprising as it might now seem, early performances of *Tosca* often confused audiences and were excoriated by critics. One of the latter wrote:

> The sonatinas and cantatas from the wings, and the organ, and the Gregorian chant, and the drums that announce the march to the scaffold, and the bells, and the cow bells, and the rifle shots, and the cannon fire, which at times constitute essential elements in the development of the opera, are not enough to fill the holes left by the lack of music.[15]

Another was sure of the opera's fate:

> In thirty years . . . *Tosca*, together with all the other operas of its type, will be an obscure and uncertain memory of a time of confusion in which music was subtracted, by the logic of history, from its own dominion, from its own laws, and from common sense.[16]

Most mysterious of all is a review of the first London performance that once more takes issue with raw sounds:

> *Tosca* is too artificial, and when the composer wishes to be most intense, there is little save irritating noise – much sound with little musical sense. This remark applies chiefly to the second act. There are some who say that they best enjoy Wagner's music at the theatre by shutting their eyes, and not being worried by what is taking place on the stage. In the second act of *La Tosca*, on the contrary, it is the sound of the music which seems to interfere with the undoubtedly strong dramatic situation.[17]

The mystery, of course, is why the musical noise, which is one of the most profoundly realistic gestures in opera, is here dismissed as 'too artificial' – as if opera as a genre had so firmly established its unique blend of naturalness and artifice that common sense can no longer apply. Of course, we can now smile at these critics if we choose, just as we can dismiss those who found nothing but recitative in the letter scene in *Onegin*, or thought its libretto a domestic bore. It may, though, be more productive to take their complaints seriously. The various attempts at operatic realism towards the end of the nineteenth century were indeed radical and unsettling, challenging as they did long-held ideas about music's proper place in the operatic spectacle. But our second critic's confident prediction, that such innovations would soon fade away, could not have been further from the mark. In realism's wake some of opera's strangest and noisiest moments were about to break confusingly on to the scene.

17
Turning point

In 1893, a French composer decides to write an opera. He is classically trained, a product of the Paris Conservatoire and winner of the prestigious 'prix de Rome' composition prize. He has already finished one opera in draft form, a three-act giant in a historical-Spanish-chivalric setting. This fulfils any lingering *grand opéra* responsibilities that inhabit his nationalist conscience, and he becomes unhappy with it. One night he attends a spoken play by the Belgian dramatist Maurice Maeterlinck (1862–1949) and daringly decides to use this play as the text of an opera – without turning it into poetry, without even restructuring the sections he takes from it in any significant way, aside from some cutting and line editing. The play has only one brief passage that in any way lends itself to becoming an operatic set piece, a song for the heroine. Everything else is freeform conversation and random musing.

This new opera takes two years to write, orchestration not included, and is then extensively revised before finally being performed in 1902. The venue is Paris's Opéra-Comique. For much of the earlier nineteenth century, anything performed at the Opéra-Comique would – by law – have had passages of spoken dialogue interspersed among the numbers; but by now this rule had evaporated and the theatre was happy to stage operas containing no speech. With this new Maeterlinck opera, the Opéra-Comique had a *succès de scandale* that became a flashpoint for debates about the past and future of French music. It premiered a piece that for some opera-goers to this day remains an inexplicable bore, hardly an opera at all, with no great melodies and only a few instances where the orchestra plays at anything approaching full volume.

In brief, this is the story of *Pelléas et Mélisande*, a *drame lyrique* in five acts by Claude Debussy (1862–1918) and the single most innovative opera to emerge at the *fin de siècle*. Despite the indecisive princes and other sensitive flowers that populate its dramatis personae, and despite its generally languorous pace and extreme musical informality, it excited great passions. Maeterlinck and Debussy fought bitterly over the casting of the heroine Mélisande. At one point the playwright – although a wilting aesthete on the page, he was evidently a decent swordsman in real life – roared into the composer's flat and challenged him to a duel. The opera's reception was mixed. The young Maurice Ravel went to every single performance in the initial run. In 1908, Henry Adams was looking forward to seeing a revival but arrived at the theatre to find that Massenet's *Manon* was on instead. A letter he wrote after the fact says merely 'My wrath was deep.'[1] At the other end of the spectrum, critics wrote dismissively of 'rhythm, song, and tonality [being] three things unknown to M. Debussy'.[2] For some, rhythm and tonality were the least of its problems. Camille Bellaigue saw civilization itself under threat:

> after listening [to *Pelléas*] one feels sick . . . one is dissolved by this music because it is in itself a form of dissolution. Existing as it does with a minimum of vitality, it tends to impair and destroy our existence. The germs it contains are not those of life and progress, but of decadence and death.[3]

The director of the Paris Conservatoire issued an edict prohibiting his students from attending performances. Decades later, Pierre Boulez railed against conductors who tried to make *Pelléas* boring with 'discretion worthy of a footman', interpretations in which 'the many contrasts in the work were reduced to a minute scale and . . . robbed . . . of their potency and violence'.[4] In short, *Pelléas* is for some unbearable in its tedium while for others it is the most beautiful edifice in sound ever to involve characters, libretto and costumes.

It's important to start with this account of *Pelléas* because so much about the opera is strange, new or unusual. For one thing, opera libretti adapted from spoken dramas had before this point almost invariably undergone restructuring by professional librettists: men of letters who slashed and burned, and who then put what remained into verse, neatly packaged to suit the conventional musical forms of opera's past. For a composer himself to turn a pre-existing play into an opera, and to do little more than cut here and there for the sake of brevity, was almost unheard of. Parts of Musorgsky's *Boris Godunov* were done this way, and it is a famous earlier example. Debussy knew the piece. He had spent apprentice years in Russia, as a musician in the personal entourage of Tchaikovsky's patroness, Nadejda von Meck. An opera with a text like *Boris* or *Pelléas* – in German they would be called *Literaturoper*, works whose words are taken directly from a spoken drama – is a frighteningly blank slate. Where does one start, musically? How to fashion regular melodies from unmetred prose? What can mark the musical points of articulation when there is so little in the words to say where such points might reasonably lie?

This is not the only conundrum raised by *Pelléas*. For much of the nineteenth century, composing opera in the central Western European traditions was a particular kind of job. If you were good at it, you rarely ventured into other genres; and if you were a fine instrumental composer, perhaps even outstanding in solo song, you dabbled in opera at your peril. Examples abound: curiosities such as the largely unperformed operatic œuvre of Franz Schubert, or Robert Schumann's *Genoveva* (1850) or Hugo Wolf's *Der Corregidor* (1896). Brahms, Bruckner and Mahler, three of the greatest German instrumental composers, hardly even tried. Of course, there were a few Western European exceptions, Saint-Saëns being perhaps the most obvious. And several who hailed from outside Italy, Germany and France – composers such as Dvořák or Tchaikovsky – were polymaths, writing orchestral works, operas and chamber music with equal fluency. But the extent to which operas in the nineteenth century were the products of specialists is still remarkable. The giants, Verdi and Wagner, are the paradigmatic cases.

By 1900 this was changing. In the twentieth century it becomes difficult to think of anyone aside from Puccini who fits the old, specialist pattern and made a success of it. This is important for several reasons. On a practical level it underlines that new operas were declining in number and importance. It proved ever more difficult, even with much-improved copyright protection, to make a decent living by composing exclusively for the stage. But the rise of the twentieth-century operatic dabbler also had consequences for the kinds of opera composed. When composers brought up as specialists in instrumental genres chose to write opera, their efforts were often suffused with an alternative musical universe, one with its own habits and sounds, its own methods of acoustic theatricality. When he started *Pelléas*, Debussy was already an orchestral radical whose sonic imagination resembled little else in music of the time, and whose harmonic vocabulary was recognized as avant-garde. He was also an attentive and often caustic observer of the French operatic milieu, and harboured a particular critical distaste for imitation. 'There is nothing more deplorable', he wrote a little later, in 1906, 'than that neo-Wagnerian school in which French genius is obscured by a lot of imitation Wotans in long boots and Tristans in velvet jerkins'.[5]

In this neo-Wagnerian department, there were a great many to deplore. Ernest Reyer produced a *Sigurd* in 1884 featuring Brünnhilde, Siegfried, Gunther and Gutrune, all spelled differently; his music, though, is more *grand opéra* than grand Bayreuth. An increasing number of libretti in French began to involve tragic medieval love affairs (Emmanuel Chabrier's *Gwendoline*, 1886, or Ernest Chausson's *Le Roi Arthus* – King Arthur, 1903) or misty legends (Vincent d'Indy's *Fervaal*, 1897). Nor were the long boots and velvet jerkins confined to France. To the south, Ruggiero Leoncavallo planned a massive trilogy (to his own libretto, of course, and entitled – with embarrassingly deliberate Wagnerian overtones – *Crepusculum*, 'twilight' in English, 'Dämmerung' in German). It was to be set in the Italian Renaissance – Italy's answer to Nordic myth. *I Medici*, the first instalment, was premiered in 1893 but was received so coolly that its composer wisely shelved the two sequels, instead trying vainly to beat Puccini at the box office with an alternative version of *La bohème*. To the east, Peter Cornelius unsuccessfully tried his hand at *Gunlöd* (1869–74), which features Odin (aka Wotan, tenor) and a triangle resembling Hunding, Siegmund and Sieglinde. Richard Strauss's first two operas, *Guntram* (1894) and *Feuersnot* (1901), struggle through multiple Wagnerian attractions and anxieties, being respectively a medieval-religious tragedy about renunciation and a folk-Bavarian comedy. The Russians, too, were vulnerable. Nikolay Rimsky-Korsakov's *The Legend of the Invisible City of Kitezh* (1907) mates Slavic and Teutonic mythology, featuring all-knowing forest birds (à la *Siegfried*) and a half-mystical, half-ecclesiastical redemptive transfiguration at the end (à la *Parsifal*). Before that he had dabbled in an *Odyssey* opera, and even a trilogy of works based on Russian epic poems;[6] both ideas petered out at the sketching stage.

While it would be wrong to assume that every late-nineteenth-century opera with medieval knights was aping *Lohengrin* (there had been many such knights before Wagner), Nordic gods are harder to explain away. But libretto trends are only a minor symptom. Wagner's fundamental innovations in operatic music, especially the sheer attraction of his sound, proved extraordinarily hard to ignore. His operas resonated around Europe and beyond whether you shunned them or stared them boldly in the face. They resonated even if you lampooned them – many a French operetta composer would try this route, and Emmanuel Chabrier's wry piano-duet quadrilles on themes from *Tristan*, called *Souvenirs de Munich*, are not to be missed. Debussy's ironic reference to *fin-de-siècle* operas swarming with Wagnerian revenants, characters mired in the Middle Ages or the fjords, only begins to illustrate the dilemma: what style to adopt in the wake of Bayreuth?

For some, a way out was to renounce words altogether. There are a whole series of French post-Wagnerian operas in which soprano or mezzo-soprano siren calls represent danger in direct proportion to the absence or meaninglessness of their words. In the previous chapter, we touched on Saint-Saëns' *Samson et Delila* and Massenet's *Esclarmonde*, both of whose heroines exercise this charm. More famous still, at least in concert renderings, is an aria from the second act of Léo Delibes's *Lakmé* (1883). An upstanding British officer is betrayed when he responds to the eponymous heroine's singing voice, which is for him an object of fascination. The fatal lure is Lakmé's 'Bell Song', a *locus classicus* of hyper-ornamentation functioning as hyper-seduction. At such moments, the singer, vocal part and character combine to overcome all resistance. Here, for instance, is a suitably hyperbolic and erotically charged account of Lily Pons as Lakmé, from a review of 1929:

> But whatever may be the amazing power of her high soprano, the caress of the middle register, there is her ideal incarnation of these heroines, the artistic intoxication of youth that bursts forth from her heart like a blaze of love, now in accents of terror, like an Aeolian harp, like the light and burning perfume of the great mimosas in the forest consecrated to Brahma. I have no memory of greater enchantment than her Bell Song heavy with an indefinable exotic seduction.[7]

Such extreme coloratura is textless almost by definition, but the same effects can occur when the words are present but are of little consequence. In a strange, typically refracted way, a shard of this singing style reached *Pelléas*, part of whose radicalism is its unusually slavish, meticulous musical attention to the rhythms of words. A strange, elliptical exchange between Pelléas and Mélisande summarizes the degree to which the female voice, even with words, can still be taken as birdsong or siren bells. Mélisande sings to her lover, Pelléas, 'Je ne mens jamais, je ne mens qu'à ton frère' (I never lie, I only lie to your brother), a statement that is, like so much in Maeterlinck, simultaneously disturbing and mystifying. But Pelléas does not react to this uncertainty of meaning, instead going into ecstasies over her vocal timbre: 'Oh! comme tu dis cela! Ta voix, ta voix! Elle est plus fraîche et plus franche que l'eau' (Ah, how you say that! Your voice, your voice! It is cooler and clearer than water). Throughout the opera, the hero rhapsodizes in similar terms over the heroine's voice, which rivals her long hair as his chief erotic fixation: just as, not coincidentally, Carmen's voice was for Don José, or Dalila's for Samson.

In this particular sense, elements of *Pelléas* are directly in line with far more conventional French operas of the later nineteenth century. Debussy dealt with the problem not by indulging it to excess – with too much coloratura and open vowel sounds – but by enquiring into it philosophically. Mélisande certainly fascinates her lover, but never for a moment does she sing without words, and never does she sing with any particular virtuosity. Nonetheless, accounts of the singers who performed Mélisande can become as rapturous as those concerning Lakmé, suggesting that the seductive effect could be analogous. Mary Garden, the first Mélisande and a famous operatic interpreter, could be called 'a condor, an eagle, a peacock, a nightingale, a panther';[8] another excited commentator said that her voice as Mélisande had the ability to:

> shape and colour the significant and haunting phrase, to thread her way through an iridescent web of them . . . at moments her singing is like a new and strange speech – as new and strange as Debussy's music. The listener feels the captivating fascination and the penetrating suggestion, and leaves the tests of cold technical blood until after the spell has passed.[9]

THEATRE OF THE ALMOST-ABSURD

Maeterlinck specialized in a style of theatre called 'symbolist', which was related to an anti-realist movement in art and poetry (Mallarmé and Verlaine were standard-bearers) that favoured addressing the largest human issues by indirect means, often through fantasy and dreams. True to its label, *Pelléas* is characterized by an overriding sense that human beings will always, ultimately, be submerged by those giant, impersonal forces of fate constantly bearing down on them. It is a drama of halftones and mystifying epigrams, peopled by actors who efface their individual personalities the better to reflect the symbols they represent. The setting is a fictional long ago, a castle in the kingdom of Allemonde – *alle* is German for 'entire' and *monde* is French for 'world'. While out hunting in a forest, Prince Golaud (baritone), a widower and the heir of his grandfather, King Arkel (bass), stumbles on a girl (soprano) weeping by a well. She refers enigmatically to her past but mostly refuses to answer his questions, revealing only that her name is Mélisande. All subsequent scenes take place in or around Arkel's castle, where Golaud brings Mélisande after marrying her. There she meets Golaud's younger half-brother, Pelléas (high baritone or low tenor), and the remainder of the opera involves a string of vignettes, mostly between Pelléas and Mélisande, who are thrown together with what proves to be tragic frequency. Arkel drifts in and out representing noble antiquity; Pelléas and Mélisande play emotional games and fall in love; Golaud's young son, Yniold (boy soprano), has a solo scene in which one of his toys, a golden ball, becomes trapped and in which a flock of weeping sheep pass by; Golaud kills Pelléas when he discovers the couple in a lovers' tryst. In the final act, Mélisande dies, fading away inexplicably after a minor injury, having (we are told) given birth to a daughter. Riddles concerning minor events in the plot abound. Does Mélisande deliberately lose her wedding ring when she drops it into a fountain? Why is Golaud thrown from his horse at exactly that moment? Why does Golaud take Pelléas to visit an underground cave? Who is the mysterious shepherd (not to mention his weeping sheep) whom Yniold encounters while trying to dislodge his golden ball?

Such indeterminacy is typical of symbolist literature, in which the signs and secrets of fate remain self-consciously impossible to decode. The point is to create, in the reader or spectator, a feeling that meanings are all-powerful but elusive, that behind each object or phrase lie infinite possibilities that cannot be pinned down. In this respect, Wagner was often an explicit hero and model of symbolist poets and dramatists. But what they adored in Wagner – and what they tried to capture in words – was a quality they found not in his libretti but in his music. It was music that seemed to well up from an unseen, transcendent realm, representing neither pure, abstract form nor self-evident emotional expression. This in turn accounts for much of the strangeness of symbolist texts. If words rather than music were to articulate their artistic projects, the words had to evoke an equivalent mystery, as half-references or dissolved meaning; they became like music by retreating from sense and approaching pure sound.

On the surface, this aesthetic gave rise to an art of suggestion rather than statement. In Maeterlinck's play, events can often seem detached from one another, as if we are witnessing causes without effects or consequences without origins. And it was just these features that became Debussy's inspiration for the radical operatic music he conceived in *Pelléas*. Often the characters barely intone their lines, with music so austere as to be next door to silence. Phrases often funnel down into pure orchestral resonance, with the harp or another deep instrument playing a single note that decays into echoes in an empty space. The drowned causality in Maeterlinck's play becomes Debussy's model for a musical equivalent. Scenes are assembled out of individual musical sections which are unique and very beautiful, but which are largely separate from each other – as unrelated as the enigmatic events that occur without motivation in the play. These are also the idiosyncrasies that make *Pelléas* fundamentally a musician's opera, and a fastidious musician at that. The piece has little to say to people who like narrative thrust, self-contained arias and the satisfying bray of cadential closure with trumpet and drum. In 1910, Thomas Beecham revived *Pelléas* at Covent Garden, and it was greeted with great pleasure after a season of Richard Strauss:

> It came along at the right moment: blood and thunder had exhausted [Strauss's] appeal; there was something akin to an unspoken demand for a work of pure beauty. London responded immediately; a large gathering assembled to hear Debussy's masterpiece. The antagonism between the early Victorians, who regard *La traviata* and *Lucia di Lammermoor* as works of art, and their grandchildren, who know better, seemed to have faded before the season of Peace on Earth . . . if Mr. Beecham has reconciled London to *Pelléas and Mélisande* by his production of operas like *Tiefland* and *Salome*, he will not have laboured in vain.[10]

And note that by 1910, eight years after its premiere, *Pelléas* is a masterpiece. Its divided reception lasts to this day; but it was, like most great operas, hardly an unrecognized wallflower in its debutante period.

OLD KLINGSOR

Wagner was never far from Debussy's mind when he composed *Pelléas*. He went to Bayreuth in the summers of 1888 and 1889, and heard *Parsifal*, *Meistersinger* and *Tristan*. He heard *Lohengrin* in Paris in 1887 and again in 1893, and was at the first Paris performance of *Die Walküre*, also in 1893. In the spring of that last year he had assisted at a strange lecture-performance, held on the stage of the Opéra, with Catulle Mendès discoursing on the *Ring* while Debussy, a second pianist and six soloists did their best to serve up excerpts from *Das Rheingold*. One tries in vain to imagine *Rheingold*'s sustained opening E♭ as executed by two pianos, four hands. Did they open the lids and pluck the string? Afterwards Debussy said: 'It is good to have done with the Rhine. The performance was a terrible bore.'[11] But much that Debussy wrote about Wagner took a scornful tone that may well indicate an emotion too deep, or a debt too heavy for comfort. As he put it in 1903:

> It is not my concern to discuss Wagner's genius here. His force was undeniably dynamic. But its effect was all the greater because the way had been prepared by cunning magicians whose guile knew no bounds. . . . Perhaps it is the extraordinarily anguished groaning in his music that is responsible for the deep impression made by Wagner on the contemporary spirit: he has awakened the secret thirst for the criminal in some of the most famous minds of our age [Debussy added a wry footnote here about Richard Strauss]. To conclude, Wagner's works suggest a most striking image: Bach is the Holy Grail, Wagner is Klingsor, who wants to destroy the Grail and take its place. Bach reigns . . . Wagner vanishes. A fearsome darkness, black as soot.[12]

The drift of the metaphors is striking. German composers are magicians – the predecessors include Bach. Wagner is a magician too, but a different kind. He is a criminal sorcerer like Klingsor, the infertile nihilist from Wagner's *Parsifal*. Indeed, almost every polemical statement Debussy made about opera took aim at Wagner: 'I shall not imitate the follies of the lyric theatre where music insolently predominates and where poetry is relegated to second place. In the opera house they sing too much.'[13] But the rejection was much easier to announce polemically than it was to translate into musical practice. At one early point in its genesis, Debussy made elaborate sketches for a scene in *Pelléas* but then realized that 'the ghost of Klingsor, alias R. Wagner', had appeared; he felt obliged to rip out the offending pages.[14] Perhaps to inoculate himself and his opera from further unwelcome visits, he scattered through the score little clues relating to his obsession. At one point Mélisande, with a characteristic show of enigma, says, 'je suis heureuse, mais je suis triste' (I am happy, but I am sad), and on that word 'triste' the *Tristan* chord punningly appears, a ghost whose presence could be tolerated only (one assumes) because swathed in irony.

Such caution towards Wagnerian enthusiasms might at first seem compromised by *Pelléas*'s opening, which introduces a sequence of contrasting musical ideas that will all return later as leitmotifs. First come four bars of low, modal music, almost like plainchant, which will be attached to the antique ambience of Allemonde and perhaps also to the dense forest in which the action begins. This gives way to, and then alternates with, a restless idea later associated with Golaud, in the middle register and based on the whole-tone scale. And then, high up, *doux et expressif*, comes a lyrical idea that will later belong to Mélisande, based on the more densely chromatic octatonic scale. The message would seem clear. Three musical 'calling cards' are here propped up on the *Pelléas* mantelpiece in the first minute of the opera, as if in homage to Wagnerian practice. But there are crucial differences. For one thing, although these three ideas are strongly differentiated in register, harmony, rhythm and texture, they appear in sharp juxtaposition, with hardly any attempt at transition from one to another. In that sense, they represent an antithesis to the Wagnerian praxis, in which leitmotifs succeed each other and even transform into one another without seams. Debussy's leitmotifs, self-sufficient and isolated, foreshadow in microcosm his opera's overarching aesthetic, the unmediated shifts from one musical atmosphere to another. Equally important, though, the three initial ideas in *Pelléas* constitute virtually its entire leitmotivic substance, and none of them recurs with any regularity. A symphonic web of recurring ideas? Hardly.

The score is also un-Wagnerian in more noticeable ways. There is little loud noise, since the orchestra is unusually deployed in groups and at modest dynamic levels. Although the sound-world Debussy creates – the orchestral web is a continuous presence behind the singers, with its own musical matters to pursue – channels the spirit of Wagner, the musical surface rarely sounds anything like him. 'Old Klingsor' is kept firmly at bay. Consider Act 2, scene 3. Pelléas and Mélisande make a night-time visit to a vaulted grotto by the edge of the sea. Mélisande has lied to Golaud about her wedding ring, saying that she lost it there and will return to search for it. Before any singing, we are treated to the vaulted grotto in orchestral form. Over a pianissimo rumble in the lowest registers, the woodwind play a quiet, phantasmal fanfare, and then they repeat it to show where we are – in a place where sound bounces and echoes. A cymbal is brushed by a feather, tremolo strings hover in the heights. A strange combination of brass instruments plays a single chord, then an odder mix – muted instruments – plays it again, showing the same view from a different angle, or the same object in a different light. When the lovers appear, they hesitate outside; but once they pass over the threshold, the music accompanying their initial appearance is repeated with its acoustic wrapper entirely different, because when you walk into a cave the ambient sound changes.

The scene is a monologue for Pelléas, who describes in detail the dark grotto they walk through, his vocal line shaped to the music of the orchestra. There is a spectacular *coup de théâtre*. The moon suddenly floods the cave with its radiance. Pelléas cries in ecstasy, 'Oh! voici la clarté!' (Oh! here is the light!); the orchestra instantly stops what it is doing in order to create musical light, harp glissandos up and down, the woodwinds in a circular, melancholy motif heard earlier. But this only lasts a moment, because the pair catch sight of three starving, white-haired paupers who have crept into the cave for shelter. The gorgeous moon-sounds disappear, to be replaced by a single oscillating figure, two notes repeated over and over again, with a bleak melodic fragment above. 'There is a famine', sings Pelléas, 'they are asleep.' Mélisande wants to flee but refuses Pelléas's arm to help her climb. Everything audible begins to wind down. Motifs heard earlier in the scene pass like shades, and last of all comes the woodwind echo-fanfare from the start, now voiced very low in the cellos and basses. The music doesn't end so much as pass beyond the threshold of hearing, as if we ourselves are getting further from the grotto's sound-shifting ambience.

Debussy's genius for the music of ambient sounds predated his opera, and was not limited to it. He would write brilliant orchestral tone poems like the *Prélude à l'après-midi d'un faune* (1894) and *La Mer* (1905). More important in terms of operatic tradition is the scene's assembly. The musical sections succeed one another without transition; something different always comes along, and the mystery that results is to be savoured. This novel structure was in many way inspired by the words. Maeterlinck's idiosyncratic libretto helped spring Debussy from the *fin-de-siècle* French opera trap. His earlier, abandoned *grand opéra* – *Rodrigue et Chimène* – resembles Massenet. *Pelléas et Mélisande* is, and has remained, unclassifiable.

SALOME, TOWARDS THE EXTREME

The parallels between the early operatic careers of Debussy and Richard Strauss (1864–1949) are immediately arresting. Strauss also first came to prominence as a specialist in orchestral tone poems, and also wrote journeyman operas that suffer from derivative libretti and the operatic models they suggest. What the examples of both Debussy and Strauss indicate is that freeing one's voice as an opera composer around 1900, at least in France and Germany, often involved finding a different kind of libretto. The various cast-offs from and rehashes of nineteenth-century operatic manners, especially when obviously cloned from Wagner, were of little help, since they led, inexorably, along old musical roads. A solitary exception was the unexpected success of Engelbert Humperdinck's fairy-tale opera *Hänsel und Gretel* (whose premiere in 1893 was conducted by Strauss). Unashamedly Wagnerian in orchestral and harmonic language, it managed to harness these unwieldy musical attributes to a fast-moving plot, also incorporating some of the realistic touches that were, to the dismay of nationalists and others, making Leoncavallo and Puccini so successful in Wagner-saturated Germany at that time. Strauss praised the score, declaring it 'original, new and so authentically German!' and also saying (with a disparaging reference to the new Italian craze) that it had 'given the Germans a work they hardly deserve'.[15]

No one felt the operatic problems more keenly than Strauss. Of all the opera composers who came of age around 1900, he was closest to Wagner and seemed most fated to continue in the Master's footsteps. Nearly an adult when Wagner died, he got to know the operas intimately through an early apprenticeship to Hans von Bülow in Meiningen (von Bülow called him 'Richard the Third' – after Wagner there could of course never be a worthy 'Richard the Second'). Strauss became a virtuoso conductor, hired by Wagner's widow Cosima to direct *Tannhäuser* at Bayreuth in 1894 and going on to conduct almost all Wagner's mature operas during his long career. He also became a friend of the Bayreuth clan, with all the obeisance and indoctrination that could entail. Small wonder that he steered away from operatic composition. His initial creative persona was established by the 1890s as a master of the Germanic symphonic poem, a genre he injected with wholly new energy and orchestral brilliance. By contrast, and as we have already said, his first operas, *Guntram* and *Feuersnot*, were haunted.

Strauss waited patiently, and was already forty when early in 1903 he attended a performance in Berlin of Oscar Wilde's play, *Salomé* (1891), translated into German by Hedwig Lachmann from the original French and staged by the young Max Reinhardt. Strauss had read the play a little earlier, and may have been sketching themes already, but it was the staging that fired his imagination. He decided to use Lachmann's translation as the text for his opera, like Debussy fashioning his own libretto simply by means of cuts and line editing. Wilde may himself have owed a tiny debt to *grand opéra*, since his biblical setting and Oriental exoticism, complete with Judean *femme fatale*, is reminiscent of *Samson et Dalila* and other Gallic epics. However – the similarity with *Pelléas* is significant – the play's language was nothing like old-style libretto-speak. Nor would its frankness about sexual obsession, necrophilia and the nude female form have possibly passed the censors of an earlier era.

In England, which admittedly had special problems with Wilde, the Lord Chamberlain banned the *Salomé* play altogether, and it was not allowed to cross the Channel until 1931. The opera, though, was staged in London as early as 1910 – we have already cited one reviewer's note about how Thomas Beecham followed *Salome* with a course of *Pelléas* for the Christmas season that year. Public sensibilities were admittedly somewhat protected in the 1910 London staging: the decapitated head of John the Baptist, brought to Salome on a silver tray near the end of the drama, was replaced by a (relatively innocuous) bloody sword. But the fact that the opera was palatable long before the play underlines music's tendency to defuse words and images which otherwise might be thought to go too far. A protective umbrella spreads out over all operas by virtue of their music, and in acknowledgment of the labour that goes into their production. Back in the Victorian era, Alexandre Dumas's play *La Dame aux camélias* (1852) was subjected to censure and censorship in England, but the opera based on it, *La traviata* (1853), was praised for its artful delicacy. Sober, highly accomplished people are responsible for performing opera, typically at great expense. Scandal is always prone to be smothered by gravitas, even when the composer was, like Strauss, being as outrageous as possible.

Salome the opera is relatively short. A single act depicts the court of King Herod on Lake Galilee at the time of Jesus and his disciples. Herod (tenor) has imprisoned John the Baptist (called Jokanaan, baritone) in a cistern below the terrace of his palace. His stepdaughter, the princess Salome (soprano), daughter of Herodias (mezzo-soprano), is sixteen years old, bored, beautiful and innocent – Strauss insisted on this last quality. Herod lusts after her with quivering intensity, as do, we are led to believe, numerous others in his court. But she disdains them all. After an opening scene involving one such lovelorn soul (Narraboth, Captain of the Guard, tenor), Salome hears Jokanaan's voice emanating from the cistern and is bewitched by it. She persuades Narraboth to bring the prophet up from his cell. As soon as Jokanaan appears it becomes clear that Salome has developed an erotic fixation; she praises in turn his ivory body, his mane of black hair and, finally, his red mouth. When Jokanaan recoils and curses her for her evil thoughts, she turns angry and sullen. He retreats to the sanctity of his cistern. Herod and Herodias appear, and Herod begins wheedling, trying to persuade Salome to dance. Fired up by her refusals, he offers her whatever she desires, if only she will dance. Salome agrees to the bargain and performs the infamous Dance of the Seven Veils, all seven falling as contracted to the floor. She then claims as her reward, with due innocence of tone, the severed head of Jokanaan, to be brought to her on a silver tray. An executioner is sent down, does the deed, appears with the head. Salome seizes it, addresses it tenderly, reproaches it, kisses it on the mouth and discovers a bitter taste on its lips. By this stage Herod, although himself no stranger to decadence, has had enough. He orders his soldiers to kill Salome; they crush her beneath their shields as the curtain falls.

One of the shock elements in *Salome* is not so much that insanity and perversion are presented for viewing pleasure, but that these states are couched in flowery phrases full of highly perfumed poetic metaphor and imagery. Another is that a female protagonist treats her male antagonist as an object, waxing hideously lyrical about his body, his hair, his mouth. Up to now in operatic history, such lyricism had been heard often enough, but the prerogative of dominance had been confined to men, and the object-status confined to women. One could argue that Wilde's play was merely homoerotic in its rhapsodies over a male form, and that the admiring words are put by a male author into the mouth of a girl for the sake of misdirection. But this biographical nuance is far removed from the opera, in which the rhapsodizing soprano is easily the most powerful vocal presence on stage. Her voice fills the theatre, particularly when she addresses for the last time her male antagonist, now no more than a bloody fetish served up on silver.

Fundamentally, the libretto released Strauss's operatic fantasy not because it was daring per se, but because Salome, as a soul in torment overmastered by passion, suggested an extreme role for music in opera. Such music would be neither commentary nor scene painting. It would not pretend to be objective. It would instead trace in intimate detail Salome's and the other characters' morbid thoughts, the multiple and violent disturbances of their disordered minds. So Strauss, who had the experience of several raucous tone poems behind him, let things rip. The levels of dissonance, of orchestral volume, of sheer, cacophonous musical noise in *Salome* are unprecedented. Unsavoury characters such as Herod quaver and pipe, shriek and snarl; his nagging wife Herodias is if anything even less given to lyricism. And although Salome is supposed to be sixteen, her singing impersonator must, in Strauss's words, have the voice of an Isolde. It speaks volumes that the most controlled, even ironic, music in the entire opera is the orchestral episode that accompanies Salome's dance. Although this interlude cites some earlier leitmotifs associated with the heroine, it mostly seems to deal in routine exoticism, of a type explored in abundance by earlier French and Russian opera composers.[16] This might seem strange as an accompaniment to the erotic climax of the opera, but is less so when we recall that the dance functions as stage music. It exists within the fiction and for this reason doesn't bear the weight of expressing any of the characters' interior states of mind – states that range in a narrow band from the obsessive to the fanatical to the delusional to the frankly insane.

Strauss used many devices he learned from Wagner, most obviously some complicated games with leitmotifs. When Jokanaan takes leave of Salome, he cries out to her, 'Du bist verflucht, du bist verflucht' (You are cursed, you are cursed). He sings this to a four-note motif, with the first three notes on the same pitch and the last a minor third higher. In the long instrumental transition between his departure and Herod's arrival, the orchestra repeats this motif, but turns it into something else. The original four notes are followed by a sequence of five new ones that send the motif (now played by a horn) upward to end in disquieting harmony. The orchestra is clearly saying something here: as it turns out, something that is surfacing in Salome's mind. When much later, with her seventh veil shed, she makes her demand to Herod 'Ich will den Kopf des Jochanaan' (I want the head of Jokanaan), the nine notes that articulate her statement are the very same. The earlier orchestral transition is, in other words, the trail of Salome's inner evolution, as Jokanaan's curse rings in her head, and the ringing generates a resolve that causes the opera's bloody denouement.

Jokanaan is the only major character unburdened by sin, and what he sings from the cistern – mostly prophecies of redemption – is stable and harmonious, with distinct, Lutheran-leaning chorale undertones, all boomed out in a warm, strong baritone. This sonorous hum is of course what we hear in the theatre; but it also conveys Salome's experience of his vocal presence. She apostrophizes his voice after he is dead, telling the decapitated head, 'Deine Stimme war ein Weihrauchgefäss, und wenn ich dich ansah, hörte ich geheimnisvolle Musik' (Your voice was an incense vessel, and when I looked at you, I heard mysterious music). As she sings this phrase a ghostly echo comes from the orchestra, a motif that Jokanaan had indeed sung earlier during his conversation with her. This close alliance – between the orchestral music and Salome's perceptions of it – is made clearest in the interlude during which the executioner goes down into the cistern. Salome tries to hear what is happening, and as it turns out she misreads the sounds. Strauss uses orchestral tricks in order to suggest these multiple acoustic delusions. A solo double-bass plays a very high note, misleading us into thinking that it's a violin; instrumental cracks and whispers obviously imitate noise, but they avoid giving us any sense of what that noise could be.

ELEKTRA, ERWARTUNG, BLUEBEARD: THREE ROUTES TO MODERNITY

Strauss's *Salome* is often called 'expressionist', a term primarily associated with the visual arts in Germany around this period (Schiele, Kokoschka and Kandinsky are prime suspects here) but also found in literature (Trakl, Kafka), film (Fritz Lang) and other arts. It was a movement in which phenomena, both human and non-human, are characteristically distorted in order to increase the emotional temperature of their representation, tracing an intense subjectivity that typically favours negative emotions. One of the reasons Strauss's music is labelled expressionist is that its frequent lingering on extreme perceptions and mental states has a shattering effect on audiences. In the early days, such effects were often negative, even among those who in general respected Strauss's undoubted musical skills. The French dramatist Romain Rolland, who had been an enthusiastic supporter of *Pelléas*, wrote a letter to Strauss in which he put the blame firmly on Oscar Wilde:

> Wilde's poem . . . has a nauseous and sickly atmosphere about it: it exudes vice and literature. This isn't a question of middle-class morality, it's a question of health . . . Wilde's Salomé, and all those who surround her, except the poor creature Jokanaan, are unwholesome, unclean, hysterical or alcoholic beings, stinking of sophisticated and perfumed corruption. In vain do you transfigure your subject, increase its vigour a hundredfold and envelop it in a Shakespearean atmosphere . . . you transcend your subject, but you can't make one forget it.[17]

Even today, good performances of *Salome* tend to be received with moments of stunned silence. There is a sense that, having been dragged into these demented inner worlds by musical means, we need a pause before returning to the outside, the places we usually inhabit.

Operatic expressionism is indeed a devastating riposte to operatic realism, a riposte in which female characters seem especially prone to mental disorder. The sufferings of nineteenth-century Italian opera heroines, for all their glorious emoting, offer greeting-card sentiments by comparison. To put this another way, Italian and French opera's increasingly fragile fantasy was to imagine that madness could be an aesthetic state represented by volleys of perfect coloratura and lyric control; that overwhelming emotion was properly represented by beautiful, warmly expressive music. The late nineteenth century was a time when the pathology of mental suffering was being researched and codified. Jean-Martin Charcot, a neurologist at the Salpêtrière Hospital in Paris from 1862 to 1893, staged clinical demonstrations with hysterical patients, ones that Sigmund Freud attended in 1885–6. Freud and Josef Breuer published their *Studies on Hysteria* in 1895. According to these *fin-de-siècle* theories, hysteria did not express itself in well-modulated song, but in defects of language, bizarre paralyses and physical ills. The public and scientific explorations of psychosis made conventional theatrical suffering, such as that of Donizetti's Lucia or even Verdi's Violetta, appear quaint; the cultural aftershocks in all the arts were obvious.

While Strauss was working on *Salome*, he visited Reinhardt's theatre in Berlin again, this time for a new play, *Elektra*, freely adapted from the Greek by the Viennese poet Hugo von Hofmannsthal (1874–1929). While writing the play, Hofmannsthal had read and absorbed the lessons of Freud and Breuer's hysteria book, particularly the claim that hysterics repeated certain verbal formulae as protective talismans. Gertrud Eysoldt, who had played Reinhardt's Salome, now starred as his Elektra. Reinhardt thus played a critical supporting role in Strauss's operatic evolution. He was the most important theatre director in Germany for the first three decades of the twentieth century, and his innovations included rhythmic choreographing, so that crowds seemed to flow like insect swarms over the stage sets, and re-imagining the body language of actors, asking for long frozen moments and sudden kinetic explosions. This was all very far from the ambulate-and-gesture traditions of conventional acting at the time, and was an obvious sign that nineteenth-century habits were waning. It is in this sense significant that Strauss did not fully grasp the potential of Wilde's *Salomé* until he saw Reinhardt's staging; and he was so struck by *Elektra* that the idea of using it persisted throughout his work on *Salome* – he wrote to Hofmannsthal in 1906 for permission to proceed, thus beginning a collaboration that extended to five further operas and ended only with Hofmannsthal's death in 1929.

Elektra (1909) continued the *Salome* aesthetic. Based on Sophocles' play of the same name, it puts a mad, ragged, dirty, cunning, tragic heroine at centre stage for ninety uninterrupted minutes. Elektra (soprano) broods obsessively over the murder of her father, Agamemnon. Other characters appear, including her sister, Chrysothemis (soprano); her stepfather, Aegisthus (tenor), who makes a brief but memorable transit to his doom; her mother, Clytemnestra (mezzo-soprano), who provides the occasion for opera's most awful mother–daughter chat; and her beloved brother, Orestes (baritone), believed dead, who arrives out of exile to avenge Agamemnon's long-ago death and brutally murders Clytemnestra and Aegisthus. A buried axe once used to cleave open Agamemnon's skull figures as the most important prop. The opera ends with Elektra executing a wild dance of triumph and then falling lifeless to the ground.

Given this plot, it comes as no surprise that *Elektra* is often raucously dissonant; as with *Salome*, it embraces this style primarily because its music seems to issue directly from the consciousness of the shrieking, groaning, tortured characters, above all from the protagonist, who never leaves the stage. As Elektra puts it, 'Ob ich die Musik nicht höre? Sie kommt doch aus mir' (How could I not hear the music? The music comes from me). The aphorism could stand for operatic Expressionism *tout court*. But Strauss also worried about the potential similarity between the two one-act operas. He wanted to do something new and, typically for the times, 'new' meant more advanced in harmonic language and sheer orchestral din. This experimentation comes to a cacophonous climax in the heroine's final, fatal dance, in which a triumphant major (C major, no less) is constantly interrupted by a mysterious, distantly related minor triad – a fracture maintained even in the final, brutal, fortissimo cadence.

By the time of *Salome* and *Elektra*, Strauss was thought by many to be at the apex of operatic modernism. However, the year of the latter, 1909, saw the composition of a thirty-minute 'monodrama' called *Erwartung* (Expectation), whose concentration on the extremes of human emotion were clearly related to those of Strauss, but which made his efforts look conservative by comparison. Its composer was Arnold Schoenberg (1874–1951), unlike Strauss a minor and occasional opera composer. But Schoenberg resembled Strauss in being someone who in other genres had already made a reputation for the uncompromising embrace of musical extremes. Indeed, it is certain that Strauss was for some time one of Schoenberg's models. Gustav Mahler gave Schoenberg a score of *Salome* soon after its premiere, and one of Schoenberg's pupils recalled him saying that 'Perhaps in twenty years' time someone will be able to explain these harmonic progressions theoretically',[18] a statement of non-comprehension that could count, in the atmosphere of the time, as a powerful endorsement. *Erwartung*'s libretto is a strange, fragmentary stream-of-consciousness, patching together impressions emanating from an unnamed woman (soprano), who is (possibly, it may all be an elaborate nightmare) on the edge of a dark wood, searching for her lover, whose mutilated body she eventually stumbles over. It was written by a young doctor called Marie Pappenheim, and had been influenced by contemporary developments in psychiatry even more obviously than had Hofmannsthal and Strauss. Pappenheim had, though, never before written for the stage, and probably for this reason opted for a kind of interior monologue rather than anything more conventional. Whatever the case, her drama did not, like Strauss's, dress up the expressionist extremes in exotic or classical subjects. The *mise-en-scène* of *Erwartung* was to be nothing more nor less than the human psyche, bereft of time and place – Central Europe before the Great War – whose downward arc was evident.

Let us pause to sample the invective that has greeted Schoenberg's 'sound' almost from the moment he put pen to paper. Here is a representative screed:

> The leader of cacophonists is Arnold Schoenberg. He learned a lesson from militant suffragettes. He was ignored until he began to smash the parlor furniture, throw bombs, and hitch together ten pianolas, all playing different tunes, whereupon everybody began to talk about him. In Schoenberg's later works, all the laws of construction, observed by the masters from Bach to Wagner, are ignored, insulted, trampled upon. The statue of Venus, the Goddess of Beauty, is knocked from its pedestal and replaced by the stone image of the Goddess of Ugliness.[19]

Or, if not a suffragette, perhaps he is a naval munitions expert, 'Arnold Schoenberg is the musical Von Tirpitz of Germany. Having failed to capture a hostile world by his early campaign . . . he began to torpedo the eardrums of his enemies, as well as neutrals, with deadly dissonances.'[20] Fighting words: Schoenberg's music is anhedonistic, allowing for no pleasure or aesthetic warmth, and is understood as an act of aggression against the audience. But such ugliness is no more than proper to *Erwartung*'s spare devastations. An ancient operatic credo – that the music be expressive in just measure to the drama – has been affirmed.

Even for Schoenberg, *Erwartung* was an acoustic extreme. Had his contemporary critics known of atomic bombs, they would doubtless have rushed to embrace the metaphor. Strauss's use of dissonance was always intended to express peculiar states, and could comfortably reside next to passages of relatively stable tonality (such as Jokanaan's music in *Salome*). Schoenberg, though, had precisely in these years (1908–11) decided to abandon tonality as an organizing force within his musical language, and had done so under the influence of an overtly expressionist credo. As he wrote in a famous letter to his friend Kandinsky, 'art belongs to the *unconscious!* One must express *oneself!* Express oneself *directly!*'[21] In his *Harmonielehre* (Theory of Harmony, 1911), he questioned the antithesis between 'consonance' and 'dissonance', suggesting that musical evolution would soon make them irrelevant; elsewhere in the book he heralded the appearance of 'tone-colour melodies', in which variations of pitch would be less important than those of tone colour, a mode that would heighten 'in an unprecedented manner the sensory, intellectual and spiritual pleasures offered by art'.[22] *Erwartung* is in many ways an illustration of these emerging principles. Although there are fleeting moments of tonal reminiscence, most of the score is written in the rapidly codifying *lingua franca* of free atonality. In arguments certainly influenced by Schoenberg's own theorizing, critics used to claim that *Erwartung*'s harmonic language was, like its literary text, an unfettered stream-of-consciousness, with no connecting threads or discernible system. But the determined avoidance of anything that might smack of tonal direction or even tonal anchor produced in its turn a pronounced gravitation towards alternative chordal anchors. *Erwartung* favours the perfect fourth plus the augmented fourth, a sonority that became for atonality something close to a cliché – a trusted and reliable standby when invention flagged.

In its angular extremes, the vocal part in Schoenberg's opera might be described as Kundry plus Salome *in excelsis*, and he makes that ancestry explicit by sketching in fleeting but quite recognizable quotations from both formidable predecessors. Their tendencies to scream and whisper are explored to the full, within an anti-melodic vocality unimaginable in the models. In this context it is something of a surprise (particularly in the light of his own, barely representational sketches for the setting) to learn that Schoenberg tried to insist on staged productions with a degree of naturalism, in particular with a nice, recognizable forest. Such naturalism would today be disjunctive in the extreme, particularly as – to most listeners, at least – Schoenberg's music sounds no less alien and ungraspable now than it did a century ago. But it may also remind us that, in dramatic terms, his heroine had obvious links to the immediate past.

To read comparisons between Strauss and Schoenberg – sometimes even in histories of opera, within which Strauss might seem self-evidently of enormously greater significance – can emphasize how far the story of twentieth-century music still tends to rely on narratives of progress. Schoenberg, we are often told, 'went further' than Strauss in harmonic terms and thus deserves pride of historical place. *Salome* and *Elektra* may get the performances, but *Erwartung* should nevertheless take the musicological medals. This argument was brewing even at the time. Not long after *Erwartung*, Strauss wrote a letter of recommendation for Schoenberg (it was addressed to Gustav Mahler's widow). In it, he showed himself to be part of the uncertain times in his care not to dismiss out-of-hand the atonal revolution, 'since one never knows what posterity will think about it'. He nevertheless voiced strong personal opinions, suggesting that Schoenberg would 'do better to shovel snow instead of scribbling on music paper'.[23] Schoenberg, who got to know about the letter, was quick to respond in kind, saying that Strauss 'is no longer of the slightest artistic interest to me, and whatever I may once have learnt from him, I am thankful to say I misunderstood'.[24] Of course, by that time Strauss had turned away from his *Salome* and *Elektra* manner, and – as we shall see in the next chapter – had embarked on a route that made the antagonism between the two even more pronounced. A mutual lack of sympathy would set in. But the passing of time usually encourages historians to enfold such squabbles into a larger picture. In this case, with hindsight, the *querelle* between the two composers might be thought a good illustration of the creative turmoil of the time. However, this historical readjustment hasn't taken place. The investment of music history in a particular, forward-looking strand of its modernist past has, until very recently, proven too intense.

Historians of modernism thus struggle with Béla Bartók (1881–1945), whose one-act opera *A kékszakállú herceg vára* (Bluebeard's Castle), written in 1911, was first performed in Budapest in 1918. The text, originally a play but with an operatic setting already in mind, was by fellow Hungarian Béla Balázs. He took the plot from Perrault's fairy tales, but added various national elements, in particular the insistent rhythms of Hungarian folk ballads – what he called 'dark, weighty, uncarved blocks of words'.[25] But Balázs had also imbibed from Maeterlinck and the symbolist movement generally. As he later stressed, 'My ballad is the "ballad of inner life". Bluebeard's castle is not a real castle of stone. The castle is his soul. It is lonely, dark and secretive: the castle of closed doors.'[26] He might have been describing Maeterlinck and Debussy's Allemonde – or, although he could not have known it, Pappenheim and Schoenberg's dark wood. The plot has a further resemblance to *Pelléas* in its strange, ritualistic, mostly unmotivated action. Bluebeard (baritone) brings his new wife, Judith (soprano), back to his castle. They stand in a Gothic hall that has seven large doors. Judith asks for them to be unlocked; Bluebeard is reluctant; she insists. The first two doors reveal a torture-chamber and an armoury, both stained with blood; the next three, with gathering light, show Bluebeard's treasury, his garden and, to an enormous orchestral climax, his vast lands. But each scene again becomes blood-soaked. Gloom descends as the last two doors are opened: the sixth is a lake of tears and the seventh a procession of Bluebeard's three past wives. Judith is constrained to accompany the wives back through the seventh door. Bluebeard is left alone.

Bluebeard, one of the great early twentieth-century operas, seems in many ways to mediate between Debussy and Strauss. Bartók, too, came to opera with successes as an instrumental composer, and this circumstance again becomes embedded in the fabric of the opera. For example, a rigid tonal scheme (which one might expect in a purely instrumental piece, but has always been rare in opera) accompanies the 'arch' structure of the tale. The journey from darkness to light to darkness is mirrored by a tonal movement from F♯ to C major (the fifth door) and then back to F♯. The opera's inheritance from Bartók's instrumental imagination is evident above all in the music for the seven doors. The sonic world behind every new door is fashioned as a miniature orchestral tone poem, as if in each case a special chamber orchestra were lurking in there alongside the horrors. There are muted brass fanfares for the armoury; a solo violin rhapsodizing at the riches of the treasury;

harp arpeggios, horn calls and flute trills for the gardens; and an *Also sprach Zarathustra*-like C-major tutti (organ and all) for the fifth door and its domains. The elephantine chords of door five may be orchestrally Straussian, but harmonically they move through a sequence of parallel triads, thus rehearsing a Debussy signature heard most famously in piano pieces such as 'La Cathédrale engloutie' (The Submerged Cathedral) from the first book of *Préludes* (1910).

Few composers at this time ignored leitmotif, and *Bluebeard* includes one at its core. Each time the stain of blood invades the stage picture, the orchestral ensemble is coloured by a 'blood' motif, a grating minor second, shrill and strident in the woodwind. But this is a surface gesture. The opera is *Pelléas*-like in being formed from a series of vignettes, just as its vocal manner is for the most part determinedly syllabic and faithful to spoken rhythms. Only towards the end, in one of the bleakest finales in all opera, does a more connected vocal idiom emerge. As Bluebeard grasps the inevitability of each door giving up its secrets, his resignation and awareness of loss bring forth the lyricism that had before been impossible. Eventually, even he becomes mute. The orchestra makes the ending, returning us to instrumental austerity, where we had begun.

OUTSIDE THE RADIOACTIVE ZONE

What does opera history make of outsiders, composers and works that have no apparent genetic ties or compositional debts to the central tradition? Perhaps a better question would be: given that opera outside the German, Italian or French traditions, circa 1900, quickly found idiosyncratic ways to evade the Wagnerian curse, is that because any such curse can extend only so far geographically? Consider the opera known in the West as *Jenůfa*, written between 1894 and 1904 by Leoš Janáček (1854–1928), a Czech (or, more properly, a Moravian) who spent most of his life as no more than a local celebrity in Brno, and whose remarkable late flowering as an international opera composer will be considered in Chapter 19. Janáček's first operas are conventional enough in their mixture of Romantic and nationalist elements, but in the early 1890s he came across a play by Gabriela Preissová called *Její pastorkyňa* (Her Stepdaughter). Just like Debussy before him and Strauss a few years later, the experience of this spoken drama was inspirational enough to generate experiments with a new kind of opera – one that set the text directly to music. What captured Janáček's imagination is clear, because although Preissová's play has a folk-like setting its action is anything but traditional. Act 1 opens with Jenůfa (soprano) in love with and secretly pregnant by Števa (tenor), who owns the local mill. But she is loved by Števa's half-brother, Laca (tenor), who in a fit of jealous rage slashes her cheek with a knife. In the second act, half a year later, Jenůfa has been hidden away by her stepmother, the Kostelnička (soprano), and has just given birth to a son; Števa has deserted her. When Laca arrives to enquire about her, the Kostelnička admits that she has had a baby, but tries to reassure him by saying that it has died. Laca leaves, and the Kostelnička takes the baby out into the winter night and drowns it in the millstream. In Act 3, two months later, Jenůfa has agreed to marry Laca, but as the stream thaws the villagers discover the dead child. Jenůfa fears it is her son, and the crowd close on her threateningly, believing she is the murderer. But the Kostelnička confesses and is led off. Jenůfa, after great struggles, forgives her, and in a finale of gathering musical intensity accepts Laca's love.

Part of the reason the opera took so long to write is that Janáček changed his objectives over time. While attracted to the violent, *verismo* elements of the plot, he rightly felt he needed a new musical language to make the opera work dramatically. Parts of Act 1, the first to be written, still bear traces of his older, nationalist vein, with lively, modal folk choruses in syncopated rhythm and even some recognizable arias and ensembles. But during that same period Janáček, previously a dedicated collector of folk music, began to collect what he called 'speech-melodies', fragments of Czech spoken discourse that he would notate rhythmically and melodically, in the process finding the musical building blocks from which he would construct a new operatic style. The extreme realization of this technique would occur in his later operas; in *Jenůfa* the effect is more sporadic, and interacts with an older, more familiar language (which is probably why it has remained his most popular work).

The drama thus grows out of an accretion of musical miniatures – often based on speech-melody fragments or small, mimetically inspired melodic gestures. This gift for assembling a mountain from pebbles is evident right from the start of the opera, and makes Janáček's idiom unmistakable. In the brief orchestral prelude to Act 1, an obsessively repeated rhythmic idea, clearly meant to mimic the turning of the mill that looms continuously over the action, is not so much developed as explored in multiple sonorities: first restrained and rather gentle, then in full orchestral flood, then with a solo violin. We are, in other words, presented with an orchestral tour through the emotions that will soon crowd on to the stage. As the characters are introduced and the action develops, more and more of these miniatures are established and then explored. It is as if the orchestra savours the words or brief phrases a character has just declaimed, turning them over without altering them, just repeating them again and again. Such assemblages, so very different from the gradual musical transformations of Wagner and his followers, mystified many when the opera was first performed. It was not until 1916, with Janáček sixty-one years old, that *Jenůfa* had a major revival in Prague, and not until the 1920s and 1930s that it became an accepted – if eccentric – work, and even then it was mostly performed in German translation.

Only with time has *Jenůfa* become a staple of the repertoire. By the mid twentieth century, operatic developments elsewhere made its innovations less perplexing, allowing audiences to understand what a tremendous vehicle for musical drama Janáček's special idiom could be. The end of the opera is justly famous. After the melodrama of the Kostelnička's confession, poor, disfigured, bereft Jenůfa and patient, violent Laca are left alone onstage. As the heroine finds a route to forgiveness, a last musical idea emerges in the orchestra – a magnificent, pulsing, full-orchestral chord, with trumpet arpeggios sounding forth. It is as if the obsessive repetitions on which the opera has been built have at last found a goal, a wall of sheer musical sound that moves nowhere and, like the characters onstage, celebrates sheer survival.

LATE *VERISMO*

A vital aspect of Bartók's and Janáček's operas is that they show how the works of Debussy and the early, expressionist Strauss – both in their different ways seeming like end-points, unrepeatable extremes – might be points of departure. However, an even earlier sign that Wagnerism might not be an everlasting obsession came to Germany quite soon after Wagner's death, and was also felt in France and elsewhere. The source of this awakening was all the more threatening because of its unexpected origin. Wagnerian complexity and profundity had been thought by many to have conquered once and for all the Italian tradition represented by Verdi. Many German intellectuals thought Verdi's masterpieces from the early 1850s ridiculously old-fashioned (albeit still disturbingly popular), while the more sophisticated fruits of his old age, *Otello* (1887) and *Falstaff* (1893), were judged modern and improved, the result of salutary Wagnerian influences. But then, in the early 1890s, operatic Europe found itself in the grip of an entirely new kind of Italian opera, one in which up-to-date harmonies and orchestration were grafted on to realistic plots oozing with steamy passion, enlivened by brief but show-stopping, singer-grateful arias. Mascagni's *Cavalleria rusticana* (Rustic Chivalry, 1890), Leoncavallo's *Pagliacci* (Clowns, 1892) and, most dangerous of all because most obviously sophisticated, Puccini's *Manon Lescaut* (1893) became international successes. Anxious Teutonic glances were once again cast southwards across the Alps.

The glances were in fact being cast both ways. Even though Puccini enjoyed unprecedented fame in the first decade of the twentieth century, he was constantly aware that more advanced music from France and Germany carried greater intellectual prestige; he paid close attention to musical innovation there – searching as always for new dramatic means. Debussy was more to his taste than Strauss. He praised the orchestration and 'extraordinary harmonic qualities' of *Pelléas*, even though 'it never carries you away, lifts you; it is always sombre in colour, as uniform as a Franciscan's habit'.[27] About Strauss he was more circumspect. He attended a famous revival of *Salome* in Graz in 1906, putting him in the company of a host of other celebrities of the present and future, including Mahler, Schoenberg and his pupil Alban Berg, and – if his later recollections were correct – a struggling, music-obsessed young Austrian called Adolf Hitler.[28] Puccini confided to a friend, 'Salome is the most extraordinary, terribly cacophonous thing. There were some brilliant musical effects, but in the end it's very tiring. Extremely interesting spectacle, though.'[29] Puccini and Strauss were, however, linked in another important way. Much more so than today, when original-language performances are the norm and singers tend to specialize in either the German or the Italian repertory, they wrote for the same female stars – Maria Jeritza, Emmy Destinn, Selma Kurz and Lotte Lehmann were all famous for both their Strauss and Puccini roles.

Did this Puccinian sampling of the ultra-modern have any effect on his later operas? As his remarks suggest, both Debussy and Strauss, in their very different ways, were too extreme and monochromatic for a composer who prized variety above all. He never attempted a prose libretto, despite their vogue in his later years; to do so would have been to renounce the vocal lyricism that was so critical a side of his musical personality. But his later libretti did become increasingly prose-like, while space for arias or grand, singing-together ensembles become rarer. *La fanciulla del West* (The Girl of the West, 1909) is a case in point. It is set in the Californian gold rush of 1849 and features a fiercely independent, gun-toting heroine, a handsome, tough-but-sensitive hero, and a cruel antagonist (*lo scheriffo*, the sheriff, no less). Given such extroverted dramatis personae, it's surprising that there is virtually no trace of exportable, concert-style arias, even though the hero's role was created especially for Enrico Caruso. What's more, the second act ends in something close to spoken drama, a tense poker-game played out between the heroine and the antagonist (the prize will be, in antique Italian-opera mode, the heroine's honour), with cards violently slapping the table as the dominant sound effect.

Not everyone was happy about it. In 1924, the year of Puccini's death, one irritated Englishman summarized the composer's creative arc as follows:

> No living composer is more despised and execrated by the leaders of musical opinion today in every country. . . . What we really resent, if we take the trouble to analyse our feelings, is that, however detestable his music may be, particularly on paper, it is impossible to deny that it generally 'comes off' exasperatingly well in performance, where other and better music fails disastrously. . . . Some of his later work is by no means as contemptible as many suppose. For although his operas from *Manon Lescaut* onward reveal a constantly growing preoccupation with theatrical effect and a correspondingly marked decline in musicianship – a melancholy progression in which *La fanciulla del West* represents the culminating point or rather the nadir – his recent partial recovery, as exemplified in the so-called *Trittico*, is all the more welcome because it was so wholly unexpected.[30]

What is more, this 'decline' – which begins from day one with *Manon Lescaut* – is laid at an interesting door:

> Puccini's artistic development suggests an analogy with Verdi. He seems to have set himself to Italianize modern composers in precisely the same way Verdi. . . . Italianized Wagner. But while the latter's attempt to prolong the existence of the old Italian tradition which was lying gasping and emaciated upon its death-bed, by means of a kind of artificial rejuvenation or transfusion of blood from a younger and more vital organism, resulted in the production of two supreme masterpieces, *Otello* and *Falstaff* . . . the former's operation, performed by a less skilful and steady hand, has hardly tuned out so successfully.[31]

This 'young and vital organism' that saved Italian opera circa 1890 is once more none other than R. Wagner (dead at the time). The unnamed 'modernist composers' Puccini turned to a generation later are deemed incapable of working the same trick. *La fanciulla* does indeed have its fair share of advanced harmonic and orchestral effects, 'transfusions' from the moderns. But what is it about *Il trittico* (The Triptych, 1918), a sequence of three one-act operas, that signals Puccini's ascent out of perdition? To choose one-act operas suggests the model of *Salome* and all those other, self-consciously modern works. The first opera of the three, *Il tabarro* (The Cloak), is a grim melodrama about adultery set on a barge on the Seine, with an atmospheric introduction cast as an advanced orchestral tone poem. The opening chords, depicting the relentless swell of the river, are built on fourths and with their delicate orchestration sound almost in homage to Debussy; a distant car motor horn and tugboat siren add to the realistic effect. A little later, there are allusions to Stravinsky (both in orchestration and harmony) in a strangely dissonant imitation of an old, out-of tune organ.

In some ways, though, the last panel of *Il trittico*, the comic piece *Gianni Schicchi*, is the most radical. Written during the dark days of the First World War, its story is derived from Dante, *the* literary icon of the Italian past, and noisily celebrates the cultural and economic energies of the Renaissance, a period when Italians led the world. The plot concerns a venal family group who gather at the deathbed of a relative to discover that he has left a will not at all in their favour. They engage a wily merchant, Gianni Schicchi (baritone), to help them; he impersonates the deceased relative, successfully alters the will, but in the process awards the choicest items to himself. The love interest is supplied by Schicchi's daughter, Lauretta (soprano), and Rinuccio (tenor), both of whom have well-defined arias. Rinuccio's famous 'Firenze è come un albero fiorito' (Florence is like a tree in flower) is delicately poised between irony and sincerity, part nostalgic travelogue, part bombastic celebration of local pride. Puccini's setting, with its march-like theme and uncomplicated harmonies, is very different from his usual, lachrymose tragic solos. The macho optimism is put into cultural perspective, and its musical mood matched, by his embarrassing 'Inno a Roma' (Hymn to Rome), which he wrote soon after the premiere of *Il trittico*, and which was premiered during a gymnastics competition in Rome (training 'the soldiers of tomorrow'), pealed forth by a chorus of 5000, accompanied by the massed brass bands of the carabinieri. (The 'Inno' was a great hit in the decades to come, particularly when recast as the 'Inno al Duce'.)

Moments such as this highlight the fact that nationalistic sentiments became more strident over much of Europe after the First World War. But other passages in *Schicchi* are within hail of atonality, with curious disjunctions in the musical argument. Even openly parodic sections cast a shadow, particularly the sinister foxtrot, 'In testa la cappellina!' (On his head the little cap), a *marche funèbre* for modern times that would not be out of place in a Brecht–Weill collaboration. Critics seem for the most part to have passed over these passages without comment, perhaps thinking them merely innocent fun. Nor was any sinister resonance felt in Schicchi's warning to the relatives that their stratagem risks a grisly punishment, amputation of the hand and exile. He underlines the point by singing a little ditty ('Addio, Firenze, addio cielo divino' – Farewell, Florence, farewell, divine skies), its flowery ornamentation in imitation of Renaissance vocal style as he raises a handless sleeve in mock farewell. The relatives repeat the tune, and its threat prevents them from exposing Schicchi when he takes for himself the most enticing parts of their inheritance. Again: all innocent fun? In 1918 in Italy, after years of brutal conflict, with wounded, limbless soldiers returning to every town? Perhaps the echoes were just too close to contemplate.

Just as did Verdi's *Falstaff*, Puccini's comic masterpiece ends with an address to the audience that carries with it a clear nationalist message. In Verdi's case there is an energetic fugue in celebration of the world's folly, perhaps not least the folly that had led young Italians to neglect such learned musical forms and to rush in search of dangerous, foreign idioms. In *Gianni Schicchi*, Puccini (once a prime example of those Italian upstarts) plays another card: with a last, fleeting reference to

Rinuccio's bombastic celebration of Florence, the protagonist conjures up 'il gran padre Dante'. As one early, fervently nationalist critic put it, this ending was meant to release the 'purest word of the race'. The tone of such praise is now jarring, even alienating, but it can also be instructive. In *Gianni Schicchi* we can if we so choose merely enjoy the blue sky and the Renaissance sunshine; but not far beneath this surface we may also find other, darker colours, not least a remembrance of times past in Italian history and, perhaps still more disturbing, an anticipation of times soon to come.

18
Modern

In the autumn of 1910, without much sense that he was doing anything particularly novel, Richard Strauss started writing his second opera to a libretto by Hugo von Hofmannsthal. They had decided on a comedy, a period piece set in eighteenth-century Vienna, and Hofmannsthal wrote the text directly as an opera libretto. This would not be a matter of adopting a pre-existing play, as with *Elektra* a few years earlier. To understand the opera that emerged, *Der Rosenkavalier* (The Knight of the Rose, 1911), we need to get a sense of the tone that pervades Hofmannsthal's comedies for the spoken theatre, pieces that were not intended to metamorphose into libretti and never did. This tone is more complex than simple nostalgia, but any attempt at evocation or précis seems to make such works sound like mere kitsch.

Der Schwierige (The Difficult Character, 1921) is set in near contemporary times – Vienna during the First World War. The protagonist is Count Kari Bühl, a diffident, whimsical character who finds it hard to say what he thinks. One of his whims in Act 1 is to declare that he will visit the circus rather than attend the soirée demanded by social duty. In Act 2, having arrived at the soirée after all, he discusses the circus and its famous Italian clown, Forlani, with Countess Helene Altenwyl (he loves her, but cannot bring himself to declare it). The conversation demonstrates their apartness and grace at a gathering in which the vulgar and *arriviste* prefer to discuss Goethe and other heavy cultural fare. Hofmannsthal's tongue-tied hero and heroine are delighted by a clown, and this illustrates – as does their airborne disquisition on his performance – what is to be mourned about their kind vanishing for good. The dramatic means are small and indirect, but the sadness is sharp. Hofmannsthal's gift was to make stage characters, whose travails can engross us for a few hours, and whose voices and bodies are so obviously present, seem at the same time to be already lost and gone.

For decades, the reception of *Der Rosenkavalier* was characterized either by naïve enthusiasm or the disdain of avant-garde purists. Enthusiasts saw the opera as a guidebook to a lost civilization. The forgotten tribe in question was distant not geographically but temporally: they were the charming (and not so charming) nobility of Imperial Austria, around the time of Maria Theresa, as updated by Hofmannsthal. For the disdainful, the problem was summed up by the opera's starring prop, a fake silver rose drenched in oil of roses to disguise its metallic tang. The central plot rigmarole – that, among the nobility of eighteenth-century Vienna, before a bridegroom could show up for a first meeting with his fiancée, the latter had to be formally presented with a silver engagement rose by a high-born emissary – was all fabricated. Enthusiasts have to maintain a suspension of disbelief that joins hands with the false authenticity of the opera's exotic milieu. The disdainful can nurse Puritan discomfort at such fakery and silliness, or even at the idea that aristocrats can be interesting. And then, to complicate matters further, there is Strauss's music: some of it surpassingly (or dangerously) beautiful and famously (or shamefully, or notoriously) easy to listen to.

Artifice, which makes *Der Rosenkavalier* unusual for its moment in 1911, can give us an avenue into the operatic years from 1910 to the Second World War – years that marked the genre's wildest efflorescence at the moment it was becoming a thing of the past. Horticulturists will recognize the phenomenon. In the spring of the year in which a tree is stressed, there are hundreds of blossoms; in the autumn the branches bend under the weight of fruit. The tree is reacting to the fact that it has no future, and the unnatural abundance marks this self-knowledge. As one of the first works of this late, terminal operatic efflorescence, *Der Rosenkavalier* is in many ways a landmark in German opera. It is funny, artificial, alternately conveying self-consciousness about history (using musical pastiche and parody as a reference to the past) and achieving a paradoxical state of ironic bliss.

Der Rosenkavalier also raises questions about opera in the twentieth century, specifically about how opera – an extraordinarily long-lived genre – remade itself by means of modernist idioms and ideologies. How many other musical genres originating in the early seventeenth century were still active, creative magnets in the early twentieth? The instrumental genres that rose up in the late eighteenth and nineteenth centuries, and that were opera's great musical rival, were comparatively easy to modernize: symphonies, string quartets and piano sonatas could be made pleasingly up to date with novel harmonies, complex rhythms and ingeniously fragmented forms. But updating opera could not rest solely on musical manipulations. Up to and including the early twentieth century, opera remained a fundamentally expressive art: characters had feelings and they uttered them; the music was there to help get the message across. Everything happened in the present, right there on stage. This was the case even in operas proclaiming themselves at the vanguard of musical progress. When the tortured, psychotic heroine of Schoenberg's notoriously dissonant, free-form *Erwartung* sang fractured successions of intervals rather than beautiful melodies, the expressive means and ends create a calculus that says dissonant expression equals tortured heroine. The sound may have shocked many, but the correspondence, even the redundancy, between musical mood and character's condition were essentially no less conventional than, say, Puccini's *La bohème*. In Strauss's *Der Rosenkavalier* this alignment – and with it, the very idea of sincere, unmediated expression in opera – starts to fragment.

Hofmannsthal's self-consciously fictional eighteenth century was the perfect place to begin the experiment. Mozartian prototypes and authentic eighteenth-century theatrical characters lurk behind each person. The opera involves a romantic triad: in Act 1, we meet the Marschallin (soprano), who as the curtain rises is in bed with – indeed, if the whooping horn calls in the Prelude have told us anything, was just a moment ago having sex with – her many-years-younger paramour, Octavian. Octavian is cast as a mezzo-soprano playing an amorous boy, a type best known as Cherubino in Mozart's *Le nozze di Figaro* (1786). What is more, the Marschallin, in both her time-obsessed melancholy and her weakness for adolescent males, strongly evokes Mozart's Countess Almaviva.

The Marschallin and Octavian are, however, designed to confound the audience in excess of their Mozartian prototypes. Yes, the plot says they are opposite sexes. But given the *in flagrante* opening tableau, most performances will invite another view, one based entirely on our consciousness of the *singers*. Beyond the woman and the young man, we're seeing a more interesting and, for 1911 at least, more scandalous union between two women. In *Le Deuxième Sexe* (The Second Sex, 1949), Simone de Beauvoir devoted several long passages to this kind of older woman plus younger man-or-woman amorous pair. What stands out about her heterosexual examples is that they all derive from the Enlightenment, even though she is making no particular historical point. It's as if, by the 1940s, the eighteenth century has unconsciously become the assumed natural habitat of such beings, the Cherubinos of history. Moreover, Beauvoir moves between matron-male and matron-female pairs without hitting a single speed bump:

> Her attitude toward women was precisely that of Rousseau with Mme de Warens, of the young Benjamin Constant with Mme de Charrière: sensitive and 'feminine' adolescents, they also turned to motherly mistresses. We frequently meet with the lesbian, more or less markedly of this type, who never identified with her mother . . . but who, while declining to be a woman, wishes to have rather the soft delight of feminine protection . . . she behaves like a man, but as a man she is fragile, and this makes her desire an older mistress; the pair will correspond to that well-known heterosexual couple, matron and adolescent.[1]

At that point, Beauvoir's English translator notes the Marschallin and Octavian as a further example. In one sense they are the ultimate example of Beauvoir's ideal type, since, embodied in a performance, they represent both cases at once.

In the original 1911 Dresden production, the bedroom set was permitted, but in the Berlin premiere of the opera (also 1911) any combination – matron plus boy, matron plus girl, bedroom – was deemed too risqué, so the set for the opening act was changed to the Marschallin's dining room. For the London premiere, the Lord Chamberlain instructed Thomas Beecham that either the bed had to be taken out of the set, or the text had to be rewritten to remove all references to it, and the singers forbidden to approach the offending object.[2] The 1925 silent film of *Der Rosenkavalier* went ever further. The part of Octavian was given to a young male actor, Jacques Castelain, and his interactions with the Marschallin include a decorous tête-à-tête on a park bench. Indeed, in Hofmannsthal's original script for the film – which was almost entirely set aside by the filmmakers – Octavian pursues the Marschallin, but she being a married woman rejects him. So much bowdlerizing, taking so many forms, suggests at the very least that every single scandalous implication of the opera's opening tableau was evident right from the start.

Hofmannsthal's plot motor is the silver rose, which lends its name to the opera's title. In Act 1, Octavian jokingly agrees to act as the Rose-Bearer for the Marschallin's distant relative, the distinctly oafish Baron Ochs auf Lerchenau (bass), who blusters his way into the Marschallin's boudoir. The threat of discovery necessitates a quick change into servant girl's clothing for Octavian, who will, like Cherubino, spend some of the opera disguised as a bashful country lass, here called 'Mariandel'. Ochs is an elderly aristocratic vulgarian aiming to shore up his finances by marrying a rich young girl, Sophie von Faninal (soprano) – for this, read Doctor Bartolo and young Rosina in Rossini's *Il barbiere di Siviglia* (1816). In Act 2 Octavian presents the famous fake rose to Sophie in the magnificent setting of her father's town house, and they fall instantly in love. The remainder of the act shows us Sophie's horror at her boorish fiancé, Octavian's embroilment in the matter and the beginnings of a plot to unseat Ochs. Octavian as 'Mariandel' sends him a letter suggesting an assignation in a cheap hotel: when, Octavian reasons, the Baron is discovered *in flagrante*, the scandal will annul his engagement. Most of Act 3 (set in a private room at the hotel) is pure farce: drunkenness, slammed doors and mistaken identity. But at the point of greatest chaos, when everything threatens to unravel into hopeless misunderstanding and shame, the Marschallin appears like an Enlightenment *deus ex machina*. She sets everything right, renounces her claim on Octavian and sadly ushers him into Sophie's arms. The scene in which this happens is among the most formally conservative in the opera: Sophie, Octavian and the Marschallin converse in recitative and, when the time comes for them to react to their dilemma, they pour forth their feelings in a set-piece trio.

In a 1927 essay on the libretto's genesis, Hofmannsthal described how his text was conjured in an instant, during conversations with his friend Count Harry Kessler. He makes it clear that the idea began as a set of operatic archetypes – whom he and Kessler initially referred to simply as 'the Buffo', 'the Lady' and 'the Cherubino' – and how 'the plot per se arose out of the eternal and typical relationships of such characters to one another, without our precisely knowing how it happened'.[3]

In reviving Mozartian characters, in inventing the ritual of the rose, in having Enlightenment aristocrats talk like Viennese nobility circa 1910, Hofmannsthal set up conflicting time lines, in a drama where anachronism is not (as in most opera libretti) an error to be tolerated, but an aesthetic device. The strata of anachronism have a distancing effect, one that in turn has musical consequences. Characters so elaborately layered cannot inhabit the usual operatic aesthetic of immediate, sincere expression. Another kind of music is required. As with that closing formal trio in Act 3, part of Strauss's solution was to make self-conscious reversions to ancient operatic patterns and devices. But he also evolved a musical flavour that was every bit as complex as Hofmannsthal's idiosyncratic evocation of present loss, or of the present as past.

The music Strauss invented for *Der Rosenkavalier*, since in part it involves creating distance through pastiche, is necessarily tied to farce and comedy. In Harry Kessler's diaries, we glimpse a contemporary analysis of that music from George Bernard Shaw, whom Kessler visited in London in 1912. Shaw is quoted:

> About Mozart, Shaw said he had kept his music flowing by little impulses, sforzando passages, 'little kicks'. When the completely different broad melodies of Beethoven and Wagner arose, the directors played Mozart as well in this style and killed him. Only Richard Strauss, whose style is related to Mozart's, rediscovered the correct style to present Mozart.[4]

Note the matter-of-fact claim that Strauss's style derives from Mozart's, and is far removed from Wagner's. But the truth is more complex: the origins of the *Rosenkavalier* sound were too many for its music to be tied to any one past master.

DISTANCE, THE NEW MOOD

Der Rosenkavalier's new operatic aesthetic seemed to appear simultaneously in German and French comic opera. Strauss's opera depends on musical devices that include tricks with time, an embrace of artifice, and layering musical pasts over the musical present. *L'Heure espagnole* (Spanish Notions of Time, 1911) by Maurice Ravel (1875–1937) is in this sense *Der Rosenkavalier*'s French companion. In Ravel's opera, Concepción (soprano), wife of the clockmaker Torquemada (tenor), has to juggle the visits of her two lovers – the banker Don Iñigo Gomez (bass) and the poet Gonzalve (tenor) – while her husband is out of the shop. She stuffs them into grandfather clocks to hide them from one another, and orders a brawny muleteer, Ramiro (baritone), to haul the loaded clocks from room to room as extra insurance against discovery. Gonzalve expresses himself in proper poetic verses, and Ravel sets them to musical Iberianisms that pour forth in opium-dream cascades. Ramiro's usual mode is huffing, accompanied by horns and trombones thumping in imitation of his heavy tread.

Much of the dialogue in *L'Heure espagnole* is free-form, orchestrally accompanied recitative. But in one scene Ramiro finds himself alone among the ticking clocks, which appear to him as lullaby-singers promising bliss and peace. He becomes lyrical and the orchestral accompaniment pours forth with unironic generosity. The sad jest is in the reversal. The automata, the clocks, offer forms of solace and sympathy lacking among the human characters. Ravel and his librettist, Franc-Nohain (Maurice Étienne Legrand), were among the first operatic modernists to revive the eighteenth-century moralizing coda, the final number in which characters comment on what has happened in the drama – as they do at the end of Mozart's *Don Giovanni* (albeit in that case minus the protagonist, who is otherwise engaged). The modern difference in *L'Heure espagnole* is that the characters have disappeared altogether. The five singers who gather for Ravel's commentary refer to the parts they have played in the third person, unmasking, demonstrating the artificiality of their stage personae. What is interesting – and this remains a central precept in such codas – is that the mask is not taken off in musical terms. The music doesn't suddenly convey sincere expression or apparent guilelessness. The moralizing quintet is done as an Introduction-and-Habañera that combines the Iberian with the fantastic to make for unalloyed musical joy. But first, before the Habañera begins, the five principals are silent for a moment. The sustained high string chords that accompany this pause, and precede the Habañera's first loud stamp, produce a complicated effect. On the one hand, this is a clichéd orchestral signal for transfiguration and here marks the singers' unmasking. On the other, it is simply a pause that promises fun, like a drawn-in breath before laughter.

COMEDY IN LAYERS

Comedy, then, freed both Strauss (experienced opera composer) and Ravel (operatic novice), allowing them to restore to opera fixed forms and stock genre pieces. But these devices are not as they were in earlier opera: to compose a recitative and trio in the nineteenth century was still a compositional given, business as usual, just as to cite an exotic sound – like Spanish-ness or antique charm – was limited to local colour, often in a performance-within-the-opera. There are good examples of the latter in the mock-Mozart pastoral opera performed in Act 2 of Tchaikovsky's *Queen of Spades*, or in the gypsy numbers that turn up in a romantic tragedy such as Verdi's *La traviata* (1853), or in countless bewigged musical episodes in Massenet's *Manon* (1882) or Puccini's *Manon Lescaut* (1893). But in operas like *Der Rosenkavalier* and *L'Heure espagnole*, the fixed forms are not business as usual but markers for artifice and manner; the exotic sounds have been liberated from their cages to become pervasive, in the process also becoming a form of melancholy.

There was one imposing nineteenth-century model for a self-conscious reversion to musical formality. This was Richard Wagner's only mature comedy, *Die Meistersinger von Nürnberg* (1868), which – as well as leitmotifs, long orchestral interludes and free-flowing sound-webs – has arias, chorales, strophic songs and even a full-scale, justly famous quintet. But what makes *Die Meistersinger* rather simple, whereas Strauss and Ravel are intricate, is that Wagner's reversion to operatic numbers does not entail any departure from conventional operatic expressiveness: when the characters in his quintet sing out their innermost feelings, the impression of unmediated and directly expressed emotion is no different from that in, say, *Les Troyens* (1856–8) or *Il trovatore* (1853). In other words, *Die Meistersinger* is conventional in the sense that its old-fashioned operatic numbers are marked and symbolic rather than simply a compositional given. To make the most obvious point, their elaborate formality harmonizes with the morals of the plot. They remind us that tradition and innovation combine to form high art; that there is value in antique art forms; and, incidentally, that older, experienced men – the hero, Hans Sachs – are not without their romantic attractions. Wagner's comedy is typical of its operatic era in that the genre pieces are not ironic: they produce no sense of estrangement, and do not complicate the sincerity-and-authenticity effect that is the hallmark of nineteenth-century opera.

Strauss and Hofmannsthal nonetheless drew on Wagner's comedy for subtle touches. For one thing, the erotic triad is similar – older, wiser man/woman painfully renouncing younger girl/boy and facilitating her/his nuptials with more appropriately aged ingénu/ingénue. In both, the big number that follows the Act of Renunciation is a formal ensemble in D♭ that begins with a solitary soprano holding forth; in *Der Rosenkavalier* it is the favourite excerpt in an otherwise rather dense opera, not without its wordiness and longueurs, and at times rambling on without sharp edges. What is more, the very fact that Strauss and Hofmannsthal left space for the conjuring up and citation of earlier operas suggests a central dilemma in the era of opera's last efflorescence: the *history* of opera is no longer irrelevant when you come to write one yourself. Musical gestures towards that past create the same effect as Kari and Helene's conversation about the clown: although the material is present, placed before us, it has also already disappeared.

There are some passages in *Der Rosenkavalier* that sum all this up in grief-stricken accents. In Act 1, the Marschallin delivers her most famous monologue, a long, unflinching meditation about the passing of time. She is talking to Octavian: 'Between you and me, Quinquin, time flows again, soundlessly, like an hourglass.' For her, Octavian is young enough to be an unchanged, beautiful image. The wording is strange, and seems to refer not so much to a human being as to something in the memory. As you age, you leave objects further and further behind; they remain in existance, but eventually they become so distant as to be almost invisible. Strauss's music for this monologue gestures towards two different dances, like a double exposure. One is a waltz, the typical Viennese dance of the nineteenth century, but slow and in a minor key. Of course, waltzes have no business in an eighteenth-century plot – the dance hadn't yet become popular. And of course waltzes were old-fashioned by 1911, the time of the opera's first performance. But this is precisely the point: there is a multiple timeline in the music, a future-plus-past that disorientates the listener and muddies the chronology. The second dance type, which is laid over and under the waltz, is a siciliano, something associated with the eighteenth century. Indeed, the siciliano had acquired a rich history in operatic parlance: Mozart used it especially in tragic situations, as in Pamina's mourning aria ('Ach ich fühl's') in Act 2 of *Die Zauberflöte*. So the Marschallin's monologue exists in multiple periods: both literally, in waltz-time and siciliano-time, and figuratively, since its music combines the eighteenth, nineteenth and early twentieth centuries.

But the amalgam sounds nothing like the eighteenth or nineteenth century in the end, since the layering effect – which includes strange harmonic slides away from and back to the home key – is contemporary. The same could be said about an aria inserted into Act 1, sung by an Italian Tenor who has been sent, peruke, brocade and all, to entertain the Marschallin while her hair is being arranged. This aria (which the Tenor is 'reading from a sheet of music') was, from the first, intended to be a rare, alien jewel. Its text is in the florid Italian libretto-speak of the old Metastasian school:

Di rigori armato il seno
Contro amor mi ribellai,
Ma fui vinto in un baleno
In mirar due vaghi rai.
Ahi! Che resiste puoco
Cor di gelo a stral di fuoco.

[With a heart armed by severity / I rebelled against love, / but I was overcome in a flash / by gazing on two lovely eyes. / Ah! A heart of ice cannot / resist that fiery flash.]

Over an orchestra reduced to chamber size, Schubertian lyricism collides with late-Italian *bel canto* (there are shades of 'Già nella notte densa', the love duet at the end of Act 1 of *Otello*), with some intricate rhythmic sleight-of-hand involving displaced downbeats making an exquisite walled garden in sound, out of time or place. Although you can visit such gardens, you will always be forced to leave, probably sooner than you might wish. Strauss underlines the point by having a second verse sung as background while Ochs argues sotto voce with the attorney negotiating his marriage contract. Ochs finally shouts out and bangs a table with his fist; this instantly cuts the aria off, in the process fashioning a little acoustic parable about beauty's defeat by noisy philistinism.

One way to judge the avant-garde quality of Strauss's layered time is by the howls it drew from those who had loved him in his Romantic era, as the composer of *Tod und Verklärung* (Death and Transfiguration, 1890) and other such massive tone poems. Invective along these lines is not hard to find, comparing Old Strauss with New Strauss:

> The one had a burning and wonderful pressure of speech. The other seems unable to concentrate energy and interest sufficiently to create a hard and living piece of work. The one seemed to blaze new pathways through the brain. The other steps languidly in roadways well worn. He is not even amusing any longer. The contriver of wonderful orchestral machines, the man who penetrated into the death-chamber and stood under the gibbet, has turned to toying with his medium, to imitating other composers, Mozart in 'Der Rosenkavalier', Handel in 'Josephslegende', Offenbach and Lully (a coupling that only Strauss has the lack of taste to bring about) in 'Ariadne auf Naxos'. He has become increasingly facile and unoriginal, has taken to quoting unblushingly Mendelssohn, Tchaikovsky, Wagner himself, even. His insensitivity has waxed inordinately, and led him to mix styles, to commingle dramatic and coloratura passages, to jumble the idioms of three centuries in a single work, to play all manner of pointless pranks with his art.[5]

Pranks. This resistance to frivolity is a symptom. In the Weimar era, the notion of 'divine frivolity' – which was Nietzsche's comment on Offenbach in *The Will to Power* – was imbued with positive value, as a bulwark against the deadly Teutonic gravitas associated with, among others, Richard Wagner.[6] And it was exactly this frivolity, the very wit embodied in *opéra comique* or Offenbach or Hofmannsthal, that became anathema in Germany: especially so after 1933, once the regime had changed.

MOZART PRANKS

One of the most layered and in some ways disquieting musical gestures in the score of *Rosenkavalier* is attached to Ochs. He is a difficult character to nail down. He's not the most appalling person in the opera – that prize goes to the two Italian intriguers, Annina and Valzacchi, as full of guile as they are empty of loyalty. But he is hard to place because Strauss wasted very few beautiful phrases or turns of poignant harmony on him. He comes closest to amiability at the end of Act 2 when, slightly tipsy and cocooned in one of the Ländler (rustic waltzes) that Strauss devises for him, he almost – almost – starts to seem like a welcome antidote to the high-minded aesthetic delicacy everywhere else on display. In 2001, those waltzes ended up in the film score for Steven Spielberg's fantasy *A.I. Artificial Intelligence* – where they accompany the main characters' visually dizzying entrée into Rouge City, capital of worldly delights. Is there, then, something to be said for Ochs as the personification of Dionysian directness? This effect is strongest when Ochs is played by a singer whose other roles might run to Sarastro in *Die Zauberflöte* or King Philip in *Don Carlos*: a bass, that is, with significant pulling-power. One early Viennese critic caught this when he called Ochs 'a Falstaff of the manure heap, a Don Juan of the cesspool'.[7] Until quite late in the genesis of the opera, Strauss and Hofmannsthal used the working title *Ochs auf Lerchenau*. If they had kept this title, might the whole affair suddenly seem quite different? Where would we look, with whom would we sympathize, with what special attention?

The disquieting musical gesture, which is a very big Mozart prank, involves Ochs's personal leitmotif (such as it is): the music heard when he first waddles onstage in Act 1. It's a bluff-sounding, C-major march theme, with timpani quietly thumping the bass, some not-too-loud brass chords and low strings playing a simple melody that just goes up the C-major scale, C-D-E, then E-F-G; the first note in the pattern is ornamented by a little 'turn', a filigree winding over and under, a bit of eighteenth-century frou-frou. But if you listen carefully – and mentally transpose the low string melody into a solo flute, keep the muffled timpani on the bass notes, keep the quiet brass – you realize you're hearing a sly reference to one of the most exalted, most solemn moments in German operatic history: the strange C-major march that accompanies Pamina and Tamino as they undergo their ultimate, perilous Trials by Fire and Water in Act 2 of *Die Zauberflöte*.

This musical jest seems to drag Mozart into bad company, and in doing so brings back everything one might want to purge from his late masterpiece: its low origins, our knowledge that its composer enjoyed scurrilous, vulgar jokes. But it also does something opposite. By placing *Die Zauberflöte* in the vicinity of Ochs, we are reminded not to over-value the fastidious gallantry of the other main characters, and to recall that humane empathy for the unlovable is the most rare form of nobility. It may even be – as Strauss and Hofmannsthal's endlessly fascinating correspondence suggests – that the composer wanted to assert his own terms as distinct from those of Hofmannsthal, and to pour musical cold water on any impulse to sentimentalize. Make sure, the composer tells us, that your heart will retain the severity it needs, to rebel against impossibly beautiful people and overwhelmingly beautiful sounds.

Strauss's Mozart prank is indeed what has come to be called an 'estrangement effect'. Pervasive effects like these became the fundamental building material in the works of the German playwright Bertolt Brecht (1898–1956), as they were in his musical-theatre pieces with Kurt Weill almost two decades after *Der Rosenkavalier*. It was Brecht who coined the term by which they are known in German theatre, *Verfremdungseffekte*. In Brecht's theory, the playwright or composer should strive constantly to remind the audience that it is seeing a fiction or construction, whether through elements of staging or performance style, or through literary means such as inserted commentaries on the action and characters. There should be musical means to enforce that edict as well, and Weill, for instance, used harsh mock-ups of popular song styles to that end. If the characters are so patently artificial, if the actors make it clear they are not the persons they are enacting, then the audience cannot be bamboozled into sympathy or identification or other forms of delusion. A sceptical, thoughtful and above all teachable observer can thus be *produced* by a theatrical experience. Anything further from Wagner's or, for that matter, the later Verdi's ideal of an absorbed and enchanted listener is hard to imagine, and that was the point.

There are, however, some knowing quotations, some self-conscious anachronisms, that simply cannot be estranging. The most celebrated piece in *Der Rosenkavalier* is that set-piece trio near the end of Act 3, in which the Marschallin ushers Octavian into the arms of Sophie. 'Hab' mir's gelobt, ihn lieb zu haben in der richtigen Weis' (I have chosen to love him in the right way): the Marschallin sings this to herself, and then the other two sopranos join in, each musing privately and thus creating that world of shared soliloquy so emblematic of ancient operatic ensembles. While the formal setting and frozen manner are archaic, the musical substance is poised between contrasting styles. In some ways, as we have said, the trio gestures towards its Wagnerian model in *Die Meistersinger*: the clear tonality (and the shared key of D♭), the waves of sound, the climactic overlapping voices. But the combined sound of three sopranos, that monochrome embarrassment of lyrical riches, also transports us to the pan-soprano world of eighteenth-century *opera seria*, a world of obvious make-believe. And then, at the end, as tonal closure seems inevitable, Strauss injects the trio with one of his trademark chromatic uplifts, a precipitate burst of bright E major (with soprano high Bs ringing repeatedly), an overwhelming harmonic contrivance that would have been unthinkable before the twentieth century.

The Marschallin exits, leaving the stage to Octavian and Sophie. Their ensuing duet, which closes the opera, has always been controversial. Discussing an earlier moment for the two lovers, Hofmannsthal had been nervous about what style of music might emerge: 'What I should wish to avoid at all costs is to see these two young creatures, who have nothing of the Valkyries or Tristan about them, bursting into a Wagnerian kind of erotic screaming'.[8] He need have had no fears in this instance. The closing duet is one of the opera's most unambiguous turns to Mozartian language: the two lovers warble together in parallel intervals and predictable phrases, accompanied by disarmingly simple orchestration. 'Ist ein Traum, kann nicht wirklich sein' (It is a dream, can it really be true), sings Sophie, and the conventionality of the sentiments is equalled in the music.

But then something extraordinary happens, a little interruption from another world. Faninal re-enters with the Marschallin on his arm; he pats Sophie's cheek, uttering a friendly homily to the Marschallin: 'They're always the same, aren't they, the young people?' 'Yes, yes', she responds very quietly. She sings music heard before, notably at the end of Act 1 when she dismissed Octavian, for the moment, and told him what her day will be: 'Now, I am going to church, and afterwards, I'll go over to Uncle Greifenklau's, he's old and lame, and that will cheer him up. And in the afternoon, I shall send a footman to you, to say whether I'll be driving in the Prater. And if I am, and if you would like to, you can come into the Prater too, and ride next to my coach.' The turn to minor at 'in the afternoon', the long falling interval in the voice, the music setting those chained subjunctives of a happiness known to be fragile and finite – this is what returns when she says, 'Yes, yes' in Act 3.

Before and after this interruption the orchestra has returned to its Straussian harmonic and melodic range, and when Faninal and the Marschallin depart there emerges one of the largest and most expansive orchestral climaxes of the entire evening. The lovers, as if oblivious, then settle down to what becomes the second verse of their little Mozartian duet; but now their phrases are fragmented and interrupted by the brittle, chromatic motif that had earlier characterized the presentation of the rose, a litany of unconnected triads glitteringly high in the orchestral register on celesta, harp, flutes and solo violins. Mozart is getting further and further away: he had reappeared in the wake of Strauss's huge orchestra but is now retreating into the distance, seen through increasing layers of acoustic frosted glass.

The music that begins with the long recitative-like scene before the trio, and ends here, used to occupy Side 8 on most LP recordings of the opera. Both its cumulative effect, and the knowledge that this very effect is suspect, is summed up in a 1957 *New Yorker* cartoon. We see a husband sick in bed, bags under his eyes, saying to his ministering spouse, 'I know the doctor said this is only a bad cold, but in case he's mistaken I'd like to hear side eight of "Der Rosenkavalier" one last time.'

OFFENBACH PLUS LULLY, BAD TASTE BY WHOSE ACCOUNT

Strauss's next opera with Hofmannsthal was *Ariadne auf Naxos* (Ariadne on Naxos, 1912; revised and expanded 1916). It was clearly part of the same project as *Der Rosenkavalier* and its plot was briefly outlined in Chapter 5, since one if its funnier moments involves the horror a dedicated *opera seria* composer feels on being told that he has to make room for comedy. *Ariadne* started life as an 'intermezzo' during a performance of Molière's play *Le Bourgeois gentilhomme* (The Bourgeois Gentleman, 1670), but was then revised into a full-scale piece comprising a Prologue and then the Opera. The action occurs in the house of 'the richest man in Vienna' during the nineteenth century. A magnificent banquet is taking place, due to be followed by a series of entertainments: first a serious opera called *Ariadne auf Naxos*, then a comic divertissement, then fireworks. In the Prologue the Composer (mezzo-soprano) fusses about the fact that a *commedia dell'arte* troupe, led by Zerbinetta (soprano), will follow his solemn work of drama; Zerbinetta mocks the seriousness of the Composer's art. Pandemonium is caused when the Major-domo announces that, because of time pressures, both the opera and the *commedia* must be played simultaneously. The Opera is set on the island of Naxos. Ariadne (soprano) has been abandoned by Theseus and longs for death. Zerbinetta, Harlequin (baritone) & Co. periodically invade and lampoon her sentiments. The god Bacchus (tenor) arrives and, in a passionate duet, he and Ariadne declare their love. Just before their closing peroration, Zerbinetta appears from the wings, points to Bacchus and Ariadne, and says, with enigmatic grace: 'When the new god approaches, we surrender without a word'.

As with *Der Rosenkavalier*, the musical options are astonishingly broad. At the start of the second part, the *opera seria* proper, there are styles from and allusions to virtually all of operatic history. Three nymphs sing a nature-music trio ('Ach, wir sind es eingewöhnet') with elaborate coloratura, close in style to Wagner's Rhinemaidens yet interweaving that recent model with an earlier prototype proper to the eighteenth-century frame narrative, the trio of sirens in Handel's *Rinaldo*. Harlequin sings a neo-classical pastiche, complete with wrong notes and over-mechanical accompaniment, as if he's a serenade-singer out of Mozart with a few quite audible twentieth-century quirks. Or, maybe he's Cochenille, the comic valet from Offenbach's *Les Contes d'Hoffmann*, whose little Act 1 aria seems close at hand. Echo, the mythological nymph belonging to the *opera seria*, develops an inappropriate liking for Harlequin's singing and at one point decides to repeat his refrain. Strauss lunges into the grand symphonic style and manages the trick of over-doing the Wagnerian motivic development without falling into parody. And finally, Ariadne's intense, almost atonal opening soliloquy flirts with Viennese modernism, a grave gesture that gets deflated when her backing group (the nymphs) repeat Ariadne's dissonant, advanced melodic intervals perhaps once too often.

The use of various aspects of Wagnerian language, all bordering on irony in the mock-serious operatic context, suggests that Strauss, who is often accused of passively remaining Wagnerian while other, truer moderns managed to escape, may have come to terms with the looming past more successfully than is usually granted. As we have seen, in *Salome* and then in *Der Rosenkavalier* he proved himself more than adept at dealing inventively with that central pillar of the late Wagnerian stylistic edifice, the leitmotif. But here in *Ariadne* he goes even further. One illustration comes in the opening of the Prologue, which was written for the second version and thus when many of the motifs of the opera proper (mostly taken over from the original version of the score) were already intact. It is certainly a complex orchestral exposition of some of the main motifs of the work, but is presented in the most un-Wagnerian way possible; each motif gives way to the next by means of a precipitate cadence, more in the manner of a Verdian *potpourri* overture than a Wagnerian prelude. This has a complicated effect later in the drama, when those same motifs are used in a more conventional Wagnerian manner, in a sense serving subtly to undermine (or at least ironize) the entire Wagnerian project from within.

Theodor Adorno would have been appalled by our approving gestures towards the composer as, at least in some ways, a progressive. Adorno (the pupil of Berg, the defender of Schoenberg) *had* to disapprove of Strauss, and argued strongly that his art, especially in the post-*Rosenkavalier* works, had lost its way:

> Strauss's turning towards Hofmannsthal marks the caesura of his development. Although in terms of content it bound Strauss even more intimately to the art of his era, which was directed towards mere life, the encounter with Hofmannsthal defines the moment at which the artist Strauss came up against an outer threshold of life that he hesitated to push back down into it, even though he experienced it in an aesthetically veiled, mild form embedded in convention.[9]

But the last part of the essay is curiously ambiguous, especially when it talks of *Ariadne*:

> Zerbinetta . . . is finally right about her new god, since the world of Bacchus, as a world of mere sensuous ecstasy, is just as much appearance as the *buffo* world above which it wishes to elevate itself. . . . [Strauss] has collected all the brilliance of temporal life and makes it shine forth out of the mirror of his music; he has perfected appearance in music and made music transparent as glass.[10]

For Adorno this transparency was, ultimately, Strauss's great failing. It was proof that he was not in the vanguard. But his sympathy with Zerbinetta's final comment puts him in a difficult position, as it is clear that 'the mirror' effect of Strauss's music was something he understood. Whatever one's conclusions, the final duet in *Ariadne* is a luminous example of Strauss's achievements under these restraints. The orchestra is little larger than that used by Mozart and his contemporaries, albeit with the addition of harmonium, celesta and piano. But it is used with such extraordinary skill as to seem authentically of the early twentieth century. In some ways, as befits the solemn close of what is, in the larger fiction, a serious opera, the final stretches of *Ariadne* are openly Wagnerian. When we hear a full orchestra in crescendos and decrescendos on a final chord, departing softly, we're hearing exactly the effect of the sound waves that end *Tristan und Isolde*. But in the end there is only a seeming openness in the homage. The celesta stands sentinel over the reference. Celestas are never heard in Wagner, and they have a time-honoured operatic function of referring to the magical and the illusory. The celesta's timbre, the delicacy of Strauss's *trompe l'oreille* orchestration, reminds us that layers of frosted glass stand between transfiguration here and now and the version we were allowed to enjoy without irony in the past.

WOZZECK, *LULU* AND THE ART OF NOSTALGIA

The severe aspect of the modernist avant-garde in Germany and Vienna was embodied in expressionist atonality. Schoenberg's operatic experiment *Erwartung* (1909), discussed in Chapter 17, exploits atonality's sounds and fundamental psychological effects – high anxiety and intimations of wrongness or madness – to underpin the drama. *Erwartung* is a masterly, free-flowing collection of musical shrieks and groans, with both the orchestra and the singer doing the shrieking and groaning, since Schoenberg wrote for the voice as if it were little more than another instrument. Occasionally resurrected, the opera sounds as strange and unapproachable as it did when first performed more than a hundred years ago: a formidable passage of incomprehension, which might be a prime exhibit in the argument that the kind of expressionism and atonality explored in pieces like *Erwartung* simply doesn't work when applied to the necessarily long stretches of time and narrative development that opera requires. However, such conclusions are strongly challenged in two operas written by Schoenberg's prize student, Alban Berg (1885–1935). Although based on similar compositional techniques, they are so different that their origins, and the shock of their unexpected beauty, can seem perpetually mysterious.

Berg was Schoenberg's student, but also his protégé and disciple. In public he praised his teacher in lavish terms. In an essay in 1912, published in a *Gedenkschrift* (commemorative volume) for Schoenberg, Berg called him 'the teacher, the prophet, the Messiah; and the spirit of language which understands the essence of the genius far better than those who abuse it, gives the creative artist the name "Master", and says of him that he created a "school"'.[11] Naturally the real relationship was more ambivalent. Berg's modest family wealth meant composition was not his entire livelihood. He inhabited a cultivated artistic milieu in Vienna, and was tall and handsome. He wrote only around twenty works in the course of his life. The first handful – during his apprenticeship with Schoenberg – were journeyman pieces, albeit remarkably accomplished ones, couched in a highly unstable tonal idiom. Much of his career was spent in illness, service in the Austrian army during the First World War, romance, melancholy, infidelity and just sheer existence. His overwhelming gift was for dramatic music, for the pacing and variety of music appropriate to the theatre.

He wrote two operas that are among the greatest produced in the twentieth century, *Wozzeck* (finished 1922, premiered 1925) and *Lulu* (left largely finished, but with its third act un-orchestrated, at Berg's death in 1935). Berg followed one trend of the time by himself adapting both libretti from previously existing spoken dramas. *Wozzeck* is based on an 1879 edition of fragments of a play entitled *Woyzeck*, which the great German playwright Georg Büchner left incomplete at his death in 1837. In fifteen scenes over three acts, the opera depicts miserable vignettes from the life of Wozzeck (baritone), a poor, tormented soldier enlisted in a nameless army in a nameless town, and his common-law wife, Marie (soprano). He eventually murders Marie in a jealous fit, and drowns himself in madness and remorse. In a desolate final vignette, Marie's little son (treble) is left riding his hobbyhorse, seemingly indifferent to taunts that his mother is dead, singing 'hopp, hopp' to himself.

Lulu was adapted from a recent two-part play by Frank Wedekind. Set in *fin-de-siècle* Vienna, it traces the rise and fall of Lulu, femme fatale and Earth Spirit, as men and women fall in love with her, are murdered and ruined by her, and die for her. In the final scene she has been reduced to prostitution and is murdered by Jack the Ripper. The opera's most disquieting literary feature is the disappearance of any frame. The libretto (like the source play) begins with an allegorical prologue in which a circus ringmaster invites the audience into the Big Top and describes the wild animals they will see. Each animal is a character in the plot. Lulu's lovers are the ape, the tiger and the camel. Lulu is the snake ('created to make trouble') and the singer playing her is actually carried on by assistants and exhibited. However, no circus master returns at the end to tell us that what we have seen was 'just a story' – we are drawn in, the fiction becomes real and we are left at the end staring at a windowless garret with no survivors. This kind of apocalyptic ending is characteristic of twentieth-century operatic tragedy, often (as in *Wozzeck*) with one disquieting voice left in the wilderness. Ferruccio Busoni's *Doktor Faust* (unfinished at Busoni's death in 1924), an erratic, ambitious opera, ends this way in some editions. Mephistopheles, posing as a nightwatchman, strolls the deserted streets at midnight and proclaims the approach of winter. He stumbles on Faust's body, and makes a cold little joke: 'Sollte dieser Mann verunglückt sein?' (Has this person come to grief?).

One way to understand Berg's genius, and his operatic accomplishment, is to say that while he embraced compositional techniques and sound worlds acquired from Schoenberg, he never used them to exclude or banish listeners. While Schoenberg founded a Society for Private Musical Performance in 1918, and could be dogmatic about suppressing musical ideas, particularly harmonic ones, familiar from the musical past, Berg never was. Both his operas contain expressive tonal music from time to time, and both thread in dance hall music, cabaret idioms, marches and songs, all composed to sound as if heard through a disorientating haze, moving in and out of focus. In Act 1, scene 3 of *Wozzeck*, Marie comforts herself and her child by singing a lullaby. It is a strange one, whose subject is Marie's own wretched life ('Mädel, was fangst Du jetzt an?' which roughly translates as 'Girl, what are you thinking of?'). Berg re-imagines the traditional, slow 6/8 lullaby metre in snappier form, and the accompaniment has a few wrong notes; yet it retains a lullaby's lilt, the rocking quality intact. When Marie gets to the refrain, 'Eiapopeia, mein süßer Bu'' (Lullaby, lullaby, my sweet child), everything slows down, her voice opens out into lush, full-voiced consolation. The second verse then appears, unsentimental and brisk again, as if returning her to reality.

Both Schoenberg and Berg adored classical instrumental forms – sonata, fugue, passacaglia, theme and variations – as organizational aids in a new world unanchored by tonality and its points of departure and arrival. But the message each delivers by means of these techniques is very different. Schoenberg deploys them to impose order, but also in a bid for cultural prestige: a way of positioning himself as the inevitable successor to those German masters who used them before, above all to Bach, Beethoven and Brahms. It's a way of saying: You see? This music may sound strange, but it has age-old musical credentials. For Berg, the fixed forms demonstrate nothing. When used thus unsentimentally, they are simply a good way to parcel out and organize operatic scenes, similar in that sense to the old slow movement plus cabaletta or the strophic song or the 'da capo' aria.

Wozzeck, then, wears its learning lightly; but it is still a hyper-structured piece, ordered and symmetrical on many levels. Each act has five scenes, and each has its own internal progress. The first act is a series of five character pieces (suite, rhapsody and hunting song, march and lullaby, passacaglia, rondo); the second is a symphony in five movements; the third is a set of inventions (or pseudo-improvisations) on very basic musical elements. Berg plays games with symmetries around the exact centre of the fifteen scenes, which is Act 2, scene 3. That scene takes place on a gloomy day in the street outside Marie's house. It is an existential confrontation between Wozzeck and Marie, and is scored for a small chamber orchestra whose instrumentation – in another homage to the master – exactly matches that of Schoenberg's Chamber Symphony, Op. 9. The second and fourteenth scenes, equidistant from this centre (that is, Act 1, scene 2 and Act 3, scene 4) are uncanny twins. The imagery of Act 1, scene 2 (rhapsody) derives from one of Büchner's strangest notions, that the earth had only a very thin crust, a thin skull over an incalculable morass. Wozzeck, in a field outside town, hallucinates: he hears noises from beneath the earth, and whispers, 'es wandert was mit uns da unten!' (something is shadowing our steps, down under there!) A sunset is burning the world. In Act 3, scene 4 (invention on a six-note chord) Wozzeck returns to the scene where he murdered Marie, a pool in a forest, obsessed with finding the knife he used as a weapon. Moonrise appears as blood, and he wades into the water ('I must wash the blood off') and drowns.

What are all these instrumental forms doing in the theatre? The answer is that we hardly notice them. What Berg instinctively realized was that opera had always done well on brevity and musical containment: on what is in effect a series of 'numbers' of modest size. He was (unlike so many of his operatically inclined fellow travellers during the period) aware that the new, tonally unmoored language could not sustain a lingering narrative: he knew that individual scenes should be short and well contrasted, and should come to a decisive end.

He was canny in other ways. Even though, like everyone else of his generation, he used recurring motifs freely – it was the Wagnerian given – his command of musical recurrence, both of motifs and what he came to call *Leit-sektionen* (best translated as 'recurring sections of music') rarely sounds routine, and can make for powerful, moving effects. In the *Lulu* prologue the Ringmaster addresses the Lulu-figure, 'My sweet beast, don't be offended: you have no right to spoil the primordial image of Woman with hissing and meowing'. Berg sets these lines to a gorgeous sequence, pairs of downward shifting chords that end when the Ringmaster's voice breaks out into a *bel canto* peak and cadence at 'Urgestalt des Weibes' (primordial image of Woman). The words are cynical and mocking, but the music is heartrending. Berg then keeps this idea in his pocket through most of the opera, saving it for moments that require an embodiment of longing, and rely on the music's beauty in ways that complicate its dramatic meaning.

A good instance occurs in Act 2. A silent-film interlude shows how Lulu (soprano) has been incarcerated for murdering her third husband, Dr Schoen (baritone), and how Countess Geschwitz (mezzo-soprano), infatuated with Lulu, takes advantage of a cholera outbreak to switch places with her in the isolation ward of the prison. Lulu returns home, walks through the door, and the Ringmaster's rhapsody suddenly pours forth from the orchestra: but what Lulu sings, at the *bel canto* moment, is 'O Freiheit! Herr Gott im Himmel!' (Oh freedom! God in heaven!) So the music's effect now also refers to something at once human and abstract, the blessing of liberty, a sentiment as moving as the Prisoners' chorus in *Fidelio*. The final recurrence of the motif is at the very end of the opera. Lulu and the remains of her entourage have landed in London. Lulu is a fledgling prostitute, and the clients that appear are doubles of her dead husbands. Last of all comes Jack the Ripper reincarnating Dr Schoen. She is desperate that he should not leave: 'ich habe Sie so gern. Lassen Sie mich nicht länger betteln' (I adore you. Don't make me beg any longer). Now the words are sordid, but that heartrending music appears again. What is its effect this time? Since Lulu and Jack are symbolically re-enacting a traumatic past in which Dr Schoen (so she claimed) was Lulu's only true love, the music functions as a memory. But Berg may also be showing us that Lulu is the Earth Spirit, beyond morality, whom men love no matter what she is, or does, or says. Both *Wozzeck* and *Lulu* favour musical recurrence and reminiscence to enhance the particular effect of conjuring up longing, nostalgia, memory.

In both works another distinct operatic quality involves the way in which the numerous fixed forms and technical devices interact with the conversations and confrontations – the unfolding story of human interaction and reaction. The virtuoso showpiece in this regard is Act 3 of *Wozzeck*, written as a series of inventions. Berg-style inventions are a difficult musical trick – a self-contained segment is composed around one simple musical element presented in various forms and disguises. The musical element is an *idée fixe*, something that remains fixed and omnipresent; everything else is draped around it. The dramatic match in Act 3 rests on the obsessive quality of invention as a musical process, and on the fact that each scene depicts obsession: Marie's guilt over her infidelity (3/1), Wozzeck's murder of Marie (3/2), a crowd in a tavern staring at blood on Wozzeck's hands (3/3), Wozzeck's search for the knife, his compulsive washing and suicide (3/4), and finally Marie's son's dissociative, repetitive skipping and singing (3/5). These inventions have been lending libraries for film composers ever after (Hitchcock's most celebrated film composer, Bernard Herrmann, seldom saw water without hearing the six-note chordal waves of the drowning scene). Berg's virtuosity, as ever, lies in how much can be invented out of so little.

The first scene, featuring Marie's remorse, is an invention on a melody, a relatively conventional process resembling theme and variations. But the second, the murder scene, is a tour-de-force, an invention on a single pitch, B. The pitch is always present, sometimes as a stratospheric high note like ringing in the ear, sometimes growling in the lowest registers, sometimes hidden in plain sight as a middle-register note surrounded by lush string chords. Wozzeck sings it alone, without accompaniment and to the word 'Nicht', just before the moon rises. As the disaster approaches, the pitch becomes more prominent, louder and less hidden within the musical texture. For the transition to scene 3, Berg simply has the orchestra freeze twice on B, the second time with everyone in crescendo. The crescendo effect is famous, but the first freeze on B is stranger: starting from a single horn, the instruments individually add their voices, as if in acoustic analogy to heads turning one after the other to stare at something horrible.

The scene-change passages in Act 3 are mute expressions of feeling – mute in the sense that no singing occurs, and yet a collective voice (the orchestra) gives expression to the pity and empathy that characters in the fiction seldom receive from their companions. They also involve a technical trick: in each transition, the musical idea from the previous invention overlaps with the upcoming *idée fixe*, so for example between the orchestral Bs at the end of the murder scene a bass drum beats out a rhythm that is the basis for the tavern scene that will follow. The only exception is the longest and most mysterious scene-change interlude, that between Wozzeck's death and the final epilogue. Its importance is marked out by Berg, who spells out that it alone constitutes a further invention, this time on a key, D minor. This interlude has always been taken as a musical microcosm of the opera, since it piles up reminiscences of important leitmotifs and relives the horrendous twelve-note chord that had marked Marie's death. But what seems more transfixing about it is a harmonic power out of the past, a key centre used both as a bludgeon at top volume and, rather like the Ringmaster's *bel canto*, an expression of enormous loss. As so often in Berg, the most effective moments entail distorted references to the musical past.

THE RAKE'S PROGRESS

Throughout the time that Schoenberg and Berg were plotting their radical course, their great antagonist was Igor Stravinsky (1882–1971). His position as their antithesis, equally self-consciously maintained, led him for most of his career to be programmatically opposed to opera, a form that represented everything most to be avoided from the past, not least the emotional outpourings of Wagner and his followers. After the shockingly daring ballet scores of Stravinsky's early years, he turned in the 1920s to a style that has become known as 'neo-classicism', an attempt to banish the excesses of the nineteenth century and return to a cooler, more supposedly objective musical stance, one in which Bach and Mozart were the restored heroes. His only full-length opera, *The Rake's*

Progress (1951), was written very late in life (he was nearly seventy when it was premiered in Venice), and was deeply embedded in a neo-classical aesthetic that, after the Second World War, seemed increasingly to belong to an earlier age. Almost immediately after its composition, quite possibly influenced by the fact that his sojourn in Europe for the premiere (his first since 1939) had demonstrated that the current avant-garde were turning to Schoenberg and his school for inspiration, he began to move away from his neo-classical style and towards Schoenbergian serialism. Perhaps aided in no small way by this sense of untimeliness, *The Rake* turned out to be an operatic tour-de-force: a work that, although utterly different from either *Der Rosenkavalier* or *Wozzeck*, managed like them to harness a general sense of operatic nostalgia to remarkable dramatic ends.

Even though Stravinsky remained a staunch, vociferous Wagner-phobe, he followed in Wagner's footsteps in at least one obvious respect, by producing a steady stream of words to accompany his music. Any-one familiarizing themselves with *The Rake* will be bombarded with Stravinskian hints about its genesis and lineage. In the very first para-graph of a programme note written in the mid-1960s, more than a decade after the premiere at Venice's Teatro La Fenice, and with the composer deep into his last, serial period, he confided that:

> Rather than seek musical forms symbolically expressive of the dramatic content (as in the Daedalian forms of Alban Berg), I chose to cast the *Rake* in the mould of an eighteenth-century 'number' opera, one in which the dramatic progress depends on the succession of separate pieces – recitatives and arias, duets, trios, choruses, instrumental interludes. In the earlier scenes the mould is to some extent pre-Gluck in that it tends to crowd the story into the secco recitatives, reserving the arias for the reflective poetry, but then, as the opera warms up, the story is told, enacted, contained almost entirely in song – as distinguished from so-called speech-song, and Wagner-ian continuous melody, which consists, in effect, of orchestral commentary enveloping continuous recitative.[12]

Later still, he recalled that he and his chief librettist, W. H. Auden (1907–73), had interrupted their first, concentrated days of work together on the opera (which took place at Stravinsky's Californian home) by attending a two-piano performance of Mozart's *Così fan tutte*, then by no means a classic repertoire piece. The event was, he said, 'an omen, perhaps, for the *Rake* is deeply involved with *Così*'.[13]

As always, we can enjoy these scraps from the composer's table; but caution is required. Stravinsky was, with or without his latter-day amanuensis Robert Craft, as formidable a shaper of his own biography as was Wagner, and rarely wrote of himself without some obvious agenda. In this case he positions *The Rake* as part of (perhaps even the culmination of) his neo-classical phase by stressing the traditional, eighteenth-century aspects of opera; but the references to Berg (now, to 1960s Stravinsky, central to the reformed canon of twentieth-century modernism), and then to Gluck, Mozart and Wagner, suggest a high-culture, reformist attitude to the genre, one in which German-speaking composers have elevated an art form that might otherwise be dangerously, damagingly popular. Admittedly, the final caution about 'speech-song' makes it absolutely clear that, even when the opera 'warms up' (as Stravinsky puts it, with a nice show of populism), Wagnerian temperatures will never be aspired to. Intriguing, though, is the fact that Wagner remains the *bête noire* when by 1951 he had been dead for much more than half a century. Why was he still a problem?

There are numerous answers to this, but the most important is that Wagner's influence on twentieth-century music had, among modernists such as Stravinsky, consistently been seen as baleful. When Stravinsky was enjoying his first successes with the Diaghilev ballet company in the Paris of 1910–13, it was a commonplace among his circle to consider that opera was worn-out: too thoroughly tarnished by the past to be able to renew itself, above all too overblown and emotionally overt. Small surprise, then, that arch-modernist Stravinsky shunned the genre, his only stage pieces – works like *L'Histoire du soldat* (The Soldier's Tale, 1918) or *Oedipus Rex* (1927) – making a point of declaring themselves non-operatic. By the 1920s and 1930s those gloomy prognostications about opera's demise seemed to have come true. An 'opera crisis' was repeatedly declared: fewer and fewer new works were entering the repertory; impresarios and others increasingly looked to opera's past in order to fill their theatres. There had been countless attempts to revive the medium, innumerable calls to order, earnest pleas for a new kind of musical drama. *Wozzeck* had seemed to some like a new beginning, and although Berg himself, in an influential essay entitled 'The Problem of Opera', denied that he was a reformer, he still, as did many others, called for a return to simpler, more immediately effective theatrical music.[14] But the old operatic machine was frustratingly intractable. What is more, and to the dismay of many, the despised, hyper-emotional works of the nineteenth century, Wagner included, remained the mainstays of the repertory, showing themselves remarkably able – now with the help of enterprising stage directors, who could add a modern patina to the old threads – to change with the changing times.

By the late 1940s, when Stravinsky started on the *Rake*, these battles had for the most part lost their energy. In straitened, post-war circumstances it became impossible even to imagine contemporary works that might compete with the warhorses of the now-distant past. The operatic juggernaut continued on its way, increasingly displaying a museum culture. But now, with new historical additions to the repertoire, at least there was a variety of styles from which to choose. Revivals of Gluck's and, in particular, Mozart's operas (which, with the exception of *Don Giovanni*, had largely disappeared from nineteenth-century stages) began to make opera newly respectable among those of elevated taste, connecting the genre securely to the great Austro-German symphonic tradition, which still retained cultural prestige among modernist generations. In this context, it was small surprise that the operatic Stravinsky would declare himself foremost a Mozartian, and decidedly German-master-inclined for the rest of his canon (Gluck, Wagner, Berg) when it came to matters operatic.

The idea of basing an opera on William Hogarth's series of engravings (1735) was Stravinsky's, but soon took on shapes characteristic of Auden and his collaborator, Chester Kallman. The action takes place in eighteenth-century England. Tom Rakewell (tenor) is engaged to Anne Trulove (soprano). The mysterious Nick Shadow (baritone) arrives to announce that Tom has inherited a substantial fortune and must immediately depart for London. Once in town, and aided by Nick, Tom indulges himself extravagantly, then becomes bored, then – to demonstrate his freedom from 'those twin tyrants of appetite and conscience' – marries a bearded lady called Baba the Turk (mezzo-soprano). Tiring of her, he becomes caught up in a reckless financial scheme and is ruined. Nick declares himself a Mephistopheles and demands Tom's soul as wages for his service. They play a game of cards to decide Tom's fate. Tom wins, but Nick's parting gesture casts him into insanity. The final scene takes place in Bedlam. Anne, still loyal, visits Tom, who thinks himself Adonis to her Venus. She lulls him to sleep and departs. He wakes up to find her gone and dies of grief. The opera ends, *Don Giovanni*-like (and *L'Heure espagnole*-like), with an epilogue in which the characters come to the front of the stage and explain the moral message of what has transpired.

The opera's very first scene demonstrates its Mozartian allegiance. The pastoral ambience of the opening trio, 'The woods are green', makes obvious gestures, even an obeisance, to Mozart, especially to the outdoor, wind-instrument-laden Mozart of *Così fan tutte*. The similarity to Fiordiligi and Dorabella's opening scene in *Così*, 'Ah guarda, sorella', is unmistakable: not only do the numbers share the same key and orchestral sonority, but snatches of Mozart's melody, harmony and accompaniment continue to surface unexpectedly in Stravinsky's spiky version of pastoral. This well-behaved, eighteenth-century operatic brand is also, of course, present in those 'secco' recitatives that Stravinsky drew attention to in his programme note. Although his first idea for *The Rake* had been to use spoken dialogue (perhaps a look back to his old, anti-operatic days), he soon, and enthusiastically, embraced the ancient division between action (recitative) and reflection (arias and ensembles), an economy that Wagner and others in the nineteenth century had done so much to undermine. Indeed, the very first recitative tells us that we are in a determinedly non-epic world, as far as possible away from the mysterious Wagnerian mists: with a flourish of arpeggio on the antique harpsichord, Anne's father calls for his beloved daughter and tells her, in unfussy declamation, 'Your advice is needed in the kitchen'.

As we move further into the opera, the stylistic picture becomes more complicated: once Tom has been ejected from Arcadia, the operatic borrowings proliferate. Mostly, as Stravinsky suggested in his programme note, these reach even further back in time, with gestures to Purcell and to the folk idiom of *The Beggar's Opera*. But in Act 1, scene 3 something quite different happens. Anne has been left alone in her country retreat, with no word from Tom. An orchestral introduction full of sharp woodwind sounds seems to lead us back into the Mozart-tinged pastoral world of the opera's beginning, if with sparer, more mournful overtones. After indulging this for a time, though, Anne launches into a two-movement aria of startling stylistic disparity. The slow movement, 'Quietly, night, O find him and caress', features a severe canon with the bassoon; the wind-instrument sounds that had previously adorned the 'budding grove' and 'pliant stream' of scene 1 are now more sinister, encircling presences, and the overall effect is closer to Bach at his most penitential. The mood is then interrupted by a 'voice off', Anne's father calling for her, which precipitates her closing aria and her sudden decision to go to London and seek out her lover. 'I go to him. Love cannot falter', she sings, and although the first melodic ideas again gesture towards Mozart, the mood is emphatically different, much closer to a nineteenth-century idiom. Indeed, this act-ending unmistakably invokes an old-style cabaletta of the Donizetti or early Verdi school. After the requisite two verses that all cabalettas boast (perhaps ornaments should be improvised second time around? the composer sketches a few, but no one dares add more) the aria and the act end with a breathless climax and a resounding high C for the soprano.

What are we to make of this? As some have suggested, the sudden change of musical atmosphere, the excursion into un-Mozartian territory and the swerve towards a new, much more popular operatic sound, may well have had something to do with Auden and Kallman. Although Auden, in his very first letter to the composer, had taken the trouble to insist that 'it is the librettist's job to satisfy the composer, not the other way round',[15] his influence on the general tone of *The Rake* (and not just the literary tone) was considerable. In this case, for example, we have documentary evidence that the high C was added at Auden's request (Stravinsky altered Anne's line at a late stage to incorporate it). A famous Auden essay on opera ends with what seems an explicit justification of this type of vocal excess:

> The golden age of opera, from Mozart to Verdi, coincided with the golden age of liberal humanism, of unquestioning belief in freedom and progress. If good operas are rarer today, this may be because, not only have we learned that we are less free than nineteenth-century humanism imagines, but also have become less certain that freedom is an unequivocal blessing, that the free are necessarily the good. To say that operas are more difficult to write does not mean that they are impossible. That would only follow if we should cease to believe in free-will and personality altogether. Every high C accurately struck utterly demolishes the theory that we are the irresponsible puppets of fate or chance.[16]

This is a far cry from Stravinsky's careful laying out of his operatic progeny in that 1960s programme note. Although Mozart is still central, Auden's is a credo that freely embraces the popular, and indeed insists that the fulcrum of 'our' opera is the nineteenth century, when the high Cs the poet found so inspiriting were flowing in such abundance. We might also recall that, as *The Rake* was in the making, Auden and Kallman, a pair of unashamed opera buffs of the old school, sent Stravinsky, whose previous severity in writing for the human voice was well-known, an LP collection of their favourite divas and divos, hoping that the composer would use these golden-age singers as, literally, role models.

The injection of new compositional blood into Anne's *scena ed aria* has been recognized and celebrated by posterity in the most obvious way. This number is by far the most popular in the opera, finding its way into numerous vocal recitals and competitions. An impressive array of divas from the last fifty years have asserted their free will and personality by trumpeting that high C at the close. There's even a recording of the very first Anne, none other than Elisabeth Schwarzkopf, singing the aria in 1951 at the Teatro La Fenice under Stravinsky's baton. The orchestra is distinctly tentative and the tempi are slow, but the sound of Schwarzkopf negotiating the part has many resonances. We might recall immediately that the great German diva was famous for her Mozartian roles, and thus an obvious choice as Stravinsky's lead soprano. But there is no little irony in the fact that she was also much associated with Strauss's operas (she was for many years the European Marschallin of choice), operas that Stravinsky hated with a passion and refused to consider part of the operatic canon ('I would like to admit all Strauss operas to whichever purgatory punished triumphant banality. Their musical substance is cheap and poor; it cannot interest a musician today'[17]). Most revelatory, though, is the response of the live audience at La Fenice. As soon as Schwarzkopf detonates that final C, there are murmurs of approval, and the moment she finishes it there's a storm of applause, uninhibitedly drowning out Stravinsky's carefully crafted final cadences. One wonders: how many other times has a Stravinsky composition been thus invaded with 'premature' applause? It's not, after all, how you're supposed to treat an earnest, modernist work. But that high C was simply too visceral an effect: the Italian audience knew immediately that, rather than attending the prestigious world premiere of a modern masterpiece, they were, for a moment, just *at the opera*.

Of course, there are many more twists and turns in *The Rake's Progress* after that triumphant high C. The work's principals continue to swing violently between various operatic modes, some of them quite severe. Auden and Kallman's largest hint towards operatic camp, the appearance of the bearded lady, Baba the Turk, was an invitation largely ignored by Stravinsky: far from indulging in *bel canto*, she has some of his spikiest, most difficult music. But Anne, her musical personality tinged by her great moment of vocal extravagance, proves forever prone to nineteenth-century operatic idioms: there are obvious strains of Donizetti's Lucia in several places; and her great arioso in Act 2 ('How strange. Although the heart for love dare everything') is preceded by a trumpet solo uncannily reminiscent of one that introduces the lovelorn tenor in Act 2 of the same composer's *Don Pasquale* ('Cercherò lontana terra'). We have, it seems, travelled a great distance from the austere list of German opera reformers that Stravinsky quoted in his programme note. What's more, it is in large part by means of such *bel canto* music that, in spite of her continued submissiveness and lack of agency, Anne invariably collects around her the greatest audience sympathy: if we care about *The Rake*, we surely care above all about Anne.

However, Stravinsky began vocally with Mozart, and with Mozart he winds towards a close, this time with gestures to the composer's one opera that had survived in the nineteenth century. As Nick Shadow shows his true stripes at the climax of the card-playing scene, we hear the angry dotted rhythms of a famous stone guest, dragging Don Giovanni irresistibly downwards. In one sense this revenant marks the fact that Mozart's operatic genius was for Stravinsky not just a dramatic starting point: that it could provide material for the most grandiose moments. But then, with yet another twist in this infinitely surprising opera, eighteenth-century tidiness and wit are re-established in the *Rake*'s final moments; as mentioned earlier, the characters shed their masks and, with a blatant imitation of the closing ensemble from *Don Giovanni*, address the audience directly.

The history of opera after 1945 is a strange tale indeed, and one we will pursue in the last chapter of this book. In one sense it was in the rudest of health, with more live (and recorded) operas available than ever before, and with the rediscovery of Mozart's operatic genius, and then Handel's, vastly enriching the fare on offer. In another sense, though, with so few new works taking their place beside the monuments of the past, opera was caught in a continual loop, one in which 'death' was routinely pronounced and then vehemently (too vehemently?) denied. There is little doubt that *The Rake's Progress* was intimately involved in this quandary. In many ways it was a valedictory work for Stravinsky. His trip to Europe for the premiere was publicly triumphant but privately traumatic. He was goaded by the changes he saw all around him in post-war Europe, in particular by a new generation of avant-gardists who saw as their spiritual fathers Schoenberg and Webern, and who as a result no longer thought of him as the embodiment of musical modernity. In response, he spent the remainder of his life trying to restore his eminence by embracing a neo-Spartan serialist idiom. But *The Rake*, unlike virtually all other 'avant-garde' operas, stubbornly remained in the repertory. Equipped with its parade of curious reliquaries (musical and otherwise), it has always been open to new interpretations. The gestures it makes to the great past of opera, Mozart above all, but high Cs and other nineteenth-century accoutrements included, keep it alive, indeed have made it part of the history it set out to explore.

19
Speech

When does speaking become marked in opera? We are not talking about dialogue opera such as *opéra comique* or German-language *Singspiel*, in both of which speaking is an accepted part of the genre; we mean those occasions in all-sung opera when a character, usually in crisis, simply talks, or shouts, or half shouts and half sings. This is a phenomenon of the late nineteenth century and beyond, and sometimes the composer seems to encourage it, sometimes not. Carmen's final word to Don José – 'Tiens!' (Take it) – is almost always shouted rather than sung, and probably better that way. Risë Stevens' recording is a prime instance. The composer wrote notes, but the performers take some dramatic licence and speak instead. A more complex example might be Tosca's last words in Act 2 of Puccini's opera, 'E avanti a lui tremava tutta Roma!' (And all Rome trembled before him!). This is written to be intoned on low C♯, but can sound far more contemptuous when (as in Maria Callas's famous recordings) it's spoken. In this case, though, one could argue that Puccini wrote the line on one note not as an invitation for speech-like declamation, but for a precise reason. Tosca is just about to enact a little religious ritual, placing candles on either side of Scarpia's corpse – she has just stabbed him to death – and then balancing a crucifix on his chest; in other words, Puccini wrote those low repeated notes because he wants her to sound ecclesiastical at the end, as if delivering a sliver of Gregorian chant. What's more, if we rewind a bit in the *Tosca* example, to the moment where Scarpia has just been stabbed, we see in the score that Puccini does indeed specifically ask for speaking – words like 'Maledetta!' and 'Questo è il bacio di Tosca!' (This is Tosca's kiss!) are written without note heads, just stems and flags to indicate the rhythms. Singers interpret this notational instruction with a motley assemblage of gasps and rattles.

These are isolated examples from a century and more ago. But soon after the phenomenon would become less of a fluke. Speech in opera, and operatic styles that veer towards speech, marks an important development in the earlier twentieth century. The invasion of speech tells us that, true to the spirit of the age, operatic composers were experimenting with new styles and effects, just as some of them borrowed from new media, like recording, radio and film. But it also suggests that the entire business of opera, of people singing out their feelings with lyrical abandon, was becoming increasingly problematic, and at certain moments seemed hard to sustain. And real speaking in opera gets much more common when we approach 1945, as the borders between speech and singing become blurred in so many twentieth-century operas. Modern iconoclasm welcomed greater intrusions of speech and half-speech into opera as a bulwark against old-fashioned lyricism, despite the fact that the phenomenon had existed, and was extensively theorized, in the nineteenth century.

Ordinary speaking within otherwise sung operas is always special, and sometimes very special. In Schoenberg's *Moses und Aron* (written 1930–32; first performed 1954), Moses' pronouncements are spoken, as if mere singing were for idolaters and the unserious. A deep voice is of course specified. In Berg's *Lulu*, when the heroine asks Dr Schoen's son, Alwa, 'Isn't this the sofa where your father bled to death?' her speaking voice conveys dreadful matter-of-factness. There is also the phenomenon of *Sprechstimme*, which means literally speech-voice, sometimes also called *Sprechgesang*, speech-song, an eerie vocal style involving pitched speaking in which the singer hoots and intones rhythmically – with the swoops up and down guided by special notation on the page. In Berg's *Wozzeck*, the protagonist's drowning scene is written entirely in this way, Wozzeck's rhythmic wailing sounding like eighteenth-century *Melodram* from the expressionist Inferno. *Sprechgesang* is an old word. In the nineteenth century it was even used to refer to 'Wagner's song-speech', where lines are fully sung but, in the words of one early critic, 'the musician subordinates himself entirely to the poet; a free declamatory element prevails'.[1] One of the earliest books written about the *Ring* says that *Sprechgesang* is its basic idiom, as opposed to 'songs and ensemble singing'.[2] But usually the term refers to a mix of singing and speaking. A nineteenth-century biography of Carl Maria von Weber treats *Sprechgesang* as synonymous with *Melodram*, speaking over the orchestra.[3] In the *Allgemeine musikalische Zeiting* of 1877 an article on sacred music notes that 'Verdi recently used *Sprechgesang* twice in his *Requiem*, to excellent effect', presumably a reference to the soprano's intonations in the 'Libera me' movement.[4]

When we consider half-speech or sung-speech in early twentieth-century opera, we need to remember that, in spoken drama, actors often half sang their lines. They were intoning, using actual pitched notes, getting the throb in the voice that way. We know this not only through early recordings, where one famous example is Sarah Bernhardt,[5] but also because the style was parodied for its exaggerations or recalled as antique grandeur in early sound films. Some idea of what serious professional actors sounded like in, say, 1900 can be gleaned from the opening scene of the German film comedy *Viktor und Viktoria* (1933), in which an aspiring tragedian (played by Hermann Thimig) chews up the scenery in an audition. He sounds far more like Caruso than Olivier, because every syllable is delivered to a sung, voiced musical pitch. The phenomenon of *Sprechstimme* and singing declamation thus existed outside opera long before it became a special, non-singing, operatic effect. One can even make the case that Wagner's radical changes in melody, the long stretches of freely sung declamation in the *Ring*, were in part modelled on a sonorous elocution common in German acting of an earlier time, a style put into his ear by singers who passed over into half-speech as a quirk, like Wilhelmine Schroeder-Devrient.[6]

Perhaps, then, this use of speech is just another example of the way in which opera is so highly porous. There is always a temptation to account for its evolution, in the twentieth or any other century, as a self-contained system, glaring at its own past and grappling with problems of its own aesthetics. But to do this is to falsify one of its hallmarks. Sounds and tricks from other genres were always re-forming opera, and continued to do so in the modern era. We do of course occasionally pay tribute to spoken theatre and its relationship to modern opera, usually by citing libretti that were inspired by spoken actors like Gertrud Eysoldt (the heroine in the first German performances of Oscar Wilde's *Salomé*) who caught Strauss's attention on behalf of a dramatic subject. Puccini is another good instance. He got the first creative ideas for several of his operas by seeing versions of their stories in the spoken theatre:

in the case of David Belasco's play *Madame Butterfly*, he enthused about a London performance even though with hardly any knowledge of the language in which the actors were speaking.

But not long into the twentieth century there appeared another significant influence, as cinema began to talk to opera. Film historians have of course dealt extensively with the influence of opera on early film. Operatic music was used in live cinema accompaniments, and there were opera-centred extravaganzas like *Phantom of the Opera* (1925). There were biopics of Wagner and Verdi, and silent-film operas such as those in which Geraldine Ferrar starred, or the 1925 *Der Rosenkavalier*. Cecil B. DeMille saw performances of Saint-Saëns' *Samson et Dalila* in his impressionable youth, and plumbed his memories of French Orientalist operas for many a Babylonian processional. There is, though, greater resistance to seeing influence move in the opposite direction: to the idea that film – low and technological and brand-new as it was – could materially change something as hallowed and long-standing as opera. Yet film belongs to the cultural history of modern opera, as much as does expressionist theatre, or recording technology or the rise of the stage director.

Let us pose a non-canonic question: did opera composers go to the movies? Maurice Ravel was certainly an enthusiastic filmgoer, and his experience in the cinema may well have shaped his scenario for the ballet *Ma Mère l'oye* (Mother Goose, 1912), in which the protagonist, Sleeping Beauty, is shown apparitions – various fairy-tale stories – while in a drowsy state. Each story is introduced by an inter-title, two Moors bringing out a scroll. In 1912, where would the composer have experienced visual phantasmagoria, been in a dark place conducive to sleep, attended a flickering fantasy world where effects could seem magical, and where the story was explained by inter-titles? In the cinema, of course. Cinematic influence on modern music in general was widespread: the famous silent-film sequence in Erik Satie's ballet *Parade* (1918) is a single instance that can stand for scores of others. Two characters in the ballet suddenly start enacting an American silent-movie parody (cowboy, chase, gunshot, train rescue) and Satie adds sound effects to the music, shots and whistles accompanying the action, just as they were often added when silent films were screened. Ravel's operas of course drew from more than just a single well of influence. His one-act opera *L'Enfant et les sortilèges* (The Child and the Spells,

1925) began as a concept for a ballet. There are significant stretches with no singing but much dancing: teacups dance the foxtrot with teapots; wallpaper shepherds and shepherdesses tread a measure; there is a long waltz for winged insects and other fluttering creatures. The opera is arranged as a series of vignettes, in Part One involving objects and books the Child (mezzo-soprano) has destroyed in a fit of temper. They come alive and reproach him. In Part Two, after a scene change from the Child's room to the garden, it's the turn of the animals he has teased and caged. Ravel's brother, at least, seems to have noted the affinity with film, claiming that ideally the way to present the opera would be along the lines of Disney's *Snow White*, which the composer saw in 1937.[7] Dances gave Ravel a sonic background for many of the scenes, the characters singing along with and in between their music. The most heartrending of these is the lament of the Squirrel (mezzo-soprano) in Part Two, sung against a carefree waltz danced by the insects, and tallying up what he lost once caged: 'Le ciel libre, le vent libre, mes libres frères' (The free sky, the free air, my free companions). What is extraordinary is that as the Squirrel's words become more and more impassioned, his musical arc carries the waltz further and further afield. At the end he sings, 'Regarde donc ce qu'ils reflétaient, mes beaux yeux, tout mirotants de larmes' (See then what they reflect, these pretty eyes of mine, all gleaming with tears). The cadence and crescendo on these lines, which shifts the waltz into the minor mode to mark the anguish, proves what was once said of Ravel by a sage philosopher: you don't need funeral marches when you can compose devastating minuets.[8]

This technique – composing lyrical vocal lines against the backdrop of dance numbers – alternates in the opera with freer outbursts of barely sung lines. The Child's opening tantrum is an example and, as so often during this period, the reversion to naturalistic declamation is earmarked for rage or loss of control. 'Plus des leçons!' (No more lessons!), shrieks the Child, and although he sings to fixed pitches, they are written in such a way as to be anti-singing, anti-melody. But the most spectacular and enigmatic use of speech is reserved for the end of the opera, when the Child faints after having been menaced by the animals. Once his consciousness is removed, the animals can suddenly no longer sing, and the orchestra itself can barely play, uttering just a few strange tones amid long silences. The Child's imagination, it would seem, has alone given forth all the music. Then the animals start to speak, haltingly, and in a slow, brilliantly choreographed musical crescendo they teach themselves how to shout out a coherent word, 'Ma ... man!' (Mum ... my!). As they do so, they simultaneously learn how to add pitch and rhythm to their sounds, to get back to singing. Their reward is to reach the grandest of musical heights, since at the end they are able to sing a fugue, a gentle contrapuntal chorus to the words 'Il est bon, l'Enfant, il est sage' (He is good, the Child, he is wise).

ZEITOPER, OPERA UP TO DATE

At one point Ravel entertained the idea of introducing film projection into *L'Enfant et les sortilèges*, and the device was not uncommon in opera in the 1920s and 1930s. Berg, a film-crazy composer, used it in *Lulu*, which includes a silent-film interlude, to be shown between Act 2 scenes 1 and 2, and depicting Lulu's arrest, imprisonment and release. Theodor Adorno and Hanns Eisler's 1947 book *Composing for the Films* argues that Berg's operas used film-music tricks, mentioning that the twelve-note chord which accompanies Lulu's death 'produces an effect very much like that of a modern motion picture'.[9] There were other modernist composers who incorporated film episodes, such Paul Hindemith (1895–1963), whose *Hin und zurück* (There and Back, 1927) is like a film run forwards and then in reverse, since it first tells its story from beginning to end, and then tells it backwards. *Hin und zurück* is a so-called *Zeitoper* or 'Timely Opera', a sub-genre that arose in Germany during the Weimar Republic (1919–33) and attracted self-consciously iconoclastic young composers. Its attractions were fashionable technology (including sound recording and film), plots revolving around modern communication and the frantic pace of life, and arms flung open to popular music.

Ernst Krenek (1900–1991) puts the matter in a nutshell in his *Jonny spielt auf* (Johnny Strikes Up, 1927). The main characters are a serious composer, an opera singer, an African-American jazz musician and a violin virtuoso; as one review from 1929 tallied it, 'Everything that is typical in contemporary life finds a place in [Krenek's] opera ... movies, radio, loud speakers, foxtrotting, exoticism, revues, grand hotels.'[10] The plot takes place in Krenek's present, and is farcical and complicated, with scenes in a railway station, a hotel corridor, on a glacier and in urban streets. Typical productions featured flashing neon signs and film projection. Max the composer (tenor) is a sighing bore (perhaps a caricature of the arch-serialist and Schoenberg pupil Anton von Webern) who is transformed when he meets the opera singer Anita (soprano) on a glacier. He vows to lighten up and descend to the modern world, a sphere personified by Jonny, the jazz musician (baritone). As Krenek said around that time, making the message of the opera clear:

> No one can get around the fact that the existence or nonexistence of symphonies is of absolutely no consequence to the members of today's bourgeoisie. On the other hand, if the output of dance music were to cease for some reason, they would demand, through their newspapers or in some other way, the immediate resumption of its production.[11]

Now very much a curiosity, *Jonny spielt auf* was the most-often performed opera in Germany of the Weimar period – and over forty productions were mounted worldwide in its first season, including one at the Metropolitan Opera in New York, with mostly German singers. The *New York Sun* wrote: 'Krenek has set most of it to music of a modernist German opera type. This is the inevitable result of his design. His aim was to travesty the kind of recitative so often heard in very grand opera, which disguises commonplace and even silly remarks in lofty sounding phrases.'[12] But for 'recitative' one should read 'conventional operatic vocal writing' in general, since what Krenek does is compose unstructured, freely sung dialogue to a background that often includes hints of ragtime, dance-hall music and jazz. His own, much later memories underline his operatic hinterland:

> [*Jonny*] was labelled a 'jazz opera', which I felt to be a misnomer, for whatever jazz here occurs is brought in to characterize the professional sphere of the protagonist, Jonny, leader of an American combo. The music attached to the other characters, which to me were at least as important, is conceived in that early romantic idiom I had chosen as my model, occasionally touched up with dissonant spices and Italianizing Pucciniesque vocal exuberance.[13]

In one scene, though – the one in which Jonny, fleeing for America, drops his train ticket on the street – the vocal writing edges close to *Sprechstimme*, the half-spoken sounds perhaps expressing Jonny's agitation or perhaps making a sharp contrast with what comes next. Feeling lonely for home, Jonny breaks into 'Swanee River', a Stephen Foster minstrel song. But since 'Swanee River' was written in 1851, it represents the historical past, the ancient yesteryear of Jonny's own world.

WHEN EVERYDAY LIFE IS SUNG

Musicalized speech appears in *Zeitoper* but hardly sets it apart from other operas written at the same time; what's more, the device says little either about *Zeitoper*'s irreverence or its love affair with the up to date and the prosaic. Such speech was in fact *Zeitoper*'s most serious debt to the past and high culture, since the idiom's ancestry includes richly pedigreed elements – something from Wagner, something from the realist composers, Puccini's 'vocal exuberance' not excluded, and something from *Literaturoper* – in which setting a spoken drama more or less intact dictates certain freedoms in the vocal writing and its accompaniment. And we should add to these the connection between the half-sung quality of musicalized speech and classical spoken theatre's sonorous elocution in performance.

But the strangest of the half-spoken operas before the Second World War were not operas written for live performance. They were the early sound films that both imitated opera – particularly *Zeitoper* and operetta – and in turn provided opera with inspiration for some of its special iconoclastic moves. Consider, for instance, René Clair's 1931 film comedy *Le Million*. Clair knew the classical-music world from the inside and had collaborated with Satie in 1924 on the short film *Entr'Acte*. In *Le Million*, ordinary people – charladies, policemen, thieves and poor artists – frequently take it into their heads to deliver their lines by singing them freely. Sometimes they do it just by rhythmicizing their speech, sometimes by erupting into quasi-melody, sometimes by joining in an impromptu song-like ensemble or by arguing in tango rhythm. As soon as they do anything remotely musical they are magically accompanied by the Invisible Orchestra from Nowhere. Considered as opera, this surreal state where everyday life is sung, is familiar and unsurprising. In the context of early sound cinema – usually a more rigidly realistic affair – the film constituted an elaborate, avant-garde piece of absurdity. In

Germany after 1933, much of this lively cinematic experimentation was lost. The Nazi cultural crackdown effectively suppressed both the German varieties of such absurdist films, where modern-day contemporary life turned into an opera, and the operatic world they reflected and refracted. Krenek, for instance, would see *Jonny spielt auf* condemned as 'degenerate music' (*entartete Musik*) and banned from performance; he fled to America in 1938.

In France the crosswinds blew a little longer. During the war years, Francis Poulenc (1899–1963), a protégé of Satie, wrote an absurdist comic opera based on a play by Guillaume Apollinaire, *Les Mamelles de Tirésias* (Tiresias' Breasts, finished 1944, premiered 1947). The heroine Thérèse (soprano) is tired of being a housewife and turns herself into a man by releasing her breasts – two helium balloons – into the air. Renamed Tirésias, she heads off for adventure, leaving her husband (the baritone) behind. A series of improbable incidents, unrelated to one another, completes the first act. The opening of Act 2 is a musical high point: after some couples dance a sarabande, accompanied by a kitschy dance-hall orchestra, the husband arrives (with no fewer than 40,049 offspring somewhere in tow). The orchestral musicians in the pit – burly men among them, no doubt – are then required to impersonate this infant juggernaut by bawling out 'La, Lala, Lala, La-Lalala-La!' to a kind of circus-slip-on-the-banana-peel number complete with penny-whistle slide, while the husband – in desperation – urges 'Silence! Silence! SilenceSilenceSilenceSilence!' In general, Poulenc ballasts the score with vocal noise as unrelated to operatic singing as he can devise: cackling, talking, sneezing and whistling. Reverting to the obvious, he reserves one great operatic gesture – with a touch of old-fashioned French Orientalism – for Tirésias' Act 2 entrance in disguise as the Cartomancer, complete with turban, robe and high soaring voice.

By placing *Les Mamelles de Tirésias* and *Le Million* side by side, we get a sense of the affinities between comic and sardonic opera and the 1930s films that made real life into opera – so-called 'operetta' films but for the most part having nothing in common with traditional, theatre-based operetta. In one famous case, though, an opera was remade immediately as a film: *Die Dreigroschenoper* (The Threepenny Opera), by the playwright Bertolt Brecht (1898–1956) and composer Kurt Weill (1900–1950), was premiered in 1928 as a wildly successful theatre piece and was then filmed in 1930–31 as a multilingual production, with both a German and a French cast directed by G. W. Pabst. Adapted from an eighteenth-century English ballad opera by John Gay, *Die Dreigroschenoper* is a work with a purpose; artists with strong principles put it together. In line with Brecht's thinking, artifice – people breaking into song, for example – is all important as a reminder to the audience that they are watching something invented, and must not get sentimentally involved. The work thus returns to the conservative tradition of dialogue opera, with spoken scenes interrupted by numbers that are often given parodic titles: 'Das Lied von der Unzulänglichkeit menschlichen Strebens' (The Song About the Insufficiency of Human Endeavour) or 'Eifersuchtsduett' (Jealousy Duet). Weill's musical style draws from German cabaret but with strange distancing effects, often brought about by complicated harmonic tricks. He also freely parodies earlier operatic styles, and employs contradictory effects: a sarcastic, brutal text will be set to pleasantly attractive music. The actor-singers were directed to perform their numbers without real involvement, by assuming attitudes. Rather than smoothing over the abyss between speaking and singing, Brecht and Weill revel in its estranging quality.

Die Dreigroschenoper would seem not to fit the mould of this chapter in one sense. There are musical numbers, and there is talking to link them together. The work largely avoids modern opera's slide towards speech, towards the meandering, continuous music and singing, speech-turned-into-music, blurred boundaries between vocalizations that sing and those that speak. But Brecht and Weill's opera is not entirely deaf to the phenomenon. For instance, in Act 1 there is a 'Liebeslied' (Love Song) between ingénue Polly Peachum (soprano) and her murderous, unfaithful, violent husband Macheath (aka Mackie Messer or Mack the Knife; tenor or baritone). On the page, the libretto looks like a conventional opera duet, starting with dialogue and ending with simultaneously sung verse. But the dialogue is not in fact sung: it is spoken over the music, and with stiff rhythms and swooping intonation: Do you see the moon over Soho, asks Macheath. I see it, beloved, answers Polly. And this mixture – which would be called *Sprechstimme* were a Berg or a Schoenberg to have written it – was also characteristic of German cabaret in the Weimar era, where a famous singer like Gussy Holl would be called a 'diseuse' as opposed to a 'chanteuse' – a 'sayer' rather than 'singer' – because she half spoke her songs.

OLD STRAUSS

It might seem that twentieth-century opera's many ways of sliding towards speech mostly go with two prior conditions. One is a libretto based in comedy, satire or farce. The other is a librettist and composer unfazed by or even enamoured of movies, popular music, flappers, things generally that come from America and other elements never to be found, say, in French *grand opéra* or in Wagner. But that conclusion ignores the fact that the phenomenon also has distinguished European roots in *Literaturoper*, where a composer sets a play without trying to pass it through the intermediate stage of becoming a libretto.

As we saw in Chapter 17, it was through operas such as Debussy's *Pelléas* and Strauss's *Salome* that some early twentieth-century composers managed to renew an operatic tradition then thought by many to be mired in Wagnerism. They did so by writing operas whose text emerged more or less unchanged from a pre-existing spoken drama. In both cases, and with others that followed, a prose play proved liberating. It encouraged jettisoning the formality and regular musical periods that seemed dictated by conventional libretto poetry, and led to experiments with more intense styles of declamation – not to mention descents into the labyrinth of the soul that were pursued with an enthusiasm unknown even to Wagner. Prolonged explorations of this labyrinth also encouraged composers to use their previous expertise as masters of instrumental music, allowing the orchestra to take much of the burden of expression, even making it the prime mover. Both *Pelléas* and *Salome* might seem more like continuations of Wagner than rebellions; but they were so primarily in their most trivial aspects, in that both use leitmotifs in ways related to his practice. Both were also tributes in sound to Wagner's orchestral innovations, and Strauss sailed close to the Wagnerian wind in his harmonic language. But their subject matter – their composers' submission to verbal imaginations very distant from Wagner's – marked the important breakthrough.

In both cases, the experiment was unsustainable. The peculiarity and intensity of the situations Debussy and Strauss explored in these two operas were impossible to emulate, let alone surpass. After attempting just such a bigger-and-scarier sequel in *Elektra* (1909), Strauss – as we have seen – then took a very different operatic route in his eighteenth-century comic extravaganza *Der Rosenkavalier*. Debussy's case was, predictably, more tortured and hesitant. He was certainly fastidious enough to abhor the idea of repeating himself, and in 1903 wrote to fellow composer André Messager:

> Those who are kind enough to hope that I will never be able to forsake *Pelléas* are carefully averting their eyes. They simply don't understand that if that were to happen, I would immediately turn to growing pineapples in my bedroom, believing as I do that repeating oneself is the most tiresome thing.[14]

But – one of the eternal questions for twentieth-century opera composers – where was he to go next? His later life, with its series of extraordinarily inventive orchestral and solo piano works, was haunted by abandoned dramatic projects. The most extensive was a version of Edgar Allan Poe's story 'The Fall of the House of Usher', a subject which had some *Pelléas*-like features (dream-like oddity in particular), but which never got past the sketch stage. Debussy blamed his lack of success on failed musical innovation, saying that 'everything strikes me as boring and empty. For a single bar that is alive, there are twenty stifled by the weight of what is known as tradition, whose hypocritical and shameful influence I nonetheless recognize there, despite my efforts.'[15] The early years of the twentieth century, with tradition ever more heavy and the need to avoid it ever more exigent, were – as we have seen again and again – hard times in which to write an opera with ease.

Even though Debussy faltered the vogue continued, and it became a critical turn. For so long, melodious singing – the arc of the voice, the live amalgam of the beautiful line in the singer's performance – had been almost a definition of opera. The burden of expressiveness lay in that amalgam. Yet now operas in which the orchestra took over the emotional expression, and in which characters became increasingly prone to natural speech rather than lyrical songs, were becoming commonplace. Small surprise, then, that an association between speech-like opera and displeasure surfaces in the 1920s:

> Why, it might be asked, should it be considered more true to life to declaim and utter sounds which more often than not give no pleasure, than singing a beautiful melody? To have cut-and-dried airs all through an opera of today would be quite as tiresome as to have none at all; yet to exclude

> them from a score which it is reasonable to suppose is written with a view to pleasing the majority of the public is surely just as annoying. Nothing can make any theatrical performance absolutely real, and yet truth can be conveyed through beautiful melody (or airs, or tunes if you will) just as it can by beautiful language . . . the public wants what gives it pleasure. Within the last thirty years or so it would be really very interesting to know how many dozens – nay hundreds – of operas have been produced in Italy, Germany, and France, not to mention other countries, and how few have survived, and the underlying reason. This would probably be found to be lack of melody, though by this I would not be misunderstood as implying that it is owing to the absence of the old modelled type of vocal air, which would be out of place in opera of today.[16]

This, from a critic in *The Musical Times*, is not just an old lay, sung by many a bard. Here, 'melody' is standing in for a sense that expressive truth in opera is easier to fashion when the human voice is central; and that, in performance, the art or power of a particular singer will go a long way towards moving the listener in the direction of that truth. To compound the problem, speech-like opera was particularly attractive to composers who were otherwise instrumental-music specialists. As we have mentioned before, this led to a situation in which the professional opera composer – the type who spent virtually his entire life in the theatre, as had Verdi and Wagner – became a rarity. And this in turn led to twentieth-century opera becoming primarily a tale of experimental works, solitary attempts by composers whose hearts were given to purely instrumental music, to reassemble opera from the wreckage of late-nineteenth-century excess.

One of the very few who managed a continuous career in operatic composition was Richard Strauss. In a series of works after *Der Rosenkavalier* and *Ariadne*, he succeeded largely through an uneasy and partial allegiance with melody. For a time, until the poet's untimely death in 1929, he did this in collaboration with Hofmannsthal. They veered between grandiose works that seemed to return to Wagnerian seriousness and complexity, such as *Die Frau ohne Schatten* (The Woman without a Shadow, 1919), which Strauss hoped would be 'the last Romantic opera',[17] and *Die ägyptische Helena* (The Egyptian Helen, 1928); and lighter pieces such as *Arabella* (1933), in which he strove to rekindle the tone of *Der Rosenkavalier*. In all these operas, and in the five post-Hofmannsthal works that followed, Strauss maintained certain *Literaturoper* attitudes he had learned as early as *Salome*, in particular a relaxed attitude to long sections in which musical elaboration was sacrificed to convoluted dialogues in quasi-recitative. Many have enjoyed selected highlights from these works, and some have enjoyed complete performances in the theatre; few, though, have wished any of them wordier.

Strauss's last opera, premiered when the composer was in his late seventies, went deep into speech, in fact took words and music in opera as its central theme. This was *Capriccio* (1942), which Strauss called a *Konversationsstück für Musik* (Conversation Piece for Music), and which he wrote in stubborn antithesis to the destruction of the Second World War raging around him. Set in eighteenth-century France, the basic dramatic conflict is simple: the poet Olivier (baritone) and the composer Flamand (tenor) are invited to the birthday celebration of a beautiful young widow, the Countess Madeleine (soprano); both become rivals for her affection. They and various other characters go over this conundrum in allegorical terms: when words are set to music, which is more powerful? Which is the master? But added to this core are a series of small events and much – very much – discussion. In a synopsis, it is astonishing how often certain phrases recur, 'they discuss', 'they engage in a discussion', 'an argument ensues', 'the conversation grows heated', 'servants enter and comment', 'she wonders out loud'. And so the opera, which is in a single act, grew to well over two hours in performance and thus became a monumental speech opera in which conversation is elaborately celebrated. The opening music is a string sextet, played by the first desk principals, and perfectly sets the tone. Its outer sections are imbued with an elaborate nostalgia reminiscent of *Der Rosenkavalier*, while in the middle comes a sudden injection of heaving theatrical passion. The final scene of *Capriccio*, in which the Countess meditates on her conundrum in a famous soliloquy, is preceded by 'Mondescheinmusik' (Moonlight Music), an orchestral peroration that seems in some ways to return, as does much of the opera, to the energies and certainties of Strauss's earliest persona. But the Moonlight Music is – and not just in the context – imbued with unbearably poignant nostalgia for a German operatic world much of which was fast disappearing into the rubble of history. Two years later, in 1944 and with catastrophe imminent, the music critic Willi Schuh described a visit to the composer's study:

> During a conversation about our era, he took down a volume of Goethe from the bookcase to read the passage from the last letter to Wilhelm von Humboldt, written five days before Goethe's death: 'Confusing conclusions about confusing deeds dominate the world, and I have nothing more pressing to do than if possible to increase that which remains and is left to me and to keep my originality in hand.'[18]

But the *Capriccio* sextet had been given its first performance, in May 1942, at a private gathering in the Vienna house of Baldur von Schirach, former head of the Hitler-Jugend and now Gauleiter of Vienna.[19] A few months later, von Schirach would give a speech in Vienna in which he said that the deportation of the Jewish population from the city would 'contribute to European culture'.[20] With such as this, Strauss had made his rotten compromise.

BROUGHT IN FROM THE COLD

Serious, non-farcical speech-opera could be a black hole for composers in Germany, or indeed in France and Italy. Yet speech-opera thrived in the hands of composers and singers outside that circle. For this reason, the earlier twentieth century marks the moment when opera from outside, written in Hungarian or Russian or Czech or English, joins a repertory High Table once restricted to those west of the German linguistic border with an Eastern hinterland. To some extent, this was because these composers' nationalist, almost anti-colonialist impulses permitted lingering salutes to folk music and popular idioms, and to nature. This is what one critic, hauling in the Slavs to defeat the moderns, called the 'path of nature that will drive away the thick atmosphere of the theatre which surrounds the more sophisticated productions of modern European cosmopolites' – although this comment in fact looks far back in time, to the Czech composer Bedřich Smetana's *Prodaná nevěsta* (The Bartered Bride, 1866), for an antidote to *Ariadne auf Naxos*.[21]

The starring non-German proponent of 'speech melody', one of the oddest and most remarkable, was Janáček. We discussed his *Jenůfa* in Chapter 17 as an opera that runs parallel to *Pelléas* and *Salome*. As mentioned there, although *Jenůfa* was premiered in Brno in 1904, Janáček remained little more than a local celebrity in his Moravian homeland until the opera's Prague revival in 1916, when he was sixty-one years old. Even then it took another decade for the work to find a place in the international repertory (mostly via performances in German translation). But Janáček, encouraged by the gradual emergence of *Jenůfa* and further inspired by an autumnal infatuation for a young married woman called Kamila Stösslová, produced in his last decade five major operas, *Výlety páně Broučkovy* (The Excursions of Mr Broucek, 1920), *Kát'a Kabanová* (1921), *Příhody lišky Bystroušky* (The Cunning Little Vixen, 1924), *Věc Makropulos* (The Makropulos Affair, 1926) and *Z mrtvého domu* (From the House of the Dead, premiered posthumously in 1930). These works were thought eccentric and even amateurish by many at the time, yet they gradually assumed repertory status in the second half of the twentieth century, belatedly crowning Janáček as one of the greatest opera composers of the last hundred years.

Janáček's compositional use of 'speech melodies' was already evident in parts of *Jenůfa*, and faithful transcriptions of the melodic and rhythmic shapes of tiny verbal phrases would become the basic material of his late operatic language. The drama in these late works typically proceeds by means of a constantly changing series of speech-melody events, fashioned into blocks in which these melodic and rhythmic shapes (inspired by a character's verbal utterance) would not so much be developed as endlessly repeated and varied in ever-changing orchestral textures. In *Jenůfa* the technique was in its infancy and was interrupted by more conventional passages such as arias and ensembles. In his late works the alternation of blocks becomes almost continuous. The resulting fragmentation was made more complex by a well nigh constant sense of rhythmic unpredictability, caused by the fact that, in the Czech language, stress and length of syllable frequently fail to coincide, thus leading speech melodies to be based on syncopated rhythmic figures. Also characteristic is a leaner orchestral sound: there are fewer string melodies, more brass and percussion, in particular the soaring trumpet and pounding timpani known to many from the opening Fanfare of Janáček's *Sinfonietta* (1926).

The vocal lines are similarly sharpened: after *Jenůfa*, Janáček rarely indulged in prolonged lyricism. It is easy to see how this style confused audiences at the time. For those listening with symphonic ears, waiting for recurring themes and leisurely development, Janáček seemed wilfully to thwart expectations. The physical look of his autograph manuscripts hardly inspired confidence, being full of erasures, changes of mind, inconsistencies of notation and rhythmic obscurities – further testimony to the sheer difficulty of operatic composition in the post-Wagnerian world. But Janáček's strangeness was testament to the originality of his imagination. To bring into sound his special musical world required him to do battle with nothing less than the limitations of musical notation.

One of the reasons these late operas succeed is that their subject matter, unconventional by any earlier operatic standards, matches so well Janáček's highly individual musical language. *The Cunning Little Vixen* is a fantastical tale of a Vixen (soprano) who is captured by a Forester (baritone), escapes after laying waste to his hens, finds true love with a Fox (soprano) but is at the last killed by a Poacher (bass). In the final scene, years after the Vixen's death, the Forester reminisces, at first sadly but then with gathering fondness, about the countryside and its eternal rhythms. He thinks he sees the Vixen once more, but a Frog (child soprano) reminds him unsentimentally that generations have now come and gone. Although the scene is one of the most expansive in all Janáček, with an almost Straussian vocal climax (soaring horn and all) as the Forester celebrates the countryside in its 'month of love', Janáček in fact remains loyal to his technique of small musical building blocks. The relentlessly repeated orchestral ostinatos and variation points are profoundly at one with the idea of nature, endlessly prolific and teeming with life and new energy.

A very different but equally apt marriage of dramatic theme and musical technique occurs in *The Makropulos Affair*, based on a play by that great Czech original Karel Čapek (1890–1938). Čapek's play is *sui generis*, a good illustration of the quirky literary imagination that pioneered an early form of science fiction as well as writing some of the most telling anti-Nazi propaganda of the 1930s. At the centre of the opera is a mysterious diva called Emilia Marty (soprano), who fascinates every man she meets but who treats them all with cold indifference. After many twists in the plot, she reveals herself at the end as Elina Makropulos, the daughter of a sixteenth-century alchemist who gave her a potion that prolonged her life for 300 years. The potion is now at last wearing off. Elina/Emilia, although she succeeds in rediscovering the formula and so could repeat the dose, ultimately decides not to do so.

The boredom she feels, constantly seeing those she is attached to age and die, have convinced her that immortality is a curse rather than a blessing. *Makropulos* is in some ways Janáček's most complex opera, since its tortuous plot, much of it unravelling incidents that happened generations before, is matched by music that creates formidable difficulties for the performers (both orchestral and vocal). As early as the Overture – which is as formal an opening as any Janáček wrote – the idea of conflict is highlighted, with fragments of lyricism in the strings battling with uncertain, hesitant ostinato figures and a recurring, dissonant offstage trumpet fanfare. Once *Makropulos* began to be performed extensively in the West, some lamented that 'folk music' – a special, operatic gift from the Slavic hinterlands – had mostly disappeared from an opera where 'the abstract nature of the story is matched by a corresponding disinterested quality in the music'.[22] But such austerity is precisely the point, for is Emilia not indifferent, and moreover unanchored in time and place? The rebarbative surface that continues through the piece – as so often with Janáček – is redeemed by a gathering focus on the principal character, and her macabre bond with a time-honoured operatic prop: the elixirs, the potions, the poisons in the cup.

SINGING POINT BLANK

Russian opera in the nineteenth century darted among the competing realisms of Musorgsky and Tchaikovsky. The first wrote his own kind of proto-*Literaturoper* on to the historical canvas of *Boris Godunov*; the second created a realist urban opera in *Yevgeny Onegin* (Eugene Onegin), one in which intense personal emotions are channelled via a background of salon music. Musorgsky knew little of Wagner and, like Tchaikovsky, was much more obviously influenced by Meyerbeerian *grand opéra*. But soon enough, as elsewhere, Wagnerism became a commanding force, albeit not the only one. The most important figure during the Russian *fin-de-siècle* and beyond was Nikolay Rimsky-Korsakov (1844–1908), who presided over a period in which opera developed from a sporadic entertainment, under the exclusive control of the Imperial theatres at St Petersburg (the Mariinsky) and Moscow (the Bolshoy), into a lively competitive culture involving several private companies and further venues in provincial cities.

The sheer range of subject matter among Rimsky-Korsakov's fifteen operas underlines the absence of a stable Russian tradition – let alone a consensus about which among the competing styles of musical drama were most suitable in a Russian context. On the one hand are historical early works such as *The Maid of Pskov* (various versions between 1873 and 1901), which continue the manner of *Boris* with realistic word declamation, avoidance of conventional forms and vivid crowd scenes. At the opposite extreme are a series of fairy-tale operas, the most famous being Rimsky-Korsakov's last opera, *The Golden Cockerel* (1909), in which intense individual emotions are shunned in an anticipation of the overt anti-Romanticism of Stravinsky and Prokofiev. There are also *sui generis* works such as *Mozart and Salieri* (1898), which takes the Mozartian pastiche of Tchaikovsky's *The Queen of Spades* and imbues it with something close to neo-classical irony.

Scattered among these stylistic zigzags are a series of epic works that look back to the earlier nineteenth century, Russian and otherwise. At least one of them illustrates the perilous attractions of Wagnerism. The *Ring* was first performed by a travelling German company in St Petersburg in the late 1880s, and there were Russian-language performances, again at the Mariinsky, after the turn of the century; on both occasions Rimsky-Korsakov attended rehearsals with a score.[23] Although initially he seems to have embraced only Wagner's orchestral practice, we can see deeper influence in a work already mentioned in Chapter 17, *The Legend of the Invisible City of Kitezh* (1907). This strange concoction, with a plot far too complicated for more than telegraphic summary (Exotic marauding Tartars – Divine intervention – City made invisible – Tartars foiled), is often called 'the Russian *Parsifal*' and in places sounds like the missing link between Wagner and the early Stravinsky of *Firebird*. But the *Parsifal*-like descending-fourth bell sounds of the final scene (so unlike the noisy, dissonant, *Boris*-like bells of so many nationalist Russian operas), and the sprinkling of leitmotifs and occasional advanced harmonies, make odd bedfellows with the modal choruses of much of the rest. Rimsky-Korsakov was uncertain how to progress: Wagner, who might have seemed a saviour, was – as so often – fatally easy to follow but impossible to emulate.

Wagner anxiety was, though, hardly a major factor in the larger picture of Rimsky-Korsakov's eclectic operatic manners. In later life he strove above all to evade what he had earlier done so much to consolidate: the idea (unfortunately still with us, sometimes in blithely unreconstructed form) that Russian opera is profoundly different from the central European variety, and that its difference springs from some ineffable strain of national character. Near the end of his life, Rimsky was unequivocal about this:

> In my opinion, a distinctly 'Russian music' does not exist. Both harmony and counterpoint are pan-European. Russian songs introduce into counterpoint a few new technical devices, but to form a new, unique kind of music: this they cannot do. And even the number of these devices is probably limited. Russian traits – and national traits in general – are acquired not by writing according to specific rules, but rather by removing from the common language of music those devices that are inappropriate to the Russian spirit . . . To create a characteristically Russian style I avoid some devices, for a Spanish style others, and for a German style others again.[24]

Rimsky's deflation of Russianness in music only goes so far: it still upholds the idea of a 'Russian spirit', even if that very concept was largely responsible for the operatic ghettoization he seems to criticize. But his prosaic dismantling of an old cliché is still worth bearing in mind, as is his casual equivalence of a 'Russian' style with – of all things – a 'German' one, which is best seen as an engagingly mischievous tilt at the increasingly common identification of German music as the 'universal' musical language.

Rimsky's last years coincided with Russia's so-called 'Silver Age', a period in which cultural influences from Western Europe were eagerly imported, and in which the influence of Wagner was matched by that of the symbolist movement, with Alexander Skryabin (1872–1915) a prime musical mover, albeit one who wrote no operas. When Debussy's arch-symbolist *Pelléas* was first performed in Russia in 1907, it seemed to some like a homecoming. Indeed, the next twenty-five years, up to around 1935, were heady times for Russia, with the children of the Silver Age (many of them leaving the country permanently or for prolonged periods) proving influential in an emerging, pan-European musical aesthetic. At the same time, though, the tumultuous political events then unfolding inexorably led to a new period of cultural isolation for the country.

The political upheavals of these decades – the Revolutions of 1917;

the ensuing civil war and Lenin's consolidation of power; Lenin's death in 1924; Stalin's take-over and gradual assumption of dictatorial control during the late 1920s and early 1930s – were accompanied by constant debates about the proper place of art in the new, revolutionary society that Russia had proclaimed. Although the Mariinsky and Bolshoy were almost immediately brought under state control, with free tickets supplied to the workers, the position of opera – as ever, commonly seen as *the* elitist art form – was delicate. Lenin personally disapproved of an entertainment he found reeking of upper-class culture. He was also suspicious of what he saw as music's general tendency to embellish the world in beautiful sounds, and thus to paper over the injustices and inequalities of the society from which it came.

But there was a problem. Opera proved tremendously popular in the new Russia. More embarrassing still, the crowd-pullers remained those classic revenants of the despised, Tsarist nineteenth century. Out of the immediate confusion of the Revolution emerged two competing camps, both with some measure of official support. At one extreme, those collected under the group called RAPM (the Russian Association of Proletarian Musicians) wanted genuine proletarian music, an art fit to reflect and articulate the new state. This position was constantly weakened by the fact that the proletariat continued to have stubbornly bourgeois taste, and because attempts to create revolutionary music *ex novo* (usually with liberal recourse to folk idioms) often sounded suspiciously like the nationalist styles of the previous century. At the other extreme was a group called ASM (the Association of Contemporary Music), who were what we would now call progressives: they wanted to reject the old, bourgeois art of the nineteenth century and enthusiastically embrace the new musical ideas coming from Western Europe. For a time, particularly in the 1920s, the progressives seemed to gain the upper hand. Their most successful composer was initially Nikolai Yakovlevich Myaskovsky (1881–1950), who was famous above all for instrumental music; in opera the key figure was Vsevolod Meyerhold (1874–1940), a theatre director who grew up within the symbolist movement and then, in the early days of the Revolution, developed radical new expressive techniques of anti-naturalism and artificiality, many of which later became associated with Brecht. At the same time, modernist operas such as *Wozzeck* and *Jonny spielt auf* were performed, and Russian film of the 1920s became internationally recognized as an aesthetic powerhouse with significant avant-garde cachet. Emerging directly out of this milieu was the precocious talent of a young composer called Dmitri Shostakovich (1906–75).

Shostakovich's first opera, *The Nose* (1930), is based on an absurdist short story by Gogol and concerns a civil servant who misplaces his nose, pursues it around town in farcical episodes and is finally reunited with it. The work owes a great deal to Meyerhold, with whom Shostakovich was much involved at the time, not least in its decision to put on stage such a patently unrealistic, not to say unrealizable fantasy. Musically, it is a wild compendium of the most radical Western styles, with Stravinskian neo-classicism, a heavy dose of *Wozzeck*-like extreme vocal and orchestral effects, and much play with popular music idioms, particularly dance tunes. In this last regard, the debt to Weimar *Zeitoper* is clear. And, as in *Jonny spielt auf*, or indeed in Ravel's *L'Heure espagnole*, among a salad of iconoclastic effects the word-setting returns to naturalistic declamation. It is a good indication that speech-opera was by this stage virtually the default mode amongst those who wished to bring the art form into the orbit of twentieth-century radicalism. In this sense, *The Nose* marks the closing of an historical circle. Musorgsky had been one of the first to hold to natural speech as a model for operatic vocal writing, and Debussy learned the lesson from that source. French composers writing opera after Debussy kept to the programme in a new way, adding sarcasms and exoticism, and Weimar Germany ran in tandem; and then, with Shostakovich, speech-opera returned to its country of birth.

It is no surprise that proletarian groups took extreme exception to *The Nose* and succeeded in getting it removed from the stage after a brief first run. Shostakovich withdrew into ballet and instrumental music, which – being non-verbal – were a lot harder to criticize. But he soon embarked on what was probably intended as an operatic compromise: an attempt to answer his critics and write a Russian opera suited to the times. The result was *Lady Macbeth of Mtsensk* (1934), one of the most famous operas of the twentieth century, albeit often celebrated for strange reasons. A sign of Shostakovich's change of heart can be seen in an article he wrote in 1933. He declared there a distinctly un-*Nose*-like operatic aesthetic, one that could almost have come from Bellini a hundred years before: 'In opera people don't talk, they sing.

Consequently, the text must be a singing one, it must give the composer maximum possibility for freely flowing song.'[25] Such pronouncements might have sounded comforting to those who were opposed to avant-garde attitudes and styles, but they sit – to say the least – oddly with the tale on which Shostakovich decided to base his opera.

Written by the composer with the help of the librettist Alexander Preys, *Lady Macbeth*'s libretto is based on a 1865 horror story by Nicolay Leskov. Katerina (soprano) is in a loveless, childless marriage with a rich merchant called Zinovy (tenor). They live with Zinovy's father, Boris (bass). Zinovy departs on a business trip and Katerina starts an affair with one of the firm's employees, Sergey (tenor). Boris discovers the affair and beats Sergey brutally. Katerina retaliates by murdering Boris, lacing his mushrooms with rat poison. Sergey moves in, but late one night, after Katerina has had a frightening vision of the ghost of Boris, Zinovy unexpectedly returns. He suspects adultery and begins to beat Katerina. Sergey, who has been hiding, intervenes; together they overcome Zinovy, Katerina strangling him and Sergey performing the *coup de grâce* with a heavy candlestick. They hide the body in the cellar. On Katerina's and Sergey's wedding day a drunkard accidentally discovers Zinovy's body and the lovers are arrested. The final scene takes place near a bridge across a river; Katerina and Sergey are convicts en route to Siberia. Sergey has transferred his attentions to a fellow prisoner, Sonetka (contralto). He manages to trick Katerina out of her woollen stockings and gives them to his new mistress. As they all cross the river, Katerina pushes Sonetka into the freezing stream and jumps in after her. Leskov's final image describes how Katerina 'threw herself on Sonetka like a strong pike on a soft little perch, and neither appeared again'.[26]

Surprising as it may seem, this operatic version had toned down Leskov's original, in which Katerina and Sergey also finish off a young boy who turns up claiming to be Zinovy's heir. The alteration turns out to be part of a larger shift of focus: while Leskov's Katerina is indeed a kind of Lady Macbeth – constantly encouraging violence, driven by her sexual needs, staunchly unrepentant – the operatic Katerina is granted unique musical status, so much so that the audience can identify with her. An example comes at the end of Act 2, leading to Zinovy's murder. The scene is Katerina's bedroom, where she and Sergey are sleeping. The introductory music involves three tiers of string sound – a sinister low bass, a 'halo' of upper strings and an ascending melody emerging in the middle register. Katerina wakes Sergey and asks him to embrace her, the music building to a huge, Straussian cadence and lyrical climax as she utters her lover's name. We seem set for an ecstatic love duet, but instead Sergey launches into a petulant rant about his lack of status as her secret lover. He too has plenty of passion and high notes, but the orchestral behaviour is markedly different. Instead of underpinning the singer's sentiments (as it had with Katerina), the accompaniment seems blithely indifferent, with spiky rhythms on chattering woodwind, a tuba-driven bass and obsessive, mechanical ostinati. Katerina tries to calm Sergey, and the moment she sings the orchestra moves back into sympathetic mode. As she kisses him again, a beautiful, ethereally long, Mahlerian string theme takes over, the harp accompaniment emphasizing the kinship with the famous Adagietto from Mahler's Symphony No. 5.

The scene thus far has followed what we might call an ABA form, with the extreme orchestral contrasts between A and B drawing all the sympathy to one character. The remainder of the scene, although it broadens the musical horizons, repeats this effect. Sergey goes back to sleep, and the ghost of Boris appears before Katerina. There are broad hints of ancient operatic ghosts, not least of the Commendatore of Mozart's *Don Giovanni* in the enunciation of Katerina's name to a descending octave; but the orchestra is again in overdrive. Noises are heard outside; they rouse Sergey and he hides. Zinovy enters to discover signs of dual occupation, and he and Katerina indulge in a huge shouting match (one of the great marital rows in opera: Wotan and Fricka are restrained and courteous by comparison). The orchestra returns to that mood of indifferent energy that underpinned Sergey's rant. Zinovy, the least heroic character imaginable, is introduced by an ironic trumpet fanfare and even a hint of Rossini's *Guillaume Tell* overture. The relentlessly jaunty, driving rhythms continue unabated until Sergey returns and the lovers strangle and club Zinovy to death. The scene then closes, wonderfully poised between its two contrasting musical worlds. As Sergey drags Zinovy's body down to the cellar, a strange Mahlerian funeral march sounds forth, a strumming low bass, with solo clarinets and then bassoons (prime movers in the preceding bouts of woodwind chatter) now subdued but once or twice edging perilously close to joviality. There is a brief, shimmering pause and a string melody as Katerina asks Sergey to embrace her and tells him 'Now you are my husband'.

To close the scene, the funeral march reappears, now played on the trombone, this unlikeliest of instruments keeping the sheer uncanniness of the ending intact to the last moment. It is laughter in the dark made musical.

In Meyerholdian terms, which would later resonate in Brecht's theories, the audience in *Lady Macbeth* is compelled by the music into an alternation between identification and estrangement. We identify with Katerina, but we are alienated by the uniformly hideous men in her life. This constant back-and-forth continues throughout the opera. The sense of orchestra-encouraged identification is at its boldest in Katerina's solos, particularly her central monologue in Act 1, 'Zherebyonok k kobïlke toropitsya' (The foal and the filly), in which she pours out her sexual longings. The strings here sometimes come close to a conventional accompanying role, and the clarinets and other woodwind, elsewhere so cheery and impertinent, assume a melancholy, hyper-expressive function. As in Katerina's other solos, the harmonic idiom is also stable, even though she has the unnerving habit of launching angular lines into the upper extremes of her register, sometimes painfully isolated from the orchestral stability beneath. On the other hand, the seduction scene (in many ways it is closer to rape) that ensues between Katerina and Sergey is again underpinned by farcical, manically over-energetic music, even including a series of graphic, descending trombone glissandos to depict what befalls Sergey after his energetic sexual climax.

So extreme are these contrasts that questions about musical meaning inevitably crowded in. The opera was at first wildly successful in Russia, but many in the West found the mixture of violent events and trivial music inexplicable. As late as 1960, the US composer Elliott Carter declared that 'the relation of the music to the action is unaccountable'.[27] One of Russian music's acutest contemporary critics has suggested a dark interpretation. A clue is offered by Shostakovich himself in a programme note he wrote for the first performance: 'It would be fairest of all to say that [Katerina's] crimes are a protest against the tenor of the life she is forced to live, against the dark and suffocating atmosphere of the merchant class in the country.'[28] From this it would be simple to understand the opera as a reflection of what was then Soviet orthodoxy (and critics at the time indeed saw it so): in other words, Shostakovich's trivial music does a magnificent job of dehumanizing the 'merchant class' (represented by the vile Zinovy), and the heroine Katerina does her job by exterminating them.

There is little doubt that Shostakovich attempted to present his opera along these lines (there is more in the programme essay to suggest it); but, as with virtually all such political readings of operas, there are loose ends and anomalies. Most pressing is the question of why, if such a message were intended, Shostakovich chose Leskov's tale in the first place: why set to music a story whose negative portrayal of the heroine, albeit tempered, was so unmistakable? It seems as plausible to suggest that Shostakovich was attracted to the tale, at least as he adapted it, because of its possibilities for ambiguity: for a chance to indulge his lyrical vein (recall that remark about how an operatic text 'must give the composer maximum possibility for freely flowing song') without falling into pastiche or – worse still – seeming un-modern. In brief, *Lady Macbeth* allowed him to explore further that hinterland between comedy and tragedy – the chilly space inhabited by that Mahlerian funeral march at the end of Act 2.

Whatever its political intent, the most famous incident surrounding *Lady Macbeth* occurred on 26 January 1936, some two years after its first performance. A revival in Moscow was attended by Stalin, together with his political henchman Vyacheslav Molotov and his culture minister, Andrey Zhdanov. Two days later an unsigned denunciation of the opera appeared in the official Soviet newspaper *Pravda* under the title 'Muddle Instead of Music'. The article principally addressed the opera's musical style, which it overtly associated with Shostakovich's mentor, Meyerhold:

> From the first minute, the listener is shocked by deliberate dissonance, by a confused stream of sounds. Snatches of melody, the beginnings of a musical phrase, are drowned, emerge again, and disappear in a grinding and squealing roar. . . . This music is built on the basis of rejecting opera – the same basis on which leftist art in the theatre rejects simplicity, realism, clarity of image, and the unaffected spoken word – which carries into the theatre and into music the most negative features of 'Meyerholdism' infinitely multiplied. . . . The power of good music to infect the masses has been sacrificed to a petty-bourgeois, formalist attempt to create originality through cheap clowning. It is a game of clever ingenuity that may end very badly.[29]

This attack on an artist of Shostakovich's international standing was unprecedented. Indeed, perhaps his success in the West was in fact a prime motive. The penultimate paragraph reads:

> *Lady Macbeth* is having great success with bourgeois audiences abroad. Is it not because the opera is absolutely unpolitical and confusing that they praise it? Is it not explained by the fact that it tickles the perverted tastes of the bourgeoisie with its fidgety, screaming, neurotic music?[30]

The attack may have resulted simply from Stalin's personal disapproval, but this *Pravda* article sent a signal to Soviet artists, one that they would disregard at their peril. The experimental, Western-influenced movement went into retreat. Those in official favour but with progressive sentiments, such as Myaskovsky and Khachaturian, avoided opera altogether, leaving it to be peopled with earnest, song-laden pieces about Soviet achievement. Meyerhold was arrested in 1939; he was tortured, 'confessed' to crimes of espionage and was executed early the next year. Shostakovich made patient attempts to rehabilitate himself, famously with the Fifth Symphony (1937).

Many celebrated works followed, but Shostakovich never again attempted an opera. Works involving 'confused streams of sounds', speech turned into music rather than conventional operatic singing and formal tidiness, had been officially identified as perilous, possibly even fatal to their creators. In André Gide's *Retour de l'URSS* (Return from the USSR, 1937), one interlocutor, prodded by Gide to account for Shostakovich's fall, put the matter in terms that have resounded for centuries, and might just as well have been said of Rameau:

> 'You see', explained X, 'it wasn't at all what the public asked for; not at all the kind of thing we want nowadays. Before this he had written a very remarkable ballet which had been greatly admired.' (*He* was Shostakovich, whom I had heard praised in terms usually reserved for geniuses). 'But what is the public to do with an opera that leaves them with no tunes to hum when they come out?'[31]

Decrying a loss of melody – tunes to hum – is the universal protest of the operatic hedonist. Yet in some times, in some places, this critique could have a dark side, and did not always represent benign hankering after opera's older forms, or their pleasures. We are left wondering how to evaluate competing losses – how to judge those who make the laments. Not all unmelodious operas, operas with speech patterns instead of song, are heroic metaphors for contemporary political defiance, as proven by *Capriccio*. But by 1945, opera's great undertow – the expressive power inherent in the melodic arc, as performed by a human voice – was demanding a faith that for many composers was beginning to look blind.

20

Revenants in the museum

The mark of opera's twentieth-century metamorphosis was the birth of self-consciousness. As we have seen often in the last few chapters, writing opera in its fourth century was rarely about just making music for a story. It was often about opera's history, about its silliness or greatness or sheer longevity. Richard Strauss was the first laureate of this tendency, and – as we saw in Chapter 18 – *Ariadne auf Naxos* was its classic illustration. But *Ariadne*, which is a comic opera, doesn't deal with a perennial staple of its tragic sister, which is Death. Death scenes, as it turns out, would become a test case for modernist composers' attitudes towards the legacy they had inherited.

On-stage death had mostly been shunned for reasons of theatrical propriety in opera's first 200 years and more. After that, though, an impressive tally of operatic characters start dying on stage; between (say) 1830 and 1900 they do so horribly or beautifully, quickly or slowly, from daggers or disease, sometimes courtesy of exotic exits via castle battlements or vats of boiling oil. But it is unusual for other characters to mourn these deaths extensively once they have occurred, to reflect by means of elaborate singing on the person just departed. For Don José, post-mortem analysis lasts around sixty seconds: 'You can arrest me ... it's me who killed her. Ah Carmen! my adored Carmen!' Rigoletto may even beat José to the tape: 'Gilda! my Gilda! she's dead! ... Ah! the curse!!'

Among the exceptions, one is a stock in trade: the moralizing epilogue of eighteenth-century opera, most famously at the end of *Don Giovanni*. This is the kind of scene ironically revisited in Stravinsky's *The Rake's Progress*, in which a mixture of gloating and character analysis is directed at the departed villain. The nineteenth century, nearer our time and mood, started to see some exceptions on the tragic side, and several are famous. Isolde's final monologue is Exhibit A, and, in *Götterdämmerung,* Siegfried's death is followed by a famous orchestral funeral march. There are no voices or words, but leitmotifs take their place as a kind of aide-mémoire, encouraging the audience to reflect on the deceased. A parallel instance occurs in Act 4 of Verdi's *Don Carlos*, but here the situation is a little more complex and needs further explanation.

Near the close of the act, the Marquis of Posa, *Don Carlos*'s baritone hero-in-waiting, is shot by a mysterious man, an emissary of the Inquisition. While dying he then charms the audience with a lengthy and beautiful *romance*. This singing-while-dying was of course a Romantic commonplace: Siegfried also indulges us; one of Verdi's most famous early tenors was even nicknamed 'il tenore della bella morte' – the tenor of the beautiful death.[1] But Posa's operatic death breaks from tradition in also being reflected upon immediately after it happens. The baritone's last breath is followed by an elaborate mourning ensemble, a leisurely episode in B♭ minor, the dark key often favoured for mourning in the nineteenth century. This *Trauermusik* takes the form of a duet (with chorus) between King Philip and Carlos, and became a famous instance of operatic recycling. Verdi dropped the episode from *Don Carlos* some time before the work's premiere at the Paris Opéra in 1867. It was jettisoned even before a notorious dress rehearsal in which – to get the work down to manageable length – he hacked various large and disturbingly beautiful chunks from the score. Its disappearance was perhaps hastened because the singer playing Posa, the great baritone Jean-Baptiste Faure, objected to lying on stage pretending to be dead while two rival colleagues were having such a grand time pealing forth his noble qualities.[2] But whatever the reason, Verdi made no attempt to reinstate the ensemble in later revisions of the opera, nor is there any record of him complaining about its disappearance. His seeming indifference reinforces the point that long, leisurely reactions to death were not typical in opera of this period. Someone dies and we move on, or the curtain falls. When, some years later, Verdi found a new use for his discarded duet, it was outside opera altogether: he used the melody to launch the 'Lacrymosa' section of his *Messa da Requiem* (1874).

Soon after the turn of the twentieth century this once-rare phenomenon, the post-mortem commentary, experienced an upswing. The dead are more readily mourned in music, and the devastation of these modern funerary scenes – we will discuss some below – cannot be accounted for merely as sadness over a character's demise. To be sure, there were still many quick and unelaborated deaths à la Carmen or Gilda, with certain schools of operatic modernism even making a speciality of brutal demises. Some are aestheticized via music, like those of the nuns in Poulenc's *Dialogues des Carmélites* (1957): guillotined one by one, they go singing ecstatically to their doom. Other modernist operas greet death with brief emotional outbursts or psychotic indifference. In Janáček's *Kát'a Kabanová* (1921), the heroine's body, having been dragged from the river where she drowned herself, is sobbed over for seconds only. In Busoni's *Doktor Faust* (first performed 1925), Faust collapses in a snowy Wittenberg street and the only comment – from Mephistopheles – is an insolent enquiry, spoken not sung: 'Has this person come to grief?'

But extended post-mortem elaboration now takes hold as a counterpoise. When a dramaturgical convention appears in this way, the question 'why?' cannot be answered simply. Large cultural shifts clearly played some role. In Europe in those early decades of the century there was widespread dancing on multiple political volcanoes, and elaborate theatrical reflections on endings and mortality might thus be thought an apt reflection of the circumstance. But the mourning scenes, viewed less globally, might also be connected to creative anxieties about opera's very future: about whether it was itself a dying art form, ready for its own funeral. In this more local context, the phenomenon could clearly be allied to librettists' and composers' new self-consciousness *about* opera (we might also recall that in the earlier twentieth century operas about artists and composers in crisis became newly fashionable).

In certain instances, the metaphorical import of the funerary moment is obvious. Ravel's *L'Enfant et les sortilèges*, already mentioned in the previous chapter, has a scene in which the child's ripped storybook comes to life; there had been a tale about a Princess, but it will never be finished now, because the pages have disappeared. The Princess materializes and sings to the child. At first we hear only her voice and a solo flute, weaving melodic lines around each other, perhaps in a distant gesture to the voice and flute duet from the mad scene of Donizetti's *Lucia di Lammermoor*. The orchestra returns towards the end as the Princess falls into conjecture: who knows what might have happened to me? She disappears and the child mourns her loss in an exquisite little aria, 'Toi, le cœur de la rose' (You, the heart of the rose), lamenting that only a scent, a trace, is left. Just as the Princess's music toyed with past moments of operatic glory, so does the child's song, in this case gesturing to Massenet's wistful farewell aria, 'Adieu, notre petite table' (Farewell, our little table), in Act 2 of *Manon*. We have witnessed the sad futility of any attempt to gather the shards of an operatic tradition now irretrievably fragmented: as the child sings, there is nothing more than 'les débris d'un rêve'.

A second example involves Puccini's *Turandot* (premiered posthumously in 1926). *Turandot*'s penultimate scene contains the last music Puccini ever completed: he travelled to a Brussels cancer clinic with nothing more than sketches for the opera's finale, and never finished it. In this penultimate scene, the slave girl Liù (soprano), unable to bear the pain of torture, directs a lament at Turandot, 'Tu che di gel sei cinta' (You who are girded with frost), then stabs herself and dies. Liù's blind companion, Timur (bass), told of her death, lets out a savage howl of grief (one of opera's greatest inarticulate cries) and takes up her lament in a funeral march. This desperately sad moment expresses the dull weight and grief of a great loss; to extend and deepen the pathos Timur is joined by the chorus. Onlookers who had, only moments before, been baying for Liù's blood suddenly appear as inconsolable as the suffering bass.

What is striking is that a secondary, sentimental character assumes such symbolic force post mortem. The chorus's final words make the transformation of the person into a metaphor for Art utterly explicit: 'Liù, goodness, Liù, sweetness. Sleep! Forget! Liù! Poetry!' During the world premiere of *Turandot*, at La Scala, Milan, in 1926, the conductor, Arturo Toscanini, stopped the performance after Liù's funeral dirge, turned to the audience and said something like (he has been variously reported): 'The opera is ending here because at this point the composer died.'[3] The closing minor triad of the dirge, played quietly but involving the extreme outer registers of orchestral sound, is repeated three times. These three chords resemble the solemn ending of *La bohème*, written thirty years earlier and so near the start of Puccini's career. But for us now, looking back over all of operatic history, they might also invoke an ancient acoustic signal, the three loud knocks with which theatres of the seventeenth and eighteenth centuries signalled the start of the entertainment: the omega referencing the alpha.

To these two instances could be added others: Countess Geschwitz's rhapsody to murdered Lulu in Berg's opera, for example, or the eerie chorus of planets that salutes Johannes Kepler's passing in Hindemith's *Die Harmonie der Welt* (first performance 1957). These episodes are like a colour change on litmus paper, a signal that something has come over opera as a genre and as an experience. That 'something' included the self-consciousness that began to flower before the First World War, which was closely tied to concerns about the burden of Mozart, Verdi and Wagner, as well as to anxieties about producing (or not producing) Eternal, Enduring Operatic Works, or even about writing opera at all.

The sea changes that marked opera's fourth century were many, and they mean that telling the history of opera's latest decades requires a changed strategy. It would be wilful and blithely utopian to narrate a march of progress and revolutionary masterpieces. If we are to present the recent history of opera as it is, and not as we might wish it to be – to avoid telling that false tale of optimism and continual healthy expansion – we will need new strategies. We need to account both for the changed cultural circumstances under which new operas were, and are, created in the later twentieth and twenty-first centuries, and for the ways in which composers confront their legacies from an operatic past. The most sociologically significant change during this time has been what is probably an irrevocable mutation: the conversion of operatic culture into a species of museum.

THE LIVING MUSEUM: REPERTORY

For at least two centuries, while France and Germany and all the rest had their share of operas, Italy, only Italy, had Opera. As the Verdi scholar Julian Budden put it: 'In Italy, empires might rise and empires might fall, but La Scala, Milan, and the Teatro la Fenice, Venice, still needed their two *opere d'obbligo* [new operas] for the winter season.'[4] Italy alone retained for centuries the unproblematic sense of an unbroken, unending procession. Individual composers would come and go, leaving contributions large and small, noble and trivial. But even the greatest of them would eventually be absorbed, becoming a mere constituent in the larger, unceasing march of Opera. From the perspective of the here-and-now, with major Italian opera houses closing or curtailing their seasons for lack of audience interest or absence of state funding, this equivalence between Italy and Opera seems to be at a uniquely problematic moment. But it was almost a century ago when the *compositional* tradition was in collapse, when the supply of new Italian works began to seem so insignificant that the idea of an unbroken succession was unsustainable.

The death of Puccini in 1924 has often proved a convenient terminus. As we saw a moment ago, Puccini died leaving the final scene of his last opera as little more than scribbled-out tunes and fugitive harmonies. What he had always imagined as *Turandot*'s final, climactic love duet – between questing Prince Calaf and reluctant but finally yielding Princess Turandot – was still in tatters. At one crucial passage in these sketches, a moment that should have been the clinching musical event of the duet, notation breaks off entirely and, in poignant recognition of the looming classics of the past, Puccini simply wrote 'poi Tristano' – then Tristan. According to this version of the story, Italian opera's great flow didn't become gently interrupted, gradually sinking into the sand. Quite the reverse: it underwent a series of ever more infrequent but ever more violent convulsions. And then finally, as Puccini's doctor said in that Brussels clinic where they tried vainly to operate on his throat cancer: 'C'est le cœur qui ne résiste pas.'[5] According to other interpretations, Italian opera's convulsions continued on past *Turandot*. But perhaps it's better to see those now-forgotten works by Mascagni, Respighi and others in the 1930s, with their grandiose, state-sponsored premieres and dictator-rich audiences, as already dead: inert presences whose inflated torsos and rouged cheeks lent them merely the simulacrum of vitality. By either account, sometime during these decades before the Second World War, Italian opera's great procession fragmented irremediably.

Although this story is most poignantly told about Italy and its centuries-long operatic tradition, the same scenario played out on other international stages during roughly the same period. Everywhere the sheer difficulty of writing new operas – financial, musical, aesthetic – began to weigh on those whose business it was to keep the show moving. The crisis had been threatening for many decades, perhaps for as long as a century. In the seventeenth and eighteenth centuries, almost all opera was new – composed especially for the occasion. Revivals might occur, but it was more prestigious to have a brand-new work; what's more, as we saw in the first chapters of this book, willing composers were on hand to produce them with unfailing regularity. Around the time of Rossini, though, this privileging of the new was slowly eroded by a body of works that travelled across Europe and beyond, being revived again and again, season after season, surviving changing fashions and serving as a forbidding benchmark for new creations. By the later nineteenth century, a large standard repertory was in place. Verdi had it just right when he boasted that *Il trovatore* would be seen 'in the heart of Africa and the Indies'.[6] What's more, new print technologies and the success of the piano as a domestic instrument meant that the most famous operas invaded domestic as well as public life, taking their places in a broader cultural imagination. There is good reason why the Liebig Bouillon Company could from the 1890s onwards profitably market its products by means of opera-scene collector's cards (see Figure 22).

At first, this standard repertory existed comfortably alongside newly composed operas, the latter still attracting greater cachet. But by the early twentieth century contemporary operas seemed less and less able to compete with older works for attention and funding. Reasons for such large-scale cultural shifts are always complex. The anti-hedonism of a certain strand of modernist music – mostly associated with Schoenberg and his followers – played a part. To write self-consciously unmelodious and difficult operas conferred a measure of prestige, but only a rare talent could make it work. Alban Berg's creation of two now-standard repertory operas within this hyper-austere tradition remains a remarkable feat.

Another reason why repertory operas began to trump new commissions was simple economics, the fearful expense of producing an opera entirely from scratch. Money generated at the box office could not pay for the composer's and the librettist's time, as well as for the star singers and the chorus and the orchestra and the stage designers and the costume fitters and the marketing department and all the rest. Someone or something has to stand behind the enterprise financially, and be equipped with the deepest of deep pockets. Until the middle of the nineteenth century this 'backer' role would typically be taken by a king, prince or petty duke still hanging on to the vestiges of absolute power in Europe, a figure for whom the prestige of opera was worth the expenditure. Increasingly, though, such characters became merely one element within a mixed economy, their money often underwriting the losses risked by an entrepreneurial impresario. But a large contingent of this ruling class was permanently forced out by either by the 1848 revolutions or, two decades later, by the unification of the German and Italian nation states.

In America and other, newer operatic landscapes outside Europe, opera continued to be funded by a loose consortium of the wealthy, as a form of social capital; but in the European operatic economy the place of independent backers was usually taken by support from the public purse. Then as now, such subsidy was unpredictable, ultimately dependent on the goodwill of those who vote in elections. When times were good, the fact that public money sustained an entertainment now enjoyed only by a favoured few was tolerated. But in the twentieth century times were often not good; subsidy would be reduced, making the purveyors of opera cautious and adverse to risk. Given their proven failure rate for centuries, the most perilous venture of all was to commission a new opera. Why not stage *Il trovatore* instead? A living museum is safer.

THE LIVING MUSEUM: EXCITEMENT

At first sight a museum may seem inert, a place where relics are merely housed, a collection of gravestones. But the best museums have never been like that: they constantly evolve, moving with the times in the way they present their artefacts to an ever-changing audience. In the same way, the operatic museum has proved remarkably able to renew itself creatively. One significant sign of this renewal appeared in 1920s Germany, a prime location of what was increasingly referred to as the 'opera crisis'. During that decade, many cities saw evidence of a 'Verdi renaissance': instead of, or by the side of, yet more revivals of the eight or so great Verdi warhorses, the thought came to explore anew some of his forgotten works.[7] This was partly a reaction against Wagner, conventionally seen as Verdi's antithesis; but more basically it reflected the fact that embarrassingly few new works were displaying any sign of longevity. People still wanted to go to the opera: radio and recordings, both of them routinely accused during the period of hastening the demise of the art form, were if anything expanding audiences.

What is more, spectators enjoyed novelty; they were committed patrons of newness in certain guises. But in general they found modern works uncongenial. So difficult and largely unperformed late Verdi pieces such as *Simon Boccanegra, La forza del destino* and *Don Carlos*, and also – more surprising – a number of his long-dormant early works, were exhumed. Later still, spreading from Germany to elsewhere in Europe (Britain and Italy in particular), revivals of earlier nineteenth-century Italians (Rossini, Bellini and Donizetti) started to appear. This renewal of the repertory by means of digging into the past has continued inexorably: in the last few decades Handel's operas have become commonplace, while Monteverdi, Rameau and others have all established a foothold. It is a story which parallels that of the 'historically informed performance' movement generally, and thus of classical music as a whole. Generated by impressive curatorial energy and often advocated with missionary zeal, it is nevertheless sustained by cultural pessimism – by a recognition of the fact that, musically, we now enjoy novelty principally when it comes from the past rather than from the present.

Along with this expanded historical repertory has come another symptom of our modern operatic condition: *Regieoper*, the German term for operatic productions whose excitement and sense of renewal are based on a strong (and preferably unprecedented) interpretation that rethinks an opera's meaning via innovative staging and décor. This technology-fuelled movement started in the 1920s as an attempt to smooth the path during opera's retreat into its past, to make newly revived works in outmoded idioms more relevant to audiences. *Regieoper*'s new visual habits were often influenced by modernist painting, or by innovative theatre producers such as Edward Gordon Craig (in Britain), Adolphe Appia (in central Europe) and Vsevolod Meyerhold (in Russia). It blossomed almost everywhere after the Second World War and has now become the default means of reinterpreting opera generally, giving new heft and relevance to repertory works otherwise thought too well known to communicate any contemporary message.

Regieoper can be wild and wonderful, upending expectations of what we thought we knew about plots and music that, through repeated performance, had become thirsty for renewal. A select few such productions have, via mechanical reproduction, recently formed into an alternative canon: Patrice Chéreau's Marxist dystopian *Ring* (Bayreuth, 1976) is now a classic; others might include Jonathan Miller's Mafia-themed *Rigoletto* (English National Opera, 1982), or Hans Neuenfels's

Die Entführung aus dem Serail, in which both a singer *and* an actor played each role (Stuttgart, 1998), or Robert Wilson's slow-motion cerements-of-the-grave *Aida* (Royal Opera House, 2003). One of the present authors adored Peter Konwitschny's *Lohengrin*-in-a-high-school (Barcelona, 2006); the other loved Stefan Herheim's *Les Vêpres siciliennes*, in which ballerinas invaded not just the customary Act 3 *divertissement*, but also the gestural vocabulary of all the characters (Royal Opera House, 2013). Opera buffs of all vintages will have their favoured contestants saddled and ready, from any time up to yesterday.

With rare exceptions, *Regieoper* does not meddle with the musical text. The fact that music alone is assumed to be sacrosanct is a relatively recent philosophical judgement (up until the early nineteenth century, opera was more commonly thought a theatrical rather than a musical genre); but the new classification is now passionately felt. Whenever a director dares to change something in the musical text, curses will abound. When Konwitschny staged *Don Giovanni* in 2008 at the Komische Oper in Berlin there was critical outrage, not because of on-stage naughtiness (there was plenty) but because, at the very end, the orchestra gradually dropped out of the great moralizing finale, leaving the voices trailing alone in a vast void, by this means creating a profound disturbance that was in some ways magical. In a larger context the vehement critical reaction might seem odd. After all, any staging is ephemeral. It will not be there in the next town, and will anyway disappear when the production is replaced. Mozart's work famously endures: you can see *Don Giovanni* elsewhere or at the flick of a button with the finale intact.

One indication that the stage director as *auteur* is now routinely at the centre of the operatic enterprise is newspaper reviews that relegate comments about the singers, the orchestra or its conductor – let alone any discussion of the work itself – to a brief addendum, the main agenda being to consider at length the directorial input, the staging, costumes, sets and lighting. Musical execution per se, it seems, cannot renew an antique work. But it is well to remember that one can make things new by performing them so differently in acoustic terms that they seem previously unheard. By the 1950s, 'historically informed performance' aimed to make ancient musical objects meaningful, adding to them a patina of cool modernity that, although it claimed authority from the past, was in many senses aligned aesthetically with the radical, modernizing stage directors.[8] Every once in a while, a conductor will rethink so comprehensively the acoustic presence, instrumental balance, tempi and general sound of a famous opera that you feel you have encountered some alternative version, heretofore unknown. This was the case with Simon Rattle's famed interpretations of *Pelléas et Mélisande* (performed in several opera houses, with different orchestras, in different stagings, beginning in 2007). The museum can pulse with excitement.

ENDURING MODERNISM: BRITTEN

In any long view of the operatic museum and opera's history in the later twentieth century, Benjamin Britten (1913–76) is *sui generis*, since in terms of repertory presence he is such an exception among postwar composers as to be quasi-miraculous. At the website operabase.com, he is by an immense margin the most regularly performed opera composer born in the twentieth century. As we write, he ranks at 13th, between Offenbach and Humperdinck; the next composer born after 1900 is Shostakovich at 39th.

Britten began his career in the 1930s as a prolific and precocious composer in practically every field except opera. As he admitted, for an impecunious young composer trying to make his way in the world, an operatic project would have been the height of impracticality. In 1939 he went to the USA for a prolonged visit, possibly to emigrate; but in 1942, in the midst of the Second World War, he and his companion Peter Pears decided to return home. By this stage Britten had an opera in mind based on a poem by George Crabbe (1754–1832) and set in a rough, seafaring community. This opera became *Peter Grimes*, premiered in London in 1945 with Pears in the leading role. It proved so successful that Britten was able to dedicate much of his future energy to opera – to make it, as he said at the time, his 'real metier'.[9] He was aware of the strangeness of this decision: the 'professional' opera composer, the specialist, had long since disappeared. As Britten reportedly said to fellow composer Michael Tippett: 'I am possibly an anachronism. I am a composer of opera, and that is what I am going to be, throughout.'[10]

Between 1945 and 1954 Britten produced seven operas, two of

which – *Billy Budd* (1951) and *The Turn of the Screw* (1954) – almost rivalled *Grimes* in popularity. After that, he turned away from opera, at least on anything like the grand scale. As well as writing more instrumental and chamber music, he essayed genres such as ballets, 'church parables' and children's pieces. His only return during the next fifteen years was for the Shakespeare adaptation *A Midsummer Night's Dream* (1960). During the 1960s, as he became a national monument, various grand operatic projects were mooted, including a *King Lear* and an *Anna Karenin*, but they were left unrealized. Towards the end of his life he wrote the television opera *Owen Wingrave* (1970) and, at the last and plainly valedictory, an opera based on Thomas Mann's novella *Death in Venice* (1973).

Grimes, though, was the breakthrough, and in retrospect becomes an ever more important moment in the history of twentieth-century opera. As with so many such works of that century, its possible place in history seemed immediately fraught. One of the most prominent aspects of the early *Grimes* reception is an anxious concern about the operatic past and Britten's placement within it.[11] Was he a follower of Verdi or Wagner? How did he relate to modernism? What about his national roots? What about popular influences?

Answers came readily but were often contradictory. To the first question, the reply was emphatically the late Verdi of *Otello* and *Falstaff*, where only shards of arias, duets and ensembles could be found, yet where the orchestra generally deferred to the voice. Then again, *Grimes* also boasted recurring motives, and subjected them to orchestral development, so Wagner was not entirely absent. The question about his modernist credentials also generated confusion. Everyone could hear that *Grimes* was tonal and had few leanings towards the atonality or serialism then in mainland European vogue. On the other hand, aspects of the opera – not least its use of elaborate orchestral interludes, its grim subject matter and its unconventional, outsider protagonist – were clearly influenced by Berg and German expressionism. In the matter of Englishness the position was again not clear, mostly because there was virtually no operatic tradition to refer to. Britten's harmonic idiom often seemed to veer into a modal writing that has resonances with British composers such as Gustav Holst and Ralph Vaughan Williams.

But in terms of specific operatic models, Britten himself emphasized the national void preceding him: he even declared that part of his task was 'to restore to the musical setting of the English language a brilliance, freedom and vitality that have been curiously rare since the death of Purcell'.[12] Thus the suspicion arose that a part of *Grimes*'s success derived from the fact that its composer was less encumbered by operatic tradition than were his contemporaries elsewhere, being free to indulge his eclectic tendencies. To emphasize this further, some of the public scenes in *Grimes* plainly evoked popular musical styles, perhaps filtered through Gershwin's *Porgy and Bess* or influenced by Britten's early work in the film industry.

These varied musical influences were matched by a story that was hard to define and again proved resistant to easy interpretation. Crabbe's original 1810 poem, called *The Borough*, had few such equivocations. The section devoted to Grimes presents a bleak portrait of a fisherman who murders three young apprentices through violence and neglect, and then dies delirious and terrified, pursued by their spirits. Britten and his librettist Montagu Slater fleshed out this tale, but in the process made Grimes (tenor) as much a victim as a villain. Although prone to violence, he shows a gentler, visionary side in his dealings with the retired sea captain Balstrode (baritone), with the schoolteacher Ellen Orford (soprano), and above all in his poetic reactions to the wild seascape that surrounds him. Fundamentally he is an outsider, and disliked as such by the pompous town worthies. After the death of an apprentice (accident, not murder), he is hunted by the townspeople; driven mad by their persecution he takes his boat out to sea to commit suicide.

Peter Grimes is, in short, a protagonist about whom we can never feel secure, and to project that insecurity in music demanded subtle treatment. In the opening scene, as he is sworn in at an inquest investigating the death of his first apprentice, his slow, gentle repetition of the oath is in stark contrast to the woodwind-rich, impatient chatter of the accusing townsfolk; this contrast has often been compared to the way Bach singles out Christ's utterances in his passion narrative. The same gentle declamation on a reciting tone comes in Act 1, scene 2, in Grimes's visionary aria 'Now the Great Bear and Pleiades'. But near the end of this lyrical set piece he erupts into shocking musical violence. What, then, is his true nature? The violence escalates at the start of Act 2, when he strikes Ellen and utters the lines 'And God have mercy upon me!' to a jagged motif that deteriorates into a bass-register growl.

The final scene of the opera is laid out as an old-fashioned set piece that, in Britten's own words, can 'crystallise and hold the emotion of a dramatic situation'.[13] In this sense, it harks back to many an operatic mad scene of the past, as far distant as Donizetti's *Lucia di Lammermoor*, which it resembles in its play with distorted, half-remembered musical fragments from earlier scenes. The meaning of these remembrances is subject to a sophisticated game involving reality and delusion. In the previous scene, the townspeople had stoked their anger by repeatedly screaming out Grimes's name. Now these cries, punctuated by a distant foghorn, resonate in the distance, but have mutated into a gentle tonal hum, outlining the sounds that had underpinned the protagonist's first words in the opera. This parallel raises a question many opera composers have posed in writing music for distraught characters: where do such distant sounds come from? Are they real, or do they emanate from Grimes's disordered mind? Ellen appears and tries to comfort him, and his last, lyrical re-voicing of the earlier music parallels a transformation of the townsfolk's distant cries into a lamenting commentary on his tragic fall.

Britten might have taken Verdi's *Otello* as his model and ended the opera there, with a broken hero singing to the last. But he evidently felt something more was needed. At the start of a coda, there is unadorned speech; Balstrode approaches Grimes and utters words that could hardly be more prosaic: 'Sail out till you lose sight of land. Then sink the boat. D'you hear? Sink her. Goodbye Peter'. Then, according to a lengthy and elaborate scene direction:

> Together they push the boat down the slope of the shore. Balstrode comes back and waves goodbye. He takes Ellen who is sobbing quietly, calms her and leads her carefully down the main street home. The men pushing the boat out has been the cue for the orchestra to start playing again.

Those two adverbs – *quietly*, *carefully* – deserve scrutiny. They seem to be telling the performers that no histrionics, nothing remotely attention-seeking, nothing *operatic*, should take place. Ellen and Balstrode should not claim too much of the audience's attention because something far more evocative occurs at that point: a long reprise of the opera's first orchestral interlude. This brilliant, shimmering seascape, uncannily realistic with its high, keening strings, harp arpeggios and low brass chords, signals the end. The townspeople give up their manhunt and begin their dawn routine. Some minor characters exchange desultory words about a boat out at sea – is it sinking? The chorus herald the cold beginning of another day. The orchestra sinks into a cavernous low register, where three deep punctuations signal the end.

After the success of *Grimes*, Britten's operatic subject matter mostly continued in the same vein – personal, interior dramas featuring restraint and ambiguity, above all nothing epic (a problematic exception being his 'coronation' opera *Gloriana,* 1953). What is more, his love of letting the orchestra take the burden of communication at critical moments, as heard in those last minutes of *Grimes*, became a persistent impulse. In *Billy Budd* (1951) the central confrontation is the scene between the condemned sailor Billy Budd and Captain Vere, who announces to Billy his sentence of death. This confrontation is not sung at all, but represented entirely by means of the orchestra, which moves through a sequence of tonal and instrumental combinations in a succession of thirty-four chords. *The Turn of the Screw* (1954), like *Grimes*, gains much of its individuality from a series of orchestral interludes connecting an otherwise fragmentary succession of short scenes. If anything, Britten's compositional range became more boldly modernist as time went on: the interludes in *Turn of the Screw* were even styled as variations on a twelve-note 'row', albeit one constructed and deployed in a way that maximizes its tonal possibilities.

What lesson is there to be read from Britten's operatic popularity? He was born in 1913, but in the twenty-first century is more often performed than Bellini, Janáček, Massenet, Gluck or Weber.[14] Are his operatic ways and means to be regarded as a model for success in the operatic future, with composers enjoined to think how Britten would have done it? Here it may be wise to remember Claude Debussy's celebrated bon mot concerning the afterlife of Richard Wagner: Wagner, he said, was 'a beautiful sunset that was mistaken for a dawn'.[15] Debussy wrote this in 1903, and would probably have stood by it to his dying day. The operatic world – composers, performers, theorists and audiences – saw matters differently. Wagner may have made the writing of opera harder, the attrition greater, but a remarkable range of individual composers, Debussy included, were productive after the Wagnerian moment, and often precisely because Wagner had shown what really new things were possible. But sunsets and dawns can often look alike. Appearing just as the Second World War was coming to a close, *Peter Grimes* was immediately hailed as a new beginning, and the opera ends with a famous orchestral dawn, delicately poised (*quietly, carefully*) between weary acceptance and hope. But this time, even given Britten's enduring success, the message has turned out to be mostly about sunset.

THREE LIONS

By no measure can Britten be deemed an avant-garde composer. Yet three recently deceased avant-garde lions of the postwar era, all of whom prospered into the twenty-first century, have also continued to figure in existential debates concerning contemporary opera, even though they are, like Britten, now part of history. Hans Werner Henze (1926–2012) wrote more than twenty operas and is routinely proclaimed Germany's greatest postwar opera composer; he is also one the most regularly performed, enjoying forty-one revivals in the five years from 2008/9 to 2012/13.[16] Although he first came to prominence in the late 1940s in the avant-garde atmosphere of the Darmstadt New Music Summer School, his explicit rejection of this ambience is in one sense signalled by the fact that he wrote so many operas in the 1950s and 1960s – at a time, that is, when most card-carrying musical radicals saw the art form as desperately moribund.

In this and other ways, Henze might be compared to Britten; but there is little doubt that Darmstadt also left a considerable mark. His first great success came with *Boulevard Solitude* (1952), yet another remake of Abbé Prévost's Manon Lescaut story, which had engaged Massenet and Puccini more than half a century earlier. The Schoenberg lineage is declared in the twelve-tone harmonic idiom, and also in the use of vocal extremes, the post-Wagnerian surface of prevailing musical dialogue and the elaborate, attention-seeking orchestration. However, Henze's sense of dramatic economy ensures that one scene follows another with brisk dispatch. What is more, and apart from the expressionist orchestral interludes with their obsessive rhythmic motives, he shows a willingness to respond creatively to nineteenth-century operatic manners, with vintage techniques like text repetition, duets in parallel intervals and even coloratura vocal delivery. Good examples of this response can be found in the exchanges between Manon and her brother. It may, though, be significant that whenever the siblings sing in concordance, they are at their most deceptive and oily within the plot – as if making a moral point that such echoes of the operatic past, hence of the pleasure it supplies, are highly suspect.

Luciano Berio (1925–2003) is in many ways a more typical product of the postwar avant garde. He was also connected with Darmstadt in his early years, and his musical-theatre works of the 1950s–1970s are aggressively 'anti-opera'. But then, as part of what seems to have been a more widespread rapprochement with the ancient art form, he collaborated in the early 1980s with the novelist Italo Calvino, producing two much more conventionally shaped operas (*La vera storia*, 1981, and *Un re in ascolto*, 1984), albeit both of formidable postmodern credentials.[17] The fact that Berio's last operatic venture was a new completion of Puccini's unfinished *Turandot* adds further weight to the rapprochement thesis, if also to the ambivalence routinely surrounding it. Berio, for example, proclaimed an immediate distaste for the brashness of Puccini's planned ending, in which the proud, icy Princess is 'melted' by means of a violent kiss from virile tenor Calaf; still more did he castigate Franco Alfano's ending (the one usually performed today), in which this kiss is celebrated musically by a huge orchestral dissonance and heavy bangs on the bass drum. In its place he wrote a complex orchestral interlude in high-modernist vein, complete with exotic percussion and quotations from Mahler and Schoenberg: an attempt, that is, to resituate the opera within a dominant instrumental tradition.[18] Instead of Puccini's idea of bringing down the curtain to triumphant reiterations of Calaf's aria 'Nessun dorma' (which has, at least after 'The Three Tenors', become a brash symbol of opera's flirtation with popular culture), Berio finished with yet more delicate orchestral filigree and fleeting leitmotivic reminiscences of past themes: as unemphatic an ending as is possible to imagine. It would be hard to think of a more pointed modernist commentary, in musical form, on the defects of the core operatic repertory.

The last of our already-historical postwar giants presents a similar trajectory to that of Berio. The Hungarian composer György Ligeti (1923–2006) also served his time at Darmstadt, and also avoided opera for much of his career. However, he too embraced the rapprochement, and in his fifties wrote *Le Grand Macabre* (1977; revised 1996), a work that relies extensively on the operatic past while projecting a devil-may-care attitude, injecting immense humour and energy into the programme. Set in 'Breughelland', with an expressionist/pantomime action, the opera mines what Ligeti called 'deep-frozen' music from history but – like Henze's best work – benefits from a happy awareness that no scene or musical attitude should linger long.[19] The sheer promiscuity of the musical borrowings is exhilarating – or bewildering. A staccato prelude for twelve motor horns (a perfect palindrome, hat tip to serialism, but also an obvious gesture to Monteverdi's *Orfeo*) introduces the entwined lovers, Amando and Amanda (sopranos), who warble together with madrigalesque lasciviousness and ornamentation. They are interrupted by a drunken idiot shouting the 'Dies Irae'; and so it goes on, with Britten-like trebles (or counter-tenors), wild coloratura sopranos bringing down the house, speaking roles, Beethoven pastiches, Offenbachian galops and much more. If this is the way opera ends, Ligeti seems to be telling us, it does so in ludic chaos. Or perhaps the whole idea of opera's life versus afterlife is up for challenge: can we know the difference? Not for nothing is the character Nekrotzar, the nihilistic impresario whose name invokes Necropolis, given a knockout entrance, a cortège with blaring brass and a disquieting rhythmic energy that rivals Clytemnestra's arrival in *Elektra*.

Le Grand Macabre has enjoyed several successful revivals in the last two decades. In 2010, for example, it was performed to tremendous acclaim by the New York Philharmonic, not in an opera house but – semi-staged – in Avery Fisher Hall. The multi-media effects, with video projections, entrances up the aisles and musicians scattered through the hall (one of the present authors found herself seated in proximity to several brass instruments) played to a younger audience ready to enjoy absolutely everything on offer. Perhaps one reason Ligeti's opera has started to endure is that in some indefinable way it provides ample the room for glee. The openness of the 2010 production, the fact that the lights were up in the house, that one could read the libretto, drink bottled water and go in and out with (relative) freedom may have played a part in assuring the largely under-forty audience that this was something very far from their grandmothers' operatic experience. Whether that assurance, along with the young audience it recruited, is transferable to conventional opera houses, with their different rules and habits, remains to be seen. But it is a lesson that could be learned.

BEAUTY AND/OR THE POLITICAL

These three lions, along with the tale of their operatic achievements, illustrate the degree to which opera had a troubled relationship with the postwar avant-garde. For many 'serious' European composers born in the earlier decades of the twentieth century, the idea of writing grand opera was only to be confronted with distaste, if not representing outright anathema. After all, one thing the Second World War was meant to have burned from the playbook was allegiance to regressive bourgeois genres. There is an oft-told tale that vividly illustrates the pattern. When the great French modernist Olivier Messiaen (1908–92) was approached at age sixty-three by the Paris Opéra, his initial reaction was to refuse instantly. Yet temptation had been offered, and over many years he produced *Saint François d'Assise* (first performance 1983), a speech-imbued opera with glorious, complicated instrumental sounds and a veritable catalogue of bells. The vocal writing, which relies on intonation more than melody, has far more liturgical than operatic sound in its DNA. What is, though, profoundly operatic about *Saint François* is the massive musical resources it requires, and the expense demanded by its production. In recent years it has, in recognition of its acoustic wonders and grandeur, been reappraised, with a handful of new productions mounted over the last decade.

The last thirty or so years have demonstrated that such visceral reactions against opera were generational and temporary. And while many operas written since 1980 are unmistakably the progeny of twentieth-century musical modernism, they exhibit different, more open attitudes to opera's history, along with a degree of optimism about how heavily that history need weigh on the genre's present-day viability. These are composers for whom a later birth has proven a liberating benison.

John Adams (b. 1947) remains a polarizing figure, whose immense popular success over decades has come about primarily with operas that are conspicuous for the immediacy of their subject matter. *Nixon in China* (1987), written in collaboration with Alice Goodman (libretto) and Peter Sellars (direction and 'concept'), used as its source material the US president's historic diplomatic mission to China, which had occurred less than two decades earlier. In taking the path of such *actualité*, Adams went against the grain of post-1945 operatic fashion. Of course, there had been up-to-date operas in the past, but almost all of them were comic. *Opera buffa* of the eighteenth and nineteenth centuries tended to be set in near-contemporary times (Mozart's *Le nozze di Figaro* is a classic case, Donizetti's *L'elisir d'amore* another), where social critique could function with maximum clarity. As we saw in the last chapter, the 'opera-crisis' of 1920s Germany also produced a string of *Zeitopern*, in which the machines – and attitudes – of modernity were defiantly paraded, again usually for comic effect. But *Zeitoper* was a short-lived fashion, perhaps because operas that celebrate the here-and-now would seem, at first glance, to invite their own datedness. Write a *Zeitoper* about current events and, pretty soon, you will not be current.

Given this circumstance, and also given the ignominy with which Nixon's tenure as president ended, the fact that Adams's *Nixon* treated the visit to China as an epic rather than comic encounter gave audiences and critics quite a shock – for some perhaps even greater than the extravagant sexual antics of *Le Grand Macabre*, premiered only a decade earlier. Opera, Adams seemed to tell audiences, *does* have a future, *can* address head on contemporary society's concerns. On the other hand it is difficult, given the nature of his musical language, to imagine any aesthetic outcome other than epic, timeless distance. Adams used as his starting point the so-called 'minimalist' style of composers such as Steve Reich and Philip Glass, a technique going back to the 1960s and 1970s, in which superimposed sequences of endlessly repeated musical figures form dense blocks of internally active sound, which shift gradually to other blocks over long stretches of time. Glass's operas, perhaps particularly *Satyagraha*, shimmer somewhere behind *Nixon*. Adams imitates the block construction, but his blocks move more frequently, in the process varying in orchestration (sometimes piquant, Stravinsky-reminiscent combinations, sometimes big-band-inspired) and gaining harmonic direction (often with chord progressions a major or minor third apart). The effect is close to film music, especially the kind of film music that accompanies grand outdoor vistas. Characters and prominent choral groups declaim the text with rigorous fidelity to natural accentuation, but with melodic shapes that derive from the sonorous orchestral backdrop. There are even da capo arias – knowing gestures towards opera's past. This warm bath of vast, slow-changing sound is no place to find comedy; even Richard Nixon becomes heroic by default, simply by being present in the soundscape.

The experience of seeing events within living memory, narrated in an unmistakably high style but wrapped in a familiar musical idiom, proved irresistible at the box office. Although some critics complained about the musical manners, and although more austere composers were predictably dismissive, Adams brought a new audience to the opera house, many of them visitors from cinema and other mass media. Small wonder that he and his collaborative team were soon commissioned again. The result, *The Death of Klinghoffer* (1991), was even more up to date: it takes as its theme the 1985 takeover by Palestinian terrorists of an Italian cruise ship and the subsequent murder of Leon Klinghoffer, a disabled Jewish-American passenger. *Klinghoffer* is, as one might expect, darker in tone than *Nixon*; but not much so. The outdoor music and epic stance are in many ways identical. The opera begins with a pair of choruses: first of Exiled Palestinians, then of Exiled Jews; the sense of a balanced, even-handed approach to the opposing forces is established by a detached, oratorio-like atmosphere that continues throughout. As with *Nixon*, Adams's musical characteristics mean that onstage action is hardly possible; even the most obvious events have to be delivered through elaborate narration.

The perceived lack of musical differentiation – probably inevitable given Adams's compositional style – caused a controversy. While few were concerned when Richard Nixon was ennobled by immersion in a minimalist hum, Palestinian terrorists were another matter. Accusations that the opera was anti-Semitic or condoned terrorism soon appeared, and have continued even decades after the premiere, reaching new levels of intensity when the opera was staged at New York's Metropolitan Opera in 2014.[20] Adams was hurt by the controversy, and seemed surprised that his opera could have raised such passions. As he said in one interview during the 1990s: 'All of us did a lot of research . . . I read a great deal of Edward Said's writings. I know Alice Goodman [the librettist] read most of the Koran.'[21]

This reference to Said, a literary critic of great distinction and up to his death in 2003 one of the most powerful pro-Palestinian voices in the Israel–Palestine conflict, takes us back to issues aired in Chapter 15, in particular of opera playing a cameo role in what, in the wake of Said, has become known as post-colonial criticism. Adams seemed to be using Said as a kind of guarantor of respectability; it is thus worth knowing that Said himself, who had a significant second career as a music critic, wrote at some length about the opera. In general he found it even-handed; but, as he pointed out, that was because he judged the musical style incapable of taking any strong position, or indeed of expressing any meaningful dramatic contrast. As Said put it, '[the] music . . . frequently sounds strangely retrospective, vaguely or only partially convinced of where it's going.'[22] Famously, it is only with the final aria, sung by Marilyn Klinghoffer, that specific and personal grief breaks into a musical idiom that has otherwise distanced itself from events.

It is interesting – especially after the 2014 protests in New York City – to indulge in a thought experiment, an experiment that queries the role music plays in opera. Periodically through opera's history we come across the phenomenon of substitute libretti being invented for existing musical scores. Political censorship could require retitling of operas, relocating their action and renaming their characters. Verdi's *Un ballo in maschera* is an example: if the hero who gets murdered is the real King Gustav III of Sweden, and his presence is forbidden, then just move the plot to Massachusetts and call him Riccardo, Count of Warwick. The opera is marvellous in either circumstance; the frisson of depicting a real historical murder (or not) has no bearing on the composer's ability to pack in the public and move them to tears, because the music has an alchemy that survives alterations to the libretto. If the libretto of *The Death of Klinghoffer* were changed, to become a story about – say – the murder of a longshoreman by Teamsters in the 1920s, would the music be able to recruit equally passionate attention for this less controversial plot? The very impossibility of the substitution suggests the degree to which contemporary 'political' opera can depend on its narrative – its topicality – to make a mark.

Adams can be viewed as a foundational figure for a new form of *Zeitoper*, with recent works such as Mark-Anthony Turnage's *Anna Nicole* (2011), Nico Muhly's *Two Boys* (2011) and Philip Glass's *The Perfect American* (2013) all demonstrating how real-life scandal and celebrity make excellent operatic subjects. Yet in the wake of the *Klinghoffer* controversy Adams himself retreated for a time to instrumental music and oratorio. He has since returned, in particular with *Doctor Atomic* (2005), which features J. Robert Oppenheimer as its protagonist and involves the making of the first atomic bomb. Whether this will enjoy *Nixon*'s fate is a riddle for time to solve.

THE HERE-AND-NOW AND THE MYTHICAL PAST

In spite of the successes of Adams and others, most contemporary operas do not rely on real life or topical headlines, preferring to access a very different and venerable convention for operatic subjects: the world of myth and antiquity, the treasury of spoken drama from centuries past. The British composer Thomas Adès (b. 1971) wrote his first grand opera, *The Tempest* (after Shakespeare, but to a modernized English libretto by Meredith Oakes), in 2004. It was immediately hailed as a major event. Although adapting Shakespeare quite freely, Oakes kept the bare bones of one of his most famous inserted songs, which becomes a song-within-the-opera. Ariel (soprano) sings it to lure Ferdinand to Prospero's shore:

> Five fathoms deep your father lies,
> Those are pearls that were his eyes,
> Nothing of him that was mortal is the same,
> His bones are coral,
> He has suffered a sea change,
> Into something rich and strange,
> Sea nymphs hourly ring his knell:
> I can hear them: ding dong bell.

Songs-within-the-opera are time-honoured, and are usually, as here, set apart musically and formally – simple and hyper-melodious in relation to the surrounding context. When such rules are adhered to, beautiful singing and well-formed melody become antiquated styles: inserted songs can, in other words, constitute a brief aesthetic vacation – for composers as well as listeners.

Although modernized in diction and vocabulary, Shakespeare's poem remains basically intact, a precious object within a libretto that radically restructures most of its dramatic source. Adès responds by giving the song a colour apart. Elsewhere, the opera's predominant musical ancestor is the expressionism of speech-opera c. 1930, a technique that originated in early twentieth-century modernism with roots in Wagner and Musorgsky. Prospero (baritone) often sings along these lines, tending to atonal anguish articulated atop loud, elaborate orchestral ideas.

Ariel is a coloratura role with a tessitura so high as to seem physiologically dangerous, and when she's in Prospero's musical orbit she squeaks eerily in his image, as if she's Lulu on helium.

But her real musical voice, as manifest in the song-within-the-opera, comes from the spirit world, which is evidently a quieter place. 'Full fathom five' was already an uncanny poem in its Shakespearean incarnation, with its image of a body under the water undergoing metamorphosis into nacreous matter and gems. On cue, several magical things happen in the music, the most audible of which is a strange low sonority – a kind of vibration made from strings and barely audible percussion – which conjures up the bells. We hear it tolling on 'nymphs', '[hour]ly' and 'knell', a sound at the lowest end of the audible spectrum, contrasting across a voided middle with Ariel's stratospheric vocal line. Since Ariel is mischievous, she sings the four syllables of 'I can hear them' as the Westminster chimes, as if she's a miniature Big Ben. And three times, as foil to the three quiet knells, a single syllable is blasted out over dissonant orchestral wreckage for an alarming fortissimo instant, '*fath*[oms]', '*are* [coral]' and '[ding]-*dong*'.

Throughout the song, Ariel's vocal line is suspended against pianissimo high strings shifting among beguiling orchestral sonorities. As well as the pleasure their beauty gives, another major departure from the opera's standard musical progress involves its word–music relationship: Ariel intones each of her syllables slowly, lovingly, voice to the fore; and to a regular pulse, each syllable the same length, slow-motion steps in melodic arches adding up to regular phrases. This is powerfully unlike the staccato syllabic declamation elsewhere in *The Tempest*, which uses the metric-meander technique characteristic of speech-opera. In the song there is a sense that, within Ariel's gentle pulse, we have gained a breathing space, a place of repose.

The end of *The Tempest* recaptures the otherworldly suspension that characterized Ariel's song. This reprise is fitting, since Prospero cedes the stage ('Farewell, farewell. / Now I've no art. / Pity, take my part') and Caliban, shorn of darkness, is given the final lines. But Ariel remains as an invisible presence, her voice transformed into wordless sonority echoing Caliban's singing:

> In the gleam of the sand, Caliban,
> In the hiss of the spray
> In the deep of the bay,
> In the gulf, in the swell, Caliban.

The opera ends on a single bass note held seemingly for ever, with a three-note motif ('Ca-li-ban') whispered between the siren voice, piccolos and flutes, celesta, harp – all instruments of the afterworld.

Although set apart from the often spiky musical exterior heard elsewhere in the opera, the ending of *The Tempest* does indeed belong to a type, but the tradition to which it gestures has a very different pedigree. The use of wordless female voice (or voices) is an ancient musical code for transcendence and transfiguration, as are immobile or slow-shifting sonorities. Whole treatises could be written on stasis and operatic choruses singing 'Ah-ah' or 'Oh-oh'. Such conceits were much in vogue in Orientalist works of the nineteenth century, in the strange female Ah-ing of the 'Immenso Fthà' episode in Verdi's *Aida* or the Indian dance scenes in Delibes's *Lakmé*. *Aida* is also pertinent for pioneering a favourite type of late twentieth-century operatic finale, what we might call the blissed-out ending. The 'Evening Song' that ends Philip Glass's *Satyagraha* (1979), with its endlessly rising Phrygian scales, is a numinous example. Harmonic activity ceases, tonal stasis sets in, everything becomes very quiet as lights and life flicker out; choruses (sometimes present, often offstage) reduce to a hum, and an assortment of old-world and afterworld instruments repeat melodic fragments, circling and circular, with lazy flutes, little bells chiming or harps pinging serenely. Such atmospheres imply that the music is not really ending, just departing into a faraway realm beyond the senses, like a ship disappearing into the mist.

L'Amour de loin (2000), a debut opera by the Finnish composer Kaija Saariaho (b. 1952), generously distributes acoustic delights of this kind. The libretto by Amin Maalouf is assembled from mysterious vignettes centring on Jaufré Rudel (baritone), a twelfth-century French troubadour. Jaufré encounters a nameless Pilgrim (mezzo-soprano), who tells him of Clémence (soprano), a beautiful lady in Tripoli in the mysterious East, to whom Jaufré journeys, only to die in Clémence's arms. This is French symbolist theatre for a new century. Saariaho writes soundscape or 'spectral' music (a technique in which compositional decisions are informed by computer analysis of timbre), massing rich sonorities – instrumental booming, ringing, apparitional chord clouds, trilling like birdsong – into a mutable acoustic tapestry. Jaufré's music also channels medieval chanson or chant into triple-metre vocal phrases with simple accompaniment and small vocal ornaments against harp strokes. But 'spectral' is an apposite word in another sense, because his chanson is perpetually heard through a filter of distance, producing uncanny resonances.

At the beginning of Act 2, the Pilgrim travels back over the sea to Tripoli, and an interlude representing the journey and arrival at Clémence's palace calls on wordless choruses for its power. Against low-frequency rumbles, harmonies that have no centre of gravity and a further collection of afterworld instruments, the chorus's repeated 'Ah-ah' conveys pure awe, as if invisible spectators cannot remain silent in the face of some great mystery. It is a sound-world strongly resembling Bernard Herrmann's extraordinary score for Henry Levin's 1959 film *Journey to the Center of the Earth*: an acoustic of wonderment, with tremendous power to move the listener. The comparison might seem heretical to some. When quizzed publicly about her operatic genealogy, Saariaho referred to only two works, Messaien's *Saint François* and Debussy's *Pelléas et Mélisande*. This strikes a note of high-art authenticity, but the genealogy could in fact be writ much more broadly. Indeed, perhaps her soundscapes attract us and seem meaningful in part because they call up multiple memories of music that has referenced the otherworldly: certainly to earlier composers who translated the whispers of the natural world into musical form (Debussy); but also to popular evocations of distant planets (in classic science fiction films) and to other disquieting soundscapes (Brian Easdale's score for Powell and Pressburger's film *Black Narcissus*, 1947).

Written on Skin by the British composer George Benjamin (b. 1960) was also a debut grand opera. It appeared in 2012, has already seen multiple revivals and is programmed into several future opera seasons. Alex Ross in *The New Yorker* announced it as Benjamin's 'long-awaited masterpiece', and 'the work of a genius unleashed'.[23] Its libretto, by Martin Crimp, again retells a medieval story. A wealthy Protector (bass-baritone) employs a young man, here called simply the Boy (counter-tenor), to create an illuminated manuscript celebrating his family and achievements. The Protector's wife, Agnès (soprano), becomes interested in the Boy, perhaps seeing him as a route to sexual awakening. The scene is thus laid for a classic operatic triangle in the manner of Wagner's *Die Walküre* (Act 1), or Debussy's *Pélléas et Mélisande*, or Puccini's *Il tabarro*; perhaps a closer comparison, though, is to Britten's *Billy Budd* (an older man, assailed with repressed homoerotic attraction to a pure youth who has entered his domain). The denouement, though, is more violent even than Puccini's cadaver-under-the-cloak: the Protector, mad with jealousy, murders the Boy and forces Agnès to eat his heart; defiant to the last, she leaps to her death from the balcony of their house.

Crimp's libretto language has many narrative quirks. The text is full of oblique gestures and distancing effects, in particular by having characters enunciate their own stage directions, typically set by Benjamin in rapid staccato asides, or refer to themselves and others in the third person. The action is set even further at a distance by being framed: a trio of Angels (mezzo, tenor and a counter-tenor who doubles as the Boy) comment on the characters from the perspective of the present day – as they say in the opening scene, 'Cancel all flights from the international airport and people the sky with angels.' The final grim pursuit and suicide is not sung and acted out by Agnès and the Protector, but rather described by the Boy-as-Angel, who makes it into an illustration in his book, 'See how her body has dropped from the balcony – how I pause her in mid-fall – at the exact centre of the page.'

The musical language makes occasional gestures to medieval practice, hocket-like textures and other *ars antiqua* revenants, and the orchestra includes a viola da gamba: such borrowings from early music are yet another compositional device the opera shares with *L'Amour de loin*. But Benjamin's orchestra responds with far greater alacrity – indeed, with startling, virtuosic invention – to images in the libretto. There is, for instance, a wonderful word-painting moment in Act 1, scene 4, when light shimmering through water is brought to our ears via a phalanx of percussion. Underneath these ornamental elements, however, the opera bears a rich resemblance to the hundred-year-old *Erwartung*/*Wozzeck* template, the gold standard of atonal modernist music drama. *Erwartung* is powerfully evoked by Agnès at moments (there are many) of expressionist angst and erotic sickness. One moment where the echo is loud occurs in the climactic penultimate scene. The heroine's final words are 'Nothing, nothing, not if you strip me to the bone with acid, will ever take the taste of that Boy's heart out of my mouth.' To match the horror vocally, her line has huge, angular leaps, with a prolonged high C on 'mouth' (her last utterance in the opera).

The *Wozzeck* model, which was mentioned by numerous reviewers, is obvious on many other levels: *Written on Skin*, like its famous antecedent, is made up of three roughly thirty-minute acts, each divided into five scenes; in spite of its largely atonal idiom, there are frequent pitch anchors (mostly in the form of pedal points in the orchestra) to orientate both singers and listeners; there are orchestral interludes between the scenes, forbidding any opportunity for applause that might break the dramatic flow, and also encouraging a sense that the work is at base an orchestral one with vocal accompaniment. These gestures to modernist tradition, the fact of their familiarity, surely contribute to the enthusiasm with which audiences have reacted. But there may also be a more uncomfortable reason: *Written on Skin* brings back once again a familiar modernist muse, a female protagonist whose released sexuality leads inexorably to her objectification and, ultimately, to retribution of extreme violence. Think of Salome, or of Shostakovich's Katerina Ismailova. Watching women being represented as writhing sexual creatures, then watching them being punished, is something that – it seems – never fails to please a segment of the public.

There is, finally, another side to Ross's bestowal of those epithets 'masterpiece' and 'genius': the sense that, as loaded words, they lead us back to the comfort zone of the historical canon rather than propel us forward into the future. In this context, we might ponder the following distinction. *Wozzeck* and *Written on Skin* sound in many ways rather similar, even though separated by nearly a century. But Wagner in the 1850s was not writing operas that people extolled by saying they wonderfully evoked or significantly resembled works from the 1750s. *Tristan* does not sound like late Handel or early Gluck. The years 1759 to 1859 saw such a flow of invention, metamorphosis, formal earthquakes, expansions of operatic ways and means, that the end point, even if you substitute another composer for Wagner, bears but faint resemblance to the beginning. By the twenty-first century, the imagined possibilities and inventions, the acoustic surprises, the gorgeous variations on the past themes, are no longer proliferating in this way, so profusely and at such speed. Operatic time, so to speak, has slowed to *lento*.

The Tempest, *L'Amour de loin* and *Written on Skin* were all premiered within the last two decades and have all been revived many times – not just dutifully but with true enthusiasm. As so often in the past, the novelty of very new opera, the energy of the *succès d'estime,* itself generates elation and animation. The interesting question is whether these works will resonate when they are in a changed context and with an audience not yet born when they were premiered. That is a question about marvellous ephemerality and the entrance ticket to the museum, one that at present we cannot answer. What *is* clear, though, is that all these operas embrace an ambience at some considerable distance from our own, as do many recent works. One is also struck by some curious parallels. Why twelfth-century troubadours and artists (*L'Amour*, *Written on Skin*)? Why Mediterranean sea travel (*Tempest*, *L'Amour*)? Perhaps timelessness is alluring because there remains some pervasive uneasiness about opera's fragile position in contemporary culture. But, that notwithstanding, all these living composers have given hope to those who believe that opera as a cultural institution can survive by means of new works, by transcending the museum. To assess how realistic or how pious that hope may be – indeed to investigate opera's survival as the twenty-first century rolls on – is among the concerns of our final chapter.

21

We are alone in the forest

The Second World War was not far distant and opera was entering old age when René Clair's film comedy *Le Million* (1931) appeared. To appreciate its homage to opera, we need to know the plot. An Italian tenor has purchased a jacket from a second-hand shop. Unbeknownst to him, in the jacket pocket is a winning lottery ticket belonging to Michel, a poor artist whose girlfriend, Béatrice, a ballet dancer at the Opéra Lyrique, gave Michel's jacket away. Michel thus has an excellent reason for being very angry indeed with Béatrice. The two temporarily estranged lovers, together with others eager to acquire the winning ticket, end up at the opera, where the Italian tenor, donning the jacket as his costume, has been quarrelling backstage with his nemesis, a large blond soprano. The curtain goes up. Standing around in a forest are brigands, led by the head brigand, the soprano's admirer (baritone), who objects to the soprano's liaison with his arch-enemy. The brigands clink goblets, and sing the melody of the Soviet national anthem to the words, 'À nous l'ivresse! / à nous les caresses / d'une ravissante maîtresse!' (Give us drunkenness! Give us the caresses of a ravishing mistress!) At the end of this chorus, tenor and soprano stroll onto a scene in which brigands are in plain sight everywhere. The tenor launches into a recitative, announcing 'Nous sommes seuls, bien aimée! Viens avec moi dans la forêt parfumée!' (We are alone, beloved! Come with me into the scented forest!) 'We are alone' is priceless: brigands a couple of feet away look at him in bewilderment, as well they might (see Figure 45).

There is, in the entire corpus of cinema, no greater or more delicate expression of affection for opera, of delight in its absurdities and faith in its transformative powers, than *Le Million*. The powers are demonstrated most obviously by a love duet heard just before the brigand scene, a number in which the warring tenor and soprano are united in the temporary bliss of singing together. It also cures once and for all the anger and resentment between Michel and Béatrice, who have become accidentally trapped behind a piece of scenery just as the curtain rises for the duet, and thus are forced – cold and distant at first – to stay in place and listen. Tenor and soprano seat themselves on a rustic bench, and begin: 'Nous sommes seuls enfin, ce soir!' This evening we are alone at last! At last we are free to speak openly! Far from the world and its agony! The tenor begins a solo passage: what sorrow clouds thy sense? What, my love, is my offence? And Michel, hearing this, gestures silently with the same message to Béatrice. The heroine demurs in song, Béatrice demurs in pantomime. The hero entreats vocally, Michel entreats silently. The tenor's voice soars, the soprano competes, Michel mimes eternal devotion and Béatrice at last smiles. The duet ends 'nous sommes seuls dans la fôret' (we are alone in the forest), and both couples embrace. A stagehand, a busy working man, one of the small army needed to create this onstage magic, throws rose petals down from the catwalks, but this unmasking of artifice does nothing to dull the effect. Whether or not the lottery ticket is retrieved, we are morally certain that all will be well with Michel and Béatrice. We know this because opera has done its work.

From the 1930s through to the 1950s, at a time when writing a new opera for the theatre would become an ever-harder task, the *institution* of opera was so high on the popular radar in America and Europe that it was thought completely reasonable to make and expect profit from opera-themed movies. In 1930, the American baritone Lawrence Tibbett starred in *The Rogue Song*, the first of several films built around his sublime voice and not inconsiderable masculine charm. The film's plot (drawn from a Léhar operetta) is idiotic but, as one contemporary review put it, 'When Mr Tibbett sings, one cares not why.'[1] In 1935, Tibbett would star in *Metropolitan*, a comedy about a vengeful diva who, scorned by the Metropolitan Opera, decides to open her own opera company on a shoestring. In *Maytime* (1937), Jeanette MacDonald plays a glamorous opera singer whose love is divided between her career and Nelson Eddy, and who makes the wrong choice (career). The same year saw *Hitting a New High*, starring the coloratura soprano Lily Pons as a nightclub singer who dreams of performing opera and who is willing, clad only in feathers, to impersonate a primitive diva from the

South American rainforest to further her cause. The Marx Brothers' *A Night at the Opera* (1935), mentioned in Chapter One, casts opera in a double light. Opera *going* clearly represents stuffy high culture, the province of the rich and privileged. But operatic *singing* is a joy that can be experienced by anyone, by those doing it as well as those hearing it, and in whatever venue.

As if to demonstrate that truth, the great Danish tenor Lauritz Melchior appeared in two feature films, *Two Sisters from Boston* (1946) and *Luxury Liner* (1948), both of which include movie-star ingénues (Kathryn Grayson and Jane Powell respectively) whose characters' governing passions are to become opera singers. Melchior is seen recording the Prize Song from *Die Meistersinger von Nürnberg* in the former and performing the Spring Song from *Die Walküre* in the latter. In *Mad About Opera* (*Follie per l'opera*, 1949), set in post-Blitz London, a roguish Italian named Guido Marchi wants to rebuild a church, and decides that organizing an opera gala is his best chance of funding the enterprise. A Disney cartoon short from 1946, *The Whale Who Wanted to Sing at the Met* (voice work by Nelson Eddy), shows that in the century past young children were assumed to be connoisseurs of *Il barbiere di Siviglia*, *Tristan und Isolde*, tragedy, comedy and *Moby-Dick* all at once. Nor should we forget Mario Lanza in *The Great Caruso* (1951), and especially in *Serenade* (1956), where – just to heighten already fraught clashes between high and low, Italian and Aryan, poor and rich – his character performs the Italian Tenor's aria from Richard Strauss's *Der Rosenkavalier*.

The social role played by opera in such concoctions was not entirely straightforward. Opera could stand for cultural hauteur, set in opposition to the more down-to-earth future, the nightclub music in *Hitting A New High* or the smoky music-hall joints that Kathryn Grayson must work in to finance her singing lessons in *Two Sisters*. But operatic *singing* was another matter, and it invariably had the magical force it was given in *Le Million*: to assuage ill, for a few moments to enchant and transform ordinary existence into paradise. That the glorious singing is often done by silly people, perhaps too old or too fat, perhaps with eccentricities that somehow set them apart, is a feature of its spell. Opera appears in almost completely positive forms, as something that – even when stuffy – is a source of delight.

After the 1950s, the commercial film industry largely stopped producing humane comedies that took grand opera and opera singers as prime subject matter. After that point, when commercial cinema did (and does) make films about opera, the art form, along with operatic singing, is often no longer endearing and benign. In extraordinary ways, to track 'opera' in cinema over the course of the twentieth and early twenty-first centuries is to see a kind of seismographic trace of its place in culture. The seismograph shows opera's fates and fortunes in modern society, marks the periods in which it was ordinary and unexceptional to know and care about opera, and those – nowadays – in which 'opera' is often seen as a bizarre object from dubious and dying places, above all a representative of European-based elitism. This is what happens in Anthony Minghella's *The Talented Mr. Ripley* (1999), in a scene where Ripley, a novice murderer, attends a performance of Tchaikovsky's *Yevgeny Onegin* in Rome. The opera-house scene underlines Ripley's newly acquired fondness for expensive European high culture: he has just murdered a friend to provide himself with the wealth necessary to indulge his new appetites. At the same time, 'opera' is not purely ornamental in *Ripley*. It adds psychological intensity, since the extract we see performed – Lensky's death by Onegin's bullet – becomes for Ripley a traumatic reminder of the murder. A tear of regret descends his cheek as he watches Lensky expire. This is a relatively nuanced deployment of 'opera', which is once more assigned the power to move its listeners, even (or perhaps especially) when they are otherwise deemed unmovable. In worst-case scenarios, and there are many from the 1980s and 1990s, opera simply defaults into the reliable cinematic signifier of kitschy decadence, or a cliché of gay-ness – as in Patrick Conrad's 1987 film *Mascara*, which features scary transvestites who do opera karaoke for fun; or *Philadelphia* (1993), in which Tom Hanks does tragic-opera karaoke to a recording of Maria Callas.

Films in which opera and operatic singing are friendly elements gave way to those in which opera-house scenes become ornamental places to conjure up alien grandeur. This says something important about attitudes towards the genre, as well as the audience it is imagined to address, and the news is not good. The movie seismograph whispers to us that there were several decades earlier in the twentieth century when large numbers of ordinary citizens were familiar with opera, felt positive about its value, supported its consumption and continuation. It would be extraordinarily bold to claim, in the second decade of the twenty-first century, that this is still the case. Indie cinema occasionally delivers a throwback to the old ways, as does István Szabó's *Meeting Venus* (1991), a backstage drama depicting a performance of Wagner's *Tannhäuser* rescued from disaster, or Dustin Hoffmann's comedy *Quartet* (2012), which features endearing opera-singer oldsters making mischief in a retirement home. But the newer truth was exemplified as far back as Federico Fellini's *The Ship Sails On* (*E la nave va*, 1983), set on the eve of the First World War, which features a ship of fools peopled by opera singers and aristocratic fanatics, benighted and mad on the whole; it has a scene in which a famous Russian bass demonstrates the magical power of operatic singing by hypnotizing a chicken with his low notes.

THE PARADOX OF EASY ACCESS

If the movie seismograph is correct this falling-away on the part of the general public has been going on for more than fifty years. But, in one specific sense, a decline in knowledge and affection for opera is paradoxical. Popular regard for opera has shrunk during the very years in which experiencing opera – in the form of recordings – has become more and more effortless. We now have an unparalleled archive of operatic performances from the past and present at our disposal – compared to the 1950s the treasury is vast and ridiculously easy to access. If there is no longer widespread general knowledge about opera, this is not because it has become more difficult to find or more expensive to consume. Indeed, the operatic experience now involves not so much live performance (still costly to attend, still a rare thing for most), not recordings that we have had to buy and can then hold in our hands (a dying technology), as it does extraordinary online collections like the streaming services offered by large opera houses or the free mass archive of YouTube, an ever-growing repository. In one of YouTube's many rooms, we can see and hear operas otherwise virtually unknown, assessing for ourselves whether they might one day find a place in the repertory. In another we can be taught that opera in performance is a constantly changing art. We can now easily compare legions of singers from the distant past: not only hear their voices but in some cases also see how they acted, assess their body language and gestures, thus appreciating how operatic 'realism' constantly changes with the changing times. The Comments facility on YouTube additionally acts as a barometer of the obsessions and passionate identity-formation that opera so often inspires.

An example, taken virtually at random from among countless thousands, can demonstrate what has been gained. The great French tenor Georges Thill (1897–1984), whose 1932 recording of 'Unis dès la plus tendre enfance' from Gluck's *Iphigénie en Tauride* is posted several times, offers an object lesson in a kind of French diction that has all but disappeared (numerous modern renderings, both amateur and professional, can serve as ready comparison, and we can even compare and contrast with Fritz Wunderlich's German-language version). We may also discover something about the mutability of early recordings as they are now passed down to us: the CD transfer is, it seems, at a different speed from the original 78, which makes for a noticeable modification of effect. This last snippet of information comes via the Comments facility, where we can learn from and, if the spirit so moves, participate in a multi-lingual celebration of Thill and this recording, a carnival that is mostly joyous but can on occasions be testy in the extreme (the operatic Internet, with all those passionate identities in dialogue, can be a surprisingly angry place). In short, YouTube enables and then gives voice to a new operatic community, one that may have started life in a public forum but that can now make use of the archive for many intimate functions, not least providing a means by which opera lovers can share links privately among themselves, conversing through music even when separated physically.

Another form of mass sharing for the operatic community has come into being with the phenomenon of HD opera broadcasts, pioneered by the Metropolitan Opera in late 2006 and now imitated by numerous companies across the globe. These provide, via a network of participating cinemas, 'live' or delayed transmissions of real-time performances. There is no doubt that the total audience for opera in the theatre could in theory be markedly increased by such broadcasts. But has this been the case? Are there droves of new recruits – people who come into the HD cinema broadcast not knowing about opera and who leave eager to find out more? Or is it rather that a slice of the public already consuming opera has merely discovered a less expensive and easier-access form? That the latter situation prevails is suggested not just by the demographics of the HD audiences (which seem largely to match those of opera-house audiences), but by the fact that HD cinema audiences typically observe the protocols of theatrical attendance: silent attention, a prohibition against coming and going in mid-performance, the interval drinks, even the persistence of cathartic applause at the end. The suspicion arises that ever-easier access to opera may do little to ameliorate an overall attrition in the numbers of those who care whether opera exists at all.

THE CINEMATIC TURN

For any account of opera that poses difficult questions about its consumption and dissemination in recent decades, the issue of opera and video recording is critical. The presence of opera *within* film, which has been going on for more than a hundred years, has been joined by a newer counterpart, the wholesale conversion of opera *into* an audio-visual media phenomenon, consumed via screens both small and large. Besides HD broadcasts of live events, and the DVD performance archive, there is the strange case of studio-filmed opera. The heyday of studio-filmed opera came in the 1970s and 1980s, and it has since largely disappeared. This eccentric byway in the history of opera and modern media nonetheless includes several classic films by fabled directors, among them Ingmar Bergman's *Magic Flute* (1975), Joseph Losey's *Don Giovanni* (1979) and Franco Zeffirelli's *Otello* (1986). In all such films, the singers (or sometimes actors) lip-synch to a studio recording of the piece. Studio-filmed opera of the 1970s and 1980s looked back to two foundational works, Michael Powell and Emeric Pressburger's *Tales of Hoffmann* (1951), and (discussed in Chapter 15) Clemente Fracassi's *Aida* (1953), which starred Sophia Loren as Aida-on-screen, with Renata Tebaldi supplying the voice. *Tales of Hoffmann* remains, with Bergman's *Flute*, the most visually imaginative instance of the form.

There is a sense in which the true history of opera in the late twentieth and early twenty-first centuries is not in a roll call of new works and their parade of styles, nor even an account of the evolution of their staging by strong interpretative moves; it is rather in opera's ever-more-intense dance with recording and media culture. This new pattern of consumption, which began with recordings and radio broadcasts – sound-only media – and culminates today in HD broadcasts and a DVD recording culture, has upended the practices of opera-going and the acquisition of operatic knowledge, but it has also had profound influences on opera's visual manifestations. With mounting sophistication, staging is now often conceived with the cameras in mind, and sometimes privileges the camera above the view from Row M in the stalls. One recent example: the Metropolitan Opera's new *Ring* staging (2010–12), widely disliked, sometimes placed singers downstage in a shallow trench, a design element that, to those in most parts of the theatre, made them appear cut off at the knees. But this in-house experience was not the point. Hidden cameras for the HD broadcasts could do artful up-angles from within the trench, so that cinemagoers could see entire figures dramatically framed and foreshortened.

To take another obvious example, video recording has made newly problematic opera's traditional generosity about some singers' lack of conventional physical beauty. Opera may remain, as we put it in our first chapter, one of the few contemporary spectacles in which what you look like counts for less than how you sound, a marvellous exception to the tyranny of gorgeousness. But the constraints are narrowing because the close-ups made possible by camerawork are unforgiving. The more we consume opera on screen, in forms that are shaped by cinematic techniques such as elaborate micro-acting with eye movement and facial gestures, the more we expect operatic experience to conform to the terms of mainstream cinema.

Nowadays, when we see a video recording of a performance such as the Metropolitan's 1982 *Lucia di Lammermoor* (which even then was a time capsule from the 1960s: Joan Sutherland and Alfredo Kraus were the stars), we are struck by the artifice. There is a blissful insouciance with regard to acting (the occasional glare will suffice), a noble disregard for moving around on stage. Singing – focused musicality emerging directly from the human body – carries the day completely. We are left with a kind of hyper-consciousness of the performance: put in positive terms, a consciousness of our distance from the plot, and freedom from being absorbed by it. The media era in which we now reside forces us to confront anew some fundamental questions about the source of our pleasure in opera. When we experience an opera, are we to be – should we strive to be – absorbed in the fictional world, suspending disbelief? Or is part of opera's bliss a consciousness that art is being performed – often with great virtuosity, but sometimes with tongue in cheek even in the most tragic works – by real human beings?

BURN EVERYTHING

The vast YouTube archive, opera houses' recent efforts to record and then disseminate their every product, the pileup of artefacts in opera's living museum – all these things can be celebrated, but they do also have a disquieting underside. As the archival tonnage increases, there is a sense in which its contents can become an obsession and a distraction. Repeated visits to the treasury of recordings are, as a gesture, analogous to our museum-like approach to the operatic repertory, in which the old is fervently and lovingly preserved, and far more often performed than any new work. But beyond this, ever-evolving recording technologies may lead to the impression that nothing operatic need be ephemeral: that everything can be and should be preserved, for repeated enjoyment and, we might fondly imagine, for the edification of future listeners. This new sense of all-encompassing permanence is of course comforting, but it encourages us to forget that ephemerality is in some ways the essence of the theatrical. It is the forest fire that clears the terrain for new growth, a purging that even ancient practices constantly need. As we have noted throughout this history, new operas appeared in dazzling profusion precisely in those eras when the past was utterly fungible and when the ephemeral held no terrors. Opera's survival in the era of recordings turns out to be full of strategic complications.

Richard Wagner, although certainly not lacking a lively sense of his own world-historical importance, nonetheless considered as early as the 1850s the possibility that permanence and ephemerality could become entwined in a dance of death. In those years, in exile from Germany, he was at work on the four libretti of what would become *Der Ring des Nibelungen*; by 1856 he had finished the music for *Das Rheingold* and *Die Walküre*. The epic scope of the *Ring* was now clear, but Wagner found himself in the alienating position of working entirely in the abstract. There was no foreseeable opportunity for a performance: indeed, there would be no staging of the entire *Ring* for a further two decades. Being no stranger to the consolations of a sudden philosophical impulse, he turned necessity into virtue, and began to imagine radical alternatives to the drear weight of conventional operatic production. In 1850, writing to Theodor Uhlig about *Siegfrieds Tod* (a libretto he had yet to set to music), he proposed a kind of temporary, one-time-only event:

> Here, in Zurich, where I now chance to be, and where many conditions are far from unfavourable, I should erect a rough theatre of planks and beams, according to my own plans, in a beautiful meadow near the city, and furnish it merely with the scenery and machinery necessary for *Siegfried*. Then I would select the best available artists and would invite them to come to Zurich. I should go about selecting my orchestra in the same way ... When everything was in order, I should give three performances of *Siegfried* in the course of a week; after the third, the theatre would be pulled down and the score burned.[2]

In 1855, he conceived of a *Ring* taking place on Lake Lucerne, to be staged on an archipelago of barges strung together especially for the performances, which would be dismantled and floated away afterwards.[3] A threat to burn the *Ring* scores, with allusions to their transcending normal performance standards, recurs through the 1850s and 1860s, as in this letter to Franz Liszt from March 1855:

> What I am creating at present shall never see the light except in perfectly congenial surroundings; on this I will in future concentrate all my strength, my pride, and my *resignation*. If I die before having produced these works, I shall leave them to you; and if you die without having been able to produce them in a dignified manner, you must burn them: let that be *settled*.[4]

Much of this was, of course, posturing mingled with self-pity. Wagner would not seriously have advocated that his work be consigned to oblivion, and the only reply open to his interlocutors was immediate and rallying protest. Yet it is still worth pausing over Wagner's radicalism, so contrary to the conservationist impulses already invading opera by 1850. As we have seen in earlier chapters, by this point in opera's history a repertory of past works in present performance was starting to be established. The idea of unassailable operatic masterpieces from the past – by Mozart and Beethoven in certain areas (especially where German was spoken), by Rossini, Bellini, Donizetti and Verdi everywhere else – was taking hold.

So Wagner's proposal calls forth a question: was there some alternative to this preservationist tendency, to the beginnings of the operatic museum; and if so what might it be? Wagner's al fresco *Ring* that would float away on the gentle swells of Lake Lucerne, his threats to burn scores rather than see them realized imperfectly, are fantasies. But there is a salutary irritant embedded in them. The optimism of earlier operatic eras, the practitioners for whom impermanence held few terrors: were they on to a strange truth? By the mid nineteenth century, that optimism was disappearing. By the mid twentieth century, halfway between Wagner and today, it had all but vanished. We live nowadays in an operatic time that is culturally pessimistic, one symptom of which is that transmission of works from the past is central to the enterprise.

Besides tending an ever-larger archive of video recordings and sound documents, curatorial fervour also manifests itself in the continuing industry of scholarly editions (of Handel, Mozart, Berlioz, Verdi, Wagner and many others). There are, admittedly, good arguments in favour of these editions. Occasionally they resurrect operas – or parts of operas – that were simply not performable before, because no scores were available (Rossini's *Il viaggio a Reims*, for example, or the original French version of Verdi's *Don Carlos*). And even when new editions do little more than lightly inflect the texts of works that have long been part of the repertoire (perhaps with new performance instructions or adjusted instrumentation), they may nevertheless suggest bracing new approaches. The irony is that the ancient operatic practice these editions purport to make available was often close to the opposite of careful and preservationist: it could be thrillingly lax and last minute, with a ready indulgence of cuts, re-scorings and pragmatic accommodations that would be unthinkable today. This chaotic situation is, after all, why so many operatic classics come down to us in such a messy, inconclusive state: why there can be no single authentic or definitive *Carmen* or *Don Carlos* or *Boris Godunov* or *Les Contes d'Hoffmann*; why these and many other operas – indeed, *most* other operas before the twentieth century – exist in competing versions, presenting a surplus of authorial and other intentions. The question then arises: to what ideal should authenticity be directed? To an ideal version of an opera, established through modern musicological methods of sifting and editing? Or to the original spirit of the enterprise?

Our desire to cling to the operatic past, finally, is not limited to mere revival of past works. We could even say that this particular conservatism is neither the most pervasive nor the most influential aspect of operatic nostalgia. What stands out even more dramatically is a ritual aspect in the ways and means by which new operas are commissioned by major houses in Europe and America, the rhetorical armament that surrounds the idea of contemporary opera. This ritual is full of irony. Those involved in opera production, as well as critics whose livelihood depends on novelties being steadily supplied, tend to preach that such activity is essential to opera's future, its very lifeblood, a matter of survival. Simple contentment with the repertory and its treasury is, they assert, insufficient. But the metaphorical field we encounter in talk about new operatic composition is strangely antique, or at least constantly gestures back in time: we must encourage the next Mozart, the next Verdi. On 3 January 2014, the *New York Times* music critics published a collective article about the most successful contemporary operas of recent decades; it bore the headline 'Tomorrow's Valhalla' – as if aesthetic achievements might be measured by residence in the Care Home of the Gods, with proximity to Richard Wagner a prime marker of desirability.[5] In this context, today's prestigious operatic commissions could be seen less as the necessary road to the future, more as yet another attempt to hold on to the past – not this time in the form of its products, but rather in the form of its rituals and behaviour, its aura. In 1831, Milan's Teatro alla Scala commissioned Bellini's *Norma*, now a stalwart of the operatic repertory; 150 years later the same theatre commissioned Luciano Berio's *La vera storia* (1982). What continuity! What noble lineage!

But the endlessly repeated question – posed at the opening of the *New York Times* 'Valhalla' story – remains the same: 'Will it find a place in the repertory?' That question is a prime example of using the past as a measuring stick, even a cudgel. Another, more brutal form of it would be: 'Will it find a place of permanence, as *Figaro*, or *La traviata* or *Die Meistersinger* have?' The answer will in almost all cases be a resounding 'no'. But is joining the repertory the only exam worth passing? For long stretches of history, operas were written to be enjoyed for a season and then cast aside to make way for other and possibly better ones. Operas were disposable, and that very disposability was a sign of fervency and creativity.

CURATORSHIP BY THE NUMBERS

The last fifty years have actually witnessed a global increase in numbers of opera houses, with new institutions springing up in many venues that, while they may have had such theatres in the nineteenth century, then lost them in the early twentieth. This has been the case in the UK and the USA, with revived regional opera houses in the former, and newer institutions such as Santa Fe Opera or Glimmerglass in the latter. Opera is also renewing its global reach, spreading again (as it did in the nineteenth century) in newly prosperous Asian countries – as evinced by the Guangzhou Opera House, which opened in 2010. Asian film nowadays features opera in much the same way as Western film did in earlier times, as a source of emotional openness and a setting for romance. In Farhan Akhtar's *Dil Chahta Hai* (The Heart Desires, 2001), the Hindi-speaking hero and heroine visit the Sydney Opera House and swoon to an opera especially invented for the film but seemingly in imitation of French *tragédie lyrique*.

This fresh globalization of opera, the increasing numbers of opera venues around the world, has been accompanied by an expansion of the repertory. But the 'new' operas that have been thus assisted into the repertory are typically works rescued from opera's past. The database at operabase.com provides invaluable numbers – inevitably incomplete but the best we have. During a recent five-year stretch (from the 2009/10 to the 2013/14 seasons), there were c. 18,500 opera productions globally (a third of them in Germany), in c. 750 cities (Vienna, Berlin, Paris and Moscow at the head; neither London nor New York, let alone any city in Italy, can at present compete with these elite four) in around sixty countries. The picture is clear: the primary creative energies of this global industry were dedicated not to creating new works; they were to interpreting masterpieces from the past. The top three composers (again measured in numbers of productions of their operas rather than total numbers of performances) are Verdi (3323), Mozart (2386) and Puccini (2322); Wagner (1170), Rossini (1086) and Donizetti (1058) are the next three. These are the bedrock of the present-day operatic repertory, and they constitute a large proportion of the total (far more than half). The first living composer to enter the list, Philip Glass with seventy-nine revivals, comes in at 40th and he is way out in front among the race of the living: next – at joint 73rd – come Jake Heggie (b. 1961) and Peter Maxwell Davies (b. 1934), both with twenty-nine revivals. True, there were around 300 world premieres during the five-year period, and around 500 living composers saw their operas performed; but the vast majority of these composers had only one or two premieres or revivals. As we saw in Chapter 20, when a recent work like George Benjamin's *Written on Skin* is taken up by multiple theatres in a very short space of time, the phenomenon makes headlines.

Many people whose business is opera, and who thus make their living from its present, history-soaked existence, find it tragic, even morally reprehensible, that new operas do not compete successfully with Verdi's, Mozart's and Puccini's. Here is David Pountney, a distinguished opera director of the last thirty years, speaking at the dawn of the new millennium:

> Those who do nothing more than live like parasites off the past I cast into a particularly unpleasant circle of hell. There is no greater betrayal of custodianship than that. Therefore, the future of opera for me is not about how many more performances of *La Bohème* there will be in the next century, nor about whether this *Bohème* is dressed up as something else. It is about which stories we would like to tell in our new century, and what music we will tell them with, and which audience will we find to listen to our stories . . . I am talking about new work. I am talking about a hard and rigorous truth that unless you are feeding the new, you have no right to live off the old. Sadly, there are very few opera houses anywhere in the world who could hold up their hands and claim to fulfil that condition. So let me say it again, loud and clear: what we inherit is an incredible cornucopia. Those who exploit it without adding to it are betraying the heritage of which they purport to be the custodians, and they should be cast out![6]

There are strong words here, but the remedies Pountney suggests later in his piece have a familiar ring. Embracing ephemerality as a positive phenomenon is too radical to make even the tiniest appearance. Instead, we find suggestions for guaranteeing popularity and endurance. Composers should espouse more approachable idioms, divesting themselves of modernist sympathies and a love of complexity. Theatre managements should be tougher, insisting on works the public will enjoy. Above all there should be much more subsidy: governments, regions, cities and private institutions should pay generously and often, ensuring that every theatre can provide the elaborate life-support systems new operas require.

What Pountney does not face is that one aspect of the operatic industry – its affection for the past in *all* its forms – is self-evidently a blockade of sorts, even in the most physical sense. Our newest opera houses are impressive indeed, but like almost all those that have survived from the past they are overwhelmingly geared towards the consumption of certain kinds of now-ancient opera. Their auditoria suit nineteenth-century works with large orchestras and with singers powerful enough to penetrate to the furthest reaches. New creations, written to be premiered in these spaces, are thus pre-ordained by architecture to attempt the same manner, a task for which few composers have immediate models, and in which their past experience (almost inevitably with 'pure' instrumental music of much smaller proportions) is often a hindrance. Several years ago, we talked to a composer who was about to complete a commission for a major US opera house. He freely admitted that he found many recent operas unbearable, and said straight out that works subjecting listeners to hours-long exposure to atonal idioms were doomed from the outset (he recalled how short *Wozzeck* is, how rapidly its scenes change). He was also aware that his particular enterprise had soaked up approximately $2m of other people's money, and that he had no experience of writing extended works for the stage. He remained, though, optimistic: he passionately believed that his opera would be – must be – different from what had gone before; he was convinced that it would communicate to audiences when countless others had failed. His attitude was extraordinary testimony to the personal conviction required to undertake anything of this creative magnitude. Just as extraordinary, though, was the extent to which hope could triumph over the collective experience.

If the blockade-like force of the institutions and their attitudes, the rhetoric and the rituals, the scholarly editions, the treasury of recordings and all the other features of the museum, are given only negative value, what is the alternative? Would it be possible to imagine a future in which opera regained some form of cultural optimism? Perhaps the marvellous 'operas' yet to be written will be those that do not resemble any of its past forms, just as an avant-garde, all-staged, part-electronic, sung-without-vibrato wonder such as Glass's *Einstein on the Beach* is interesting and engrossing precisely in being a non-opera. Perhaps such renegade pieces are the fireflies, the workshopped, performance-art operas that challenge the limits of the very word: Rinde Eckert's *And God Created Great Whales* (2000) is another case in point.

The arch-radical Pierre Boulez, patrolling the streets at the high noon of modernism, would certainly have none of the past, even architecturally. In 1967, he despaired of the fact that

> the new German opera houses certainly look very modern – from outside; but inside they have remained extremely old fashioned. It's nearly impossible to produce a work of contemporary opera in a theatre in which, predominantly, repertory pieces are performed. It is really unthinkable. The most expensive solution would be to blow the opera houses up. Don't you think that would also be the most elegant solution?[7]

The various air forces of the Second World War had of course made significant progress in that direction (see Figure 46), but – two decades later – Boulez wanted a more complete denouement. And he was surely right about one thing: that any new form of cultural optimism must be based on relinquishing at least some aspects of the museum. Insisting on the hoary ritual of commissioning new operas (works that are inescapably Grand Opera raised from the dead) would only be effective if it came with a corollary that virtually no one – perhaps these days not even Boulez – seems to want: the limiting or radically altering or simply forgetting of old operas, and of the spaces, mostly so redolent of the nineteenth century, in which they are performed.

Why is the operatic situation so different from the relatively buoyant one in sister arts? Think of the media frenzy and potential financial rewards circulating around the Turner Prize, or the brisk enterprise of new spoken drama in the West End or on Broadway. The answer is both too obvious and too fraught. By now, we have enough distance from 1945 to be able to look back at the postwar years and identify the main sustainers of the modernist repertory; several of them have been discussed in the previous chapters. But anomalies aside (the result of chronological oddity, such as Stravinsky or Poulenc writing opera late in life, or of geographical oddity, such as an English radical making his own operatic microclimate in chilly East Anglia), how many operas have 'entered into Valhalla' since the Second World War? It is much easier to make a list of high-profile ephemera between, say, 1950 and

1980. Here are ten, all by composers with formidable reputations, all premiered (or commissioned to be premiered) at the highest level, most with eminent literary associations:

L'incantesimo (Enchantment, 1943/1952) by Italo Montemezzi (1875–1952); broadcast premiere (NBC Symphony Orchestra) in 1943; stage premiere at the Arena di Verona in 1952.

Troilus and Cressida (1954) by William Walton (1902–83), based on Chaucer; premiere at Covent Garden, conducted by Sir Malcolm Sargent; US premiere (1955) at San Francisco Opera, then seen at New York City Opera (1955) and La Scala (1956).

Assassinio nella cattedrale (Murder in the Cathedral, 1958) by Ildebrando Pizzetti (1880–1968), after T. S. Eliot's play; premiere at La Scala.

Don Rodrigo (1964) by Alberto Ginastera (1916–83); commissioned by the city of Buenos Aires and premiered there at the Teatro Colón. Plácido Domingo sang the title role at the US premiere (New York City Opera, 1966).

Miss Julie (1965) by Ned Rorem (1923–), after Strindberg; commissioned by and premiered at the New York City Opera.

Antony and Cleopatra (1966) by Samuel Barber (1910–81), after Shakespeare, with a libretto by Franco Zeffirelli; premiered (enormous cast, enormous expense) at the opening of the new Metropolitan Opera House. It was dropped from the Met's repertory after the initial performances and has had only sporadic revivals since.

Der Besuch der alten Dame (The Visit of the Old Lady, 1971) by Gottfried von Einem (1918–96); premiered at the Vienna Staatsoper; German premiere at the Deutsche Oper, Berlin (1972).

Yerma (1971) by Heitor Villa-Lobos (1887–1959), after Federico García Lorca; written in 1955–6, premiered by the Santa Fe Opera fifteen years later.

Lord Byron (1972) by Virgil Thomson (1896–1989); commissioned by the Ford Foundation for the Metropolitan Opera, but never produced there; amateur premiere at the Juilliard School in New York City.

Paradise Lost (1978) by Krzysztof Penderecki (1933–), after Milton; premiered at the Lyric Opera, Chicago, then given at La Scala (1979).

Is it tragic or morally reprehensible that such works are not revived? There are doubtless beautiful moments in many of them; but they were brought into existence and then fell silent.

We have stressed that brief existence has been the absolute norm for operatic works throughout history, but the moment has come to tease out the more uncomfortable historical lessons from this fact. Even when the operatic repertory began to become fixed in the mid nineteenth century, a glance at (say) Paris Opéra posters will remind us that huge, dead-on-arrival hopefuls regularly littered the landscape. Louis Niedermeyer's *Marie Stuart*, to take a random example from 1844, had a star cast, a fashionable plot and a hit song, and even earned for its composer enlistment in the *Légion d'honneur*; all to no lasting avail. Nor was this just at the hidebound Opéra: the repertory of the coming Parisian venue of the 1850s and 1860s, the Théâtre Lyrique, contains many now-forgotten premieres, mixed with a small number of new successes and revivals of legendary works like *Don Giovanni*.[8] But, here and now, the moral to be taken from such historical givens becomes uncertain. For one thing, beginning in the later twentieth century, the numbers changed in significant ways. Nowadays the proportion of successful new arrivals in comparison with repertory revivals has grown so minuscule as to constitute an immense gulf.

We could, of course, use this circumstance as an argument for profligacy, suggesting that sheer numbers of trials form a necessary base from which the rare diamond will emerge, that we must continue to commission new operas because we seek a one-in-a-thousand hit. Instead, though, it might be salutary to confront a more difficult thought: the thought that opera's heyday might be finite. Opera once flourished, and diamonds appeared in significant numbers; but that was in past times, in cultures that no longer exist. Why assume that our present times, which are so radically different, so alien to those of the past, will constitute equally fertile ground for this strange art?

The mystery of the rare diamond is complicated. At the Théâtre Lyrique, in among all the non-starters, there also occurred the premiere of Gounod's *Faust* (1859), which would become over the next century one of the most often-played operas in the world. What's more, *Faust* established itself as a repertory piece almost immediately; although it was certainly innovative, there was never a sense that the work needed time and effort on the part of general audiences. The *Faust* story has, then, a different moral to teach. It is that the works which persist – which stand out, are revived and repeated, recalled with relish, thought worth any expense – do so because they supply pleasure to the many, not just to the few. If this is the case, the statistics about contemporary opera tell us that many of the newest works fall down on that very specific job, while doing another – satisfying the elite and the insiders – quite well.

FRAGMENTS AND THE LOSS OF MEANING

After around 1950, repertory opera became a script for *Regieoper*, for a marvellous and entertaining parade of reinterpretations. As we have seen, it also had a complicated life as a theme and a source of musical material in films. There has also been a wide dissemination of opera into true mass culture, but this tends to involve particles, the tiniest operatic scraps, fragments from opera that have small shards of meaning. Do such fragments recruit anyone in the mass audience to the enjoyment of opera per se? In Pixar's animated film *Finding Nemo* (2003), a clownfish searching for his lost son is urged on his way by mackerels who, by singing with vibrato and schooling to form the shape of the Sydney Opera House, tell him wordlessly where he needs to go. In 2010–11 the child phenomenon Jackie Evancho (b. 2000) made a fortune by holding a microphone very close to her mouth and using rolled 'r's and vibrato to imitate operatic singing. Evancho, the youngest solo artist ever to have an album go platinum, can be heard on her CD *Dream With Me* singing an eerie 'Nessun dorma'. The version shows how far her vast audience is from worrying about Puccini's last work. 'Nessun dorma' sexless? Recall the text: 'Oh Princess . . . On your mouth I will whisper my name when dawn breaks, and my kiss will dissolve the silence that makes you mine!' When this aria is sung, in only vaguely approximate Italian, by a prepubescent girl soprano wearing a white dress with sash, what's bewildering is not the child performer or her profits, it is rather the burial rite for opera's ground note of adult passion, the loss of meaning and context.

That question about potential new customers sounds a grim note. Although the second half of our last century saw new opera companies spring up in many parts of the globe, recent signs are not always cheering. As the second edition of this history goes to press, the New York City Opera has gone dark, lost to a bankruptcy that some blamed on its embrace of 'difficult' new operas. The Metropolitan is also facing serious financial troubles, awash in tickets it cannot sell (many blame the HD broadcasts for keeping the core audience away) and facing costs that were only appropriate to a Gilded Age when the cultural capital granted by opera was thought to be worth its high price. Lacking the government subsidies that cushion institutions through bad financial times, opera in America may be the canary in the global mine, its breath beginning to falter. The question is whether this predicts outcomes elsewhere in the world, particularly in Europe (still the overwhelming source of most operas and opera performances), where subsidies as well as a deeper cultural investment in high art might mean a different outcome.

EVOLUTIONARY TURN

Is there nevertheless some cause for optimism? As we said a little earlier, perhaps the most beautiful and transfixing operas still to be written might not be 'opera' at all in any previous sense of the word. There are many hybrids and new creatures we could consider. In this category fall many works by Glass (note the operabase.com statistics, quoted earlier, which make him by such a margin the most popular living opera composer), whose brilliance in writing music for drama extends to musical stage spectacles, multi-media theatre like *Einstein on the Beach*, and operas like *Satyagraha* and *The Voyage* (1992), with their hypnotic allure. Glass's minimalism involves treating voices as chant, sometimes in repeated melodic cells, sometimes as solo voices but often as a vocal collective that seems like one voice multiplied into many. His harmonic idiom, those gradual changes rung on chord progressions, mysteriously and perpetually moving, conform to no previous historical operatic precedent; nor does his vocal writing. Both the present authors recall experiences of his operas as forms of acoustic delight that, in involving leisurely metamorphoses and frequent intervals of peace, were transfixing. But it may be important that Glass's operatic music does not demand utter attentiveness at every moment. By allowing the audience the freedom to drift, such music recaptures a very ancient operatic virtue: the composer offers, if you will, an *invitation* to listen and be charmed, not an *edict*. It is in this sense no accident that Glass is also a successful film music composer. His music for opera and film, while beautiful and emotionally astute, is also modest in the sense that it knows how to make room for other theatrical components: for what is seen; for words, characters, their actions and mental states; for the listener's participation. Good film music composers know when to be silent, when not to have music at all. One thing that good opera composers need to have is an analogous though not completely parallel wisdom about music – as a collaborator and not a dictator.

Indeed, it may even be that opera is undergoing a significant evolutionary turn via the 'cinematic', becoming a form of art-for-the-screen. This does not simply mean that the most common mode of operatic consumption in the twenty-first century is through Internet streaming of video clips, DVDs and HD broadcasts; or that the primacy of attendance at the theatre (rather than the cinema) has been challenged. Nor does it simply mean that – as mentioned a short time ago – the comforts and conventions of cinema and TV have begun to inflect its staging. More radical still is that this new evolutionary turn has begun to impinge on the basic conception of new operas. Screen media are entering the genetic makeup of the genre.

As a test case, we might reconsider Benjamin's *Written on Skin*, discussed in terms of its operatic heritage in Chapter 20. What is immediately striking about its staging as manifested via DVD (a version released soon after the premiere, and based on that premiere's staging) is the degree to which we see advanced cinematic vocabulary put to use in a live performance, creating a strange hybrid form, a new operatic flavour. There are carefully composed medium shots, in which the camera is positioned where no theatre-spectator eye could possibly exist, seeming to be right there among the characters on stage. There are shot/reverse shot edits. The singers have been coached to act with eye movements and glances, something that would not be legible from the usual theatrical distance. Most significant of all, there is a particular camera shot – the set and characters seen from above, in a bird's eye view – that is Hitchcockian in its odd menace. In those shots the camera is far above the action, but the voices and orchestra are still heard as if one's ear were down there in the house. This leads to a disquieting cognitive split between sight and hearing: it suddenly seems as if we are looking at a movie scene but hearing a separate opera soundtrack, an effect enhanced by the fact that in the bird's eye view you see only the tops of the singers' heads, not their mouths moving. The DVD is taping a live performance, but this staging has been imagined to create something chimerical specifically for the recording medium: a live movie.[9]

That's merely the result of a too-artful DVD, one might say: it's still a traditional opera. But then the libretto sometimes recalls clichés of serial-killer talk – dissociative addressing of one's victim in the third person, for example – as in films like *The Silence of the Lambs* (1991), not to mention woman-as-erotic-maniac and other cinematic treats. There is even a quality in the music's frequent word-painting that aligns it with one of film and TV music's great glories: so-called rendered sound, musical heightening of an image or noise. The difference is that in film we *see* what is being imitated in sound (trembling water becomes shimmering percussion), while in *Written on Skin* the objects imitated in music are verbally *described*. The alchemy is mysterious, but although the piece is conventionally modern-operatic in many respects, there's a sense of a new species emerging: one for which the DVD, in using film techniques, becomes the work's truest, best home. Only in the DVD do all the connections emerge. The package affirms the degree to which the new species has been shaped – in its use of music, in its ways of enticing an audience, by modern, non-operatic media.

THAT'S OPERA. JUST A LOT OF PEOPLE IN COSTUMES FALLING IN LOVE AND DYING

Opera has always been a peculiar form of drama, and will remain for ever so. It took shape gradually in the seventeenth century, and for around 200 years was a dominant – if not, by the nineteenth century, the most elevated – form of elite culture. The monuments of the operatic tradition continue to fascinate us, and have proved themselves remarkably well able to adapt to changed cultural and political circumstances; indeed, the fact that operas have continued to be composed for so long, and that the art form is expanding its global dissemination at a time when other types of 'classical' music are severely threatened, should surely be a cue for jubilation. Even if this particular form of drama with music is now mostly a museum of past musical works – as are the madrigal and motet, or for that matter the four-movement symphony – dystopian prognostications about its endurance are probably unfounded. And to take the longest historical views, far longer than opera's last 400 years, is to realize that the arts in which actions and passions go hand in hand with music – with or without singing – have endured for millennia, and show no signs of present collapse. Drama has, at most times and in most cultures, always enjoyed more or less elaborate musical accompaniment – a circumstance that, as we saw many chapters ago, stimulated the first operatic experiments. As we write these lines, and as you read them, acres of music are being created around the world to accompany drama, whether in films or TV or for the stage or to underpin proliferating forms of virtual entertainment. Most of it will be transitory and soon forgotten. Sometimes even the media that stimulate it will disappear; this too has always been the case. Other technologies, other phenomena will replace them. Opera has been part of this larger history of drama and music, and a magnificent one – one that above all celebrates the human singing voice. So long as we have theatrical spaces suited to the purpose, and performers willing to devote themselves to realizing its complex glories, operas will continue to be performed, and will continue to articulate some of the drama and complexities of human experience in ways no other art form can match. Many of the trees in this vast forest are very old and very grand. Their beauty and the shadows they cast are immense.

References

1. INTRODUCTION

1. Paul Robinson, 'A Deconstructive Postscript: Reading Libretti and Misreading Opera', in Arthur Groos and Roger Parker, eds., *Reading Opera* (Princeton, 1988), 328–46; here 345.
2. Enrico Fubini, *Music & Culture in Eighteenth-Century Europe: A Source Book* (Chicago, 1994), 209.
3. Richard Wagner, 'Der Freischütz: To the Paris Public', in William Ashton Ellis, trans., *Richard Wagner's Prose Works vol. 1: The Art Work of the Future, and Other Works* (1895; repr. Lincoln, 1993), 169–82; original in French in *Gazette musicale de Paris*, 23 and 30 May 1841.
4. Robert Bailey, 'Siegfried or Tristan?', in *Prelude and Transfiguration from Tristan und Isolde: The Norton Critical Score* (New York, 1986), 5–6.
5. Karl Gustav Fellerer, 'Mozarts Zauberflöte als Efenoper', in *Symbolae Historiae Musicae*, eds. Friedrich Wilhelm Riedel and Hubert Unverricht (Mainz, 1976), 229–47.
6. Philip Gossett, *Divas and Scholars: Performing Italian Opera* (Chicago, 2006), 124.
7. Michael Barron, *Auditorium Acoustics and Architectural Design* (London, 1993), 318.
8. *The New York Times*, 14 October 1883.
9. Anthony Tommasini, *The New York Times*, 1 January 2007.
10. Denis Forman, *The Good Opera Guide* (London, 1996), 264.
11. Alessandro Luzio, ed., *Carteggi verdiani*, vol. 1 (Rome, 1935), 111.
12. Francesco Milizia, *Complete Formal and Material Treatise on the Theatre* (1794); cited in Fubini, *Music & Culture in Eighteenth-Century Europe*, 255.
13. Max Winkler, *A Penny from Heaven* (New York, 1951), 238.
14. Richard Osborne, *Rossini*, 2nd edn (Oxford, 2007), 152.
15. Gaetano Cesari and Alessandro Luzio, eds., *I copialettere di Giuseppe Verdi* (Milan, 1913), 26.

2. OPERA'S FIRST CENTENNIAL

1. For a classic iteration, see Donald Jay Grout, *A Short History of Opera* (1947; 4th edn, with Hermine Weigel Williams, New York, 2003).
2. Henry Maty, *A New Review, with Literary Curiosities and Literary Intelligence* (London, 1783), 133.
3. Waldo Selden Pratt, *The History of Music: A Handbook and Guide for Students* (New York, 1927), 151–2.
4. Richard Wagner, *Opera and Drama* (1851), trans. William Ashton Ellis (repr. New York, 1995), 26.
5. Gottfried Wilhelm Fink, *Wesen und Geschichte der Oper* (Leipzig, 1838), 89, 98.
6. Ellen Rosand, *Opera in Seventeenth-Century Venice: The Creation of a Genre* (Berkeley, 1991), 35.
7. F. W. Sternfeld, *The Birth of Opera* (Oxford, 1995), 87–8.
8. Thomas Forrest Kelly, *First Nights: Five Musical Premieres* (New Haven, 2000), 49.
9. Cristoforo Ivanovich, *Minerva al tavolino* (1681), cited in Piero Weiss, *Opera: A History in Documents* (New York, 2002), 39.
10. Rosand, *Opera in Seventeenth-Century Venice*, 223–5.
11. Charles Burney, *A General History of Music* (London, 1776–89), Vol. III, 790.
12. John Rosselli, *Singers of Italian Opera: The History of a Profession* (Cambridge, 1992), 12.
13. Ibid., 13.
14. Rosand, *Opera in Seventeenth-Century Venice*, 232.
15. Denis Stevens, *The Letters of Claudio Monteverdi* (Cambridge, 1980), 117.
16. Rosand, *Opera in Seventeenth-Century Venice*, 22.
17. Ibid., 45.
18. Saint-Évremond, letter to the Duke of Buckingham (1669 or 1670), quoted in Weiss, *Opera*, 53.
19. Rosand, *Opera in Seventeenth-Century Venice*, 133–5.
20. *Giasone* is discussed by Rosand, *Opera in Seventeenth-Century Venice*, 346–8 and 358–9; also by Susan McClary, 'Gender Ambiguities and Erotic Excess in Seventeenth-Century Venetian Opera', in Mark Franko and Annette Richards, eds., *Acting on the Past: Historical Performance Across the Disciplines* (Hanover, NH, 2000), 177–200; and by Roger Freitas, *Portrait of a Castrato* (Cambridge, 2009), 143.
21. Memoirs of Jean-Jacques Bouchard, cited in Weiss, *Opera*, 33.
22. See Bettina Varwig, 'Schütz's *Dafne* and the German Imagination', in Nikolaus Bacht, ed., *Music, Theatre and Politics in Germany: 1848 to the Third Reich* (Aldershot, 2006), 115–35.

23. See the entry on 'Masque', *The New Grove Dictionary of Opera* (London, 1992), vol. 3, 253.

3. *OPERA SERIA*

1. Ellen Rosand, *Opera in Seventeenth-Century Venice: The Creation of a Genre* (Berkeley, 1991), 22.
2. John Rosselli, *Singers of Italian Opera: The History of a Profession* (Cambridge, 1992), 56.
3. Ibid., 122–3.
4. Charles de Brosses, quoted in Piero Weiss, *Opera: A History in Documents* (New York, 2002), 85.
5. Suzanne Aspden, '"An Infinity of Factions": Opera in Eighteenth-Century Britain and the Undoing of Society', *Cambridge Opera Journal*, 9/1 (1997), pp. 1–19; here 8.
6. Charles de Brosses, quoted in Weiss, *Opera*, 85.
7. Aspden, 'An Infinity of Factions', 11–13.
8. Moreschi's 1904 version of the Bach/Gounod 'Ave Maria' is available on http://www.archive.org/details/AlessandroMoreschi.
9. Rosselli, *Singers of Italian Opera*, 39.
10. Rosand, *Opera in Seventeenth-Century Venice*, 400 (translation adapted slightly).
11. Ibid., 275 (translation adapted slightly).
12. Weiss, *Opera*, 53.
13. Joseph Kerman, *Opera as Drama* (1956; rev. edn, Berkeley, 1988), 39–57.
14. Lorenzo Bianconi and Giorgio Pestelli, eds., *Opera on Stage* (Chicago, 2002), 71.
15. Otto Erich Deutsch, *Handel: A Documentary Biography* (New York, 1955), 33.
16. Mark W. Stahura, 'Handel's Haymarket Theater', in Mark A. Radice, ed., *Opera in Context: Essays on Historical Staging from the Late Renaissance to the Time of Puccini* (Portland, Ore., 1998), 103.
17. Ibid., 104.
18. Christopher Hogwood, *Handel* (London, 2007), 63–4.
19. *The Spectator*, 6 March 1710.
20. Entry on 'Orlando', *The New Grove Dictionary of Opera* (London, 1992), vol. 3, 757.

4. DISCIPLINE

1. Charles Burney, *The Present State of Music in France and Italy* (London, 1773), 225.

2. John Rosselli, *Singers of Italian Opera: The History of a Profession* (Cambridge, 1992), 83.
3. Samuel Richardson, *Pamela*, iv.111–12.
4. John Mainwaring, *Memoirs of the Life of the Late George Frederic Handel* (London, 1760), 110.
5. Piero Weiss, *Opera: A History in Documents* (New York, 2002), 98–9.
6. Ibid., 102.
7. Ibid., 73.
8. Enrico Fubini, *Music & Culture in Eighteenth-Century Europe: A Source Book* (Chicago, 1994), 203.
9. Lorenzo Bianconi and Giorgio Pestelli, eds., *Opera Production and Its Resources* (Chicago, 1998), 247.
10. Ibid., 249
11. Charles Burney, *A General History of Music* (London, 1776–89), vol. 4, 547.
12. Charles Burney, *An Account of the Musical Performances . . . in Commemoration of Handel* (London, 1785), 33.
13. Fubini, *Music & Culture in Eighteenth-Century Europe*, 209–10
14. Ibid., 215.
15. Weiss, *Opera*, 108.
16. Julie Ann Sadie, ed., *Companion to Baroque Music* (Berkeley and Los Angeles, 1990), 138.
17. Weiss, *Opera*, 119.
18. Fubini, *Music & Culture in Eighteenth-Century Europe*, 238.
19. Ibid., 249.
20. Weiss, *Opera*, 98.
21. Burney, *A General History*, vol. 4, 495.
22. Simon Goldhill, 'Who Killed Chevalier Gluck?', in Goldhill, *Victorian Culture and Classical Antiquity* (Princeton, 2011), 92.
23. Adolf Bernhard Marx, *Gluck und die Oper* (Berlin, 1863), 313.
24. Charles Burney, *Music in Germany* (1775), cited in Patricia Howard, C. W. *Gluck: Orfeo* (Cambridge, 1981), 57.
25. Jean-François Marmontel, *Essay on the Progress of Music in France* (1777), cited in Fubini, *Music & Culture in Eighteenth-Century Europe*, 370.
26. Goldhill, 'Who Killed Chevalier Gluck?', 87.
27. Ibid., 98.
28. E. T. A. Hoffmann, 'Ritter Gluck', in *Tales of E. T. A. Hoffmann*, eds. and trans. Leonard J. Kent and Elizabeth C. Knight (Chicago, 1969), 9–10.
29. Letter to Leopold Mozart, 8 November 1780; in Eric Blom, ed., *Mozart's Letters* (Harmondsworth, 1968), 148.
30. Ibid., 147.
31. Alfred Einstein, *Gluck*, trans. Eric Blom (London, 1936), 151.

5. *OPERA BUFFA* AND MOZART'S LINE OF BEAUTY

1. Piero Weiss, *Opera: A History in Documents* (New York, 2002), 89.
2. Thomas Busby, *A General History of Music from the Earliest Times to the Present*, vol. 2 (London, 1819), 447–8. The specific sentence about the 'merit' of Galuppi's opera surpassing any other '*burletta* in England' is plagiarized from Charles Burney's *General History of Music from the Early Ages to the Present*, vol. 4 (London, 1776), 474.
3. Goethe, *Italian Journey*, trans. Robert H. Heitner, in *Goethe's Collected Works*, ed. Victor Lange, Eric A. Blackall and Cyrus Hamlin, vol. 6 (Boston, 1989), 64; discussed in Mary Hunter, *The Culture of Opera Buffa in Mozart's Vienna* (Princeton, 1999), 44.
4. 7 May 1783; in Eric Blom, ed., *Mozart's Letters* (Harmondsworth, 1956), 208.
5. Nicholas Till, *Mozart and the Enlightenment* (London, 1992).
6. 17 December 1781; in Blom, *Mozart's Letters*, 186–7.
7. This is one of the theses of Joseph Kerman's treatment of operatic history in his *Opera as Drama* (1956; rev. edn, Berkeley, 1988).
8. Mark Everist, 'Enshrining Mozart: Don Giovanni and the Viardot Circle', in *19th-Century Music*, 25/2–3 (2001), 165–89; here 176.
9. For an extensive account of *Don Giovanni* fervour from the 1780s to the 1850s, see Otto Jahn, *Life of Mozart* (1856–9), trans. Pauline D. Townsend, vol. 3 (London, 1882), 134–45. For more recent fervour, see Bernard Williams, 'Don Giovanni as an Idea', in Julian Rushton, ed., *W. A. Mozart: Don Giovanni* (Cambridge, 1981), 81–91.
10. Cited in Enrico Fubini, *Music & Culture in Eighteenth-Century Europe: A Source Book* (Chicago, 1994), 388.
11. Excerpt from *Either/Or* cited in Weiss, 151.
12. Jahn, *Life of Mozart*, vol. 3, 134–45.
13. Hermann Abert, *W. A. Mozart* ([1923–4] New Haven, 2007), 632.

6. SINGING AND SPEAKING BEFORE 1800

1. Richard Wagner, *Opera and Drama* (1851), trans. William Ashton Ellis (repr. New York, 1995), 112–13.
2. Cited in Thomas Betzwieser, *Sprechen und Singen: Ästhetik und Erscheinungsformen der Dialogoper* (Stuttgart and Weimar, 2002), 1. The source is an 1816 review by Hoffmann of Méhul's *Ariodant* (1799).
3. Thomas Baumann, ed., *Mozart: Die Entführung aus dem Serail* (Cambridge, 1987), 77.
4. Royal Opera House production, directed by Elijah Moshinsky; first seen in May 2001.

5. Betzwieser, *Sprechen und Singen*, 75.
6. Letter dated 26 September 1781; in Eric Blom, ed., *Mozart's Letters* (Harmondsworth, 1968), 181.
7. Piero Weiss, *Opera: A History in Documents* (New York, 2002), 137–8.
8. John T. Scott, ed., *Jean-Jacques Rousseau: Essay on the Origin of Language and Writings Related to Music* (Dartmouth, 1999), 497.
9. Emily Anderson, *Letters of Mozart and His Family* (London, 1985), 631.

7. THE GERMAN PROBLEM

1. Howard Bushnell, *Maria Malibran: A Biography of the Singer* (University Park and London, 1979), 196.
2. Richard Wagner, *Pilgrimage to Beethoven and Other Essays*, trans. William Ashton Ellis (repr. New York, 1994), 36.
3. Herbert Weinstock, *Rossini: A Biography* (New York, 1968), 118.
4. Carl Dahlhaus, *Nineteenth-Century Music* (Berkeley, 1989), 8–15.
5. Edmond Michotte, *Richard Wagner's Visit to Rossini* (Paris, 1860), trans. and ed. Herbert Weinstock (Chicago, 1968), 98.
6. Mark Everist, 'Enshrining Mozart: Don Giovanni and the Viardot Circle', in *19th-Century Music*, 25/2–3 (2001), 165–89; here 178.
7. Peter Mercer-Taylor, *The Cambridge Companion to Mendelssohn* (Cambridge, 2004), 19.
8. Richard Wagner, *Prose Works*, Vol. 7, trans. William Ashton Ellis (London, 1898), 179.
9. John Warrack, ed., *Carl Maria von Weber: Writings on Music* (Cambridge, 1981), 338.
10. Entry on '*Der Freischütz*', in *The New Grove Dictionary of Opera* (London, 1992), vol. 2, 299.

8. ROSSINI AND THE TRANSITION

1. Stendhal [Henri Beyle], *Life of Rossini*, trans. Richard N. Coe (London, 1956), 1.
2. Giovanni Pacini, *Le mie memorie artistiche* (Florence, 1865), 64.
3. Richard Osborne, *Rossini*, 2nd edn (Oxford, 2007), 126.
4. Ibid., 35.
5. Giuseppe Mazzini, *Filosofia della musica* (1836), ed. Marcello de Angelis (Florence, 1977), 53–4.
6. Ibid., 56.
7. Ibid., 56.
8. Stendhal, *Life of Rossini*, 65.

9. Philip Gossett, 'Introduction', Critical Edition of Vocal Score of *Tancredi* (Pesaro, 1984), xix.
10. Gossett, *Tancredi*, xvii.
11. Stendhal, *Life of Rossini*, 396.
12. Herbert Weinstock, *Rossini: A Biography* (New York, 1968), 345–7.
13. Paolo Fabbri, 'Rossini the Aesthetician', *Cambridge Opera Journal*, 6 (1994), 19–29; here 27.
14. Stendhal, *Life of Rossini*, 452.
15. Ibid., 239–40.
16. Ibid., 252.
17. Ibid., 237.
18. Ibid., 239.
19. Ibid., 251.

9. THE TENOR COMES OF AGE

1. Raymond Edward Priestley, *Antarctic Adventure: Scott's Northern Party* (New York, 1915), 93–4.
2. James Davies, '"Veluti in speculum": The Twilight of the Castrato', *Cambridge Opera Journal*, 17/3 (2005), 271–301; here 276.
3. Ibid., 271.
4. Ibid., 271.
5. Heather Hadlock, 'On the Cusp between the Past and the Future: The Mezzo-Soprano Romeo of Bellini's *I Capuleti*', *Opera Quarterly*, 17/3 (2001), 399–422; here 400.
6. Gilbert-Louis Duprez, *Souvenirs d'un chanteur* (Paris, 1880), 75.
7. Entry on 'Duprez', in *The New Grove Dictionary of Opera* (London, 1992), vol. 1, 1281.
8. This and all subsequent quotations in the paragraph are from Annalisa Bini and Jeremy Commons, eds., *Le prime rappresentazioni delle opere di Donizetti nella stampa coeva* (Rome, 1997), 344–55.
9. Carmelo Neri, ed., *Lettere di Vincenzo Bellini (1819–1835)* (Palermo, 1991), 287.
10. Ursula Kramer (with Peter Branscombe), entry on 'Unger, Caroline', in *The New Grove Dictionary of Music* (London, 2001), vol. 26, 72–3.
11. Guido Zavadini, *Donizetti: vita, musiche, epistolario* (Bergamo, 1948), 379.
12. Susan McClary, *Feminine Endings: Music, Gender and Sexuality* (Minneapolis, 1991), 93–9.
13. Mary Ann Smart, 'The Silencing of Lucia', *Cambridge Opera Journal*, 4/2 (1992), 119–41.
14. Romana Margherita Pugliese, 'The Origins of *Lucia di Lammermoor*'s Cadenza', *Cambridge Opera Journal*, 16/1 (2004), 23–42.

15. Gustave Flaubert, *Madame Bovary*, Part 2, Chapter 15, trans. Eleanor Marx-Aveling (New York, 2007), 292–3.
16. Herbert Weinstock, *Donizetti* (London, 1964), 200.
17. Smart, 'The Silencing of Lucia', 34.
18. Weinstock, *Donizetti*, 262.
19. Heinrich Heine, 'Heinrich Heine's Musical Feuilletons (Concluded)', eds. O. G. Sonneck and Frederick H. Martens, *The Musical Quarterly*, 8/3 (1922), 435–68; here 468.
20. Stendhal [Henri Beyle], *Life of Rossini*, trans. Richard N. Coe (London, 1956), 378.
21. Gaetano Cesari and Alessandro Luzio, eds., *I copialettere di Giuseppe Verdi* (Milan, 1913), 416.
22. Ibid., 416.
23. David Kimbell, *Vincenzo Bellini: Norma* (Cambridge, 1998), 63.
24. Ibid., 93.
25. John Rosselli, *The Life of Bellini* (Cambridge, 1996), 43.
26. Ibid., 54–5.
27. Kimbell, *Vincenzo Bellini: Norma*, 92.

10. YOUNG VERDI

1. Most standard histories of the early twentieth century follow this line; see for example Donald Jay Grout, *A Short History of Opera* (1947; 4th edn, with Hermine Weigel Williams, New York, 2003), 401–2. It is largely repeated, albeit with a great deal more sophistication, in Joseph Kerman, *Opera as Drama* (1956; rev. edn, Berkeley, 1988), 144–8.
2. Julian Budden, *The Operas of Verdi*, 3 vols. (London, 1973, 1978, 1981), vol. 2, 61.
3. Ibid., vol. 1, 111.
4. Pierluigi Petrobelli, *Music in the Theater* (Princeton, 1994), 33.
5. William Weaver, *Verdi: A Documentary Study* (London, n.d.), 13 (translation adapted).
6. Carlo Gatti, *Verdi nelle immagini* (Milan, 1941), 236.
7. Charles Reid, *The Music Monster: A Biography of James William Davison* (London, 1984), 181.
8. Gabriele Baldini, *The Story of Giuseppe Verdi* (Cambridge, 1980), 74.
9. Marcello Conati, *Interviews and Encounters with Verdi* (London, 1984), 109.
10. Budden, *The Operas of Verdi*, vol. 1, 270.
11. David Rosen and Andrew Porter, *Verdi's* Macbeth*: A Sourcebook* (New York, 1984), 7.
12. Ibid., 67.
13. Ibid., 71.

14. Budden, *The Operas of Verdi*, vol. 1, 477.
15. Ibid.
16. Ibid., 479.
17. Abramo Basevi, *Studio sulle opere di Giuseppe Verdi* (Florence, 1859), 197.

11. GRAND OPERA

1. Susanna Pasticci, '*La traviata en travestie*: Rivisitazioni del testo verdiano nella musica strumentale ottocentesca', *Studi verdiani*, 14 (1999), 118–87.
2. Hervé Lacombe, 'The "Machine" and the State', in David Charlton, ed., *Cambridge Companion to Grand Opera* (Cambridge, 2003), 21–42, here 29; other unattributed details in this paragraph come from the same source.
3. Marian Smith, 'Dance and Dancers', in Charlton, *Cambridge Companion to Grand Opera*, 93–107; here 106.
4. Julian Budden, *The Operas of Verdi*, 3 vols. (London, 1973, 1978, 1981), vol. 3, 22.
5. John Sanderson, *Sketches of Paris: in Familiar Letters to His Friends* (Philadelphia, 1838), 30.
6. Joseph d'Ortigue, *La Balcon de l'Opéra* (Paris, 1833), 122–3.
7. Heinrich Heine, 'Über die französische Bühne'; quoted in Jürgen Maehder, 'Historienmalerei und Grand Opéra: zur Raumvorstellung in den Bildern Géricaults und Delacroix und auf der Bühne der Académie royale de Musique', in Sieghardt Döhring and Arnold Jacobshagen, eds., *Meyerbeer und das europäische Musiktheater* (Laaber, 1999), 58–87.
8. Richard Wagner, *Opera and Drama* (1850); in *Richard Wagner's Prose Works*, trans. William Ashton Ellis (repr. Lincoln, Neb., 1993–95), vol. 2, 95.
9. Simon Williams, 'The Spectacle of the Past in Grand Opera', in Charlton, *Cambridge Companion to Grand Opera*, 58–75; here 61.
10. Ibid., 64.
11. Bayreuth, Nationalarchiv der Richard-Wagner-Gesellschaft, Ms B II a 5, 55: 'Ein Traum (Paris). Mit Herwegh. Menschen umringen und singen uns an. H. verwundert. *Ich*: hat sich das nicht auch Gessler im Tell gefallen lassen müssen?' (A dream. Paris. With Herwegh. People surround us and sing at us. H. is amazed. *I*: didn't Gessler in Tell also have to put up with that?)
12. Edmond Michotte, *Richard Wagner's Visit to Rossini* (Paris, 1860), trans. and ed. Herbert Weinstock (Chicago, 1968), 69.
13. Frederick Niecks, *Frederick Chopin as Man and Musician*, vol. 1 (London, 1890), 226, 227.
14. David Charlton, 'The Nineteenth Century: France', in Roger Parker, ed., *The Oxford Illustrated History of Opera* (Oxford, 1994), 122–68; here 138.

15. Sandy Petrey, '*Robert le diable* and Louis-Philippe the King', in Roger Parker and Mary Ann Smart, eds., *Reading Critics Reading: Opera and Ballet Criticism in France from the Revolution to 1848* (Oxford, 2001), 137–54; here 143.
16. Cormac Newark, 'Ceremony, Celebration, and Spectacle in *La Juive*', in Parker and Smart, *Reading Critics Reading*, 155–87; here 185.
17. A classic iteration comes in the discussion of French Grand Opera in Donald Jay Grout, *A Short History of Opera* (1947; 4th edition, with Hermine Weigel Williams, 2003), 354: 'Musical forms and idioms were mingled in a luxuriant eclecticism, the object being to dazzle popular audiences who demanded thrills and for whom the aristocratic restraints of the eighteenth century had no meaning. The inevitable consequence was an inflated style ... of striking and brilliant musical numbers inadequately motivated by the dramatic situation.'
18. Heinrich Heine, 'Über die französische Bühne'; quoted in Tom Sutcliffe, *The Faber Book of Opera* (London, 2000), 303.
19. David Cairns, *Berlioz*, 2 vols. (London, 1989, 1999), vol. 2, 239.
20. Stuart Spencer, *Wagner Remembered* (London, 2000), 31.
21. Thomas S. Grey, *Wagner and His World* (Princeton, 2009), 335.
22. Guido Zavadini, *Donizetti: vita, musiche, epistolario* (Bergamo, 1948), 494–5.
23. Andrew Porter, '*Les Vêpres siciliennes*: New Letters from Verdi to Scribe', *19th-Century Music*, 2 (1978–9), 95–109; here 97 (translation amended).
24. Budden, *The Operas of Verdi*, vol. 2, 171.
25. Gaetano Cesari and Alessandro Luzio, eds., *I copialettere di Giuseppe Verdi* (Milan, 1913), 578.
26. Ibid., 220.
27. J. Moynet, *L'Envers du théâtre, machines et décorations* (1875; 3rd edn, Paris, 1888), 282.

12. YOUNG WAGNER

1. *Eberhardt's Allgemeiner Polizei-Anzeiger*, vol. 23, no. 47 (July 1853), 280.
2. A copy of the original arrest warrant poster of 1849 is in the Deutsches Theatermuseum Munich.
3. Rosemary Lloyd, ed., *Selected Letters of Charles Baudelaire* (Chicago, 1986), 145.
4. Catulle Mendès, *Richard Wagner* (Paris, 1886), ii. On medical diagnoses of Wagner's uninterruptible speech, which circulated even during his lifetime, see Nicholas Vazsonyi, *Richard Wagner: Self-Promotion and the Making of a Brand* (Cambridge, 2010), 2.

5. Thomas S. Grey, *The Cambridge Companion to Wagner* (Cambridge, 2008), 25.
6. Thomas S. Grey, *Wagner and His World* (Princeton, 2009), 342.
7. Richard Wagner, 'A Communication to My Friends', in *Prose Works*, vol. 1, trans. William Ashton Ellis (London, 1892), 370 (translation adapted).
8. Grey, *Wagner and His World*, 252.
9. '*Das Liebesverbot*: Report on a First Performance' (1871), in *Richard Wagner Prose Works*, vol. 7, trans. William Ashton Ellis (London, 1898), 8.
10. Ibid., vol. 8 (London, 1899), 67–8.
11. Roger Nichols and Richard Langham Smith, *Debussy: Pelléas et Mélisande* (Cambridge, 1989), 193.
12. *Richard Wagner's Prose Works*, vol. 7, 81.
13. *Musical Review and Gazette* (16 April 1859), 116.
14. *The Aeolian Quarterly*, vol. 1, no. 2, 7.
15. The authors' names are pseudonyms for The Honourable Julian Henry Charles Fane and Edward Robert Bulwer-Lytton, first Earl of Lytton, not to be confused with Edward George Bulwer-Lytton, first Baron Lytton, author of the novel *Rienzi, The Last of the Roman Tribunes* (1835).
16. Samuel Holland Rous, *The Victrola Book of the Opera* (4th rev. edn, New York, 1917), 478.
17. *Marcel Proust: Selected Letters 1880–1903*, ed. Philip Kolb, trans. Ralph Manheim (New York, 1983), 91.
18. Hugh Reginald Haweis, reporting on the first London performances of the opera in 1876, in *My Musical Life*, vol. 2 (London, 1884), 547.
19. Review of *Tannhäuser*, London, 14 February 1882, in *The Theatre. A Monthly Review of the Drama, Music, and the Fine Arts*, vol. 5 (Jan–June 1882), 166.
20. 'The Destiny of Opera', in *Richard Wagner Prose Works*, vol. 5, trans. Ellis, 141.
21. Theodor W. Adorno, *In Search of Wagner* (London, 2005), 2.

13. *OPÉRA COMIQUE*, THE CRUCIBLE

1. Mark Everist, 'Jacques Offenbach: The Music of the Past and the Image of the Present', in Everist and Annegret Fauser, eds., *Music, Theater, and Cultural Transfer, Paris 1830–1914* (Chicago, 2009), 72–98.
2. Heinrich Heine, 'The Musical Season of 1844', in *The Works of Heinrich Heine*, trans. Charles Godfrey Leland, vol. 4 (New York, 1906), 442 (translation slightly adapted).
3. *Galignani's New Paris Guide* (Paris, 1839), 462.
4. Monika Hennemann, '"So kann ich es nicht componiren": Mendelssohn, Opera, and the Libretto Problem', in John Michael Cooper and Julie D.

Prandi, eds., *The Mendelssohns: The Music in History* (Oxford, 2002), 181–202; here 185.
5. Hector Berlioz, *Critique musicale 1823–1863*, ed. Yves Gérard (Paris, 1998), 551–5.
6. David Charlton, 'Opéra Comique: Identity and Manipulation', in Roger Parker and Mary Ann Smart, eds., *Reading Critics Reading: Opera and Ballet Criticism in France from the Revolution to 1848* (Oxford, 2001), 13–45; here 23.
7. Delphine Mordey, 'Auber's Horses: *L'Année terrible* and Apocalyptic Narratives', *19th-Century Music* 30/3 (2007), 213–29.
8. *The Victrola Book of the Opera* (Camden, NJ, 1915), 329; this statistic appears only in the 1915 edition; it is not in the 1912 and 1913 editions, and was omitted in later (post-First World War) editions.
9. Statistics at www.operabase.com.
10. Siegfried Kracauer, *Jacques Offenbach and the Paris of His Time*, trans. Gwenda David and Eric Mosbacher (New York, 2002), 206–7.
11. Ibid., 211.
12. Édouard Noël and Edmond Stoullig, *Les Annales du théâtre et de la musique, Première année 1875* (Paris, 1876), 108, 'Madame Galli-Marié fait du personage effronté de Carmen l'une de ses meilleures creations. Il est impossible de render avec plus de talent cette étrange figure de bohémienne: voyez-la se balançant sur ses hanches comme une pouliche des haras de Cordoue ... Quelle vérité, mais quel scandale!'
13. This tale seems to have spread widely after being repeated in an article by Charles Tenroc in *Le Courrier musical* (1 March 1925); for the history of the anecdote see Winton Dean, *Bizet* (London, 1975), 117.
14. *The Case of Wagner: Turin Letter of May 1888*, in Walter Kaufman, trans. and ed., *Basic Writings of Nietzsche* (New York, 1968), 613.
15. Cited in Michael Kennedy, *Richard Strauss: Man, Musician, Enigma* (Cambridge, 2006), 286.
16. *Saturday Evening Post*, vol. 195 (5 August 1922), 36.

14. OLD WAGNER

1. John Deathridge, *Wagner beyond Good and Evil* (Berkeley and Los Angeles, 2008), 119.
2. Laurence Dreyfus, *Wagner and the Erotic Impulse* (Cambridge, Mass., 2010), 143.
3. Jean-Jacques Nattiez, *Wagner Androgyne* (Princeton, 1993), 163–72.
4. Charles Reid, *The Music Monster: A Biography of James William Davison* (London, 1984), 210.
5. Dreyfus, *Wagner and the Erotic Impulse*, 134.
6. Diary entry of December 1875; cited in Nancy B. Reich, *Clara Schumann: The Artist and the Woman* (Ithaca, NY, 1985), 203.

7. *Richard Wagner an Mathilde Wesendonck* (Berlin, 1904), 20.
8. *The Theater*, vol. 5 (January–June 1882), 293–4.
9. Dieter Borchmeyer, *Richard Wagner: Theory and Theater*, trans. Stewart Spencer (Oxford, 1991), 13.
10. Theodor W. Adorno, *In Search of Wagner* (London, 2005), 142.
11. *Richard Wagner Prose Works*, Vol. 6, trans. William Ashton Ellis (London, 1897), 184.
12. Ibid., Vol. 2 *(Opera and Drama)* (London, 1900), 96.
13. 'The Destiny of Opera', in ibid., Vol. 5 (London, 1896), 134.
14. Carolyn Abbate, 'Opera as Symphony, a Wagnerian Myth', in Carolyn Abbate and Roger Parker, eds., *Analyzing Opera* (Berkeley and Los Angeles, 1989), 122–3.
15. Friedrich Nietzsche, 'Attempt at a Self-Criticism', 1886 preface to *The Birth of Tragedy*, in *Basic Writings of Nietzsche*, trans. and ed. Walter Kaufmann (New York, 1968), 22–5.
16. Nietzsche, *The Birth of Tragedy*, 127.
17. Mark Twain, 'At the Shrine of St. Wagner', in *What is Man and Other Essays* (London, 1919), 226.
18. Saul Friedländer, 'Hitler und *Wagner'*, in *Richard Wagner im Dritten Reich*, eds. Saul Friedländer and Jörn Rüsen (Munich, 2000), 165–78.
19. Friedrich Kittler, 'World Breath: On Wagner's Media Technology', in David Levin, ed., *Opera through Other Eyes* (Stanford, 1994), 224.

15. VERDI – OLDER STILL

1. Roberta Montemorra Marvin, 'Andrea Maffei's "Ugly Sin": The Libretto for Verdi's *I masnadieri*', in Stephen A. Crist and Roberta Montemorra Marvin, eds., *Historical Musicology: Sources, Methods, Interpretation* (Rochester, NY, 2004), 280–301; 296–7
2. Ibid., 232.
3. John Sanderson, *Sketches of Paris: In Familiar Letters to His Friends* (Philadelphia, 1838), 151–2.
4. Gaetano Cesari and Alessandro Luzio, eds., *I copialettere di Giuseppe Verdi* (Milan, 1913), 220.
5. Hans Busch, *Verdi's 'Aida': The History of an Opera in Letters and Documents* (Minneapolis, 1978), 34.
6. Edward Said, 'The Empire at Work', *Culture and Imperialism* (London, 1994), 133–59; here 156.
7. Cesari and Luzio, *I copialettere di Giuseppe Verdi*, 572.
8. Julian Budden, *The Operas of Verdi*, 3 vols. (London, 1973, 1978, 1981), vol. 2, 112.
9. Frank Walker, *The Man Verdi* (London, 1962), 449.
10. Budden, *The Operas of Verdi*, vol. 3, 307.

11. Ibid., 309.
12. Ibid., 328.
13. Hans Busch, *Verdi's 'Otello' and 'Simon Boccanegra' in Letters and Documents*, 2 vols. (Oxford, 1988), vol. 1, 310–11.
14. James Hepokoski, *Giuseppe Verdi: Falstaff* (Cambridge, 1983), 34.
15. Ibid., 34.
16. Ibid., 140.
17. Budden, *The Operas of Verdi*, vol. 3, 299.
18. Cesari and Luzio, *I copialettere di Giuseppe Verdi*, 323.
19. Ibid., 702.
20. Ibid., 633.
21. Ibid., 629–30.
22. Budden, *The Operas of Verdi*, vol. 3, 470–71.
23. Karen Henson, 'Verdi, Victor Maurel and *Fin-de-siècle* Operatic Performance', *Cambridge Opera Journal*, 19/1 (2007), 59–84.
24. Mary Jane Phillips-Matz, *Verdi: A Biography* (Oxford, 1993), 756.

16. REALISM AND CLAMOUR

1. Linda Nochlin, *Realism* (London, 1971), 13.
2. Letter to Matilde Wesendonck, 29 October 1859, in Barry Millington, ed., *Selected Letters of Richard Wagner* (London, 1987), 475.
3. Robert William Oldani, 'Musorgsky, Modest Petrovich', in *The New Grove Dictionary of Music and Musicians* (London, 2001), vol. 17, 541–55; here 544.
4. Richard Taruskin, *Defining Russia Musically* (Princeton, 1997), 531.
5. Constantin Stanislavski and Pavel Rumyantsev, *Stanislavski on Opera* (New York, 1998), 334.
6. Astrid Varnay, with Donald Arthur, *Fifty-Five Years in Five Acts: My Life in Opera* (Boston, 2000), 309.
7. *The New Quarterly Musical Review*, Vol. 1 (May 1893), 126.
8. Léon Daudet reports on Massenet's behaviour in his *Souvenirs des milieux littéraires, politiques, artistiques et médicaux* (6 vols., 1913–22), translated as *Memoirs of Léon Daudet* (New York, 1925), 14–16.
9. 'Gallery of Players', *The Illustrated American*, No. 3, ed. Austin Brereton (New York, 1894), 4.
10. *The Musical Times* (1 March 1884), 135.
11. Quoted in Ethan Mordden, *Opera Anecdotes* (Oxford, 1985), 244.
12. Philip Hale, 'Of Realism in Opera', in *The Looker-On*, vol. 3 (July–December 1896), 65–6.
13. Gaetano Cesari and Alessandro Luzio, eds., *I copialettere di Giuseppe Verdi* (Milan, 1913), 624.
14. Michele Girardi, *Puccini: His International Art* (Chicago, 2000), 331.

15. Arman Schwartz, 'Rough Music: *Tosca* and Verismo Reconsidered', *19th-Century Music,* 31/3 (2008), 228–44; here 235.
16. Ibid., 235.
17. *The Athenaeum* (July–December 1900), 96.

17. TURNING POINT

1. Letter of 12 May, in Henry Adams, *Selected Letters*, ed. Ernest Samuels (Cambridge, Mass., 1992), 498.
2. Roger Nichols, *The Life of Debussy* (Cambridge, 1998), 106.
3. Jann Pasler, 'Paris: Conflicting Notions of Progress', in *Music and Society: The Late Romantic Era*, ed. Jim Samson (London, 1991), 397–8.
4. Pierre Boulez, *Orientations: Collected Writings*, ed. Jean-Jacques Nattiez, trans. Martin Cooper (London, 1986), 315.
5. Richard Langham Smith, *Debussy on Music* (London, 1977), 224.
6. Marina Frolova-Walker, *Russian Music and Nationalism* (New Haven, 2007), 214 and 370 (n.92).
7. *Lily Pons: A Centennial Portrait*, ed. James R. Drake and Kristin Beall Ludecke (Portland, Ore., 1999), 34.
8. James Huneker, *Bedouins* (New York, 1920), 4.
9. Henry Charles Lahee, *The Grand Opera Singers of Today* (Boston, 1912), 181.
10. *The Sketch: A Journal of Art and Actuality*, vol. 72 (December 1910), 396.
11. Edward Lockspeiser, *Debussy: His Life and Mind* (Cambridge, 1978), vol. 1, 91.
12. *Gil blas*, 19 January 1903; cited in Langham Smith, *Debussy on Music*, 97.
13. Robert Orledge, *Debussy and the Theatre* (Cambridge, 1982), 49.
14. Ibid., 52.
15. Willi Schuh, *Richard Strauss: A Chronicle of the Early Years 1864–1898* (Cambridge, 1982), 341.
16. Davinia Caddy, 'Variations on the Dance of the Seven Veils', *Cambridge Opera Journal*, 17/1 (2005), 37–58; here 54.
17. Derrick Puffett, *Richard Strauss: Salome* (Cambridge, 1989), 131–2.
18. Willi Reich, *Schoenberg: A Critical Biography* (New York, 1971), 25.
19. Henry T. Finck, 1923, cited in Nicolas Slonimsky, *Lexicon of Musical Invective* (repr. New York, 2000), 159.
20. Review in the *New York Evening Post*, 1915, ibid., 159.
21. Daniel Albright, *Modernism and Music: An Anthology of Sources* (Chicago, 2004), 170.
22. Ibid., 66–7.
23. Michael Kennedy, *Richard Strauss: Man, Musician, Enigma* (Cambridge, 1999), 173.
24. Ibid., 173.

25. Piero Weiss, *Opera: A History in Documents* (New York, 2002), 273.
26. Ibid., 274.
27. Michele Girardi, *Puccini: His International Art* (Chicago, 2000), 265.
28. Alex Ross, *The Rest is Noise: Listening to the Twentieth Century* (London, 2008), 311 and 575.
29. Girardi, *Puccini: His International Art*, 267.
30. Cecil Gray, *A Survey of Contemporary Music* (London, 1924), 240–41.
31. Ibid., 241.

18. MODERN

1. Simone de Beauvoir, *The Second Sex*, trans. H. M. Parshley (New York, 1980), 416. The 'her' in the first sentence is Sarolta Vay, 'Count Sándor', a female cross-dresser discussed by Krafft-Ebbing.
2. Alan Jefferson, *Richard Strauss: Der Rosenkavalier* (Cambridge, 1985), 90.
3. Hugo von Hofmannsthal, 'Der Rosenkavalier: Zum Geleit' (1927), in *Hugo von Hofmannsthal: Gesammelte Werke*, vol. 5 (Frankfurt am Main, 1979), 149.
4. *Journey to the Abyss: The Diaries of Count Harry Kessler 1880–1918*, ed. and trans. Laird Easton (New York, 2011), 578.
5. Paul Rosenfeld, *Musical Portraits: Interpretations of Twenty Modern Composers* (New York, 1920), 41–2.
6. *The Will to Power*, trans. Walter Kaufmann and R. J. Hollingdale, ed. Walter Kaufmann (New York, 1967), aphorism 834 (p. 439).
7. Julius Korngold, quoted in Bryan Gilliam, ed., *Richard Strauss and His World* (Princeton, 1992), 351.
8. Hans Hammelman and Ewald Osers, *The Correspondence between Richard Strauss and Hugo von Hofmannsthal* (London, 1961), 49.
9. Gilliam, *Richard Strauss*, 413.
10. Ibid., 414–15.
11. Walter Frisch, ed., *Schoenberg and His World* (Princeton, 1999), 259.
12. Paul Griffiths, *Igor Stravinsky: The Rake's Progress* (Cambridge, 1982), 63.
13. Igor Stravinsky and Robert Craft, *Memories and Commentaries* (Berkeley, 1981), 158.
14. Daniel Albright, *Modernism and Music: An Anthology of Sources* (Chicago, 2004), 124–6.
15. Stravinsky and Craft, *Memories and Commentaries*, 155.
16. W. H. Auden, 'Some Reflections on Opera as a Medium', *Tempo* (Summer, 1951), 6–10; here 10.
17. Robert Craft and Igor Stravinsky, *Conversations with Igor Stravinsky* (London, 2009), 75.

19. SPEECH

1. *Dwight's Journal of Music*, vol. 39 (1879), 196.
2. Karl Reinhold von Köstlin, *Richard Wagners Tondrama Der Ring des Nibelungen: seine Idee, Handlung, und Komposition* (Tübingen, 1877), 86.
3. Hermann Gehrmann, *Carl Maria von Weber* (Berlin, 1899), 87.
4. *Allgemeine musikalische Zeiting*, vol. 12 (1877), 233.
5. A recording of her reciting from Edmond Rostand's play *La Samaritaine* is available on YouTube.
6. David Trippett, '"Bayreuth in Miniature": Wagner and the Melodramatic Voice', *Musical Quarterly*, 95 (2012), pp. 71–138.
7. Cited in Madeleine Goss, *Bolero: The Life of Maurice Ravel* (New York, 1945), 197.
8. Vladimir Jankélévitch, *Ravel* (Westport, Conn., 1976), 133.
9. Theodor Adorno and Hanns Eisler, *Composing for the Films* (1947; London, 2007), 24.
10. *The Survey: A Journal of Constructive Philanthropy* (December 1929), 634.
11. Susan Cook, *Opera for a New Republic* (Rochester, 1988), 201.
12. William H. Seltsam, *Metropolitan Opera Annals: A Chronicle of Artists and Performances* (New York, 1947), 500.
13. Ernst Krenek, *Horizons Circled* (Berkeley, 1974), 26.
14. David Grayson, 'Debussy on Stage', in Simon Trezise, ed., *The Cambridge Companion to Debussy* (Cambridge, 2003), 81.
15. Robert Orledge, *Debussy and the Theatre* (Cambridge, 1982), 118–19.
16. Claude Trevor, 'Cant in Music', *The Musical Times*, vol. 61 (1 August 1920), 530.
17. Entry on 'Strauss', *The New Grove Dictionary of Music and Musicians* (London, 2001), vol. 24, 514.
18. Bryan Gilliam, ed., *Richard Strauss and His World* (Princeton, 1992), 293.
19. Michael Kennedy, 'From Casti to *Capriccio*: Strauss's Theatrical Fugue', in David Rosen and Claire Brook, eds., *Words on Music: Essays in Honor of Andrew Porter* (New York, 2003), 171–91; here 190.
20. Robert S. Wistrich, *Who's Who in Nazi Germany* (London 2002), 223.
21. Daniel Gregory Mason, *The Art of Music*, vol. 9 (New York, 1916), 439.
22. Bernard Stevens, 'Czechoslovakia and Poland', in Howard Hartog, ed., *European Music in the Twentieth Century* (London, 1957), 303.
23. Marina Frolova-Walker, *Russian Music and Nationalism* (New Haven, 2007), 212.
24. Ibid., 207.
25. Caryl Emerson, 'Back to the Future: Shostakovich's Revision of Leskov's "Lady Macbeth of Mtsensk District"', *Cambridge Opera Journal*, 1/1 (1989), 59–78; here 69.
26. Ibid., 62.

27. Richard Taruskin, *Defining Russia Musically* (Princeton, 1997), 504.
28. Ibid., 500–501.
29. Piero Weiss, *Opera: A History in Documents* (New York, 2002), 302.
30. Ibid., 303.
31. Julien Steinberg, ed., *Verdict of Three Decades: From the Literature of Individual Revolt against Soviet Communism 1917–1950* (New York, 1950), 307–8.

20. REVENANTS IN THE MUSEUM

1. This was Napoleone Moriani (1806–78); identified as such in Frank Walker, *The Man Verdi* (1962; repr. Chicago, 1982), 88.
2. This speculation is made by Julian Budden, *The Operas of Verdi*, 3 vols. (London, 1973, 1978, 1981), vol. 3, 141.
3. Eugenio Gara, ed., *Carteggi pucciniani* (Milan, 1958), 563.
4. Julian Budden, *The Operas of Verdi*, vol.1, 3. (London, 1973, 1978, 1981), vol. 1, 3.
5. Gara, *Carteggi pucciniani*, 563.
6. Budden, *The Operas of Verdi*, vol. 2, 112.
7. For an extensive discussion of the Verdi 'renaissance', see Gundula Kreuzer, *Verdi and the Germans* (Cambridge, 2010),138.
8. Richard Taruskin, *Text and Act* (Oxford, 1995).
9. Donald Mitchell, Philip Reed and Mervyn Cooke, eds., *Letters from a Life: The Selected Letters and Diaries of Benjamin Britten. Vol. 3 (1946–51)* (Berkeley, 2004), 100.
10. Humphrey Carpenter, *Benjamin Britten: A Biography* (London, 1992), 193–4.
11. For an account of the reception of the opera, see Philip Brett, *Benjamin Britten: Peter Grimes* (Cambridge, 1983).
12. Paul Kildea, ed., *Britten on Music* (Oxford, 2003), 50.
13. Ibid., 50.
14. The comparative popularity comes from operabase.com.
15. Richard Langham Smith, *Debussy on Music* (London, 1977), 164.
16. Statistics are from operabase.com.
17. Statistics are from operabase.com.
18. For these and many other details about Berio's completion, see Marco Uvietta's '"È l'ora della prova": Berio's Finale for Puccini's *Turandot*', *Cambridge Opera Journal*, 16/2 (2004), 187–238.
19. György Ligeti, *György Ligeti in Conversation* (London, 1983), x.
20. For an account of this latest round of protests, which even spread to the entire season in which the opera was staged, see 'Klinghoffer takes the stage to chorus of boos', *Guardian* (22 October 2014), 20.
21. David Beverly, 'Klinghoffer and the Art of Composing', interview on 25

October 1995, printed on John Adams's website, http://www.earbox.com/inter003.html (accessed 12.12.09).
22. Edward Said, *Music at the Limits* (New York, 2008), 136.
23. Alex Ross, 'George Benjamin's Long-Awaited Masterpiece', in *The New Yorker*, 25 March 2013.

21. WE ARE ALONE IN THE FOREST

1. Mordaunt Hall, review of *The Rogue Song*, *The New York Times*, 29 January 1930.
2. Wagner to Theodor Uhlig, 20 September 1850, *Richard Wagner's Letters to His Dresden Friends*, trans. J. S. Shedlock (London, 1890), 67–8.
3. Max Fehr, *Richard Wagners Schweizer Zeit* (Aarau, 1934–54), vol. 2, 21.
4. Richard Wagner to Franz Liszt, March 1855, in *Briefwechsel zwischen Wagner und Liszt. Zweiter Band: Vom Jahre 1854 bis 1861* (Leipzig, 1887), 60.
5. http://www.nytimes.com/2014/01/05/arts/music/critics-weigh-in-on-standout-operas-of-recent-decades.html.
6. David Pountney, 'The Future of Opera' (lecture given at the Royal Opera House, 13 February 2000); published at http://www.rodoni.ch/OPERNHAUS/novembre/intervistapountney.html.
7. From a 1967 interview with the composer in *Der Spiegel*, quoted in David J. Levin, *Unsettling Opera: Staging Mozart, Verdi, Wagner, and Zemlinsky* (Chicago, 2007), 18, n.38.
8. http://www.artlyriquefr.fr/dicos/Theatre-Lyrique%20creations.htm.
9. *Written on Skin*'s DVD was released in 2013 on the Opus Arte label (OA 1125D). While the original stage director was Katie Mitchell, the DVD is billed as 'produced and directed for the screen by Margaret Williams'.

General Bibliography

I. INTRODUCTION

Complete histories of opera are not numerous these days. For a long time, the standard work was Donald Jay Grout, *A Short History of Opera* (1947; 4th edn, with Hermine Weigel Williams, New York, 2003); this has been periodically updated, although it still bears the stamp of its musicological period of creation, in which most Italian opera of the nineteenth and twentieth centuries was suspect (to say the least). The opera sections of Richard Taruskin's *Oxford History of Western Music*, 6 vols. (Oxford, 2005), are far more up to date and reliable, not to mention bracingly controversial at times. An excellent recent survey, albeit one concentrating on the social aspects of the story, is Daniel Snowman's *The Gilded Stage* (London, 2009). In the field of opera criticism Joseph Kerman's *Opera as Drama* (1956; rev. edn, Berkeley, 1988) still retains its power, even though it condemns almost all eighteenth-century opera (and, implicitly, much of the nineteenth-century repertoire) to what Kerman calls 'the dark ages'. Gary Tomlinson's *Metaphysical Song* (Princeton, 1999) is in some ways a modern version of Kerman, albeit with a much broader purview. Bernard Williams's *On Opera* (New Haven, 2006) is a typically thought-provoking reflection by a leading philosopher.

Other worthwhile general histories include: Lorenzo Bianconi and Giorgio Pestelli, eds., *Opera Production and Its Resources* (Chicago, 1998), and the same authors' *Opera on Stage* (Chicago, 2002), both of which take a very broad view of Italian opera; John Rosselli, *Singers of Italian Opera: The History of a Profession* (Cambridge, 1992); Susan Rutherford, *The Prima Donna and Opera, 1815–1930* (Cambridge, 2007); Thomas Forrest Kelly, *First Nights at the Opera* (New Haven, 2004); Roger Parker, ed., *The Oxford Illustrated History of Opera* (Oxford, 1994); and Piero Weiss, *Opera: A History in Documents* (New York, 2002). The various *Grove Dictionaries* offer the most reliable factual compendia; Amanda Holden, ed., *The Penguin Opera Guide* (London, 2002) is also excellent.

2. OPERA'S FIRST CENTENNIAL

John Butt and Tim Carter, eds., *The Cambridge History of Seventeenth-Century Music* (Cambridge, 2008), provides an up-to-date introduction to the period, and contains several fine essays on opera. Lorenzo Bianconi, *Music in the Seventeenth Century* (Cambridge, 1987), remains important, particularly in its coverage of the Italian scene. For the period before 1600, see Frederick W. Sternfeld, *The Birth of Opera* (Oxford, 1993). On Monteverdi generally, see especially: Denis Stevens, *The Letters of Claudio Monteverdi* (Cambridge, 1980); Gary Tomlinson, *Monteverdi and the End of the Renaissance* (Berkeley, 1987); and John Whenham and Richard Wistreich, eds., *The Cambridge Companion to Monteverdi* (Cambridge, 2007). Directly concerned with Monteverdi's operas are: John Whenham, *Claudio Monteverdi: Orfeo* (Cambridge, 1986), and Tim Carter, *Monteverdi's Musical Theatre* (New Haven, 2002). For Venetian opera, the standard work is Ellen Rosand, *Opera in Seventeenth-Century Venice: The Creation of a Genre* (Berkeley, 1991). For Cavalli, see Jane Glover, *Cavalli* (London, 1978); for Purcell, see Curtis Price, *Henry Purcell and the London Stage* (Cambridge, 1984). Beth L. Glixon and Jonathan E. Glixon, *Inventing the Business of Opera: The Impresario and His World in Seventeenth-Century Venice* (Oxford, 2006), offers a document-rich account of the business of Italian opera in the period.

3. OPERA SERIA

For Italian *opera seria* in the eighteenth century, the place to start is Martha Feldman's *Opera and Sovereignty: Transforming Myths in Eighteenth-Century Italy* (Chicago, 2007), which is the most thoroughgoing attempt to connect the genre to broader intellectual currents. Reinhard Strohm's *Dramma per musica. Italian Opera Seria of the Eighteenth Century* (New Haven, 2007) is also very good, while Michael F. Robinson's *Naples and Neapolitan Opera* (Oxford, 1972) covers the minor figures. Enrico Fubini, *Music & Culture in Eighteenth-Century Europe: A Source Book* (Chicago, 1994), offers a valuable compendium of contemporary sources on opera. Those wishing to know more about castrati should consult Patrick Barbier, *The World of the Castrati: The History of an Extraordinary Operatic Phenomenon* (London, 1998); see also Angus Heriot, *Castrati in Opera* (London, 1956). Well-written general books on Handel include Jonathan Keates, *Handel: The Man and His Music* (London, 2008), and Christopher Hogwood, *Handel* (London, 2009). On Handel's operas, the standard work is Winton Dean, *Handel's Operas* (vol. 1, Oxford, 1987; vol. 2, Woodbridge, 2006); see also Reinhard Strohm, *Essays on Handel and Italian Opera* (Cambridge, 1985).

4. DISCIPLINE

Charles Burney, *A General History of Music* (London, 1776–89) and Burney, *The Present State of Music in France and Italy* (London, 1773), offer wonderful contemporary viewpoints on opera (and opera's history). For a general history of the period, with ample cultural context, see Daniel Heartz, *From Garrick to Gluck: Essays on Opera in the Age of Enlightenment*, ed. John A. Rice (Hillsdale, 2004). Downing A. Thomas, *Aesthetics of Opera in the Ancien Régime, 1647–1785* (Cambridge, 2002), is good on the French context. On Gluck, see Bruce Alan Brown, *Gluck and the French Theatre in Vienna* (Oxford, 1991); useful insights can also still be found in Ernest Newman, *Gluck and Opera. A Study in Musical History* (London, 1895). On *Orfeo*, see Patricia Howard, *C. W. Gluck: Orfeo* (Cambridge, 1981); on Gluck's reception in the nineteenth century, see Simon Goldhill, *Victorian Culture and Classical Antiquity: Art, Opera, Fiction, and the Proclamation of Modernity* (Princeton, 2011). On Rameau, see Charles Dill, *Monstrous Opera: Rameau and the Tragic Tradition* (Princeton, 1998). For general books on Mozart, see the bibliography to Chapter 5; for *Idomeneo* in particular, see Julian Rushton, *W. A. Mozart: Idomeneo* (Cambridge, 1993).

5. *OPERA BUFFA* AND MOZART'S LINE OF BEAUTY

The intellectual background that helped to form Mozart's mature comedies has been the subject of several excellent books. See in particular Daniel Heartz, with contributing essays by Thomas Bauman, *Mozart's Operas* (Berkeley and Los Angeles, 1990); Mary Hunter, *The Culture of Opera Buffa in Mozart's Vienna* (Princeton, 1999); and Thomas Bauman and Marita Petzoldt McClymonds, eds., *Opera and the Enlightenment* (Cambridge, 2006). For insightful discussions of the operas, see David Cairns, *Mozart and His Operas* (London, 2006); Ivan Nagel, *Autonomy and Mercy: Reflections on Mozart's Operas*, trans. Marion Faber and Ivan Nagel (Cambridge, Mass., 1991); Andrew Steptoe, *The Mozart–Da Ponte Operas: Cultural and Musical Background to Le nozze di Figaro, Don Giovanni, and Così fan tutte* (Oxford, 1988); and Nicholas Till, *Mozart and the Enlightenment: Truth, Virtue and Beauty in Mozart's Operas* (London, 1992). For book-length treatments of individual Da Ponte operas, see: Tim Carter, *W. A. Mozart: Le nozze di Figaro* (Cambridge, 1987); Lydia Goehr and Daniel Herwitz, eds., *Don Giovanni Moment: Essays on the Legacy of an Opera* (New York, 2006); Julian Rushton, *W. A. Mozart: Don Giovanni* (Cambridge, 1981); and Bruce Alan Brown, *W. A. Mozart: Così fan tutte* (Cambridge, 1995).

6. SINGING AND SPEAKING BEFORE 1800

The best general introduction to the issues in this chapter are the relevant chapters of John Warrack, *German Opera: From the Beginnings to Wagner* (Cambridge, 2001). For more detailed studies of the German operatic landscape, see Thomas Baumann, *North German Opera in the Age of Goethe* (Cambridge, 1985), and Matthew Riley, *Musical Listening in the German Enlightenment* (Aldershot, 2004). For the French perspective, see David Charlton, *Grétry and the Growth of Opéra comique* (Cambridge, 1986). In addition to the general Mozart literature mentioned in the bibliography to Chapter 5, books that particularly concern Mozart's German operas include: Thomas Baumann, *W. A. Mozart: Die Entführung aus dem Serail* (Cambridge, 1987); Peter Branscombe, *W. A. Mozart: Die Zauberflöte* (Cambridge, 1991); and David Buch, *Magic Flutes and Enchanted Forests: The Supernatural in Eighteenth-Century Musical Theater* (Chicago, 2008).

7. THE GERMAN PROBLEM

Edmond Michotte, *Richard Wagner's Visit to Rossini* (Chicago, 1968), is the most reliable account of the fateful meeting between those two composers. The best general introduction to Beethoven is Lewis Lockwood's *Beethoven: The Music and the Life* (New York, 2003). Glen Stanley, *The Cambridge Companion to Beethoven* (Cambridge, 2000), offers a reliable introduction to the music; for *Fidelio* in particular, see Paul Robinson, *Ludwig van Beethoven: Fidelio* (Cambridge, 1996). For the French background, see Malcolm Boyd, ed., *Music and the French Revolution* (Cambridge, 1992); Victoria Johnson, *Backstage at the Revolution. How the Royal Paris Opera Survived the End of the Old Regime* (Chicago, 2008); and Jean Mongrédien, *French Music from the Enlightenment to Romanticism 1789–1830* (Huddersfield, 1996). For Cherubini, the English-language source is still Basil Deane, *Cherubini* (Oxford, 1965). There are two excellent compendia on E. T. A. Hoffmann: Abigail Chantier, *E. T. A. Hoffmann's Musical Aesthetics* (Aldershot, 2006), and David Charlton, *E. T. A. Hoffmann's Musical Writings* (Cambridge, 1989). The best general introduction to Weber remains John Warrack, *Carl Maria von Weber* (2nd edn, Cambridge, 1976). More specific to his operas are: Michael C. Tusa, *Euryanthe and Carl Maria von Weber's Dramaturgy of German Opera* (Oxford, 1991), and Stephen C. Mayer, *Carl Maria von Weber and the Search for a German Opera* (Bloomington, 2003).

8. ROSSINI AND THE TRANSITION

A good general introduction to the period can be found in the relevant chapters of David Kimbell, *Italian Opera* (Cambridge, 1994). Richard Osborne's *Rossini* (2nd edn, Oxford, 2007) is the best available life-and-works, although Herbert Weinstock, *Rossini: A Biography* (New York, 1968), has abundant documentary information. Stendhal (Henri Beyle), *Life of Rossini*, trans. Richard N. Coe (London, 1956), is highly idiosyncratic (and often unreliable), but it is also full of passion and delightful exaggeration. Recent scholarly attitudes are collected in Emanuele Senici, *The Cambridge Companion to Rossini* (Cambridge, 2004).

9. THE TENOR COMES OF AGE

John Rosselli, *The Opera Industry in Italy from Cimarosa to Verdi: The Role of the Impresario* (Cambridge, 1984), provides an excellent introduction to the Italian opera 'industry'; just as the same author's *Music and Musicians in Nineteenth-Century Italy* (London, 1991) sets the broader cultural scene. With Donizetti, the place to start is William Ashbrook, *Donizetti* (Cambridge, 1982); Herbert Weinstock, *Donizetti* (London, 1964), has further information about Donizetti's *milieu*. Bellini's life is succinctly dealt with in John Rosselli, *The Life of Bellini* (Cambridge, 1996), while David Kimbell, *Vincenzo Bellini: Norma* (Cambridge, 1998), offers a good introduction to Bellini's most famous opera. For a stimulating account of one particular genre in this repertoire, see Emanuele Senici, *Landscape and Gender in Italian Opera: The Alpine Virgin from Bellini to Puccini* (Cambridge, 2009). For fascinating insights into the musical-gestural language, see Mary Ann Smart, *Mimomania: Music and Gesture in Nineteenth-Century Opera* (Berkeley, 2004).

10. YOUNG VERDI

The classic account of Verdi's operas remains Julian Budden's magnificent three-volume study, *The Operas of Verdi* (London, 1973, 1978, 1981), the first of which takes us up to *Rigoletto*. The same author's one-volume treatment in the 'Master Musicians' series, *Verdi* (3rd edn, Oxford, 2008), also includes a section on the life. For a briefer account of Verdi's life and works, see Roger Parker, *The New Grove Guide to Verdi and His Operas* (Oxford, 2007). The classic biography remains Frank Walker, *The Man Verdi* (London, 1962), although John Rosselli's brief *Life of Verdi* (Cambridge, 2000) is more up to date. William Weaver's *Verdi: A Documentary Study* (London, n.d.) offers an excellent compendium of pictorial evidence. Scott Balthazar, ed., *The Cambridge Companion to Verdi* (Cambridge, 2004), is generally reliable. Volumes dedicated to the early operas in particular include Gabriele Baldini, *The Story of Giuseppe Verdi* (Cambridge, 1980), David R. B. Kimbell, *Verdi and the Age of Italian Romanticism* (Cambridge, 1985), and David Rosen and Andrew Porter, *Verdi's* Macbeth*: A Sourcebook* (New York, 1984).

11. GRAND OPERA

There are several stimulating and up-to-date general books on French Grand Opera, which is, it seems, much more popular with musicologists than with opera-house managers and audiences. Among the best are: David Charlton, *The Cambridge Companion to Grand Opera* (Cambridge, 2003); Jane Fulcher, *The Nation's Image: French Grand Opera as Politics and Politicized Art* (Cambridge, 1987); Anselm Gerhard, *The Urbanization of Opera: Music Theater in Paris in the Nineteenth Century* (Chicago, 1998); and Sarah Hibberd, *French Grand Opera and the Historical Imagination* (Cambridge, 2009). Benjamin Walton's *Rossini in Restoration Paris: The Sound of Modern Life* (Cambridge, 2007) is excellent on the cultural background of Rossini's last operatic phase. Berlioz is also very well served: see in particular David Cairns's fine biography, *Berlioz*, 2 vols. (London, 1989, 1999), and the same author's edition of the *Memoirs of Hector Berlioz* (London, 1969). A book-length account of Berlioz's largest Grand Opera is provided by Ian Kemp, *Hector Berlioz: Les Troyens* (Cambridge, 1989). On Meyerbeer, see Heinz and Gundrun Becker, *Giacomo Meyerbeer: A Life in Letters* (London, 1989), and Mark Everist, *Giacomo Meyerbeer and Music Drama in Nineteenth-Century Paris* (Aldershot, 2005). A variety of cultural backgrounds are explored in Mark Everist and Annegret Fauser, eds., *Music, Theatre, Cultural Transfer: Paris 1830–1914* (Chicago, 2009). Cormac Newark, *Opera in the Novel from Balzac to Proust* (Cambridge, 2011), presents a fascinating tour through grand opera's novelistic appearances.

12. YOUNG WAGNER

Those wishing to explore the Wagner bibliography will find a famously crowded field. William Ashton Ellis, ed. and trans, *Richard Wagner's Prose Works*, 8 vols. (London, 1892–1912) offers a translation, now very dated, of most of the important prose works. Also valuable here is Richard Wagner, *My Life*, trans. Andrew Gray (Cambridge, 1983), and Stewart Spencer and Barry Millington, *Selected Letters of Richard Wagner* (London, 1988). The standard life remains Ernest Newman, *The Life of Richard Wagner*, 4 vols. (Cambridge, 1976), although there are reliable briefer treatments by Derek Watson, *Richard Wagner: A Biography* (London, 1979), and Barry Millington, *Wagner* (Princeton, 1992). There are numerous recent volumes of collected essays: Barry Millington, ed., *The Wagner Compendium: A Guide to Wagner's Life and Music* (London, 1992); Ulrich Müller and Peter Wapnewski, *The Wagner Handbook* (Boston, 1992); Thomas S. Grey, *The Cambridge Companion to Wagner* (Cambridge, 2008); and the same author's *Wagner and His World* (Princeton, 2009). Monographs on the composer and his operas are also legion. Among the most stimulating are: Theodor Adorno, *In Search of Wagner*, trans. Rodney Livingstone (London, 1981); Carl Dahlhaus, *Richard Wagner's Music Dramas* (Cambridge, 1979); Michael Tanner, *Wagner* (London, 1996); Joachim Köhler, *Richard Wagner: The Last of the Titans* (London, 2004); and John Deathridge, *Wagner beyond Good and Evil* (Berkeley, 2008). Thomas S. Grey, *Richard Wagner: Der fliegende Holländer* (Cambridge, 2000), offers a book-length treatment of one of the early operas. Patrick Carnegy's *Wagner and the Art of the Theatre* (New Haven, 2006) offers the best recent account of the history of Wagner staging.

13. *OPÉRA COMIQUE*, THE CRUCIBLE

A good general introduction to the period, with much about *opéra comique*, is provided in Hervé Lacombe, *The Keys to French Opera in the Nineteenth Century* (Berkeley, 2001). For Bizet, the most reliable account of the life and works remains Winton Dean, *Bizet* (3rd edn, London, 1975); see also Mina Curtis, *Bizet and His World* (New York, 1974). On Bizet's most famous opera, see Susan McClary, *Georges Bizet: Carmen* (Cambridge, 1992). On Offenbach, the best general introduction is still Siegfried Kracauer, *Offenbach and the Paris of His Time* (London, 1937); see also Alex Faris, *Jacques Offenbach* (Boston, 1980), and Heather Hadlock, *Mad Loves: Women and Music in Offenbach's 'Les Contes d'Hoffmann'* (Princeton, 2000).

14. OLD WAGNER

(For Wagner books in general, see the bibliography to Chapter 12.) Friedrich Nietzsche, *The Birth of Tragedy and The Case of Wagner*, trans. with commentary by Walter Kaufmann (New York, 1967), presents the original texts of a famous controversy. For books that specifically address the later works, see: John Warrack, *Richard Wagner: Die Meistersinger von Nürnberg* (Cambridge, 1994); Roger Scruton, *The Death-Devoted Heart: Sex and the Sacred in Wagner's 'Tristan und Isolde'* (New York, 2004); Arthur Groos, *Richard Wagner: Tristan und Isolde* (Cambridge, 2011); and Lawrence Kramer, *Opera and Modern Culture: Wagner and Strauss* (Berkeley, 2004).

15. VERDI – OLDER STILL

(For Verdi books in general, see the bibliography to Chapter 10.) The second and third volumes of Julian Budden's *The Operas of Verdi* (London, 1978, 1981) cover the operas of this later period. For books that specifically address the later works, see: Hans Busch, *Verdi's 'Aida': The History of an Opera in Letters and Documents* (Minneapolis, 1978), and the same author's *Verdi's 'Otello' and 'Simon Boccanegra' in Letters and Documents*, 2 vols. (Oxford, 1988); James Hepokoski, *Giuseppe Verdi: Otello* (Cambridge, 1987); and the same author's *Giuseppe Verdi: Falstaff* (Cambridge, 1983). Marcello Conati, *Interviews and Encounters with Verdi* (London, 1984), provides a fascinating account of the manner in which Verdi projected his image to journalists and others in the second half of his career. Gundula Kreuzer, *Verdi and the Germans: From Unification to the Third Reich* (Cambridge, 2010), presents a revealing account of Verdi's reception in Germany from 1870 onwards.

16. REALISM AND CLAMOUR

Three excellent recent books about the Russian operatic background are: Richard Taruskin, *Defining Russia Musically* (Princeton, 1997); Marina Frolova-Walker, *Russian Music and Nationalism* (New Haven, 2007); and Richard Taruskin, *On Russian Music* (Berkeley, 2009). For Musorgsky in general, see Caryl Emerson, *The Life of Musorgsky* (Cambridge, 1999), and Richard Taruskin, *Musorgsky: Eight Essays and an Epilogue* (Princeton, 1993). For *Boris* in particular, see Caryl Emerson and Robert W. Oldani, *Modest Musorgsky and Boris Godunov: Myths, Realities, Reconsiderations* (Cambridge, 1994). For general introductions to three important *fin-de-siècle* opera composers, see: David Brown, *Tchaikovsky: The Man and His Music* (New York, 2007); Stephen Huebner, *The Operas of Charles Gounod* (Oxford, 1990); and Demar Irvine, *Massenet: A Chronicle of His Life and Times* (Portland, 1994). Alan Mallach, *The Autumn of Italian Opera: From Verismo to Modernism, 1890–1915* (Chicago, 2007), offers a good introduction to the post-Verdi phase of Italian opera. For Puccini in particular, see: William Ashbrook, *The Operas of Puccini* (Ithaca, 1985); Mosco Carner, *Puccini: A Critical Biography* (London, 1974); Michele Girardi, *Puccini: His International Art* (Chicago, 2000); Julian Budden, *Puccini: His Life and Works* (Oxford, 2002); and Alexandra Wilson, *The Puccini Problem: Opera, Nationalism and Modernity* (Cambridge, 2007). Two of Puccini's early operas are treated at book length in Arthur Groos and Roger Parker, *Giacomo Puccini: La bohème* (Cambridge, 1986), and Mosco Carner, *Giacomo Puccini: Tosca* (Cambridge, 1985).

17. TURNING POINT

The effect of Wagner is discussed in David C. Large and William Weber, eds., *Wagnerism in European Culture and Politics* (Ithaca, 1984). For Wagner-obsessed France, the best place to start is Steven Huebner, *French Opera at the 'Fin de Siècle': Wagnerism, Nationalism, and Style* (Oxford, 1999); see also Robin Holloway, *Debussy and Wagner* (London, 1979). Many of Debussy's writings are collected in François Lesure, ed., *Debussy on Music* (Ithaca, 1988). Recent multi-author books about the composer include: Jane Fulcher, ed., *Debussy and His World* (Princeton, 2001), and Simon Trezise, ed., *The Cambridge Companion to Debussy* (Cambridge, 2003). Robert Orledge's *Debussy and the Theatre* (Cambridge, 1982) is a valuable introduction to the composer's broader theatrical enthusiasms. Books devoted to his great opera include: David Grayson, *The Genesis of Debussy's Pelléas et Mélisande* (Ann Arbor, 1986), and Roger Nichols and Richard Langham Smith, *Claude Debussy: Pelléas et Mélisande* (Cambridge, 1989). General introductions to Strauss include: Michael Kennedy, *Richard Strauss: Man, Musician, Enigma* (Cambridge, 1999); Bryan Gilliam, *The Life of Richard Strauss* (Cambridge, 1999); and Bryan Gilliam, ed., *Richard Strauss and His World* (Princeton, 1992). For in-depth accounts of his two first operatic successes, see: Derrick Puffett, *Richard Strauss: Salome* (Cambridge, 1989), and the same author's *Richard Strauss: Elektra* (Cambridge, 1990). For Bartók, see Peter Laki, ed., *Bartók and His World* (Princeton, 1995), and Carl S. Leafstedt, *Inside Bluebeard's Castle: Music and Drama in Béla Bartók's Opera* (Oxford, 1999). For the rich post-Wagnerian atmosphere in Vienna, see Carl Schorske, *Fin-de-Siècle Vienna: Politics and Culture* (New York, 1980). On Schoenberg, see Joseph Auner, *A Schoenberg Reader: Documents of a Life* (New Haven, 2003), and Carl Dahlhaus, *Schoenberg and the New Music* (Cambridge, 1987). For Janáček, see: John Tyrrell, *Czech Opera* (Cambridge, 2005); the same author's *Janáček's Operas: A Documentary Account* (London, 1992); and Michael Beckerman, *Janáček and His World* (Princeton, 2003).

18. MODERN

For an introduction to and contemporary sources concerning early Modernism, see: Daniel Albright, *Untwisting the Serpent: Modernism in Music, Literature, and Other Arts* (Chicago, 2000); the same author's *Modernism and Music: An Anthology of Sources* (Chicago, 2004); and Christopher Butler, *Early Modernism: Literature, Music and Painting in Europe 1900–1916* (Oxford, 1994). The general Strauss literature is listed in the bibliography to Chapter 17. For *Rosenkavalier*, see Hans Hammelman and Ewald Osers, *The Correspondence between Richard Strauss and Hugo von Hofmannsthal* (London, 1961), and Alan Jefferson, *Richard Strauss: Der Rosenkavalier* (Cambridge, 1985). For Berg in general, see Anthony Pople, *The Cambridge Companion to Berg* (Cambridge, 1997). For *Wozzeck*, see Douglas Jarman, *Alban Berg: Wozzeck* (Cambridge, 1989); even more in-depth analysis of both Berg's operas (emphatically not for the fair-hearted) is offered in George Perle, *The Operas of Alban Berg*, 2 vols. (Berkeley, 1980, 1989). Stephen Walsh, *Stravinsky: The Second Exile: France and America, 1934–1971* (London, 2006), gives a biographical context for *The Rake's Progress*. See also Jonathan Cross, *The Cambridge Companion to Stravinsky* (Cambridge, 2003), and Paul Griffiths, *Igor Stravinsky: The Rake's Progress* (Cambridge, 1982).

19. SPEECH

Alex Ross's *The Rest is Noise: Listening to the Twentieth Century* (London, 2008) provides a perceptive and enjoyable introduction to this period and its discontents. On Ravel, see Vladimir Jankélévitch, *Ravel* (London, 1959), an individual, highly poetic view of the composer, still worth reading. Deborah Mawer, *The Cambridge Companion to Ravel* (Cambridge, 2000), provides a recent compendium. On Weill and Krenek, see: Bryan Gilliam, ed., *Music and Performance during the Weimar Republic* (Cambridge, 1994); Lys Symonette and Kim H. Kowalke, eds., *Speak Low (When You Speak of Love): The Letters of Kurt Weill and Lotte Lenya* (Berkeley, 1996); Stephen Hinton, *Kurt Weill: The Threepenny Opera* (Cambridge, 1990); Ernst Krenek, *Horizons Circled: Reflections on My Life in Music* (Berkeley, 1974); and John L. Stewart, *Ernst Krenek: The Man and His Music* (Berkeley, 1991). On Shostakovich, see: Rosamund Bartlett, *Shostakovch in Context* (Oxford, 2000); Laurel Fay, *Shostakovich: A Life* (Oxford, 1999); and the same author's *Shostakovich and His World* (Princeton, 2004).

20. REVENANTS IN THE MUSEUM

For a series of (mostly) optimistic essays on opera's last complete century, see Mervyn Cooke, *The Cambridge Companion to Twentieth-Century Opera* (Cambridge, 2005). General books on Britten include Humphrey Carpenter, *Benjamin Britten: A Biography* (London, 1992), and Mervyn Cooke, *The Cambridge Companion to Benjamin Britten* (Cambridge, 1999). A sceptical view is offered in Heather Wiebe, *Britten's Unquiet Pasts: Sound and Memory in Postwar Reconstruction* (Cambridge, 2012). On *Peter Grimes*, see Philip Brett, *Benjamin Britten: Peter Grimes* (Cambridge, 1983). The literature of John Adams is increasing;

see in particular Thomas May, ed., *The John Adams Reader: Essential Writings on an American Composer* (Pompton Plains, NJ, 2006).

21. WE ARE ALONE IN THE FOREST

On recent trends in opera production, see Thomas Sutcliffe, *Believing in Opera* (London, 1996), Marcia Citron, *Opera on Screen* (New Haven, 2000), and David J. Levin, *Unsettling Opera: Staging Mozart, Verdi, Wagner, and Zemlinsky* (Chicago, 2007).

Index